PARTY AUTONOMY IN PRIVATE INTERNATIONAL LAW

This book provides an unprecedented analysis and appraisal of party autonomy in private international law – the power of private parties to enter into agreements as to the forum in which their disputes will be resolved or the law which governs their legal relationships. It includes a detailed exploration of the historical origins of party autonomy as well as its various theoretical justifications, and an in-depth comparative study of the rules governing party autonomy in the European Union, the United States, common law systems, and international codifications. It examines both choice of forum and choice of law, including arbitration agreements and choice of non-state law, and both contractual and non-contractual legal relations. This analysis demonstrates that while an apparent consensus around the core principle of party autonomy has emerged, its coherence as a doctrine is open to question as there remains significant variation in practice across its various facets and between legal systems.

ALEX MILLS is Reader in Public and Private International Law at the Faculty of Laws, University College London. He is the author of *The Confluence of Public and Private International Law* (Cambridge University Press, 2009) and was awarded the American Society of International Law Private International Law Prize in 2010. He has Directed Studies in Private International Law at the Hague Academy of International Law, and he is a member of the Academic Research Panel of Blackstone Chambers and the Editorial Board of the *International and Comparative Law Quarterly*.

PARTY AUTONOMY
IN PRIVATE
INTERNATIONAL LAW

ALEX MILLS

University College London

CAMBRIDGE
UNIVERSITY PRESS

University Printing House, Cambridge CB2 8BS, United Kingdom

One Liberty Plaza, 20th Floor, New York, NY 10006, USA

477 Williamstown Road, Port Melbourne, VIC 3207, Australia

314-321, 3rd Floor, Plot 3, Splendor Forum, Jasola District Centre, New Delhi - 110025, India

79 Anson Road, #06-04/06, Singapore 079906

Cambridge University Press is part of the University of Cambridge.

It furthers the University's mission by disseminating knowledge in the pursuit of
education, learning and research at the highest international levels of excellence.

www.cambridge.org
Information on this title: www.cambridge.org/9781107079175
DOI: 10.1017/9781139941419

© Alex Mills 2018

First published 2018

A catalogue record for this publication is available from the British Library

Library of Congress Cataloging in Publication data
Names: Mills, Alex.
Title: Party autonomy in private international law /
Alex Mills, University College London.
Description: Cambridge, United Kingdom ; New York, NY, USA :
Cambridge University Press, 2018.
Identifiers: LCCN 2018011055 |
ISBN 9781107079175 (hardback)
Subjects: LCSH: Conflict of laws. | Liberty of contract. |
BISAC: LAW / International.
Classification: LCC K7068 .M55 2018 | DDC 346.02—dc23 LC record
available at https://lccn.loc.gov/2018011055

ISBN 978-1-107-07917-5 Hardback
ISBN 978-1-107-43741-8 Paperback

To my wife, in loving appreciation of her tireless
support and belief.

CONTENTS

ACKNOWLEDGEMENTS

This book is the product of almost a decade of wrestling with these issues (I leave it to the reader to decide who, if anyone, has emerged victorious), drawing on the support of colleagues at the University of Cambridge and University College London, as well as the broader global community of private international lawyers. I am particularly grateful to the organisers of and participants in the following conferences or seminars, at which aspects of the research, as indicated, have been presented and discussed:

- 'Implied and Imputed Choices of Law in Contract', *The Rome I Regulation*, Trinity College Dublin, October 2009
- 'The Limits of Party Autonomy in Contractual Choice of Law and Choice of Forum', *Kurt Lipstein Memorial Law Colloquium*, Clare College, University of Cambridge, May 2010
- 'The Foundations and Limits of Party Autonomy: Private International Law and Non-State Regulation', *International Law Association Biennial Conference*, The Hague, August 2010
- 'Party Autonomy in Non-Contractual Private International Law Disputes', *Journal of Private International Law Conference*, Milan, April 2011
- 'The English Ambivalence to Law and Dispute Resolution Beyond the State', *Commercial Law Seminar Series*, Queen Mary University of London, March 2013
- 'Choice of Non-State Law in Practice and Theory: Legitimacy Within and Beyond the State', *Journal of Private International Law Conference*, University of Cambridge, September 2015
- 'Recent International Developments in Private International Law', *SCIL Year in Review*, Sydney Law School, February 2017
- 'The Hague Choice of Court Convention and Cross-Border Commercial Dispute Resolution in Australia and the Asia-Pacific', Melbourne Law School, April 2017

I also carried out part of the research for this book as a visiting scholar at Sydney Law School, and I am very grateful for the warm hospitality of its international lawyers, particularly Professor Timothy Stephens and Professor Chester Brown, and for the support of the UCL Global Engagement Fund. This book also benefited from helpful research assistance from Camelia Aknouche, Ali Auda, Joseph Crampin, Ira Lakhman, and Simon Tysoe. Finally, I am very grateful to Finola O'Sullivan and all at Cambridge University Press who have helped steer this book through to publication.

1

Introduction

When can parties enter into binding agreements as to the forum in which their disputes will be resolved, or the law that governs their legal relationships? To what extent should parties have the power to make such agreements? To put this another way, to what extent should courts or arbitral tribunals respect and enforce such agreements? These are the principal questions of party autonomy in private international law, which has become an increasingly important and widely accepted part of the global legal landscape. Even non-lawyers are likely to be familiar with (even if they are not likely to read) the clauses in the fine print of contracts that specify the forum and law to govern disputes arising under the contract. Such clauses are often – wrongly – considered merely part of the 'boiler-plate' of standard contracting, rather than key terms to be carefully negotiated for a particular relationship. The use of such clauses is ubiquitous, flourishing as an apparent international consensus around at least certain core questions of their validity and effectiveness has emerged and been consolidated. The Hague Convention on Choice of Court Agreements 2005 has, for example, been developed by the main international organisation responsible for harmonising private international law, the Hague Conference on Private International Law. It has come into effect for the Member States of the European Union, Mexico and Singapore, has been signed by the United States, the People's Republic of China, Ukraine, and Montenegro, and is under consideration by other states.[1] In 2015 the Hague Conference also adopted the Hague Principles on Choice of Law in International Commercial Contracts, a soft law instrument which seeks to influence and promote international adoption of party autonomy in the context of the law applicable to contracts.[2] Recent European and Chinese regulation in private international law has also extended the scope of party autonomy in choice of law beyond its traditional focus on contract law into

---

[1] See further Section 3.1.
[2] See further Section 7.2.7.

other areas of law such as non-contractual obligations, property law, succession, and family law.[3] Scholars argue that party autonomy has become, or at least is in the process of becoming, close to universal and incontestable as a "unifying principle"[4] of modern private international law, "the one principle in conflict of laws that is followed by almost all jurisdictions",[5] or a "rule of customary law".[6] It has even been argued that party autonomy is so central to private international law that the subject should be rethought, so that party autonomy provides its entire foundation.[7] Party autonomy is so accepted in practice that there is a tendency to suggest, somewhat alarmingly, that it does not require theoretical justification.[8] Party autonomy is indeed such an omnipresent feature of modern contracting practice as to appear quite banal. It is difficult to imagine a book being published that presented an argument rejecting party autonomy altogether – it would be considered too far out of step with established practice.

This is not, however, cause to doubt whether a book offering an examination and appraisal (not a work of either opposition or advocacy)[9] of party autonomy is necessary – at least, this is the view of the author of this book, and it is hoped that even the sceptical reader will not leave this book entirely unconvinced otherwise. Scholarship opposing or advocating party autonomy also of course has its place. It is indeed hoped that the analysis in this book may serve as a platform for such engagement, by analysing and evaluating the features of party autonomy as a matter of both theory and positive law. As will be seen throughout this book, despite the apparent consensus that has developed around party autonomy there are numerous controversial questions which still remain unresolved or which are dealt with inconsistently in different jurisdictions. Questions also arise concerning whether the rules governing party autonomy are consistent with its theoretical and policy justifications, and whether the rules

---

[3] See further Chapter 8.
[4] Symeonides (2014), p.346.
[5] Lehmann (2008), p.385.
[6] Lowenfeld (1994), p.256 ("support of party autonomy is by now so widespread that it can fairly be called a rule of customary law"). See also Nygh (1999), p.45.
[7] See e.g. Peari (2013) (in respect of choice of law); Karayanidi (2017) (in respect of jurisdiction).
[8] Muir Watt (2010), pp.252–3, n.5 (criticising the "tendency to consider freedom of choice as so natural as to need no justification").
[9] It may be noted that Peter Nygh's seminal work *Autonomy in International Contracts* (1999) expressly aimed (at p.vii) "to argue for a further development and extension of the principle of autonomy unhampered by historical notions of territoriality and sovereignty which hitherto sought to restrain it".

governing different aspects of party autonomy are (or should be) consistent with each other, as discussed further in Section 1.4. Party autonomy in private international law is also a worthy object of study simply because it has extremely important – even dramatic – effects. It gives private parties a (limited) power to determine the extent of the jurisdiction of state courts and the scope of application of state law. Private international law has long been understood as being concerned with the allocation of regulatory authority in matters of private law between states, in terms of both institutional authority (jurisdiction) and substantive regulatory authority (applicable law).[10] This allocation is indeed an important part of global governance, which is also served by rules of jurisdiction in public international law (and by jurisdictional prohibitions such as rules of state immunity).[11] Importantly, the allocation of regulatory authority must also be understood as a form of regulation, albeit a higher level function – it concerns the regulation of regulation. What is distinctive and even remarkable about party autonomy is that it allows private parties to determine the distribution of private law authority themselves, thus essentially privatising an important allocative function of global governance. Even more significantly, where a non-state forum (arbitration) or non-state law is chosen, the effect can be viewed as a double privatisation, not just of the allocative function but also of the regulatory function. Private parties can allocate regulatory authority not only between states but also to other private actors, again in terms of both institutional regulatory authority (disputes may be resolved by arbitrators, who are also 'private' actors in the sense that they are often acting under obligations of confidentiality) and substantive regulatory authority (disputes may be resolved through the application of privately generated legal rules).

1.1   Perspectives on Party Autonomy

While party autonomy has become close to ubiquitous and incontestable over the course of the twentieth century, the origins of and justifications for this development, examined in Chapter 2, remain relatively obscure. While a book opposing party autonomy would today be difficult to imagine, only a century ago many courts and scholars viewed party autonomy as impossible. Although support for party autonomy has long been a feature of at least some private international law reasoning, many scholars

---

[10] See further Muir Watt and Fernández Arroyo (2014); Mills (2009a).
[11] See further Mills (2014).

have found it difficult to reconcile such apparent private power with the sovereignty of states. Indeed, party autonomy has never sat comfortably with traditional conceptions of state jurisdiction under public international law. Party autonomy is therefore in the unusual position of being apparently ubiquitous and banal, but also incongruous and exceptional. The theoretical underpinnings of private international law remain underdeveloped – although the various aspects of party autonomy (choice of state and non-state forums, and choice of state and non-state law) have all received significant consideration in academic books and journal articles, this has tended to be fragmented, particularised, or technical in focus rather than examining questions of underlying principle. This is not to understate the importance of practical work on the drafting and interpretation of such clauses, but simply to note that there has been limited academic engagement with party autonomy as a general phenomenon.

Although this may not be apparent at first glance, this book complements the author's previous book on *The Confluence of Public and Private International Law*.[12] That book explored the links between private international law and public international law, examining the extent to which rules of private international law can be considered as manifestations of broader principles of public international law, including the jurisdictional rules which bind states. It dealt with party autonomy,[13] but inevitably in a limited way given the aims of the book, which focused more on the underlying purpose of private international law and the types of connection that justify the power of a forum or the application of a law in the absence of party choice. This book approaches the subject of private international law essentially from the opposite direction. Rather than viewing it from the perspective of its relationship with public international law, focused on the rights and powers of states, this book focuses on the rights and powers of private parties.[14] These opposing perspectives are complementary in addressing the range of theoretical foundations of private international law. It is indeed part of the attraction and perhaps even mystique of private international law that it engages such a wide variety of interests, from the powers of states in international law to the rights and interests of disputing private parties.

---

[12] Mills (2009a).
[13] Mills (2009a), p.291ff.
[14] For a similarly private-centred perspective on public international law jurisdiction, see Mills (2014).

It is worth noting, however, that party autonomy appears radically different depending on the perspective from which it is approached – a point introduced further immediately below, and developed in Chapter 2. This is at least in part because private international law functions at two discrete levels. First, it is concerned with the exercise of regulatory authority by one or more states, raising the question of whether that exercise of power is legitimate under international law. Second, it is concerned with the relationship between national courts and two or more disputing private parties, including of course the regulation by the court of the private law relationship between those parties. This raises the question of whether the exercise of power meets standards of fairness to private parties (criteria which can generally be satisfied where those parties have consented to the exercise of power), or whether it balances protecting the interests of the defendant and claimant, alongside third party and public interests. This in turn begs the further question of where these standards of fairness should come from. Different national systems have different conceptions of what is fair or just, and traditional private international law can be understood as engaged instead with the distinct question of how regulatory authority should be allocated (fairly and justly) in the context of a pluralism of conceptions of 'justice'.[15] These perspectives are not irreconcilable, but there is an unresolved tension between them in the history and theory of private international law, in which various conceptions of power and fairness have long vied for influence. As discussed below and throughout this book, these competing perspectives also explain why party autonomy has at times been viewed as incompatible with the foundations of private international law, and at other times as central to those foundations.

1.1.1   Party Autonomy from a State-Sovereigntist Perspective

Traditionally in international law (at least since the nineteenth century) it is states that are exclusively recognised as possessing sovereignty on the international plane, and state governments who exercise that sovereignty through law, including both private law and private international law. As discussed further below and in Chapter 2, the existence of party autonomy has thus sometimes been viewed as a seemingly intractable problem for theorists who have sought to reconcile rules of private international law with public international law – indeed historically some scholars denied the existence of party autonomy precisely because they considered that

---

[15] Mills (2009a), p.3ff.

individuals could not have power over sovereigns, and thus could not have control over the allocation of their regulatory authority. Denying party autonomy has not proven a durable approach in practice, however, and thus some means of reconciliation has long been sought. The solution generally adopted (from this traditional perspective) is to view party autonomy as merely a privilege granted by states and contingently conferred on individuals. Put simply, individuals only have the power to determine which court or law governs their legal relations to the extent that states give them that power (through their domestic law), and states could just as readily take away that power.[16] In the words of the US Second Restatement of Conflict of Laws:

> There is nothing to prevent the forum from employing a choice-of-law rule which provides that, subject to stated exceptions, the law of the state chosen by the parties shall be applied to determine the validity of a contract and the rights created thereby. The law of the state chosen by the parties is applied, not because the parties themselves are legislators, but simply because this is the result demanded by the choice-of-law rule of the forum.[17]

From this perspective, what appears to be an exercise of party autonomy is really no more than parties expressing a preference, stating as a matter of fact which court or law they would prefer. It is states that agree to give effect to that preference in certain circumstances. The justifications for party autonomy, in this model, must be traced to states – looking to the reasons why states support party autonomy and why they constrain it. This argument does not, therefore, in fact provide a 'justification' for party autonomy, but more an explanation as to *how* party autonomy can be adopted – through the private international law of states. There is, in this view, a superficial quality to the 'autonomy' exercised by private parties, because it is entirely contingent on the largess of states, although even from this perspective the fact that states have almost universally chosen to confer this power is significant in and of itself.

The legitimacy of an exercise of party autonomy, viewed from this perspective, derives from the legitimacy of the exercise of state power through which it is recognised. As already noted, this raises the question of whether party autonomy is compatible with public international law constraints on state power, which are principally set out in the international law on jurisdiction. If a state court exercises jurisdiction or applies its law in civil proceedings based purely on consent by the parties, this is obviously difficult to reconcile with the traditional public international law requirement that

---

[16] See e.g. Zhang (2006a), p.555ff; Nygh (1999), p.32ff.
[17] Section 187, comment (e).

jurisdiction must be justified by a substantial objective connection, typically of territoriality or nationality.[18] Faced with this argument, three alternative responses have generally been presented. First, rejecting the idea that private international law is about the allocation of regulatory authority between states – denying any connection between public and private international law, thus rejecting the application of public international law jurisdictional rules to civil disputes, leaving them unrestricted except under national law. The difficulty with this response is that it would leave the exercise of civil jurisdiction unlimited also in the absence of party autonomy, which is inconsistent with state practice[19] and normatively undesirable as it would greatly increase the risk of parallel proceedings and conflicting judgments and fail to recognise the regulatory significance of private and procedural law. Second, making (unrealistic) arguments against party autonomy, a response taken perhaps most famously under the First Restatement of Conflict of Laws in the United States. As examined further in Section 2.2.2, this response was inconsistent with the predominant practice of the courts even at the time, and is now simply untenable. Third, accepting party autonomy, but limiting the choice of the parties to those states that have an objective connection which would justify the exercise of jurisdiction under public international law. As discussed further in Sections 3.4 and 7.3, it is notable that practice in some states has particularly tended to limit party autonomy on these grounds, thus viewing it as a rule of selection (where multiple states are connected to a legal relationship, determining which of them gets to exercise regulatory authority) rather than a rule through which the parties can themselves confer such authority. However, the practice of most states does not restrict party autonomy in this way.

None of these approaches is, therefore, entirely satisfactory, and a fourth approach may be suggested as a preferable alternative – to accept that the rules on public international law are applicable, but to reformulate our account of the rules so that it is consistent with party autonomy. This requires accepting that party agreement is itself a connecting factor that justifies the exercise of jurisdiction by a state. A court may hear a case or apply a law based purely on the agreement between the parties, with no objective connecting factors (connections of territoriality or nationality) to justify the national exercise of jurisdiction as a matter of public

---

[18] See further Mills (2014).

[19] See e.g. the submissions of the European Commission and (jointly) the United Kingdom and the Netherlands in *Kiobel* v. *Royal Dutch Petroleum*, 133 S. Ct. 1659 (2013), discussed further in Mills (2014), p.225ff.

international law. However precisely this argument is formulated, it is difficult to contest in light of the widespread practice that states have agreed that the recognition of an exercise of party autonomy is consistent with the applicable principles of public international law.[20]

1.1.2   Party Autonomy from a Party-Sovereigntist Perspective

From a contrasting private party-centred perspective, it might be argued that private parties have an inherent autonomy, particularly where they act beyond the boundaries of a single legal order, and it is states that are recognising that underlying reality in accepting the freedom of private parties to choose a forum or law. From this more 'radical' perspective, party autonomy is a direct challenge to the predominance of state sovereignty, perhaps even suggesting instead the co-existence of 'individual sovereignty' alongside the sovereignty of the state. Horatia Muir Watt, noting the dominance of the state-sovereigntist approach discussed above, has argued that the "representation of party freedom as being subordinate to state authority appears to have survived both the demise of the liberal state in the domestic sphere and the decline of the Westphalian model in international relations"[21] – but that survival is increasingly coming under challenge, as "party autonomy has evidently ceased to imply subordination of private actors to state authority, but actually reverses this relationship".[22] An analogy might be drawn here with developments in international human rights law, and the contested question of whether such rights are merely the contingent creations of states, or a new foundation of international law itself (beyond the Westphalian model), operating as a fundamental and permanent constraint on state sovereignty. This may be more than an analogy – some have argued that the foundations of party autonomy in private international law should lie in a 'human right' of personal freedom, which is itself prior to the state, particularly since the sovereignty of the state may be viewed as deriving from an exercise of individual autonomy through the form of a social contract.[23] This argument is, of course, much

---

[20] As noted above, it has been argued that party autonomy has itself attained the status of a rule of customary international law: Lowenfeld (1994), p.256; Nygh (1999), p.45.

[21] Muir Watt (2010), p.258.

[22] Ibid.

[23] See e.g. Basedow (2013a), p.182 ("If State sovereignty for its part can be attributed to the will of the individual, the exercise of this will as regards the applicable law in a conflict-of-laws scenario cannot be attacked as an infringement on the sovereignty of the State."). See further discussion in Section 2.3.1.

less persuasive when it comes to legal entities like companies, for whom the idea of innate legal (let alone 'human') rights would appear paradoxical, since they are creations of state law. This may, however, overstate the role of law, in particular of any national law in regulating a transnational enterprise, and the limited reality of legal personality in a corporate group formed of a fluid constellation of different national legal persons. Another version of this argument is to see private parties as exercising a form of law-making authority when they make a contract – a posture famously adopted in French law[24] – and thus as themselves 'sovereign' in a sense that encompasses at least private international law party autonomy. The French expression for party autonomy, *autonomie de la volonté*, pointedly suggests such a foundational role for the will of the parties.

From this perspective, when rules of private international law accept party autonomy, they are merely *recognising* the autonomy of private parties, rather than making a contingent choice to give effect to party preferences. Under this perspective, the justifications for party autonomy and the reasons for its constraint should focus on private parties themselves. As discussed further in Section 2.3.1, the legitimacy of an exercise of party autonomy derives (in this approach, somehow) *directly* from the agreement of the parties, rather than from its recognition in national law – the fact of the agreement itself justifies its effectiveness and makes its effectiveness just. As a result, private international law rules do not only involve mediating between the principles of justice embodied in systems of national law, but also invoke principles of justice that are not embodied in national law. In the words of Matthias Lehmann:

> Party autonomy can only be justified if one ignores the state relations that have so far been the focus of the classic theory. One needs to accept that the parties are the center of the conflicts problem. They are allowed to choose the applicable law because it is their dispute that is in question.[25]

Those examining the question from a state-sovereigntist perspective might respond to this claim by arguing that the agreement between the parties is in turn derivative from national law, as it is national law that confers upon it the status of a contract. However, in its strongest form, the argument from a party-sovereigntist perspective rejects the contention that to be effective an agreement must be conferred the status of contract under national law, positing either a contract without law, or simply that an agreement alone is sufficient. The context in which this argument is

---

[24] French Civil Code 2016, Art.1103 (previously Art.1134); see Nygh (1999), p.7 and p.35ff.
[25] Lehmann (2008), p.415.

most often made is in relation to arbitration (and it is no coincidence that it is most associated with French law and scholars),[26] where the claim is commonly (but still controversially) made that the authority of an arbitral tribunal derives solely from the agreement between the parties, and not from any national legal order. The agreement itself is, under this approach, considered to be a source of rights and obligations.[27]

This perspective is even more difficult to reconcile with traditional principles of international law than the state-sovereigntist perspective discussed above, because it requires recognising that individuals are themselves a source of normative authority – that international jurisdiction is not merely a matter of the rights and powers of states. An argument can be made, however, that this is indeed the case, through the increased recognition of individuals as subjects of international law.[28] In the striking words of the Court of Appeal of England and Wales:

> a fundamental change has occurred within public international law. The traditional view of public international law as a system of law merely regulating the conduct of states among themselves on the international plane has long been discarded. In its place has emerged a system which includes the regulation of human rights by international law, a system of which individuals are rightly considered to be subjects.[29]

If an acknowledgement is made of an 'individual sovereignty' that is balanced against that of the state, the widespread recognition of party autonomy – even viewed as deriving from the parties themselves rather than national law – can be considered to be compatible with norms of public international law jurisdiction.[30] The apparent incompatibility arises only as a result of traditional and now arguably outmoded conceptions of public international law jurisdiction, which conceive of jurisdiction as purely a matter of (territorial or nationality-based) state rights and powers. Party autonomy provides an argument for an evolution in these ideas of jurisdiction, to encapsulate the idea of jurisdiction as a matter of individual right. Another way of expressing this idea is that the right to be

---

[26] See further Section 6.2.
[27] Discussed further below and in Chapter 6.
[28] See generally e.g. Mills (2014).
[29] *Belhaj* v. *Straw* [2014] EWCA Civ 1394, [115].
[30] The deference to party autonomy in private international law was long ago described as reflecting "the sovereign will of the parties" by Judge Bustamente in his Separate Opinion in the *Serbian Loans Case, France* v. *Yugoslavia* (1929) PCIJ Ser A, No 20, Judgment 14, p.53. Note also the recognition of the affinity between international norms and private international law rules on party autonomy in the Basel Principles (1991).

subject to jurisdiction only in accordance with traditional international law limitations (based on connections of territoriality or nationality) is a right that may be waived, not only by states, but seemingly by individuals themselves. However it is expressed, this idea suggests that the adoption of party autonomy in private international law is a reflection of broader developments in international ordering, under which international law is no longer just the law between states, but is more broadly conceived as the global law of humanity.[31] As Hans Van Loon has perceptively observed:

> Where the nation-State is no longer its sole anchor space, private inter-national law must transcend its traditional boundaries, and, adapting its methodologies while preserving its integrity, orient itself towards the idea of an emerging global community.[32]

1.1.3   Congruence or Competition

This analysis is developed further in Chapter 2 – the main point to note for present purposes is simply that party autonomy in private interna-tional law can be viewed from the radically different perspectives explored above. A central complexity of party autonomy in private international law is that these explanations appear to co-exist in an uneasy truce. On the one hand, party autonomy is indeed evidently the product of national legislative processes (albeit based in some cases on international codifica-tion), through which limited rights are conferred on private parties. Part of the reality of *how* party autonomy is given effect is through national law, even if this does not engage with the question of *why* national legal orders would permit such a choice. On the other hand, multinational par-ties engaging in cross-border activity may not view their choices of court, arbitral tribunal or law as a product of any particular national legal order, but rather as an exercise of an autonomous power, under which their pri-vate agreement designates the applicable legal order. While these differ-ent approaches may be in tension, they are not necessarily so – states may for a variety of reasons (explored throughout this book) be interested in facilitating the autonomy of private parties, rather than constraining it. However, as discussed further in Section 2.3, these different approaches suggest an alignment with different theoretical foundations for party autonomy. As a result, there are likely to be boundaries to this coincidence of interests, reflected in the legal limits on party autonomy.

---

[31] See e.g. Teitel (2011); Peters (2009); Tesón (1992); Sohn (1982).
[32] Van Loon (2016), p.45.

These contrasting perspectives run throughout the different aspects of party autonomy, but perhaps the most obvious area where they have come into direct conflict is choice of non-state dispute resolution and law. There is widespread agreement among states – principally in the form of the New York Convention on the Recognition and Enforcement of Foreign Arbitral Awards 1958 – that parties should be free to grant exclusive jurisdiction over their private disputes to *non-state* methods of dispute resolution, such as arbitral tribunals, to the (at least partial) exclusion of state judicial jurisdiction. This development is subject to two contrasting and incompatible readings, each of which is both widely adopted and heavily contested. The first is that it simply reflects the acceptance by states of arbitration as a form of alternative dispute resolution, backed up by state courts, but lacking any normative power of its own. The second is the more radical proposition that it implies the acceptance by states of a non-state form of ordering, alongside and competing with national courts – that arbitral tribunals are privately constituted courts, sometimes even applying privately constituted (non-state) private law. This revolutionary idea would certainly represent a further challenge to traditional conceptions of jurisdiction, recognising individual party freedom not just between state laws or adjudicative bodies, but beyond them, through the recognition of private (non-state) legal forms of ordering, or of legal pluralism beyond the state.[33] It would thus also be a serious challenge to the idea that jurisdiction in public international law is only concerned with the powers of states, as it would involve accepting not just individual jurisdictional power, but also jurisdictional power created and conferred by individuals on private institutions – not just privatisation of the regulatory function of private international law, but also privatisation of the regulatory functions of substantive private law and national courts. Whether this is indeed taking place, or has already taken place, remains one of the great contested issues of the international legal order.

1.2   Comparative Scope

Questions of private international law are both global concerns and matters that have been dealt with through a diverse range of national, sub-national, and supra-national approaches. Any general study on a subject of private international law, including that of party autonomy, faces the unavoidable difficulty that a degree of comparison is essential, but being

---

[33] See further discussion in Sections 6.2 and 10.1.

truly comprehensive would be impossible both as a matter of expertise and practicality.[34] This book takes as its focus four main sources of private international law:

(1) International private international law, including in particular the treaties or soft law instruments prepared under the auspices of the Hague Conference on Private International Law (such as the Hague Convention on Choice of Court Agreements 2005 and the Hague Principles on Choice of Law in International Commercial Contracts 2015), and also including the New York Convention on the Recognition and Enforcement of Foreign Arbitral Awards 1958.

(2) European Union private international law, the harmonised rules which have been adopted by the European Union and developed by the Court of Justice (CJEU)[35] to facilitate the more efficient functioning of the internal market, and that have replaced significant parts of the national private international law of the EU Member States.

(3) The common law, historically dominated by English/British/UK courts and law, but represented around the globe by various national traditions (including in Australia, Canada, Hong Kong, India, Ireland, Kenya, New Zealand, Pakistan, and Singapore). These traditions, while mutually influential and sharing a common heritage, have become increasingly independent of English law, particularly as private international law in the United Kingdom has become increasingly regulated by EU law – this book focuses particularly on English law, but includes analysis of varying approaches in other common law jurisdictions.

(4) The private international law of the United States, which has developed from common law foundations to adopt a very distinctive and rich tradition of scholarship and practice, across the diverse state and federal courts.

---

[34] There are some notable and laudable exceptions. For a global comparative overview of choice of law codifications, see Symeonides (2014), with a particular focus on party autonomy in Chapter 3. For a very broad international study of private international law in general, see also Basedow et al. (2017), an encyclopaedia with 195 authors contributing and eighty national reports. For an analysis of party autonomy in Asia, see Nishitani (2016). For further comparative analysis of party autonomy, see also generally the Preliminary Documents to the Hague Convention on Choice of Court Agreements 2005 (available at www.hcch.net/en/instruments/conventions/publications1/?dtid=35&cid=98), and the Preparatory Work to the Hague Principles on Choice of Law in International Commercial Contracts 2015 (available at www.hcch.net/en/instruments/contracts-preparatory-work).

[35] The modern terms 'EU' and 'CJEU' are used throughout, favouring consistency over historical accuracy.

These four categories of sources provide the majority of the material for the analysis undertaken in this book. They are not listed in any hierarchical order – the order of treatment in different parts of the book varies depending on which arrangement will support the clearest analysis. Sources from other national traditions (including a particular focus on Chinese and Brazilian choice of law rules) are referred to at various times where they offer a distinctive approach on the issue under examination, but are not taken as principal objects of study. No claim is made that these sources are representative of all the approaches or legal traditions of the world, nor that their perspectives on party autonomy are exhaustive. These various legal systems do, however, account for the majority of world cross-border trade in goods and services.[36]

1.3 Distinctions and Exclusions

At this point, the casual reader may be fearing for the scope of this book. It may then be a timely source of reassurance to set out some matters that might be considered as related to party autonomy, but which are distinguishable from it and thus excluded from these pages. This is not because these are unimportant or entirely unconnected with the issues to be discussed in this book, but because they are considered to raise sufficiently distinct questions as to require separate treatment. This section thus not only serves the negative function of carving out what is not covered in the book, but also the positive function of defining party autonomy more precisely by distinguishing it from other related aspects of private international law.

1.3.1 Party Autonomy and Indirect Choice of Forum or Law through Control over 'Objective' Factors

Many traditional rules of private international law operate through identification of an objective connecting factor. In the context of choice of law in particular, these are often referred to as 'objective' choice of law rules, as opposed to the 'subjective' choice of law that is exercised by the parties through party autonomy. For a claim in tort, for example, the courts of the domicile of the defendant and the courts of the place of the tort are likely to have jurisdiction, and the law of the place of the tort is likely to govern.

---

[36] See generally e.g. World Trade Organization, 'World Trade Statistical Review 2017' (available at www.wto.org/english/res_e/statis_e/wts2017_e/wts17_toc_e.htm).

In a sale of goods contract, the courts of the domicile of the defendant and the courts of the place of delivery of the goods may be given jurisdiction, and choice of law rules might for example specify that the law of the place of residence of the seller will govern. In some contexts, these objective factors are outside the control of the parties. A party committing a tort is unlikely to have any capacity to plan or control where the tort is located. Questions of nationality are principally within the control of states, rather than individuals. In other contexts, these objective factors may be within private control. For example, the parties to a sale of goods contract can determine where the goods are to be delivered, and thereby at least partially determine which court will have jurisdiction over disputes arising under their contract. More broadly, both natural persons and companies may have at least some control over their residence or domicile, as they may have the power to choose where they customarily live (although for natural persons at least this is only the experience of a privileged minority). There is a sense, therefore, in which private international law rules that rely on these objective connecting factors are giving indirect effect to party choices, where the factor relied on is within the control of one or more parties.[37] It has been suggested, for example, that the oldest recorded example of party autonomy is:

> A decree issued in Hellenistic Egypt in 120–118 BC [which] provided that contracts written in the Egyptian language were subject to the jurisdiction of Egyptian courts, which applied Egyptian law, whereas contracts written in Greek were subject to the jurisdiction of the Greek courts, which applied Greek law. Thus, by choosing the language of their contact, parties could directly choose the forum and indirectly the governing law.[38]

Strictly speaking this is not party autonomy, but in relying on the language of the contract, the rule would readily be open to indirect party choice, at least for those parties capable of contracting in more than one language. If a choice of law rule relies on a factor within the control of one party or both parties (such as the place of execution of a contract, or the place of residence of the parties), it thus gives individuals greater control over the law applicable to their legal relations, and thus also in certain contexts their personal identity from a legal perspective.

Such rules are not, however, true examples of party autonomy, which involves the parties contractually choosing the forum in which their disputes will be heard or the law to govern their legal relations, rather than

---

[37] See generally Basedow (2013a), p.239ff.
[38] Hay, Borchers, and Symeonides (2010), p.1086.

choosing the objective factors under which such a determination will take place. An exercise of party autonomy may be direct, or may even rely on objective factors to indicate the choice – such as a contractual clause conferring exclusive jurisdiction on the courts of the place of delivery of goods. This remains distinct from simply relying on jurisdictional rules that apply in the absence of a choice, even if the outcome might in some cases be the same. There is a practical reason to draw this distinction, which is that choice of forum or law will rarely be the basis on which parties agree on these objective factors. It is difficult to imagine parties to a sale of goods contract agreeing on an inconvenient place of delivery, purely for the purposes of manipulating the potentially available court or applicable law.[39] But even where parties might act on such a basis, there is something significantly different in principle about what happens when they do, from the perspective of private international law. The parties are accepting and subjecting themselves to the rules governing the allocation of regulatory authority that are adopted by the relevant states, and are merely adapting their behaviour to those rules in order to achieve the desired result; they are making choices based on the law, rather than making a choice of forum or law. There is no sense in which the parties are themselves directly determining how regulatory authority is allocated, as they do in a true exercise of party autonomy.

It is not, however, claimed that this issue is entirely distinct from party autonomy in a broader sense. In some cases, a rule of party autonomy may be disguised through permitting the parties to agree on a fictional connecting factor – such as the French concept of 'elected domicile' in jurisdiction.[40] More broadly, one argument for party autonomy might be that if, in at least some circumstances, parties can manipulate objective factors such that they are in effect choosing the forum or governing law for their disputes, the law should permit them to do so directly rather than requiring such choices to be made indirectly. As examined in Section 2.2, this argument influenced the historical emergence of party autonomy – if parties could determine the governing law by choosing the place of performance of their contractual obligations, it could readily be argued that they should simply be able to choose the law directly. On the other hand, this may equally suggest that some constraints on party autonomy should apply where the parties are 'engineering' an objective connection for the purposes of evading the law that would otherwise be applicable – these

---

[39] But see e.g. C-106/95 *MSG* v. *Les Gravieres Rhenanes* [1997] ECR I-911.
[40] French Civil Code, Art.111.

are discussed further in Chapter 9. Peter Nygh, by contrast, argued that party autonomy in choice of law should be accepted because it would be hopeless to try to stop the parties from effecting such a choice indirectly through their selection of objective connecting factors.[41] There is, however, something of the tail wagging the dog about this argument. Party autonomy as a general matter is not necessarily required by the fact that some parties can adapt their behaviour to the law to ensure desired results. Adopting party autonomy might however be justified if there were some unfair advantage that those parties were gaining compared with other parties. A multinational company with offices in many jurisdictions might, for example, have more freedom to determine where goods it purchases are delivered, because they could potentially be delivered to any one of its offices. This could offer some support for a private international law rule that extended this freedom to all parties through party autonomy, for the sake of equality of arms in cross-border transacting. This is, however, not the most persuasive of justifications for party autonomy – a subject this book addresses in greater detail in Section 2.3. Although the two phenomena are related, the possibility for the parties to indirectly affect the forum or law through selection of an objective connecting factor should thus be distinguished from the recognition of direct party choices through an exercise of party autonomy.

1.3.2   Party Autonomy and Submission to a Forum

In the context of jurisdiction, a further distinction should be drawn between the exercise of party autonomy through a choice of court agreement and submission to a forum. Once again, it should be emphasised that these doctrines are not unrelated. A choice of court agreement may be viewed as accepting a forum in advance, where submission involves accepting the forum after the proceedings have been commenced. In some cases, a choice of court clause will be expressed as an agreement to submit, or will include, in addition to specifying the chosen forum, a promise to submit to the jurisdiction of the court if it is seised. Despite the use of the language of submission, such clauses should be viewed as choice of court

---

[41] Nygh (1999), p.2 ("No State can hope effectively to control international contracts … Even if parties were denied any freedom to choose the applicable law, they could not be denied the freedom to 'localise' their contract by choosing such connecting factors as the place of contracting, the place of performance, of payment and the currency of the contract. Any attempt therefore to restrict the autonomy of the parties beyond internationally accepted parameters would be worthy of King Canute.").

agreements, and not as themselves constituting submission. However, although submission issues arise at a different point in time (after proceedings have been commenced), submission might be viewed as a sort of quasi-contractual process, where a claimant in commencing proceedings in a particular forum 'offers' for the dispute to be settled in that forum, an offer that the defendant 'accepts' by submitting to the forum, giving rise to an agreement as to forum. There is no doubt that submission raises many of the same issues that are raised by party autonomy, such as questions about whether and to what extent the parties can confer jurisdiction on a court that would otherwise not appear to have regulatory power, and that the answer to these questions may also be closely related. These connections may be illustrated by the fact that the exclusive subject-matter rules on jurisdiction under Article 24 of the Brussels I Regulation provide limitations on the power of the parties to submit to another forum (under Article 26) as well as their power to agree on another forum through a choice of court agreement (under Article 25), as discussed in Section 5.4.

Submission will, however, not be addressed significantly in this book. One reason for this is simply space limitations. Another more substantive reason is that submission raises distinct concerns, which arguably suggest that different considerations are at play in evaluating the rules that should apply. Rules on submission are, for example, partly motivated by more procedural concerns – they are at least in part designed to ensure that challenges to the jurisdiction of a court must be made at the commencement of proceedings. There are two reasons why such an objective might be supported. First, *efficiency* – it is wasteful if a court starts hearing proceedings on the merits, and then later determines that it should not have done so. Second, *fairness* – a party should not be able to argue on the merits but then dispute jurisdiction if it appears their case is not going as well as they had hoped. Thus, a party who appears or presents arguments on the merits is considered to have submitted to the jurisdiction of the court. Even if this may in some cases be viewed as a kind of implied agreement to accept the court's jurisdiction, there is something fictional about adopting such an analysis. While the defendant may through their conduct be considered to have accepted the court's jurisdiction, this does not involve an inquiry into whether they have genuinely consented or otherwise to the power of the court – an express statement that they do not intend to submit may not defeat an argument that they have in fact submitted through their conduct. These points are contestable and worthy of further discussion, but to discuss them any further here would somewhat defeat the purpose of this section, which is primarily to note that they are excluded from consideration in this book.

1.3.3 Party Autonomy and a Unilateral Undertaking to Submit to a Forum

A further related exclusion from the scope of this book is the effect of a unilateral undertaking to submit to a court. A context in which this might regularly occur is where proceedings are commenced before the courts of a common law jurisdiction, and those courts are considering whether to exercise jurisdiction pursuant to the related doctrines of *forum conveniens* or *forum non conveniens*, examined in Section 3.4. One important factor that is taken into account in this consideration is whether there is an available alternative forum that could hear the case, which includes the question of whether an alternative forum would have a basis of jurisdiction. In some cases, the defendant seeking to persuade the court not to exercise jurisdiction may voluntarily agree to submit to the alternative forum, as a means of ensuring that it will have jurisdiction. This is not a choice of court agreement, nor does it on its own establish such submission. It is an undertaking to one court to submit to proceedings in a foreign court. It does not on its own provide a basis of jurisdiction for the foreign court, and as such should be considered distinctive from either a jurisdiction agreement or submission to that court. Should the party making the undertaking ultimately refuse to accept the jurisdiction of the foreign court, the court initially seised is likely to hear the case and may impose additional penalties, particularly in relation to costs. Even if an injunction is ordered requiring the party to submit to the foreign forum, in accordance with the undertaking, this will still not establish the jurisdiction of the foreign court, and any penalty for non-compliance with the injunction will be a matter for the court first seised. As this type of undertaking does not itself provide a basis of jurisdiction, it should clearly be distinguished from an exercise of party autonomy (or indeed submission to a forum), and it will not be considered further in this book.

1.3.4 Party Expectations as a Justification for an Objective Choice of Law Rule

Party autonomy is concerned with the agreed wishes of the parties, as expressed in a contractual clause. It is not concerned with the presumed wishes or the expectations of the parties. Choice of law rules in particular are sometimes justified on the basis that they meet those supposed expectations. It may be argued, for example, that parties to a tort would normally expect that the law which would govern the proceedings would be the law of the place of the tort (the *lex loci delicti*), because of the usual expectation that territorial law governs standards of behaviour. Of course, as examined in Section 8.3, the law of the place of the tort is not applied invariably – choice of law rules sometimes look to the law common to the parties, or another more closely connected law – but the *lex loci* is typically the basic choice of law rule. In any case, although this rule may be justified by reference to party expectations, it is clearly distinctive from an exercise of party autonomy. The applicable law is not determined by the subjective agreement of the parties, but instead the presumed wishes or expectations of the parties are relied on to support an objective choice of law rule.

This is not to say, however, that the two are unconnected, a point explored further in Chapter 2. If choice of law rules were motivated solely by the desire to give effect to the expectations of the parties, and there is evidence in the form of a choice of law clause that the parties had particular expectations, that might appear to support giving effect to their agreement – adopting a choice of law rule that permits party autonomy. There is, however, doubt as to whether this link is as strong as it may appear. First, it is not the case that objective choice of law rules are motivated solely by the desire to give effect to the expectations of the parties, although this is sometimes considered an important factor. Choice of law rules are also shaped by broader principles of territoriality and other connecting links, long recognised in both public and private international law as justifying the exercise of authority by a state. Second, party expectations are shaped by the law, as much as the contrary.[42] If choice of law rules clearly provided that, for example, the law of the place of contracting applied, without any exception for party autonomy or otherwise, the expectations of the parties would certainly be that this law would govern, and for well-informed parties this expectation would still apply even if they had a choice of law clause in their contract in favour of a different system of law, because they would rightly expect that the clause would be ineffective. References to the expectations of the parties as a justification for a particular objective choice of law rule are thus importantly distinct from party autonomy. They are not truly a rule based on the subjective agreement between the actual parties, but rather a justification for an objective choice of law rule that is based on the claim that, if there were no choice of law rules, this is the law that parties would expect to be applied. They are thus once again importantly distinct from the exercise of party autonomy, and will not be examined further in this book, except in relation to the influence played by party expectations in the historical development of party autonomy examined in Chapter 2.

---

[42] See Mills (2009a), p.8ff; Lehmann (2008), p.392.

1.3.5   *Party Autonomy and Contractual Autonomy*

This book is about party autonomy in private international law, not party autonomy in contract law. The latter governs questions that arise within a legal order, even for purely domestic contracts, and concerns the question of what limits there are to the freedom of contract of the parties.[43] The former, the subject of this book, is concerned with prior or higher level questions, including which system of private law applies to the legal relations between the parties. The scope of contractual party autonomy is determined by the applicable law. Party autonomy in the context of choice of law may be part of determining that applicable law, and thus which rules of freedom of contract apply. It is a freedom to choose between different freedoms – the diverse degrees of contractual autonomy available in different national systems of private law. Contractual party autonomy is limited by the public policy or mandatory rules of a national system of contract law; private international law party autonomy is limited by the public policy or mandatory rules of private international law. The claim that "As part of [their] freedom to determine the terms and conditions of their contract, the parties also have the freedom to choose the applicable law"[44] misleadingly conflates these two forms of autonomy.[45] The parties' freedom of contract is determined by a system of national law. To say that their choice of law is part of that freedom of contract is to ignore the particular function of private international law as a prior set of 'secondary rules',[46] unless the bolder (and equally problematic) claim is made that there is "a general principle of freedom of contract which allows the parties to choose the applicable legal system and which precedes national law".[47] This is not to deny that a choice of law agreement or choice of court agreement is or can be analysed as a contract (although as discussed in Chapters 3 and 7, the point is not entirely without contention), and that as a contract it is bound by a system of contract law. It is rather to emphasise that the choice involved in a choice of law or choice of court agreement is distinctive from the normal choices of substantive terms involved in contract law, which take place within the scope of contractual party

---

[43] For a comparative study see Bermann (2005).
[44] Nygh (1995), p.297; see similarly Nygh (1999), p.8.
[45] Note also similarly Symeonides (2016), p.361 ("The principle of party autonomy is simply the 'external' side of a domestic law principle, usually referred to as 'freedom of contract'"); Keyes (2009), p.182 ("The fundamental justification [for party autonomy in private international law] is that the parties' freedom to contract should be respected by enforcing their agreements"); Briggs (2008), p.12; Zhang (2006a), p.552.
[46] Mills (2009a), p.19ff.
[47] Lehmann (2008), p.390.

autonomy.[48] As will be seen throughout this book, questions regarding the exercise of party autonomy in choice of forum and choice of law are regulated both by particular rules of private international law as well as by general rules of contract law provided by the governing law for the agreements through which the parties have exercised their autonomy.

This is once again not to say that there is no influence between the doctrine of contractual party autonomy and private international law party autonomy – such an influence can certainly be detected in the historical and theoretical origins of private international law party autonomy, as examined in Chapter 2. If parties are able to exercise a very wide degree of contractual party autonomy, it becomes more difficult to argue that they should be precluded from choosing a foreign legal order to govern their legal relations. The greater the degree of contractual autonomy, the more the function of contract law may be considered to be merely providing default rules to govern the relations between the parties. If this is the function of contract law, then choosing a foreign legal order to govern those relations may be viewed as merely a more efficient means of opting out of those default rules in favour of a different set of default rules. Providing default rules is not, however, the sole function of contract law – rules of contract law can limit the exercise of contractual autonomy, as well as support it, through mandatory provisions of contract law and rules of public policy.[49] Such rules are, however, importantly different from the private international law concepts of mandatory rules and public policy, as they apply as part of a system of private law, delimiting the scope of its contractual autonomy, not as an overriding application of the law of the forum. As will be examined in Chapter 9, the equivalent private international law concepts operate as constraints on the exercise of party autonomy in choice of law, not on the exercise of contractual autonomy. There are thus important differences between the two doctrines – party autonomy operating between legal orders, and contractual autonomy operating within a legal order. This distinction is important for the purposes of analysis of the

---

[48] See Hook (2016) for a sophisticated exploration of the consequences of this for choice of law agreements, viewing them as subject to a "framework that fuses principles of choice of law and contract" (p.12). The idea that these sources of law are 'fused' is, however, arguably an unnecessary complication – it is perhaps simpler just to accept that choice of law agreements (like choice of court agreements, at least in some legal systems) are both subject to rules of private international law (to determine their effectiveness) and rules of contract law (to determine their validity and interpretation). This important distinction is discussed further in later chapters.

[49] See generally Bermann (2005); Nygh (1999), p.28ff; Jaffey (1984), p.538ff.

private international law doctrine, even if it has not always been clearly recognised in practice, and for this reason contractual autonomy is largely excluded from consideration in this book except by way of emphasising its distinctiveness.

1.3.6   *Party Autonomy and the Incorporation by Reference of Rules of Law*

A final and closely related distinction should be made between party autonomy and the practice of incorporating by reference terms that are taken from a particular legal system. For example, it is possible (although relatively unusual) for parties to a contract to include a provision that states that the contract includes a set of rules taken from national law or from a non-state law codification – those rules are incorporated by reference as terms of the contract. A clause of this type is merely a shorthand way of drafting the contract, equivalent in legal effect to cutting and pasting the text of those rules into the pages of the contract. On its own, such a provision may determine the *content* of the contract – it is an exercise of contractual autonomy – but not the law that governs the contract. It is thus not an exercise of party autonomy, at least not in the private international law sense of the term. As explained in the comments to the Second Restatement of Conflict of Laws in the United States:

> The parties, generally speaking, have power to determine the terms of their contractual engagements. They may spell out these terms in the contract. In the alternative, they may incorporate into the contract by reference extrinsic material which may, among other things, be the provisions of some foreign law. In such instances, the forum will apply the applicable provisions of the law of the designated state in order to effectuate the intentions of the parties. So much has never been doubted.[50]

It is not entirely clear whether this comment purports to be an explanation of the general rule on party autonomy in the Second Restatement, or an aside about the effectiveness of incorporation by reference, or perhaps a slightly confused conflation of the two.[51] The term 'generally speaking' in this analysis is another point of obscurity – masking the fact that the contractual autonomy of the parties is not unlimited, and its extent is in itself a legal question. Whether the inclusion of certain terms in the contract is

---

[50] Section 187, comment (c).
[51] See e.g. Lehmann (2008), p.391.

permissible or not will depend on the law that governs the contract, which may or may not be the same as the law from which the terms incorporated by reference are sourced.

This is, once again, not to deny that these concepts are related, nor to claim that they are always clearly distinguished in practice – a point amply demonstrated in later chapters. For example, parties who incorporate by reference terms from a particular legal order may well have in mind that those terms will be interpreted and applied consistently with the practice in that order. The inclusion of statutory provisions as part of a contract is thus a strong indicator of a possible implied choice of law agreement, and it is treated as such by the courts (as examined further in Section 7.2). But the link between the two is evidentiary rather than logical – the incorporation by reference of statutory terms from a national (or non-state) legal order does not necessarily imply a choice of that system of law to govern the contract, and there is nothing incoherent about an express choice of a different law, or the courts finding that no implied choice can be identified in the circumstances.

An illustration of the confusion between these concepts in practice may be taken from an old US Supreme Court decision, *Pritchard* v. *Norton* (1882).[52] The Court was concerned with the validity of an appeal bond that had been entered into in New York, relating to litigation in Louisiana. In analysing the choice of law question, the Court noted that:

> in case of contract, the foreign law may, by the act and will of the parties, have become part of their agreement, and in enforcing this, the law of the forum may find it necessary to give effect to a foreign law which, without such adoption, would have no force beyond its own territory.[53]

Thus far, this appears to be recognition of an exercise of contractual autonomy through incorporation by reference. Terms of foreign law have become part of the agreement between the parties, and so must be given effect in order to enforce the agreement. The court, however, went on to argue that:

> This, upon the principle of comity for the purpose of promoting and facilitating international intercourse and within limits fixed by its own public policy, a civilized state is accustomed and considers itself bound to do, but, in doing so, nevertheless adheres to its own system of formal judicial procedure and remedies. And thus the distinction is at once established between the law of the contract, which may be foreign, and the law of the procedure and remedy, which must be domestic and local.

---

[52] 106 US 124 (1882).
[53] At 129.

This appears more to analyse the situation as an example of private international law party autonomy – foreign law is recognised as a matter of comity, not simply as a matter of enforcing the contract. As examined further in Section 2.2, this blurring between the concepts of contractual autonomy and party autonomy is an important part of the history of the emergence of party autonomy in private international law.

1.4   Five Questions of Consistency

Taking account of the distinctions and exclusions set out above, this book examines the full range of aspects of party autonomy in private international law: both its historical and theoretical foundations (the focus of Chapter 2) and their doctrinal implementation; across both choice of forum (the focus of Chapters 3–6) and choice of law (the focus of Chapters 7–10); including state and non-state forms of law and dispute-resolution (both courts and arbitral tribunals, and state and non-state law); and dealing with contractual and non-contractual disputes. The theoretical and doctrinal aspects of this book are intended to inform each other – the theoretical foundations are partly identified through analysis of practice, but also inform critical analysis of particular rules that have been adopted in different legal systems. Practice may not always be consistent with theory, and where this is the case this should generate a productive tension, but whether it is theory or practice or both that adjusts as a result may always be contested (the theory may be criticised as unrealistic, or the practice as unprincipled). Through this analysis, the book aims to identify and analyse the key principles that justify and define the limits of party autonomy in private international law, in both theory and practice. The wide focus of the book allows it to address a fundamental question: whether party autonomy is or should be consistent across this range of different contexts – choice of forum and choice of law, contractual and non-contractual relationships, and state and non-state forums and laws. To put this in another way, one theme of the book is the question whether there really is (or should be) one doctrine of party autonomy, or whether it is a bundle of different (even if related) rules; whether the different rules of party autonomy should aspire to coherence, or rather specialised adaptation to their particular contexts.

To set out these considerations clearly up front, this book can be viewed as concerned (among other things) with five questions of consistency. (These are examined again as part of the conclusions of this book in Chapter 11.) In most contexts, there is both an analytical or descriptive question – is the law consistent – and a normative or theoretical question – whether it should be.

1.4.1   Consistency between Party Autonomy in
Choice of Forum and Choice of Law

Choice of forum and applicable law may be made independently, or in conjunction. They are not logically connected, although they are frequently connected in a more practical sense. If parties choose a national court and a national law, typically they will choose the same for both, as this is likely to enhance the efficiency and predictability of any dispute resolution. If the parties choose both a forum and its law to govern their legal disputes, it might be expected that both choices would be effective in the same circumstances and to the same extent, so that the chosen forum will always apply its own law, and conversely, that only the courts whose law is chosen will have jurisdiction. The first question of consistency that this book examines is to ask whether this is indeed achieved in practice, and whether it should be.

1.4.2   Consistency between Party Autonomy in
Contract and in Other Areas of Law

Party autonomy is almost always exercised as a term of a contract – a choice of court or choice of law clause – and naturally enough, it has emerged primarily through the private international law of contracts. In recent years, however, as noted already above and explored particularly in Chapters 4 and 8, party autonomy has increasingly been influential in other areas of private international law, such as non-contractual obligations and claims in property. This invites a further question of consistency. Is the treatment of party autonomy consistent whether a claim is brought in contract, or as a tort or proprietary claim, or in some other form? Is consistency a virtue here, so that the outcome does not depend on the way the cause of action is framed, or should the effectiveness of a party choice of forum or law vary in different substantive legal contexts, to reflect the different policy considerations of those contexts?

1.4.3   Consistency between the Choice of Non-State
Forums or Law and the Choice of State Forums or Law

Two of the most significant developments in party autonomy are the extension of choice of forum beyond state courts, and the much-debated potential extension of choice of law beyond state law. The former development concerns arbitration (the subject of Chapter 6) – the extent to which parties can opt out of national courts in favour of private dispute resolution mechanisms. The latter (the subject of Chapter 10) has long been considered a potential consequence of this first development – that an arbitral tribunal, as a private dispute resolution mechanism, is not beholden to any national law but should rather resolve the dispute in accordance with the parties' contractual agreement, which may direct the tribunal to apply non-state law. In more recent years, it has also been queried whether a choice of non-state law should be accepted by national courts. This then invites a third question of consistency – whether a choice of a non-state forum or law is or should be treated consistently with a choice of a state court or law. Both choice of arbitration and non-state law raise fundamental questions about the scope of party autonomy. They raise the possibility that private parties might not only choose between different national courts or legal systems, but might also choose privately constituted alternatives – private parties are potentially given the power not just of choice, but of creating the object of their choice.

1.4.4   Consistency between Party Autonomy in Practice and Party Autonomy in Theory

In a broader sense, as already noted above, this book is concerned with the question of whether theory and practice are consistent in the field of party autonomy in private international law. Unlike the other consistency questions noted above, the issue here is purely analytical rather than normative – theory and practice should of course be consistent. The scope of what is covered in theory and practice need not, however, be coextensive. Practice may raise problems and provide solutions to questions that are not addressed or at least not directly addressed in theory, and thus may lead to the greater development of theory. On the other hand, if new problems arise in practice, theory can provide a solid foundation for the development of a solution. To the extent that theory and practice are coextensive, a further question arises as to whether they correspond. Do the limits on party autonomy in practice match up with its theoretical justifications? To the extent that this is not the case, should theory or practice or both be revised?

1.4.5   Consistency between Legal Systems

A final question of consistency is whether the approaches to party autonomy in the various legal systems examined comparatively in this book (as set out in Section 1.2) are the same. As noted above, party autonomy has been presented as a universal or unifying principle in private international law – this consistency question asks whether, on closer examination, different legal systems have the same understanding of party autonomy and its limits. This is principally an analytical rather than normative question, although it undoubtedly has a normative dimension that relates to the perennial issue of whether rules of private international law should strive for international harmonisation or to be a reflection of local policies and preferences.

2

Historical and Theoretical Foundations of Party Autonomy

2.1 Introduction

This chapter considers two related but distinct foundational questions concerning party autonomy in private international law. The first is the question of the *historical* foundations of party autonomy (Section 2.2). Where, when and how did party autonomy emerge as a practice, and how did it become so widely (although not quite universally) accepted around the globe? The second is the question of the *normative* foundations of party autonomy (Section 2.3). Why (and thus in what circumstances) should choice of law or choice of forum agreements be effective? What justifications are or can be offered for giving effect to party choices of law or forum? Both questions approach what are broadly the same key issues, but from a distinct angle – why and how has party autonomy become so widely accepted?

The answers to each of these questions are critically important for the foundations of party autonomy and also for the analysis in this book. Present attitudes to party autonomy must be understood as partly the product of historical development and context – without a temporal dimension, legal analysis can only provide a snapshot of the law at a moment in time, with no appreciation of its context or dynamics, the trends or momentum in the development of the law. A second major reason to examine the history and theory of party autonomy is the fourth 'question of consistency' discussed in Section 1.4.4 – the question of whether the rules giving effect to party autonomy are consistent with its theoretical foundations. Any critical examination of the rules of party autonomy in any particular legal system requires a conception of what party autonomy is and ought to be aiming to achieve, and (as developed in Section 2.4) what limits should be imposed on party choices.

2.2   Historical Foundations of Party Autonomy

The history of party autonomy in private international law is a puzzling combination of two features, each of which is itself puzzling. On the one hand, the idea of party autonomy has a long history, and recurs in a range of contexts throughout that history. It is an idea whose longevity demonstrates its enduring power and appeal, at least in the scholarship of those advocating its adoption. This is, however, despite the fact that party autonomy does not obviously seem consistent with broader prevailing approaches or theories in private international law throughout that history, and often during that history the justifications offered for party autonomy have been at best vague and uncertain. On the other hand, party autonomy is also very much a modern development, which in the twentieth century went from a highly contested and controversial proposition to perhaps the most universally accepted aspect of private international law (although perhaps that also says as much about the uncertain foundations of private international law generally as it does about party autonomy). This is, however, again despite the fact that there has not obviously been any particular change in private international law theories or approaches that would justify or support this widespread acceptance, nor has a particularly clear new justification been offered for party autonomy in this period. Nevertheless, as Horatia Muir Watt has pointed out, party autonomy has become so accepted – "its centrality in the European tradition is so taken for granted" – that "astonishingly little attention has been paid to the function with which it is henceforth invested – or rather, the function being implicitly accepted, the steps which led there – within a vastly changed economic and political environment".[1]

This section first considers the historical origins of party autonomy in matters of choice of forum, before turning to the historical origins of party autonomy in choice of law. As discussed in Section 1.2, the comparative analysis in this book focuses on four key sources – international codifications, EU law, the common law, and US law. International codifications and EU law are relatively modern developments – for the historical analysis of both choice of forum and choice of law, the primary focus is thus on the evolution of the common law in England and its subsequent or parallel adaptation in the United States, while drawing also on the broader European legal traditions that have influenced their development and the development of EU and international private international

---

[1] Muir Watt (2010), p.253.

law codifications. This is evidently not a complete analysis of the history of party autonomy across all legal systems, which would require at least an entire book of its own. It is also primarily a doctrinal history rather than one focused on situating the rise of party autonomy within broader economic and social developments (although some points of particular significance are noted), which would require yet another book. The purpose of this section is primarily to highlight the key arguments and issues that have been significant in the emergence of party autonomy in legal doctrine, by way of providing background for the theoretical and comparative analysis carried out in this book.

2.2.1   Historical Origins of Party Autonomy in Choice of Forum

To situate party autonomy in choice of forum in its historical context, it is necessary to offer a basic account of the general approach to jurisdiction. This limited account purports only to be reflective of the key principles – perhaps most significantly, it highlights that party autonomy is (at least historically speaking) an exceptional basis of jurisdiction because it is not based on an objective factual connection between the parties or their dispute and a territorial legal order.

Under the Roman law tradition, three distinct types of jurisdiction over civil disputes – all still broadly recognised under modern law – were long established. First, the general rule that a plaintiff might bring any suit in the place of domicile of the defendant.[2] A variation of this rule in some legal systems gives jurisdiction to the place of nationality of the defendant.[3] Second, proceedings can be brought in the place where a contract was made or to be performed, or in the place where the act (including a tortious or delictual act) giving rise to the claim was done, at least in certain circumstances.[4] Third, proceedings concerning title to property can be brought 'in rem' in the place where the relevant property is located.[5] In some legal systems, such as Germany, this basis of jurisdiction has been broadened to permit proceedings that do not directly concern title to the property, except by way of a possible remedy to satisfy the claim at hand – thus jurisdiction can be based on the mere presence and attachment of property of the defendant in the territory.[6]

[2] See e.g. Story (1834), s.532.
[3] See e.g. French Civil Code, Art.15.
[4] See e.g. Story (1834), s.536.
[5] See e.g. Story (1834), s.532.
[6] See e.g. Story (1834), s.549.

In the common law tradition, by contrast, initially all proceedings could only be brought in the courts of the location of the relevant acts or events. This was because in civil proceedings (as in criminal proceedings) judgments were rendered by a jury who were selected from the local area, and might be witnesses to the events, know one or both parties, or make their own inquiries as to the facts. This was an obstacle to the English courts ever hearing cases involving foreign events, as no local jury could be impanelled, but it became accepted that the requirement for a local jury could be surmounted by a legal fiction (the pleading and acceptance that the events, although foreign, had taken place in an English county).[7] The impracticality and inconvenience of the traditional rule, together with the evolution of the idea of an independent jury assisted by separate witnesses, lead to the gradual abandonment of the idea that a local jury would be necessary in most cases. The requirements for a local jury were reduced, and statutory reforms[8] provided that a judgment would not be invalid if jurors were not drawn from the required location. This left open, however, the question of where proceedings could be commenced. A further distinction evolved between actions in which there was a particular local connection that required the empanelling of a local jury, and other actions that did not. The former were known as real or local actions, and the latter as personal or transitory actions.[9] If a claim was brought for title to immovable property, for example, this was a local action that could only be brought in the location of the relevant property – thus, if the dispute concerned title to foreign immovable property, no action could be brought. This was relied on as the basis for the *Mozambique* doctrine in the common law,[10] which is further reflected in modern rules of exclusive jurisdiction that constrain party autonomy, as discussed in Section 5.4. Transitory or personal actions, such as claims for breach of contract or non-property torts,

---

[7] *Mostyn* v. *Fabrigas* (1774) 98 ER 1021, 1030 ("So all actions of a transitory nature that arise abroad may be laid as happening in an English county ... the law has in that case invented a fiction; and has said, the party shall first set out the description truly, and then give a venue only for form, and for the sake of trial, by a videlicet, in the county of Middlesex, or any other county. But no Judge ever thought that when the declaration said in Fort St. George, viz. in Cheapside, that the plaintiff meant it was in Cheapside. It is a fiction of form"). See further discussion in *British South Africa Co* v. *Companhia de Mozambique* [1893] AC 602, 618. English courts have thereby accepted, for example, that Hamburg (*Ward's Case* (1625) 82 ER 245) is in London, which may help or complicate matters post-Brexit.

[8] Stat 16 & 17 Charles II c 8 (1664). See also 4 & 5 Anne c 3 (1705).

[9] See generally e.g. Wicker (1925); Kuhn (1918).

[10] *British South Africa Co* v. *Companhia de Mozambique* [1893] AC 602, 619ff.

could be brought in any court possessing jurisdiction over the defendant.[11] The focus in the general law of jurisdiction thus (gradually) shifted from the question of the location of the events to the location of the defendant. The general foundation of jurisdiction became the question of whether the courts could command the defendant to appear before the court, which could only be done if the defendant was present in the territory (and perhaps also for defendants who were resident but not present), but did not require that the relevant events had taken place in the territory.

These traditional approaches to jurisdiction under both Roman law and common law have a key feature in common – each relies on a territorial or personal connection to justify a state exercising regulatory authority over a defendant or a dispute. They view jurisdiction as a matter of state power (exercisable at the discretion of each state), and thus do not allow any role for individual autonomy. In England in the eighteenth and nineteenth centuries, through landmark decisions such as *Kill* v. *Hollister* (1746),[12] *Gienar* v. *Meyer* (1796)[13] (discussed further below) and *Scott* v. *Avery* (1856),[14] it thus became established that individuals could not confer or take away the jurisdiction of a court, whether through agreements on jurisdiction or arbitration. In a domestic sense, this reflected the idea that national court jurisdiction was an exercise of public authority. This meant that rules of national court jurisdiction for international cases were also conceived as connected with principles of 'jurisdiction' in the broader public international law sense, under which a state can only exercise regulatory authority where it has such a territorial or personal connection to justify the exercise of its public power.[15]

Over time, this sense of a close connection between private international law jurisdiction and questions of public authority (as well as public international sovereignty) became eroded,[16] opening the space for the interests of private parties to play a greater role. Perhaps the earliest recognition of this in the common law may be found in the decision of *Gienar* v. *Meyer* (1796),[17] in the context of maritime law. In this case the court affirmed that

---

[11] See e.g. Story (1834), s.554; *Mostyn* v. *Fabrigas* (1774) 98 ER 1021, 1029–30.

[12] (1746) 95 ER 532. See further generally e.g. Lorenzen (1934).

[13] (1796) 126 ER 728, 730 ("no persons in this country can by an agreement between themselves exclude themselves from the jurisdiction of the King's courts").

[14] (1856) 10 ER 1121 (permitting, however, the parties to make completion of arbitration a condition precedent to litigation); see further Tweeddale and Tweeddale (2011); see also discussion in Section 6.4.2.

[15] See further Mills (2014).

[16] Although it has re-emerged in many federal systems – see Mills (2009a), Chapter 4.

[17] (1796) 126 ER 728.

parties could not oust the jurisdiction of the courts by agreement,[18] but nevertheless determined that English proceedings would be stayed in light of an agreement entered into between the master and seamen of a ship, all Dutch, that the seamen would only bring suit in the Netherlands. This was because the agreement was understood (whether or not correctly) to be effective under Dutch law, and it was determined to be "more reasonable to send the parties to their own country, there to pursue their remedy".[19] This decision came at least very close to party autonomy, and was followed in other cases on similar facts,[20] but it does not appear in the short term to have influenced the law outside the maritime context (which was considered to require a particular approach because of the interests of international commerce). It also concerned a decision not to exercise jurisdiction, rather than an agreement serving as a basis of jurisdiction. The decision was thus compatible with the traditional idea that jurisdiction is a matter of sovereign discretion, but with the novelty that a private agreement was considered to help justify the exercise of discretion not to hear the claim.

A further phase of the erosion of the 'public power' perspective on jurisdiction emerged through the acceptance that proceedings could be brought against "foreigners ... who have submitted to the jurisdiction, wherever the law allows its exercise".[21] This basis of jurisdiction, which (as discussed in Section 1.3.2) should be carefully distinguished from party autonomy, became firmly established in the nineteenth century.[22] There are two main reasons for the emergence of jurisdiction based on submission. The first is that territorial jurisdiction over foreign nationals was often described as justifiable because although foreign nationals were not 'subjects' of the local sovereign, they had similarly and implicitly 'subjected' themselves to the authority of the sovereign in choosing to reside in (or in some cases even merely enter into) the territory.[23] If territorial jurisdiction was thus based on a theory of implied submission, it would potentially follow that express submission should also provide a basis of jurisdiction. The second is that this change reflected a shift in focus in the principles of private international law jurisdiction – away from concerns of international law and inter-state power, and towards concerns of fairness to individual defendants. Jurisdiction based on genuine submission

---

[18] See note 13.
[19] At 731.
[20] See e.g. *Johnson* v. *Machielsne* (1811) 170 ER 1300.
[21] Story (1834), s.552.
[22] See generally Dickinson (2017a).
[23] See e.g. Story (1834), s.541.

by a defendant would always satisfy considerations of fairness to that defendant – and such a basis of jurisdiction thus became increasingly widely accepted as considerations of state interest were sidelined.

In the early nineteenth century, associated with the development of this doctrine, there are also suggestions of what would become party autonomy in choice of forum. In his influential 1849 treatise Savigny argued, for example, that jurisdiction could be exercised by the "forum of the obligation", and that this "depends on the voluntary submission of the parties, which, however, is generally indicated, not in any express, but in a tacit declaration of will, and is thus always excluded by an express declaration to the contrary".[24] While this may appear (and has been claimed) to constitute recognition of party autonomy, the true position is perhaps less clear. Savigny goes on to argue, for instance, that the courts of the place of performance of a contractual obligation should have jurisdiction, on the basis that "the whole expectation of the parties is directed [to this place]; and it is therefore part of the essence of the obligation that the place of fulfilment is conceived as the seat of the obligation, that the special forum of the obligation is fixed at this place by voluntary submission".[25] Under this formulation, it appears that the 'voluntary submission' which is attributed to the parties is merely their act of contracting – by choosing to enter into a contract to be performed in a particular place, the parties are in a sense choosing the 'seat' (and thus for Savigny the forum) for their legal obligations. As discussed in Section 1.3.1, this falls short, however, of party autonomy in its modern understanding and the sense in which it is used in this book.

Through the course of the late nineteenth century, the interests of private parties received increased recognition in the law of jurisdiction. This was particularly evident in decisions to decline jurisdiction where a foreign court or arbitral tribunal had been agreed on by the parties, which broadened beyond the maritime context discussed above. Curiously, in England these developments did not originate in private international law – in section XI of the Common Law Procedure Act 1854, courts were permitted to stay proceedings where the parties had entered into a binding arbitration agreement. This was not targeted at cross-border disputes, but rather at accepting arbitration as a means of alternative dispute resolution, although the Act applied whether or not the arbitration was to be conducted in England. In *Law* v. *Garrett* (1878),[26] it was remarkably held that

---

[24] Savigny (1849), p.152.
[25] Savigny (1849), p.153.
[26] (1878) LR 8 Ch D 26 (CA).

the reference to 'arbitration' agreements in the Act should also be understood to encompass exclusive jurisdiction agreements in favour of foreign
courts.[27] It was not made *obligatory* to stay proceedings commenced contrary to such an agreement – the private agreement still could not oust the
jurisdiction of the courts[28] – but the court was empowered to do so, and
increasingly (but not invariably)[29] viewed it as appropriate to enforce the
agreement between the parties (by exercising the discretion not to exercise
jurisdiction) in the absence of exceptional circumstances.[30]

At the end of the nineteenth century, however, under the common law
the mere agreement of the parties was still considered generally to be
insufficient to *establish* the jurisdiction of the courts. In *The British Wagon
Company* v. *Gray* (1896),[31] for example, the parties' contract provided that
the defendant, a Scottish resident, "hereby submits to the jurisdiction of the
High Court of Justice in England",[32] but the defendant later contested the
jurisdiction of the English courts. The court approached this as a question
of the limits of its powers under the applicable rules (Order XI of the Rules
of the Supreme Court 1883), finding that "The Court is forbidden to exercise the jurisdiction which it is now asked to exercise, and cannot regard
the contract of the parties as to the extent of its jurisdiction."[33] The principal difficulty facing the court here was that the English common law had
historically required the presence of the person of the defendant before

[27] This interpretation continued under the equivalent provision (s.4) of the *Arbitration Act
1889* – see e.g. *Austrian Lloyd Steamship Company* v. *Gresham Life Assurance Society,
Limited* [1903] 1 KB 249 (staying proceedings on the basis of an exclusive jurisdiction
agreement in favour of the courts of Budapest).

[28] See e.g. *Hoerler* v. *Hanover Caoutchouc Gutta Percha and Telegraph Works* (1893) 10 TLR
103 (giving permission to commence proceedings despite a foreign jurisdiction agreement,
although on the facts also determining that the agreement was non-exclusive); *The Cap
Blanco* [1913] P 130, 136 ("Although, therefore, this Court is invested with jurisdiction,
I order that the proceedings in the action be stayed, in order that the parties may litigate in
Germany, as they have agreed to do.").

[29] See e.g. *The Fehmarn* [1957] 2 Lloyd's Rep 551.

[30] See e.g. *Kirchner & Co* v. *Gruban* [1909] 1 Ch 413, 418 ("prima facie it is an agreement by
which the parties are bound and upon which the Court must act, unless for some good
cause there is reason to think that the matter ought to be determined otherwise than by
the tribunal to which the parties have deliberately agreed to submit their differences."); *The
Cap Blanco* [1913] P 130, 136 ("In dealing with commercial documents of this kind, effect
must be given, if the terms of the contract permit it, to the obvious intention and agreement
of the parties. I think the parties clearly agreed that disputes under the contract should be
dealt with by the German tribunal, and it is right to hold the plaintiffs to their part of the
agreement.").

[31] [1896] 1 QB 35 (CA).

[32] At 35.

[33] At 37.

proceedings could be commenced (on the basis that civil proceedings had historically involved seizure of the person of the defendant, or that the summons was a sovereign command which could only be exercised within the territory of the state).[34] This limitation had gradually been overcome, including through statutory reform (sections XVIII–XIX of the Common Law Procedure Act 1852, Order XI of the Supreme Court of Judicature Act 1875, and Order XI of the Rules of the Supreme Court 1883[35]), but the starting point remained that jurisdiction over a person outside the territory was prohibited unless expressly permitted, and in 1896 the Order made no provision for defendants who had contractually agreed to accept the jurisdiction of the court.

This approach seems implicitly to view jurisdiction as a matter of state power, leaving little room for party autonomy. This may be to overstate the matter, however. It had, for example, been accepted that presence in the territory could be established through contractual nomination of a local agent to accept service.[36] In addition, submission by the defendant (to the court, and thus to the sovereign) was during this period considered enough to establish jurisdiction in English courts, even in response to a writ issued in excess of the court's authority,[37] and a similar position had long been recognised in US courts. One justification offered for this was that "the appearance of the defendant ... waived all objection to the irregularity of the return [of the writ]".[38] This approach suggested a partial shift in focus in principle towards fairness to the defendant, rather than the powers of courts or states. Another aspect of this shift in the English

---

[34] See generally Dickinson (2017a).

[35] See generally Piggott (1892).

[36] *Tharsis Ltd* v. *La Société des Métaux* (1889) 58 LJ (QB) 435 (also contractually agreeing on a deemed 'domicile' in the territory for jurisdictional purposes); see also *Montgomery, Jones and Co* v. *Liebenthal and Co* [1898] 1 QB 487.

[37] See e.g. *Edwards* v. *Warden* (1873–4) LR 9 Ch App 495; *Boyle* v. *Sacker* (1888) 39 Ch D 249; Dicey (1896), General Principle IV and Rule 42. Dicey argued (at p.224) that this encompassed party autonomy, on the basis that "This submission may take place in various ways", including where a person "has made it part of a contract that questions arising under the contract shall be decided by the Court", but this was not in fact the position at the time, as held by *The British Wagon Company* v. *Gray* [1896] 1 QB 35 (CA) (and noted by Dicey on p.225, fn.2).

[38] *Wood* v. *Lide*, 8 US 180, 181 (1807). See also *Penhallow* v. *Doan's Administrators*, 3 US 54, 87 (1795); *Pennoyer* v. *Neff*, 95 US 714, 733 (1878) – "To give such proceedings any validity, there must be a tribunal competent by its constitution – that is, by the law of its creation – to pass upon the subject matter of the suit; and if that involves merely a determination of the personal liability of the defendant, he must be brought within its jurisdiction by service of process within the State, or his voluntary appearance."; *Cooper* v. *Reynolds*, 77 US 308, 317–8 (1869); *Galpin* v. *Page*, 85 US 350, 368 (1873); *In re Moore*, 209 US 490 (1908).

courts was the recognition, in *Rousillon* v. *Rousillon* (1880),[39] that a foreign judgment obtained on the basis of not only submission but also a jurisdiction agreement would be capable of recognition.[40] But at least in *The British Wagon Company* v. *Gray* (1896) it was considered that submission before the English courts needed to take place through the appearance of the defendant before the court – that the parties could not by contract extend the jurisdictional powers of the court.[41] As noted in Section 1.3.2, this reflects the fact that submission, while similar to party autonomy, is distinct because it arises after proceedings have been commenced and is justified principally by the need to avoid abuse of the court's procedure.

Amendments to Order XI of the Rules of the Supreme Court were, however, introduced in 1920, to expand the range of circumstances in which the courts might give permission for a claimant to commence proceedings against a defendant outside the jurisdiction. Most significantly for present purposes, they provided (in Order XI, Rule 2a) that the parties to a contract may agree that the court would have jurisdiction over claims arising under the contract, either directly or through nomination of a place of service within England.[42] It was later established that such jurisdiction would ordinarily be exercised, even in the absence of connections with England.[43] Further consequences followed from the recognition of such agreements as binding, including the possibility of an anti-suit injunction to restrain foreign proceedings commenced in breach of a jurisdiction agreement,[44] and even an anti-enforcement injunction should the foreign court nevertheless award a judgment.[45]

These reforms thus completed a notable shift in focus in the law of jurisdiction in England – from historical foundations that were based

---

[39] *Rousillon* v. *Rousillon* (1880) 14 Ch D 351, 371 ("The Courts of this country consider the defendant bound ... where he has contracted to submit himself to the forum in which the judgment was obtained").

[40] See also e.g. *Feyerick* v. *Hubbard* (1902) 71 LJKB 509; *Jeannot* v. *Fuerst* (1909) 25 TLR 424; *Emanuel* v. *Symon* [1908] 1 KB 302.

[41] The decision in *Copin* v. *Adamson* (1875) 1 Ex D 17, under which an English shareholder in a French company was found to be properly subject to the jurisdiction of the French courts on the basis of a constructive domicile in the company's articles of association, may arguably be an exception.

[42] Dicey and Keith (1922), p.272ff (noting that "this rule was made to remove the inconvenience resulting from the decision in *British Wagon Co* v. *Gray*"); Dickinson (2017a).

[43] See e.g. *Unterweser Reederei GmbH* v. *Zapata Off-Shore Co* [1968] 2 Lloyd's Rep 158 (the English case which paralleled the US decision in *The Bremen* v. *Zapata Off-Shore Co.*, 407 US 1, 14 (1972), discussed below).

[44] See e.g. *The Angelic Grace* [1995] 1 Lloyd's Rep 87.

[45] *Ellerman Lines Ltd* v. *Read* [1928] 2 KB 144; see further Section 3.4.3.

exclusively on conceptions of territorial sovereignty, requiring the presence of the defendant, to flexible rules allowing for the assertion of jurisdiction against parties outside the territory in a range of circumstances, including where there is an agreement consenting to the jurisdiction of the English courts. Aside from jurisdiction agreements, the rules establishing jurisdiction over a party outside the territory still require a territorial or similar connection to justify their exercise, but this may be indirect – for example, the fact that the contract was made or breached in England. This expansion in jurisdiction was counterbalanced by the development of the doctrine of *forum conveniens* (discussed further in Section 3.4.3) under which such exercises of jurisdiction are discretionary, based on considerations of fairness and appropriateness. The loosening of requirements for a territorial connection for the exercise of jurisdiction has thus been part of a broader shift away from traditional ideas of territorial sovereignty towards questions of fairness in the law of jurisdiction. The acceptance of the positive and negative effects of exclusive choice of forum agreements, even in the absence of objective connections with the chosen forum, is thus perhaps the ultimate expression of this change – the agreement of the defendant is considered sufficient in itself to satisfy considerations of fairness and thereby to establish jurisdiction, as well as to render litigation in any other forum presumptively unfair. The context for this shift is evidently the economic globalisation of the nineteenth and twentieth centuries, under which cross-border commercial activity proliferated and increasingly asserted independence from state sovereign regulation. The legal developments that gave rise to party autonomy in England are also at least arguably a reflection of legislative and judicial responsiveness to the needs of this increasingly globalised commercial practice. Party autonomy facilitated the management of litigation risks in cross-border commerce, which might otherwise establish a variety of territorial connections and thus potential forums.

A similar shift took place in the United States from the late nineteenth to the mid-twentieth century. This was also the result, at least in part, of a movement away from questions of state power in the law of jurisdiction, as in older cases such as *Livingston* v. *Jefferson* (1811)[46] and *Pennoyer* v. *Neff* (1878),[47] towards a focus on fairness to defendants. In *Livingston* v. *Jefferson*, former President Jefferson was sued in Virginia for trespass to land in Louisiana, but the Virginia court concluded (with some reluctance)

---

[46] (1811) 1 Brock 203.
[47] 95 US 714 (1878).

that as this was a local action (following the distinction between local and transitory actions adopted in the English common law, noted above), he could only be sued in Louisiana. As Louisiana law only permitted proceedings to be commenced against a defendant present in the territory of the state, Jefferson was able to avoid the proceedings simply by avoiding visiting Louisiana. In *Pennoyer* v. *Neff*, proceedings were brought in Oregon in a dispute over title to Oregon land, and it was similarly held by the Supreme Court that jurisdiction was only permitted over persons or property actually present in the territory (and the latter only *in rem*), in the absence of submission by the defendant (which, as noted above, was considered as a form of territorial presence or a waiver of jurisdictional irregularities). The movement away from this approach was exemplified by decisions such as *Hess* v. *Pawloski* (1927),[48] in which it was held that a Pennsylvanian resident driving in Massachusetts (but no longer in the territory by the time of commencement of proceedings) had, simply by driving on the road, implicitly submitted to the jurisdiction of the courts of Massachusetts. The device of an 'implied submission' (which must be distinguished from actual submission)[49] was used to overcome the restrictions of *Pennoyer*, and forms the conceptual basis for many 'long arm' statutes, which permit US courts to hear claims against absent defendants where the dispute has sufficient connection with the territory. The connections are not themselves considered to justify jurisdiction, but rather, their implication that the defendant may be considered to have implicitly submitted to the forum. The modern law was established in *International Shoe* v. *Washington* (1945),[50] under which it was held that a state may exercise jurisdiction over an absent defendant, so long as the defendant has "minimum contacts with it such that the maintenance of the suit does not offend 'traditional notions of fair play and substantial justice.'"[51] State sovereignty considerations have never entirely departed from US law on jurisdiction, but the focus on fairness has meant that (despite *International Shoe* and some later Supreme Court authority)[52] these still tend to be framed in terms of whether a defendant has implicitly submitted to a jurisdiction through their conduct (rather than simply whether the state's power extends to that

---

[48] 274 US 352 (1927).
[49] See Section 1.3.2.
[50] 326 US 310 (1945).
[51] At 316, citing *Milliken* v. *Meyer*, 311 US 457, 463 (1940).
[52] See e.g. *McGee* v. *International Life Ins Co*, 355 US 220, 222 (1957); *Burnham* v. *Superior Court of Cal., County of Marin*, 495 US 604, 618 (1990); see further discussion in Section 3.4.1.

conduct), which has also led to a focus on questions of foreseeability for the defendant.[53] Most recently, the Supreme Court has again emphasised that "The principal inquiry in cases of this sort is whether the defendant's activities manifest an intention to submit to the power of a sovereign",[54] expressly rejecting fairness as the central concern (because "jurisdiction is in the first instance a question of authority rather than fairness")[55] but still viewing that authority as established based on an implicit (or explicit) submission.[56]

As examined further in Section 3.4.1, however, the acceptance of the effectiveness of choice of forum agreements in US law took longer, particularly in relation to their derogation ('ouster') rather than prorogation ('conferral') effects, and has been both more contested and less universal. Forum selection agreements were viewed not as giving rise to a form of submission, but rather as an attempt by the parties to regulate matters that were not properly part of their contract (unlike, for example, stipulations that claims had to be brought within a certain time period), but rather of the public law of the state.[57] Similar to the analysis of the common law set out above, in *Home Insurance Company* v. *Morse* (1874),[58] the US Supreme Court analysed forum selection agreements as an improper attempt to oust the jurisdiction of a public authority, and viewed jurisdictional rights as non-waivable,[59] citing House of Lords authority such as *Scott* v. *Avery* (1856).[60] US practice did not, however, track the developments in England

---

[53] *Asahi Metal Industry Co* v. *Superior Court of California*, 480 US 102 (1987).

[54] *J. McIntyre Machinery, Ltd* v. *Nicastro*, 564 US 873 (2011) (per Kennedy J).

[55] Ibid.

[56] For criticism of the 'implicit submission' doctrine, see the dissenting judgment of Justice Ginsberg in *Nicastro*.

[57] *Slocum* v. *Western Assur. Co.*, 42 F 235, 235 (DCNY 1890) ("a stipulation inserted in a contract limiting the remedy for a breach of the contract to a particular forum is not a valid stipulation"); *Nute* v. *Hamilton Mut. Ins Co*, 6 Gray 174 (Mass. 1856) ("there is an obvious distinction between a stipulation by contract as to the time when a right of action shall accrue and when it shall cease, on the one hand; and as to the forum before which, and the proceedings by which an action shall be commenced and prosecuted. The one is a condition annexed to the acquisition and continuance of a legal right, and depends on contract and the acts of the parties; the other is a stipulation concerning the remedy, which is created and regulated by law."). But for a contrary view on time limits see *French* v. *Lafayette Ins Co*, 9 F Cas 788, 789 (CC Ind. 1853).

[58] 87 US 445 (1874).

[59] At 451 ("Every citizen is entitled to resort to all the courts of the country, and to invoke the protection which all the laws or all those courts may afford him. A man may not barter away his life or his freedom, or his substantial rights … agreements in advance to oust the courts of the jurisdiction conferred by law are illegal and void").

[60] (1856) 10 ER 1121.

discussed above, under which statutory support for the effectiveness of arbitration agreements was considered by implication to justify the effectiveness of foreign choice of court agreements. Despite the adoption of the Federal Arbitration Act in 1925, in 1930 it was considered to be "well settled" that a foreign choice of court agreement was not effective to exclude the jurisdiction of a US court.[61] As discussed in Section 3.4.1, while exceptions to this perspective arose, it was not until the Supreme Court's decision in *The Bremen* v. *Zapata Off-Shore Co.* (1972)[62] that the validity of choice of court agreements was firmly established under US federal law.

As noted above, another way of analysing these developments is as a shift from public concerns towards private interests – the law of jurisdiction was, in both England and the United States, refocused away from public questions of state power, towards private questions of fairness to (or submission by) the parties. If jurisdiction is approached as such a private law question, then a jurisdiction agreement, as a contract, is likely to be viewed as decisive. This increasing emphasis on jurisdiction as a matter of the rights or interests of private parties, rather than a question of the extent of state power, is a key element in the historical emergence of party autonomy in choice of forum. An alternative framework for analysing this is that it was an evolution in the question of the legitimacy of state court jurisdiction, reflecting the growing recognition of the significance of private actor interests.[63] Instead of the legitimacy of an exercise of jurisdiction being evaluated from the perspective of another state (has this state purported to regulate matters that are beyond its authority?), it is evaluated through the eyes of the parties (has this state acted unfairly in exercising authority over the defendant?). From this second perspective the consent of the defendant, in the form of a choice of court clause, thus provides a basis of legitimacy for the exercise of jurisdiction.

The development of party autonomy in choice of forum was evidently not limited to the common law and US jurisdictions examined above. Historically, civil law systems also tended to view questions of jurisdiction as public law matters concerned with the powers of governmental authorities. They were, for that reason, reluctant to accept prorogation or derogation of jurisdiction, as such questions of public authority could not

---

[61] *Wood Selick* v. *Compagnie Generale Trans*, 43 F.2d 941, 942 (2d Cir. 1930) ("We may at the start lay aside the clauses in the bills of lading, which apparently were intended to confine any litigation over the contracts to a French court. The respondent does not pretend that, so construed, these would be valid, and it is of course well settled that they would not.").

[62] 407 US 1 (1972).

[63] See Section 1.1.

be affected by private agreement.[64] In some civil law systems, for example, attempts to derogate from the jurisdiction of national courts were impermissible if one or more parties were resident nationals of the forum state – perhaps viewing a right of access to national courts as a non-waivable right.[65] This approach thus mirrored the early scepticism of US and English courts towards party autonomy, as discussed above. As party autonomy became more widely accepted, the limitations of this approach were sometimes overcome through legal fictions, such as permitting the parties to establish a 'deemed' domicile through contractual agreement, which could be used to establish the jurisdiction of the French courts.[66] During the twentieth century, however, the trend also mirrored developments elsewhere towards greater acceptance of choice of court agreements and both their positive and negative effects on jurisdiction. This was expressly characterised by the French courts as a finding that rights of access to courts are in fact waivable.[67] The increasingly widespread adoption of party autonomy in the context of jurisdiction was also reflected in the emergence of international instruments providing for the effectiveness of choice of court agreements,[68] such as the Hague Convention of 15 April 1958 on the jurisdiction of the selected forum in matters relating to the international sale of goods,[69] and the Hague Convention of 25 November 1965 on the choice of court.[70] It has been noted that the national law of every EU Member State (still applicable in cases not covered by the Brussels I Regulation or Hague Convention on Choice of Court Agreements 2005) now accepts the principle that jurisdiction should not generally be exercised where the parties have derogated from national jurisdiction through a foreign exclusive jurisdiction agreement.[71] This may, however, be subject to safeguards, for example if declining jurisdiction would deny the

---

[64] See further e.g. Lenhoff (1961).

[65] See e.g. Italian Code of Civil Procedure 1942, Art.2 (since modified by the Italian Private International Law Statute 1995, Art.4.2), discussed in Nygh (1999), p.22.

[66] See e.g. French Civil Code, Art.111.

[67] See further e.g. Cutler (1985), p.114ff.

[68] For further historical and comparative material on party autonomy in choice of forum, see the Preliminary Documents to the Hague Convention on Choice of Court Agreements 2005, available at www.hcch.net/en/instruments/conventions/publications1/?dtid=35& cid=98. See further Van Loon (2016), p.33ff; Nygh (1999), p.22ff.

[69] See www.hcch.net/en/instruments/conventions/full-text/?cid=34; not in force.

[70] See www.hcch.net/en/instruments/conventions/full-text/?cid=77; not in force.

[71] See generally e.g. Nuyts (2007), p.73ff.

claimant a forum because the chosen court is not available or would not comply with requirements of procedural fairness.[72]

As discussed further in Chapter 6, the idea of jurisdiction as a matter of private law would receive further – perhaps ultimate – expression later in the twentieth century, with the widespread acceptance that parties might choose private dispute resolution through arbitration rather than a state court to resolve their disputes, internationalised through the New York Convention 1958. Under such clauses, it is not merely the form of agreement that is private, but also its object – the establishment of private processes of dispute resolution to complement or replace those of states. However, as noted above, it is a curiosity that in both the common law and the United States the recognition of such agreements actually predated the recognition of foreign choice of court agreements. Historically speaking, it is therefore not accurate to view arbitration as an expansion of the available forums from which the parties might choose – it was rather the acceptance of arbitration that prompted recognition that the parties might alternatively choose a foreign state court.

2.2.2   Historical Origins of Party Autonomy in Choice of Law

Some element or aspect of party autonomy in choice of law in contract has long been a feature of private international law. This is, however, somewhat anomalous, because party autonomy has often been at least apparently incompatible with the prevailing theories that have supposedly provided the foundations for choice of law.

Perhaps the oldest example of this phenomenon may be identified in the early European middle ages, when the application of law was generally based on tribal or ethnic affiliation, rather than territorial location.[73] The reliance on personal status as a determinative factor reflected the importance of personal identity in legal relationships, and this identity was generally viewed as an objectively identifiable question of fact – whether or not an individual was a member of a particular community legal order (or a subject of a particular law-maker). It is difficult to see any room that this approach would leave for party autonomy, because subjection to a legal order was part of the 'social contract' under which individuals would gain protection or status. Despite this, it appears to have become accepted

---

[72] See e.g. Nuyts (2007), pp.74–6.
[73] See generally e.g. Mills (2009a), Chapter 2; Mills (2006a).

that in civil disputes a party could make a declaration of their ethnicity,[74] known as a *professio iuris*,[75] and thereby (at least to some extent) determine themselves which law governed their legal relations. It is not, however, entirely clear whether such a declaration was truly permissible without consequence for the individual – whether claiming the application of a tribal law would have necessitated accepting obligations under that law unrelated to the particular contract at hand.[76] It is also unclear whether the declaration could be fictitious, or was merely a matter of clarifying whether the law of their origin or the law of their place of residence would apply.[77] This is thus perhaps not quite party autonomy in its modern form, which is an agreement rather than a matter of unilateral declaration, and in most (but not all)[78] cases may involve selecting a law without connection to the parties or their legal relation. It may nevertheless be recognised as its most significant early ancestor, and it would have been possible for parties to make mutual declarations in this form. It is unclear whether this occurred in practice, although the *professio juris* was not limited to court proceedings but can be found also in written documents from this period, suggesting a role more akin to a choice of law agreement.[79] To the extent that party autonomy was thus given effect, it took place in the shadows as a legal fiction, in order for it to be compatible with the theory that regulatory power rested in 'sovereign' tribal leaders. Even in this early period, this nevertheless reflected the idea that personal status could or should be a matter of individual freedom. This was arguably both a point of principle and also a practical solution to the difficulties in determining questions of personal identity in an era where large population movements occurred after the collapse of the Roman Empire – precursors to some of the modern principled and practical arguments for party autonomy discussed below. It may thus be understood as providing the simplest solution where

[74] For an expression of doubt over whether the historical evidence supports the general view, see Faulkner (2016), p.12.

[75] This term is now predominantly used to refer to a unilateral choice of law, such as that made by a testator of the law to govern his or her succession – such a choice is given effect in some legal systems, including under the Hague Succession Convention 1989 (not in force) and the EU Succession Regulation, as discussed in Section 8.8.1. It is, however, also occasionally used to refer to the exercise of party autonomy in choice of law in contract.

[76] If so, it may be more an example of party control over an objective connecting factor – see Section 1.3.1.

[77] It may have begun in the latter form, but apparently evolved to incorporate the former – Basedow (2013a), p.210ff; Juenger (2001), p.7; Juenger (1992), p.10; Juenger (1985), p.139.

[78] See further Section 7.3.

[79] Kalenský (1971), p.49.

(as a result of population movements and varying levels of integration into different social groups) questions of individual identity were difficult to determine as a matter of objective fact.[80]

Another important and distinct approach to private international law emerged in later statutist medieval scholarship, which developed the idea that each statute could be identified as belonging to one of two categories – 'personal' or 'territorial'.[81] If a law was personal, it 'attached' to certain persons (typically those with a relationship of subject-hood to the law-maker)[82] and applied to them even outside the territory of the statutory authority. If a law was local (or 'real', meaning territorial), it 'attached' to the land, and applied only within the territory of the statutory authority, but to all persons (whether or not subjects) within that territory. It is again difficult to see any role for party autonomy in this approach, which is based purely on the recognition of two forms of state power. Indeed, party auton-omy does not appear to feature in early statutist scholarship, although party choices could be given some indirect recognition. For example, it was generally argued that a contract should be governed by the law of the place of contracting (as regards form and matters relating to the contract itself) or the law of the place of performance (as regards matters relating to the performance of the contract).[83] While these are matters potentially within the choice of parties (for example, since performance could be the designated place where goods had to be delivered), such rules are not, however, true examples of party autonomy (as discussed in Section 1.3.1), which involves the parties choosing the law or forum to govern their legal relations, rather than choosing the objective factors under which such a determination will take place. The growth of state law – with personal or territorial effect – may be understood to have displaced the concept of tribal law that had previously operated, including its protean conception of party autonomy.

The idea of party autonomy in choice of law would re-emerge as the sta-tutist approach was further developed in France in the sixteenth century. One of the most important scholars in this period was Dumoulin, who broadly followed the statutist approach, but with an additional emphasis

---

[80] Vischer (1992), p.130; Basedow (2013a), p.210ff.

[81] See further Mills (2009a), Chapter 2; Mills (2006a).

[82] This idea of 'subjecthood' predates the modern notion of the 'citizen', but similarly reflects an idea that individuals may owe personal obligations of obedience to a 'sovereign' that are not territorially based.

[83] See Bartolus, 'Commentary upon Justinian's Code' (date of publication unknown, lived 1314–57), translated in Beale (1914), p.18ff, p.74.

on the importance of party agreements (such that Dumoulin is often considered as a founder of modern 'party autonomy').[84] Indeed, Dumoulin went so far as to argue that party agreement was the foundation of all determinations of which statutes should apply to a particular legal relation – finding that the interpretation of the relevant statutes reflected a fictional 'tacit agreement' between the parties. Although Dumoulin is generally considered part of the statutist tradition, there is an important and subtle shift in emphasis here, away from considerations of state power (the territorial or personal authority of medieval law-makers), towards considerations of individual fairness or giving effect to private agreement. Dumoulin sought to justify the application of foreign law based on considerations internal to the parties themselves – not based on the powers of sovereigns over them. Thus, under his approach, two English parties who entered into a contract to be performed in France might be considered to have submitted to the authority of the rules of French contract law, if their expectations were that French law would govern the performance of their contract. While in this form the rule adopted is not in fact an example of party autonomy, but appears rather to be a justification for an objective 'law of the place of performance' rule, it has been suggested that Dumoulin also recognised the validity of an express choice of law by the parties.[85]

It is difficult to understand how in this form the rule could be compatible with Dumoulin's commitment to the statutist method – how the express agreement of the parties as to the law to govern their contract might affect the intended scope of application of the statutes that might potentially govern the legal relation between the parties. Private parties cannot, by agreement, retrospectively affect the intentions of legislators. It is, however, less difficult to understand why the focus in Dumoulin's approach on justifying choice of law by reference to party intentions might lead him in this direction – if the applicable law were indeed justified based on meeting presumed party expectations, then an *express* statement of those expectations might be viewed as trumping such a presumption. But the problem with this argument is that the presumption itself was a legal fiction, dealing with the expectations of hypothetical parties, designed to justify the appropriateness of an objective rule (the law of the place of

---

[84] See e.g. Zhang (2006a); Nygh (1999), p.4; Niboyet (1927), p.9ff.

[85] Zhang (2006a), p.516ff; Yntema (1966), p.16; Wolff (1950), p.26, p.29; Von Bar (1892), p.34; Westlake (1880), p.16ff; Juenger (1992). But see Nygh (1999), p.4, arguing that Dumoulin only used implied agreement as a justification for selecting the law of the place of performance of the contract rather than the place of contracting; see also similarly Nishitani (2016).

performance of the contract) – there is a slip in reasoning to accepting that the expectations of *actual* parties are important or relevant.[86] Party expectations have, in this approach, implicitly moved from being one justification for a rule, to being a rule in themselves. The choice of law rules generally followed by Dumoulin (in accordance with the statutist method) were not based on meeting the expectations of the parties, but rather on considerations of the express or presumed intentions of the *legislators* – the intended scope of application for their laws. However, it has been argued that Dumoulin also advocated party autonomy in its modern sense, on the basis that "the supreme law in the sphere of the law of contracts was the will of the parties".[87] The influence of this justification for party autonomy, which views it as an extension of the autonomy of contracting parties who are themselves viewed as 'law-makers', is considered further below. Why should Dumoulin have made such a leap in apparent logic (if indeed he did)? One proffered practical explanation is that "Dumoulin's teachings reflected the interests of the merchants since they enabled their representatives to overcome legal particularism by private agreement; thus the customs observed in Paris as a centre of commerce could be applied in Brittany, Normandy and other provinces which lagged behind in their economic and legal developments".[88] If true, this arguably attributes to Dumoulin the development of two additional justifications for party autonomy (each discussed below) that have had a significant modern influence – the idea that the parties can choose the law that is best suited to their relationship, and perhaps even that the consequent regulatory competition would encourage progressive law reform.

Dumoulin's apparent support for party autonomy, while influential, was not undisputed. The French scholar D'Argentré (from the strongly independent province of Brittany) led a reaction to his approach, rejecting Dumoulin's emphasis on the will of the parties in favour of a reassertion of local territorial law (and thus the powers of the provinces).[89] Following this trend, the development of private international law theory is usually traced through Dutch scholars in the seventeenth century, particularly Paul Voet, Johannes Voet, and Huber. These scholars moved the focus away from the presumed or inferred intention of statutes towards a broader consideration of reconciling the application of foreign law with

---

[86] See further Section 2.3.1.
[87] Kalenský (1971), p.65.
[88] Lunts (1952), p.52, cited in Kalenský (1971), p.67.
[89] See further Mills (2009a), Chapter 2; Mills (2006a).

the emergent principle of territorial sovereignty (although Johannes Voet also supported a more limited party autonomy). Huber provided the most compelling and influential version of this reconciliation, determining that the laws of a sovereign should apply within its territory, including in relation to aliens even temporarily within the territory, but that states "will so act by way of comity" to recognise "rights acquired within the limits of a government".[90] A (somewhat precarious) distinction was thus drawn between the application of a foreign law and the recognition of rights acquired under that law. In any case, the clear focus in Huber's account of private international law was on the territorial sovereignty of states, with 'comity' serving as an ambiguous justification for recognition between states of each other's territorial sovereignty. There is, once again, little scope to see how party autonomy could be supported under such an approach – Huber strongly emphasises that contracts should be governed by the law of the place of contracting, as one might expect under a doctrine of territorially 'acquired rights'.[91] And yet Huber also, at least in appearance and by repute, took the view that the intentions of the parties were determinative of the law applicable to their contract – that a contract should be governed by the law of the place "the parties had in mind".[92] This apparent support for party autonomy could be explained on the basis that Huber viewed party autonomy as a natural extension of freedom of contract (an argument discussed further below), and thus that parties were capable of creating a 'vested right' under a foreign legal order. In a more practical sense, Huber's acceptance of party autonomy might also be a consequence of the fact that the place of contracting was increasingly arbitrary in the conduct of international trade – although this argument might equally support the selection of the law of the place of performance. But there is cause for serious doubt as to whether Huber was really intending to express anything more than an acknowledgement of the role of the law of the place of performance of the contract, as a law that the parties would or should have 'had in mind' – an approach that appears similar to that of Dumoulin. Following the reference cited above to the place the parties "had in mind",

---

[90] Cited and translated in Lorenzen (1919), p.403. See further Mills (2009a), Chapter 2; Mills (2006a).

[91] "Contracts made in accordance with the law of the place where they are entered into will therefore be supported everywhere, in court as well as out, even in those places where contracts entered into in such manner would not be valid." – cited and translated in Lorenzen (1919), p.406.

[92] "The place, however, where a contract is entered into is not to be considered absolutely; for if the parties had in mind the law of another place at the time of contracting the latter will control." – cited and translated in Lorenzen (1919), p.412.

Huber offers as an authority a citation taken from the Digest stating that "Everyone is deemed to have contracted in that place, in which he is bound to perform".[93] This suggests that his apparent support for party autonomy is more debatable than is usually considered.[94]

Huber's approach to private international law had a direct and power-ful influence on the subject, including in English and US law. In England, his influence was felt in the courts in the eighteenth century, particularly through Scottish civil-trained lawyers such as Lord Mansfield. In the foundational case of *Robinson* v. *Bland* (1760), Lord Mansfield recognised the significance of choice of law principles, holding that "the general rule established *ex comitate et jure gentium* is, that the place where the con-tract is made, and not where the action is brought, is to be considered in expounding and enforcing the contract".[95] However, he also held that in this case the disputed contract, entered into in France but to be performed in England, was governed by English law because "The parties had a view to the laws of England", citing Huber as principal authority for this propo-sition.[96] Again, the law of the place of performance is chosen as reflecting the agreed expectations of the parties. Once again, it was at least somewhat ambiguous as to whether that law applied because those *particular* parties expected that law to apply (an expectation that would be defeated by a con-trary choice of law agreement), or because parties in their position would *generally* expect that law to apply, as the law of the place of performance (an objective test that would not be defeated by a contrary choice of law agreement). The long acceptance in both English and US law that as "a principle of universal law ... in every forum a contract is governed by the law with a view to which it was made"[97] thus perhaps provided a founda-tion for party autonomy, but did not itself necessarily entail it.

The uncertain status of party autonomy in choice of law is also reflected in the most prominent early nineteenth century private international law scholars. Perhaps the most influential scholar in the United States and common law world was the US judge and academic Joseph Story, who was in turn highly influenced by Huber.[98] Story started, like Huber, from an

---

[93] Ibid., citing the Digest of Justinian, 44.7.21.

[94] See also Nygh (1999), p.5.

[95] (1760) 96 ER 141.

[96] (1760) 97 ER 717, 718, also holding that "The law of the place can never be the rule, where the transaction is entered into with an express view to the law of another country, as the rule by which it is to be governed." See also Nygh (1999), p.5.

[97] *Wayman* v. *Southard*, 23 US 1, 48 (1825).

[98] See e.g. Story (1834), s.23, s.29.

acceptance of the territorial sovereignty of states – that "every nation possesses an exclusive sovereignty and jurisdiction within its own territory".[99]
As a direct consequence of this, he argued, "the laws of every state affect
and bind directly ... all contracts made and acts done within it".[100] Again,
similarly to Huber (and in turn Lord Mansfield), Story thus gave a central role to the law of the place of contracting, although accepting that a
role might also be played by the place of performance of the contract in
some circumstances.[101] Story's approach seems, however, even more difficult than Huber's to reconcile with party autonomy. He argued that the
correct ground for this doctrine is not that parties have implicitly submitted to the law of the place where they contract, but rather that "the law of
the place of the contract acts upon it, independently of any volition of the
parties, in virtue of the general sovereignty possessed by every nation to
regulate all persons, property, and transactions within its own territory".[102]
An 'implicit submission' justification would have appeared more open to
a different understanding being expressly adopted by the parties themselves. While Story did subsequently suggests that where two foreigners
contract in an arbitrary place the law that the parties had in mind might be
applied instead of the law of the place of contracting, he appeared to limit
this possibility to the place of performance of the contract, and indeed
cited *Robinson* v. *Bland* in support of his approach.[103] Party intentions
were thus, once again, given an ambivalent role here – arguably serving
as a justification for a law of the place of performance of the contract rule,
rather than party autonomy serving as a rule in its own right. Story himself clearly states that his approach adopts a 'lex loci contractus' rule, but
with a double meaning – "it may indifferently indicate the place, where
the contract is actually made, or that, where it is virtually made according
to the intent of the parties, that is, the place of performance."[104] Under the
influence of Huber, the foundation of choice of law for Story was again the
doctrine of comity, whose focus on inter-state relations left relatively little
room for the expressed wishes of the parties to affect the governing law.

---

[99]   Story (1834), s.18.
[100]   Story (1834), s.18, s.242, s.260ff.
[101]   Story (1834), s.233.
[102]   Story (1834), s.261.
[103]   Story (1834), s.273, s.280 ("where the contract is either expressly or tacitly to be performed
       in any other place [than where it is made], there the general rule is, in conformity to the
       presumed intention of the parties, that the contract, as to its validity, nature, obligation,
       and interpretation, is to be governed by the law of the place of performance.").
[104]   Story (1834), s.299. See further Nygh (1999), p.6; Yntema (1955), p.51ff.

A similar approach was later endorsed by Savigny in his 1849 treatise, although his position is perhaps even less clear. Savigny does argue that "The local law for every legal relation is liable to be very extensively influenced by the freewill of the persons interested, who may voluntarily subject themselves to the authority of a particular law, although this influence must not be regarded as unlimited."[105] In a later section, the position is perhaps put even more strongly, in arguing that:

> Voluntary subjection to a local law is manifested in various kinds and degrees. Sometimes it consists in the free choice of a local law to regulate a matter where another law might have been preferred; as, for example, in obligatory contracts, in which the freely elected local law is itself to be regarded as part of the contract.[106]

However, this apparent (albeit qualified) endorsement of party autonomy is less evident in other passages. Savigny expressly rejects the language of 'autonomy' in this context, arguing that it would be as improper as suggesting that a party chooses their law because they may choose their domicile.[107] In the specific context of determining the law applicable to a contract, Savigny focuses on the law of the place of performance, determined either expressly in the contract or as a matter of presumption, on the basis that the parties are presumed to have submitted themselves to this law.[108] But then this in turn is qualified by the statement that "The territorial law ... ceases to apply when the presumption of voluntary submission is excluded by an expressed contrary intention".[109] Savigny's writing is certainly not without ambiguity on this point, but there is at least some evidence that he makes a subtle but decisive shift – from the intentions of the parties being used as a justification for a particular choice of law rule (that the law of the place of performance of the contract accords with their intentions), to party intentions becoming themselves foundational (so that an expressed intention may override one that is merely a legal presumption).[110]

---

[105] Savigny (1849), p.89.
[106] Savigny (1849), p.90.
[107] Savigny (1849), pp.91–2. On this distinction see further Section 1.3.1.
[108] Savigny (1849), p.175.
[109] Savigny (1849), p.176.
[110] See further e.g. Peari (2014); Zhang (2006a), p.518; Reimann (1999), p.595 ("Savigny postulated that the parties to a contract should be allowed to select the applicable law. To be sure, this was not his original idea, but he nonetheless made it the centerpiece of his entire approach.").

Despite the arguments of Savigny, and the apparent support for party autonomy in some cases dealing with contracts of marriage[111] or ante-nuptial contracts[112] in the mid-nineteenth century, the ambiguous status of party autonomy found in Story (and earlier in *Robinson v. Bland*) was generally continued in subsequent English authorities. In *Lloyd v. Guibert* (1865),[113] for example, the court observed that "it is necessary to consider by what general law the parties intended that the transaction should be governed, or rather to what general law it is just to presume that they have submitted themselves in the matter".[114] These two questions, equated by the court, are of course not necessarily the same – the former suggests a subjective test, and the latter an objective one. In this case and others, the courts were again generally focused on choosing between the law of the place of the contract and the law of the place of its performance, and references to party intentions were made largely in support of one of these positions. In *The Peninsular and Oriental Steam Navigation Company v. Shand* (1865),[115] for example, the court held that

> The general rule is, that the law of the country where a contract is made governs as to the nature, the obligation, and the interpretation of it. The parties to a contract are either the subjects of the Power there ruling or as temporary residents owe it a temporary allegiance: in either case equally they must be understood to submit to the law there prevailing, and to agree to its actions upon their contract. It is, of course, immaterial that such agreement is not expressed in terms; it is equally an agreement in fact, presumed

---

[111] An early case suggesting acceptance of party autonomy in marriage is *Este v. Smyth* (1854) 52 ER 44, although it is unclear whether the court was accepting party choice of the law to govern the marriage contract, or merely accepting that the marriage may be governed by the intended domicile of the parties. Such an approach had been supported by Huber on the basis that the intended domicile was the place of performance of the marriage contract. Huber's approach is also cited with approval in *Brook v. Brook* (1861) 11 ER 703, 710; see also similarly *Van Grutten v. Digby* (1862) 54 ER 1256, 1259.

[112] In *Earl of Stair v. Head* (1844) 6 D 904, two Scottish parties temporarily resident in England entered into an antenuptial contract which included the provision that "it is declared that, although the parties happen to be at present in England, where they have the prospect of remaining some time ... yet they intend, when circumstances shall permit, to return to Scotland, and fix their residence there; and, therefore, it is agreed that the import and effect of this contract, and all matters and questions connected with their intended marriage, shall be construed and regulated by the law of Scotland." The majority gave effect to this choice of law (and rejected the possibility of a *renvoi* in favour of English law), although there is a degree of uncertainty in some of the judgments as to whether the agreement between the parties actually selected the law governing their contract, or simply indicated a Scottish domicile despite English residence.

[113] (1865–6) LR 1 QB 115.

[114] At 120–21.

[115] (1865) 16 ER 103.

de jure, and a foreign Court interpreting or enforcing it on any contrary rule defeats the intention of the parties, as well as neglects to observe the recognized comity of nations.[116]

This argument appears to conflate the subjective agreement of the parties 'in fact' with their presumed agreement 'de jure'. It leaves unanswered the key question: what if these particular parties in fact have an intention, expressed in their contract, which is different from the intention that the law presumes to apply to them? As well as drawing on the intention of the parties, the court relied on the comity of nations, perhaps suggesting a further dependence on territorial sovereignty as articulated by Huber, under which it is difficult to situate party autonomy. Other cases in this period appeared to distinguish between the governing law for the purposes of contractual interpretation, which should be the law selected by the parties, and the governing law for the purposes of contractual validity, which could not be determined by the parties themselves, but in general the distinction between these issues (and the issue of incorporation by reference discussed in Section 1.3.6) was not clearly expressed.[117]

As late as 1880, Westlake cited *Robinson v. Bland* (1760) for the proposition that the governing law of a contract is the law of the place with the 'most real connection' to the contract (generally the place of performance), regardless of the actual intention of the parties.[118] As he wrote, however, this position was coming under direct challenge. In *Chamberlain v. Napier* (1880),[119] the court suggested that "The parties may contract that the deed shall be construed in accordance with a law other than the lex loci, but such contract must be, and that is not the case here, so expressed."[120] Three years

---

[116] At 110.

[117] Thus, e.g., in *The Halley* (1867–9) LR 2 PC 193 the Court states that "in many cases the Courts of England inquire into and act upon the law of foreign countries, as in the case of a contract entered into in a foreign country, where, by express reference, or by necessary implication, the foreign law is incorporated into the contract, and proof and consideration of the foreign law therefore becomes necessary to the construction of the contract itself."

[118] Westlake (1880), p.237 ("Lord Mansfield can have meant by 'an express view' to [a law] nothing special to the case, but merely that tacit expectation which may always be said to be directed to the place of fulfilment, even when the result of appealing to that place is to defeat the specific intentions of the parties").

[119] (1880) 15 Ch D 614.

[120] See similarly *Greer v. Poole* (1880) 5 QBD 272, holding (at 274) that "It is no doubt competent to an underwriter on an English policy to stipulate, if he think fit, that such policy shall be construed and applied in whole or in part according to the law of any foreign state, as if it had been made in and by a subject of the foreign state, and the policy in question does so stipulate as regards general average, but except when it is so stipulated the policy must be construed according to our law and without regard to the nationality of the vessel."

later, in *Chartered Mercantile Bank of India* v. *Netherlands Co.* (1883),[121] the court held that "The question what the contract is, and by what rule it is to be construed, is a question of the intention of the parties, and one must look at all the circumstances and gather from them what was the intention of the parties." Party intentions had moved from a supporting role to the leading light in determining the law applicable to a contract. Similarly, in *Jacobs, Marcus & Co.* v. *The Crédit Lyonnais* (1884),[122] the court held that "where a contract is made in England between merchants carrying on business here, as this is, but to be performed elsewhere, the construction of the contract, and all its incidents are to be governed by the law of the country where the contract is made, unless there is something to shew that the intention of the parties was that the law of the country where the contract is to be performed should prevail."[123] The law of the place of performance was, under this formulation, not to be applied because that would be consistent with presumed party expectations, but only where it would *in fact* be consistent with party expectations. The emphasis became even stronger a few years later in *In Re Missouri Steamship Company* (1889),[124] in which the court at first instance held that:

> Although the law of *Massachusetts* would ... hold these stipulations void, I cannot find any sufficient reason for saying it would hold them void in the case of a contract made within the state for the carriage of goods where the performance of the contract was (as in the case before me) to take place mainly outside the state, if it were declared expressly on the face of the contract that for all purposes the contract was to be governed by the law of the country to which the ship belonged, and the law of such country allowed the stipulations to be valid.[125]

Although Justice Chitty noted that "The contracts before me do not contain any such express declaration", the judgment nevertheless essentially invited parties to adopt such declarations – choice of law clauses – in future cases.[126] In the Court of Appeal, Lord Halsbury expressed his support for Justice Chitty's approach, but re-articulated it as a rule that "you must have regard to the law of the contract, by which I mean the law which

---

[121] (1883) 10 QBD 521.

[122] (1884) 12 QBD 589.

[123] At 596–7. Similarly, at 600, "the law of a country where a contract is made presumably governs the nature, the obligation and the interpretation of it, unless the contrary appears to be the express intention of the parties".

[124] (1889) 42 Ch D 321.

[125] At 325–6.

[126] Such a clause is present in, for example, *The British Wagon Company* v. *Gray* [1896] 1 QB 35 (discussed in Section 2.2.1).

the contract itself imports is to be the law governing the contract".[127] This even more strongly suggested that a contract could determine its own governing law – or rather that the parties could select the law through the terms of the contract. A similar approach was emphasised in *Hamlyn* v. *Talisker Distillery* (1894),[128] which held that:

> It is not necessary to enter upon the inquiry, which was a good deal discussed at the bar, to which of these considerations the greatest weight is to be attributed, namely, the place where the contract was made, or the place where it is to be performed. In my view they are both matters which must be taken into consideration, but neither of them is, of itself, conclusive ... In this case, as in all such cases, the whole of the contract must be looked at and the rights under it must be regulated by the intention of the parties as appearing from the contract. It is perfectly competent to those who, under such circumstances as I have indicated are entering into a contract, to indicate by the terms which they employ, which system of law they intend to be applied to the construction of the contract and to the determination of the rights arising out of it.[129]

It is notable that these practical judicial developments were out of step with the prevailing theoretical support for the idea of 'vested rights', inherited and advanced by Dicey in England (and through his influence, Beale in the United States).[130] Under this approach (discussed further below in relation to Beale), foreign law was indirectly applied because an act in the foreign territory had created an obligation under that law, which should be recognised by the local legal order. Although Dicey was too practical and empirical in his approach to reject a doctrine accepted by the courts, and thus endorsed party autonomy,[131] it is difficult to understand how under a 'vested rights' approach parties might 'self-vest' through a choice of foreign law. Nevertheless, by the early twentieth century, the intention of the parties had gone in England from being one justification for a particular objective rule to the very foundation of choice of law in contract, such that the law selected would be determined by the parties' express, implied, or 'imputed' intention.[132] Party intentions had by 1937 been transformed from a justification to a rule:

---

[127] At 336.

[128] [1894] AC 202.

[129] At 208.

[130] See further e.g. Mills (2013).

[131] Dicey (1896), p.540 (defining the proper law of a contract as "the law or laws to which the parties intended, or may fairly be presumed to have intended, to submit themselves").

[132] See also Dicey (1896), p.567.

> The legal principles which are to guide an English Court on the question of the proper law of a contract are now well settled. It is the law which the parties intended to apply. Their intention will be ascertained by the intention expressed in the contract if any, which will be conclusive. If no intention be expressed the intention will be presumed by the Court from the terms of the contract and the relevant surrounding circumstances.[133]

In the leading modern English case of *Vita Food Products Inc.* v. *Unus Shipping Co. Ltd* (1939),[134] it was similarly held that:

> where there is an express statement by the parties of their intention to select the law of the contract, it is difficult to see what qualifications are possible, provided the intention expressed is bona fide and legal, and provided there is no reason for avoiding the choice on the ground of public policy.[135]

While these developments were taking place in the English common law, similar developments were occurring elsewhere in the world. As with the parallel developments in the law of jurisdiction, examined above, it is no coincidence that this corresponded with a period of economic globalisation, and the increased assertion of the independence of cross-border commercial activity and global markets from sovereign regulation. Once again, courts and legislators appear to be responding to the needs of commercial parties increasingly engaged in cross-border commercial activity that might give rise to more than one territorial connection, and thus otherwise more than one applicable law. In the United States, the law of the place of the contract rule favoured by Story and the courts was gradually modified, as choice of law clauses were given increasing effect by the courts from the late nineteenth century. In 1875, it appeared clear from the US Supreme Court that the law of the place of the contract governed (meaning either or potentially both (with distinct roles) the place of contracting and the place of performance).[136] However, there was separate authority that suggested that the parties could themselves determine whether it was the law of the place of contracting or the law of the place of performance that governed (at least with regard to statutory limitations on interest rates),[137]

---

[133]   *R* v. *International Trustee for the Protection of Bondholders A.-G.* [1937] AC 500, 529.

[134]   [1939] AC 277.

[135]   At 290. See further Section 7.2.1.

[136]   See e.g. *Scudder* v. *Union National Bank*, 91 US 406, 412–13 (1875) ("Matters bearing upon the execution, the interpretation, and the validity of a contract are determined by the law of the place where the contract is made. Matters connected with its performance are regulated by the law prevailing at the place of performance.").

[137]   See, for example, *Andrews* v. *Pond*, 38 US 65, 78 (1839) ("if the interest allowed by the laws of the place of performance, is higher than that permitted at the place of the contract, the parties may stipulate for the higher interest"). See also e.g. *Miller* v. *Tiffany*, 68 US 298

suggesting a limited concept of party autonomy as a means of choosing between the two competing contractual choice of law rules. This case law culminated in the Supreme Court decision of *Pritchard* v. *Norton* (1882).[138] Although this case concerned the validity of a bond of indemnity that did not in fact contain a choice of law agreement, the court held generally that:

> in case of contract, the foreign law may, by the act and will of the parties, have become part of their agreement, and in enforcing this, the law of the forum may find it necessary to give effect to a foreign law which, without such adoption, would have no force beyond its own territory.[139]

On its own, this statement would offer only ambiguous support for party autonomy. It might, for example, be interpreted as discussing only incorporation by reference, or as compatible with the idea that it is merely the act of the parties in determining the place of performance of their contract that is effective to determine the governing law, under an objective law of the place of performance rule (as discussed in Sections 1.3.1 and 1.3.6). Indeed, most of the judgment appears to support a strict application of the 'lex loci solutionis', the law of the contract, "used in a double sense, to mean sometimes the law of the place where a contract is entered into, sometimes that of the place of its performance".[140] However, the court went on to hold that:

> The law we are in search of, which is to decide upon the nature, interpretation, and validity of the engagement in question, is that which the parties have, either expressly or presumptively, incorporated into their contract as constituting its obligation.[141]

There is a still a limited ambiguity in this statement, because the reference to a law 'incorporated into' a contract might again indicate the selection of a place of performance, or even the 'incorporation by reference' of terms rather than the selection of a governing law, neither of which is genuinely a matter of party autonomy.[142] The more natural reading of this statement is, however, in support of party autonomy, albeit with a degree of ambiguity – the Supreme Court itself appeared to consider the question undecided in

---

(1863); *Arnold* v. *Potter*, 22 Iowa 194 (1867) (Supreme Court of Iowa) (expressly ruling out, however, free choice of law by the parties in general (at 200)); *Cromwell* v. *County of Sac*, 96 US 51 (1877).

[138] 106 US 124 (1882). See e.g. discussion in Zhang (2006a), p.529ff.

[139] At 129.

[140] At 136.

[141] Ibid.

[142] See Sections 1.3.1 and 1.3.6.

1888.[143] Again, party autonomy shifts, this time apparently even within a single judgment, from being a justification for the application of a particular objective law (the law of the place of contracting or contractual performance), to being the fundamental rule itself, with an express agreement overriding any presumed intention. It is not the presumed intentions of the parties or of parties in their position, but the actual intentions of the parties, including as expressed in terms of the contract, which are viewed as determinative of the laws that will govern even those intentions themselves. This view was further endorsed in *London Assurance* v. *Companhia de Moagens do Barreiro* (1897),[144] in which the parties did not expressly choose English law, but the contract (of marine insurance) stated that it should be interpreted in accordance with the "usages of Lloyd's". The court held that:

> the interpretation of the contract was intended by the parties to depend upon the principles of English law as they obtained and were recognized in England by the usages prevailing at Lloyd's. This is what the parties expressly stipulated for, and it is no injustice to the company to decide its rights according to the principles of the law of the country which it has agreed to be bound by, so long as, in a case like this, the foreign law is not in any way contrary to the policy of our own.[145]

In *The Kensington* (1902),[146] the Supreme Court, considering a contract with an express choice of Belgian law, suggested that such a choice would ordinarily be binding. The court affirmed generally that "It is true as a general rule that the *lex loci* governs, and it is also true that the intention of the parties to a contract will be sought out and enforced",[147] although found

---

[143] *Liverpool and Great Western Steam Co.* v. *Phenix Insurance Co.*, 129 US 397 (1888), noting (at 462) that "The present case does not require us to determine what effect the courts of the United States should give to this contract, if it had expressly provided that any question arising under it should be governed by the law of England". The court otherwise held (at 458) that the law of the place of contracting should govern, "unless the parties at the time of making it have some other law in view", or "unless the parties, when entering into the contract, clearly manifest a mutual intention that it shall be governed by the law of some other country".

[144] 167 US 149 (1897).

[145] At 161.

[146] 183 US 263 (1902). See also similarly *Mutual Life Insurance Company of New York* v. *Tine Cohen*, 179 US 262 (1900) (although this case appears to conflate a choice of law clause with the incorporation by reference of a statutory provision); *Pinney* v. *Nelson*, 183 US 144, 148 (1901) ("parties in making a contract may have in view some other law than that of the place, and when that is so that other law will control. That the parties have some other law in view and contract with reference to it is shown by an express declaration to that effect.").

[147] At 269.

that this rule (and the choice in the case at hand) was subject to contrary considerations of public policy.[148]

The practice of US courts was far from clear or consistent,[149] however, and many private international law scholars in the United States were initially opposed to these developments. Most prominent among these was Joseph Beale, an influential Harvard professor and the author of the First Restatement of Conflict of Laws in 1934, who rejected party autonomy[150] on the basis that it purported to attribute to individuals a power over states, arguing that "The fundamental objection to [party autonomy] in point of theory is that it involves permission to the parties to do a legislative act."[151] Beale's opposition to party autonomy was not at the time necessarily considered an extreme position (although he himself noted that there was some judicial practice to the contrary)[152] – his approach derived from the theory of vested rights, taken from Dicey in England, which (despite being rather vulnerable to the criticism that it is obviously circular)[153] was both influential and supported by broader scholarship. Beale simply followed that theory more fully through to its natural conclusion than Dicey, as did others under his influence or the influence of the same theoretical framework.[154] Supreme Court Justice Oliver Wendell Holmes Jr., for example, (despite being one of the foundational thinkers of the legal realist movement which would reject 'vested rights'[155]) observed in 1904 that:

> The theory of the foreign suit is that, although the act complained of was subject to no law having force in the forum, it gave rise to an obligation, an *obligatio*, which, like other obligations, follows the person, and may be enforced wherever the person may be found ... But as the only source of this obligation is the law of the place of the act, it follows that that law determines not merely the existence of the obligation ... but equally determines its extent.[156]

[148] See similarly *Oceanic Steam Nav. Co. v. Corcoran*, 9 F.2d 724 (1925).
[149] See Beale (1909b) and (1910a); Yntema (1955).
[150] See Beale (1909a) and (1910b); First Restatement of Conflict of Laws, ss.332 and 358 (applying a combination of the laws of the place of contracting and place of performance).
[151] Beale (1935), p.1079; also in Beale (1910b), p.260; Beale (1896), p.170; see further discussion in Mills (2013); Yntema (1955), p.54ff.
[152] See further Symeonides (2014), p.113.
[153] See further Mills (2013).
[154] See e.g. Lorenzen (1921), p.658 ("The validity or invalidity of a legal transaction should result from fixed rules of law which are binding upon the parties. Allowing the parties to choose their law in this regard involves a delegation of sovereign power to private individuals."); see discussion in Yntema (1955), p.57ff.
[155] See e.g. Holmes (1897), p.466.
[156] *Slater v. Mexican National Railroad Co.*, 194 US 120, 126 (1904).

On a similar basis, in *Louis-Dreyfus* v. *Paterson Steamships* (1930),[157] Judge Learned Hand[158] held in the Second Circuit (citing a draft of the First Restatement in support) that:

> the validity of a provision in a contract of carriage ... was to be determined by the law of the place where the contract was made, and this is well-settled law (section 366, Tentative Restatement No. 4, Conflict of Laws; American Law Institute), even when the parties expressly stipulate that all questions shall be decided according to some foreign law, which would require a different result.[159]

A year later, Judge Learned Hand similarly held in *E. Gerli & Co* v. *Cunard SS Co.* (1931)[160] that:

> People cannot by agreement substitute the law of another place; they may of course incorporate any provisions they wish into their agreements – a statute like anything else – and when they do, courts will try to make sense out of the whole, so far as they can. But an agreement is not a contract, except as the law says it shall be, and to try to make it one is to pull on one's bootstraps. Some law must impose the obligation, and the parties have nothing whatever to do with that.[161]

The rejection of party autonomy, even by such influential figures, did not however halt its rise in practice.[162] Courts generally remained more attuned to the interests of those engaged in cross-border commercial activity, and increasingly gave effect to their choice of law agreements. The disconnect between theory and practice created as a consequence served largely to undermine Beale's First Restatement, encouraging scepticism about private international law rules and scholarship more broadly, and contributing to the rise of the American realist challenge to private international law.[163] This in turn led to a proliferation of new choice of law approaches in the United States, under many (but not all) of which party autonomy has become strongly accepted,[164] and Beale's theoretical objections have been

---

[157] 43 F.2d 824 (1930).

[158] Who, it may be noted, studied at Harvard Law School in the 1890s and thus was likely taught by Beale.

[159] At 826. Incorporation by reference was, however, carefully distinguished at 827 ("the parties cannot select the law which shall control, except as it becomes a term in the agreement"). See further Section 1.3.6.

[160] 48 F.2d 115 (2d Cir. 1931).

[161] At 117.

[162] See e.g. Yntema (1955).

[163] See generally Mills (2013).

[164] See further Section 7.2.4.

overcome or at least sidelined. As noted in the comments to the Second Restatement of Conflict of Laws, adopted in 1971:

> An objection sometimes made in the past was that to give the parties this power of choice would be tantamount to making legislators of them. It was argued that, since it is for the law to determine the validity of a contract, the parties may have no effective voice in the choice of law governing validity unless there has been an actual delegation to them of legislative power. This view is now obsolete and, in any event, falls wide of the mark. The forum in each case selects the applicable law by application of its own choice-of-law rules. There is nothing to prevent the forum from employing a choice-of-law rule which provides that, subject to stated exceptions, the law of the state chosen by the parties shall be applied to determine the validity of a contract and the rights created thereby. The law of the state chosen by the parties is applied, not because the parties themselves are legislators, but simply because this is the result demanded by the choice-of-law rule of the forum.[165]

Party autonomy has thus become established in theory as well as in practice, although not completely in either case. The modern status of party autonomy in choice of law in the United States is discussed in Chapters 7–10.

Part of the explanation for the rise of party autonomy in choice of law is that choice of law clauses increasingly became viewed as ordinary contractual terms, and ordinary contractual terms increasingly became viewed as themselves having a quasi-legislative character. This meant that Beale's objection – that choice of law clauses put the parties in the position of legislators – failed to resonate. Peter Nygh, for example, argued that party autonomy emerged, at least in part, because "Whereas originally [a contract] was seen as an obligation imposed on the parties by the general law arising out of their transaction, it came to be seen as an obligation created by the parties themselves."[166] If contractual obligations are viewed as a product of state law, then it appears circular to argue that the parties should be free to choose which law governs their contract – such a choice is only effective if a law permits it, but it is difficult to see which law is in a position to do so. If a contract merely contains party-generated obligations, however, then there is no obvious reason in principle why the parties

---

[165] Section 187, comment (e).

[166] Nygh (1999), p.7. See further Muir Watt (2010), p.257 ("according to traditional discourse, the empowerment of private actors to choose the law governing their relationship is a natural consequence, and indeed the mirror image, of freedom of contract in the domestic sphere"). On the distinction between contractual party autonomy and private international law party autonomy, see further Section 1.3.5.

might not choose to generate their obligations by reference to a system of law of their choice. This latter perspective may be traced to the Napoleonic Code – Horatia Muir Watt has argued that

> the idea of contract as 'private legislation', so elegantly codified as such in the Napoleonic Code (now 1134 Code civil),[167] certainly originated as much a means to justify binding the parties to their word – and no doubt in the French post-revolutionary context, to keep the judge at bay – as to empower them to create their own brand of law.[168]

In any case, party autonomy may be understood as an internationalisation of freedom of contract. Just as party freedom to 'legislate' the terms of their contracts expanded within liberal economies throughout the twentieth century, so did their freedom to choose between national legal orders, as actors independent of states participating in a globalised economy – possessing autonomy and perhaps even what might be described as a form of sovereignty.[169] Although this is strictly speaking a conflation of contractual autonomy and private international law autonomy (as discussed in Section 1.3.5), the blurring of this distinction has undoubtedly been influential in the development of party autonomy. Even today, the Second Restatement of Conflict of Laws argues that party autonomy in choice of law in contract is justified by "the fact that, in contrast to other areas of the law, persons are free within broad limits to determine the nature of their contractual obligations".[170]

In the civil law tradition, support for party autonomy also gradually gained acceptance from the nineteenth century. An early choice of law rule giving effect to party autonomy was adopted in the 1865 Civil Code in Italy, with its supporters including (perhaps surprisingly) the Italian scholar Mancini, more closely associated with advocating the use of nationality as a connecting factor in private international law.[171] It has, however, been suggested that for Mancini this was also a product of conflating contractual party autonomy with private international law party autonomy, as

---

[167] Now Article 1103 in the French Civil Code 2016.
[168] Muir Watt (2010), p.257 n.29. Muir Watt notes, however, the argument of Samuel (2010), p.54, that "one might note that contract was enforceable at common law not as a form of private legislation, despite the consistent emphasis during the 19th century on the doctrine of freedom of contract".
[169] See Section 1.1.2.
[170] Section 187, comment (e).
[171] See Nygh (1999), pp.8–9; Giuliano-Lagarde Report, p.16; Yntema (1952).

discussed above.[172] Support for party autonomy was, however, countered by opposing movements that (including under the influence of Mancini) emphasised the role of the nation state as the sole determinant of law. This was particularly the case in the post-colonial experience of Latin American states forging national identity in the late nineteenth century, in which "the doctrine of autonomy was firmly rejected" because "due to unfortunate past experiences at the hands of North American and European creditors, [they were] anxious to maintain territorial sovereignty".[173] Party autonomy was not accepted, for example, in the Bustamente Code 1928 which has been influential in the Americas.[174] Party autonomy was also given only partial or wavering support as a principle in Germany, France, and the Netherlands in the early twentieth century,[175] perhaps also reflecting the influence of nationalist conceptions of sovereignty. In the decision of the Permanent Court of International Justice in the Serbian and Brazilian Loans cases, however, the Court observed somewhat tentatively that determining the applicable law for the relevant contracts must be decided "by reference to the actual nature of the obligations in question and to the circumstances attendant upon their creation, though it may also take into account the expressed or presumed intention of the Parties".[176] After the Second World War, an international consensus around party autonomy in choice of law emerged as part of the movement of economic international-ism, reflected for example in Article 2.1 of the 1955 Hague Convention on the Law Applicable to the International Sale of Goods,[177] and in the further developments discussed in Chapter 7.

---

[172] See e.g. Nishitani (2016), p.307 ("Mancini, however, failed to provide a logical and theo-retical basis for party autonomy, as he did not strictly distinguish between freedom of con-tract in substantive law and freedom of choice of law in private international law").

[173] Nygh (1999), p.9. For further discussion of these issues in the context of the 1889 and 1940 Montevideo Civil International Law Treaties, see Albornoz (2010), p.32ff; Juenger (1997); Yntema (1952).

[174] See e.g. Lorenzen (1930).

[175] See generally Rühl (2007a); Nygh (1999), p.9; Yntema (1952); Niboyet (1927) (critiquing the adoption of party autonomy on the basis that it treats the parties as 'sovereign' – simi-larly to Beale's First Restatement approach). The recognition of party autonomy in choice of law in contract in France is usually attributed to *American Trading Co.* v. *Quebec Steamship Co.*, Cass. (civ.), 5 December 1910, s.1911, 1, 129, which accepted both an express and implied choice of law. See Lorenzen (1928). However, under the dominant approach party autonomy played a more restrictive role in French choice of law (as only one among a num-ber of connecting factors localising a contract) until the adoption of the Rome Convention 1980 – see Nygh (1999), p.9.

[176] *Serbian Loans Case, France* v. *Yugoslavia* (1929) PCIJ Ser A, No 20, Judgment 14, 41; *Brazilian Loans Case, France* v. *Brazil* (1929) PCIJ Ser A, No 21, Judgment 15, 121.

[177] See discussion in Van Loon (2016), p.32ff.

2.2.3   *Conclusions*

The primary focus of later chapters in this book is on the modern law of party autonomy. The purpose of this historical analysis has been to highlight certain notable features of the way in which party autonomy has emerged, to put the modern law in context. Party autonomy is both an old and a new phenomenon. It has a long history (although not as long or unambiguous as is often claimed by those seeking to establish its credentials), but its emergence as a dominant and uncontested principle is a product of the late nineteenth and early twentieth centuries. How it emerged to have this position is unclear, and thus the historical foundations of party autonomy are perhaps surprisingly tenuous. In both choice of forum and choice of law, there is no single theoretical or doctrinal development that marked the emergence of party autonomy. Rather, in each case there was a slow slide from which a rule in favour of party autonomy gradually emerged. In the context of choice of forum, this was a gradual shift in the rules of jurisdiction, from emphasising the limitations of state power over a defendant (based on respect for the equal sovereignty of other states) to emphasising questions of fairness to defendants themselves. Here, party autonomy emerged primarily (in respect of prorogation) from the rules regarding submission to a forum which were considered to overcome any concerns about fairness, as well as (in respect of derogation) an acceptance that private agreements should justify a refusal to exercise jurisdiction. In the context of choice of law, party intentions went from being relevant as a justification for an objective rule (generally the place of performance of a contract, as the law the parties actually or must have 'had in mind'), to becoming the foundation of choice of law in general (such that a specific agreement would override any presumed intention of the parties). This move was also partly supported by enhancements in freedom of contract, and a blurring between contractual party autonomy and private international law party autonomy.

It is particularly notable that these two processes do not appear to have been conceptually or practically linked. There was no single or coherent push for the adoption of party autonomy as a general principle, but rather two different and independent processes through which the different forms of party autonomy emerged. In both cases, however, part of the background to these transformations is a shift in the conception of private international law, from being situated as part of international law (with a focus on international limitations on the regulatory authority of states, based on connections of territory or nationality), to being situated as part of private law (with a focus on fairness and doing justice between the parties), with choice of law and choice of court agreements being viewed as simply ordinary contractual terms. It might thus be argued that the rise of the individual as a 'sovereign' under party autonomy is associated with the declining influence of the powers and limitations of state sovereignty on the development of private international law. Indeed, the rise of party autonomy arguably reflects a broader decline in the influence of state sovereignty, as it mirrors and has contributed to the establishment of the global private markets that have become characteristic of the modern economy, as discussed further below.

2.3   Normative Foundations of Party Autonomy

Why should choice of court or choice of law agreements be given effect? This deceptively simple question might prompt a simple response – because that is what the parties have agreed. It might thus be argued that choice of law and choice of forum agreements are or should be enforced simply because they are contracts, an approach that has perhaps been particularly associated with the common law.[178] But as discussed further below, this is question-begging; an agreement is (at least conventionally) only a contract if a state has decided to make it legally enforceable. Contracts exist not only to serve the parties but also to serve broader public interests, such as promoting the efficient functioning of economic relations by putting state enforcement resources behind private promises. States *choose* whether to view expressions of party autonomy (choice of forum or choice of law clause) as enforceable contracts – indeed, as noted above, such agreements were historically often not enforced, and some states still treat at least some types of these agreements as unenforceable (although the evident trend in private international law is towards giving more rather than less effectiveness to exercises of party autonomy). Choice of law and forum agreements are thus not simply contracts – they are special, because they purport to take the parties outside (or bring the parties inside) the institutions and governing law of the legal system that evaluates them and that confers the status of contract.[179] They are private legal acts that seem, almost paradoxically, to claim a status higher than the laws of the states

---

[178] See generally e.g. Briggs (2008); Yntema (1955), p.47 ("In cases of conflict of laws, it is thus a natural inference from the principle of contract that the law contemplated by the parties should apply in situations where their rights are to be measured by their agreement"). See further discussion in Chapters 3 and 7.

[179] See e.g. *Northwestern National Insurance Co. v. Donovan*, 916 F.2d 372 (7th Cir. 1990).

that give such private acts their legal character. As discussed in Section 1.3.5, an exercise in private international law party autonomy is different from an exercise in contractual autonomy. This distinctiveness might be viewed as a good reason to treat such agreements differently from other contracts (or contractual terms) – to refuse to enforce them. So the question remains, why choose, in principle, to make choice of law and forum agreements enforceable?

There is no single, widely accepted articulation of the justification or justifications for party autonomy in private international law. Indeed, there is surprisingly little scholarship that directly addresses the normative question of why party autonomy ought to be given effect.[180] Much private international law scholarship on this topic has tended to simply accept the reality of party autonomy, and explore its contours purely as a question of positive law – a field to be navigated by practitioners. There is no doubt that such work is of great importance and utility. However, any critical discussion of the rules determining the scope and limitations of party autonomy – any evaluation of party autonomy, in theory or practice – requires a conception of what the supposed objectives or benefits of party autonomy actually are.

A range of competing justifications for party autonomy may be identified – this section categorises them into two general types of arguments, one private and unilateral (itself divided into two sub-types, deontological and consequentialist), and the other public and systemic. While these are distinct, they also overlap significantly, and from them key common principles may arguably be identified for the foundations and limits of party autonomy. Each may be understood and is described below as a form of 'libertarianism' – it is not intended to import with this term its unfortunate modern political loading, but rather the philosophical tradition that places foundational emphasis on individual autonomy in various ways.

2.3.1   Party Expectations and Private-Unilateral Justifications

As examined above, under the modern common law private international law has been primarily viewed as concerned with private rights, a flexible and frequently discretionary set of rules focused on doing justice in

---

[180] See e.g. Basedow (2013a), p.164 ("Party autonomy is generally considered as a universally accepted bedrock principle of the international law of contractual obligations despite the fact that its theoretical foundations continue to remain elusive.") – but then providing probably the most thorough analysis of those foundations.

individual cases and meeting the needs of the parties. Under this framework, it is usually argued that party autonomy is respected because it corresponds with party expectations. As noted above, a particular form in which this argument is commonly presented is that choice of law and choice of court agreements should be given effect as a matter of contract law. Enforcement of such clauses, it is argued, will advance the general purposes of contract law, including allowing the parties to establish a legal framework for their relationship. In its strongest form, it is often claimed that such clauses are ordinary contractual terms, and enforcing them follows simply and directly from the policy of enforcing contractual bargains. Historically, the adoption of party autonomy thus often appeared to follow as a 'natural' consequence of freedom of contract, as explored in Section 2.2. As state regulation of contract law increasingly took the form of optional 'default' rules, which the parties could opt out of through the adoption of specific terms in their contract, it became more difficult to resist the argument that the selection of a foreign legal system with different default rules should be given similar effect. The comments to the Second Restatement rule giving effect to choice of law clauses, for example, explain that:

> Giving parties this power of choice is also consistent with the fact that, in contrast to other areas of the law, persons are free within broad limits to determine the nature of their contractual obligations.[181]

Where the adoption of party autonomy has been resisted, the converse argument has been made: that such clauses are procedural in nature, or concerned with state power rather than private rights, and thus the question of their enforceability should not be simply a matter of the law of contract.

It is important to recognise that agreements on choice of law and jurisdiction may indeed form part of the bargain between the parties – that a preferred court or governing law may be selected as part of a trade-off involving substantive contractual terms, and refusing to enforce part of that trade-off would risk unbalancing the contract. As examined above and in later chapters, such considerations have been particularly prominent under the common law approach to party autonomy.[182] There is, however,

---

[181] Second Restatement, s.187, comment (e).

[182] See e.g. *The Bremen v. Zapata Off-Shore Co.*, 407 US 1, 14 (1972) ("There is strong evidence that the forum clause was a vital part of the agreement, and it would be unrealistic to think that the parties did not conduct their negotiations, including fixing the monetary terms, with the consequences of the forum clause figuring prominently in their calculations.").

something circular about this reasoning. If well-advised parties knew that choice of court and choice of law clauses were unenforceable, they would not negotiate for them as terms of a contract – they would not trade away other potential contractual rights in exchange for their supposed benefits. It is only because such clauses are generally enforceable that the parties view them as desirable. Obviously what the law should not do is to hold out that such clauses will be enforceable and then fail to enforce them, but of course no one suggests such an approach. The argument that choice of court and choice of law agreements should be enforced simply because they are part of the bargain between the parties thus risks circularity – it justifies giving effect to such agreements, because the law provides and thus parties expect that such agreements will indeed be given effect.

Part of the answer to this issue is that when party expectations are referred to in this context, this may not mean the actual expectations of the parties, which are likely to differ in a dispute, and which (as already discussed in Section 1.3.4) in any case are or should be shaped by existing rules of private international law. If party autonomy were clearly not accommodated in the law, well informed parties would not expect their wishes as to jurisdiction or applicable law to be taken into consideration, and their expectations would be met by *failing* to give effect to any such wishes. Surely different rules should not apply depending on whether it may be realistically presumed that the parties are sophisticated enough to know the law.[183] As this author has argued previously elsewhere,[184] party expectations in this context might instead mean one of two possible things. First, it might mean the mere (subjective) wishes of the parties – viewing choice of law or forum agreements as an expression of those wishes. But this leaves us with a further secondary question as to why such wishes should be fulfilled, and a general sense that the law should be in the business of wish-fulfilment is not a satisfactory justification because the law will often not enforce the wishes of parties, such as where there are opposing public policies or interests. Second, it might mean the (more objective) reasonable expectations of a reasonable party, if there were no rules of private international law – viewing choice of law or forum agreements as giving rise to a legitimate and reasonable expectation, when considered from behind a 'veil of ignorance' as to the present legal position. Such an argument may leave us little the wiser as to why such agreements do give rise to expectations that are legitimate and reasonable, except perhaps based

---

[183] See generally Hepple (1970).
[184] See further Mills (2009a), p.8ff.

on the idea that expectations created by agreements should generally be considered legitimate, because agreements should generally be enforceable – an intuition commonly expressed through the roman (and international) law maxim 'pacta sunt servanda'. Under either of these approaches, the appeal to party expectations is revealed to be really little more than an appeal to an intuition that, in the absence of compelling reasons, the state should generally enforce rather than obstruct the wishes or freely made agreements of private parties. But this is itself a proposition that requires justification, rather than being sufficient to provide strong foundations for party autonomy on its own. Even if choice of court and choice of law clauses are understood to be 'binding' on the parties, they do not bind the court that must determine their effectiveness, or at least do not do so for the same reasons. Other stronger justifications for party autonomy have however been developed from this base, in various forms, as explored in the following sections.

2.3.1.1   Deontological Libertarianism

The intuition that the state should generally enforce rather than frustrate private agreements, while opaquely expressed in private international law scholarship as simply 'meeting party expectations', may nevertheless still indeed reflect or provide an important justificatory foundation for party autonomy in private international law. The focus on individual freedom required or suggested by this argument means that we might characterise it as a form of 'deontological libertarianism'. This is because it starts from the position that the autonomy of the individual is inherently valuable, and it is an interference with this autonomy, not the autonomy itself, which requires justification. A choice of law or forum may then be viewed as "a necessary expression of individual autonomy",[185] or as a product of "the natural will of the individual along with the corollary right to craft such will by virtue of the individual's innate freedom".[186] There is a long philosophical tradition that can be drawn on in support of this perspective, in which the work of Immanuel Kant may be singled out as particularly influential in positing autonomy as a moral good in itself in facilitating individual self-fulfilment.[187] It is difficult to see why Kant's idea of autonomy as reflecting individual moral agency should extend to corporate actors

---

[185] Lehmann (2008), p.417.
[186] Basedow (2013a), p.196.
[187] See further generally Basedow (2013a), p.196ff; Peari (2013); Schneewind (1997). For a variation based on the work of John Rawls, see Pontier (1998).

motivated at least primarily by shareholder profit, unless accompanied by a belief in 'The Virtue of Selfishness',[188] an idea that is antithetical to Kant's own account of autonomy and whose influence primarily reflects its convenience. Nevertheless, the Kantian ideal of individual autonomy is frequently drawn on in the context of private international law party autonomy. Peter Nygh argued, for example, that "For idealists [party autonomy] is an expression of the human right of individuals to arrange their personal and economic lives as they see fit, subject only to such constraints as are necessary to maintain public order and prevent the exploitation of the weak".[189] Party autonomy in private international law may thus be justified not because of any perceived beneficial *consequences* of its adoption, but because it is considered to be the 'default' position, unless overriding party autonomy is justified in the circumstances of a particular case. Where a legal relation crosses borders it may particularly be argued that no state has an overriding claim to regulate that relationship, and that party autonomy emerges as a residual claim:

> From a legal perspective, too many contradictory rules with equal right to be followed create a void. Thus, we are back in a state of nature, or more precisely, in a 'modern state of nature', where there is no objectively applicable law – paradoxically because of an abundance of law. In this context, the parties regain their residual power to regulate their relationships. Party autonomy means nothing more than that people can take care of their own affairs.[190]

This perspective is thus 'private' and 'unilateral' in character, focused on the freedoms of individual 'self-ordering'. It suggests that the scope of party autonomy should (somehow) be derived from a conception of the innate freedoms of individuals. As already noted in Section 1.1.2, it is no coincidence that some advocates of this approach have analysed an exercise of party autonomy as an exercise of 'human rights',[191] an area of law

---

[188]   The title of a 1964 collection of essays by conservative thinker Ayn Rand.

[189]   Nygh (1999), p.258.

[190]   Lehmann (2008), p.414 (footnote omitted – strikingly, this is to the libertarian philosopher Robert Nozick, *Anarchy, State, and Utopia* (1974); note also the citations of Kant, Hayek, and Nozick on p.418). See also similarly Basedow (2013a), p.200.

[191]   See e.g. Basedow (2013a), p.200 (although he mixes deontological and consequentialist approaches: "The parties can determine the assignment to a national legal system by virtue of their natural will since the alternative, namely assignment according to a national conflict-of-laws regime, varies from country to country and thus cannot guarantee the parties that their legal relationship will be subject to one and the same legal order across all the global fora that may eventually be seised of the case."); Jayme (1991). See discussion in Maultzsch (2016), p.476.

that undoubtedly recognises the value of 'personal autonomy'.[192] The claim is strongest in relation to questions of family law and personal identity, as discussed in Section 8.8. It is much more difficult to see how autonomy in commercial matters can be justified on such grounds, or how legal persons (such as companies) can make a convincing claim to have legal (let alone human) rights inherently, when they derive their (legal) existence from systems of national law. Unsurprisingly, however, this approach may often be identified with the perspective of powerful private actors, particularly multinational corporations, whose view of the world is shaped by the reality of their own economic power, coexisting alongside the formal sovereign power of states, and not necessarily perceived as subsidiary to them.

In essence, this approach arguably involves a recognition of a form of individual sovereignty alongside or perhaps even prior to the sovereignty of the state.[193] Such a perspective is difficult in some ways to reconcile with the state-centric traditions of public international law, even if it makes allowance for countervailing state interests that may serve to restrict party autonomy. Indeed, as noted in Section 1.1, the usual account of public international law rules on 'jurisdiction' makes no allowance for private party choice of law or forum, depending instead on traditional objective connections based on territoriality and personality (nationality, residence, or domicile).

Of course, critics of this perspective may argue that this notion of 'individual sovereignty' is unnecessary, because individual autonomy derives purely from state law – that party choices are only effective because and to the extent that the state allows them to be, through national rules of jurisdiction and choice of law. This is, indeed, the classic response to the argument raised by scholars such as Beale, as discussed above, that party autonomy should be rejected because it "involves permission to the parties to do a legislative act".[194] As noted in Section 2.2.2, for example, the comments on the Second Restatement of Conflict of Laws explain:

> The forum in each case selects the applicable law by application of its own choice-of-law rules. There is nothing to prevent the forum from employing a choice-of-law rule which provides that, subject to stated exceptions, the law of the state chosen by the parties shall be applied to determine the validity of a contract and the rights created thereby. The law of the state chosen by the parties is applied, not because the parties themselves are

---

[192] See e.g. *Pretty v. United Kingdom* – 2346/02 [2002] ECHR 427, [61].

[193] See Section 1.1.2; Zhang (2006a), p.553 ("the importance of granting autonomy to the parties lies with the belief that the will of the parties is sovereign in the field of contract").

[194] Beale (1935), p.1079; see also similarly Beale (1910b), p.260; Beale (1896), p.170.

legislators, but simply because this is the result demanded by the choice-of-law rule of the forum.[195]

This offers a state-sovereigntist response to the 'how' question, but not the 'why' question. Those who adopt this response must rely on some other justification for party autonomy, which supports the state decision to allow private parties to make choices of forum or law – the idea of individual sovereignty discussed above may thus still be required to play a justificatory role, if not a legal one. Even if we understand states to be conferring the legal right to exercise party autonomy, this autonomy may also reflect a prior normative claim.

Other advocates of party autonomy would simply embrace the claim that this perspective cannot be reconciled with the state-centric traditions of international law, and argue that it is part of a broader paradigm shift – already discussed briefly in Section 1.1.2 – with legal as well as normative consequences. The widespread recognition of party autonomy as a principle in private international law, from this perspective, represents an evolution of traditional jurisdictional rules, to accommodate the rise of the individual in international law – just as (in the view of many scholars) the direct recognition of individual human rights has transcended the traditional sovereignty of states. The individual autonomy at the heart of the development of human rights finds a distinct but parallel expression here, in the private international law 'party autonomy' of individual or commercial actors which has been widely accepted by states themselves. State support for party autonomy does not, in this view, require a justification – it is state restraint of party autonomy that would require a justification. Whether party autonomy should extend to private forms of ordering, through acceptance of a choice of a state or non-state law or forum, is under this view simply a question of the scope of individual autonomy – although there is a tradition of libertarian thinking that would readily be open to the emergence of non-state law.[196]

The strength of this argument is in its intuitive appeal to individual freedom as the foundation of the particular legal freedom that is party autonomy. Its weakness is in its articulation as to why individual freedom in a general philosophical sense ought to have this particular implication. Individual freedoms are frequently constrained by other interests. Why should individual freedom mean the freedom to choose whichever law you want (possibly even non-state law) to govern your private legal

---

[195] Second Restatement, s.187, comment (e).
[196] See e.g. Trakman (2011); Petsoulas (2001); Hayek (1973); Hayek (1960).

relations? It is perfectly possible to be committed to a broad conception of contractual autonomy within the state, but not committed to party autonomy in terms of selection between (or beyond) the laws of different states. Selection between different state laws allows the choice of legal systems that have more (or less) contractual freedom than those in which a contract may be formed or performed – commitment to a particular standard of contractual freedom would thus ordinarily be *incompatible* with the idea that parties should be able to select variable standards of contractual freedom themselves. As discussed in Section 1.3.5, the choice of law question, to put this another way, is not the same as the question of contractual freedom itself. It is a 'meta' question, a question concerned with the potential applicability of different legal orders, each of which contains a distinct conception of contract law and of the scope of contractual autonomy. If the purpose of contract law were merely to provide default rules, in the absence of a party choice of alternative rules to govern their private relations, then this distinction would fall away – if the parties can freely choose *any* rules to govern their contractual relations, there is no reason to exclude particular rules because they derive from foreign law. Contract law, however, also embraces other purposes – it pursues state policy interests, which sometimes constrain contractual party autonomy – and to the extent that it does so, it is not self-evident why the parties should have the power, as a matter of private international law party autonomy, to determine which legal system imposes those constraints. Nevertheless, it must be noted that many arguments for private international law party autonomy depend expressly or implicitly on the idea that the autonomy of individuals is in some way a matter that arises independently of state support or constraint, and it is this prior autonomy that demands the recognition of party autonomy in national rules of private international law.

2.3.1.2   Private Consequentialist Libertarianism

An alternative private-unilateral justification for party autonomy may be found in arguments focusing on the beneficial effects of recognising individual choice (rather than the inherent value of individual freedom), which might be characterised as a form of 'consequentialist libertarianism'. It may be argued that individuals should be free to choose the forum or law for their disputes not because of any inherent autonomy they possess, but because giving them that freedom has useful consequences for them. This instrumental justification is more closely aligned with the perspective of states, because it views private party autonomy as conditional rather than inherent, but it remains focused on the benefits of such autonomy to the parties themselves. For example, one often cited reason why choice of forum and choice of law agreements might be enforced is the complexity and difficulty of the rules that apply in the absence of any party choice.[197] An exclusive choice of court agreement in particular may have the benefit of replacing multiple potential courts with a single forum, making jurisdiction more predictable. In both choice of court and choice of law, divergencies in private international law rules between states can multiply the uncertainties. As the Commentary to the Hague Principles on Choice of Law in International Commercial Contracts 2015 notes, "Determination of the law applicable to a contract without taking into account the expressed will of the parties to the contract can lead to unhelpful uncertainty because of differences between solutions from State to State".[198] If the rules on choice of law or choice of court are otherwise difficult to predict, giving effect to party autonomy allows the parties to simplify them and thus to order their relationship. Choice of law rules that depend on an unpredictable judicial determination are highly undesirable for private parties, as the law governing contractual relationships is not only the law applied to resolve disputes, but much more importantly is the law that the parties must themselves interpret and apply in planning their transactions, exercising their rights, and carrying out their obligations. If the forum in which any disputes will be heard is unpredictable, differences in choice of law rules between jurisdictions make the determination of the law that must govern the decisions of the parties doubly unpredictable.[199]

One of the key benefits of party autonomy may thus be a product of (or depend on) its widespread adoption – as a principle that has gained broad (but not invariable) international support, it offers the prospect of ensuring consistent treatment of choice of court and choice of law agreements, increasing legal certainty for the parties in cross-border transactions and reducing incentives for (the harmful version of) forum shopping.[200] This objective, which has long been a fundamental goal for private international law, is often described as 'decisional harmony'. Other harmonised rules of private international law could of course achieve much of the same

---

[197]   See e.g. Maultzsch (2016), p.476; Basedow (2013a), p.193; Nagy (2012), p.579 ("One of the merits of party autonomy is that the question of the applicable law is not left to the intricacies of conflicts law"); Lehmann (2008), p.385 ("More and more states allow parties to cut the 'Gordian knot' of conflict of laws by choosing the applicable law themselves."); Nygh (1999), p.3.

[198]   At [1.2].

[199]   See generally Brand (2013a).

[200]   See further discussion below, and see e.g. Pertegás and Marshall (2014), p.977.

benefit, but none has in practice attracted the breadth of support of party autonomy. In the words of the Second Restatement of Conflict of Laws:

> Prime objectives of contract law are to protect the justified expectations of the parties and to make it possible for them to foretell with accuracy what will be their rights and liabilities under the contract. These objectives may best be attained in multistate transactions by letting the parties choose the law to govern the validity of the contract and the rights created thereby. In this way, certainty and predictability of result are most likely to be secured.[201]

The Reporter for the Second Restatement similarly argued in academic writing that party autonomy "is the only practical device for bringing certainty and predictability into the area of multi-state contracts".[202] In the similar words of the US Supreme Court, "A contractual provision specifying in advance the forum in which disputes shall be litigated and the law to be applied is ... an almost indispensable precondition to achievement of the orderliness and predictability essential to any international business transaction".[203] The flip side of this private benefit is the public gain that "the court is spared the pains of decision" in relation to the difficult issue of private international law,[204] although the 'pain' is merely transferred to the private parties themselves, who (at least in theory) must conduct a comparative analysis of different procedural and substantive laws before making a choice of forum or law. Without party autonomy, harmonisation of substantive law between jurisdictions would of course also potentially spare a court (or the parties) 'the pains of decision' as to what law would apply – this is indeed an alternative strategy in promoting cross-border activity, but one that comes at the significant cost of legal diversity, and thereby without the benefits of systemic competition discussed below.[205]

A further potential consequence of party autonomy in choice of forum and law is that it allows parties to properly cost and indeed reduce their litigation risks, which is in turn likely to lead to more efficient dispute settlement, as commercial parties are less likely to litigate rather than settle a dispute if their legal positions are clear.[206] Giving effect to party autonomy

---

[201] Section 187, comment (e).
[202] Reese (1960), p.51.
[203] *Scherk* v. *Alberto-Culver Co.*, 417 US 506, 516 (1974). See also e.g. *The Bremen* v. *Zapata Off-Shore Co.*, 407 US 1, 13–14 (1972) ("The elimination of all such uncertainties by agreeing in advance on a forum acceptable to both parties is an indispensable element in international trade, commerce, and contracting.").
[204] Reese (1960), p.51.
[205] See further e.g. Coyle (2011); Mills (2010).
[206] See generally e.g. Rühl (2007a); Whincop and Keyes (2001).

may also allow parties to choose a law or court that is very familiar to them, or most effectively or efficiently adapted to their particular relationship or to the types of disputes that they anticipate might arise between them, again reducing the costs and risks of dispute settlement.[207] This may also suggest permitting a choice of non-state forum (arbitration) or non-state law, as this will increase the capacity of the parties to customise dispute settlement processes and permit the parties to choose from a broader range of applicable laws – including laws designed specifically for transnational problems.[208] The Commentary to the Hague Principles on Choice of Law in International Commercial Contracts 2015 also notes, for example, that "parties to a contract may be in the best position to determine which set of legal principles is most suitable for their transaction".[209] If party autonomy is applied not only to contractual issues but also to non-contractual issues, that may further remove the uncertainty and complexity that might be raised by the problem of characterisation – the same law or court will have authority regardless of how the claim is framed or categorised.

Some of the potential efficiency gains from allowing parties to determine the best law or forum for their relationship can, however, only be achieved to the extent that the parties are able to successfully anticipate what issues their choice of law or forum agreements may affect – parties may not in fact have chosen an efficient forum or law if the type of dispute that arises is one that they did not anticipate. The achievement of such efficiencies also presumes that the parties are negotiating from a relatively equal position, such that their agreement will select a fair, neutral and efficient forum, rather than one that will favour the anticipated interests of one of the parties. As discussed further below, the bilateral nature of the agreement reached through choice of forum and choice of law agreements distinguishes the negotiation of those agreements from 'forum shopping', a term that is used (generally critically) where one party has the power to choose the forum (and potentially, through that choice, the applicable law), and their choice will be driven by strategic advantages rather than efficiency. The forum shopping facilitated by party autonomy may be viewed as essentially a form of delegated decision making – leaving it to the parties to determine what is the most appropriate forum or law for their disputes, rather than attempting to adopt a rule that decides this objectively on their behalf. (It might therefore be argued that party

---

[207] See e.g. Rühl (2007a); Guzman (2002); O'Hara and Ribstein (2000).
[208] See e.g. Radicati di Brozolo (2012a); Muir Watt (2010), p.263ff; Juenger (2000).
[209] At [1.3].

autonomy should only operate where objective rules do not provide a clear answer.[210]) As such, it may also be justified on the grounds of a general principle of subsidiarity – that it is the parties themselves who are best placed to make this determination – although this of course must be balanced against any other interests that the parties are not best placed to consider or protect, including third party and public interests.

Giving the parties a choice over the law or forum that governs their relationship may be further justified not only as a practical matter of efficiency, but also as a matter of legitimacy. It may be argued that for a cross-border relationship or dispute, party autonomy provides the most legitimate way of determining which court or system of law should have regulatory power, because its legitimacy is derived from the consent of the parties themselves.[211] The necessity for such a determination arises in part because public international law lacks rules of priority to deal with overlapping jurisdictional claims by states, and thus has no clear answer to the question of whose regulatory authority should govern a cross-border relationship that gives rise to more than one jurisdictional entitlement.[212] In private international disputes, as discussed further below, this risks incentivising a race to the preferred courtroom rather than negotiated dispute settlement. By giving exclusive jurisdiction to one forum (and thereby also exclusive effect to its choice of law rules), party autonomy may eliminate such incentives, conferring priority on the chosen court, although this would perhaps suggest a model of party autonomy in which the parties are limited to choosing between courts or systems of law with an objective connection to their legal relationship. Alternatively, it may be argued that this lack of priority between national systems, and the focus in each legal order on developing solutions to domestic problems, means that no national system is adequate (or legitimate) to deal with cross-border disputes, and thus recourse to arbitration and non-state law should be made available as necessary or at least desirable alternatives. In any case, the idea that party autonomy itself serves as a legitimising criteria for the exercise of jurisdiction or application of law is evidently in tension with other modes of legitimising the application of law – such as the idea that the application of law is legitimised through being the product of national democratic processes.[213]

---

[210] See e.g. Kegel and Schurig (2004), p.653.
[211] Brilmayer (1989), p.1298ff.
[212] See further e.g. Mills (2014).
[213] See further Muir Watt (2010).

2.3.2   Public-Systemic Justifications – Public Consequentialist Libertarianism

Party autonomy in private international law may also be justified through arguments that focus more on the *systemic* or *public* effects of recognising party autonomy, rather than its effects on individuals – a distinct form of 'consequentialist libertarianism'. It may be argued that individuals should be free to choose the forum or law for their disputes because this has benefits not necessarily for them as individuals, but rather benefits the society or legal system as a whole (this might be framed as a benefit for a state, a region, or for the global economy at large). For example, it may be argued that enforcing choice of forum or choice of law agreements will encourage cross-border activity by reducing litigation risk, with the increase in economic activity leading to greater public welfare.[214] Peter Nygh argued, for example, that "For pragmatists [party autonomy] may be seen as the necessary accompaniment of the globalisation of international trade and commerce".[215] This distinct form of instrumental or 'utilitarian' justification[216] is particularly prevalent in the context of European Union private international law rules, which are motivated more by their systemic implications for the internal market (promoting cross-border economic activity) than by the concerns of doing justice, meeting expectations, or benefiting parties in individual cases. Such arguments are most likely to be raised by state actors, as this justification for party autonomy is the one under which it is most conditional on the public benefits supposedly engendered by supporting the doctrine, and under which it remains most squarely within the power and control of states. This is, however, not necessarily the case – as noted above, advocates for this form of party autonomy may support it from an internationalist perspective rather than that of particular states. Some recent expressions of this type of justification have articulated it as an argument that party autonomy should be recognised in order to create a 'law market' regarding both procedural law (choice of forum) and substantive law (choice of law).[217] At least in the commercial context, party autonomy may thus be inherently linked to both the globalisation

---

[214] Basedow (2013a), p.194.

[215] Nygh (1999), p.258.

[216] Muir Watt (2010), p.256 ("its dominant justification is essentially utilitarian, linked to the needs of international trade"); see further Muir Watt (2016); Muir Watt (2004); Wai (2002).

[217] Muir Watt (2010), p.258 ("By allowing parties to cross jurisdictional barriers unhindered, the principle of free choice generates a competitive market for legal products and judicial services."). See further e.g. Eidenmüller (2011); Coyle (2011); Smits (2011); O'Hara and Ribstein (2009); Rühl (2007a); Muir Watt (2004); Muir Watt (2003).

of private markets in practice, and the internationalisation of the theory of market regulation, as domestic freedom of contract is transposed to the higher level question of a choice between the institutions and substantive rules of different national legal orders.[218] Whether and to what extent private international law should be put at the service of such interests is at the heart of disputes over the foundations and limits of party autonomy.

In the context of choice of court, the public consequential justification for party autonomy advocates a type of 'forum shopping' by the parties in their contractual negotiations, selecting the most favourable or efficient forum for any disputes that they anticipate may eventuate. This mode of forum shopping is, however, very different from the (generally disparaged) forum shopping permitted by broad and overlapping jurisdictional rules, and encouraged by differences in procedural law or choice of law rules.[219] This latter (negative) type of forum shopping is unilateral – the selection of an advantageous forum by a claimant, which may not lead to the most efficient allocation of the dispute because it is likely to be driven by strategic interests ("unseemly and mutually destructive jockeying by the parties to secure tactical litigation advantages"[220]) rather than efficiency. The type of forum shopping enabled by party autonomy is mutually agreed by the parties in advance, and therefore may be generally assumed not to advantage either party excessively (in the absence of significant bargaining disparities, as discussed further below). Rather, as examined above, the selection is likely to be made by the parties on the basis of familiarity and thus predictability, or on the basis of what they agree is the most appropriate forum to hear any dispute, for reasons that might include expertise or neutrality. In either case, this type of forum shopping will tend, at least in theory,[221] to lead to greater efficiency, not less, not just in terms of the individual parties and their dispute, but because of systemic efficiencies which are enhanced through competition between state legal institutions.[222] Effective forum shopping in advance (a sensibly negotiated exclusive choice of court or arbitration agreement) may even preclude the harmful form of forum shopping, by limiting litigation to a single forum, further increasing the efficiency of dispute resolution processes. The justification for giving effect to party autonomy under this approach is thus not derived from its respect

---

[218] Muir Watt (2010). On the link (and the distinction) between contractual party autonomy and private international law party autonomy, see further Section 1.3.5.

[219] See generally Bell (2003).

[220] *Scherk v. Alberto-Culver Co.*, 417 US 506, 517 (1974).

[221] For a more sceptical view, see, however, Johns (2008).

[222] See e.g. Whincop and Keyes (2001).

for any idea of individual sovereignty, or even focused on benefits to be achieved by the parties themselves, but rather from expected efficiency benefits for the state or region in which such choices are permitted, or indeed the perceived benefits to the global economy from adopting such rules internationally. Put in internationalist terms, such arguments are not necessarily supportive of the idea that party autonomy should remain under state sovereign control, granted only where the consequences are beneficial to the state. Put in more sovereigntist terms, however, this analysis may mean that different views on the scope of party autonomy are adopted depending on whether a state views foreign parties litigating in their courts as a business opportunity (as in the English commercial courts)[223] or a potential burden on local institutions and citizens (as is more common in the United States).

In the context of choice of law, the public-systemic justification for party autonomy advocates a similar form of 'law shopping'. Here, the choice of the parties is, however, less focused on 'appropriateness', because practical considerations such as the location of evidence or witnesses are only relevant to choice of forum (although choice of law may follow from (or dictate) choice of forum, because it is likely to be most efficient for a court to apply its own law). Aside from such considerations, the focus in this context will largely be on which legal system has the rules that are the fairest as well as the most efficient and helpful to the parties, as discussed in Section 2.3.1. The distinction here is the theory that the ability for parties to select among a variety of applicable laws should similarly lead to 'regulatory competition'[224] – the existence of a law market creates incentives for legal systems to improve their effectiveness and thus their attractiveness to parties, in order to increase their scope of application. (It is less clear whether this theory is supported by practice.[225]) As noted above, a choice of law will also allow the parties to choose a law that they are familiar with (perhaps they might even have litigated similar issues under it previously) and that

---

[223] Note, for example, the famous brochure published by the Law Society of England and Wales in 2007, entitled 'England and Wales: The jurisdiction of choice' ("This brochure sets out the reasons for our success and lets people know why it is in their own interests to use English law and to settle their disputes here." – Foreword, p.5).

[224] See further references in Eidenmüller (2013); Basedow (2013a), p.107ff; Eidenmüller (2011); Rühl (2007a); Mills (2009a), p.202ff; O'Hara and Ribstein (2000); Ogus (1999).

[225] Vogenauer (2013) (concluding at p.77 that "the emergence of regulatory competition in the relevant fields cannot be observed anywhere in the real world. There is no empirical evidence that parties choose the applicable contract law or the forum on the basis of the quality of specific legal rules and that lawmakers improve the quality of these rules to attract more users."). For further empirical analysis see Cuniberti (2014).

is appropriate for their relationship, reducing transaction costs and again leading to efficiencies. An additional public benefit of a party autonomy approach is that the cost of determining the 'better law' for the parties is borne by the parties themselves, rather than by the court.[226] The primary concern here is, however, again principally with the efficiency benefits for the state or region as a whole, or indeed the global economy, including those caused by increased competition between national laws. It might then even be argued that these competition effects should be enhanced through increasing the number of available choices by permitting a choice of non-state law – that "non-national rules should be allowed to compete with national law".[227]

Choices of law are typically in the form of agreed clauses in contracts, but a special form of unilateral party autonomy may be noted at this point. Occasionally choice of law rules may provide that one party is free to select the governing law from a limited number of options – this approach is particularly followed in tort law in some legal systems, to favour 'victims'. For example, under Article 7 of the Rome II Regulation (discussed further in Section 8.3.4):

> The law applicable to a non-contractual obligation arising out of environmental damage or damage sustained by persons or property as a result of such damage shall be the law determined pursuant to Article 4(1) [i.e. the place of the damage], unless the person seeking compensation for damage chooses to base his or her claim on the law of the country in which the event giving rise to the damage occurred.

In this context, the claimant is given a choice of law in the assumption that they will choose the law most beneficial to their individual position,[228] which is the law that will maximise environmental protection. By giving the claimant this choice, the market of potentially applicable laws is distorted in favour of a substantive policy objective that is aligned with maximising the interests of environmental tort claimants. This could also be achieved by a rule that requires the court to determine which of the potentially applicable laws would maximise environmental protection, but by giving this power to the claimant the law also allocates the cost of making this determination to a private party. This particular mode of party

---

[226] Compare, for example, Leflar (1966a,b).

[227] Radicati di Brozolo (2012a), p.19.

[228] Note also, e.g., Art.6(3)(b) of the Rome II Regulation, giving the claimant a limited choice of law in unfair competition claims.

autonomy is thus supported by a distinctive form of public consequential-ist justification.

Another way of conceptualising the procedural and substantive 'law markets' is to consider that they operate like a 'virtual' free movement principle – virtual because the change in forum or applicable law may be made by party choice, rather than requiring any kind of physical move-ment, which would be required if the forum or law were chosen based on some party territorial connection.[229] Advocates of regulatory competition in the EU have supported, for example, the idea that companies should be able to easily incorporate (or reincorporate) in any Member State, with-out requiring any physical change in the location of their central adminis-tration, and then conduct business across Europe governed only by their 'country of origin', on the basis that this will create competition between the laws of the different Member States, leading to overall improvements in efficiency.[230] A similar theory operates in the context of party autonomy in private international law – that the selection of a forum or law by the parties creates competition between the legal institutions and systems of the different Member States – and indeed potentially globally, to the extent that party autonomy is more widely recognised. Such regulatory competi-tion is able to operate virtually because states will commonly apply for-eign private law rules (unlike rules of foreign public law). For competition between public law rules, free movement principles are required – it might be considered, for example, that such a form of competition may loosely take place in terms of tax law regulation, with individuals and corpora-tions basing themselves (to the extent that they have an otherwise free choice) in a country whose tax law they find most attractive. But competi-tion between private law rules is enhanced because the 'movement' may be virtual – companies may base themselves in one jurisdiction, but choose for their contracts to be governed by a foreign system of law which they find more acceptable, allowing them to disaggregate the public and private choices of law and make independent choices of the most beneficial law in each context.

Historically, the global law market has often worked in favour of the application of English courts and law.[231] Parties have selected English courts and law in contracts with limited or no connections to England

---

[229]   See e.g. Muir Watt (2010), p.255.
[230]   See further e.g. Mills (2009a), p.200ff; Michaels (2006); Muir Watt (2005); Roth (2003); Ballarino (2002); Basedow (2000).
[231]   Cuniberti (2014).

because they are at least perceived as being fair and sophisticated, particularly in technical areas such as insurance and shipping law. This is also likely to be a consequence of network effects (or 'choice overload'),[232] which may operate to undermine the effectiveness of the law market as a small number of frequently chosen jurisdictions or systems of law become viewed as market-leading 'standards'.[233] It is no coincidence that the common law evolved a particularly open approach to party autonomy, to encourage and protect this development. The favourable disposition towards party autonomy in English law is thus both a cause and an effect of the rise of London as an international centre of dispute resolution.

2.4   Theoretical Concerns and Limits

These different theoretical justifications for party autonomy in private international law will, to a great extent, support each other – they each offer a justification for basic rules of party autonomy. This is not least because the deontological and consequentialist forms of libertarianism may be viewed as sharing some common foundations. The scope of a 'law market' may be viewed not just as an issue of economic efficiency or outcomes, but as a philosophical question of when individuals should be able to choose their own normative framework, and when the public interests of a society should override their individual freedoms. However, the different justifications for party autonomy also each require a slightly distinct analytical focus, looking variously at the sovereignty of the individual, the efficiency benefits for the parties and the resolution of their disputes of recognising individual choice, and the systemic benefits of regulatory competition. They may therefore be taken to provide slightly distinct answers to the question of *when* party autonomy should be given effect – what are the circumstances in which party agreements on a forum or applicable law should or should not be enforced. They may thus be associated with the different perspectives on party autonomy already introduced in Section 1.1. Justifications that focus on private-unilateral aspects of party autonomy – particularly the deontological version which considers party autonomy as the exercise of an inherent freedom by private parties – are evidently more closely associated with a party-sovereigntist perspective. Justifications that focus on the public benefits purportedly generated by permitted exercises of party autonomy are evidently more

---

[232] Low (2013).
[233] See generally e.g. Druzin (2009).

closely associated with a state-sovereigntist perspective. Arguably the same is true for justifications that look at the benefit for individuals (the private consequentialist perspective), rather than seeing individual choice as a matter of the exercise of an inherent freedom, although such perspectives are perhaps best viewed as a hybrid because they involve both considerations of public power and private interest.

Despite this variety of theoretical justifications, the analysis of the different approaches above suggests a number of key common principles or concerns that might be taken into consideration in determining the limits on party autonomy. These themes, which will recur throughout this book, will now be considered in turn.

2.4.1   Authenticity

In some circumstances there may be doubts over whether a real choice of forum or law has actually been made by the parties. Under each of the justifications for party autonomy examined above, a choice must be genuine for it to be justified.[234] A choice asserted by one party but which is not genuinely a matter of agreement will not be an exercise of the parties' inherent freedom, will not involve a mutually beneficial determination of law or forum by the parties, and will not generate a functional law-market (indeed if the supposed 'choice' is actually just asserted by one party, it could constitute an exercise of unilateral forum-shopping with the negative consequences discussed above).

Doubts as to whether a choice is genuine may arise for evidentiary reasons – whether there is really sufficient evidence to support the determination that the parties have chosen the law or forum, as determined by the courts. Special rules such as writing requirements, or requirements that attention be particularly drawn to certain clauses in the process of contracting, may therefore be adopted as requirements for the formal validity of exercises of party autonomy. Curiously, as discussed particularly in Sections 5.2 and 7.2, such formal constraints are much more common in relation to choice of court clauses than they are in relation to choice of law clauses.

Doubts may also arise for principled reasons as to whether an apparent choice by the parties is actually a free and mutual decision – the

---

[234] O'Hara and Ribstein (2000), p.1151 ("To the extent practicable, parties should be able to choose their governing law, subject to possible procedural protections designed to ensure that the choice is real.")

acknowledgement of bargaining inequalities (including informational asymmetries)[235] involved in certain negotiations, such as the protection of consumers or employees. Such decisions would not be genuine expressions of individual sovereignty, and such a choice will be likely to reflect the relative power of the two parties rather than the most efficient or appropriate forum for the dispute, and thus will also not give rise to beneficial market effects. A running theme throughout the analysis in this book will thus be the question of what standards are applied to review the material validity of a 'choice' apparently made by the parties – the authenticity of their exercise of party autonomy. This is not to suggest that 'authenticity' is necessarily given priority over other values. As discussed in Section 3.4.1, the analysis of consumer choice of forum agreements in the United States, for example, tends to take into account not only the fairness of the agreement itself, but also the potential wider benefits in legal certainty to the supplier, which in turn may benefit consumers through lower prices.

2.4.2   Foreseeability

A second issue that may raise doubts as to the benefit of giving effect to party autonomy arises in respect of disputes or potential disputes that are unforeseeable – where the choice made by the parties may thus be considered blind. Considerations of foreseeability would have the strongest role in the justifications for party autonomy examined above, which are based on private or public outcomes – public and private variations of 'consequentialist libertarianism'. An uninformed choice is certainly unlikely to be of great benefit to the parties, and will not give rise to efficient market outcomes as the rationality of the parties' decision can only reflect factors that they know or may reasonably anticipate at the time of law or forum selection.

A choice that is blind and uninformed may also not be viewed as a genuine choice, and thus not truly reflect an exercise of individual freedom, as party autonomy may be considered under the 'deontological libertarianism' justification examined above. This is, however, a relatively weak argument – adherents of a deontological libertarian approach are likely to take the position that parties should generally be free to make even uninformed choices, because it is the act of choosing itself rather than any beneficial consequences of empowering individual choice that is valued. Foreseeability would also be a relatively insignificant consideration if the

---

[235] See e.g. Rühl (2014), p.343ff; Rühl (2007a), p.177ff.

justification for party autonomy is allowing parties to simplify the determination of questions regarding choice of court or choice of law – under
this approach it is the mere act of *making* a choice that confers the benefit
on the parties, not necessarily any advantage of the court or law that is
chosen.

The general concern here is whether giving individuals decisional
power through private international law party autonomy will actually
lead to beneficial outcomes, either for themselves or for public interests.
If party autonomy is a delegation of decision-making power from states to
individuals, then the issue is whether or when individuals are really able to
exercise that power (relying on party autonomy) better than states (relying on traditional territorial or personal connecting factors). These factors perhaps contribute to explaining why party autonomy has (at least
traditionally) had a much more limited effect when dealing with non-
contractual disputes, where the disputes are less likely to be foreseeable –
an issue discussed further in Chapters 4 and 8. For present purposes, it
is sufficient to note that the question of whether a choice of law or forum
is limited to matters that were foreseen or foreseeable to the parties at
the time when they made their choice is likely to be a contentious issue,
because it is a point whose relevance varies under different justifications
for party autonomy.

2.4.3   Public Interests and Values

Third, there may be overriding public values that must be balanced against
and may trump individual 'sovereignty' – norms that parties should not be
able to evade through contractual choice, however freely entered into, or
possible 'externalities' (effects on third parties or on the public at large)[236]
that are unlikely to be taken into consideration by a private bargain but
that nevertheless should influence matters. One of the underlying issues
at stake in determining when these considerations apply is the question of public interest in private arrangements – the danger that private
agreements may evade public scrutiny, a concern sometimes described
as 'regulatory escape'. Without restrictions, party autonomy would risk
undermining the interests of states in regulating private legal relationships.

---

[236] See e.g. Rühl (2007a), p.177ff; Muir Watt (2010), p.281 ("Promoting party autonomy ...
entails the risk that exclusive attention to private interests might neglect more general soci-
etal values in a world which lacks other forms of regulation – at least beyond regulatory
competition through party choice"); Wai (2002).

The European Parliament has, for example, raised the concern that "the promotion by the Hague Conference of party autonomy in contractual relations worldwide has such serious implications from the point of view of the evasion of mandatory rules as to warrant its being debated and reflected upon in democratic fora worldwide".[237] In the recent words of the Canadian Supreme Court:

> forum selection clauses divert public adjudication of matters out of the provinces, and court adjudication in each province is a public good.[238] Courts are not merely "law-making and applying venues"; they are institutions of "public norm generation and legitimation, which guide the formation and understanding of relationships in pluralistic and democratic societies" (T.C.W. Farrow, *Civil Justice, Privatization, and Democracy* (2014), at p.41). Everyone has a right to bring claims before the courts, and these courts have an obligation to hear and determine these matters.
>
> Thus, forum selection clauses do not just affect the parties to the contract. They implicate the court as well, and with it, the court's obligation to hear matters that are properly before it.[239]

This may raise particular concerns as to whether exercises of party autonomy are appropriate for all types of disputes, particularly non-contractual claims. Another possible concern relates to resource allocation – when and how public resources, like courts, should be put at the service of private parties. Should it merely be up to private parties to decide which courts (and thus which state's public resources) are put to work in resolving their dispute? The basic and rather classical problem here is balancing the interests of the individual (or the free market) against the interests of state regulation. The determination of the limits on party autonomy in private international law is thus, in a small way, part of the balance that must be struck between the individual and the collective, the 'liberal' and the 'society', in any liberal society.

When dealing with expressions of party autonomy that choose between the laws and courts of different states, the issue concerns *which* public authority has the opportunity to impose its norms on the substantive contractual bargain between the parties. The question is which national

---

[237] European Parliament resolution of 23 November 2010 on civil law, commercial law, family law and private international law aspects of the Action Plan Implementing the Stockholm Programme (2010/2080(INI)), [38].

[238] Note, however, the "profound disagreement" with this statement of the dissenting judges in this case, expressed at [161]: "The overwhelming weight of international jurisprudence shows that, far from being a subterfuge to deny access to justice, forum selection clauses are vital to international order, fairness and comity."

[239] *Douez* v. *Facebook, Inc.*, 2017 SCC 33, [25]–[26].

system of private law (determined by the choice of law question), and which national procedural law, public policy and mandatory rules (determined at least primarily by the choice of forum question), may have a role to play. One difficulty here is determining the priority of the public constraints and private choice – should any public court seised of a dispute be free to impose its own constraints on the choice of the parties, or should the choice by the parties itself be effective to determine which public constraints may be brought to bear on the validity of that choice? Neither option appears entirely satisfactory, as explored in later chapters. A further complication arises when dealing with 'transnational' party autonomy – the selection of a non-state law or forum (such as an arbitral tribunal). Here, the issue is whether *any* public authority will have the opportunity to impose its norms on the parties' contractual bargain. This question thus presents a particular challenge for the justification and limits of party autonomy, which is explored in Chapters 6 and 10.

2.4.4   Justifiability

A further and related consideration that may arise in relation to party autonomy is whether its effectiveness should depend on whether the choice by the parties is *in fact* justifiable or appropriate. Justifications for party autonomy that focus on the exercise of an inherent freedom by the parties – deontological libertarian approaches – are unlikely to suggest that any such review is appropriate. Other forms of justification may, however, leave open the possibility of such review. For example, if party autonomy is justified based on the idea that parties can benefit by choosing the best court or law for their legal relationship, this might be subject to review if in fact in the circumstances the parties have chosen a forum or law that is disadvantageous or inappropriate. This would not be a necessary feature of rules based on this justification – parties might instead be entirely trusted to choose for themselves – but since the justification is based on the idea that party choice leads to a beneficial outcome in each particular case, this raises the possibility that a court might not sanction a choice that did not in fact lead to such an outcome.

One variation of this might be a restriction that did not permit parties to choose a law or forum unconnected to their legal relationship. Such a choice might be discounted either because it represents an inappropriate selection by the parties, or because it also takes into account the importance of traditional objective connections (such as territorial or personal links with the parties or their legal relationship) to justify the exercise of jurisdiction or application of law by a state. This might alternatively be considered a further recognition of public values – the interests of states in allocating their judicial resources or in asserting their regulatory authority. Party autonomy may thus, in this context, be viewed as a rule of priority rather than a source of jurisdictional authority in its own right – a perspective that, as seen in later chapters, does appear to influence the law in some states.

2.4.5   Cross-Border Element

A final and once again related issue arises as a consequence of the fact that under some formulations of the justifications for party autonomy, it appears that it is necessary for the dispute or relationship to have a cross-border character. For example, one justification is that if a legal relationship touches more than one state, the best way to determine which law applies, either as a matter of efficiency or legitimacy, is to allow the parties to choose themselves. If, however, the legal relationship does not have a cross-border element, under this approach there is no justification for permitting party autonomy – there is no uncertainty as to which law applies in the absence of a party choice.

Other justifications – that party autonomy is a free exercise of individual sovereignty that is 'prior' to the state, or that party autonomy creates an effective 'law market' that leads to regulatory competition which improves the quality of law and judicial services – do not, however, appear to require this element. For these justifications to function, it is not necessary that the relationship be connected objectively to more than one legal system – although that condition might still be imposed for other reasons, such as the protection of domestic public values. This analysis suggests that whether or not a cross-border element is necessary for party autonomy to be effective is likely to be a contested question, as indeed is shown in later chapters.

3

Choice of Court Agreements:
Effects and Effectiveness

3.1 Introduction

A choice of court agreement (also known as a jurisdiction agreement, choice of forum agreement, or a forum selection clause) is a contract, or a clause in a contract, under which the parties agree that a particular court may hear a dispute or a category of disputes – often but not necessarily disputes related to or arising out of a contract containing the clause. These clauses may be expressed as a form of submission by the parties ('The parties agree to submit any disputes arising under this contract to the English courts, and waive any entitlement to object to the jurisdiction of the English courts'), or more simply, as a declaration ('Jurisdiction: New York courts'). Such clauses very often feature as part of the 'boilerplate' in contractual negotiations, and as part of the terms and conditions of standard form contracts, but any assumption that these clauses fully resolve questions of jurisdiction significantly understates the complexity of the issues that can arise concerning their effects and effectiveness in practice.

This chapter examines the general consequences of jurisdiction agreements, focusing on claims in contract – the extent to which such agreements are recognised by national courts, and the ways in which they are given direct and indirect effect. It examines first the distinction between exclusive and non-exclusive jurisdiction agreements (Section 3.2), before considering the approaches to determining the law governing the interpretation and validity of jurisdiction agreements (Section 3.3). The positive and negative effects of jurisdiction agreements in different jurisdictions are then analysed (Section 3.4), before two recurring problems are examined: the validity of asymmetrical jurisdiction agreements (Section 3.5) and the impact of a jurisdiction agreement on third parties (Section 3.6). Chapter 4 continues the analysis by examining the extent to which jurisdiction agreements are effective in relation to non-contractual claims, such as claims in tort, property or equity. Chapter 5 further examines the formal and subject-matter restrictions that may apply to choice of court agreements. Chapter 6 concludes the analysis of party autonomy in juris-diction by considering agreements in favour of dispute resolution through arbitration, looking at the distinct issue of what limitations are imposed on the powers of the parties to exclude national courts altogether in favour of private dispute resolution, and how questions of validity are approached in relation to arbitration agreements.

As will be evidenced generally below, the unmistakable trend has been towards wider enforcement of choice of court agreements, both in terms of the number of legal systems in which they are recognised, and the degree of effectiveness that is given to them. Brazil, which has long been highlighted as the most prominent objector to party autonomy,[1] has recently recog-nised the effectiveness of choice of court agreements.[2] Chinese law has also increasingly recognised the effectiveness of foreign choice of court agree-ments for foreign-related contracts.[3] A further marker of this trend is the adoption in 2005 of the Hague Convention on Choice of Court Agreements, at the Hague Conference on Private International Law, discussed in Section 3.4.4.[4] The purpose of this Convention is to enhance the effectiveness of choice of court agreements in favour of the courts of Convention states. It is notable that this Convention arose out of a broader project that has (so far) failed to reach agreement on a convention dealing with jurisdiction and the recognition and enforcement of judgments. The decision to focus on the Convention as a narrower product of this work could suggest that choice of court agreements were perceived to be the least controversial aspect of contemporary civil jurisdictional rules.[5] The Convention, which came into effect in 2015, has been ratified by the European Union on behalf of all its Member States except Denmark, as well as Singapore and Mexico, and has been signed but not yet ratified by the United States,[6] the

---

[1] On the traditional position see further Albornoz (2010), p.56ff (noting also Uruguay as adopting a similar approach); Stringer (2006).

[2] Articles 22 and 25 of the new Code of Civil Procedure (L.13.105/15), effective 15 March 2016. This is subject to areas of mandatory Brazilian jurisdiction under Article 23.

[3] Civil Procedure Law, Art.34; Supreme People's Court 'Interpretation of Civil Procedure Law' Zhu Shi [2015] No. 5, Arts.29–30, 531; see generally Tang, Xiao and Huo (2016), p.63ff. The meaning of 'foreign-related contract' is noted in Sections 5.3 and 9.3. See generally e.g. Bath (2016). For prior practice see Tang (2012); Tu (2007).

[4] See further www.hcch.net/en/instruments/conventions/specialised-sections/choice-of-court.

[5] See generally e.g. Teitz (2005). The broader project has now been revived and has made significant progress in relation to the recognition and enforcement of judgments: see www.hcch.net/en/projects/legislative-projects/judgments.

[6] Difficulties have arisen in terms of questions of constitutional competence to implement the convention in the United States: see Brand (2013b); De la Torre (2013).

People's Republic of China, Ukraine, and Montenegro.[7] The Convention rules are discussed in this chapter alongside those of various national legal systems and the European Union, as they represent an attempt to establish an international consensus on choice of court agreements. As examined below, they already have an important impact in relation to certain choice of court agreements in favour of Convention states – the Convention overrides both European Union and national law rules of jurisdiction to the extent of any inconsistency, although the Convention will only prevail over the Brussels I Regulation where one of the parties to a jurisdiction agreement is resident in a Contracting State to the Convention that is not a European Union Member State.[8] The Convention rules may also have a significant influence on the future development of the law either directly (as more states ratify the Convention)[9] or indirectly (as its rules are likely to serve as an inspiration for national law reform, even if not directly adopted). As analysed in this chapter, however, the Convention is not necessarily reflective of existing practices in the legal systems under examination.

3.2   Exclusive and Non-Exclusive Jurisdiction Agreements

It is well known and widely accepted that jurisdiction agreements may be either non-exclusive (also known as 'permissive') or exclusive (also known as 'mandatory') in their effect. A non-exclusive jurisdiction agreement expresses the intention of the parties to submit a selected range of possible disputes to a particular court, without precluding the possible jurisdiction of any other court. Its purpose is to enhance flexibility – enabling litigation to take place in the nominated forum, in addition to any other court that may have jurisdiction. An exclusive jurisdiction agreement, by contrast, is not only intended to confer jurisdiction on the nominated court (often referred to as 'prorogation'), but also to exclude the possibility of any other court exercising jurisdiction over the covered subject matter of

---

[7] For current status see www.hcch.net/en/instruments/conventions/status-table/?cid=98. Denmark has since acceded to the Convention, effective 1 September 2018.

[8] Article 26(6)(a).

[9] The Hague Conference reports that the Convention is under consideration by a number of further states: see Hague Conference on Private International Law, Council on General Affairs and Policy of the Conference, 'Suggested Further Work in Support of Forum and Law Selection in International Commercial Contracts' (2017) Preliminary Document No.5 of January 2017, available at https://assets.hcch.net/docs/a357a94b-5bac-44c5-9fa3-4f1a079b2411.pdf. See also e.g. Mills (2017a) and Marshall and Keyes (2017) (discussing Australia's proposed accession).

the agreement (often referred to as 'derogation'). Its purpose is to enhance certainty – it is intended to ensure that litigation will only take place in the designated forum. There is thus a very clear logical and functional distinction between these two types of jurisdiction agreements, although 'jurisdiction agreements' are often analysed as a single aspect of party autonomy.[10]

The discussion of distinct types of jurisdiction agreements collectively might risk confusion or conflation of their different functions and effects, particularly where they are regulated by a single rule or article. The dual effect of Article 25 of the Brussels I Regulation in the European Union is illustrative here – as explored further below, it may be a basis for both an exclusive ground of jurisdiction (when applied to an exclusive jurisdiction agreement) and a non-exclusive ground of jurisdiction (when applied to a non-exclusive jurisdiction agreement). These functions give Article 25 two very different hierarchical positions in the logic of the Regulation. An exclusive jurisdiction agreement precludes the applicability of the general rules on jurisdiction (principally contained in Articles 4, 7, and 8), giving Article 25 a hierarchically superior relationship to those Articles. A non-exclusive jurisdiction agreement, by contrast, supplements the general rules on jurisdiction. With such an agreement, Article 25 operates along-side the general rules, in a relationship of logical equivalence, as an additional alternative forum in which a claimant may choose to commence proceedings. The non-exclusive function of Article 25 is in fact not evident from the drafting of the Regulation – it might have been better to have separate articles dealing with exclusive and non-exclusive jurisdiction agreements, to clarify their distinct effects. Their combination has presented little practical difficulty, however, as the courts have, on this point at least, taken a sensible purposive approach to the interpretation of Article 25.[11]

This simple division of jurisdiction agreements into exclusive and non-exclusive is, it must be noted, not one that applies clearly in all cases in practice.[12] The parties to a choice of court clause may, for example, agree that any disputes may be submitted to the English or French courts, as

---

[10] The Hague Convention on Choice of Court Agreements 2005 does clearly distinguish between the effects of exclusive jurisdiction agreements (which are the principal focus of the Convention) and non-exclusive jurisdiction agreements (dealt with only through an optional mechanism of reciprocal declarations under Article 22).

[11] See e.g. *Antec International Ltd* v. *Biosafety USA Inc.* [2006] EWHC 47 (Comm), [3]; *Insured Financial Structures Ltd* v. *Elektrocieplownia Tychy SA* [2003] EWCA Civ 110; *Kurz* v. *Stella Musical Veranstaltungs GmbH* [1992] Ch 196.

[12] See further e.g. Briggs (2012).

alternatives, but to the exclusion of any other courts. The evident intention of such an agreement is partially non-exclusive and partially exclusive in its effects. Arguably, an agreement that purports to confer jurisdiction exclusively on the courts of the United Kingdom should be interpreted similarly – as conferring jurisdiction on the courts of England and Wales, Scotland, and Northern Ireland, as alternatives but to the exclusion of any other courts – in the absence of any evidence that a particular court was intended.[13] In general, it may be noted that courts will usually emphasise the importance of giving effect to the intentions of the parties, and thus find ways of adapting the applicable jurisdictional rules where necessary to give effect to such hybrid clauses; some examples of this adaptation are discussed below.[14] The Supreme Court of the People's Republic of China has, however, held that a jurisdiction agreement in favour of more than one court is thereby invalid,[15] although it is unclear whether this remains the modern approach, and an agreement that selects a different court exclusively for each party has been held to be valid.[16] An agreement may also (purport to) be exclusive for one party, but non-exclusive for another. As discussed further in Section 3.5, decisions of the French and Russian courts have cast doubt on the validity of such agreements in recent years, although it is not clear that these are based on persuasive reasoning. A jurisdiction agreement might also, unusually, purport to have only a 'derogation' effect – the parties might agree that no proceedings can be commenced in the courts of France, but without limiting the availability of other courts – the effectiveness of such an agreement would be unclear under most jurisdictional rules, which do not contemplate such a negative choice, but there seems no reason of principle why such a choice could not be made. The intended effects of a particular jurisdiction agreement require careful interpretation. Despite their variety of possible forms, however, the majority of jurisdiction agreements will fall relatively straightforwardly into the categories of exclusive and non-exclusive (or some combination of the two), and these remain useful conceptual reference points in evaluating the effect of such agreements.

This chapter identifies and examines five direct and indirect effects of jurisdiction agreements (with a principal focus on the first two, which are the most significant). The first effect is the question of whether

---

[13] Internal UK law will then determine which court exercises jurisdiction – on which see Cheshire, North and Fawcett (2017), p.317ff.

[14] See further Section 3.5.

[15] Supreme People's Court, Judicial Interpretation No. 22 [1992], Art.24.

[16] See further Section 3.5.

a jurisdiction agreement will be viewed by the chosen court as 'conferring' jurisdiction upon it – this applies to both exclusive and non-exclusive jurisdiction agreements. The second is whether a jurisdiction agreement will be viewed by a non-chosen court as 'removing' its jurisdiction or justifying a refusal to exercise that jurisdiction – this possible effect evidently only arises for exclusive jurisdiction agreements. The third is whether an exclusive jurisdiction agreement will be enforced through an anti-suit injunction or award of damages for its breach. The fourth is whether a jurisdiction agreement will be indirectly given effect through recognition and enforcement of a judgment from a foreign court, where the judgment court based its jurisdiction on a choice of court clause – this might apply to both exclusive and non-exclusive jurisdiction agreements. The fifth is whether an exclusive jurisdiction agreement may be relied on as a defence against the recognition or enforcement of a foreign judgment obtained in breach of the agreement. Before turning to these questions, Section 3.3 addresses the preliminary issue of what law governs a jurisdiction agreement, which may affect both its validity and interpretation, including the question of whether it is exclusive or non-exclusive.

3.3   Interpretation and Validity

Which type of jurisdiction agreement the parties have entered into, as well as what types of disputes are covered by that agreement, are matters of interpretation. The interpretation of a jurisdiction agreement may, however, not be an ordinary question of contract law, for two reasons which are examined below. First, the possible existence of special interpretive presumptions, which may affect the exclusivity or scope of the agreement.[17] Second, the principle of severability, which may affect the law governing the jurisdiction agreement, not only for the purposes of its interpretation but also for assessing its validity.

3.3.1   Presumptions Regarding Exclusivity

The interpretation of a jurisdiction agreement may be affected by special private international law rules. One such rule is found in Article 25 of the Brussels I Regulation, which establishes (in relevant part) that:

> If the parties ... have agreed that a court or the courts of a Member State are to have jurisdiction to settle any disputes which have arisen or which may

---

[17] The issue of the scope of jurisdiction agreements is examined further in Section 4.2.

arise in connection with a particular legal relationship, that court or those courts shall have jurisdiction ... Such jurisdiction shall be exclusive unless the parties have agreed otherwise.

Jurisdiction agreements that satisfy the conditions of the Brussels I Regulation (as discussed further below, and in Chapters 4 and 5) are thus rebuttably presumed to be exclusive in effect. This may be viewed as an overriding EU rule of 'contractual' interpretation for jurisdiction agreements. Alternatively, it might be viewed as a rule giving jurisdiction agreements a presumptive exclusive effect (as the rule specifies that the jurisdiction, rather than the agreement, shall be exclusive). In any case, the justification for this rule is not entirely clear. It is true that exclusive jurisdiction agreements tend to create greater certainty and predictability for the parties, and that these are values generally endorsed by the Regulation. However, it is less obvious that these values should be imposed on parties who may not themselves place them above the competing value of flexibility that would be enhanced by a non-exclusive jurisdiction agreement, even if such parties form a minority. The presumption of exclusivity thus risks undermining the foundation of Article 25 in giving effect to party autonomy, as it tends to suggest that the court should not examine the intentions of the actual parties to the agreement, but apply an objective rule of interpretation based on their presumed intention.

These risks should, however, not be exaggerated, provided the presumption remains rebuttable, and parties have a reasonable opportunity to present evidence that establishes that their agreement, although ambiguous, was not in fact intended to be exclusive. The parties to an exclusive jurisdiction agreement may benefit significantly in terms of legal certainty, and it is not unreasonable for that benefit to give rise to an interpretative presumption that parties to commercial contracts will ordinarily have the intention of achieving exclusivity when nominating a forum. Well-advised commercial parties will also take the rule in Article 25 into consideration in drafting choice of forum clauses, and may be rightly presumed to have intended exclusivity where their clause is not clearly non-exclusive. For other parties, the key question is ensuring that the right balance is struck between the weight given to the presumption, as an objective rule of interpretation, and the opportunity parties should be given to demonstrate different subjective intentions – too much weight risks imposing objective policies on the parties rather than giving effect to their exercise of autonomy. The Hague Convention on Choice of Court Agreements 2005 adopts a similar and perhaps even stronger rule, under which jurisdiction agreements are "deemed" to be exclusive in the absence of express provision to the contrary,[18] which might perhaps suggest a growing international acceptance of a presumption in favour of exclusivity.[19]

There is, however, some debate concerning whether any similar interpretative presumptions operate at common law. Traditionally, the English courts have not presumed in favour of or against exclusivity, or a broader or narrower interpretation of the scope of a jurisdiction agreement, treating the interpretation of jurisdiction agreements as subject to ordinary interpretative rules and principles.[20] Recent case law dealing with dispute resolution clauses – initially focused on arbitration but with a potentially wider impact – may, however, suggest a different approach. In *Fiona Trust* v. *Privalov*, discussed further in Section 6.3, the House of Lords held that "the construction of an arbitration clause should start from the assumption that the parties, as rational businessmen, are likely to have intended any dispute arising out of the relationship into which they have entered or purported to enter to be decided by the same tribunal."[21] In context, this presumption was concerned with the scope of an arbitration agreement (the range of disputes that it should be understood to cover) rather than its exclusivity, but it is arguable that it may impact on both, and may also extend to jurisdiction agreements. Since *Fiona Trust*, the same principle has indeed been applied by lower courts in the context of the interpretation of the scope of choice of court clauses.[22] It is unclear whether this is an interpretative presumption of English contract law, applicable only if the jurisdiction agreement is governed by English law,[23] or an interpretive

---

[18] Hague Convention on Choice of Court Agreements 2005, Art.3(b): "a choice of court agreement which designates the courts of one Contracting State or one or more specific courts of one Contracting State shall be deemed to be exclusive unless the parties have expressly provided otherwise".

[19] See also e.g. *Cathay United Bank* v. *Gao*, Shanghai High Court, (2016) Hu Min Xia Zhong No 99; but see Tang, Xiao and Huo (2016), pp.64–5.

[20] See, for example, *Sinochem International Oil (London) Ltd* v. *Mobil Sales & Supply Corp* (No.2) [2000] 1 Lloyd's Rep 670, [32] ("The test which has been developed for distinguishing an exclusive from a non-exclusive jurisdiction clause is whether on its proper construction the clause obliges the parties to resort to the relevant jurisdiction, irrespective of whether the word 'exclusive' is used"); see also *Austrian Lloyd Steamship Co* v. *Gresham Life Assurance Society Ltd* [1903] 1 KB 249.

[21] *Fiona Trust* v. *Privalov* [2007] UKHL 40, [13].

[22] *Starlight Shipping Company* v. *Allianz Marine & Aviation Versicherungs AG* [2014] EWCA Civ 1010, reversed on other grounds at [2013] UKSC 70; *UBS* v. *HSH Nordbank AG* [2009] EWCA Civ 585, [82]; *Maple Leaf Macro Volatility Master Fund* v. *Rouvroy* [2009] EWHC 257 (Comm), [199]. But see *Ryanair Ltd* v. *Esso Italiana Srl* [2013] EWCA Civ 1450. See also Section 4.2, on whether jurisdiction agreements are interpreted to encompass non-contractual claims.

[23] Each of the cases cited in the previous footnote involved English jurisdiction agreements.

presumption of the English law of jurisdiction that would be applied to jurisdiction agreements governed by foreign law (typically, foreign jurisdiction agreements, as discussed below). The better view is that interpretation should be left to the governing law of the agreement.[24] For jurisdiction agreements governed by English law at least, the main implication of this principle is that they will be interpreted broadly. Thus, a clause providing that any disputes arising 'under this contract' should be heard exclusively by the English courts should also cover, for example, any disputes relating to the validity of the contract. Such an approach was not always adopted in the past.[25]

The argument for applying a similar presumption in favour of exclusivity is slightly distinct – a non-exclusive jurisdiction agreement merely preserves a flexible choice of forum at the time of commencing litigation, and is not incompatible with ensuring that only a single forum will, in the end, hear all related claims.[26] It is thus perhaps not quite so obvious, as noted above, that parties would necessarily wish to constrain their litigation options in favour of achieving greater certainty in this manner. At least in a commercial context, however, such an interpretive presumption may nevertheless be appropriate, as adopted under Article 25 of the Brussels I Regulation, if it remains reasonably open to the parties to demonstrate the contrary. There is thus a reasonable case for suggesting that under the English common law the courts will, guided by this authority, tend to find a commercial jurisdiction agreement governed by English law to be exclusive – applying a special rule of contractual interpretation derived from the presumed intentions of 'rational businessmen'.[27] Australian law has not yet clearly adopted such a presumption, however, but instead interprets

---

[24] See e.g. Dicey, Morris and Collins (2012), [12–105].

[25] See the discussion of previous case law in *Fiona Trust* v. *Privalov* [2007] UKHL 40, [11], and see further Section 4.2.

[26] See further Section 3.4.3.

[27] For support for this approach see further e.g. *Sohio Supply Co* v. *Gatoil (USA) Inc.* [1989] 1 Lloyd's Rep 588 ("To my mind, it is manifest that these business men intended that clause to apply to all disputes that should arise between them. I can think of no reason at all why they should choose to go to the trouble of saying that the English courts should have non-exclusive jurisdiction. I can think of every reason why they should choose that some court, in this case the English court, should have exclusive jurisdiction. Then, both sides would know where all cases were to be tried."); *British Aerospace plc* v. *Dee Howard Co.* [1993] 1 Lloyd's Rep 368; *Continental Bank* v. *Aeakos Compania Naviera SA* [1994] 1 Lloyd's Rep 505, 509 ("In our judgment it would be a surrender to formalism to require a jurisdiction clause to provide in express terms that the chosen court is to be the exclusive forum."); *Hin-Pro International Logistics Ltd* v. *Compania Sud Americana De Vapores SA* [2015] EWCA Civ 401 (establishing also that this leaves little room for a presumption against the interests

jurisdiction clauses on their own terms (focused on whether mandatory words are used), taken in context. For example, if the court chosen would in any event have had jurisdiction, this is a factor taken to indicate exclusivity.[28] Under Indian law, a slightly stronger presumption applies: the courts have indicated that the express inclusion of a particular jurisdiction in a choice of forum clause should generally imply the exclusion of other possible forums for the litigation, although this has controversially (in this context) been based on applying the interpretative maxim *expressio unius est exclusio alterius*.[29]

Under US law, the practice on whether jurisdiction agreements (commonly referred to as forum selection clauses) should be presumed exclusive or non-exclusive has historically been mixed[30] – if anything there has traditionally been a presumption *against* exclusivity,[31] although some analysis suggests that this may be changing to a presumption *in favour of* exclusivity.[32] US courts have split over the related question of whether they should take into consideration the substantive applicable law in interpreting a forum selection clause, some finding that it is essential to give effect to the intentions of the parties (particularly if the parties have chosen

---

of the drafter, unlike the approach under US law discussed below – for criticism of this decision see Chan (2016)).

[28] See generally Garnett (2013a). But see e.g. *Global Partners Fund Ltd* v. *Babcock & Brown Ltd (in liq)* [2010] NSWCA 196.

[29] See e.g. *M/S Swastik Gases P.Ltd* v. *Indian Oil Corp. Ltd* (2013) 7 SCR 581 (Supreme Court of India); *ABC Laminart* v. *AP Agencies, Salem* (1989) 2 SCC 163 (Supreme Court of India).

[30] Heiser (2010), p.1015 ("There does not appear to be a uniform approach to this important determination. Some courts are reluctant to find that a forum selection clause is exclusive, requiring an agreement that designates one forum to also contain specific language that clearly excludes jurisdiction elsewhere") (footnotes omitted). See further e.g. Weintraub (2008), pp.300–301.

[31] Wright (2011), pp.1635–6 ("the general rule is that a forum-selection clause is treated as mandatory (hereinafter 'exclusive') only if it contains clear, unambiguous language of the parties' intent to make the specified forum compulsory and exclusive. Therefore, a clause that merely authorizes jurisdiction in a specified forum, but does not clearly prohibit litigation elsewhere, will be interpreted as permissive (hereinafter 'non-exclusive')") (footnotes omitted); Yackee (2004), p.61; Brand (2002), p.87; *IntraComm, Inc.* v. *Bajaj*, 492 F.3d 285, 290 (4th Cir. 2007); *Docksider, Ltd* v. *Sea Technology, Ltd*, 875 F.2d 762, 764 (9th Cir. 1989) ("When only jurisdiction is specified the clause will generally not be enforced without some further language indicating the parties' intent to make jurisdiction exclusive.") *Hunt Wesson Foods, Inc.* v. *Supreme Oil Co.*, 817 F.2d 75, 77–8 (9th Cir. 1987).

[32] See e.g. Borchers (1992), p.82; *HSBC* v. *Suveyke*, 392 F.Supp.2d 489 (EDNY 2005) (citing to the Hague Convention presumption in favour of exclusivity); Hay, Borchers, and Symeonides (2010), p.535 (a "mild preference" for exclusivity).

foreign law to apply to their contract),[33] others finding that the decision whether or not to give effect to a forum selection agreement is purely a question of US federal procedural law,[34] and others suggesting that it is a hybrid of both.[35] Perhaps the safest conclusion is that generally no clear presumption of exclusivity or non-exclusivity is likely to apply, and that the focus of US courts will be on determining the actual intention of the parties, principally from the language they have chosen to use in their agreement (but potentially construing ambiguous terms against the party who drafted the provision).[36] The absence of any presumption may lead to greater fidelity to the intentions of the parties, although it is perhaps more likely that a lack of presumption in favour of exclusivity simply reflects the traditionally more cautious attitude under US law towards whether exclusive jurisdiction agreements are legitimate or an impermissible attempt to 'oust' the authority of a judicial body that would otherwise possess authority over the parties, as discussed further below.

3.3.2 Severability and the Applicable Law

The second reason why the interpretation of a jurisdiction agreement may not be an ordinary question of contractual interpretation is that the law governing a jurisdiction agreement may be different from the law governing the remainder of the contract of which it is a term. (It is, of course, possible for the parties to enter into a jurisdiction agreement separately from any contract – as might take place, for example, if the jurisdiction

---

[33] *EnQuip Technologies Group* v. *Tycon Technoglass*, 986 N.E.2d 469 (Ohio Ct. App. 2012) (finding a choice of Italian courts to be exclusive on the basis of the applicable Italian law rules on interpretation, found in the Brussels I Regulation); *Albermarle Corp.* v. *AstraZeneca UK Ltd*, 628 F.3d 643 (4th Cir. 2010) (finding that an English forum selection clause governed by English law should be interpreted to be exclusive, as it would be by an English court pursuant to the Brussels I Regulation); *Yakin* v. *Tyler Hill Camp, Inc.*, 566 F.3d 72, 76 (2d Cir. 2009); *Mazda Motors of Am., Inc.* v. *M/V Cougar ACE*, 565 F.3d 573, 580 (9th Cir. 2009); *Sterling Forest Assoc., Ltd* v. *Barnett-Range Corp.*, 840 F.2d 249, 251 (4th Cir. 1988); *Yavuz* v. *61 MM, Ltd*, 465 F.3d 418, 428 (10th Cir. 2006); see further Yackee (2004).

[34] *Manetti-Farrow, Inc.* v. *Gucci America, Inc.*, 858 F.2d 509, 513 (9th Cir. 1988) ("because enforcement of a forum clause necessarily entails interpretation of the clause before it can be enforced, federal law also applies to interpretation of forum selection clauses").

[35] See e.g. *Phillips* v. *Audio Active Ltd*, 494 F.3d 378, 385 (2nd Cir. 2007). See further discussion in Taylor (1993).

[36] See e.g. *John Boutari & Son, Wines & Spirits, SA* v. *Attiki Imps. & Distribs. Inc.*, 22 F.3d 51 (2nd Cir. 1994); *HSBC* v. *Suveyke*, 392 F.Supp.2d 489 (E.D.N.Y. 2005); *JP Morgan Chase Bank, NA* v. *Reijtenbagh*, 611 F.Supp.2d 389 (S.D.N.Y. 2009); *Caldas & Sons, Inc.* v. *Willingham*, 17 F.3d 123 (5th Cir. 1994). See generally e.g. Force (2011).

agreement is entered into after the parties have established a legal relationship – but this is exceptional in practice.) This follows from the doctrine of 'separability' or 'severability', similar to that applied in the context of arbitration (as discussed in Section 6.3), under which a jurisdiction agreement should be viewed as a distinct contract from any broader agreement as part of which it was executed.

3.3.2.1   The Autonomy of a Jurisdiction Agreement

Severability does not only affect the governing law of a jurisdiction agreement. Perhaps the most important consequence of this doctrine – applied commonly in English[37] and US law,[38] and also expressly affirmed as part of the Hague Convention on Choice of Court Agreements 2005[39] and of the Brussels I Regulation in the European Union[40] – is that the *validity* of the jurisdiction agreement must be assessed independently from the agreement of which it forms part. Thus, challenges to the validity of the contract as a whole do not *necessarily* affect the validity of the jurisdiction agreement, which may therefore remain effective to determine which court can determine the outcome of those challenges. Termination of a contract will similarly not terminate its jurisdictional provisions.

The key question is then whether a challenge to validity affects the jurisdiction agreement itself, rather than the substantive terms of the contract. If an issue of validity arises that is specifically targeted at the jurisdiction agreement (for example, if the jurisdiction agreement was fraudulently added to the contract), then evidently that may be considered by *any* court examining the validity of the jurisdiction agreement. By contrast, if it is alleged that the contract as a whole is invalid because its financial terms were affected by bribery, this may affect the validity of the substantive agreement but is unlikely to undermine the jurisdiction agreement. The

---

[37] *Deutsche v. Asia Pacific Broadband* [2008] EWCA Civ 1091; Dicey, Morris and Collins (2012), [12.112]; Cheshire, North and Fawcett (2017), p.415ff.

[38] See e.g. *Preferred Capital, Inc. v. Associates in Urology*, 453 F.3d 718, 722 (2006) ("[g]eneral claims of fraud ... do not suffice to invalidate the forum selection clause"); *Afram Carriers, Inc. v. Moeykens*, 145 F.3d 298 (5th Cir. 1998); *Richards v. Lloyd's of London*, 135 F.3d 1289 (9th Cir. 1998). The validity of jurisdiction agreements under federal law and under the law of many states is instead governed by the test established in *The Bremen v. Zapata Off-Shore Co.*, 407 US 1 (1972), as discussed below – see e.g. *Scherk v. Alberto-Culver Co.*, 417 US 506, 519 (1974).

[39] Hague Convention on Choice of Court Agreements 2005, Art.3(d): "an exclusive choice of court agreement that forms part of a contract shall be treated as an agreement independent of the other terms of the contract. The validity of the exclusive choice of court agreement cannot be contested solely on the ground that the contract is not valid."

[40] Brussels I Regulation, Art.25(5); see e.g. Cheshire, North and Fawcett (2017), p.233ff.

principal consequence of this, compelled perhaps more by practical benefit than logical necessity, is that it is usually the court chosen by the parties
that should hear any dispute as to the validity of the contract as a whole,
even where that hearing might ultimately determine that no substantive
contract was formed between the parties.[41] The more difficult issue arises
where an invalidity issue is not specifically targeted at the jurisdiction
agreement, but may affect whether any contract has been formed at all
(for example, where it is alleged that the entire contract was forged or was
induced by misrepresentation). The better view is that the validity of the
jurisdiction agreement should be affected in the same way as the substantive terms in these circumstances.[42] To require the jurisdiction agreement
to be specifically affected would be to enforce it despite its potential invalidity, which would no longer be a matter of giving effect to party autonomy.[43]
This does, however, increase the risk that jurisdiction agreements might
be undermined through tactical pleading – an issue that has been particularly contentious in the EU, as discussed in Section 3.4.2 – and so in
practice some courts will give effect to a jurisdiction agreement even if the
existence of any contract at all between the parties is disputed.[44]

3.3.2.2   Are Jurisdiction Agreements
Procedural or Substantive?

As noted above, a jurisdiction agreement (as a severable contract) may be
governed by a different applicable law from that which governs the remainder of the legal relationship between the parties. In fact, many courts have
historically tended to approach the validity of a jurisdiction agreement as
a 'procedural' issue, governed by the law of the forum,[45] although as will
be explored below there has been some (but by no means universal) movement towards the approach of viewing a jurisdiction agreement as a 'substantive' issue governed by the law selected by the choice of law rules of the
court that it designates (in the absence of an express choice of its governing law).[46] The procedural approach is more protective of the parties and

---

[41] See e.g. *Mackender* v. *Feldia AG* [1967] 2 QB 590, 602.
[42] *Fiona Trust* v. *Privalov* [2007] UKHL 40, [17].
[43] See e.g. Symeonides (2015), p.338ff; Merrett (2009a), p.548. See also *Mackender* v. *Feldia
     AG* [1967] 2 QB 590, 598 (per Lord Denning), 602–3 (per Diplock LJ); *Crédit Suisse First
     Boston (Europe) Ltd* v. *Seagate Trading Co Ltd* [1999] 1 Lloyd's Rep 784.
[44] See e.g. Hay, Borchers, and Symeonides (2010), p.539.
[45] This remains the position in Australia: see e.g. *Jasmin Solar Pty Ltd* v. *Trina Solar Australia
     Pty Ltd* [2015] FCA 1453; *Oceanic Sun Line Special Shipping Co Inc.* v. *Fay* (1988) 165 CLR
     197, 202, 225, 256, and 260.
[46] See generally Yackee (2004).

restrictive of party autonomy, while the substantive approach gives greater effect to the parties' choices and reduces the risk of conflicting decisions arising. The possibility that a jurisdiction agreement may, because of its severability and procedural characterisation, be governed by a different law from that governing the remainder of the contract mirrors the possibility, examined further in Section 6.3, that an arbitration agreement may be found to be governed by the law of the seat of the arbitration rather than the substantive law of the underlying contract.

In the United States, this issue has not often been discussed directly.[47] Instead it has tended to be obscured by the focus on whether federal courts exercising diversity jurisdiction (where the claim involves one or more foreign or interstate parties)[48] should apply federal or state law to the question of the validity of a choice of court agreement – the former being the applicable procedural law and the latter providing either the applicable choice of law rules or the substantive law.[49] Whatever the explanation, it appears that most US practice adopts a procedural approach, and simply applies the law of the forum to determine the validity of a choice of court agreement in favour of a foreign or other US state court. This is the case even where the contract contains a foreign choice of law clause, although the chosen law is applied more often to the question of the interpretation (rather than the validity) of the clause.[50] Another way of understanding this approach is that it views the constraints on choice of court agreements as mandatory rules, placing greater emphasis on the importance of giving effect to forum restrictions on party autonomy rather than giving effect to a choice of foreign forum and law. By contrast, the practice in the common law is to view jurisdiction agreements as matters of substantive law, which may (or may not) be the same as the law governing the contract as a whole, and may (or may not) be the law of the forum.[51] Whether jurisdiction agreements are viewed as procedural or substantive terms, the

---

[47] But see e.g. *Yavuz v. 61 MM, Ltd*, 465 F.3d 418, 428 (10th Cir. 2006); Symeonides (2017a), p.56ff; Symeonides (2017b); Symeonides (2016), Chapter 11; Clermont (2015); Yackee (2004).

[48] 28 US Code s.1332.

[49] See further discussion in Section 3.4.1. The issue has also arisen in the context of determining whether a jurisdiction agreement is exclusive or non-exclusive – see discussion in Section 3.3.1.

[50] See e.g. Symeonides (2017a), p.56ff; Symeonides (2017b); *Weber v. PACT XPP Technologies, AG*, 811 F.3d 758 (5th Cir. 2016); *Martinez v. Bloomberg LP*, 740 F.3d 211 (2nd Cir. 2014); Yackee (2004).

[51] See e.g. *Astrazeneca UK Ltd v. Albemarle International Corp* [2010] EWHC 1028 (Comm); *OT Africa Line Ltd v. Magic Sportswear Corporation* [2005] EWCA Civ 710, [60].

law governing the validity of a jurisdiction agreement may be different from the law governing the remainder of the contract, although under a substantive approach this would ordinarily be an unusual result[52] unless the parties have specified it directly. Even if the jurisdiction agreement is a separate contract, it might be expected that the same choice of law rule would be applied to determine the governing law for the jurisdiction agreement and to the substantive contract, leading to the same applicable law either directly or indirectly through a principle that related contracts should be presumed to be governed by the same applicable law.[53]

In the European Union, however, the possibility that the law governing a jurisdiction agreement might differ from the law governing the contract in which it is found is enhanced by the fact that 'choice of court agreements' are excluded from the operation of the Rome I Regulation, which (as examined in Section 7.2) ordinarily determines the law governing a contract when proceedings are brought in any Member State. This exclusion is at least in part a consequence of the historic disagreement over whether the validity of a jurisdiction agreement should be viewed as a procedural or substantive legal question. The former would suggest applying the law of the forum (either that hearing the case or that chosen by the parties), while the latter would suggest applying the substantive law of the contract. The Giuliano-Lagarde Report on the drafting of the Rome Convention 1980 itself noted majority support (after "lively debate") for the view that "the matter lies within the sphere of procedure and forms part of the administration of justice (exercise of State authority)",[54] evidently rejecting a purely private law substantive characterisation of choice of court agreements. The exclusion of jurisdiction agreements from the Rome I Regulation means that in EU Member States the choice of law rules applicable to a jurisdiction agreement are not, at least directly, the same as the choice of law rules applicable to the substantive terms of the contract of which it forms part, increasing the likelihood that the jurisdiction agreement will have a different governing law. Indeed, the law governing a jurisdiction agreement will be determined through the application of national choice of law rules, which may lead to different outcomes for jurisdiction agreements in favour of different EU Member States (though

---

[52] For example, in *Phillips* v. *Audio Active Ltd*, 494 F.3d 378, 386 (2nd Cir. 2007), the Court suggested that "we cannot understand why the interpretation of a forum selection clause should be singled out for application of any law other than that chosen to govern the interpretation of the contract as a whole".

[53] See further Section 7.2.

[54] Giuliano-Lagarde Report, p.11. See also Merrett (2009a), p.555; Nygh (1999), p.82ff.

because of Article 25 of the Brussels I Regulation, at least in theory, not different outcomes for the same jurisdiction agreement, as discussed below).

A further part of the explanation for the exclusion of jurisdiction agreements from the Rome I Regulation is that Article 23 of the Brussels I Regulation 2001 and its predecessor, Article 17 of the Brussels Convention 1968, were intended to function as a partial uniform 'code' for jurisdiction agreements.[55] The CJEU long took the view that jurisdiction agreements may only be assessed in accordance with the requirements set down in Article 23 (or Article 17), holding that:

> A jurisdiction clause, which serves a procedural purpose, is governed by the provisions of the [Brussels] Convention, whose aim is to establish uniform rules of international jurisdiction. In contrast, the substantive provisions of the main contract in which that clause is incorporated, and likewise any dispute as to the validity of that contract, are governed by the *lex causae* determined by the private international law of the State of the court having jurisdiction.[56]

The intention was evidently that assessing the validity or effectiveness of a jurisdiction agreement should thus not require a determination of the substantive law applicable to the contract between the parties,[57] but should instead reflect a 'European procedural' characterisation. The application of this principle was (and is) relatively straightforward in relation to the requirements for formal validity, which were clearly set out in the Brussels Convention and now Regulation (and, in relation to the current Article 25 of the Brussels I Regulation, are discussed further in Section 5.2.1). In relation to substantive questions as to whether there is a genuine jurisdiction agreement, the application of the principle was highly problematic. Article 23 did not, of course, set out substantive contract law doctrines such as lack of authority, mistake, or fraud, which might be relied on to establish whether a jurisdiction agreement is invalid. While this might have tempted a court to refer to such doctrines under national law, it was clear from the jurisprudence of the CJEU that Article 23 was intended to function as an independent code, making it unnecessary to determine

---

[55] This was not clear, however, from the Jenard Report, OJ C 59/37, 5 March 1979.

[56] C-269/95 *Benincasa* v. *Dentalkit* [1997] ECR I-3767; see also C-543/10 *Refcomp SpA* v. *AXA Corporate Solutions Assurance SA* EU:C:2013:62, [21]; C-159/97 *Trasporti Castelletti* v. *Hugo Trumpy* [1999] ECR I-1597; C-214/89 *Powell Duffryn Plc* v. *Petereit* [1992] ECR I-1745, [13]–[14]; *Antonio Gramsci Shipping Corporation* v. *Lembergs* [2013] EWCA Civ 730.

[57] *Deutsche* v. *Asia Pacific Broadband* [2008] EWCA Civ 1091; Case 150/80 *Elefanten Schuh* v. *Jacqmain* [1981] ECR 1671. See generally e.g. Cheshire, North and Fawcett (2017), p.232ff; Hartley (2013b), p.145ff; Merrett (2009a); Camilleri (2011).

the applicable substantive law, with a view to ensuring that Article 23 functioned identically in each Member State. The CJEU instead focused on the requirement in Article 23 that the parties "have agreed" on the choice of forum clause, interpreting this as requiring that "real consent" must be established, again without recourse to national law principles.[58] The effect of all this was that a jurisdiction agreement regulated by Article 23 of the Brussels I Regulation 2001 was *a contract governed by European law*, at least in terms of its validity and its interpretation as exclusive or non-exclusive. The CJEU thus appeared to set itself the task of establishing European principles governing when consent should be considered to have been given to a jurisdiction agreement, and when that consent might be vitiated by, for example, lack of authority, mistake, or fraud.

Perhaps in recognition of the immensity of the legal and political challenges presented by this undertaking, the 2012 Recast of the Brussels I Regulation made an abrupt about-turn on this issue by providing (in Article 25(1)) that a jurisdiction agreement should be given effect "unless the agreement is null and void as to its substantive validity under the law of [the chosen] Member State".[59] This is further clarified by Recital 20, which provides that:

> Where a question arises as to whether a choice-of-court agreement in favour of a court or the courts of a Member State is null and void as to its substantive validity, that question should be decided in accordance with the law of the Member State of the court or courts designated in the agreement, including the conflict-of-laws rules of that Member State.[60]

This is, effectively, a complex choice of law rule, somewhat curiously buried in the Brussels I Regulation (which is otherwise exclusively focused on jurisdiction and the recognition and enforcement of judgments), and which essentially adopts *renvoi* (choosing a set of choice of law rules rather than a substantive law), despite the exclusion of that principle in other EU choice of law instruments, including the Rome I Regulation on choice of law in contract.[61] The 'European' choice of law rule adopted in Article 25(1)

---

[58] C-106/95 *MSG* v. *Les Gravières Rhénanes SARL* [1997] ECR I-911, [17]; C-159/97 *Trasporti Castelletti* v. *Hugo Trumpy* [1999] ECR I-1597, [19]. See also *Joint Stock Company 'Aeroflot-Russian Airlines'* v. *Berezovsky* [2013] EWCA Civ 784, and further discussion below.

[59] See further discussion in Herranz Ballesteros (2014); Ratković and Zgrabljić Rotar (2013), p.252ff.

[60] Brussels I Regulation, Recital 20.

[61] Rome I Regulation, Art.20. An argument could be made that this is technically not *renvoi*, because Article 25 is a rule of European law, and there is no possibility of a reference back from national choice of law rules to European law as the governing law for the contract. But see Hartley (2013b), p.166ff.

and Recital 20 is that the substantive validity of a jurisdiction agreement is in turn referred to the choice of law rules of the legal system whose courts have been nominated by the parties. This approach at least ensures that a jurisdiction agreement is governed by the same law, regardless of which Member State court is hearing the dispute – although it does potentially mean differential treatment of jurisdiction agreements in favour of different Member States. It might be viewed as an adaptation of the approach that the CJEU has noted should be applied to jurisdiction agreements in favour of non-Member States – suggesting that, as such agreements fall outside the scope of Article 25 of the Regulation, their validity should be determined by their governing law, itself determined by the choice of law rules of the court making the evaluation.[62] In that case, however, this was not a choice of law rule, but simply the consequence of the fact that choice of court agreements in favour of non-Member State courts were not governed by either the Brussels I Regulation or Rome I Regulation. The rule also did not point to the choice of law rules of the court nominated by the parties, but to those of the forum, and thus did not adopt *renvoi*.

It is not entirely easy to understand the thinking behind the modified extension of this rule to jurisdiction agreements that do fall within the Brussels I Regulation, as provided by Article 25(1) and Recital 20. In part this may be explained as an adaptation of the rule adopted in Article 5(1) of the Hague Convention on Choice of Court Agreements 2005, in anticipation of the EU becoming bound by that Convention (as it did in 2015),[63] which provides that:

> The court or courts of a Contracting State designated in an exclusive choice of court agreement shall have jurisdiction to decide a dispute to which the agreement applies, unless the agreement is null and void under the law of that State.

It was not, however, strictly necessary to make this adaptation, because the Convention applies directly as part of EU law and overrides the Regulation to the extent of any inconsistency. The approach adopted in both instruments arguably reflects an acceptance that the question of whether a choice of court agreement is procedural or substantive cannot be resolved and should be left to national law, but in a way that minimises the risk of inconsistent decisions arising. Consistently with the Convention rule, the Regulation provides that the law of the chosen court should be applied to the question of the validity of a jurisdiction agreement both by the

---

[62] C-387/98 *Coreck Maritime GmbH* v. *Handelsveem BV* [2000] ECR I-9337, [19].
[63] See further discussion below.

chosen court itself, and also by the courts of any other Member State.[64] In the former case, the law designated is both the *lex fori* and also the law of the forum chosen by the parties, and is thus an obvious selection, while in the latter case it is a perhaps slightly less obvious choice between the two. Indeed, the exclusive application of the law of the chosen court under the Brussels I Regulation rule may not quite reflect the more subtle rule adopted in the Hague Convention. Under the Convention, the courts of states other than the chosen court apply a hybrid of the law of the chosen court (to determine whether the agreement is 'null and void') and their own *lex fori* (to determine whether the parties lacked capacity),[65] which seems a preferable rule. It does appear that the Hague Convention rule is also (like the rule adopted in the Brussels I Regulation) intended to adopt *renvoi*,[66] requiring the application of the choice of law rules of the chosen court to determine the law that governs questions of the validity of the choice of court agreement. Like the Brussels I Regulation rule, this leaves it open to particular states to decide whether choice of court agreements in favour of their courts should be viewed as substantive (and thus governed by the law that governs the choice of court agreement, which is likely to be but is not necessarily the law that governs the contract as a whole), or procedural (and thus governed by forum law), while requiring other states to give consistent effect to that characterisation. The use of *renvoi* would not be necessary to deal with the possibility that the parties would have wanted incidental issues such as questions of capacity to be governed by their 'home' laws rather than the law of the nominated forum, given that capacity is already dealt with through separate provisions.[67] On the other hand, perhaps this at least partially explains why it was necessary to adopt a doctrine similar to *renvoi* in Article 25(1) and Recital 20 of the Brussels I Regulation – in the absence of a special provision dealing with questions of capacity, it would not be appropriate to suggest that all aspects of the validity of a jurisdiction agreement should be governed by the law of the chosen forum.

In any case, it is not difficult to identify significant problems with this choice of law rule (or perhaps 'choice of choice of law rule') – it is, for

---

[64] See Hague Convention on Choice of Court Agreements 2005, Art.6(a).

[65] Hague Convention on Choice of Court Agreements 2005, Art.6(b).

[66] Hague Convention Explanatory Report, [125].

[67] But see e.g. Ratković and Zgrabljić Rotar (2013), p.258. Issues of capacity are in fact dealt with separately under the Hague Convention, precisely because it is not clear that the law of the chosen court should govern exclusively – see Hague Convention Explanatory Report, [126] n.161.

example, unclear how it should operate if the clause nominates a different court for each party, or gives one or more parties a choice of possible forums.[68] It is not evident whether a single law should be chosen (and if so how), or whether different laws should be applied to different parties or aspects of a single clause (disaggregating a complex clause into a series of distinct agreements). If the latter, it is not clear whether the laws should be applied discretely or concurrently, and if so whether a single invalidity should affect the clause as a whole. Nevertheless, the general principle now appears established that under the Recast of the Brussels I Regulation, jurisdiction agreements should be analysed as being subject to a hybrid of the *European* rules of formal validity and interpretation (as to exclusivity) in Article 25, together with whatever *national* rules on substantive validity apply under the law governing the jurisdiction agreement, determined through application of the national choice of law rules of the state designated in the agreement.

What about questions of interpretation other than those relating to exclusivity? As noted above, Article 25 only provides an interpretive rule for the question of whether the agreement is exclusive or non-exclusive, and a choice of law rule for whether it is "is null and void as to its substantive validity". It thus remains unclear to what extent a national governing law must also be referred to when it comes to interpreting the scope of application of the jurisdiction agreement.[69] The same issue arises in relation to the Hague Convention, which as noted above also specifies the law that governs the validity of a choice of court clause, but not the law that governs its interpretation. Even under the Brussels Convention 1968 and Brussels I Regulation 2001, some CJEU authority suggested that reference to national law may be necessary on this point,[70] which might invite drawing on any national law authority that supports an expansive or narrow approach to interpretation (including the English authority discussed above). This was difficult to reconcile with the jurisprudence of the CJEU in relation to questions of validity under Article 23 of the Brussels I Regulation 2001 – that it should not be necessary to refer to national law to determine the validity of a jurisdictional agreement – which would be to some extent compromised if reference to national law was required

---

[68] See further Section 3.5; see also e.g. *Commerzbank Aktiengesellshcaft* v. *Liquimar Tankers Management* [2017] EWHC 161 (Comm), [79]–[80].

[69] See further Section 4.2.

[70] C-214/89 *Powell Duffryn Plc* v. *Petereit* [1992] ECR I-1745; C-269/95 *Benincasa* v. *Dentalkit Srl* [1997] ECR I-3767; see also e.g. *Roche Products Ltd* v. *Provimi Ltd* [2003] EWHC 961 (Comm).

in order to interpret the scope of the agreement. The development of European principles of contractual interpretation to displace national law in this context would seem equally controversial, particularly now in light of the reforms in the Recast Brussels I Regulation which instead point to the application of national law for questions of validity. The better view is thus that national law should govern the interpretation of a choice of court agreement, but it remains unclear whether this national law should be forum law, or determined by application of the choice of law rules of the forum or of the chosen court. The CJEU has suggested (albeit primarily in older cases) that what is now Article 25 of the Regulation should be interpreted narrowly, as an exceptional rule of jurisdiction.[71] This is different from suggesting that jurisdiction agreements should *themselves* be interpreted narrowly in scope, although if the scope of effect of Article 25 is narrowed this is potentially to similar effect. An alternative view could perhaps be that no presumption as to scope should apply, either as a matter of European or national law, but rather that jurisdiction agreements should simply be interpreted on their own terms. That would, however, probably still require the implicit development of European rules as to interpretation. The better approach is simply to accept the need to apply national law, as supported by Article 25 of the Recast Brussels I Regulation. The most satisfactory rule is likely to be that the law applicable to the validity of the jurisdiction agreement also determines its interpretation, but this will require judicial clarification.

The apparent reliance on European law to govern jurisdiction agreements under Article 23 of the 2001 Regulation (and perhaps still to some extent under Article 25 of the Recast Regulation) thus provides at best only a partial explanation for the exclusion of jurisdiction agreements from the choice of law rules in the Rome I Regulation, as noted above. For jurisdiction agreements that do not satisfy the criteria in Article 25 – most obviously, those in favour of non-Member States – the picture is even less clear. As noted above, such clauses must be evaluated and interpreted entirely according to national law, determined by relevant choice of law rules,[72] but this also requires a reversion to traditional national choice of law rules

---

[71] See e.g. Case 24/76 *Estasis Salotti di Colzani* [1976] ECR 1831, [7]; Case 25/76 *Galeries Segoura* [1976] ECR 1851, [6].

[72] C-387/98 *Coreck Maritime GmbH* v. *Handelsveem BV* [2000] ECR I-9337, [19] ("Article 17 of the Convention does not apply to clauses designating a court in a third country. A court situated in a Contracting State must, if it is seised notwithstanding such a jurisdiction clause, assess the validity of the clause according to the applicable law, including conflict of laws rules, where it sits.").

since the Rome I Regulation also excludes these agreements (not just agreements covered by Article 25 of the Brussels I Regulation). National courts might at least partially circumvent this issue by finding that such jurisdiction agreements are presumed to be governed by the same law as the remainder of the contract, which law may be determined by application of the Rome I Regulation, but such sleight of hand is more convenient than satisfactory.

It would evidently be better if jurisdiction agreements were not excluded from the Rome I Regulation at all. To the extent that Article 25 of the Brussels I Regulation reintroduces the need for jurisdiction agreements to be governed by national law, there is no obvious reason why this should be determined in accordance with traditional national choice of law rules, rather than consistently between the different Member States applying a single rule under the Rome I Regulation. Consistency of decision making between different Member State courts is hardly enhanced if they take different views on what law governs a jurisdiction agreement and therefore on its validity or applicability. For jurisdiction agreements that are not covered by Article 25, their exclusion from the Rome I Regulation is arguably still harmful to uniformity of jurisdiction, assuming that non-Member State jurisdiction agreements are to be given some degree of 'reflexive effect', as discussed below.[73] If jurisdiction agreements were brought within the auspices of the Rome I Regulation, it would not even appear necessary to include any particular special rule to deal with them – under existing rules, for example, a court may view a jurisdiction agreement as a severable contract, which ought to be subject to a distinct analysis in order to determine its applicable law.[74] However, at least in the absence of an express choice of law clause for the jurisdiction agreement (and perhaps even in the presence of such a clause), contentious issues are likely to arise as to whether the agreement is presumed to be governed by the law of the forum (as a procedural matter) or the substantive applicable law of the contract, or some combination of both (perhaps distinguishing between questions of validity and interpretation, as in some US approaches discussed above). Agreeing that jurisdiction agreements should be governed by the Rome I Regulation is much simpler than agreeing on what choice of law rules or presumptions should be adopted to govern them, which is a much more fundamental question going to the heart of how a choice of court by the parties is to be understood. As discussed

[73] See Section 3.4.2.
[74] See e.g. Camilleri (2011).

above, the underlying question that makes choice of law issues for jurisdiction agreements so complex remains whether such agreements should
be characterised as procedural or substantive.

3.4   Positive and Negative Effects of Jurisdiction Agreements

This section examines the general effects of jurisdiction agreements, both
exclusive and non-exclusive. As discussed above, exclusive jurisdiction
agreements intend to have dual effects – both conferring jurisdiction on
the chosen court (sometimes referred to as prorogation), and excluding or
ousting the jurisdiction of other courts (sometimes referred to as derogation). Non-exclusive jurisdiction agreements are intended to have only the
former effect. The extent to which both the intended positive and negative
effects are actually implemented is examined in this section in relation to
different jurisdictions.

3.4.1   United States

As noted above, the dual regulation of exclusive and non-exclusive jurisdiction agreements through Article 25 of the Brussels I Regulation is perhaps symptomatic of a tendency to discuss exclusive and non-exclusive
jurisdiction agreements collectively (as varying forms of jurisdiction
agreements, or different aspects of party autonomy), despite the fundamental distinction between them. The importance of this distinction is
evident in the history of party autonomy in choice of forum, examined in
Section 2.2.1, and perhaps emerges most clearly in the US jurisprudence
on the effectiveness of choice of forum agreements. US courts have tended
to distinguish more sharply between 'conferral' and 'ouster' clauses – the
former category essentially covering all, including non-exclusive, jurisdiction agreements, and the latter (a subset of the former) covering exclusive
jurisdiction agreements. Non-exclusive jurisdiction clauses are alternatively sometimes described as 'permissive', and exclusive jurisdiction
clauses as 'mandatory'.[75] Regardless of terminology, the key point is that
the different categories and effects of different jurisdiction agreements are
clearly recognised.

   As a preliminary point, it should be noted that questions of jurisdiction are a matter for each court, and thus different approaches to party
autonomy may operate in US federal and state courts. Although generally

---

[75] See e.g. *Snapper, Inc. v. Redan*, 171 F.3d 1249, 1262 n.24 (11th Cir. 1999).

foreign parties can have cases removed to the federal courts (on the basis of diversity jurisdiction),[76] this is not always the case as 'complete diversity' (no claimant and defendant can be from the same US state) is generally (although not always) required.[77] Removal from a state court will thus not be permitted if, for example, a foreign party defendant has a local subsidiary that is a proper party to an action brought by a local claimant. Removal will also not generally be permitted where there is a jurisdiction agreement in favour of the state court, as the statutory right of removal is considered to be waived by such an agreement (consistent with the general approach discussed below).[78]

3.4.1.1   Prorogation (Conferral)

The positive effect of a jurisdiction agreement has traditionally been analysed in the US as a form of consent to jurisdiction – or, to put this another way, a particular (contractual) form of waiver of any right the defendant may have to object to the personal jurisdiction of a court over them. As discussed in Section 2.2.1, US courts have long recognised the effectiveness of such waivers in other forms, such as through entering an appearance, and this appears to have led to the acceptance of a contractual waiver (without great consideration of the distinction between submission and party autonomy discussed in Section 1.3.2).[79] Some courts in the US have traditionally gone even further than permitting consent to jurisdiction: they have permitted the parties to consent to an immediate judgment for liquidated damages, through what is known as a 'cognivit' agreement or a 'confession of judgment', thus apparently allowing a defendant to waive any

---

[76] 28 US Code s.1332 and s.1441 – note that (under s.1332) the claim must be valued at more than $75,000. See further e.g. Heiser (2010), p.1022ff.

[77] 28 US Code s.1441. See e.g. *Caterpillar, Inc.* v. *Lewis*, 519 US 61 (1996); *Newman-Green, Inc.* v. *Alfonzo-Larrain*, 490 US 826 (1989); *Strawbridge* v. *Curtis*, 7 US 267 (1806).

[78] Heiser (2010), p.1023.

[79] See e.g. *Petrowski* v. *Hawkeye-Security Co.*, 350 US 495 (1956) (waiver through stipulation in proceedings accepting personal jurisdiction); *National Equipment Rental* v. *Szukhent*, 375 US 311, 316 (1964) ("parties to a contract may agree in advance to submit to the jurisdiction of a given court"). Although this principle was clearly expressed in sufficiently broad terms to encompass a jurisdiction agreement, it is notable that *Szukhent* actually concerned 'submission' through appointment of a local agent, which might be better characterised as an indirect or constructive presence in the territory. See discussion in Weintraub (2008), p.212. Under the English common law, appointment of a local agent is also sometimes viewed as constituting 'submission', although again this might be better characterised as constructive presence: see e.g. *The Society of Lloyd's* v. *Richard A Tropp* [2004] EWHC 33 (Comm); Cheshire, North and Fawcett (2017), p.333.

right to make substantive objections as well as jurisdictional objections.[80] Such (extraordinary) measures remain controversial, even in the commercial context. Submission to jurisdiction through an ordinary waiver in the form of a jurisdiction agreement has, however, been accepted for some time in US federal courts,[81] and is also generally (although less consistently) accepted in US state courts.[82] Some state legislatures welcome a choice of the local forum as a means of dispute settlement for foreign parties, particularly in order to attract business to the local legal industry. New York is perhaps the paramount example here – the New York Code expressly provides that:

> any person may maintain an action or proceeding against a foreign corporation, non-resident, or foreign state where the action or proceeding arises out of or relates to any contract, agreement or undertaking for which a choice of New York law has been made in whole or in part ... and which (a) is a contract, agreement or undertaking, contingent or otherwise, in consideration of, or relating to any obligation arising out of a transaction covering in the aggregate, not less than one million dollars, and (b) which contains a provision or provisions whereby such foreign corporation or non-resident agrees to submit to the jurisdiction of the courts of this state.[83]

Thus, parties involved in large commercial disputes governed by New York law with a New York forum selection agreement are given special access to the New York courts. Other choice of court clauses may also be effective,[84] but the clear intent here is to privilege those cases that will likely be beneficial to the New York economy – suggesting a public consequentialist perspective on party autonomy (where the relevant 'public' is New York).[85]

---

[80] See e.g. *D.H. Overmyer Co., Inc.* v. *Frick Co.*, 405 US 174 (1972). This must, however, be subject to a substantive review process: see e.g. *Henry County Bank* v. *Stimmels, Inc.*, 2013-Ohio-1607 (2013).

[81] See e.g. *National Equipment Rental* v. *Szukhent*, 375 US 311, 316 (1964); *The Bremen* v. *Zapata Off-Shore Co.*, 407 US 1, 11 (1972); *Ultracashmere House, Ltd* v. *Madison's of Columbus, Inc.*, 534 F.Supp. 542 (SDNY, 1982); *Northwestern National Insurance Co.* v. *Donovan*, 916 F.2d 372 (7th Cir. 1990). See further Weintraub (2008), p.211ff.

[82] Among numerous authorities, compare e.g. *McRae* v. *J.D./M.D., Inc.*, 511 So.2d 540 (Fla. 1987) (holding that a forum selection clause cannot establish personal jurisdiction over an objecting non-resident defendant); *Datronic Rental Corp.* v. *DeSol, Inc.*, 474 N.W.2d 780 (Wis.App. 1991) (holding that personal jurisdiction can be conferred purely by consent); *National Union Fire Ins. Co. of Pittsburgh, Pa.* v. *Worley*, 690 N.Y.S.2d 57 (1999) (holding that a forum selection agreement conferred personal jurisdiction and waived any basis to dispute jurisdiction).

[83] New York Code, s.5-1402(1). Note also s.5-1401 (relating to choice of law – discussed in Section 7.3.1).

[84] New York Code, s.5-1402(2).

[85] See further Section 2.3.2.

US federal courts (and most other US courts that recognise forum selection clauses) do not generally require any 'objective' connection between the chosen forum and the parties or their dispute[86] – a forum may indeed be chosen because of its neutrality, and such a choice does not appear to violate constitutional due process requirements, which ordinarily require minimum contacts before a court may exercise jurisdiction over a dispute.[87] The choice is given effect both through accepting it as a basis of jurisdiction, and also indirectly through accepting that the court should (generally) not stay proceedings commenced on the basis of an exclusive jurisdiction clause (as discussed further below).[88] The conferral of jurisdiction on foreign courts (exclusively or non-exclusively) is also widely recognised and given indirect effectiveness by US courts, through accepting such conferred jurisdiction as a basis for recognition and enforcement of a foreign judgment.[89]

It is notable that consent to jurisdiction has generally been described and accommodated by US courts indirectly as a form of 'waiver' of the right to contest jurisdiction, rather than as a direct recognition of any right or power of individuals to choose the forum to hear their disputes.[90] As discussed further below, the mode through which this power is indirectly recognised in US law thus accepts party autonomy while maintaining the view that jurisdiction is exclusively a matter of public power – an example of the ambiguous accommodation of party autonomy by states in a way

---

[86] A principle arguably established in *Neirbo Co.* v. *Bethlehem Shipbuilding Corp.*, 308 US 165, 167–8 (1939).

[87] See generally *International Shoe Co.* v. *Washington*, 326 US 310 (1945); *Hanson* v. *Denckla*, 357 US 235 (1958); *J. McIntyre Machinery, Ltd* v. *Nicastro*, 564 US 873 (2011); *Goodyear Dunlop Tires Operations, SA* v. *Brown*, 564 US 915 (2011); *Daimler AG* v. *Bauman*, 571 US 20 (2014). The acceptance of jurisdiction based on a choice of court agreement reflects the modern US focus on 'fairness' rather than 'power' in jurisdiction, as discussed in Section 2.2.1. But see e.g. *McRae* v. *J.D./M.D., Inc.*, 511 So.2d 540 (Fla. 1987) (holding that consent alone does not obviate the need for minimum contacts).

[88] See discussion in Heiser (2010), p.1019ff.

[89] Federal courts exercising diversity apply state law on the point. Most US states apply either the Uniform Foreign-Country Money Judgments Recognition Act 2005, section 5(a)(3), or Uniform Foreign Money-Judgments Recognition Act 1962, section 5(a)(3), which each establish in almost identical terms that the personal jurisdiction of the judgment court may be based on a prior agreement to submit the subject matter of the dispute to that court. See discussion in Heiser (2010), p.1024ff.

[90] This approach is also partly explained by the fact that in the US, federal, and state courts operate in parallel, with constitutional limitations on their jurisdiction. Some US case law is thus concerned to emphasise that private parties cannot overcome those restrictions, for example by attempting to confer state subject-matter jurisdiction on a US federal court – see e.g. Hay, Borchers, and Symeonides (2010), p.381.

that attempts to preserve the exclusivity of state authority, as discussed in Chapters 1 and 2.

Although a non-exclusive jurisdiction agreement can be analysed purely in terms of such consent or 'waiver', an exclusive jurisdiction agreement cannot. Its intended effect is to address not only any rights of the defendant to contest the jurisdiction of the nominated court, but also the entitlement of the claimant to invoke the jurisdiction of any other court – it therefore aims to deprive alternative courts of any jurisdiction that they may otherwise have had. An exclusive jurisdiction agreement in favour of a particular US court may well therefore have indirect negative effects in terms of how such a court perceives the exercise of jurisdiction by another court. Such negative effects might in principle be enforced through an anti-suit injunction issued by the nominated court, to protect its jurisdiction.[91] Unlike the English courts, however (as discussed further below),[92] US courts do not necessarily view an anti-suit injunction as an ordinary remedy (an order for contractual specific performance) for breach of an exclusive jurisdiction agreement. They tend to be more tolerant of allowing parallel proceedings, and look instead for evidence of vexatious and oppressive conduct.[93] The question of whether damages may be available as an alternative (or additional) remedy for a breach of a forum selection agreement is controversial under US law,[94] arguably reflecting the unsettled question of whether such agreements should be characterised as procedural or substantive (as discussed in Section 3.3.2). Another indirect negative effect of an exclusive jurisdiction agreement is that breach of such an agreement is generally considered a strong reason to refuse to recognise or enforce a foreign judgment.[95]

---

[91] See e.g. *E. & J. Gallo Winery* v. *Andina Licores SA*, 446 F.3d 984 (9th Cir. 2006); *Indosuez International Finance, B.V.* v. *National Reserve Bank*, 758 N.Y.S.2d 308 (N.Y. App. Div. 2003). See discussion in Force (2011), p.441ff; Tan (2005a); Bermann (1990).

[92] See Section 3.4.3.

[93] The standard for issuing an anti-suit injunction in US courts is, however, unclear, with no Supreme Court guidance and the different circuits taking distinct approaches. See e.g. *General Electric Co.* v. *Deutz AG*, 270 F.3d 144 (3rd Cir. 2001) ("injunctive power must be exercised sparingly; parallel proceedings are ordinarily permitted to proceed simultaneously, at least until one has reached the stage where its ruling becomes *res judicata*"); *Kaepa, Inc.* v. *Achilles Corporation*, 76 F.3d 624 (5th Cir. 1996), *cert. denied* 519 US 821 (1996); *China Trade & Development Corp.* v. *M. V. Choong Yong*, 837 F.2d 33, (2nd Cir. 1987); *Quaak* v. *Klynveld Peat Marwick Goerdeler Bedrijfsrevisoren*, 361 F.3d 11 (1st Cir. 2004); Force (2011), p.441ff.

[94] See e.g. Tan (2005b).

[95] See e.g. Heiser (2010), p.1029.

3.4.1.2   Derogation (Ouster)

In the United States, the more controversial question has been what effect should be given to exclusive jurisdiction clauses by courts other than the nominated court. As discussed in Section 2.2.1, such clauses were traditionally analysed in the US as an attempt to 'oust' the jurisdiction of a judicial body, and were thus generally (although not without exceptions)[96] viewed as ineffective or impermissible.[97] In the often-quoted words of a 1958 Second Circuit opinion, "agreements in advance of controversy whose object is to oust the jurisdiction of the courts are contrary to public policy, and will not be enforced."[98] In more recent years, however, most US courts have grown more comfortable with ouster clauses, viewing them (again) as not directly effective in taking away the powers of courts, but rather as a persuasive reason for the courts to exercise their *own* power to decline to exercise their jurisdiction over a dispute, usually through the doctrine of *forum non conveniens*.

It is important at this point to note that this doctrine is formulated slightly differently under US law than it is in most common law systems including English law (discussed further in Section 3.4.3), because it requires not only consideration of the private interests of the parties (whether the court seised is an appropriate and convenient forum *for them* to resolve their dispute), but also consideration of public interest concerns including

---

[96] See e.g. *Central Contracting Co.* v. *Maryland Casualty Co.*, 367 F.2d 341 (3rd Cir. 1966); *Wm. H. Muller & Co.* v. *Swedish American Line Ltd*, 224 F.2d 806 (2nd Cir. 1955); *Krenger* v. *Pennsylvania R. Co.*, 174 F.2d 556, 560–1 (2nd Cir. 1949), per Judge Learned Hand ("courts have for long looked with strong disfavor upon contracts by which a party surrenders resort to any forum which was lawfully open to him ... In truth, I do not believe that, today at least, there is an absolute taboo against such contracts at all; in the words of the Restatement [of Contracts, s.558] they are invalid only when unreasonable"); *US Merchants' & Shippers' Ins. Co.* v. *A/S Den Norske Afrika Og Australie Line*, 65 F.2d 392 (2nd Cir. 1933), per Judge Learned Hand; *Mittenthal* v. *Mascagni*, 66 N.E. 425 (Mass. 1903).

[97] See e.g. *Nute* v. *Hamilton Mutual Insurance Co.*, 6 Gray 174, 184 (Mass. 1856) ("The rules to determine in what courts and counties actions may be brought are fixed, upon considerations of general convenience and expediency, by general law; to allow them to be changed by the agreement of parties would disturb the symmetry of the law, and interfere with such convenience"); *Insurance Company* v. *Morse*, 87 US 445, 451 (1874); *Prince Steam-Shipping Co.* v. *Lehman*, 39 F. 704 (S.D.N.Y. 1889); *Slocum* v. *Western Assurance Co.*, 42 F. 235, 235 (S.D.N.Y. 1890) ("a stipulation inserted in a contract limiting the remedy for a breach of the contract to a particular forum is not a valid stipulation"); *Mutual Reserve Fund Life Ass'n* v. *Cleveland Woolen Mills*, 82 F. 508 (6th Cir. 1897).

[98] *Carbon Black Export, Inc.* v. *The Monrosa*, 254 F.2d 297, 300–301 (5th Cir. 1958), *cert. dismissed*, 359 US 180 (1959); see further Brand (2002), p.59; Karayanni (1996); Reese (1964), p.187 ("One thing can be said with certainty. In the United States the effect of a choice of forum clause dealing with future controversies is uncertain.").

"court congestion, local interest in the matter, interest in having the trial at home with the law that governs, avoidance of conflict-of-law problems or application of foreign law, and unfairness in burdening local citizens with jury duty."[99] An exclusive foreign choice of forum agreement will ordinarily be decisive (or at least influential – the weight given varies in different US jurisdictions)[100] when it comes to questions of private interest or convenience. If the parties have selected the forum, they have determined that it is available and appropriate to deliver justice, and any inconvenience for one party is considered to be part of the agreement (absent a fundamental and unforeseeable change in the nature of the foreign legal system).[101] Similarly, an exclusive local choice of forum agreement will ordinarily be decisive (or at least influential) in establishing that there is no other more convenient foreign court. Neither will, however, affect the public interest considerations noted above. This suggests that US courts will be slightly less likely than English courts to enforce exclusive jurisdiction agreements, because as part of their version of *forum non conveniens*, US courts take into account additional factors that may operate against giving effect to such agreements, balancing the private agreement of the parties with considerations of public interest (or third party interest – for example, to consolidate proceedings against multiple defendants or by multiple claimants).[102] Such cases are, however, still likely to be exceptional – and as noted above the general trend has been towards greater recognition of the need to give effect to forum selection clauses in most circumstances.

---

[99]   *Wong* v. *PartyGaming Ltd*, 589 F.3d 821, 832 (6th Cir. 2009); see further *Gulf Oil Corp.* v. *Gilbert*, 330 US 501 (1947); *Piper Aircraft Co.* v. *Reyno*, 454 US 235 (1981).

[100] See e.g. Hay, Borchers, and Symeonides (2010), p.558ff; Buxbaum (2004); Brand (2002), p.64ff.

[101] See e.g. *McDonnell Douglas Corp* v. *Iran*, 758 F.2d 341 (8th Cir. 1985).

[102] See e.g. Force (2011), p.434ff; Heiser (2010), p.1020; Taylor (1993) (suggesting that such 'public' considerations may only be applicable in cases covered by the federal venue transfer statute – see discussion below – but advocating their relevance in all cases); but see *AAR International, Inc.* v. *Nimelias Enterprises SA*, 250 F.3d 510, 524–5 (7th Cir. 2001), holding that "where the parties to an international dispute have agreed to a mandatory forum selection clause, the usual *forum non conveniens* analysis no longer applies, and the only question remaining for the district court to determine is whether the forum selection clause is enforceable under the standards set forth in *Bremen* v. *Zapata Off-Shore Co.*", thus suggesting that 'public' considerations will not play a role in determining the effectiveness of an exclusive jurisdiction agreement. The court also indicated that the usual *forum non conveniens* analysis should still apply in relation to a non-exclusive jurisdiction agreement, perhaps unless the parties have expressly waived the right to make *forum non conveniens* objections – see further e.g. *Blanco* v. *Banco Industrial de Venezuela, S.A.*, 997 F.2d 974, 979–80 (2nd Cir. 1993).

It may also be noted at this point that a choice of *law* clause can only indirectly affect the question of the jurisdiction of US courts. Consider, for example, contracting parties who have not entered into a choice of court agreement, but have chosen Californian contract law to govern their contract. (We may presume for present purposes that the choice is valid and effective – on which see further Chapter 7.) Unlike in the English courts (as discussed below), the choice of Californian law will not itself serve as a basis of jurisdiction for the Californian courts, but where another basis of jurisdiction exists, the fact that the contract concerned is governed by Californian law is likely to be strong factor in favour of the dispute being heard by the Californian courts (or federal courts sitting in California), as disputes are generally resolved most efficiently by a court applying its own law. The Supreme Court has also held that a choice of law clause is itself a 'contact' that is relevant for determining whether the Californian courts have sufficient 'minimum contacts' to exercise jurisdiction.[103] There is thus an important link between the exercise of party autonomy in choice of law and that in choice of forum – a choice of law agreement is not the same as a choice of court agreement, but may be effective to persuade the court whose law is chosen to exercise jurisdiction. There is even some authority that supports the stronger position that a *forum non conveniens* stay is not available if local law governs the case – thus a choice of a foreign court may not be given effect (depending on the facts) if it is not accompanied by a choice of foreign law.[104]

The seminal case in the recognition of jurisdiction agreements under federal law was the Supreme Court decision in *The Bremen* v. *Zapata Off-Shore Co.* (1972)[105], which concerned a claim arising out of damage to an offshore oil rig owned by Zapata while under tow (from Louisiana to Italy) by the vessel *The Bremen*. The towage contract provided that "Any dispute arising must be treated before the London Court of Justice", but Zapata commenced proceedings in federal admiralty jurisdiction in Florida (where *The Bremen* had put into port following the accident), alleging both negligent towage[106] and breach of contract. The Supreme Court held that

---

[103] *Burger King Corp.* v. *Rudzewicz*, 471 US 462, 482 (1985); see also e.g. *Sunward Electronics, Inc.* v. *McDonald*, 362 F.3d 17 (2nd Cir. 2004).

[104] "If domestic law is applicable to the case, the *forum non conveniens* doctrine is inapplicable." – *Yavuz* v. *61 MM, Ltd*, 576 F.3d 1166, 1178 (10th Cir. 2009); *Gschwind* v. *Cessna Aircraft Co.*, 161 F.3d 602 (10th Cir. 1998); *Rivendell Forest Products, Ltd* v. *Canadian Pacific Ltd*, 2 F.3d 990, 993 (10th Cir. 1993).

[105] *The Bremen* v. *Zapata Off-Shore Co.*, 407 US 1 (1972).

[106] The claim was thus partly in tort, giving rise to the further issue of whether forum selection agreements are effective in relation to non-contractual claims – see further Section 4.3.3.

the Florida court ought not to have accepted jurisdiction, finding that this gave insufficient effect to the agreement between the parties. In so doing, the Court recognised the importance of party autonomy for international business – applying a public consequentialist justification for party autonomy[107] – finding that "The expansion of American business and industry will hardly be encouraged if, notwithstanding solemn contracts, we insist on a parochial concept that all disputes must be resolved under our laws and in our courts."[108] The rule established was therefore that 'forum selection' clauses "are prima facie valid and should be enforced unless enforcement is shown by the resisting party to be 'unreasonable' under the circumstances",[109] in particular (although perhaps not exclusively)[110] because of "fraud, undue influence, or overweening bargaining power".[111] The first two of these qualifications (fraud and undue influence) are doctrines that would, if established, invalidate the jurisdiction agreement as a matter of general contract law, and so are relatively uncontroversial limitations on party autonomy (although determining which law governs such questions may raise complications, as discussed in Section 3.3). The third (overweening bargaining power) could be a special further restriction on choice of forum agreements, but in practice this requirement has been interpreted narrowly by the courts.

This may be illustrated by a later Supreme Court decision on forum selection clauses, *Carnival Cruise Lines, Inc.* v. *Shute* (1990),[112] which concerned a claim brought exclusively in tort for an accident that occurred aboard a cruise ship.[113] Proceedings were commenced in Washington State, the claimant passengers' place of domicile. The cruise ticket included the following clause (printed on its reverse): "It is agreed by and between the passenger and the Carrier that all disputes and matters whatsoever arising under, in connection with or incident to this Contract shall be litigated,

---

[107] See Section 2.3.2.

[108] *The Bremen* v. *Zapata Off-Shore Co.*, 407 US 1, 9 (1972).

[109] Ibid.

[110] The courts have also refused to enforce forum selection agreements where some unforeseeable change in circumstances has affected the appropriateness of the chosen forum: see e.g. *McDonnel Douglas Corp.* v. *Islamic Republic of Iran*, 758 F.2d 341 (8th Cir. 1985). See further e.g. *Haynsworth* v. *The Corporation*, 121 F.3d 956, 963 (5th Cir. 1997), *cert. denied*, 523 US 1072 (1998))

[111] *The Bremen* v. *Zapata Off-Shore Co.*, 407 US 1, 12 (1972).

[112] *Carnival Cruise Lines, Inc.* v. *Shute*, 499 US 585 (1990). See further e.g. Borchers (1992); Mullinex (1992).

[113] Again giving rise to the issue of whether forum selection agreements are effective in relation to non-contractual claims – see Section 4.3.3.

if at all, in and before a Court located in the State of Florida, U.S.A. to the exclusion of the Courts of any other state or country." The Court held that the parties should be bound by the jurisdiction agreement, notwithstanding the fact that the agreement was not and could not have been negotiated, noting in particular that the cruise line had a legitimate interest in limiting the courts in which it could potentially be sued, and that this interest would operate not only to the benefit of the cruise line but also its customers in the form of increased legal certainty and lower prices.[114] The Court thus interestingly shifted from the purely public consequentialist justification for party autonomy adopted in *The Bremen*, to also include a variation of a private consequentialist justification[115] – it was not only the interests of American business and consumers in general that justified the effectiveness of jurisdiction agreements, but the interests of the cruise line and its contracting parties in particular. The Court did emphasise that "forum selection clauses contained in form passage contracts are subject to judicial scrutiny for fundamental fairness"[116] (endorsing in particular the suggestion in *The Bremen* that a choice of a significantly inconvenient forum chosen to frustrate possible litigation would not be given effect),[117] although it held that there was nothing unfair about limiting litigation to the courts of the headquarters of the cruise line in this case. The Court's approach here does not appear to signify any special treatment of jurisdiction agreements – under US law, all form contracts ('contracts of adhesion') are generally subject to "scrutiny for reasonableness"[118] – and thus the decision does not appear to establish that 'overweening bargaining power' will frequently justify invalidating a forum selection agreement, even in the case of non-negotiable consumer contracts.[119]

In each of these decisions, the Court emphasised that the effect given to jurisdiction agreements was not in recognition of any power of private

---

[114] *Carnival Cruise Lines, Inc.* v. *Shute*, 499 US 585, 593–4 (1990).

[115] See further Section 2.3.1.

[116] *Carnival Cruise Lines, Inc.* v. *Shute*, 499 US 585, 595 (1990).

[117] *The Bremen* v. *Zapata Off-Shore Co.*, 407 US 1, 17 (1972) ("the serious inconvenience of the contractual forum to one or both of the parties might carry greater weight in determining the reasonableness of the forum clause"). In *Carnival Cruise Lines*, the court held (at 595) that "there is no indication that petitioner set Florida as the forum in which disputes were to be resolved as a means of discouraging cruise passengers from pursuing legitimate claims".

[118] *Carnival Cruise Lines, Inc.* v. *Shute*, 499 US 585, 600 (1990), per Justice Stevens (dissenting, although not on this point).

[119] See also *Wong* v. *PartyGaming Ltd*, 589 F.3d 821, 829–30 (6th Cir. 2009).

parties to confer or oust the jurisdiction of states, but rather a decision by the courts that such agreements should generally be given effect for policy reasons. The Second Restatement of Conflict of Laws (which shortly pre-dated the decision of the Supreme Court in *The Bremen*) similarly provides that "The parties' agreement as to the place of the action cannot oust a state of judicial jurisdiction, but such an agreement will be given effect unless it is unfair or unreasonable."[120] In the commentary to this provision, it is argued that:

> Private individuals have no power to alter the rules of judicial jurisdiction. They may not by their contract oust a state of any jurisdiction it would otherwise possess. This does not mean that no weight should be accorded a provision in a contract that any action thereon shall be brought only in a particular state. Such a provision represents an attempt by the parties to insure that the action will be brought in a forum that is convenient for them.

This suggests that party autonomy is given effect because of the convenience to the parties themselves – a private consequentialist justification. This is, however, slightly different from the justifications ordinarily relied on by US courts, which (as noted above) tend to emphasise public consequentialist reasons in favour of supporting party autonomy. In *The Bremen*, for example, the Court stated directly that:

> The argument that such clauses are improper because they tend to 'oust' a court of jurisdiction is hardly more than a vestigial legal fiction. It appears to rest at core on historical judicial resistance to any attempt to reduce the power and business of a particular court, and has little place in an era when all courts are overloaded and when businesses, once essentially local, now operate in world markets. It reflects something of a provincial attitude regarding the fairness of other tribunals. No one seriously contends in this case that the forum selection clause 'ousted' the District Court of jurisdiction over Zapata's action.[121]

There is, of course, scope for argument here in identifying the 'legal fiction'. It might equally be contended (adopting a deontological perspective on the justifications for party autonomy)[122] that the recognition of party autonomy by states is a reflection of the realities of private power in a

---

[120] Second Restatement of Conflict of Laws, s.80.
[121] *The Bremen* v. *Zapata Off-Shore Co.*, 407 US 1, 12 (1972).
[122] See further Section 2.3.1.

globalised economy, and the claim by courts that they recognise choice of forum agreements purely to pursue their own policy objectives might thus also be characterised as a convenient legal fiction. This is simply one example of a general conceptual difficulty presented by the rise of party autonomy, as discussed in Chapters 1 and 2 – the difficulties in reconciling recognition of individual power to select a forum or governing law with traditional conceptions of state sovereignty.

Both Supreme Court decisions discussed above concerned disputes in federal admiralty jurisdiction.[123] The law regarding jurisdiction agreements that was established by the Court in these cases was thus initially limited to federal admiralty jurisdiction, although it was subsequently extended to include cases heard on the basis of any federal statute ('federal question' jurisdiction).[174] If, however, a federal court is exercising 'diversity jurisdiction' over parties from different states (including foreign states) – the third major source of US federal court jurisdiction – the analysis is somewhat more complicated. If the dispute concerns a possible transfer between federal courts, then the decision is governed by federal procedural law.[125] The test under these rules is similar to the approach in *The Bremen* – the selection of another court by the parties is viewed as a very significant factor in favour of transferring the case – but the mechanism to give effect to jurisdiction agreements is the statutory forum transfer test rather than the common law *forum non conveniens* doctrine.[126] The strength of the forum selection clause as a consideration in this analysis (echoing an argument made more generally above in relation to *forum non conveniens*) has recently been emphasised by the Supreme Court in

---

[123] See also *Kawasaki Kisen Kaisha Ltd* v. *Regal-Beloit Corp.*, 561 US 89 (2010) (finding an exclusive Japanese forum selection clause in a bill of lading to be effective to justify staying US proceedings).

[124] *Stewart Organization, Inc.* v. *Ricoh Corp.*, 487 US 22, 29–30 (1988); see also e.g. *Phillips* v. *Audio Active Ltd*, 494 F.3d 378 (2nd Cir. 2007); *Slater* v. *Energy Services Group International, Inc.*, 634 F.3d 1326 (11th Cir. 2011).

[125] 28 US Code s.1404.

[126] See *Stewart Organization, Inc.* v. *Ricoh Corp.*, 487 US 22, 25–6 (1988); *Belfiore* v. *Summit Federal Credit Union*, 452 F.Supp.2d 629, 631 (D. Md. 2006). See further e.g. Wright (2011); Heiser (2010), p.1020ff; Taylor (1993); Borchers (1992).

Atlantic Marine Construction Co., Inc. v. United States District Court for the Western District of Texas,[127] finding that:

> a court evaluating a defendant's §1404(a) motion to transfer based on a forum-selection clause should not consider arguments about the parties' private interests. When parties agree to a forum-selection clause, they waive the right to challenge the preselected forum as inconvenient or less convenient for themselves or their witnesses, or for their pursuit of the litigation …
>
> As a consequence, a district court may consider arguments about public-interest factors only.[128]

The effect of the clause is thus to disqualify consideration of any private interests – viewing those as decisively determined by the parties themselves through their agreement – leaving the court solely to consider the potential public interests affected by the forum for the litigation. If a transfer is made between federal courts based on a forum selection clause, the transferee court must (contrary to usual practice under such transfers) apply the state law of the place where it is sitting, rather than the law of the state in which the transferor court is sitting – reflecting the fact that the initial commencement of proceedings (contrary to the clause) is considered to be illegitimate.[129]

If the dispute concerns a possible transfer to a state court or a foreign court, the Supreme Court has not decided whether it is federal or state law that should govern (in essence, whether forum selection clauses are 'substantive' or 'procedural'),[130] although the view adopted by most federal circuit appellate courts is that it is a procedural question governed by federal

---

[127] *Atlantic Marine Construction Co., Inc. v. United States District Court for the Western District of Texas*, 134 S.Ct. 568, 581 (2013), holding that "When the parties have agreed to a valid forum-selection clause, a district court should ordinarily transfer the case to the forum specified in that clause. Only under extraordinary circumstances unrelated to the convenience of the parties should a §1404(a) motion be denied." The court also clarified that in general a forum selection clause in favour of a different part of the US should be given effect through a venue transfer under s.1404 rather than a dismissal under s.1406.

[128] At 582.

[129] *Atlantic Marine Construction Co., Inc. v. United States District Court for the Western District of Texas*, 134 S.Ct. 568, 581 (2013); *Ferens v. John Deere Co.*, 494 US 516 (1990).

[130] See e.g. discussion in *Barnett v. DynCorp International, LLC*, 831 F.3d 296 (5th Cir. 2016); Wright (2011); Hay, Borchers, and Symeonides (2010), pp.543–4.

law and thus the rule from *The Bremen*.[131] The situation regarding jurisdiction is thus (arguably) distinct from that regarding choice of law, in which federal courts exercising diversity jurisdiction apply the law (including the choice of law rules) of the state in which they sit, as discussed further in Section 7.2.4. Forum selection clauses in favour of state or foreign courts will thus ordinarily be given effect in federal courts exercising diversity jurisdiction, as a matter of federal law.[132] Some courts have suggested that forum selection clauses will be given an even greater presumptive effect in international cases (as opposed to cases involving more than one US state) because of the support such clauses give to the functioning of international commerce, a factor emphasised in *The Bremen*.[133]

If a question regarding the effectiveness of a jurisdiction agreement arises in a US state court (or in a federal court exercising diversity jurisdiction that takes the minority view that the effect of a forum selection clause is a matter of substance and not procedure), then the issue is a matter of state law. The *effectiveness* of a choice of forum clause is always then a matter for the forum procedural law – as discussed earlier in this chapter, in some US states the *validity* of a forum selection agreement is also viewed as a procedural question to be dealt with under forum law, although there is some authority for applying the law of the chosen court. These distinct questions are, however, rarely analysed satisfactorily in US courts. Many US states follow the rule in *The Bremen*, and thus generally give effect to an exclusive choice of a different forum.[134] This practice is not,

---

[131] See e.g. *In Re Union Electric Co.*, 787 F.3d 903, 906–7 (5th Cir. 2015); *Krenkel v. Kerzner International Hotels Ltd*, 579 F.3d 1279, 1281 (11th Cir. 2009); *Wong v. PartyGaming Ltd*, 589 F.3d 821, 827 (6th Cir. 2009); *International Software Systems, Inc. v. Amplicon, Inc.*, 77 F.3d 112 (5th Cir. 1996); *Jones v. Weibrecht*, 901 F.2d 17, 19 (2nd Cir. 1990); *Manetti-Farrow, Inc. v. Gucci America, Inc.*, 858 F.2d 509, 514 n.5 (9th Cir. 1988); Anon (2005), p.935ff, Yackee (2004), p.62ff; Lee (1997); De By (1989). The 6th Circuit has, however, also held that the effectiveness of a clause *conferring* jurisdiction on an Ohio federal court should be evaluated according to state law: *Preferred Capital, Inc. v. Sarasota Kennel Club, Inc.*, 489 F.3d 303 (6th Cir. 2007). See also e.g. *Phillips v. Audio Active Ltd*, 494 F.3d 378, 384 (2nd Cir. 2007), suggesting (*obiter*) that a forum selection clause may best be viewed as governed by a hybrid of applicable laws, with its validity determined as a matter of federal procedural law, but its interpretation governed by a substantive law chosen according to the applicable state choice of law rules – an approach which may be similar to the situation under the 2001 version of the Brussels I Regulation, as discussed above (with EU rules governing validity, and national law governing most aspects of interpretation).

[132] Heiser (2010), p.1023.

[133] See e.g. *Lipcon v. Underwriters at Lloyd's, London*, 148 F.3d 1285, 1295 (11th Cir. 1998).

[134] See e.g. Heiser (2010); Ritchie (2010); Heiser (1993).

however, universal – some state courts and state legislatures (for example, Alabama,[135] Iowa,[136] Montana,[137] North Carolina,[138] North Dakota,[139] Oklahoma,[140] and South Carolina)[141] have been sceptical or even actively hostile towards the idea that parties might contract out of their 'rights' of access to their local state courts.[142] Even among state courts that generally give effect to forum selection clauses there are differences regarding which clauses may be held to be contrary to public policy (either as a matter of common law, or through particular statutes designed to protect local parties or interests)[143] – as discussed further in Chapter 5. The analysis above

[135] Alabama now officially follows federal law standards: see *Professional Insurance Corp.* v. *Sutherland*, 700 So.2d 347, 351 (Ala. 1997), overruling *Redwing Carriers, Inc.* v. *Foster*, 382 So. 2d 554, 556 (Ala. 1980) ("We consider contract provisions which attempt to limit the jurisdiction of the courts of this state to be invalid and unenforceable as being contrary to public policy. Parties may not confer jurisdiction by consent, nor may they limit the jurisdiction of a court by consent."). But subsequent practice in fact suggests that there is residual scepticism towards foreign forum selection clauses: *Investors Guaranty Fund, Ltd* v. *Compass Bank*, 779 So.2d 185 (Ala. 2000).

[136] *Davenport Machine & Foundry Co.* v. *Adolph Coors Co.*, 314 N.W.2d 432 (Iowa 1982) ("clauses purporting to deprive Iowa courts of jurisdiction they would otherwise have are not legally binding in Iowa. We further hold, however, that under a motion to dismiss an Iowa action without prejudice on the ground of forum non conveniens, such a clause, if otherwise fair, will be given consideration along with the other factors presented, in determining whether the Iowa court should decline to entertain the suit.").

[137] See e.g. *Keystone, Inc.* v. *Triad Systems Corp.*, 971 P.2d 1240 (Mont. 1998), refusing to enforce a Californian arbitration agreement (contrary to the Federal Arbitration Act) on the basis of Section 28-2-708, Montana Code Annotated, which provides that "Every stipulation or condition in a contract by which any party thereto is restricted from enforcing his rights under the contract by the usual proceedings in the ordinary tribunals ... is void", and generally noting (at 1244) that "§ 28-2-708, MCA, has been applied to invalidate forum selection clauses that would have the effect of forcing Montana residents to litigate disputes outside of Montana." See further *Rindal* v. *Seckler Co. Inc.*, 786 F.Supp. 890 (D.Mont. 1992); *Polaris Industries, Inc.* v. *District Court*, 695 P.2d 471 (Mont. 1985). But see also more recently *Polzin* v. *Appleway Equipment Leasing, Inc.*, 191 P.3d 476 (Mont. 2008).

[138] See North Carolina General Statutes, s.22B-3 ("any provision in a contract entered into in North Carolina that requires the prosecution of any action or the arbitration of any dispute that arises from the contract to be instituted or heard in another state is against public policy and is void and unenforceable").

[139] 2015 North Dakota Century Code, s.9-08-05.

[140] Oklahoma Statutes, Title 15, s.216.

[141] A strong policy against ouster of jurisdiction is adopted in the South Carolina Code 1976, § 15-7-120(A) (effectively providing that all jurisdiction agreements in favour of courts other than those of South Carolina must be viewed as non-exclusive). See further Ritchie (2010), pp.100–1.

[142] See further e.g. Weintraub (2008), p.298ff; Ritchie (2010), p.100ff.

[143] For examples, see discussion in *Wong* v. *PartyGaming Ltd*, 589 F.3d 821, 826–7 (6th Cir. 2009) (with particular reference to the courts of Ohio). See also e.g. § 47.025, Fla. Stat. (1999).

highlights that there is a significant diversity of approaches to forum selection agreements in the United States, which reflects a variety of justifications that have been adopted for giving (or not giving) them effect.

3.4.2   EU Law (Brussels I Regulation)

As noted earlier in this chapter, the Brussels I Regulation deals with exclusive jurisdiction agreements principally through Article 25, which confers exclusive jurisdiction on a Member State court that is the 'beneficiary' of such an agreement, provided it meets certain formal requirements (discussed in Section 5.2). The effects of exclusive jurisdiction agreements in favour of EU Member State courts may also be covered by the Hague Convention on Choice of Court Agreements 2005, discussed in Section 3.4.4, where at least one party to the agreement is resident in a contracting state to the Convention that is not an EU Member State. Exclusive jurisdiction agreements in favour of non-EU contracting states may also be covered by the Convention. It is, however, surprisingly unclear whether this also requires a party to be resident in a non-EU contracting state.[144]

3.4.2.1   Prorogation

One evident effect of Article 25, in relation to both exclusive and non-exclusive jurisdiction agreements, is to serve as a basis of jurisdiction in favour of the chosen court. An exclusive jurisdiction agreement in favour of the courts of a Member State operates as one of the strongest grounds for jurisdiction under the Regulation. A non-exclusive jurisdiction agreement in favour of the courts of a Member State also establishes a potential basis for jurisdiction against a defendant domiciled in any Member State under Article 25. In this form, as noted above, Article 25 operates as one of the non-exclusive jurisdictional rules under the Regulation, in addition to Articles 4, 7, and 8.

It has been confirmed by the CJEU that Article 25 does not require any objective connection between the parties or their dispute and the forum chosen – the parties are free to choose, for example, an entirely disconnected and therefore neutral forum for their disputes.[145] The Regulation does not explain particularly clearly why jurisdiction agreements must be given effect, providing only (in Recital 19) that "The autonomy of the parties

---

[144] See Cheshire, North and Fawcett (2017), p.315.
[145] Case 56/79 Zelger v. Salinitri [1980] ECR 89.

to a contract [subject to certain exceptions] ... should be respected".[146] This does not offer any explanation why that autonomy should extend beyond contractual autonomy to jurisdictional questions,[147] which is the evident intention and effect of the Regulation. The general justification for the Regulation (as set out in Recital 4, that "Certain differences between national rules governing jurisdiction and recognition of judgments hamper the sound operation of the internal market"), suggests that a public consequentialist justification is operative here – it is the perceived benefit to the European internal market provided by certainty in litigation risk management that justifies the recognition of party autonomy.[148]

All the jurisdictional rules under the Brussels I Regulation are given indirect effect through the rules on the recognition and enforcement of judgments – judgments obtained from the courts of one Member State on the basis of these rules (or even on the basis of their traditional national rules pursuant to Article 4) must be readily recognised in other Member States. The rules governing choice of court agreements are no exception. However, it is notable that the Brussels I Regulation does not contain a rule under which breach of an exclusive jurisdiction agreement operates as a defence to the recognition and enforcement of another Member State judgment.[149] As discussed further below, this is because mutual trust between the courts of Member States has been given higher priority than the principle of party autonomy, although the Recast Regulation somewhat rebalances the equation. The enforceability of a non-Member State judgment obtained in breach of a Member State exclusive jurisdiction agreement is not dealt with directly by the Regulation, but rather covered by national law. However, there is a strong argument that such a judgment, obtained contrary to the jurisdiction agreement and thus contrary to the provisions of the Regulation, should be refused enforcement as a matter of public policy, drawn from EU law. A similar argument applies in relation to judgments against EU domiciled consumers or employees obtained from non-Member State courts – as discussed further in Section 5.5, under the Regulation these parties are effectively subject to the exclusive jurisdiction of their home courts, and a non-Member State judgment in breach of that exclusive jurisdiction should be refused enforcement under the national law of each Member State as a matter of EU public policy.

---

[146]   Note similarly Recital 15 – "the autonomy of the parties warrants a different connecting factor".
[147]   See Section 1.3.5.
[148]   See further Section 2.3.2.
[149]   See Article 45.

3.4.2.2 Derogation

Curiously, the Brussels I Regulation does not expressly include any 'negative' obligation on other Member State courts not to exercise jurisdiction if a different Member State court has been chosen exclusively by the parties. A provision to similar effect in Article 27 is limited to cases covered by the exclusive subject-matter jurisdiction provisions in Article 24 (discussed further in Section 5.4). This provision could not have been straightforwardly extended to exclusive jurisdiction agreements because of the possibility that a defendant might overcome the effect of such an agreement by submitting to another court, pursuant to Article 26 (a possibility that does not arise for jurisdiction based on Article 24).[150] Absent submission under Article 26, an obligation on the courts of other Member States not to exercise jurisdiction is, however, evidently intended to exist as part of the determination in Article 25 that "such jurisdiction shall be exclusive unless the parties have agreed otherwise", and courts have interpreted the provision purposively to give it the necessary effect. Despite the absence of a provision to this effect, it must be understood that there is an obligation under the Regulation not to exercise jurisdiction where the courts of another Member State have jurisdiction pursuant to an exclusive jurisdiction agreement.

As discussed further below, a limited degree of clarification has now been added under Article 31 of the Recast Brussels I Regulation, in providing that:

(2) Without prejudice to Article 26, where a court of a Member State on which an agreement as referred to in Article 25 confers exclusive jurisdiction is seised, any court of another Member State shall stay the proceedings until such time as the court seised on the basis of the agreement declares that it has no jurisdiction under the agreement.

(3) Where the court designated in the agreement has established jurisdiction in accordance with the agreement, any court of another Member State shall decline jurisdiction in favour of that court.[151]

There is something ostensibly puzzling about these provisions. They seem to require that where there is an exclusive jurisdiction agreement in favour of one Member State court, and that court is actually seised of proceedings, other Member State courts must stay their proceedings – temporarily until the court chosen by the parties has determined whether or not it has jurisdiction, and permanently once the court has indeed established its

---

[150] See Cheshire, North and Fawcett (2017), p.226ff.
[151] See further generally Ratković and Zgrabljić Rotar (2013), p.261ff.

jurisdiction. But surely the obligation to stay proceedings commenced contrary to an exclusive jurisdiction agreement must apply regardless of whether the nominated court has actually been seised. The solution to this conundrum lies in understanding that Article 31(2) applies to *apparent* jurisdiction agreements, not *established* jurisdiction agreements, a point confirmed by the final words of the article that clearly contemplate that the jurisdiction agreement may in the end be invalid or inapplicable. This provision is thus not about giving effect to an established jurisdiction agreement, but rather about giving the apparently designated court priority (in case of parallel proceedings) to determine the validity or effectiveness of the designation. For this rule to apply, it should not be enough merely to assert the existence of a jurisdiction agreement – there must be an apparent or *prima facie* agreement – but exactly what standard should be applied remains to be determined by the courts.[152] It is clear, however, that something less than the ordinary burden of proof in civil matters will be required. The effect is that the party asserting the existence of a jurisdiction agreement is treated more favourably than the party denying its existence – the criticism could be made that the rule is not so much supportive of choice of court agreements, as supportive of those *claiming* the existence of choice of court agreements, which is not quite the same thing.

Another point of uncertainty to note in this provision is that the words 'Without prejudice to Article 26' are not quite sufficient to explain how a court should deal with the possibility that a defendant may have submitted to its jurisdiction despite the existence of an exclusive jurisdiction agreement in favour of the courts of a different Member State. It is, however, to be expected that the existing practice of the courts, under which subsequent submission may override a jurisdiction agreement, will continue, and Article 31(2) will be inapplicable in this situation. A final uncertainty is whether this provision will apply to an asymmetrical jurisdiction agreement, such as one that is exclusive for one party but non-exclusive for the other, as discussed further in Section 3.5 – there is English authority that it does (where proceedings are commenced against the beneficiary of the exclusive agreement contrary to that agreement), which is the better approach, although it goes slightly against the wording of the provision.[153]

---

[152] See e.g. discussion in Cheshire, North and Fawcett (2017), p.452ff; Weller (2017), p.118ff; Hartley (2013a).

[153] *Commerzbank Aktiengesellshcaft* v. *Liquimar Tankers Management* [2017] EWHC 161 (Comm); *Perella Weinberg Partners UK LLP* v. *Codere SA* [2016] EWHC 1182 (Comm), [18]. In the typical scenario, Party A who has the benefit of the exclusive jurisdiction agreement in favour of e.g. the English courts (i.e. Party A can only be sued in England, but can

Under the Brussels I Regulation 2001, where two parties, neither of whom was domiciled in a Member State, entered into a jurisdiction agreement in favour of the courts of a Member State, the effectiveness of that jurisdiction agreement would ordinarily be determined pursuant to national law in accordance with Article 4 of the Brussels I Regulation 2001. Article 23(3) of the Regulation provided an overriding 'negative' rule of jurisdiction in these cases – establishing that:

> Where such an agreement is concluded by parties, none of whom is domiciled in a Member State, the courts of other Member States shall have no jurisdiction over their disputes unless the court or courts chosen have declined jurisdiction.

The Recast Brussels I Regulation alters this rule significantly, by providing that Article 25 (formerly 23) applies regardless of the domicile of the parties.[154] Under this new rule, the Brussels I Regulation is extended to disputes involving non-EU domiciled defendants who are subject to an exclusive jurisdiction agreement in favour of the courts of a Member State – providing that such agreements will be effective to confer jurisdiction on that court, and (as noted above) implicitly establishing that other courts cannot exercise jurisdiction in these circumstances. Importantly, this means that in some cases in which jurisdiction would otherwise be governed by national law (because proceedings are brought against non-Member State domiciled defendants), the Regulation precludes jurisdiction (because there is an exclusive jurisdiction agreement in favour of the courts of another Member State, and the Regulation implicitly obligates other Member State courts not to exercise jurisdiction in those circumstances). It is slightly unclear how this rule should operate in the context of non-exclusive jurisdiction agreements between non-EU domiciled parties. In these circumstances, either Article 25 may not be applicable at all (leaving jurisdiction to be determined by national law), or alternatively, it may be effective to confer jurisdiction on the chosen Member State courts, but the possible jurisdiction of other Member State courts will remain to be determined under national law. The latter approach seems more consistent with the text, but creates a complex situation where the

---

sue Party B in England or elsewhere) is instead sued in the courts of e.g. France by Party B. Party A brings proceedings in the English courts, and asks those courts to continue despite being second seised. In this situation, Party A is in fact relying on the *non-exclusive* component of the jurisdiction agreement to establish the jurisdiction of the English courts, which is not obviously what is contemplated by Article 31(2). See discussion in Keyes and Marshall (2015), p.358ff.

[154] See e.g. discussion in Ratković and Zgrabljić Rotar (2013), p.251ff.

jurisdictional rules governing a dispute are a 'hybridisation' of EU and national law.[155]

3.4.2.3 Limitations Based on Mutual Trust

In general, the Brussels I Regulation thus recognises both the positive (prorogation) and negative (derogation) effects of exclusive jurisdiction agreements. There are, however, two important practical restrictions on that recognition which have arisen through the case law of the CJEU.

The first is the effect of the decision in *Gasser* v. *MISAT* (2003).[156] In a dispute between Austrian and Italian parties, proceedings were first commenced in Italy, despite the contract containing an Austrian exclusive jurisdiction agreement. Under the Brussels I Regulation, it is clear that the Italian courts were obligated to determine that they had no jurisdiction, assuming they found the jurisdiction agreement to be valid and applicable. The issue before the CJEU concerned Austrian proceedings that were, however, commenced before any such decision had been reached by the Italian courts. The Regulation ordinarily provides (now in Article 29) for a strict *lis pendens* rule to prevent parallel proceedings and the risk of irreconcilable judgments from arising, under which any court other than the court first seised of a dispute must stay its proceedings. In these circumstances, could the Austrian proceedings continue (on the basis that the court had exclusive jurisdiction under what is now Article 25), or were they required to be stayed under what is now Article 29 (on the basis that another Member State court was first seised)? The CJEU decided that Article 29 had to take priority – the risk of irreconcilable judgments, and the obligations of mutual trust[157] inherent in the Brussels I Regulation regime, were found to outweigh the policy inherent in Article 25. To put this another way, party autonomy was viewed as having only a secondary importance as a policy objective for the Regulation – Article 25 was held to be subsidiary to Article 29. In reaching this conclusion, it was significant that breach of an exclusive jurisdiction agreement may not be relied on as a basis for the courts of a Member State to refuse recognition and enforcement of a judgment from the courts of another Member State – as noted

---

[155] Similar complexity could also arise under the Brussels I Regulation 2001, where jurisdiction over a claim brought by an EU domiciled claimant against a non-EU domiciled defendant could be governed by a hybrid of national jurisdictional rules (under Article 4) and a non-exclusive jurisdiction agreement (under Article 23).

[156] C-116/02 *Gasser* v. *MISAT* [2003] ECR I-14693; Cheshire, North and Fawcett (2017), p.450ff; Steinle and Vasiliades (2010); Fentiman (2005); Hartley (2005).

[157] On which see generally Weller (2015).

above, this form of indirect effect of party autonomy is precluded under the Brussels I Regulation.

In theory, the potential for conflicting decisions should be resolved decisively through a decision of the Italian courts that the jurisdiction agreement is or is not valid or applicable – such a decision will not only be determinative of the Italian courts' own jurisdiction, but will also be binding on the Austrian courts.[158] If the Italian court determined that the jurisdiction agreement is invalid or inapplicable and took jurisdiction over the merits, as a matter of mutual trust and indeed *lis pendens* there should then also be no basis for the Austrian courts to award damages for breach of the agreement (should they be minded to follow the practice of the English courts in awarding such damages, as discussed in Section 3.4.3) – although a recent decision of the UK Supreme Court has controversially suggested otherwise, and refused to refer the point to the CJEU.[159] If the Italian court determined that the exclusive jurisdiction agreement is valid and applicable, however, their proceedings must be ended and the Austrian courts would be free to take jurisdiction. The practical reality is, however, that the court chosen by the parties cannot hear their dispute until such time as any other court previously seised by one of the parties determines whether or not it has jurisdiction. The delay involved in such a determination may be considerable[160] – the speed of justice is not always *rapidissimo* in every European Member State – and thus as a practical matter the risk of bad faith litigation as a delaying tactic (known as an 'Italian torpedo') has presented a real obstacle to the effectiveness of exclusive jurisdiction agreements under the Brussels I Regulation.[161]

A partial response to this issue has been provided in Article 31(2) of the Recast Brussels I Regulation (as set out above), when combined with Recital 22, which establishes an exception to the normal *lis pendens* rule. The intention is that the court chosen in an exclusive jurisdiction agreement can continue to hear proceedings, even if another court has been first seised. The court first seised is, instead, obliged to stay its proceedings if the court nominated by the parties in an exclusive jurisdiction agreement

---

[158] C-456/11 *Krones AG* v. *Samskip GmbH* EU:C:2012:719.

[159] *The Alexandros T* [2013] UKSC 70; Cheshire, North and Fawcett (2017), p.446; Dickinson (2015). See further e.g. Sanchez Fernandez (2010); Steinle and Vasiliades (2010), p.579ff.

[160] This was, however, dismissed as a relevant consideration by the CJEU: C-116/02 *Gasser* v. *MISAT* [2003] ECR I-14693, [53].

[161] See further e.g. *JP Morgan Europe* v. *Primacom* [2005] EWHC 508 (Comm).

has subsequently been seised of the same proceedings.[162] As noted above, this provision should not require that an *actual* jurisdiction agreement has been established, but only that there is an *apparent* or *prima facie* jurisdiction agreement. While the applicable standard is opaque, the clear intention is that the decision on whether or not a jurisdiction agreement is valid or applicable should (in case of parallel proceedings) be made by the apparently designated court. Whether the court first seised will always be in a position to take action to stay its proceedings of its own motion, without the jurisdiction agreement being presented as evidence before it, seems doubtful in practice. Parties to a jurisdiction agreement may still, therefore, be required to appoint lawyers, appear and present evidence in another jurisdiction, which is precisely what the jurisdiction agreement was intended to avoid. If they do not, and the court first seised decides on the merits (or determines that the alleged jurisdiction agreement does not meet the threshold for the application of Article 31(2)), that decision will (despite Article 31(2)) be binding on the court nominated in the apparent agreement.[163] If the court first seised instead stays its proceedings, it is possible that the court chosen by the parties may be prepared to award damages for the costs incurred in the proceedings once they have moved to the selected forum, particularly if costs will not be awarded in the court first seised,[164] but these measures are likely to significantly mitigate rather than entirely resolve the issue of the Italian torpedo, particularly in light of the following.

The second practical restriction on the effectiveness of jurisdiction agreements under the Brussels I Regulation derives from the CJEU decision in *Turner* v. *Grovit* (2004).[165] In this dispute, Turner commenced proceedings first against Grovit in England, before Grovit commenced counter-proceedings in Spain. The English courts held that the Spanish proceedings were brought in bad faith, in an attempt to frustrate the English proceedings by forcing Turner to settle rather than face litigation on two fronts, and issued an anti-suit injunction to restrain Grovit from continuing with the Spanish proceedings.[166] It was also considered significant that, on the view of the English courts, the Spanish court was obliged

---

[162] It does not appear that Article 31(2) can be engaged if the two sets of proceedings are merely related – see Kenny and Hennigan (2015).

[163] C-456/11 *Krones AG* v. *Samskip GmbH* EU:C:2012:719.

[164] See further references in Section 3.4.3.

[165] C-159/02 *Turner* v. *Grovit* [2004] ECR I-3565; Cheshire, North and Fawcett (2017), p.477ff; Hartley (2005); Briggs (2004); Kruger (2004).

[166] See Section 3.4.3.

to stay its proceedings in accordance with the *lis pendens* rules under what is now Article 29. The CJEU held, however, that the anti-suit injunction was an improper interference with the ability of the Spanish courts to determine their own jurisdiction under the Brussels I Regulation. While the English court might be confident that the *lis pendens* rules would apply, with the litigation in England and Spain involving the same parties and same subject matter, the Spanish court should be given the opportunity to determine these questions for itself.

Although there was no jurisdiction agreement in this case, the decision established generally that no anti-suit injunction may be granted in relation to proceedings commenced in another Member State pursuant to the Brussels I Regulation. This means that even if the parties are bound by an exclusive English jurisdiction agreement, and proceedings are commenced in the courts of another Member State in breach of contract, the English courts are unable to issue an anti-suit injunction to hold the parties to their contractual bargain (effectively, providing for specific enforcement of the jurisdiction agreement). While the decision of the CJEU is supported by the obligations of mutual trust between the courts of Member States that are one of the foundations of the Regulation, it therefore nevertheless has the effect of partially depriving the English courts of one of the devices they have traditionally used to ensure that a jurisdiction agreement in favour of the English courts is effective, as discussed further in Section 3.4.3. The 'Italian torpedo' is therefore partially effective even if it is adopted subsequently to proceedings being commenced in the chosen court – the court second seised must be given the opportunity to determine its own jurisdiction, and that means that an English claimant who has commenced proceedings in England relying on an exclusive English jurisdiction agreement must still contest the jurisdiction of a foreign forum subsequently seised contrary to its contractual rights. In the absence of specific performance of those rights, the claimant can only once again rely on an expectation that they may be awarded costs in the foreign forum, or receive damages for breach of the contractual jurisdiction obligation in the English courts, to compensate them for their added expenses and inconvenience. The need to dispute the jurisdiction of the foreign court may present a significant obstacle to litigation for many parties (who may have negotiated a jurisdiction agreement for precisely these reasons), perhaps leading to an unfavourable settlement, and damages may not be available in all jurisdictions (particular those that characterise jurisdiction agreements as procedural, as discussed above).[167] While an anti-suit injunction may not be the solution to these problems, particularly as it only exists in common law Member States, the issue presents a continuing challenge to the effectiveness of jurisdiction agreements across the European Union.

3.4.2.4   Reflexive Effect

A further practical problem that has arisen in relation to jurisdiction agreements under the Brussels I Regulation is the effect that should be given to exclusive jurisdiction agreements in favour of non-Member State courts. The policy underlying Article 25 of the Regulation suggests that exclusive jurisdiction agreements should generally be enforced, but the Regulation lacks a mechanism to achieve this, because Article 25 deals only with agreements in favour of the courts of a Member State. The issue has been particularly apparent since it was determined that jurisdiction under the Regulation is mandatory, and cannot be stayed through an exercise of *forum non conveniens* discretion[168] – the English courts had previously used this as a device to circumvent the lacuna in the rules, by finding that a non-Member State jurisdiction agreement could be relied on to justify a refusal to exercise jurisdiction under the Regulation.[169] This is one aspect of a general problem with the Regulation, which is the failure for its rules to match up to its scope (both as interpreted by the CJEU) – its scope encompasses a variety of non-internal market questions and disputes, but its rules are motivated only by internal market considerations.[170] The terms of the Regulation determine its applicability principally on the basis of the 'domicile'[171] of the defendant in any civil or commercial litigation – potentially encompassing claims against EU domiciled defendants that are otherwise entirely unconnected with the internal market. However, the rules of the Regulation are drafted only with internal market problems in mind (with the sole exception of the new non-Member State *lis pendens* and related proceedings rules in Articles 33 and 34, discussed further below) – giving no consideration to the effect of jurisdiction agree-

---

[167]   See further Steinle and Vasiliades (2010), p.575ff.
[168]   C-281/02 *Owusu* v. *Jackson* [2005] ECR I-1383; see further e.g. Cheshire, North and Fawcett (2017), p.462ff; Fentiman (2006b); Briggs (2005); Cuniberti (2005); Hartley (2005).
[169]   *Re Harrods (Buenos Aires)* [1992] Ch 72.
[170]   See generally Mills (2016a).
[171]   As defined in Articles 62 and 63 of the Brussels I Regulation.

ments in favour of non-Member State courts, or other 'externalities' such as subject-matter connections with non-Member States.

The view that has attracted the support of most courts and academic literature is that some 'reflexive effect' should be given to the exclusive jurisdictional rules adopted under the Regulation – applying them to non-Member State situations in a similar or identical manner to the way in which they are applied to Member State situations.[172] Thus, an exclusive jurisdiction agreement in favour of the courts of a non-Member State should be given an equivalent effect to that provided for exclusive jurisdiction agreements in favour of Member State courts under Article 25.[173] Whether this effect should be the same, or whether an element of discretion should be introduced to take account of the fact that non-Member State courts do not demand the same level of mutual trust, remains an unresolved issue, although the better view is that a level of discretion is necessary.[174] The parties may, for example, have entered into an exclusive jurisdiction agreement in favour of the courts of a state that has since plunged into civil war, or whose judiciary has since become subject to political interference. Giving mandatory effect to their jurisdiction agreement in such circumstances would hardly seem consonant with justice, but giving no effect to non-Member State exclusive jurisdiction agreements seems equally unpalatable – leaving a discretionary rule as the only option.[175]

This issue was, perhaps surprisingly, not directly dealt with in the 2012 Recast of the Brussels I Regulation, and it remains a major concern and source of uncertainty in the jurisdictional rules of the European Union. The concerns are not limited to the context of party autonomy – possible reflexive effect arguments also arose under the 2001 Regulation in relation to the *lis pendens* rules, as well as the subject-matter exclusive jurisdiction

---

[172] See e.g. Cheshire, North and Fawcett (2017), p.473ff; Nuyts (2007), p.81ff; Fentiman (2006a). This means that a reflexive effect should not be possible contrary to the protective rules for insurance, consumer and employment contracts, discussed further in Section 5.5. This might suggest that the formality requirements in Article 25 would also need to be satisfied in relation to non-Member State exclusive jurisdiction agreements, but this is probably not the better approach – see further Section 5.2.1.

[173] See e.g. *Konkola Copper Mines v. Coromin* [2005] EWHC 898 (Comm).

[174] See e.g. *Ferrexpo AG v. Gilson Investments Ltd* [2012] EWHC 721 (Comm); Goodwin (2013).

[175] It might alternatively be argued, in support of a non-discretionary reflexive effect approach, that in these circumstances the jurisdiction agreement itself was frustrated and therefore unenforceable – this would be a matter for the contract law governing the jurisdiction agreement.

rules in what is now Article 24 of the Regulation (discussed further in Section 5.4). The lack of clarity around the effectiveness of non-Member State exclusive jurisdiction agreements is, however, a particularly important aspect of this unsatisfactory current state of affairs.[176] The Recast Brussels I Regulation does include new rules, in Articles 33 and 34, which deal with the situation of a *lis pendens* or related proceedings where the court first seised is that of a non-Member State (permitting the Member State court to stay its proceedings in favour of the court first seised in certain circumstances).[177] The fact that the Recast Regulation thus partially responds to the reflexive effect issue might be taken to indicate that the non-adoption of rules dealing with the reflexive effect of Article 25 is intended to preclude such possible effect. Support for this argument might come from two sources.

First, there is some textual support in the fact that the *lis pendens* rules permit the Member State court second seised, in deciding whether to stay its proceedings, to take into account "whether the court of the third State has exclusive jurisdiction in the particular case in circumstances where a court of a Member State would have exclusive jurisdiction".[178] If Article 25 were given reflexive effect, there would appear to be no need for this consideration to apply – the Member State court could defer to the non-Member State court on the basis of that reflexive effect (applicable regardless of which court is first seised) rather than on the basis of the *lis pendens* rules.

The second argument that might support the view that giving a reflexive effect to Article 25 is not possible is that the EU may well be deliberately refusing to give effect to foreign jurisdiction agreements for countries that are not parties to the Hague Convention on Choice of Court Agreements 2005 (discussed in Section 3.4.4). The intention may be that a refusal by EU Member State courts to give effect to such agreements in relation to claims against EU domiciled parties, unless the foreign state has signed up to the Hague Convention, will leverage states to become bound by that

---

[176] See e.g. Ratković and Zgrabljić Rotar (2013), p.247ff.

[177] This rule notably does not apply if the Member State court's jurisdiction is based on Article 25. This makes sense for *exclusive* jurisdiction agreements – if the English courts are chosen in an exclusive jurisdiction agreement they cannot stay proceedings even if the New York courts are first seised of the same or related proceedings. It is a problematic and unfortunate omission for *non-exclusive* jurisdiction agreements. If the parties have entered into a non-exclusive English jurisdiction agreement, and there are prior proceedings in New York, the English proceedings may not be stayed under this rule – the non-exclusive jurisdiction agreement is effectively treated as exclusive. See *UCP Plc* v. *Nectrus Ltd* [2018] EWHC 380 (Comm).

[178] Recital 24.

Convention and thereby also to benefit from it.[179] If this is indeed the case, only time will tell whether this somewhat curious strategy, which in the short term sacrifices party autonomy in choice of forum as a means of aspiring to promote it in the long term, will be a success.

3.4.3   Common Law

The dual aspects of an exclusive jurisdiction agreement – establishing mirrored 'positive' and 'negative' effects (with the positive effects also shared with non-exclusive jurisdiction agreements) – are also well illustrated by the common law approach to such agreements. This approach is generally shared around the common law world, although with some variation in detail.

This section focuses on the English courts, distinguishing particularly between English and foreign exclusive jurisdiction agreements. It should be noted, however, that since the Recast Brussels I Regulation came into effect in 2015, the effectiveness of almost all jurisdiction agreements in favour of the English courts is governed by the Brussels I Regulation, as discussed above, or the Hague Convention on Choice of Court Agreements 2005, discussed below. In relation to a jurisdiction agreement in favour of the English courts, the common law rules will only apply if the case falls outside the scope of the Regulation. The practice of the English courts is nevertheless discussed here, not only for cases falling outside of the Regulation, but because the scope of application of the common law may well be expanded as a consequence of an anticipated Brexit, and because the practice of the English courts on this point is broadly representative of the common law world, except as noted below.

In the English courts, exclusive jurisdiction agreements in favour of the courts of other Member States are also generally given effect pursuant to Article 25 of the Brussels I Regulation, as examined above. The effectiveness of jurisdiction agreements in favour of non-EU Member States is, however, governed by the common law if jurisdiction in the case is based on the common law rules (this will be true for most claims against non-EU domiciled defendants). If jurisdiction is based on the Brussels I Regulation (which will be the case for claims against EU domiciled defendants falling

---

[179] This has been suggested to the author by two people involved in the Recast negotiation process. See also Ratković and Zgrabljić Rotar (2013), p.249 (noting "the reasonable conclusion that the Commission's intention when not including a provision on the choice of a third-state court was to give an incentive to non-Member States to ratify the Hague Convention when and if the EU ratifies it").

within the scope of the Regulation), and there is an exclusive jurisdiction agreement in favour of the courts of a non-EU Member State, the effectiveness of that agreement will be determined by the 'reflexive effect' argument under EU law discussed above. The following table summarises this somewhat complex situation, assuming the case falls within the scope of the Brussels I Regulation; the common law rules obviously apply if the case is not regulated by EU rules.

Agreement in favour of	EU domiciled defendant	Non-EU domiciled defendant
English courts	Brussels I Regulation, Art.25	Brussels I Regulation, Art.25
Other EU Member State courts	Brussels I Regulation, Art.25	Brussels I Regulation, Art.25
Non-EU Member State courts	Brussels I Regulation, reflexive effect and/or Arts.33–4	Common law

Setting these complexities aside, the following sections examine the positive and negative effects of jurisdiction agreements under the common law, on the assumption that it is indeed applicable.

3.4.3.1   Prorogation

If an exclusive jurisdiction agreement is in favour of the English courts, the 'positive' effect of that agreement is given by the acceptance of jurisdiction. Under the common law, jurisdiction may be based on (i) the presence of the defendant in the territory, (ii) submission to the court, or (iii) permission to commence proceedings against a party who is not 'present' before the English courts, under the circumstances set out in Rule 6.36 and Practice Direction 6B of the Civil Procedure Rules.[180] An English jurisdiction agreement is not considered sufficient to establish submission – this requires that the defendant appear before the court and accept its authority over the case after the proceedings have been commenced.[181] Where a defendant is present in England, the jurisdiction agreement is

---

[180] See generally Cheshire, North and Fawcett (2017), Chapter 12.
[181] Nomination of a local address for service together with a jurisdiction agreement is sometimes considered to establish submission, but the better view is that, at least ordinarily, this establishes only presence: see Cheshire, North and Fawcett (2017), p.333.

not necessary to establish jurisdiction, but will influence the question of whether the court will stay the proceedings pursuant to the doctrine of *forum non conveniens* (under which jurisdiction is generally declined if a foreign court is a clearly more appropriate forum for the dispute).[182] Where the defendant is not present in the jurisdiction, an English jurisdiction agreement is a basis for service outside the territory under Practice Direction 6B, and thus is (and has been since 1920)[183] a ground on which permission may be sought to commence proceedings.[184] This permission is discretionary, pursuant to the doctrine of *forum conveniens*, which is closely related to the *forum non conveniens* discretion but with a greater burden on the claimant to justify the exercise of jurisdiction against an absent defendant.[185]

In the context of both *forum non conveniens* and *forum conveniens*, an English exclusive jurisdiction agreement gives rise to a very strong presumption that such an agreement will be given effect (through a refusal to stay English proceedings or the granting of permission to commence English proceedings) in the absence of unforeseeable circumstances justifying a departure from the agreement between the parties.[186] Exceptions may arise, for example, where necessary to consolidate claims against multiple defendants in a foreign court.[187] The exclusivity of the agreement is generally considered to be conclusive in establishing that the English courts are the most appropriate forum for the litigation, and will almost always lead to the exercise of jurisdiction by those courts. This is not an inevitable approach – there is no necessary reason why the judgement of the parties as to what constitutes an appropriate jurisdiction *for them* should be adopted by the courts as such a strong factor in determining what is the most appropriate forum *in general*. The decision to accord the parties' determination an almost conclusive effect reflects the strong

---

[182] See generally Cheshire, North and Fawcett (2017), p.393ff.

[183] See Section 2.2.1.

[184] Civil Procedure Rules, Practice Direction 6B, Para 3.1(6)(d); see further Cheshire, North and Fawcett (2017), p.345ff.

[185] As discussed further below, it is sometimes argued that the effect of a jurisdiction agreement is so significant that a distinct test applies, rather than the usual discretionary doctrines. This arguably reflects an ongoing uncertainty as to whether the jurisdiction agreement is procedural or substantive. See Cheshire, North and Fawcett (2017), pp.398–9.

[186] See e.g. *Donohue v. Armco Inc.* [2002] 1 Lloyd's Rep 425; *ACE Insurance SA-NV v. Zurich Insurance Company* [2001] EWCA Civ 173; *The Nile Rhapsody* [1994] 1 Lloyd's Rep 382; *British Aerospace plc v. Dee Howard Co.* [1993] 1 Lloyd's Rep 368; *The El Amria* [1981] 2 Lloyd's Rep 119; *The Eleftheria* [1970] P 94.

[187] See e.g. *Bouygues Offshore SA v. Caspian* [1998] 2 Lloyd's Rep 461.

measure of respect for party autonomy under the common law approach to jurisdiction in contract. A non-exclusive English jurisdiction agreement has a similar but weaker effect – it equally confers appropriateness on the chosen court, again in the absence of factors that were unforeseeable at the time of contracting, but does not discount the possibility that another court may be more appropriate.[188] Unlike the US practice discussed above, in determining whether to exercise jurisdiction the English courts do not take into account countervailing public interests (such as the imposition of a burden on the English courts, or whether there is a foreign interest in the dispute), making it even more likely that effect will be given to an English exclusive or non-exclusive jurisdiction agreement.[189] There is no requirement that the parties or the dispute have any connection with England.[190] In exercising jurisdiction on this basis, the English courts have not appeared to find it necessary to argue (as is common in US courts) that this conferral of jurisdiction takes place only indirectly through a contractual waiver of the entitlement to object to jurisdiction. (Jurisdiction agreements may, however, be accompanied by clauses in which a party agrees to waive any objection to the chosen court – it is unclear whether those clauses significantly impact the question of jurisdiction under the common law, as they probably do not prevent objections based on unforeseeable factors.)[191] The English approach has thus arguably been more pragmatic, making less effort to reconcile conceptually the positive effect of party autonomy with the traditional limitations on state power, although it remains true, as in the US, that a degree of overriding control for the court is retained through the *forum conveniens* and *forum non conveniens* discretions.

An English exclusive jurisdiction agreement has a further 'negative' effect, affecting English attitudes towards the exercise of jurisdiction by alternative foreign courts, which may be given effect in a number of different ways. First, through an 'anti-suit injunction' restraining a party from commencing or continuing foreign proceedings in breach of the exclusive English jurisdiction agreement. While such an injunction is inherently discretionary and fact sensitive, the English courts are particularly prepared to make the order where they consider it necessary to enforce

---

[188] See e.g. *Standard Chartered Bank (Hong Kong) Ltd v. Independent Power Tanzania Ltd* [2015] EWHC 1640 (Comm); *Cuccolini SRL v. Elcan Industries Inc.* [2013] EWHC 2994 (QB); *Amtec International Ltd v. Biosafety USA Inc.* [2006] EWHC 47 (Comm), [7].

[189] See Cheshire, North and Fawcett (2017), pp.406–7.

[190] See similarly Singapore Rules of Court, O.110, r.8(2).

[191] See discussion in *Standard Chartered Bank (Hong Kong) Ltd v. Independent Power Tanzania Ltd* [2015] EWHC 1640 (Comm).

the jurisdictional provisions of the contract between the parties.[192] In such circumstances, indeed, the anti-suit injunction is frequently considered to operate as a contractual remedy, to ensure specific performance of an English exclusive jurisdiction agreement – characterising the effectiveness of the agreement as a private law contractual matter rather than a matter of procedure. As noted earlier in this chapter, this is a contentious question, at least internationally.[193] Breach of an anti-suit injunction may further constitute contempt of court, leading potentially to punitive consequences and the award of a default judgment.

A second negative effect of an English exclusive jurisdiction agreement is the refusal of the English courts to recognise and enforce any foreign judgment obtained contrary to the jurisdiction agreement, a rule confirmed by statute.[194] The priority given to maximising the effectiveness of the agreement between the parties, in support of party autonomy, is demonstrated by the fact that the English courts always determine the question of whether there is a valid and applicable exclusive English jurisdiction agreement themselves, even if the foreign court has already 'decided' that there is no such agreement on its way to issuing the judgment.[195] If foreign proceedings in breach of an English exclusive jurisdiction agreement have continued to judgment, an order may also (exceptionally) be obtained restraining enforcement of the judgment, known as an 'anti-enforcement injunction'.[196]

A third possible effect of an English exclusive jurisdiction agreement is that the English courts may be prepared to award damages for breach of the agreement, to account for any additional costs or losses incurred by the defendant to improper foreign proceedings, such as the costs incurred in disputing the jurisdiction of the foreign court.[197] Such a remedy may be particularly sought where an anti-suit injunction is ineffective because the

---

[192] *The Angelic Grace* [1995] 1 Lloyd's Rep 87, 96 ("there is no good reason for diffidence in granting an injunction to restrain foreign proceedings on the clear and simple ground that the defendant has promised not to bring them").

[193] For the arguments for and against a contractual characterisation, see e.g. Briggs (2016); Briggs (2008); C Knight (2008).

[194] Civil Jurisdiction and Judgments Act 1982, s.32.

[195] Civil Jurisdiction and Judgments Act 1982, s.32(3).

[196] See e.g. *Ecobank Transnational Inc.* v. *Tanoh* [2015] EWCA Civ 1309; *Bank St Petersburg* v. *Arkhangelsky* [2014] EWCA Civ 593.

[197] See further e.g. *Starlight Shipping Company* v. *Allianz Marine & Aviation Versicherungs AG* [2013] UKSC 70, [38]; *Union Discount Company Ltd* v. *Zoller* [2001] EWCA Civ 1755; Takahashi (2008); Merrett (2006); Tham (2004); Tan and Yeo (2003). Such a remedy should only be available if the foreign court has not itself awarded costs – see Hartley (2013b), p.217ff.

foreign claimant is not practically susceptible to the enforcement jurisdiction of the English courts, although in such cases enforcing the damages award may present similar difficulties. Once again, this reflects a characterisation of the choice of court agreement as a matter of substantive private law, rather than a point of procedure. Alternatively, in exceptional circumstances, a claim might perhaps be brought in tort for malicious prosecution (based on the improper commencement of foreign proceedings), a form of action that is now understood to extend to civil proceedings.[198]

Finally, a fourth possible effect of an English exclusive jurisdiction agreement is that, since breach of the agreement is characterised as constituting a breach of contract, a third party might be held liable in tort for inducing such a breach. Such a claim was at the heart of the recent *AMT Futures* v. *Marzillier* litigation which reached the Supreme Court in the United Kingdom.[199] In this case, a German law firm was sued for inducing breach of an English exclusive jurisdiction agreement by encouraging its clients to sue in Germany. Although ultimately the Supreme Court held that the English courts did not have jurisdiction over the claim (as any tort had occurred in Germany, and there was no other basis of jurisdiction over the German defendant), the case remains a high profile reminder (in particular, for legal practitioners) of the possibility of such claims.

If there is an exclusive jurisdiction agreement in favour of a *foreign* court, its 'positive' effect is given by the acceptance that the foreign court's jurisdiction is thereby legitimate. A jurisdiction agreement, on its own, is considered under the common law to constitute 'submission' by the parties to the foreign court,[200] which satisfies the jurisdictional criteria for the recognition and enforcement of a judgment from that court.[201]

3.4.3.2 Derogation

A foreign exclusive jurisdiction agreement will also traditionally be given a 'negative' derogation effect under the common law – although strictly it is not considered to 'oust' any jurisdiction that the courts would otherwise have. A foreign exclusive jurisdiction agreement is rather given

---

[198] *Crawford Adjusters v. Sagicor General Insurance (Cayman) Ltd* [2013] UKPC 17.

[199] *AMT Futures v. Marzillier* [2017] UKSC 13

[200] Even though an English jurisdiction agreement does not establish submission to the English courts.

[201] See e.g. *Emanuel v. Symon* [1908] 1 KB 302, 309; *Adams v. Cape Industries plc* [1990] Ch 433, 458 (for the purposes of the English rules on recognition of a foreign judgment, "the jurisdiction of a foreign court over a defendant may be established, on a consensual basis, either by the defendant's participation in the proceedings or by the defendant's agreement to submit to the jurisdiction").

effect through a discretionary decision under (or closely related to) the doctrines of *forum conveniens* and *forum non conveniens* not to exercise jurisdiction. Although the courts will take a wide range of factors into consideration, a foreign exclusive jurisdiction agreement has the effect of rendering a foreign court a clearly more appropriate (and generally available) forum, ordinarily presumed to be capable of delivering justice to the satisfaction of the parties, in the absence of exceptional and unforeseeable circumstances.[202] The position under the common law is thus similar to that under US federal law, although without using the language of 'ouster' or 'waiver' of jurisdictional rights – an exclusive foreign jurisdiction agreement is not *necessarily* effective to limit the jurisdiction of common law courts (maintaining at least the appearance of the primacy of public over private power), but provides a highly persuasive reason why that jurisdiction should ordinarily not be exercised.

As already noted above, there is one important distinction, however, between English and US federal practice, which derives from a difference in the *forum non conveniens* test applied in each jurisdiction. Under US law, *forum non conveniens* commonly also includes consideration of public interest concerns (such as court congestion or local interest in the matter). Under English law, *forum non conveniens* is purely examined in terms of the interests of the parties – whether there is another clearly more appropriate forum to resolve the dispute between the parties, and whether the claimant would not be denied access to justice if denied access to the English courts.[203] As a jurisdiction agreement is likely to be viewed as determinative of private interest considerations – questions of which court is the more appropriate forum – there is very little scope for an English court to find that a jurisdiction agreement should not be given effect. It is very difficult for a party to argue that they would be denied justice if litigation takes place in a forum that they have chosen, unless circumstances have radically and unforeseeably changed since the choice was made.[204] One context in which the English courts have been minded not to enforce exclusive jurisdiction agreements is where a dispute involves multiple

---

[202] See e.g. *The Eleftheria* [1970] P 94; *Evans Marshall & Co Ltd* v. *Bertola SA* [1973] 1 WLR 349; *British Aerospace* v. *Dee Howard* [1993] 1 Lloyd's Rep 368; *Citi-March Ltd* v. *Neptune Orient Lines Ltd* [1996] 2 All ER 545; *Akai Pty Ltd* v. *People's Insurance Co Ltd* [1996] HCA 39 (Australia); *Akai Pty Ltd* v. *People's Insurance Co Ltd* [1998] 1 Lloyd's Rep 90; *Marubeni Hong Kong and South China* v. *Mongolian Government* [2002] 2 All ER (Comm) 873.

[203] See generally *The Spiliada* [1987] AC 460.

[204] See e.g. *Standard Chartered Bank (Hong Kong) Ltd* v. *Independent Power Tanzania Ltd* [2015] EWHC 1640 (Comm).

parties, only some of whom are subject to the agreement. The advantages to the parties and to the efficient resolution of their dispute of having all proceedings consolidated in a single forum may in some cases outweigh the desirability of giving effect to the jurisdiction agreement – potentially leading to a stay of English proceedings despite an English exclusive jurisdiction agreement,[205] or the exercise of jurisdiction by the English courts despite a foreign exclusive jurisdiction agreement.

It has long been debated whether an exclusive jurisdiction agreement should be viewed as merely one strong factor in the exercise of *forum conveniens* or *forum non conveniens*, or whether it is such an important factor that it should be considered to give rise to a separate category of case to which a different test applies.[206] In part this reflects uncertainty over the categorisation of jurisdiction agreements as procedural or substantive – the former approach suggests a focus on judicial discretion, while the latter suggests contractual obligation. The debate does not appear to be very significant in practice, as it does not appear to affect what factors are relevant to the discretion or how much weight is attached to them, although reframing the discretion as a separate rule may provide a relatively simple way of giving due emphasis to the strength of the jurisdiction agreement and recognising that the burden of proof should be on the party seeking to overcome the agreement. This issue was addressed recently in the Supreme Court of Canada. While the law of jurisdiction in Canada is now in general rather different from that under English law, as it is based on the requirement for a 'real and substantial connection',[207] the traditional common law approach to jurisdiction agreements has remained strongly influential.[208] In *Douez* v. *Facebook, Inc.* (2017),[209] the Supreme Court of Canada held (unanimously) that the existence of a foreign exclusive jurisdiction agreement required the application of a different test from *forum non conveniens*, to ensure that other factors are not given excessive weight against the agreement. The civil law jurisdiction of Quebec is an exception – under the Civil Code there is no discretion to exercise

---

[205] Although recalling that in most such cases, jurisdiction will be based on the Brussels I Regulation, and in that case proceedings may not be stayed under *forum non conveniens*.

[206] See discussion in Cheshire, North and Fawcett (2017), p.410ff.

[207] See *Morguard Investments Ltd* v. *De Savoye* [1990] 3 SCR 1077; *Club Resorts Ltd* v. *Van Breda* [2012] 1 SCR 572.

[208] See e.g. *Momentous.ca Corp.* v. *Canadian American Association of Professional Baseball Ltd* [2012] 1 SCR 359; *Z.I. Pompey Industrie* v. *ECU-Line NV* [2003] 1 SCR 450.

[209] 2017 SCC 33.

jurisdiction where there is a valid and applicable foreign exclusive jurisdiction agreement.[210]

Under Australian law, the approach to the question of whether Australian
proceedings should be stayed in light of a foreign exclusive choice of court
agreement is notably somewhat broadened by a further category of cases.
Australian courts have refused to stay proceedings despite a foreign exclusive jurisdiction agreement in some cases in which it is established that
the foreign court would not recognise rights under Australian law – such
as where the cause of action is based on an Australian statute that would
not be applied by the foreign court.[211] Australian practice on this point has
been viewed critically by some commentators and may be declining,[212] but
it should perhaps only be criticised to the extent that the Australian statutes
concerned are not categorised as mandatory rules, as discussed further in
Section 9.4.1. Another distinctive feature of the rules governing the effectiveness of jurisdiction agreements in Australia is that the intra-Australian
allocation of jurisdiction (between federal and state courts, and between
state courts) is governed (at least partially) by the cross-vesting scheme,
under which a transfer of proceedings may take place where this is in "the
interests of justice".[213] This is somewhat analogous to the US 'motion to
transfer' procedure discussed in Section 3.4.1, and like that procedure it is
a discretion under which exclusive jurisdiction agreements are likely to be
given effect, but are not on their own a decisive factor.

Distinctively among common law jurisdictions, the courts of India
have taken a restrictive approach to the effectiveness of choice of court
agreements. Under section 28 of the Indian Contract Act 1872, an agreement that restrains a party from enforcing their rights "by the usual legal
proceedings in the ordinary tribunals" is void. This does not generally
invalidate exclusive choice of court agreements, as these limit rather than

---

[210] *GreCon Dimter inc.* v. *JR Normand inc.* [2005] 2 SCR 401; Civil Code of Quebec, Art.3148.
There is, however, an exception for consumer and employment contracts under Article
3149.

[211] See e.g. *Hume Computers Pty Ltd* v. *Exact International BV* [2006] FCA 1439; *Reinsurance
Australia Corporation Ltd* v. *HIH Casualty & General Insurance Ltd (in Liq.)* [2003] FCA
56; *Commonwealth Bank of Australia* v. *White* [1999] 2 VR 681. See also discussion in Mills
(2017a); Keyes (2009), p.199ff.

[212] See e.g. Garnett (2013a); Keyes (2009); Garnett (2009), p.166; Garnett (1998).

[213] See *Jurisdiction of Courts (Cross-vesting) Act 1987* (Cth) s.5. For constitutional reasons,
state courts may not transfer proceedings to federal courts which would not otherwise
have jurisdiction. This had formed part of the original cross-vesting scheme, but this feature of the scheme was found to be unconstitutional by the High Court of Australia (*Re
Wakim ex parte McNally* (1999) 198 CLR 511).

prevent access to a court, but it has been held that an exclusive choice of court agreement in favour of a court that would not otherwise have jurisdiction is void, on the basis that it excludes the jurisdiction of all courts that would have had jurisdiction (in the absence of the clause).[214] The effect of this interpretation is that an exclusive jurisdiction agreement may only be entered into in favour of an Indian court that would, in any case, have jurisdiction over the dispute – requiring, in effect, an objective connection between the dispute or the parties and the chosen forum. It is not only derogation but also prorogation that is potentially invalidated – it has equally been held that "It is not open to the parties by agreement to confer by their agreement jurisdiction on a Court which it does not possess under the [Indian] Code [of Civil Procedure]".[215] These restrictions do not, however, apply in relation to foreign choice of court agreements, which are given effect under principles that are very similar to those of the English common law.[216]

3.4.3.3   Non-Exclusive Jurisdiction Agreements and Anti-Suit Injunctions

The analysis above has focused on the effect of exclusive jurisdiction agreements under the common law, which carry both a positive 'conferral' and negative 'ouster' implication, and also the similar positive effect of a non-exclusive jurisdiction agreement. But it is perhaps not entirely clear whether that is the limit of the effects of a non-exclusive agreement – whether it might not also confer a degree of appropriateness on the chosen court that is greater than other available alternative courts, such that it should have a mild 'negative' effect in decreasing the likelihood that other courts should exercise jurisdiction. This issue has been considered by the English courts in particular, in the form of the question of whether an English non-exclusive jurisdiction agreement might also in some way affect the possible issue of an anti-suit injunction. Two particular aspects of this may be highlighted through examination of the practice of the courts.

The first issue is whether an English non-exclusive jurisdiction agreement may be the foundation for an anti-suit injunction (other than in relation to proceedings in another EU Member State, where as noted above

---

[214] *ABC Laminart* v. *AP Agencies, Salem* (1989) 2 SCC 163; see also *Rajasthan SEB* v. *Universal Petrol Chemicals Ltd* (2009) 3 SCC 107.

[215] *Hakam Singh* v. *M/S Gammon (India) Ltd* (1971) 3 SCR 314; see also *Patel Roadways Limited, Bombay* v. *Prasad Trading Company* (1991) 3 SCR 391.

[216] See e.g. *Modi Entertainment Network* v. *WSG Cricket Pte Ltd* (2003) 4 SCC 341.

anti-suit injunctions are now prohibited).[217] Traditionally, the English
courts have taken the view that such an order will not be justified by a
non-exclusive jurisdiction agreement (at least in the absence of prior substantive English proceedings – as discussed further below), because the
agreement does not purport to oust the jurisdiction of any foreign court,
and thus the foreign proceedings are not in themselves a breach of contract.
By contrast, an anti-suit injunction has been understood to be generally
appropriate for an *exclusive* jurisdiction agreement, which itself purports
to oust the jurisdiction of foreign courts to the same effect as the anti-suit
injunction itself – and thus, as noted above, the anti-suit injunction merely
enforces the terms of the contractual bargain between the parties.[218]

The case of *Sabah Shipyard (Pakistan) Limited* v. *Pakistan*[219] might
appear at first glance to be contrary to this general approach – in this case,
the English courts issued an anti-suit injunction to restrain the continuation of prior proceedings in Pakistan, even though the only basis of jurisdiction of the English courts was a non-exclusive jurisdiction agreement.
A close examination of the case shows, however, that it remains consistent
with the principles outlined above. The prior proceedings in Pakistan were
themselves brought with the apparent sole intention of obtaining an anti-
suit injunction (as was in fact granted by the courts of Pakistan) to prevent
Sabah from litigating in England – contrary to its contractual right to do so
under the English non-exclusive jurisdiction agreement. The issue by the
English courts of an anti-suit injunction – in this case, also an anti-anti-suit
injunction – may thus be understood on these special facts to be justifiable
in order to hold the parties to their contractual bargain. If the proceedings in Pakistan had been on the merits of the case, it seems unlikely the
English courts would have had cause to restrain their continuation. The
general principle remains that a non-exclusive English jurisdiction agreement will not ordinarily justify the issue of an anti-suit injunction, because
the parties will not be breaching their contract through commencing foreign proceedings. In other words, a non-exclusive jurisdiction agreement
will (in the absence of special agreement) ordinarily not confer any priority in favour of the nominated forum over alternative courts. Some English
authority, in light of *Sabah*, has suggested that a non-exclusive jurisdiction agreement means that proceedings must, in the absence of special

---

[217] See Section 3.4.2.
[218] See e.g. *The Angelic Grace* [1995] 1 Lloyd's Rep 87; *Donohue* v. *Armco Inc.* [2002] 1 Lloyd's Rep 425.
[219] *Sabah Shipyard (Pakistan) Limited* v. *Pakistan* [2002] EWCA Civ 1643.

circumstances, take place in the nominated forum, as the parties have effectively prioritised that forum through their agreement.[220] The correctness of such approaches must be seriously doubted.

The second and related question is whether a non-exclusive English jurisdiction agreement could nevertheless justify the issue of an anti-suit injunction on other grounds, such as to protect the English courts and/ or an English claimant from 'vexatious and oppressive' proceedings that might frustrate English judicial process. It is well established that an anti-suit injunction may be granted on these grounds, even where there is no jurisdiction agreement. It would thus appear logical that an anti-suit injunction also ought to be available where the jurisdiction of the English courts is derived from a non-exclusive jurisdiction agreement – provided that the facts support a finding that the foreign proceedings are vexatious and oppressive. This is perhaps the best reading of the recent decision of the English courts in *Deutsche Bank v. Highland Crusader*,[221] in which the court found that a non-exclusive English jurisdiction agreement could not support the issue of an anti-suit injunction to restrain parallel US proceedings. The court determined (correctly) that a non-exclusive jurisdiction agreement did not have any effect of conferring priority on the chosen court, finding that there is "no cogent reason why it should automatically be assumed that nomination of a non-exclusive forum should give priority or dominance to that forum over any other".[222] In reaching this conclusion, however, the court also endorsed[223] a suggestion in the academic literature that:

> where a non-exclusive jurisdiction clause does not clearly indicate whether prior or subsequent parallel proceedings in a non-selected forum are permitted or prohibited, the best interpretation will usually be that, by contracting for non-exclusive jurisdiction, the parties have anticipated and accepted the possibility of some parallel proceedings, and as a result, only foreign proceedings which are vexatious and oppressive for some reason independent of the mere presence of the non-exclusive clause will be restrained by injunction.[224]

With respect, however, the conclusion in this case did not depend (and should not have depended) on any idea that the parties in entering into a non-exclusive jurisdiction agreement "have anticipated and accepted the

---

[220] See e.g. *BP plc v. National Union Fire Insurance Co.* [2004] EWHC 1132 (Comm).

[221] *Deutsche Bank v. Highland Crusader* [2009] EWCA Civ 725.

[222] At [108].

[223] At [105].

[224] Raphael (2008), [9.12].

possibility of some parallel proceedings". It is unrealistic to suggest that parties entering into a non-exclusive jurisdiction agreement are thereby contemplating parallel proceedings – such parties are ordinarily intending merely to keep open their options for litigation, contemplating multiple *potential* fora, not contemplating that multiple options might be exercised *simultaneously*.[225]

The better view is simply that a non-exclusive jurisdiction agreement in favour of the English courts does not (absence special facts such as those in *Sabah*) on its own justify an anti-suit injunction (in the way that an exclusive jurisdiction agreement would), because it does not establish that it is a breach of contract to pursue foreign proceedings. But the fact that the jurisdiction of the English courts is based on a non-exclusive jurisdiction agreement equally does not limit the ordinary power of the courts to issue an anti-suit injunction where foreign proceedings are vexatious and oppressive – there is nothing in a non-exclusive jurisdiction agreement, absent clear wording to the contrary, which should lead the courts to be more hesitant than usual in restraining proceedings brought by a foreign claimant, on the basis that the parties have supposedly accepted the possibility of parallel proceedings. Foreign proceedings might, for example, be vexatious and oppressive if they were brought after long-established English proceedings (regardless of the basis of English jurisdiction), for the purpose of frustrating those proceedings. Foreign proceedings should ordinarily not be capable of being considered vexatious and oppressive where they were commenced first and their commencement did not violate any contractual agreement.

3.4.3.4 Choice of Law and Choice of Forum

Under the English common law, there is another distinctive basis of jurisdiction that relates to party autonomy – the possibility of jurisdiction being exercised on the basis of a choice of the applicable law. Under Practice Direction 6B, paragraph 3.1(6)(c) of the Civil Procedure Rules, the English court may give permission to commence proceedings against a defendant not present in the territory on the sole basis that the dispute concerns a contract governed by English law. The law applicable to the contract need not have been determined on the basis of a choice of law

---

[225] Note also *Ashville Investments Ltd* v. *Elmer Contractors Ltd* [1989] QB 488, 517 (per Bingham LJ, "I would be very slow to attribute to reasonable parties an intention that there should in any foreseeable eventuality be two sets of proceedings").

agreement, but it may have been.[226] (An implied choice of English law may also arise where there is an English exclusive jurisdiction agreement,[227] but in this case the jurisdiction of the court is evidently already established on that basis.) Where the parties have a choice of English law in their contract, either express or implied, this may therefore also serve as a basis of jurisdiction for the English courts. The court must also be persuaded that the exercise of jurisdiction is appropriate pursuant to the doctrine of *forum conveniens*, as discussed above. However, the fact that English law is applicable is, in this discretion, an important factor suggesting that the English courts may be the most appropriate forum, as disputes (particularly those involving complex legal questions) are generally resolved most efficiently by the court whose law is applicable.[228] The fact that the applicable law influences jurisdiction in these two ways is an important link, perhaps uniquely strong in England, between party autonomy in choice of law and choice of forum. Under US law, the applicability of US or foreign law, including as a consequence of a choice of law clause, will affect the operation of *forum non conveniens* but will not itself provide a basis of jurisdiction.[229] In Canada it has similarly been held that a choice of law clause cannot affect whether the court has a constitutional basis of jurisdiction (pursuant to the 'real and substantial connection' requirement noted above), but can affect whether proceedings are stayed (pursuant to the doctrine of *forum non conveniens*).[230]

3.4.4 Hague Convention on Choice of Court Agreements 2005

As examined above, exclusive jurisdiction agreements are generally (although not universally) given their intended positive and negative effects. These effects are generally dealt with through the discretionary doctrines of *forum conveniens* and *forum non conveniens* under the common law and US law. The discretionary nature of these doctrines means that it is possible that in a common law or US court jurisdiction may (rarely) be declined despite an exclusive jurisdiction agreement in favour of the forum, and jurisdiction may (rarely) be exercised despite an exclusive jurisdiction agreement in favour of a foreign court. Unusual though these exceptions may be, the possibility of an exclusive jurisdiction

---

[226] See further Chapter 7.
[227] See Section 7.2.
[228] See e.g. Cheshire, North and Fawcett (2017), p.367ff.
[229] See e.g. Force (2011), p.439ff.
[230] *Christmas v. Fort McKay*, 2014 ONSC 373.

agreement not receiving enforcement may be viewed as something of a concern to private parties, for whom such agreements are a means of managing litigation risk. Another risk may apply in civil law systems, where the doctrine of *lis pendens* may be viewed as requiring the court second seised of a dispute to suspend or decline jurisdiction, even if it is of the view that an exclusive jurisdiction agreement operates in its favour, to avoid parallel proceedings. As discussed above, similar issues have arisen in relation to the Brussels I Regulation, and have been partly but not entirely addressed in the adoption of the 2012 Recast.

These concerns were part of the motivation behind the Hague Convention on Choice of Court Agreements 2005, which aims, at least to some extent, to strengthen the effectiveness of forum selection clauses, and provide an international standardisation that is similar to that provided in respect of arbitration agreements under the New York Convention 1958.[231] It should be noted that, at least generally,[232] the Convention applies only to exclusive choice of court agreements, and it only regulates the effects of agreements in favour of the courts of contracting states. An agreement that nominates more than one court (even to the exclusion of any others), or which nominates a different court for suits against each party, would not satisfy the definition of a choice of court agreement for the Convention.[233] This is not to say that such agreements would not be enforceable, but merely that their enforceability would fall outside the scope of the Convention.

3.4.4.1   Prorogation

The positive effect of an exclusive jurisdiction agreement is dealt with clearly in Article 5 of the Convention, which provides that:

> (1) The court or courts of a Contracting State designated in an exclusive choice of court agreement shall have jurisdiction to decide a dispute to which the agreement applies, unless the agreement is null and void under the law of that State.
> (2) A court that has jurisdiction under paragraph 1 shall not decline to exercise jurisdiction on the ground that the dispute should be decided in a court of another State.

---

[231] See further Chapter 6. For further background and commentary, see the Preliminary Documents available at www.hcch.net/en/instruments/conventions/publications1/?dtid=35&cid=98, which include various comparative studies on the effectiveness of choice of court agreements; the Hague Convention Explanatory Report; Van Loon (2016), p.46ff; Beaumont (2009); Brand and Herrup (2008); Teitz (2005). The current parties to the Convention are noted in Section 3.1.

[232] Non-exclusive jurisdiction agreements may be given effect as a basis for the recognition and enforcement of foreign judgments, pursuant to Article 22 of the Convention.

[233] Hague Convention Explanatory Report, [109]. See further Section 3.5.

The evident intention of this provision is to remove the discretion from a court to decline jurisdiction despite a forum selection agreement. The Convention thus prioritises party autonomy over competing policy interests – the idea that, for example, complex or multi-party disputes should be resolved in a single forum for the sake of efficiency and to minimise the risk of irreconcilable judgments arising. Different views may certainly be taken on how these policy interests should be balanced. As discussed above, common law courts, at least, have traditionally decided that refusing to give effect to party autonomy may be justified for reasons of litigational efficiency in some circumstances.[234] Perhaps, however, a loss of efficiency would be a price worth paying for the greater certainty achieved for commercial parties in general. This is evidently the position implicitly adopted in the Hague Convention itself, in its endorsement of party autonomy as an overriding principle in the determination of which court should hear a case.

The positive effect of an exclusive choice of court clause is also indirectly recognised in the Convention in the obligation to recognise and enforce a judgment from another state whose jurisdiction was based on such a clause.[235] It is notable that the Convention does not appear to be limited to monetary judgments.[236] Where a foreign judgment is obtained on the basis of a jurisdiction agreement, the Convention may thus oblige common law courts to depart from their traditional practice of not recognising and enforce non-monetary judgments, such as injunctive relief – a limitation that has already been rejected in general in Canada.[237]

A potential qualification of the effect given to exclusive jurisdiction agreements under the Convention is found in Article 19, which provides that "A State may declare that its courts may refuse to determine disputes to which an exclusive choice of court agreement applies if, except for the location of the chosen court, there is no connection between that State and the parties or the dispute." By implication, no such objective connection is ordinarily required, but under Article 19 one may optionally be imposed. As examined above, the common law, US law (with the exception of some states), and EU law have all generally accepted party autonomy in choice of court unlimited by any requirement for an objective connection between the parties or their dispute and the chosen forum, although under

---

[234] See e.g. discussion in Mills (2017a).
[235] Hague Convention on Choice of Court Agreements 2005, Art.8, subject to exceptions in Art.9.
[236] Article 4(1).
[237] See *Pro Swing* v. *Elta Golf* [2006] 2 SCR 612.

the common law and US law such considerations may have played a role in *forum non conveniens*, and they have been more directly recognised by some other legal systems (including under Indian law). Such requirements might be adopted, for example, if a national legal system wished to protect its courts from becoming overburdened, and did not believe that such burdens would be outweighed by the contribution such litigation makes to the local economy. They could, however, risk undermining some of the positive effects that party autonomy aims to achieve. This potential restriction on party autonomy under the Convention may also be viewed as an effort to balance the increased effectiveness given to party choice with the continued recognition of traditional state sovereignty and jurisdictional limits under international law – states may choose to confine party autonomy to situations in which a factual connection would justify the exercise of jurisdiction under those traditional rules. Party autonomy would thus be reconceived as a rule of priority, determining which objective connection justifies the exercise of jurisdiction in the particular case – that favoured by the parties. This clause thus indicates a notable 'pressure point' for the tension between the rise of party autonomy and the efforts to preserve traditional models of state exclusivity of public power, as discussed above and in Chapter 2.[238]

3.4.4.2   Derogation

When it comes to the negative effect of choice of court agreements, the Convention is more qualified, to take into consideration the counterbalancing concerns of access to justice for claimants. Article 6 of the Convention provides that:

> A court of a Contracting State other than that of the chosen court shall suspend or dismiss proceedings to which an exclusive choice of court agreement applies unless –
>
> (a) the agreement is null and void under the law of the State of the chosen court;
> (b) a party lacked the capacity to conclude the agreement under the law of the State of the court seised;
> (c) giving effect to the agreement would lead to a manifest injustice or would be manifestly contrary to the public policy of the State of the court seised;
> (d) for exceptional reasons beyond the control of the parties, the agreement cannot reasonably be performed; or
> (e) the chosen court has decided not to hear the case.

---

[238] See in particular Section 2.4.4.

Aside from invalidity and incapacity, which obviously nullify the agreement, there are further safeguards here to prevent injustice. It may be noted that the safeguard in point (c) applies the public policy defence, traditionally more closely associated with choice of law or the recognition and enforcement of foreign judgments, to questions of jurisdiction. This may contemplate issues of bias or corruption in the chosen court, or situations in which a claim is based on a law that will not be applied by the chosen foreign court – arguably, at least if the law is mandatory in character, it may be necessary to invalidate the choice of court agreement in order to vindicate the rights of the claimant.[239] It is perhaps also particularly notable that points (d) and (e)[240] appear to accept that the requirements of access to justice may trump the usual obligation to give effect to an exclusive jurisdiction agreement. Such an 'exception of necessity' may be understood as related to the broader concept of a 'forum of necessity', ultimately aimed at ensuring that a claimant does not suffer a denial of justice through being denied access to any court.[241]

In general, the exceptions under the Hague Convention would cover many of the circumstances in which a choice of court agreement may be refused enforcement under the common law or US law, as discussed above (although not those related to the efficient resolution of complex disputes). The breadth of these exceptions is, however, somewhat unclear, and therefore only practice will tell how exactly they strike the balance between the interests of a claimant in obtaining real access to a court, and the interests of the defendant and indeed the systemic interests of commercial parties in the legal certainty achieved by holding the parties to their contractual bargain.

3.5   Asymmetrical Jurisdiction Agreements

Many jurisdiction agreements apply identically to each party – providing, for example, that any disputes arising under a contract must be heard by the English courts. Some jurisdiction agreements are, however, asymmetrical, providing for distinct rights and obligations for the parties. Such an agreement might give each party the right to commence proceedings in a

---

[239] See the Hague Convention Explanatory Report, [153]. Such an approach has arguably been adopted by the Australian courts. See further discussion in Sections 3.4.3 and 9.4.1.

[240] Point (e) is not likely to arise frequently, since the Convention generally obliges the chosen court to exercise jurisdiction, but may perhaps apply where the nominated court lacks subject-matter jurisdiction – see Article 5(3).

[241] Hague Convention Explanatory Report, [155]. See further Mills (2014), p.221ff.

different jurisdiction – for example, allowing each party to be certain that they may only be sued in their home courts, and potentially thereby discouraging litigation by requiring each party to litigate in a foreign court.[242] Alternatively, the rights and obligations of each party may differ in kind – one party might, for example, be bound by an exclusive jurisdiction agreement, while the other may be bound only non-exclusively (to accept the jurisdiction of a particular forum), or be under no jurisdictional obligations whatsoever. These types of agreements are not uncommon in finance contracts, under which the borrower may be bound by an exclusive jurisdiction agreement in favour of the lender's preferred jurisdiction, but no equivalent restriction may apply to the lender themselves.[243] In this way, the lender maximises the predictability of venue for any litigation against them, while retaining flexibility for any suit they may wish to commence themselves – an important feature given the possibility that a borrower may move assets between jurisdictions. While the fairness of such agreements might seem questionable at first glance, the benefits of combining certainty and flexibility for the lender are likely to be reflected in the substantive terms of the loan. The interest rate set by the lender can, for example, be reduced to take into consideration their reduced risk of exposure to foreign litigation and their continuing freedom to pursue litigation themselves in any available forum. The borrower should thus benefit from the jurisdictional asymmetry in financial terms. Whether they are prepared to accept the jurisdictional 'costs' associated with an asymmetrical choice of court agreement may thus be viewed simply as part of the question of whether they are prepared to accept the commercial terms of the agreement.

One might expect, therefore, that asymmetrical jurisdiction agreements do not present any particular issues in terms of their validity – that they should be judged according to the ordinary rules applicable to choice of court agreements. This is, indeed, the position that has been clearly adopted by the English courts under both the common law[244] and EU jurisdictional rules.[245] The CJEU also confirmed early on

---

[242] See e.g. *Abbott Laboratories* v. *Takeda Pharmaceutical Co. Ltd*, 476 F.3d 421 (7th Cir. 2007).

[243] They are, for example, generally adopted in the Loan Market Association's standard documentation.

[244] See e.g. *Mauritius Commercial Bank Ltd* v. *Hestia Holdings Ltd* [2013] EWHC 1328 (Comm), discussed further below; *Law Debenture Trust Corporation plc* v. *Elektrim Finance BV* [2005] EWHC 1412 (Ch) (approving an asymmetrical hybrid jurisdiction/ arbitration clause); *NB Three Shipping Ltd* v. *Harebell Shipping Ltd* [2005] 1 Lloyd's Rep 509 (approving an asymmetrical arbitration clause). See discussion in Merrett (2018); Petch (2016); Keyes and Marshall (2015), p.373ff.

[245] *Continental Bank* v. *Aeakos* [1994] 1 Lloyd's Rep 505; see also most recently *Commerzbank Aktiengesellshcaft* v. *Liquimar Tankers Management* [2017] EWHC 161 (Comm).

that under the Brussels Convention 1968 it was possible for the parties to enter into an exclusive jurisdiction agreement that provided for different forums for each party (each having the right to be sued only in their home jurisdiction),[246] and there is no obvious reason why such agreements should not be permitted. Although as noted earlier in this chapter, Chinese courts have considered jurisdiction agreements in favour of more than one court to be invalid, this does not apply to jurisdiction agreements that select a different single court for each party – such agreements are considered valid and enforceable.[247] Such an agreement is, however, at least reciprocal – each party possesses equivalent rights. The question of the validity of a more asymmetrical jurisdiction agreement, under which only one party may be given rights, or the parties may be subject to qualitatively different obligations, has not been decided by the CJEU, although it appeared until recently that there was little cause for doubting that such agreements would be considered valid.[248] The Brussels Convention 1968 indeed appeared to provide for the recognition of asymmetrical jurisdiction agreements directly in Article 17 ("If the agreement conferring jurisdiction was concluded for the benefit of only one of the parties, that party shall retain the right to bring proceedings in any other court which has jurisdiction by virtue of this Convention"), but the interpretation of this provision was contested,[249] and it was not included in the Brussels I Regulation 2001 or the Recast Brussels I Regulation 2012. Although it may be noted that asymmetrical jurisdiction agreements are excluded from the scope of the Hague Convention, this should not be considered to cast doubt on their effectiveness, but merely to reflect the fact that they do not fit into the narrow constraints of the Convention rules.[250]

The position of asymmetrical jurisdiction agreements thus appeared secure – until 2012, when several national courts reached decisions finding that 'one-way' jurisdictional agreements were invalid.[251] The most

---

[246] Case 23/78 *Meeth* v. *Glacetal* [1978] ECR 2133.

[247] Supreme People's Court, Jing Han [1994] No 307.

[248] For example, their validity was upheld by the Italian Supreme Court in early 2012: *Grinka in liquidazione* v. *Intesa San Paolo, Simest, HSBC*, Case 5705, 11 April 2012. Chinese law has also recognised asymmetrical jurisdiction agreements in which only one party may be bound by an exclusive choice of court clause: Supreme People's Court, Jing Zhong Zi [1999] No 194.

[249] See C-22/85 *Anterist* v. *Crédit Lyonnais* [1986] ECR 1951.

[250] A jurisdiction agreement which is only exclusive for one party, or which is exclusive for each party in favour of a different jurisdiction, is not considered to be an 'exclusive' jurisdiction agreement for the purposes of the Hague Convention on Choice of Court Agreements 2005 – see Hague Convention Explanatory Report, [104]–[106].

[251] See generally e.g. Financial Markets Law Committee of London, *Issues of Legal Uncertainty Arising in the Context of Asymmetric Jurisdiction Clauses,* July 2016; Merrett (2018); Petch (2016); Keyes and Marshall (2015); Draguiev (2014); Fentiman (2013); Briggs (2013).

prominent of these was the French Cour de Cassation decision in *Soc Banque privée Edmond de Rothschild Europe* v. *Mme X*,[252] which followed similar decisions by the Supreme Court of Bulgaria[253] and by the Russian Supreme Court.[254] The decision of the Russian Supreme Court, discussed further below, was based on the argument that such clauses violated the principle of equal access to justice. In *Rothschild*, the Cour de Cassation held that a one-sided jurisdiction agreement (in favour of the courts of Luxembourg) was invalid and contrary to the object and purpose of Article 23 of the Brussels I Regulation 2001 (the predecessor to Article 25 of the current Brussels I Regulation), because of its 'potestative' character – a doctrine of French contract law under which one party may not be given unilateral control over the rights and obligations of the parties.[255] It is unclear whether the reference to the potestative character of the choice of court agreement was intended as an application of this principle of French contract law. If this is the case, it is likely that the approach was contrary to EU law given the fact, discussed in Section 3.3, that the validity of a jurisdiction agreement under the Brussels I Regulation 2001 was interpreted by the CJEU to be regulated solely by Article 23. The more generous interpretation is that the French court was relying on the doctrine to inform analysis of whether the parties 'have agreed' on the jurisdiction agreement, as that term is used for the purposes of Article 23 – although this would still be a novel interpretation of the breadth of that requirement, and place excessive weight on principles of French contract law in its (European) interpretation.

Whether or not the approach of the French courts was contrary to the requirements of the Brussels I Regulation 2001, it is important to recall that the question of the applicable law for jurisdiction agreements has been reformed in the 2012 Recast. As noted above, Article 25 of the Brussels I Regulation now provides that a jurisdiction agreement should be given effect "unless the agreement is null and void as to its substantive validity under the law of [the chosen] Member State", which (according to Recital 20) includes the choice of law rules of that state. Thus, the effectiveness of a jurisdiction agreement that confers exclusive jurisdiction on the French

---

[252] Cour de Cassation, 1st Civil Chamber, 26 September 2012, No 11-26.022 (English translation [2013] ILPr 12). This approach has since been confirmed in *ICH* v. *Crédit Suisse*, 1st Civil Chamber, 25 March 2015, No 13-27264, although without reliance on the French 'potestative' contract doctrine.

[253] Judgment No. 71 in commercial case No. 1193/2010, 2 September 2011.

[254] *Sony Ericsson Mobile Communications Rus LLC* v. *Russian Telephone Company CJSC*, Decision of the Presidium of the Supreme Arbitrazh Court of the Russian Federation of 19 June 2012, Case No. VAS-1831/12.

[255] See further discussion in Ancel, Marion and Wynaendts (2013).

courts (including one that does so only for one party)[256] is now a matter for French choice of law rules, which may well designate French substantive contract law.[257] The application of a doctrine of French contract law under which asymmetrical jurisdiction agreements are considered invalid can thus no longer be rejected solely on the basis that this is contrary to EU law.[258] In light of these reforms, further attention is required to the issue of whether the validity of such agreements should be considered questionable, and if so on what basis.

It is unclear whether the arguments relied on by the French, Bulgarian and Russian courts are persuasive reasons to invalidate an asymmetrical jurisdiction agreement under the Brussels I Regulation. The object and purpose of Article 25 and its predecessor provisions is to give effect to agreements as to jurisdiction freely entered into by the parties, not to protect the equality of rights of the parties. As noted above, an asymmetrical jurisdiction agreement can be viewed as part of the commercial bargain struck by the parties, which cannot be divorced from the broader context of the contract of which it forms part – it may, for example, have been reflected in the contract price. Also as noted above, the Brussels I Regulation appears principally to rely on a public consequentialist justification for its rules – they are designed to enhance the efficient functioning of the internal market, including in the case of choice of court agreements by allowing for a 'market of jurisdictions'.[259] If an asymmetrical jurisdiction agreement reduces litigation risk for one party, and that party is a repeat market participant (like a financial institution), that may ultimately be to the benefit of all the parties contracting with that entity. If contracting parties reach agreement on a contract that includes an asymmetrical jurisdiction agreement, there does not seem to be any basis for finding that such an agreement should be given any less respect than any other manifestation of party autonomy.

It is somewhat unclear whether the French court interpreted the one-way jurisdiction agreement to have intended merely to leave Rothschild with the power to commence proceedings in any court (in addition to

---

[256] The application of this rule to jurisdiction agreements which select difference courts for different parties is, however, entirely unclear, as noted above.

[257] Under the facts of the *Rothschild* case itself, the governing law would have been that selected by Luxembourg rather than French choice of law rules, although the law of Luxembourg is strongly influenced by French law.

[258] It may be noted, however, that French contract law has been recently reformed (see generally Rowan (2017)), leaving the status of the potestative doctrine unclear: see Merrett (2018).

[259] See Section 2.3.2.

the nominated forum) *subject to the jurisdictional rules of that court* (the normal effect of a non-exclusive jurisdiction agreement),[260] or whether it interpreted the clause as intending to constitute *submission* by Mme X to every court in the world. The latter would obviously aim to have a much broader effect, being an attempt to confer jurisdiction on all the courts of the world, rather than just to permit the exercise of whatever jurisdiction they may have. There would, in this case, be an argument that permitting such a clause would undermine the effect of the Brussels I Regulation, as it would allow the parties to contract out of its jurisdictional restrictions, potentially undermining legal certainty for one party in terms of the possible courts in which it might be sued.[261] However, even if this interpretation were correct (which seems improbable), there is an argument that it would be excessively paternalistic to prevent at least commercial parties from entering into such undertakings. When a similar argument was presented before the English High Court, the court held that the suggested interpretation (that the clause purported to confer a power on the bank to sue the lender in any court in the world) was indeed incorrect, but that even if it were the correct interpretation, that would be no reason to find it invalid.[262] It remains true that an asymmetrical jurisdiction clause might be found invalid in extreme circumstances because there was such an inequality between the parties that there was no genuine agreement reached – but such conclusions should be reached very reluctantly in the commercial context, special protection is already provided under the Regulation for weaker parties such as consumers and employees, and there is no need for a rule invalidating one-way jurisdiction agreements in general to deal with any such concerns. The approach of the English courts on this point, which has continued despite the decisions of the French, Russian and Bulgarian courts,[263] appears to be more consistent with the policy and text

---

[260] See e.g. *Lornamead Acquisitions Ltd* v. *Kaupthing Bank* [2011] EWHC 2611 (Comm), [112].

[261] This might distinguish the later decision in *Société eBizcuss.com* v. *Apple*, First Civil Chamber, 7 October 2015, Case No. 14-16898, which found that a clause permitting a party to sue in Ireland or in any place in which damage was suffered was valid. Contrast *ICH* v. *Crédit Suisse*, 1st Civil Chamber, 25 March 2015, No 13-27264. See further discussion in Keyes and Marshall (2015); Ancel, Marion, and Wynaendts (2013).

[262] *Mauritius Commercial Bank Ltd* v. *Hestia Holdings Ltd* [2013] EWHC 1328 (Comm), [43] ("If, improbably, the true intention of the parties expressed in the clause is that MCB should be entitled to insist on suing or being sued anywhere in the world, that is the contractual bargain to which the court should give effect").

[263] See e.g. *Commerzbank Aktiengesellschaft* v. *Liquimar Tankers Management Inc.* [2017] EWHC 161 (Comm).

of the Brussels I Regulation. The French approach may, however, suggest a characterisation of the jurisdiction agreement that is more focused on its procedural rather than substantive characteristics[264] – viewing it not as an ordinary part of the commercial agreement, but as an attempt to constrain the exercise of French judicial power.

In *Sony Ericsson Mobile Communications Rus LLC* v. *Russian Telephone Company*, the Russian courts (as noted above) relied on a slightly distinct approach (but arguably with a similar procedural focus), suggesting that an asymmetrical jurisdiction agreement would violate the equality of access to justice of the parties. The clause in this case was narrower and clearer in its effect – it gave Sony Ericsson the right to sue on a particular issue in the Russian courts, but otherwise all claims had to be submitted to arbitration in London. The logic of the objection to this clause is not apparent. Absent any jurisdiction agreement, jurisdictional rights between parties are very often asymmetrical, because they depend on the domicile of the defendant – in a dispute between an English and a French company, it might well be that the English company may sue the French company in France but not in England, and the French company may sue the English company in England but not in France. Jurisdictional rules thus commonly accept and affirm an inequality of access to a court, which has not been understood to offend the principle of equality of access to justice. That principle has rather generally been understood to require only access to one or more courts or tribunals, and more particularly that the procedural rules applied by a tribunal give each party equal opportunity to present their arguments. The English courts have held that even a one-way jurisdiction agreement that purported to confer jurisdiction on every court in the world for the benefit of only one party, while the other party would be subject to a single exclusive forum, would not violate the principle of equal access to justice.[265] The approach of the Russian courts may, however, again suggest greater scrutiny of choice of court agreements because of their potential procedural impact on the exercise of Russian judicial power.

As noted above, the jurisdictional obligations under the Hague Convention on Choice of Court Agreements 2005 do not apply to forms of asymmetrical jurisdiction agreement in which the clause is exclusive

---

[264] See Section 3.3.
[265] *Mauritius Commercial Bank Ltd* v. *Hestia Holdings Ltd* [2013] EWHC 1328 (Comm), [43] ("Article 6 [of the ECHR] is directed to access to justice within the forum chosen by the parties, not to choice of forum. No forum was identified in which the Defendants' access to justice would be unequal to that of MCB merely because MCB had the option of choosing the forum"). See further, e.g., *OT Africa Line* v. *Hijazy 'The Kribi'* [2001] 1 Lloyd's Rep 76.

for one party and non-exclusive for the other.[266] However, the Hague Convention Explanatory Report observes that such clauses "may be subject to the rules of the Convention on recognition and enforcement if the States in question have made declarations under Article 22"[267] (which deals with the enforcement of judgments based on non-exclusive jurisdiction agreements). A clause that is exclusive for one party and non-exclusive for the other may be analysed as having a prorogation effect in relation to both parties, which is the effect of a non-exclusive jurisdiction agreement, even if it also purports to have a derogation effect for the beneficiary of the exclusive jurisdiction clause (which effect will not be covered by the Convention). It is something of an oddity that an asymmetrical jurisdiction agreement may therefore potentially benefit from the rules on recognition and enforcement of judgments under the Hague Convention, even if the party who is the beneficiary of the exclusive jurisdiction clause is unable to rely on the Convention to give effect to that clause.

3.6 Effects of Jurisdiction Agreements on Third Parties

The analysis above has considered the effect of jurisdiction agreements on the parties who have negotiated the agreement or clause. Naturally, the starting point of analysis is that only parties to a jurisdiction agreement are bound by it or may benefit from it – reflecting the principle of privity of contract.[268] This principle commonly has limits and exceptions, however, raising the question of when a jurisdiction agreement may be binding on or benefit third parties.[269] For the purposes of illustration, in this section we will refer to the signatories of the original contract establishing the jurisdiction agreement as Party A and Party B, and to the third party as Party C. In some situations there will be an additional contract between Party B and Party C, giving rise to what we can characterise as a 'chain' of contracts. An example of such a situation is where a product manufacturer

---

[266] Hague Convention Explanatory Report, [106]. Presumably purely unilateral clauses will also not be covered. But see *Commerzbank Aktiengesellshcaft* v. *Liquimar Tankers Management* [2017] EWHC 161 (Comm), [74] ("There are good arguments in my view that the words of the definition of exclusive jurisdiction clauses in Article 3(a) of the Hague Convention cover asymmetric jurisdiction clauses").

[267] Hague Convention Explanatory Report, [106].

[268] In UK law, see classically e.g. *Dunlop Pneumatic Tyre Co Ltd* v. *Selfridge & Co Ltd* [1915] AC 847.

[269] See generally Black and Pitel (2016) (focusing on Canada and the United States); for China, see Tang, Xiao and Huo (2016), p.70ff.

(Party A) and distributor (Party B) enter into a contract, and the distributor enters into a further contract with a retailer (Party C). The question then is to what extent Party C may rely on or be bound by any limitations as to jurisdiction found in the original contract if Party C makes a claim against Party A. As examined further in Chapter 4, a jurisdiction agreement may in some circumstances still be effective even if the form of Party C's action against Party A is non-contractual.

Two general 'exceptions'[270] to privity of contract may be identified, under which jurisdictional rights or limitations from the original contract may indeed be applicable to Party C. It may be helpful to characterise these as 'collapsing the chain' or 'completing the triangle'. The first, 'collapsing the chain', describes the situation in which Party C is found to be in reality a party to the original contract. The most obvious example of this is where it is determined that Party B was acting as an agent on behalf of Party C in entering into the original contract with Party A. The chain of contracts collapses such that if Party C brings a claim against Party A, Party C is considered to be legally equivalent to Party B, and effectively subject to and a beneficiary of any limitations on jurisdiction found in the original contract. In this exception, the 'chain is collapsed' because it is determined ultimately that Parties A and C are parties to the original contract.[271]

The second exception, 'completing the triangle', describes a situation in which there is a further contract that may be identified as having arisen directly between Party A and Party C. A typical example of such an arrangement arises in a bill of lading (or in the carriage of goods more generally), in which all parties understand that Party C in accepting the bill of lading (or consignment note) is effectively entering into a contract with Party A, generally on the terms established in the underlying contract, including any limitations on jurisdiction that may be applicable under that contract (provided Party C is given notice of such terms).[272] In this exception, the 'triangle is completed' because it is determined that there is an additional contract formed between Parties A and C.

---

[270] The term 'exceptions' is used loosely – both situations describe circumstances in which privity does not restrict the claim of a non-signatory to a contract, rather than technical exceptions to privity.

[271] A similar effect could arise through statute – see e.g. *Guardians of New Zealand Superannuation Fund* v. *Novo Banco, SA* [2016] EWCA Civ 1092.

[272] See e.g. *British American Tobacco Denmark A/S* v. *Kazemier BV* [2015] UKSC 65, [26].

3.6.1   Common Law and Hague Convention on
Choice of Court Agreements 2005

In the common law, both of these exceptions to privity are recognised, including in their effect on jurisdiction agreements. The first may be established not only through agency, but also through similar doctrines such as trust (finding that Party B is a trustee for Party C, and holds its contractual rights for the benefit of Party C) and subrogation (for example, if Party C is the insurer of Party B and Party B has a claim against Party A, it might be considered that Party C steps into the shoes of Party B in making a subrogated legal claim against Party A).[273] It is notable that this approach was also approved in the drafting of the Hague Convention on Choice of Court Agreements 2005, which expressly accepts (in the Hague Convention Explanatory Report) the possibility that a third party will be governed by a jurisdiction agreement if national law provides for a substitution of rights and obligations between the parties,[274] such as in the context of subrogation under an insurance contract. In rare cases, it may even be that the agent was acting for a number of principals simultaneously, each of whom is taken to consent to (and also benefit from) the jurisdiction agreement.[275] This may be considered a narrower equivalent to the more controversial group of companies doctrine under arbitration law, discussed in Section 6.5.2. A similar consequence could also be established in some cases through estoppel, under which Party C or Party A may be found to have acted in such a way as to give rise to an equitable obligation to comply with the terms of the jurisdiction agreement in the underlying contract. Such doctrines are highly fact sensitive, and it is difficult to give a generalised account of the circumstances under which they may arise. These exceptions to privity of contract have, however, traditionally been applied restrictively under the common law. A more flexible approach may be possible where the *forum conveniens* or *forum non conveniens* discretions are being exercised. For example, if a person is alleged to have fraudulently induced another to enter into a contract containing an exclusive jurisdiction agreement, the exercise of jurisdiction over that person may be

---

[273] A party exercising subrogated rights is not, however, always considered to be bound by a forum selection clause – see further Section 6.5.2 in relation to arbitration agreements.

[274] Hague Convention Explanatory Report, [97] ("Provided the original parties consent to the choice of court agreement, the agreement may bind third parties who did not expressly consent to it, if their standing to bring the proceedings depends on their taking over the rights and obligations of one of the original parties. Whether this is the case will depend on national law").

[275] See e.g. *BNP Paribas SA v. Anchorage Capital Europe LLP* [2013] EWHC 3073 (Comm).

affected by the choice of court agreement, even if the alleged fraudster is not a party to it.[276]

A further possible argument may arise where the law permits third party beneficiaries of contractual rights to enforce a contract. If the issue arises under English law, for example, the Contracts (Rights of Third Parties) Act 1999 (UK) allows a third party beneficiary under a contract to enforce any rights, including jurisdictional rights, which may have been 'conferred' on it.[277] Thus, for example, if Party A is an insurer that enters into an insurance contract with Party B, and Party C is the named beneficiary of the insurance policy, under English law it is possible that Party C may benefit from any jurisdictional rights that Party B had under the insurance contract (such as submission by Party A to a particular forum). It has similarly been established in Australia,[278] Canada,[279] New Zealand,[280] and Hong Kong[281] that a third party to a contract may (at least in some cases) enforce a promise made for its benefit, and this has been extended to jurisdictional promises such as exclusive jurisdiction agreements.[282] It is notable that the Contracts (Rights of Third Parties) Act 1999 (UK) only deals with the enforceability of rights conferred on Party C, and does not provide for Party C to be bound by any obligations under the contract between Party A and Party B – such as any restrictions on when Party B itself could bring proceedings against Party A, the insurer. In Hong Kong, third party beneficiaries may be automatically bound by an exclusive jurisdiction clause in the underlying contract.[283] In the UK, an equivalent indirect effect may however be established through the conferral of conditional benefits – the contract between Party A and Party B may, for

---

[276] See *VTB Capital Plc* v. *Nutritek International Corp* [2013] UKSC 5 (with different views taken as to how much weight should attached to the agreement).

[277] It was initially proposed by the Law Commission that jurisdiction clauses be excluded from the Act (Law Commission Report No.242, 'Privity of Contract: Contracts for the Benefit of Third Parties', [14.14ff]), but this exclusion was dropped by parliament, and it is clear from the explanatory notes of the Act that it does indeed apply to jurisdiction agreements (see www.legislation.gov.uk/ukpga/1999/31/notes/contents), as well as arbitration agreements (on which see Section 6.5.2). See further Andrews (2001), p.374; *Petrologic Capital SA* v. *Banque Cantonale de Geneve* [2012] EWHC 453.

[278] *Trident General Insurance Co Ltd* v. *McNiece Bros Pty Ltd* (1988) 165 CLR 107; see also s.48 of the Insurance Contracts Act 1984 (Cth) (Aust.).

[279] See generally *Fraser River Pile & Dredge Ltd* v. *Can-Dive Services Ltd* [1999] 3 SCR 108.

[280] Contracts Privity Act 1982 (NZ).

[281] Contracts (Rights of Third Parties) Ordinance 2015 (Hong Kong).

[282] See e.g. *Yperion Technology SAS* v. *Luminex Pty Ltd* [2012] FCA 554; *Global Partners Fund Ltd* v. *Babcock & Brown Ltd (in liq)* [2010] NSWCA 196.

[283] Contracts (Rights of Third Parties) Ordinance 2015 (Hong Kong), s.13.

example, specify that a third party beneficiary's right to receive payment is conditional on exclusive acceptance of a nominated court, effectively establishing a bar to claims brought by Party C in any other forum.[284]

While the device of indirectly binding Party C to jurisdictional obligations through establishing conditional benefits exists in principle, there is limited case law on its operation in practice. Perhaps a partial explanation for this is the existence under the common law of alternative grounds of jurisdiction that may be relied on in such circumstances. For example, if Party A (the insurer) wished to make a claim against Party C (the beneficiary) and the insurance contract contained an exclusive English jurisdiction agreement, Party A might first commence proceedings against Party B relying on that agreement, and then add Party C as a 'necessary and proper party' to those proceedings.[285] This basis of jurisdiction, somewhat controversially, does not require any connection between Party C and England, only that there be a legitimate claim against both parties and a ground of jurisdiction over the first 'anchor' defendant.[286]

3.6.2   United States

In the United States, the approach to questions of 'privity' is in general reasonably similar to that under the English common law. Doctrines such as agency, trust or estoppel are potentially available to third parties seeking to rely on jurisdiction agreements in 'underlying' contracts.[287] However, 'necessary and proper party' jurisdiction, as recognised by the English courts, is not available in US courts, not least because it would be likely to be considered as violating US constitutional due process requirements, which require a minimum connection between the dispute or defendant and the forum.[288] Perhaps for this reason, US courts have tended to take a slightly more flexible approach in recognising the potential effect of

---

[284] Andrews (2001), p.375.

[285] Civil Procedure Rules, Practice Direction 6B, Para 3.1(3).

[286] See e.g. Cheshire, North and Fawcett (2017), p.336ff.

[287] See e.g. *Belfiore* v. *Summit Federal Credit Union*, 452 F.Supp. 2d 629, 633 (D. Md. 2006) ("Obviously when the non-party is acting as an agent of a party ... it is unquestionably covered by the choice of forum clause in the contract of the principal"); *Liles* v. *Ginn-la West End Ltd*, 631 F.3d 1242, 1256 (11th Cir. 2011) (noting that a third party may be bound by a jurisdiction or arbitration clause "under a theory of equitable estoppel, under agency or related principles").

[288] See recently e.g. *J. McIntyre Machinery, Ltd* v. *Nicastro*, 564 US 873 (2011); *Goodyear Dunlop Tires Operations, SA* v. *Brown*, 564 US 915 (2011); *Daimler AG* v. *Bauman*, 571 US 20 (2014).

jurisdiction agreements on third parties, where those third parties are beneficiaries of the contract[289] or considered to be 'closely related' to the original contractual relationship.[290] It appears that in this context the courts are prepared to apply the principle of privity of contract relatively loosely, in order to achieve the same goal which motivates English 'necessary and proper party' jurisdiction – ensuring that, wherever possible, proceedings involving multiple parties are consolidated in a single forum. There is also an element of ensuring that the rights of third party beneficiaries are protected, as under the various statutory reforms discussed above – US courts have, for example, also recognised as a matter of case law that a jurisdiction agreement may be relied on by a third party beneficiary under a contract, such as the beneficiary of an insurance policy.[291]

3.6.3   Civil Law

In civil law systems, the general absence of a requirement of 'consideration' in contract law means that a more flexible doctrine of privity of contract applies. This can provide a further mechanism through which jurisdictional rights and obligations flow to a third party, effectively through the 'completing the triangle' approach (discussed above). Under French law, for example, a chain of contracts for the sale of goods (with Party A and Party B as manufacturer and distributor respectively, and Party B and Party C as distributor and retailer respectively) may give rise to an implied contract between the manufacturer (Party A) and the retailer (Party C). Such a cause of action is characterised as contractual for the purposes of French

---

[289] See e.g. *Hatfield* v. *Halifax PLC*, 564 F.3d 1177 (9th Cir. 2009) (focused on a choice of law clause rather than a choice of court clause); *TAAG Linhas Aereas de Angola* v. *Transamerica Airlines, Inc.*, 915 F.2d 1351, 1354 (9th Cir. 1990); *Coastal Steel Corp.* v. *Tilghman Wheelabrator Ltd*, 709 F.2d 190, 204 (3rd Cir. 1983), cert. denied, 464 US 938 (1983).

[290] *Magi XXI, Inc.* v. *Stato della Citta del Vaticano*, 714 F.3d 714 (2nd Cir. 2013); *Holland America Line Inc.* v. *Wartsila North America, Inc.*, 485 F.3d 450, 456 (9th Cir. 2007) ("where the alleged conduct of the nonparties is closely related to the contractual relationship, 'a range of transaction participants, parties and nonparties, should benefit from and be subject to forum selection clauses'." (citation omitted)); *Lipcon* v. *Underwriters at Lloyd's, London*, 148 F.3d 1285, 1295 (11th Cir. 1998); *Dayhoff Inc.* v. *HJ Heinz Co.*, 86 F.3d 1287 (3rd Cir. 1996); *Hugel* v. *Corporation of Lloyd's*, 999 F.3d 206, 209 (7th Cir. 1993) ("[i]n order to bind a non-party to a forum selection clause, the party must be 'closely related' to the dispute such that it becomes 'foreseeable' that it will be bound." (citation omitted)); *Manetti-Farrow, Inc.* v. *Gucci America, Inc.*, 858 F.2d 509, 514, n.5 (9th Cir. 1988); *Coastal Steel* v. *Tilghman Wheelabrator Ltd*, 709 F.2d 190, 202–3 (3rd Cir. 1983), cert. denied, 464 US 938 (1983). See discussion in Black and Pitel (2016).

[291] See e.g. *MS Dealer Service Corp.* v. *Franklin*, 177 F.3d 942, 947 (11th Cir. 1999).

law, although the CJEU has determined that it should be considered non-contractual for the purposes of Article 7 of the Brussels I Regulation.[292] In any case, in such circumstances it is possible that under French law Party C may potentially be bound by or benefit from jurisdictional restrictions established by Party A in (or through) its contract with Party B, not as a matter of agency but because a new contract is considered to have been formed between Parties A and C.

3.6.4   EU Law (Brussels I Regulation)

Similar issues have also arisen under the Brussels I Regulation (and under its predecessor, the Brussels Convention 1968), in relation to the possible effects of jurisdiction agreements on third parties. As noted in Section 3.3, Article 23 of the Brussels I Regulation 2001 principally established formal conditions for the validity of a jurisdiction agreement (discussed further in Section 5.2). The only substantive condition was in the requirement that the jurisdiction agreement be 'agreed' between the parties. The CJEU, however, emphasised that the jurisdictional inquiry as to the validity of a choice of court agreement should (generally) not require the determination or application of a substantive national contract law.[293] This was, therefore, an area in which the CJEU effectively appeared to be developing a substantive Europeanised contract law, albeit for the narrow purpose of governing questions of the effectiveness of jurisdiction agreements. The CJEU consequently was required to develop its own jurisprudence as to when a third party may be considered to be bound by or benefit from a jurisdiction agreement, equivalent to that under the various national laws discussed above.

In two particular contexts, the CJEU established a clear approach under which choice of court agreements governed by the Brussels Convention 1968 or Brussels I Regulation 2001 might affect third parties.[294] The first was bills of lading, in respect of which the CJEU recognised that such instruments are inherently designed to establish a contractual relationship between Party A and Party C. The CJEU recognised that in these particular circumstances the requirements of what is now Article 25 could be satisfied without any direct communication between Party A and Party

---

[292] C-26/91 *Jakob Handte & Co. GmbH* v. *Traitements Mécanochimiques des Surfaces SA* [1992] ECR I-3967.
[293] See Section 3.3.2.
[294] See generally Cheshire, North and Fawcett (2017), pp.241–2; Hartley (2013b), p.149ff.

C.[295] The court therefore recognised a special rule regarding formation of jurisdiction agreements where there is a common intention between all the parties that a third party be bound by and benefit from such an agreement. Although the court's jurisprudence was not entirely clear on this point, it appeared that a third party might be party to the choice of court agreement *either* where this was established under the applicable national law,[296] *or* where the third party had met the requirements of what is now Article 25 of the Brussels I Regulation.[297]

The second context in which the CJEU accepted a special rule of contract formation applicable to jurisdiction agreements is in the context of insurance, where the court held that third party beneficiaries of an insurance policy may rely on a forum selection clause binding on the insurer,[298] although they are not limited or themselves bound by it.[299] In effect, any choice of court agreement in the underlying contract is always construed as non-exclusive and unilateral in its effect on third party beneficiaries – it provides the beneficiary with a further 'supplementary' forum in which they might pursue their claim, as permitted under what is now Article 15(2) of the Brussels I Regulation, but does not constitute consent to any particular forum by that beneficiary should the insurer bring a claim against them.

Outside of these two special contexts, under the Brussels Convention 1968 and Brussels I Regulation 2001 it was unclear what standard should be applied to determine whether a third party had sufficiently 'agreed' to a choice of court clause, such that they should be held to be bound by it. Where there was no clear common intention that a third party be bound by the jurisdiction agreement (as in the context of a bill of lading) or benefit from it (as in the context of a beneficiary under an insurance

---

[295]   C-71/83 *Tilly Russ* [1984] ECR 2417, [24]; C-159/97 *Trasporti Castelletti* v. *Hugo Trumpy* [1999] ECR I-1597, [41]; C-387/98 *Coreck Maritime GmbH* v. *Handelsveem BV* [2000] ECR I-9337, [23]-[27].

[296]   C-387/98 *Corek Maritime GmbH* v. *Handelsveem BV* [2000] ECR I-9337, [24] ("the question whether a party not privy to the original contract against whom a jurisdiction clause is relied on has succeeded to the rights and obligations of one of the original parties must be determined according to the applicable national law").

[297]   C-387/98 *Corek Maritime GmbH* v. *Handelsveem BV* [2000] ECR I-9337, [26] ("if, under the applicable national law, the party not privy to the original contract did not succeed to the rights and obligations of one of the original parties, the court seised must ascertain, having regard to the requirements laid down in the first paragraph of Article 17 of the Convention, whether he actually accepted the jurisdiction clause relied on against him").

[298]   Case 201/82 *Gerling Konzern Speziale Kreditversicherungs-AG* v. *Amministrazione del Tesoro dello Stato* [1983] ECR 2503.

[299]   C-112/03 *Société financière et industrielle du Peloux* [2005] ECR I-3707.

policy), there remained the ordinary question of whether the third party had agreed to the jurisdiction agreement in accordance with the requirements of the Convention or Regulation. Under the approach of the CJEU to Article 23 of the Brussels I Regulation 2001, this question had to be resolved as a matter of EU law rather than through recourse to national law. In one case, for example, dealing with a chain of contracts for the sale of goods, the CJEU rejected the application of any national law to the question of whether a sub-buyer could be bound by a choice of forum clause in the contract between manufacturer and distributor as leading to too much variation in the effect of such agreements. (As noted above, the approach might well be different under the common law or French law.)[300] The CJEU held that a sub-buyer of goods would (as a matter of EU law under Article 23 of the 2001 Regulation) in the absence of particular consent generally not be bound by a jurisdiction agreement in the contract between manufacturer and purchaser. The court did not, however, address the question of whether the sub-buyer might *benefit* from any consent to jurisdiction found in the underlying contract.

The CJEU's somewhat fragmentary development of an EU law of contracts to govern the validity and effectiveness of jurisdiction agreements (partially hybridised with references to national law) has thus extended to the question of when third parties might be considered bound by such agreements. As noted above,[301] however, this general approach has been reversed under the Recast Brussels I Regulation, which requires that a jurisdiction agreement should be given effect "unless the agreement is null and void as to its substantive validity under the law of [the chosen] Member State".[302] It remains to be seen whether the CJEU will view this as excluding the continued development and application of its own jurisprudence on the validity of choice of court agreements, including questions as to their effectiveness in relation to third parties. Essentially, this is the question of whether the autonomous concept of 'agreement' developed by the CJEU encompasses questions of material validity, which are now (also?) matters for national law. While reverting to national law might decrease the consistent application of Article 25 of the Regulation where different national courts are chosen by the parties, this does not inherently create an inconsistency in the application of the Regulation to the same

---

[300]   C-543/10 *Refcomp SpA v. AXA Corporate Solutions Assurance SA* EU:C:2013:62, [39]. See also e.g. *Antonio Gramsci Shipping Corporation v. Lembergs* [2013] EWCA Civ 730.

[301]   See Section 3.3.2.

[302]   Brussels I Regulation, Art.25(1); see also Recital 20.

facts by different national courts – and any uncertainty that arises may well be outweighed by the benefit of avoiding the uncertainties in the CJEU's own jurisprudence.

3.7 Conclusions

Choice of court agreements raise a range of complex issues. The most important issue is of course the question of their effectiveness as a matter of private international law. The law of jurisdiction of each state determines whether its courts will accept an exclusive or non-exclusive choice of court agreement as a basis of jurisdiction, and whether a foreign exclusive choice of court agreement precludes the exercise of jurisdiction. The practice of the legal systems analysed in this chapter is broadly to accept such prorogation and derogation effects, however this is far from uniform. There are, for example, notable exceptions in some US states, and potentially in the discretionary approach of the common law. The effectiveness of jurisdiction agreements has also been indirectly reduced by the priority given to mutual trust in the Brussels I Regulation, although less so under the Recast.

Even greater divergence is revealed in relation to a second issue, the question of the validity and interpretation of choice of court agreements. Rules of validity and interpretation may sometimes be found in private international law, such as the rules in Article 25 of the Brussels I Regulation regarding formal validity (discussed further in Section 5.2) and providing that jurisdiction agreements are presumed to be exclusive. Where private international law rules do not address questions of validity and interpretation, the question arises as to what law should govern those matters. In some legal systems, including in the United States, Australia, and in some Member States of the European Union, jurisdiction agreements are considered to have a 'procedural' character, and thus questions of their interpretation and validity are governed by forum law. In other legal systems, including under the English common law, jurisdiction agreements are viewed as contractual terms governed by a substantive applicable law, which may or may not be the same as the law of the contract of which they form part or the law of the chosen court. In the Recast Brussels I Regulation and under the Hague Convention on Choice of Court Agreements 2005, a complex choice of law rule has been adopted under which the law applicable to the validity of a jurisdiction agreement is determined by the choice of law rules of the chosen court. The effect is that the parties, in choosing a court for their disputes, also choose that court's approach to the question of whether forum or substantive law governs the validity of a jurisdiction agreement. While this is generally a helpful solution, it cannot be applied easily in all cases (such as agreements in favour of different courts) and it does not address the question of what law should govern the interpretation of a jurisdiction agreement. This may be particularly important in determining the scope of a choice of court clause, including whether it encompasses non-contractual claims, which is the focus of the next chapter.

Choice of court agreements also have a range of indirect effects, both positive and negative. They may be relied on as a basis to enforce a foreign judgment, or to refuse its enforcement. They may also potentially be relied on as a basis for an anti-suit injunction, to restrain foreign proceedings brought in breach of a contractual obligation, or for a damages award in similar circumstances. This range of effects varies in different legal systems, once again in part as a reflection of their different procedural and substantive conceptions of choice of court agreements.

Further complex issues arise in relation to the effectiveness of asymmetrical jurisdiction agreements and the effects of jurisdiction agreements on third parties. In relation to the former, the practice of different courts is again variable – whether such clauses are given greater scrutiny than other contractual terms may depend once more on whether the clause is given a procedural or substantive characterisation. The impact of jurisdiction agreements on third parties has also given rise to a variety of approaches, reflecting the range of ways in which different legal systems have addressed the constraints of privity of contract, and the balance between questions of fairness and litigational efficiency.

Choice of Court Agreements and Non-Contractual Claims

4.1 Introduction

Giving effect to a choice of forum by the parties is perhaps most intuitive in the context of contractual claims, as examined in Chapter 3, since both the claim and the jurisdictional dispute will depend on voluntarily assumed rights and obligations. This chapter examines the application of party autonomy in choice of court beyond this traditional domain, dealing with non-contractual claims. The focus in this chapter is on civil and commercial claims that may be affected by a choice of court agreement – typically, non-contractual claims arising between parties with a contractual relationship. It may be noted, however, that a limited party autonomy in choice of forum has also been adopted in the European Union under the Maintenance Regulation,[1] the Succession Regulation,[2] and the Matrimonial Property Regulation,[3] demonstrating the breadth of influence of the doctrine. These Regulations are discussed further in Section 8.8, in the context of their parallel adoption of party autonomy in choice of law.

Whether a choice of forum agreement is effective in respect of a non-contractual claim raises two distinct questions which are addressed in this chapter in turn. First, whether the agreement *purports* to affect non-contractual claims – whether non-contractual claims fall within the scope of the choice of court clause (Section 4.2). Second, whether the jurisdictional rules *implement* that purported effect (Section 4.3).

The second of these issues might involve not only interpreting and applying rules of jurisdiction, but also the exercise of characterisation

---

[1] A limited party autonomy in relation to choice of court agreements is recognised in Article 4 of the Maintenance Regulation (the choice may only be in favour of a court with an objective connection to the parties or their relationship), but is not effective with regard to disputes concerning maintenance obligations owed to a child under the age of 18.

[2] Succession Regulation, Art.5.

[3] Matrimonial Property Regulation, Arts.5 and 7.

(also known as classification), more commonly associated with the context of choice of law, but potentially equally applicable in the context of jurisdiction.[4] A claim that is purportedly non-contractual may be found by the court to in fact have at its heart the determination of contractual rights, and thereby to fall under the general rules examined in Chapter 3 – this issue arises more commonly in the absence of a jurisdiction agreement, when a court must determine whether a claim falls under the special rules of jurisdiction applicable to contractual or non-contractual claims.[5] Equally, a court may have to determine whether a claim falls within the scope of the exclusive rules of jurisdiction examined in Section 5.4, which would override the exercise of party autonomy. In practice, however, in the context of jurisdiction courts tend to approach the issues by focusing more on interpreting the scope of the choice of court agreement and the potentially applicable rules of jurisdiction, rather than a process of characterisation, although there are exceptions noted below.

4.2   The Subject-Matter Scope of Choice of Court Clauses

There are a variety of possible choice of court agreements, and determining the form of a particular agreement is a matter of interpretation. As already explored in Section 3.2, such an agreement may, for example, be exclusive (purporting to both confer jurisdiction on a court and exclude the jurisdiction of any other court) or non-exclusive (merely conferring jurisdiction on a court), or combine elements of these two categories. An agreement may also vary in the scope of the claims to which it purports to apply. A contract might, for instance, provide that:

> The parties agree to bring any claims for breach of this contract exclusively in the courts of England and Wales. (*Clause 4A*)

Such a clause can, at least if interpreted literally, have no *direct* application to a non-contractual claim arising out of the contract, which would not be a claim 'for breach' of the contract. As noted in various sections of Section 4.3, however, such a clause may possibly have *indirect* effects on non-contractual claims.

Towards the other end of the spectrum, a choice of forum agreement might specify that:

> The parties agree to submit any and all disputes of whatever nature which arise between them exclusively to the courts of England and Wales. (*Clause 4B*)

---

[4] See generally e.g. Cheshire, North and Fawcett (2017), Chapter 3; Forsyth (1998).
[5] See e.g. *Source* v. *Rheinland TUV* [1997] 3 WLR 365.

Such a clause would clearly purport to apply to all non-contractual claims as well as claims arising under the contract. It would, on its face, extend to disputes entirely unrelated to the contract or to the relationship established pursuant to the contract. Whether indeed it *would* have a direct effect on jurisdiction for all or some such claims is examined further in Section 4.3.

Although not the principal focus of this chapter, it should be noted that such broadly drafted clauses may also raise issues where two parties enter into a series of contracts. This creates the possibility that a clause in one contract may also encompass contractual claims under another contract. On its own this is not particularly problematic, but if there is an inconsistent choice of court agreement in the other contract this is likely to raise difficult issues of contractual interpretation.[6] Similar complexities arise where one contract contains a choice of court agreement, and one contains an arbitration agreement, both defined in sufficiently broad terms to encompass a dispute – or even more problematically where a single contract contains both clauses. Despite some suggestion to the contrary, there is no basis to suggest that the arbitration clause should take priority, and the issue must be resolved as a matter of interpretation.[7]

Beyond the two example clauses noted above, any number of varieties of jurisdiction agreements are possible. A contract might, for example, provide that:

> The parties agree to submit any claims relating to or arising out of the performance of this contract exclusively to the courts of England and Wales. (*Clause 4C*)

Even if such a clause were given complete effect by the jurisdictional rules of a particular state, it would only apply to disputes that fell within its purported scope of application – to disputes that relate to or arise out of the performance of the contract. This would be likely to be a narrower category of disputes than those purportedly covered by *Clause 4B*. Although it could encompass some non-contractual claims, it would appear clearly

---

[6] See e.g. *Trust Risk Group SPA* v. *AmTrust Europe Ltd* [2015] EWCA Civ 437. Recital 22 of the Brussels I Regulation provides that "where the parties have entered into conflicting exclusive choice-of-court agreements ... the general lis pendens rule of this Regulation should apply" instead of the special rule under Article 31(2). This somewhat ambiguously suggests that the determination of which jurisdiction agreement has priority should be made only by the court first seised under one of the agreements, even if that court subsequently determines that it cannot hear the case because the other jurisdiction agreement has overriding effect. See discussion in Keyes and Marshall (2015), p.358ff.

[7] See Garnett (2013b); P Tan (2011); Brekoulakis (2007). *Paul Smith Ltd* v. *H&S International Holding Inc.* [1991] 2 Lloyd's Rep 127, generally taken as authority for a pro-arbitration approach, may be better understood as merely an interpretation of the particular contract in that case.

to exclude disputes unrelated to the contract, and it might also be argued to exclude those regarding the validity or invalidity of the contract or other issues concerning its formation and perhaps even its termination. The point is not that such exclusions are inevitable, but only that it is possible that the parties may constrain the subject-matter scope of their choice of court agreement. Parties might alternatively limit their jurisdiction agreement to cover only claims arising out of certain clauses or obligations in their contract.

The general point to note is that, through detailed jurisdiction clauses, the parties may thus at least purport to define the exact limits of the effectiveness of their choice of court agreement. To the extent that the purported effectiveness of their agreement goes beyond what is permitted under the applicable jurisdictional rules, the agreement will not be effective – the limits of the party's agreement will be determined by those jurisdictional rules. An exclusive jurisdiction agreement that purported to cover all claims of any kind would for example almost certainly not be effective in relation to claims for title to immovable property located outside the territory of the state whose courts were chosen.[8] To the extent that the purported effectiveness of a choice of court agreement goes no further than what is permitted or provided for under the applicable jurisdictional rules, the limits of the party's agreement will be determined by their own voluntarily adopted restrictions.

These issues are likely to be most contentious if the jurisdiction agreement adopted by the parties is silent on its scope of application. For example, it is not uncommon to see a clause in a contract state simply:

> Jurisdiction: England. (*Clause 4D*)

Should this be understood as intending to encompass any and all disputes (like *Clause 4B*), only contractual disputes (like *Clause 4A*), or only disputes relating to the contract (like *Clause 4C*)? Identifying exactly what restrictions *have* been voluntarily adopted by the parties is ultimately a matter of interpretation – rather than a question for jurisdictional rules themselves – and thus depends on the applicable law of the jurisdiction agreement. The determination of the law applicable to a jurisdiction agreement, which is itself a contested issue, is discussed in Section 3.3. The debates over this issue reflect an underlying uncertainty over whether jurisdiction agreements should be viewed as having a procedural character, and thus be governed by the law of the forum, or whether they should

---

[8] See Section 5.4.

be viewed as substantive contractual terms, and thus potentially be governed by foreign law. There are some particular uncertainties around the question of what law should govern issues of interpretation.

For example, as noted in Section 3.3.2, it is unclear what law should govern the interpretation of the scope of a jurisdiction agreement under Article 25 of the Brussels I Regulation. The absence of guidance on this point increases the risk that different national courts may disagree on whether a particular claim falls within the scope of an exclusive jurisdiction agreement, potentially leading to conflicting judgments. The *AMT Futures* v. *Marzillier* litigation that reached the Supreme Court[9] in the United Kingdom in 2017, discussed in Section 3.4.3, is a notable example of such a risk eventuating. The proceedings concerned a claim in tort against a German law firm for inducing a breach of an English exclusive jurisdiction agreement by encouraging its clients to sue in Germany. Underlying the dispute was a determination by the German courts that the claims in Germany were not covered by the exclusive jurisdiction agreement – the English courts evidently disagreed, but the risk of conflicting judgments was averted by the absence of a basis of jurisdiction for the tort claim in the English courts. It is similarly notable that the Hague Convention on Choice of Court Agreements 2005 does not appear to offer any guidance on the principles to be applied to the interpretation of the scope of a choice of court agreement, implicitly leaving the matter for national law. As discussed in Section 3.3.2, the Convention adopts a 'choice of choice of law rule' for the determination of the validity of the agreement (the law designated by the choice of law rules of the chosen court), and there are good reasons why the same law ought to determine questions of interpretation of the agreement, but the Convention does not itself direct that this approach be followed. A range of different national interpretative approaches may, therefore, be applicable.

One approach, recently given emphasis by the English courts, is to focus on the interests of commercial parties, suggesting that such parties are likely to have a strong preference for 'one stop adjudication',[10] and thus

---

[9] *AMT Futures* v. *Marzillier* [2017] UKSC 13.

[10] See e.g. *Cinnamon European Structured Credit Master Fund* v. *Banco Commercial Portugues SA* [2009] EWHC 3381 (Ch), suggesting the application to jurisdiction agreements of Lord Hoffman's finding (in respect of arbitration agreements) that interpretation "should start from the assumption that the parties, as rational businessmen, are likely to have intended any dispute arising out of the relationship into which they have entered or purported to enter to be decided by the same tribunal" (*Fiona Trust* v. *Privalov* [2007] UKHL 40, [13]). This does not, of course, suggest that jurisdiction or arbitration agreements should be given

for interpreting ambiguous jurisdiction agreements broadly to encompass a wide range of possible disputes, including both contractual and non-contractual claims.[11] This would favour the interpretation of *Clause 4D* as either following *Clause 4B*, or in a weaker version, *Clause 4C*.[12] As noted in Section 3.3.1, it is unclear whether this is an interpretative presumption of English contract law, applicable only if the jurisdiction agreement is governed by English law, or an interpretive presumption of the English law of jurisdiction which would be applied to jurisdiction agreements governed by foreign law (typically, foreign jurisdiction agreements) – the better view is that interpretation should be left to the governing law of the agreement.

A contrasting approach, perhaps most prominently found in certain US courts,[13] takes as its starting point the view that the ordinary jurisdictional rules should only be departed from where the parties have very clearly agreed to that effect, and thus that jurisdiction agreements should be interpreted narrowly in case of ambiguity, to the likely exclusion of non-contractual claims. This approach thus favours the interpretation of *Clause 4D* as following *Clause 4A*. A third and perhaps intermediate approach, also often found in US courts[14] and traditionally applied by the English courts (although now out of favour), is to eschew interpretative presumptions, and rather focus on the specific terms and context of the

---

unlimited effect, but only that they should be given sufficient effect to cover "any dispute arising out of the relationship".

[11] See e.g. *Starlight Shipping Company* v. *Allianz Marine & Aviation Versicherungs AG* [2014] EWCA Civ 1010, [12], reversed on other grounds at [2013] UKSC 70; *UBS* v. *HSH Nordbank AG* [2009] EWCA Civ 585, [82]; *Maple Leaf Macro Volatility Master Fund* v. *Rouvroy* [2009] EWHC 257 (Comm), [199]; *Continental Bank NA* v. *Aeakos Compania Naviera SA* [1994] 1 WLR 588, 593; *Kitechnology* v. *Unicor GmbH Plastmaschinen* [1994] ILPr 568, [28] ("the express jurisdiction clauses in the present case include not only claims for breach of the relevant contract, but also other claims which are so closely connected with them that the parties can properly be taken to have intended that they should be decided by the same tribunal"). In Australia, see also similarly e.g. *Yperion Technology SAS* v. *Luminex Pty Ltd* [2012] FCA 554; *Global Partners Fund Ltd* v. *Babcock & Brown Ltd (in liq)* [2010] NSWCA 196; *Comandate Marine Corporation* v. *Pan Australia Shipping Pty Ltd* (2006) 157 FCR 45; see further Garnett (2013a).

[12] It may be noted that (as discussed above) in *Fiona Trust*, the House of Lords held that the 'one stop shop' assumption applied to "any dispute arising out of the relationship". On whether this means a 'foreseeability' restriction, the judgment is somewhat ambiguous, finding (at [27]) that "The purpose of the clause is to provide for the determination of disputes of all kinds, whether or not they were foreseen at the time when the contract was entered into", but also noting (at [28]) that "one should be slow to attribute to reasonable parties an intention that there should in any foreseeable eventuality be two sets of proceedings".

[13] See authorities in Section 3.3.1.

[14] See authorities in Section 3.3.1.

agreement between the particular parties, in an effort to resolve any ambiguity in accordance with the court's best determination of the actual subjective intentions of the parties.

Is there a preferred approach? It is not difficult to see the attractions of the English courts 'one stop shop' approach, which is likely to minimise the potential inconvenience of parallel proceedings based on different causes of action.[15] If this were the only consideration, *Clause 4B* would appear most suitable as a presumed model of interpretation. But against this approach, it is of course not always the case that claims would be brought simultaneously in contractual and non-contractual form. The claim that commercial parties would always want to ensure a single jurisdiction for all disputes, at least those relating to their contract, is also not necessarily persuasive, and despite the authority noted above there is also some indication that the English courts may be cautious in applying the 'one stop shop' presumption when it comes to non-contractual claims, at least where there is no parallel contractual claim.[16] Parties might, for example, see practical advantages in allowing proprietary claims for title to movable property to be pursued in the courts of the location of the property at the time proceedings are commenced, even if they would want contractual claims to be brought elsewhere. Similarly, if a contract is governed by English law and contains an English choice of court agreement, but a tort relating to the contract occurs in France and would be governed by French law,[17] the convenience of avoiding potential parallel proceedings (by interpreting the choice of court agreement to cover the tort) has to be weighed against the inconvenience, expense and uncertainty of proving and relying on foreign law before the English courts. Presumptions in favour of a broad interpretation of jurisdiction agreements risk at least the appearance of judges (however well intentioned) second-guessing or presuming to know what commercial parties might 'rationally' wish to agree.

The contrasting approach, which views jurisdiction agreements with suspicion and favours narrower interpretations (such as *Clause 4A*), is equally problematic. Once a court has accepted the validity and effectiveness of a jurisdiction agreement, there is little reason to presume that the parties would have wanted this agreement to have as narrow an effect as possible. Nor should interpretation of the agreement between the parties

---

[15] In favour of this approach see e.g. Briggs (2008), p.125ff.

[16] See e.g. *Ryanair Ltd* v. *Esso Italiana Srl* [2013] EWCA Civ 1450. But see *Microsoft Mobile OY (Ltd)* v. *Sony Europe Ltd* [2017] EWHC 374 (Ch).

[17] Assuming there is also no effective exercise of party autonomy in relation to the law governing the tort – on which see Section 8.3.

be affected by considerations of public interest in the 'ordinary' application of jurisdictional rules. There is a strong argument that party autonomy has itself clearly attained the status of an 'ordinary' jurisdictional rule, and should not be treated as if it were an exception to be construed narrowly. If considerations of public interest override party autonomy, they should arguably do so clearly and directly, not indirectly through presumptions of contractual interpretation that accept the agreement in general but narrow its scope.

The weaker version of the 'one stop shop' approach, presuming *Clause 4D* to be interpreted along the lines of *Clause 4C* (and thus extending only to non-contractual claims connected with the contract in some way) has more to support it. Indeed, there is a strong argument that this approach is most consistent with the justifications for party autonomy explored in Section 2.3. The parties to a contract can more readily be understood as exercising a genuine choice if that choice is constrained to matters related to the contractual relationship. To the extent that their choice encompassed unforeseeable non-contractual matters, it would be unlikely to be efficient or a genuine exercise of autonomy or to have any positive 'law-market' generating effects.

Perhaps, however, the third position discussed above – avoiding presumptions of interpretation and deferring as much as possible to the subjective intentions of the actual parties – is safest. It has the benefit at least of avoiding the appearance of judges second-guessing or only half-recognising the decisions of parties. Difficulties of course will remain if the court has little or nothing to go on to determine the actual intentions of the parties, and a focus on the specific words used by the parties is likely to have its own unsatisfactory consequences – with a risk that cases turn on marginal distinctions between disputes arising 'out of', 'under', 'from', 'in connection with', or 'in relation to' a contract,[18] perhaps resolved only by a court's favoured choice of dictionary. These types of fine linguistic distinctions have been firmly rejected by the Supreme Court in the United Kingdom, but they frequently remain the focus of analysis in other jurisdictions, such as the United States – it remains common in US case law to see careful discussion of the drafting of a clause to determine whether it is intended to encompass non-contractual claims.[19] One of the central

---

[18] See generally the analysis in Briggs (2008), p.131ff and p.184ff.
[19] See e.g. *Huffington* v. *TC Group, LLC*, 637 F.3d 18, 21–2 (1st Cir. 2011) ("the clause by its terms reaches any claim 'with respect to' the agreement and easily invites a broader application. This is confirmed by the usual sources: dictionaries and case law construing such phrases ... courts describe the phrase 'with respect to' as synonymous with the phrases 'with

reasons for the uncertainty in the case law dealing with these and similar choice of forum agreements is the ambiguity as to whether the dispute should arise 'out of', 'under', or 'from' the contract as a matter of *law* (suggesting a narrower interpretation) or *fact* (suggesting a broader interpretation). In such difficult cases, however, it is perhaps better to avoid narrow textualism not by adopting a general interpretative approach in favour of jurisdictional agreements having wide or narrow scope, but by attempting to determine the intentions of the parties through a teleological approach based on their broader contractual intentions (rather than the presumed intentions of commercial parties in general).

Regardless of the approach taken to this difficult question, the general point remains that the jurisdictional rules examined below provide only *part* of the answer to the question of whether courts will give effect to a choice of law agreement in a contract in relation to a non-contractual claim. To the extent that rules of jurisdiction permit such an effect, determining whether this possibility has indeed been exercised on the facts requires analysis and interpretation of the particular agreement between the parties, as examined in this section, as a matter of contractual interpretation. But such an analysis is ultimately redundant if the jurisdictional rules deny effect to the wishes of the parties in the context of the particular dispute. This chapter therefore now turns to examine the extent to which jurisdictional rules permit or provide for party autonomy in the context of non-contractual claims.

4.3   The Application of Choice of Forum Rules to Non-Contractual Claims

In determining whether to give effect to a choice of court agreement in relation to non-contractual claims, two points appear to be in tension. The first is that party autonomy should be respected, and that a choice of court agreement should not be easily circumvented through formulating a claim as non-contractual (such as by framing it as negligent performance

---

reference to,' 'relating to,' 'in connection with,' and 'associated with,' and they have held such phrases to be broader in scope than the term 'arising out of,' to be broader than the concept of a causal connection, and to mean simply 'connected by reason of an established or discoverable relation.'"); *Slater* v. *Energy Services Group International, Inc.*, 634 F.3d 1326, 1331 (11th Cir. 2011); *International Underwriters AG* v. *Triple I: International Investments, Inc.*, 533 F.3d 1342, 1348–9 (11th Cir. 2008); *Abbott Laboratories* v. *Takeda Pharmaceutical Co. Ltd*, 476 F.3d 421 (7th Cir. 2007).

of contractual relations, or suing for title to the property affected by a contract)[20] when it relates to the contract. The second is that the application of party autonomy beyond the field of contractual relations is more contested, for a variety of reasons including the presence of other public interests and the potential lack of foreseeability of non-contractual claims.

4.3.1   EU Law (Brussels I Regulation)

As examined in Section 3.4.2, party autonomy in choice of forum is given strong support in the Brussels I Regulation under Article 25. There are, however, three sources that might be relevant to determining whether this support extends to non-contractual obligations, which are examined in turn below. First, limitations imposed within Article 25 itself. Second, limitations imposed by the hierarchically superior rules in Article 24. Third, the question of whether jurisdiction agreements may potentially have indirect effects on non-contractual claims. The limitations imposed under Article 24 and the further limitations imposed by the rules in the Brussels I Regulation applicable to claims concerning insurance, consumer contracts, and employment contracts will also be analysed in Chapter 5.

4.3.1.1   Subject-Matter Scope of Party Autonomy in Choice of Court (Article 25)

Article 25(1) provides, in part, as follows:

> If the parties, regardless of their domicile, have agreed that a court or the courts of a Member State are to have jurisdiction to settle any disputes which have arisen or which may arise in connection with a particular legal relationship, that court or those courts shall have jurisdiction, unless the agreement is null and void as to its substantive validity under the law of that Member State.

The focus in this section is on the qualifying phrase "in connection with a particular legal relationship", which might be considered to suggest limitations to the effectiveness of Article 25. A jurisdiction agreement in a contract could evidently cover contractual claims arising out of that contractual relationship, but this phrase raises the question of whether such an agreement could, even if very broadly phrased, limit jurisdiction for claims that do not arise out of that relationship. This part of Article 25 has received surprisingly little academic or judicial consideration, and it

---

[20] It may be noted, for example, that in Chinese law the rules governing choice of forum are expressly stated to govern property disputes: see Civil Procedure Law, Art.34; Supreme People's Court 'Interpretation of Civil Procedure Law' Zhu Shi [2015] No. 5, Art.531.

is somewhat unclear whether or in what circumstances it gives force to a jurisdiction agreement that covers non-contractual claims. It would be very strongly arguable that a tortious claim for negligent performance of contractual obligations would "arise in connection with a particular legal relationship". On the other hand, if two contracting parties coincidentally had a car accident unrelated to the performance of the contract then that would not seem to have a relevant connection to their legal relationship, however broadly their jurisdiction agreement was framed. More difficult 'boundary' problems can easily be envisaged, such as an accident between two parties to a construction sub-contract in the car park at their common place of work. This raises the further question of whether the dispute must 'arise' from the relationship in a legal sense (from the performance of contractual obligations) or in a practical or causal sense.

The issue of when a dispute arises "in connection with a particular legal relationship" has been considered by the CJEU in respect of the (similarly worded) Article 17 of the Brussels Convention 1968. In *Meeth v. Glacetal* (1978),[21] the court examined the issue of whether a right of set-off could be viewed as arising from the contractual relationship between the parties. The court concluded that the claim could be brought in reliance on the jurisdiction agreement, "to avoid superfluous procedure",[22] where it is "a set-off connected with the legal relationship in dispute".[23] The emphasis on the avoidance of 'superfluous procedure' suggests a broad construction of Article 25, to ensure that it applies to any claims, contractual or non-contractual in form, arising out of a legal relationship, to avoid parallel proceedings. This decision, however, left open the question of whether a claim *unrelated* to the contract establishing the relationship could be subject to an exclusive jurisdiction agreement, if the agreement is expressed in broad enough terms.[24]

The issue arose again more directly in *Powell Duffryn v. Petereit* (1992),[25] where the CJEU found that a clause in the statutes of a company could constitute a binding jurisdiction agreement between the company and its shareholders. The Court, referring to the requirement that the claim "arise in connection with a particular relationship", held that:

> That requirement is intended to limit the scope of an agreement conferring jurisdiction solely to disputes which arise from the legal relationship in connection with which the agreement was entered into. Its purpose is to

---

[21] Case 23/78, [1978] ECR 2133.
[22] At [8].
[23] At [9].
[24] But see e.g. *Kitechnology v. Unicor GmbH Plastmaschinen* [1994] ILPr 568, [28].
[25] C-214/89, [1992] ECR I-1745. See e.g. Hartley (2013b), p.172ff.

avoid a party being taken by surprise by the assignment of jurisdiction to a given forum as regards all disputes which may arise out of its relationship with the other party to the contract and stem from a relationship other than that in connection with which the agreement conferring jurisdiction was made.[26]

Although the Court held that the validity of a jurisdiction agreement under what was then Article 17 of the Brussels Convention 1968 is a question of European law (an approach now rejected under Article 25 of the Brussels I Regulation),[27] it also held that whether in fact the particular agreement extended to the claim at hand was a matter for interpretation of the 'contract' (the clause in the company statutes) according to national law. This is the question examined in Section 4.2. Whether such an agreement would be *effective* to confer jurisdiction would, however, again be a question governed by the requirements of Article 25 – that the dispute must "arise from the legal relationship in connection with which the agreement was entered into". This limits the scope of non-contractual claims that may be affected by the jurisdiction agreement, regardless of how broadly expressed the jurisdiction agreement may be. Further support for this limitation may be found in the Opinion of Advocate General Niilo Jääskinen in the *Refcomp* case,[28] which concerned Article 23 of the Brussels I Regulation 2001, the predecessor to Article 25. The Advocate General pointed out "that Article 23 of Regulation No 44/2001 requires the agreement conferring jurisdiction to form part of a 'particular legal relationship'", and emphasised that as Article 23 provided an exceptional basis of jurisdiction, it should be interpreted restrictively, and thus "the scope of a clause conferring jurisdiction cannot be too wide".[29] A footnote to this paragraph confirms that "Accordingly, such a clause must not be worded in such a general manner as to include all possible disputes between the parties, irrespective of the contracts concluded by them."[30] The Court of Justice has affirmed more recently that, because of the requirement that a dispute arise from the particular legal relationship concerned, "the referring court must ... regard a clause which abstractly refers to all disputes arising from contractual relationships as not extending to a dispute relating to the tortious liability that one party allegedly incurred as a result of the other's participation

---

[26] At [31].
[27] See Section 3.3.2.
[28] C-543/10 *Refcomp SpA* v. *AXA Corporate Solutions Assurance SA* EU:C:2012:637.
[29] At [44].
[30] Note 35.

in an unlawful cartel".[31] Again, the Court emphasised the lack of foresee-ability of the type of litigation concerned as a reason for not extending the jurisdiction clause to encompass it.[32] Although expressed apparently as a rule of interpretation, in reality this is a rule limiting the effectiveness of a clause, however broadly it is intended to function.

There is also English authority that supports such an approach to the interpretation of the Brussels I Regulation. The courts have, for instance, held that a claim in tort arising out of the allegedly negligent manufacture of a climbing frame involved in a construction accident was not affected by an exclusive jurisdiction agreement in the terms of sale of a crane also involved in the same accident. The Court found that "None of the claims advanced in the particulars of claim arises either directly or indirectly out of the sale contract", and thus that the negligent manufacture of the climb-ing frame was insufficiently connected with the contract for sale of the crane to justify the application of what is now Article 25.[33] There remains, however, a significant lack of clarity on this issue, and there is a need for further case law to set out further what connections will be sufficient to justify the application of Article 25 to non-contractual claims.

In summary, Article 25 of the Brussels I Regulation allows for jurisdic-tion agreements to encompass some non-contractual claims, but its scope is restricted by questions of the proximity of the claim to the contractual relationship. The requirement that the parties not be "taken by surprise" suggests a focus on the foreseeability of the action, which is consistent with some of the principles underlying party autonomy examined in Chapter 2. It is clear that claimants cannot rely on a jurisdiction agreement in respect of proceedings that are entirely unrelated to that contractual relationship, however broadly it is drafted. It is, however, not clear how this 'proximity' test will be determined in practice in difficult cases. The limited effective-ness given to party autonomy under the Brussels I Regulation in respect of non-contractual claims carries the downside that it may be difficult for the parties to predict when a court will decide that a non-contractual dispute arises from their contractual relationship, negating some of the benefits of certainty which party autonomy is intended to provide.

---

[31] C-352/13 *CDC Hydrogen Peroxide SA* v. *Evonik Degussa GmbH* EU:C:2015:335, [69].

[32] At [70] ("Given that the undertaking which suffered the loss could not reasonably foresee such litigation at the time that it agreed to the jurisdiction clause and that that undertaking had no knowledge of the unlawful cartel at that time, such litigation cannot be regarded as stemming from a contractual relationship").

[33] *Hewden Tower Cranes Ltd* v. *Wolffkran GmbH* [2007] EWHC 857 (TCC), [34]–[39].

4.3.1.2   Overriding Exclusive Jurisdiction (Article 24)

As examined further in Section 5.4, Article 24 of the Brussels I Regulation establishes a number of grounds under which the courts of a Member State are to have exclusive jurisdiction. As set out in Article 25(4), such exclusive jurisdiction invalidates any contrary agreement by the parties. Each of these operates therefore as 'subject-matter' restrictions on Article 25 – defining types of disputes for which party autonomy will be ineffective. In each case, as discussed further in Chapter 5, the exclusion is based on particular 'public' interests involved in these categories of disputes.

For the purposes of this chapter, it is notable that the grounds of jurisdiction under Article 24 are broad enough to cover some non-contractual claims – indeed, they are likely to cover principally non-contractual claims. Article 24(1), for example, is concerned with "proceedings which have as their object rights in rem in immovable property" – which will generally (although perhaps not exclusively[34]) be proprietary rather than contractual claims. Similarly, Article 24(3) is likely to cover claims that are essentially proprietary in character – entries in a public register may, for example, record ownership of land or other registrable property (such as a ship or aircraft). Even more obviously, claims under Article 24(4) are likely to have a proprietary character as they concern the validity of registrable intellectual property rights. Claims concerning the violation of intellectual property rights, usually characterised as tortious, are not, however, covered by this provision unless they have as their principal concern the validity of those rights.[35] Claims covered by Article 24(2), which have as their object the validity of the constitution of a company or other legal person or of the decisions of its organs, or its nullity or dissolution, are also likely to be non-contractual in many cases, although as discussed in Section 5.4.1 such issues may be raised as defences to contractual claims, and in that context, the forum may well be designated by a choice of court agreement in the relevant contract. Finally, Article 24(5) concerns proceedings concerned with the enforcement of judgments, which are again a form of non-contractual obligation. Although the cause of action may be non-contractual in each of these cases, it remains possible, however, that there is an underlying contract between the disputing parties that purports to determine which court will have jurisdiction over the relevant dispute.

---

[34] See Section 5.4.1.
[35] C-4/03 *Gesellschaft für Antriebstechnik mbH & Co. KG (GAT)* v. *Lamellen und Kupplungsbau Beteiligungs KG* [2006] ECR I-6509.

The most significant conclusion to draw from this analysis for present purposes is that although (as argued above) Article 25 provides for party autonomy for at least some non-contractual claims, Article 24 will also cover certain non-contractual claims and thereby override that autonomy. For non-contractual claims in the covered subject-matter areas, the public interests reflected in Article 24 (and discussed further in Section 5.4) trump party autonomy in choice of court, whether the claim is brought in contractual or non-contractual form.

4.3.1.3 Indirect Effects of a Jurisdiction Agreement?

This section considers whether a jurisdiction agreement might have an indirect effect on claims that fall outside its scope under the Brussels I Regulation. Consider, for example, a contract between a party domiciled in France and a party domiciled in Germany with the following jurisdiction agreement:

> The parties agree to bring any claims for breach of this contract exclusively in the courts of England and Wales. (*Clause 4A*)

At least on its face, such a clause appears to have no application to non-contractual claims. Suppose that the contract were breached by the German party, in France, in a way that gave rise to concurrent claims in tort and contract. The contract claim would be governed by Article 25, and the English courts would therefore have exclusive jurisdiction. The tort claim would, however, not come within the agreement, and would fall to the general rules on jurisdiction. (Even if the tort claim were classified as "relating to a contract" for the purposes of Article 7(1), because it arose from contractual obligations, this would not affect the intended scope of the jurisdiction agreement itself.) This clearly invites the risk that parallel proceedings could be brought in another court, such as the court of the defendant's domicile (Germany), or the court of the location of the tort or contractual performance (both France). A claim in contract may, for example, be commenced in the English courts by the French party, while closely related non-contractual proceedings (seeking a declaration of non-liability) could be brought by the German party in the courts of France.

To avoid the parallel proceedings, the English courts might interpret the jurisdiction agreement expansively, despite its wording, although this would risk going beyond giving effect to party autonomy. Alternatively, the French courts might look to Article 30 of the Regulation. Under Article 30, the courts of a Member State seised of a dispute closely related to proceedings that have already been commenced in another Member State may decline jurisdiction over those proceedings. This provision does not, however, in any way 'confer' jurisdiction over the related proceedings (the tort claim) on the court first seised (the English courts). However, Article 30(3) provides that "actions are deemed to be related when they are so closely connected that it is expedient to hear and determine them together". It thus implicitly suggests – although may not technically require – that it should generally be invoked where the court first seised has jurisdiction over both claims.[36] Thus, it might be considered that the French courts should only refuse to exercise jurisdiction over the tort claim if the English courts had a basis of jurisdiction over that claim as well. But in our example there would be no basis for the English courts to exercise jurisdiction over the tort claim. Article 8 provides jurisdictional grounds for related claims in a number of contexts, but none of them would be of assistance here.

The counterargument is that even if the court first seised does not have such jurisdiction, there may be a benefit to delaying the proceedings in the court second seised, so that common issues between the two sets of proceedings can become *res judicata*, thereby minimising the risk of conflicting decisions. If Article 30 is interpreted in this way, it gives priority to the decisions of the court first seised. Where the basis of the jurisdiction of the court first seised is Article 25, it thus has the effect of giving that court the opportunity of determining any common issues or facts arising in the two sets of proceedings. Even where the court nominated in the jurisdiction agreement is second seised, there is an argument that Article 31(2) (discussed in Section 3.4.2) should mean the decisions of that court are given priority, although whether Article 31(2) applies to related proceedings is unclear.[37]

The conclusion of this analysis is that, under the Brussels I Regulation, an exclusive jurisdiction agreement in the form of *Clause 4A* can (if interpreted literally) have no direct effect on non-contractual claims that fall outside its scope, although it may be relied on to give priority to the chosen court at least in some circumstances. What is arguably missing from the Regulation is a rule (like that in England under paragraph 3.1(4A) of Practice Direction 6B of the Civil Procedure Rules, discussed below)

---

[36] The better view is that it also permits a temporary stay, even if the court first seised does not have jurisdiction over both claims, with the proceedings resuming once the court first seised has given judgment in the matter. This is supported by the fact that Article 30(2) permits jurisdiction to be 'declined' (rather than merely stayed) where the court first seised is able to consolidate the proceedings. See Cheshire, North and Fawcett (2017), pp.455–6.

[37] Kenny and Hennigan (2015).

that could permit the addition of related claims against a defendant, as an expansion of Article 8 of the Regulation. While such a rule could be open to abuse, it would be arguably no more so than the other headings of Article 8, and equally important to support party autonomy and address the risk of irreconcilable judgments. This analysis also highlights an important advantage of drafting a jurisdiction agreement in terms sufficiently broad to cover non-contractual claims – it will generally ensure that related contractual and non-contractual claims arising out of the same legal relationship can be heard together. It also perhaps suggests a practical wisdom in the expansive approach towards the interpretation of jurisdiction agreements which has been adopted by, for example, the English courts.[38]

4.3.2   Common Law

This section examines the possible effects of jurisdiction agreements on non-contractual claims under the common law, looking first at jurisdiction agreements in favour of the English courts and then at those in favour of a foreign court.

4.3.2.1   Jurisdiction Agreements in Favour of English Courts

As examined in Section 3.4.3, a jurisdiction agreement in favour of the English courts, exclusive or non-exclusive, has long been a distinct and sufficient basis for service of a contractual claim outside the territory, thus establishing jurisdiction without the need for any other objective connecting factor between the parties or the dispute and England. The question of whether, or to what extent, a choice of court agreement should operate to establish jurisdiction over *non-contractual* claims has, however, raised particular difficulties.

Where a jurisdiction agreement is in favour of the English courts (or the courts of another Member State), questions of jurisdiction will now, as noted in Section 3.4.3, generally be governed by the Brussels I Regulation. This is particularly because under the 2012 Recast, there is no requirement for either party to the jurisdiction agreement to be domiciled in a Member State. This section nevertheless examines the traditional practice of the English courts in relation to jurisdiction agreements, for three reasons. First, there will still be some cases that fall outside the scope of the Brussels I Regulation and are governed by the common law. Second, the practice of the English courts is broadly representative of that of other common

---

[38] See Section 4.2.

law jurisdictions, which are not affected by European regulation. Third, it is possible that the common law rules may re-expand in importance in England in light of the anticipated 'Brexit'.

Jurisdiction Based on a Jurisdiction Agreement   As noted in Section 3.4.3, the English courts may exercise jurisdiction based on (i) the presence of the defendant in the territory, (ii) submission to the court, or (iii) permission to commence proceedings against a party who is not 'present' before the English courts, under the circumstances set out in Rule 6.36 and Practice Direction 6B of the Civil Procedure Rules.[39]

Where the defendant is present in the territory, there is no need to rely on any jurisdiction agreement to commence proceedings. The agreement will, however, be relevant to the question of whether the English courts will stay proceedings commenced on this basis through the exercise of the *forum non conveniens* discretion. For present purposes, this raises the question of whether a jurisdiction agreement in favour of the English courts should be considered relevant in the exercise of this discretion where *non-contractual* claims are brought against a defendant present in England, which will be discussed further below. A jurisdiction agreement does not itself constitute submission; indeed, if the defendant has submitted to the English courts, no question of the effectiveness of a jurisdiction agreement (for contractual or non-contractual claims) arises.

The third common law basis for the jurisdiction of the English courts relates to proceedings brought with permission against a defendant who is not present in the territory. These rules have encompassed jurisdiction based on a jurisdiction clause since 1920.[40] However, this basis of jurisdiction has always been located amongst the grounds of jurisdiction dealing with claims in contract, and this has traditionally suggested that a jurisdiction agreement might not support non-contractual claims. Under the Rules of the Supreme Court (which applied until 1999),[41] jurisdiction in reliance on a contract, including a choice of forum agreement, could only be asserted if the claim was "brought to enforce, rescind, dissolve, annul or otherwise affect a contract, or to recover damages or obtain any other remedy in respect of the breach of a contract". Although not entirely certain, the view was taken in a number of cases that this condition strictly limited the effectiveness of jurisdiction agreements to contractual

---

[39] See generally Cheshire, North and Fawcett (2017), Chapter 12.
[40] See Section 2.2.1.
[41] Order 11, Rule 1(1)(d).

claims – preventing a jurisdiction agreement, however broadly drafted, from acting as a basis of jurisdiction for a non-contractual claim, however closely related to the contract, or at least requiring a direct connection between the claim and the effective enforcement of the contract.[42]

Under paragraph 3.1(6) of Practice Direction 6B of the Civil Procedure Rules (which replaced the Rules of the Supreme Court from 1999), however, jurisdiction based on a choice of court clause is only limited to claims "in respect of a contract".[43] This change has been interpreted to give potentially broader effect to jurisdiction agreements in respect of any non-contractual claim that "relates to or is connected with" a contract.[44] This has been considered to extend not only to non-contractual claims between the parties to the contract, but also even to claims involving parties who are not bound by the contract.[45] It has further been held that if a claim "has a connection with a contract ... [that] makes it a claim in respect of that contract even if it is not a claim brought under the contract", and that while "some connections with contracts are more remote than others", "the remoteness from the contract (if any) is something that can be dealt with when the court considers whether England is the proper place for a claim" under the rules dealing with *forum conveniens*.[46] Thus, where a non-contractual claim is even indirectly connected to a contract, the approach under the common law is now that a jurisdiction agreement in the contract can be relied on as a basis of jurisdiction for the non-contractual claim. However, the remoteness of the connection between the claim and the contract will be an important consideration when it comes to the decision as to whether to give permission to exercise jurisdiction on this basis.

The same approach should be applied where non-contractual proceedings are commenced against a defendant present in the territory, and there is a jurisdiction agreement in favour of the English courts. The weight to be given to the jurisdiction agreement as a factor in determining whether to stay the English proceedings pursuant to the doctrine of *forum non*

---

[42] See e.g. *Re Baltic Real Estate Ltd* [1992] BCC 629, 635 ("It is in my view material that the relevant phrase is 'or otherwise affect', in conjunction with 'enforce, rescind, dissolve, annul', and this seems to me to require some direct effect upon the relevant contract comparable with its enforcement or abrogation by one means or another"). See also *ABCI* v. *Banque Franco-Tunisienne* [2003] EWCA Civ 205; *Amoco (UK) Exploration Co* v. *British American Offshore Ltd* [1999] 2 Lloyd's Rep 772; *Compania Continental del Peru SA* v. *Evelpis Shipping Corp ('The Agia Skepi')* [1992] 2 Lloyd's Rep 467.

[43] The same wording has applied since CPR Update 14, issued on 18 April 2000.

[44] *Albon* v. *Naza Motor Trading* [2007] EWHC 9 (Ch), [27].

[45] See e.g. *Global 5000 Ltd* v. *Wadhawan* [2012] EWCA Civ 13.

[46] *Greene Wood & McClean LLP* v. *Templeton Insurance Ltd* [2009] EWCA Civ 65, [19].

conveniens should depend on how closely related the non-contractual claims are to the jurisdiction agreement, as well as the breadth of scope of the jurisdiction agreement itself, as discussed further below.

The requirement for a connection between the claim and the contract nevertheless still partially limits the effectiveness of jurisdiction agreements in respect of non-contractual claims. It has been held that "some relevant legal connection between the claim and the ... contract is required", and that if the "contract needs to be referred to and relied upon in order to assert the relevant cause of action then that requirement is likely to be satisfied since it will be a necessary part of the cause of action", but that "a mere factual connection ... is not enough".[47] Under the Civil Procedure Rules it is thus still not, for example, possible for the English courts to establish jurisdiction over a claim in tort or property unrelated to a contract and otherwise unconnected to England on the basis that the parties have a jurisdiction agreement drafted in broad enough terms to cover any tortious or proprietary liability.[48] This is an important restriction on the autonomy of the parties – they cannot choose a forum for claims entirely unrelated to the contract that contains their choice of forum. It is unclear how this restriction should be applied where, unusually, two parties enter into a jurisdiction agreement as a stand-alone contract. It is possible that in this context the jurisdiction agreement may be given a broader effect, in which case it may be advisable for parties to adopt this unusual practice if they wish their jurisdiction agreement to be effective for all claims between them, even those unrelated to a particular contractual relationship.

Paragraph 3.1(6)(d) of Practice Direction 6B, the rule specifically related to jurisdiction agreements, refers to any contract that "contains a term to the effect that the court shall have jurisdiction to determine any claim in respect of the contract". Read literally, this requirement might suggest that a jurisdiction agreement that was narrowly drafted to cover only contractual claims would not satisfy the requirements, because it would not be a term giving the court jurisdiction to determine "any claim in respect of the contract" (given how broadly "in respect of" has been interpreted by the courts). This would, however, clearly be contrary to the intended effect of the rules, to enforce both widely and narrowly drafted jurisdiction agreements. Even where a jurisdiction agreement is drafted narrowly, the rules

---

[47] *Cecil* v. *Bayat* [2010] EWHC 641 (Comm), [49] (reversed for other reasons at [2011] EWCA Civ 135).

[48] *Leond Maritime Inc.* v. *MC Amethyst Shipping Ltd ('The Anna L')* [1994] 2 Lloyd's Rep 379, 382.

should therefore not only give the jurisdiction agreement its desired effect, but will also open up the possibility that non-contractual claims may be brought pursuant to the jurisdiction agreement, where they are "in respect of" the contract containing the agreement (but not actually covered by the agreement itself). There is a danger here that the rules will actually act contrary to party autonomy, by giving the courts the power to extend the effect of a jurisdiction agreement to non-contractual claims, even if the parties have deliberately excluded such claims from the scope of their agreement. This should, once again, at least be a matter taken into consideration in determining whether to exercise jurisdiction pursuant to the *forum conveniens* discretion, discussed further below.

As noted in Section 3.4.3, in practice, well-advised parties entering into jurisdiction agreements in favour of the English courts will usually also nominate a local address for service. The view has sometimes been taken that this establishes submission to the jurisdiction of the English courts, although the better view is probably that it only establishes a form of constructive presence in the territory.[49] The rule that facilitates this practice is set out in Civil Procedure Rule 6.11, which specifies that "the claim form may be served by a method or at a place specified in the contract". However, this rule also states that this may be used as a basis for jurisdiction only if "a claim solely in respect of that contract is started". Thus, the nomination of a local address for service is once again likely (assuming a similar interpretation of the words "in respect of") to be limited to claims related to or connected with the contract in which the nomination is made.

The exclusion of non-contractual claims unrelated to an underlying contract from the effect of jurisdiction agreements may be interpreted in a number of ways, in light of the different justifications for party autonomy explored in Section 2.3. It may be viewed as a determination that in these claims (unlike those in contract) there are greater potential public interests that justify overriding party autonomy. Alternatively, it might be argued that such claims are less predictable, and thus the 'forum market' cannot operate effectively in this context – if parties cannot anticipate the types of litigation to which they may be subject, they cannot rationally choose the most efficient forum. What is notable for present purposes is that it does not appear consistent with the idea that the parties are exercising an independent autonomous freedom in choosing their forum, or that the parties may be trusted to choose the best forum for themselves – the rules clearly constrain the power of the parties to do so in certain cases.

---

[49] See e.g. Cheshire, North and Fawcett (2017), p.333.

The distinction adopted in the Civil Procedure Rules may, thus, be criticised on the basis that it denies the parties the ability to choose the forum for a non-contractual dispute which, although not related to a contract, is foreseeable and which they might rationally have taken into consideration in their contractual negotiations. Lingering doubts over the effectiveness of jurisdiction agreements for non-contractual claims may also potentially operate as an incentive for a claimant to package a claim as contractual or non-contractual simply in order to take advantage of forum shopping opportunities, although these may be limited by a more flexible approach under the doctrines of *forum conveniens* and *forum non conveniens* discussed further below. The success of such 'cause of action shopping' will also depend on how the English courts characterise the dispute, which may be independent of the form of the claim and based on whether the real issue involves interpretation of the contract.[50] It might also be argued that an exclusive jurisdiction agreement implicitly precludes either party from bringing claims in a non-contractual form in order to subvert the agreement,[51] although it is likely that such an argument would be limited to non-contractual claims that are so closely related to the contract that they could be brought in contractual form.

Indirect Effects of a Jurisdiction Agreement   While a jurisdiction agreement can thus not be relied on directly in respect of a non-contractual claim unrelated to a contract under the common law, it may, however, have possible indirect effects. As noted above, where jurisdiction under common law rules is not established based on submission, it is subject to the doctrines of *forum non conveniens* or *forum conveniens*, discretionary considerations by the court as to whether the proceedings should not be commenced or should be discontinued in favour of another clearly more appropriate forum. The courts will take into consideration a wide range of factors in making this determination.[52] As discussed in Section 3.4.3, in contractual claims the existence of a jurisdiction agreement in favour of the English courts, particularly an exclusive jurisdiction agreement, is perhaps the most powerful factor in favour of exercising (or refusing to decline) jurisdiction. It has been held that only factors that could not be foreseen by the parties at the time of contracting may weigh heavily

---

[50] See e.g. *The Sindh* [1975] 1 Lloyd's Rep 372; *The Makefjell* [1976] 2 Lloyd's Rep 29; S Knight (1977).

[51] See e.g. *Donoghue* v. *Armco* [2001] UKHL 64.

[52] See generally *The Spiliada* [1986] 3 All ER 843; Cheshire, North and Fawcett (2017), p.392ff.

against enforcing their agreement – consistently with at least some of the justifications for party autonomy examined in Chapter 2.[53]

As discussed above, it is, however, unclear how much weight (if any) should be given to a jurisdiction agreement in the exercise of a *forum conveniens* or *forum non conveniens* discretion if the claim being pursued before English or foreign courts is *not* based in contract. Such clauses are clearly given effect in at least some cases.[54] The limitation of party autonomy to claims "in respect of a contract" under the CPR would seem to approve of the use of a jurisdiction agreement as a connecting factor for such claims,[55] that is, those in which the claim is related to the contract containing the jurisdiction agreement, but disapprove of it outside that context, even where there is a free choice in respect of a foreseeable non-contractual dispute. Even if an English jurisdiction agreement were given presumptive effect in respect of a non-contractual claim, unforeseeable factors that might trump party autonomy are more likely to be present outside the contractual context.

A further indirect effect of a jurisdiction agreement in respect of non-contractual claims may arise where claims are brought concurrently in contract and in non-contractual form. Even if an exclusive jurisdiction agreement is only effective to confer jurisdiction on the English courts over the contractual claim, the fact that the courts do have jurisdiction over that claim may be a further relevant consideration in determining whether to exercise the *forum conveniens* or *forum non conveniens* discretion in respect of the non-contractual claim. In such circumstances, the courts are more likely to exercise the discretion in a way that retains jurisdiction over the non-contractual claim, to avoid fragmenting the proceedings.[56] It is true that such a discretion is most likely to be exercised in cases in which the non-contractual and contractual claims are closely related – and will therefore be unnecessary where the jurisdiction agreement is expressed in broad enough terms to cover the non-contractual claim. But this indirect

---

[53] See e.g. *Marubeni Hong Kong and South China* v. *Mongolian Government* [2002] 2 All ER (Comm) 873; *British Aerospace* v. *Dee Howard* [1993] 1 Lloyd's Rep 368.

[54] See e.g. *Unterweser Reederei GmbH* v. *Zapata Off-Shore Co.* ('*The Chaparral*') [1968] 2 Lloyd's Rep 158 (finding the jurisdiction agreement effective with respect to claims brought in both contract and tort – see discussion of the related US proceedings in Section 4.3.3).

[55] See e.g. *Donohue* v. *Armco Inc.* [2001] UKHL 64.

[56] See e.g. *Continental Bank NA* v. *Aeakos Compania Naviera SA* [1994] 1 WLR 588, 593. The same consideration supports interpreting the jurisdiction agreement as broad in scope, as discussed above – the two issues are not clearly distinguished in the *Continental Bank v. Aeakos* decision.

effect may also apply to narrowly expressed jurisdiction agreements (such as *Clause 4A* set out in Section 4.2) – although not directly applicable to a non-contractual claim, such an agreement may indirectly influence the decision of the English courts to exercise jurisdiction over that claim to avoid parallel contractual and non-contractual proceedings. For this effect to operate, however, an alternative basis of jurisdiction will be required for the non-contractual claim. This effect may thus arise, for example, where there are claims in tort and contract, and the tortious damage was suffered in England. Even if the claim in tort is not considered to be a claim "in respect of" the contract, the English courts would have a basis of jurisdiction under paragraph 3.1(9)(a) of Practice Direction 6B of the Civil Procedure Rules. The existence of the contractual proceedings in England would be an important factor in determining whether to give permission to exercise this tortious basis of jurisdiction, pursuant to the doctrine of *forum conveniens*, as the courts generally support the policy of avoiding parallel proceedings.

An alternative basis of jurisdiction for connected non-contractual claims has, since 2015, been provided by paragraph 3.1(4A) of the Civil Procedure Rules,[57] which establishes that a claim form may be served outside the territory where:

> A claim is made against the defendant in reliance on one or more of paragraphs (2), (6) to (16), (19) or (21) and a further claim is made against the same defendant which arises out of the same or closely connected facts.

The effect of this provision is that if the English court has a basis of jurisdiction over a contractual claim, pursuant to a jurisdiction agreement, it will also have a basis of jurisdiction over related non-contractual claims (arising "out of the same or closely connected facts"), even if such claims are not covered by the jurisdiction agreement, because they fall outside its intended scope. The existence of the jurisdiction agreement for the contractual claims would once again be likely to have a strong influence on the exercise of jurisdiction for the related non-contractual claims. This provision has only recently been introduced, however, and it is unclear whether its effect will be broader (or even narrower) than the existing provision under paragraph 3.1(6) of Practice Direction 6B, which already permits non-contractual claims relating to a contract to be brought pursuant to a contractual jurisdiction agreement.

---

[57] See further Cheshire, North and Fawcett (2017), p.340.

4.3.2.2   Jurisdiction Agreements in Favour of a Foreign Court

Non-exclusive jurisdiction agreements in favour of foreign courts will generally not affect the jurisdiction of the English courts, as they do not purport to preclude any jurisdiction that may exist independently of the agreement. Foreign exclusive jurisdiction agreements do, however, intend such effects, as discussed in Section 3.2. As examined in Section 3.4.3 and above, where the jurisdiction agreement is in favour of the courts of an EU Member State, or where the jurisdiction of the English courts is based on the Brussels I Regulation (as will be the case for claims against EU domiciled defendants falling within the scope of the Regulation), the effect of the jurisdiction agreement in the English courts will be governed by the Brussels I Regulation. This still leaves, however, cases governed by the common law rules (most claims against non-EU domiciled defendants) where there is an exclusive jurisdiction agreement in favour of a non-EU Member State court. The practice of the English courts in such cases is also broadly representative of that throughout the common law world, and in non-EU common law states will thus generally be applied for all foreign exclusive jurisdiction agreements. Where the English courts have a basis of jurisdiction under the common law but there is an exclusive jurisdiction agreement in favour of a foreign court, the agreement is given presumptive effect in respect of contractual claims through the doctrines of *forum conveniens* and *forum non conveniens*.[58] In this context, an agreement by the parties is taken to be a very compelling reason why a foreign court is viewed as a clearly more appropriate forum – reflecting the strong measure of respect for party autonomy under the common law approach to jurisdiction in contract.

It is, however, unclear once again in this context whether a foreign choice of court agreement should carry so much weight, if indeed it should carry any weight, if the claim being brought before the English courts is non-contractual. Since (as discussed above) jurisdiction over a claim in tort may only be based on an exclusive choice of forum agreement in favour of the English courts where the tort "relates to or is connected with" a contract, this suggests that jurisdiction over a tort that has been committed in England should only be declined because of a foreign choice of court clause where the tort is similarly connected with the contract containing the foreign jurisdiction agreement. In such circumstances a stay

---

[58] It has sometimes been suggested that a distinct test applies, because enforcement of the jurisdiction agreement constitutes specific enforcement of the contractual promise. See Section 3.4.3.

should ordinarily be granted to give effect to the agreement.[59] However, to the extent that there is a presumption that a choice of court agreement will be given effect, this is (as in the context of contractual claims) only a presumption, and it is likely to be more vulnerable to being outweighed by other factors if those factors were unforeseeable to the parties at the time of entering into the jurisdiction agreement.[60] This is more likely in respect of non-contractual disputes, suggesting that foreign choice of court agreements are more likely to be ineffective in relation to non-contractual rather than contractual claims.

4.3.3   United States

As examined in Section 3.4.1, analysis of jurisdictional rules concerning party autonomy in the United States is complicated not only by differing federal and state approaches to jurisdiction, but also by divisions among federal courts, and a lack of clear distinction between questions of venue and questions of jurisdictional power. A lack of guidance from the Supreme Court on many issues has meant that these uncertainties have remained unresolved. The modern trend is, however, for choice of forum clauses (or as they are often called in the United States, 'forum selection clauses') to generally be given both positive and negative effect, as a basis of conferral of jurisdiction and as a reason to decline jurisdiction. This trend also extends to giving these clauses effect in relation to non-contractual claims.

4.3.3.1   Direct Effects of Forum Selection Agreements

Under US law, it appears to be generally accepted that forum selection clauses, if drafted in sufficiently broad terms, will be effective to cover non-contractual claims. Indeed, two of the leading Supreme Court decisions on the general enforceability of jurisdiction agreements (both discussed in further detail in Section 3.4.1) concerned claims in tort, although neither expressly analysed the issue of whether there might be limits on the extent to which jurisdiction agreements applied to non-contractual claims.

The seminal decision of *The Bremen* v. *Zapata Off-Shore Co.* (1972)[61] concerned a claim arising out of damage to an offshore oil rig owned by

---

[59] See e.g. *Astrazeneca UK Ltd* v. *Albemarle International Corp* [2010] EWHC 1028 (Comm).

[60] See generally e.g. *Donohue* v. *Armco Inc* [2001] UKHL 64; *Import-Export Metro Ltd* v. *Compania Sud Americana De Vapores SA* [2003] EWHC 11 (Comm); *Konkola Copper Mines* v. *Coromin (No 2)* [2006] EWHC 1093 (Comm).

[61] *The Bremen* v. *Zapata Off-Shore Co.*, 407 US 1 (1972).

Zapata while under tow by the vessel *Bremen*. The towage contract provided that "Any dispute arising must be treated before the London Court of Justice", but Zapata commenced proceedings in Tampa (where the *Bremen* had put into port following the accident), alleging both negligent towage and breach of contract. Although Zapata argued before the Supreme Court that the clause should not be interpreted to cover *in rem* actions, the Court rejected this contention, finding that the clause was broad enough to cover the claims.[62] There was therefore no direct consideration of whether there are any limits on the circumstances in which a jurisdiction clause, if sufficiently broadly drafted, *should* cover non-contractual claims – it was assumed that if the clause intended to cover such claims, it would be effective to do so. The Court did find that forum selection clauses should generally be enforced, unless the party arguing against the application of the clause can "clearly show that enforcement would be unreasonable and unjust, or that the clause was invalid for such reasons as fraud or overreaching"– a requirement that has been considered relevant to the question of whether such clauses apply to non-contractual claims, as discussed below.[63]

Another important Supreme Court decision on forum selection clauses, *Carnival Cruise Lines, Inc. v. Shute* (1990),[64] concerned a claim brought exclusively in tort for an accident that occurred on a cruise ship. The claim was commenced in Washington State, the claimants' place of domicile. The cruise ticket included the following clause (printed on its reverse): "It is agreed by and between the passenger and the Carrier that all disputes and matters whatsoever arising under, in connection with or incident to this Contract shall be litigated, if at all, in and before a Court located in the State of Florida, U.S.A. to the exclusion of the Courts of any other state or country." It is clear that such a clause, on its terms, purports to determine the forum for both contractual and non-contractual claims. The clause was held to be effective and enforced in respect of the claimants' action in tort. This was, however, decided without discussion of whether or in what circumstances such clauses should *generally* be effective with respect to non-contractual claims.

The dissenting opinion of Justice Stevens, with whom Justice Marshall joined, dealt further with this issue, although again not directly. The dissent questioned whether the jurisdiction agreement effectively limited the

---

[62] At 20.
[63] At 15.
[64] *Carnival Cruise Lines, Inc. v. Shute*, 499 US 585 (1990).

ability of the claimants to continue with their claim, and thus whether it was unenforceable as a contractual attempt to limit tortious liability in negligence. Justice Stevens pointed out that "Clauses limiting a carrier's liability or weakening the passenger's right to recover for the negligence of the carrier's employees come in a variety of forms", noting that "forum selection clauses are ... designed to put a thumb on the carrier's side of the scale of justice",[65] and arguing that this contravened a US statutory rule.[66] But the dissenting opinion concluded that a forum selection clause in a standardised passenger ticket was *generally* unenforceable under prevailing US law – the opinion therefore also did not clearly distinguish between the effectiveness of such clauses over contractual or non-contractual claims.

Later cases in lower courts have also considered the question of whether contractual choice of forum clauses are applicable to non-contractual claims, but equally have tended to focus on the interpretation of the contractual clause – whether it *purported* to determine jurisdictional questions for the type of claim (the issue examined in Section 4.2) – rather than whether such a clause should be given *effect*. Thus, in analysing the effectiveness of a choice of forum agreement contained in a medical consent form in relation to a medical negligence claim, the First Circuit Court of Appeals rejected the claimant's argument "that it would be inappropriate to hold [the claimant] to the forum selection clause because their lawsuit was a tort action and not a breach of contract action", holding that "it is the language of the forum selection clause itself that determines which claims fall within its scope".[67] This analysis does not sufficiently distinguish between the issues of the intended scope of the jurisdiction clause, and its effectiveness under law.[68] The issue of intended scope is of course significant, as examined in Section 4.2. Where a choice of court agreement is limited to claims 'arising out of a contract' or 'under a contract', it may (or may not) therefore encompass non-contractual claims, depending on interpretation of the clause. However, in analysing whether a claim 'arises out of a contract', the Second Circuit Court of Appeals has emphasised that "it is inappropriate ... to depend solely on the legal labels used by plaintiff to decide if his case arises out of the contract", and that "when ascertaining the applicability of a contractual provision to particular claims,

---

[65] At p.599.
[66] 46 USC App § 183c.
[67] *Rivera* v. *Centro Medico de Turabo, Inc.*, 575 F.3d 10, 19 (1st Cir. 2009).
[68] See also similarly *Abbott Laboratories* v. *Takeda Pharmaceutical Co. Ltd*, 476 F.3d 421 (7th Cir. 2007).

we examine the substance of those claims, shorn of their labels".[69] This suggests that even narrowly expressed choice of forum agreements may cover at least some non-contractual claims – although the Court emphasised that this was a matter of contractual interpretation for each case, and indeed found in this case that certain copyright claims that were brought did not 'originate' in the contract and thus were not covered by the forum selection clause.

In a tort claim arising out of the allegedly negligent manufacture of a product, the Eighth Circuit Court of Appeals has similarly held that "Strategic or artfully drawn pleadings ... will not work to circumvent an otherwise applicable forum selection clause",[70] suggesting that such clauses should generally be interpreted to cover at least those tort claims that might have been brought in contractual form. The Court did, however, note with apparent approval the determination of the District Court in the case that, regardless of how broadly a choice of forum agreement is drafted, "it would be unreasonable to apply a broad forum selection clause contained in a contract to a lawsuit that is completely unrelated to the subject of the contract", and thus that "the claims at issue between the parties must be sufficiently related to the contract in order for the forum selection clause to apply".[71] This approach, which finds support in other authorities,[72] suggests that despite a lack of clarity in the case law, the question of whether a forum selection clause is effective in respect of a tort does in fact require consideration of the two distinct elements identified in this chapter. First, the question of whether the clause *purports* to apply to non-contractual claims as a matter of contractual interpretation – the overwhelming focus of attention in the case law. Second, the question of the effectiveness of

---

[69] *Phillips* v. *Audio Active Ltd*, 494 F.3d 378, 388 (2nd Cir. 2007). See further e.g. Hay, Borchers, and Symeonides (2010), p.546.

[70] *Terra International, Inc.* v. *Mississippi Chemical Corporation*, 119 F.3d 688, 695 (8th Cir. 1992). See also *Belfiore* v. *Summit Federal Credit Union*, 452 F.Supp.2d 629, 632 (D. Md. 2006); *Coastal Steel Corporation* v. *Tilghman Wheelabrator Ltd*, 709 F.2d 190, 203 (3rd Cir. 1983), cert. denied, 464 US 938 (1983); *Crescent International, Inc.* v. *Avatar Communities, Inc.*, 857 F.2d 943, 944 (3rd Cir. 1988) ("pleading alternate non-contractual theories is not alone enough to avoid a forum selection clause if the claims asserted arise out of the contractual relation and implicate the contract's terms").

[71] *Terra International, Inc.* v. *Mississippi Chemical Corporation*, 119 F.3d 688, 692 (8th Cir. 1992); see *Terra International, Inc.* v. *Mississippi Chemical Corporation*, 922 F.Supp. 1334, 1377 (N.D.Iowa 1996). See further Yackee (2004), p.62.

[72] See e.g. *Farmland Industries, Inc.* v. *Frazier-Parrott Commodities, Inc.*, 806 F.2d 848, 852 (8th Cir. 1986); *Manetti-Farrow, Inc.* v. *Gucci America, Inc.*, 858 F.2d 509, 514 (9th Cir. 1988) ("Whether a forum selection clause applies to tort claims depends on whether resolution of the claims relates to interpretation of the contract").

the clause – whether, assuming it purports to apply, it will be *given effect* by the applicable jurisdictional rules. In US federal law, the second question appears often subsumed under the *Bremen* test of whether "enforcement would be unreasonable and unjust", as discussed above. In the exercise of this determination, the courts have suggested that to justify giving effect to a jurisdiction agreement in a contract in respect of a claim in tort, a connection between the contract and the tort is required.[73] The effect of this is that choice of forum agreements, however broadly drafted, are only likely to have effect with respect to tort claims that are related to the contract. In some cases, the courts have expressly linked this to the consideration of 'foreseeability' (discussed in Section 2.4.2), holding for example that:

> As Plaintiff's claims do not arise directly from the ... Contract, Plaintiff could not have foreseen being bound by its forum selection clause in bringing these claims ... Accordingly, Plaintiff's choice of forum prevails unless the Swiss Defendants can establish another reason for dismissal.[74]

An express rule to similar effect is also adopted as part of New York law. As already noted in Section 3.4.1, Section 5-1402 of the New York Code expressly permits a choice of New York courts in limited circumstances:

> any person may maintain an action or proceeding against a foreign corporation, non-resident, or foreign state where the action or proceeding arises out of or relates to any contract, agreement or undertaking for which a choice of New York law has been made in whole or in part ... and which (a) is a contract, agreement or undertaking, contingent or otherwise, in consideration of, or relating to any obligation arising out of a transaction covering in the aggregate, not less than one million dollars, and (b) which contains a provision or provisions whereby such foreign corporation or non-resident agrees to submit to the jurisdiction of the courts of this state.

For present purposes, the key words are "arises out of or relates to". The provision thus only permits non-contractual proceedings in the New York courts based on a choice of court clause where the claims are connected to the contract containing the choice of court clause.

---

[73] *Lambert v. Kysar*, 983 F.2d 1110, 1121–2 (1st Cir. 1993) ("The better general rule, we think, is that contract-related tort claims involving the same operative facts as a parallel claim for breach of contract should be heard in the forum selected by the contracting parties").

[74] *General Environmental Science Corporation v. Horsfall*, 753 F.Supp. 664, 668 (N.D. Ohio 1990), approved on appeal at 25 F.3d 1048 (6th Cir. 1994), cert. denied 513 US 947 (1994).

4.3.3.2   Indirect Effects of Forum Selection Agreements

In the discussion above,[75] it was noted that the Second Circuit Court of Appeals found that certain copyright claims that were brought did not 'originate' in the contract and thus were not covered by the forum selection clause. This meant that the jurisdiction agreement (in favour of the English courts) could only be directly effective with respect to some of the claims brought by the claimant, to mandate a stay of those proceedings. This then raised the further issue as to "whether it is proper in these circumstances to dismiss one claim and retain jurisdiction over others"[76] – and thus, whether a jurisdiction agreement might have an *indirect* effect over a non-contractual claim that fell *outside* its scope, because of its effectiveness over claims *within* its scope. The Court noted in principle "that the commencement of separate proceedings in two countries is a likely inconvenience to the parties", but found that "our twin commitments to upholding forum selection clauses where these are found to apply and deferring to a plaintiff's proper choice of forum constrain us in the present context to treat [the] claims separately".[77]

The decision therefore exemplifies a tension between two policy considerations. First, the courts will generally be inclined to give indirect effect to a jurisdiction agreement in favour of a foreign court, even in respect of non-contractual claims not falling within the scope of that agreement, to avoid fragmented and parallel proceedings. Second, however, the courts will counterbalance this inclination with their general unwillingness to interference with the plaintiff's entitlement to choose the forum in which their non-contractual claims may be brought. A foreign forum selection clause may, therefore, have an indirect effect on non-contractual claims that fall outside its scope, but this is likely to depend again on how closely related the non-contractual claims are to the claims that fall within its scope, and thus the decree of 'inconvenience' that would likely be caused by the two sets of proceedings running in parallel.

Conversely, a jurisdiction agreement that *confers* jurisdiction on the forum may also have an indirect effect in respect of non-contractual claims that fall outside the scope of that agreement. Under US federal law, not only are such claims less likely to be stayed, but it is possible that the court will take jurisdiction over them merely because they are sufficiently related to other claims over which the court has jurisdiction, under the

---

[75] *Phillips* v. *Audio Active Ltd.*, 494 F.3d 378, 388 (2nd Cir. 2007).
[76] At 393.
[77] Ibid.

doctrine of 'supplemental jurisdiction'. Under this doctrine, subject to certain conditions and qualifications, "in any civil action of which the district courts have original jurisdiction, the district courts shall have supplemental jurisdiction over all other claims that are so related to claims in the action within such original jurisdiction that they form part of the same case or controversy under Article III of the United States Constitution".[78] One effect of this clause is that if parties have entered into a forum selection clause limited to contractual claims in favour of a particular federal court, and such a contractual claim has indeed been brought, related non-contractual claims not covered by the forum selection clause (including non-federal claims)[79] may also be heard by that court. This very useful added flexibility of US jurisdictional rules does not have any equivalent under the Brussels I Regulation, although it may be viewed as broadly comparable to the (recently added) paragraph 3.1(4A) of Practice Direction 6B of the Civil Procedure Rules in England, as discussed in Section 4.3.2.

4.3.4   Hague Convention on Choice of Court Agreements 2005

In defining an "exclusive choice of court agreement", the Hague Convention on Choice of Court Agreements 2005 uses terminology that appears to have been borrowed from the Brussels I Regulation. The definition states that such an agreement must be entered into "for the purpose of deciding disputes which have arisen or may arise in connection with a particular legal relationship".[80] As in the context of the Brussels I Regulation, this might suggest a limitation on the effectiveness of the jurisdiction agreement – that it may only apply to disputes connected with the legal relationship pursuant to which the jurisdiction agreement was entered into.

It is, however, unclear whether this is actually provided under the Hague Convention. If a jurisdiction agreement purported to cover all disputes between the parties, even those unrelated to the contract as part of which it was entered into, it would appear to satisfy the requirement that it cover "disputes which have arisen or may arise in connection with a particular legal relationship". The agreement is unlikely to be considered to fall outside the scope of the Hague Convention because it *also* purports to cover disputes that are not connected with the particular legal relationship.

---

[78] 28 USC 1367.
[79] See e.g. *United Mine Workers of America* v. *Gibbs*, 383 US 715, 725 (1966) ("state and federal claims must derive from a common nucleus of operative fact").
[80] Article 3(a).

The articles of the Hague Convention that set out its key obligations then do not appear to impose any constraints on the effectiveness of such an agreement. For example, Article 5 provides that "A court of a Contracting State other than that of the chosen court shall suspend or dismiss proceedings to which an exclusive choice of court agreement applies", unless certain exceptions are engaged. Article 6 similarly obliges the courts of other Contracting States to "suspend or dismiss proceedings to which an exclusive choice of court agreement applies". The only relevant limitation in these provisions is that the choice of court agreement "applies" to the dispute, not that the dispute be connected to or arise out of the contractual relationship pursuant to which the choice of court agreement was entered into. In other words, the only restriction appears to be the intended subject-matter scope of the choice of court agreement itself, rather than any constraints imposed as a matter of law.

It is, however, unclear whether this interpretation is supported by the Hague Convention Explanatory Report, which does not discuss this aspect of the Convention in great depth, but does observe that:

> [The requirement] that the designation must be for the purpose of deciding disputes which have arisen or may arise in connection with a particular legal relationship ... makes clear that the choice of court agreement can be restricted to, or include, disputes that have already arisen. It can also cover future disputes, provided they relate to a particular legal relationship. The choice of court agreement is not limited to claims in contract, but could, for example, cover claims in tort arising out of a particular relationship. Thus, a choice of court clause in a partnership agreement could cover tort actions between the partners relating to the partnership. Whether this would be so in any particular case would depend on the terms of the agreement.[81]

This appears to assume (without expressly providing) that a choice of court agreement may *only* apply to non-contractual claims connected with the relationship between the parties pursuant to which the choice of court agreement has been established.

As discussed further in Section 5.4.4, there are subject-matter restrictions on the scope of the Hague Convention that are likely to mean that it does not apply to certain non-contractual claims (unless they arise as preliminary questions or as a defence).[82] For example, the scope of the Convention excludes "claims for personal injury brought by or on behalf of natural persons", "tort or delict claims for damage to tangible property that do not arise from a contractual relationship", and "rights in rem in

---

[81]   At [101].
[82]   Article 2(3).

immovable property, and tenancies of immovable property".[83] The exclusion relating to tangible property is of particular interest, because it indirectly imposes a requirement that tort claims relating to tangible property must arise from a contractual relationship in order for them to be covered by the choice of court agreement, at least under the Hague Convention itself. The expression "a contractual relationship" is used, but presumably the intention is that the claims must arise from *the* contractual relationship pursuant to which the choice of court clause was entered into. The other two exclusions are, however, blanket restrictions, regardless of whether the dispute relates to a contractual relationship, and therefore cannot be viewed as indirectly imposing any similar requirement.

4.4   Conclusions

The possible application of party autonomy in choice of forum to non-contractual claims raises two distinct issues, which are not always clearly distinguished in practice. First, the question of the scope of the agreement – whether it was intended to cover some or all non-contractual claims – which is a matter of interpretation. Second, the question of whether jurisdictional rules will give effect to a choice of court agreement in relation to non-contractual claims. In relation to the first question, different approaches are adopted in different jurisdictions, although there is perhaps a trend towards a broad interpretation of the subject-matter scope of jurisdiction clauses. This is based on the unproven (but not improbable) proposition that commercial parties would wish to maximise the effect of the agreement to increase certainty and reduce the risk of parallel proceedings. In relation to the second question, the rules of jurisdiction examined above do not deal clearly with the issue. There appears to be general acceptance that non-contractual claims closely related to a contract containing a jurisdiction agreement should be governed by that agreement, provided they fall within its scope. Even if they do not, there are a variety of indirect effects given to choice of court agreements that may lead to similar outcomes. The question of whether courts will give effect to a jurisdiction agreement that encompasses claims unrelated to the contract of which it forms part is surprisingly unclear, but it appears that the predominant approach is that such a clause should be ineffective because it would encompass claims not anticipated by the parties. This suggests that the criterion of foreseeability plays a significant role in restricting party autonomy in choice of forum in this context.

---

[83] Article 2(2).

5

Limits on Party Autonomy in Choice of Court

5.1   Introduction

This chapter examines the four most significant potential constraints on the effectiveness of choice of court agreements. The first is the possible imposition of formality requirements, such as a requirement that such agreements must be in writing (Section 5.2). The second is the possible requirement that choice of court agreements are only valid or effective in international cases, where the dispute or the parties have existing connections with more than one state (Section 5.3). The third is the possibility that choice of court agreements may be overridden by rules of exclusive subject matter jurisdiction (Section 5.4). This includes, for example, the common rule that disputes as to the title of immovable property may only be heard exclusively in the courts of the location of the property, regardless of any choice of court agreement between the parties. The fourth is the possibility that choice of court agreements are precluded or constrained pursuant to a special jurisdictional regime that applies based on the characteristics of the parties or their contract (Section 5.5). This might include, for example, limitations on the effectiveness of choice of court agreements in relation to consumers or employees.

A fifth possible constraint on the effectiveness of a choice of court agreement was already noted briefly in Section 3.4.3. If the effect of a foreign choice of court agreement would be to avoid the application of forum mandatory rules in a case closely connected to the forum state, some courts may invalidate the choice of court agreement to ensure the effectiveness of the mandatory rules. This possibility is discussed in Section 5.5 and developed further in Section 9.4.1, which deals with mandatory rules.

5.2   Formality Requirements

Formality requirements are potentially an important restriction on the circumstances in which choice of court agreements will be given effect. Such requirements are not uncommon in practice,[1] as explored further below, but are by no means universally adopted. A requirement that a jurisdiction agreement must be in writing, for example, precludes the effectiveness of a purely oral agreement. That is the case even if there is a genuine oral agreement reflecting a common intention of the parties as to their choice of court.

That is not to say that the *purpose* of formality requirements in relation to jurisdiction agreements is to restrict party autonomy, just as the purpose of formality requirements in other areas of contract law is not to reduce the effectiveness of contracts in those areas. Such requirements are instead generally aimed at serving one or more of three other purposes. First, by increasing the formality of the contractual process they may ensure that it receives greater attention (and that the parties are more likely to benefit from legal advice), thereby increasing the likelihood that contractual obligations are intentionally created rather than imposed, imputed by law, or inadvertent, and also potentially protecting weaker negotiating parties. Second, they may increase certainty and reduce the number and cost of disputes concerning the existence of an enforceable contract, by establishing what is essentially an evidentiary requirement – if a writing requirement applies, then proving the existence of a contract requires documentary evidence, and in the absence of such evidence there is little point contending that there is a contract. Third, formality requirements may similarly increase certainty and reduce disputes concerning the terms of a contract, by requiring them to be documented with greater clarity and precision than is likely to be the case for an oral agreement.

The first of these justifications for formality requirements might be particularly influential in the context of party autonomy. Requiring that choice of court agreements be in writing might be viewed as a way of ensuring that parties do not enter into such agreements lightly. Formality requirements might also ensure that courts are not too willing to impute such an agreement to parties where they have not documented it. This issue is thus concerned both with the legitimacy of a choice by the parties, and with ensuring that party autonomy is not 'abused' by a court in finding an imputed choice of court when one has not actually been made

---

[1] In addition to the examples discussed below, note e.g. Chinese Civil Procedure Law, Art.34 (requiring a jurisdiction agreement to be in writing).

by the parties, thereby undermining the rules that apply in the absence of a choice. This is an issue that has received much greater attention in the context of choice of law, as explored in Section 7.2, where formality requirements rarely apply and it has long been a matter of controversy whether courts sometimes find an implied choice of law agreement where one was not actually entered into by the parties. It might, however, equally arise in relation to jurisdiction agreements, in the absence of formality requirements – concerns might be raised that courts were finding implied choice of court agreements to facilitate (or preclude) their own jurisdiction – although these issues do not appear prominent in practice.[2] This (perhaps theoretical) concern must be balanced against the risk (as noted above) that formality requirements could also partially undermine party autonomy because they might have the effect that some real but unwritten jurisdiction agreements are not enforced.

The second of these justifications is also likely to be influential in the context of choice of court agreements. It is widely recognised that prolonged and costly jurisdictional disputes are highly problematic, particularly as there is a risk that the court will ultimately find that it lacks jurisdiction, and the time and costs incurred will have been wasted. Imposing an evidentiary requirement that a jurisdiction agreement be in writing may also be viewed as a means of ensuring that disputes over the existence of such an agreement will be resolved largely through examination of documentary evidence, and not, for example, through hearing the testimony of witnesses to an alleged oral agreement. Although such testimony might occasionally be necessary when it comes to determining the validity of even a written choice of court agreement, requiring that the agreement itself be in writing will at least preclude some potential jurisdictional issues from argument. The third justification discussed above may also play a role in relation to jurisdiction agreements, as when such an agreement is documented it is likely that greater attention will be paid to questions such as the scope of the agreement and whether it is exclusive or non-exclusive, compared with a potential oral agreement.

---

[2] Under the common law, this may be attributed to the breadth of the rules on jurisdiction – there is no need to find, for example, that an English choice of law agreement implies an English jurisdiction agreement, if the fact that a contract is governed by English law is itself a basis of jurisdiction – Civil Procedure Rules, PD6B, Para 3.1(6)(c).

5.2.1   EU Law (Brussels I Regulation)

5.2.1.1   From the Brussels Convention
to the Brussels I Regulation

In the European Union, the Brussels Convention 1968 initially provided for relatively strict formality requirements for jurisdiction agreements. As first adopted, Article 17 of that Convention required that a court be designated "by an agreement in writing or verbal agreement confirmed in writing". The Jenard Report on the Convention explained that this approach was adopted following similar practice in earlier bilateral conventions as well as the Hague Convention of 15 April 1958 on the jurisdiction of the selected forum in matters relating to the international sale of goods (which never entered into force).[3] The reasons for adopting these requirements appear from the Report to be a mixture of the different justifications discussed above. Citing the drafters of an earlier bilateral convention between Germany and Belgium, the Report argued, for example, that the rules governing choice of court agreements should aim "to cancel out the effects of clauses in contracts which might go unread", such as "clauses in printed forms for business correspondence or in invoices", unless agreed to by the other party, suggesting a concern with identifying genuine agreements.[4] On the other hand, the Report also noted the argument that "in order to ensure legal certainty, the formal requirements applicable to agreements conferring jurisdiction should be expressly prescribed", although it cautioned against "excessive formality which is incompatible with commercial practice" (citing the preparatory work for the 1958 Hague Convention).[5]

The evident risk with adopting such strict formality requirements was that genuine jurisdiction agreements would not be given effect in some cases. In *Salotti* v. *RUWA* (1976),[6] the CJEU held that the requirements in Article 17 of the Brussels Convention 1968 must be "strictly construed",[7] because an exclusive jurisdiction agreement represented a departure

---

[3] See further www.hcch.net/index_en.php?act=conventions.text&cid=34.

[4] Jenard Report, p.37. See also Case 24/76 *Salotti* v. *RUWA* [1976] ECR 1831, [7] ("The purpose of the formal requirements imposed by Article 17 is to ensure that the consensus between the parties is in fact established"); C-221/84 *Berghoefer* v. *ASA* [1985] ECR 2699, [13] ("the purpose of Article 17 is to ensure that the parties have actually consented to such a clause and that their consent is clearly and precisely demonstrated").

[5] Jenard Report, p.37.

[6] Case 24/76 *Salotti* v. *RUWA* [1976] ECR 1831.

[7] At [7].

from the "ordinary" rules of jurisdiction.[8] It is not clear why this should have been the case – it might equally have been concluded that Article 17 should be construed broadly, because it was intended to give effect to party agreements and this would maximise legal certainty consistently with the objectives of the Convention, reflected in the priority given to Article 17 itself over other rules of jurisdiction. Perhaps this reflects a residual uncertainty about the status of party autonomy – suggesting it was at the time viewed as an exceptional rather than ordinary rule of jurisdiction – although already in 1978 the CJEU was interpreting other aspects of Article 17 broadly as "based on a recognition of the independent will of the parties to a contract".[9] In any event, the strict approach to formality requirements was followed in other cases, in which, for example, a party who had entered into an oral contract subject to another party's standard terms that included a jurisdiction agreement was held not to be bound by the jurisdiction agreement, because it was neither agreed nor confirmed in writing.[10] This led to a concern that the formality requirements might actually be out of step with commercial practice (despite the Jenard Report's note of the need to take such practice into consideration).

In the Accession Convention 1978, Article 17 of the Brussels Convention was amended to provide that a jurisdiction agreement "shall be either in writing or evidenced in writing or, in international trade or commerce, in a form which accords with practices in that trade or commerce of which the parties are or ought to have been aware".[11] This introduced additional flexibility into the rules which enabled the courts to give effect to jurisdiction agreements that formed part of the terms of oral contracts but were themselves documented in writing,[12] as well as other more unusual jurisdiction agreements, such as those binding shareholders through company

---

[8] As subsequently described in C-71/83 *The Tilly Russ* [1984] ECR 2417, [14].

[9] Case 23/78 *Meeth* v. *Glacetal* [1978] ECR 2133, [5], discussed further in Section 3.5.

[10] Case 25/76 *Segoura* v. *Bonakdarian* [1976] ECR 1851 (but suggesting, at [11], that "it would be otherwise where an oral agreement forms part of a continuing trading relationship between the parties").

[11] Accession Convention 1978, Art.11.

[12] C-106/95 *MSG* v. *Les Gravières Rhénanes SARL* [1997] ECR I-911. Note also C-221/84 *Berghoefer* v. *ASA* [1985] ECR 2699, which applied a similar interpretation to the original version of Article 17, influenced by the terms of the Accession Convention 1978 and the need "to avoid excessive formality incompatible with commercial practice" (at [10]). See generally discussion in Cheshire, North and Fawcett (2017), p.237ff.

statutes.[13] Even further flexibility was added in the Accession Convention 1989,[14] which provided that:

> Such an agreement conferring jurisdiction shall be either:
>
> (a) in writing or evidenced in writing, or
> (b) in a form which accords with practices which the parties have established between themselves, or
> (c) in international trade or commerce, in a form which accords with a usage of which the parties are or ought to have been aware and which in such trade or commerce is widely known to, and regularly observed by, parties to contracts of the type involved in the particular trade or commerce concerned.

This form of wording has also been followed under the Brussels I Regulation 2001 and now under the 2012 Recast, and thus these less restrictive but nevertheless significant formality requirements continue to apply in EU Member States. One further element of flexibility has been added, however, pursuant to Article 23(2) of the 2001 Regulation and the identical Article 25(2) of the Recast, which provide that "Any communication by electronic means which provides a durable record of the agreement shall be equivalent to 'writing'". This has been interpreted broadly to encompass an online 'click-wrapping' contract in which the parties had the opportunity to generate a durable record, even if they did not in fact do so.[15]

The evident trend in EU regulation is towards a relaxation of formality requirements. Initially, these were interpreted strictly, in order to increase legal certainty and on the basis that exercises of party autonomy were 'exceptional', and thus the relevant provisions should be interpreted narrowly. The case law and legislative developments suggest that party autonomy has been normalised, so that it is not seen as something to be narrowly confined, but rather to be promoted through amendments and interpretations that are more sympathetic to the practices of private parties. Nevertheless, these formality requirements remain a significant constraint on party autonomy, because they render purely oral jurisdiction agreements in favour of the courts of EU Member States generally unenforceable under the Brussels I Regulation (and, at least for claims against EU domiciled parties, without any residual possibility of enforcement under national law). It is perhaps striking that formality requirements have remained so influential in this context, when (as discussed in Section 7.2.2)

---

[13] C-214/89 *Powell Duffryn plc* v. *Petereit* [1992] ECR I-1745.
[14] Accession Convention 1989, Art.7.
[15] C-322/14 *El Majdoub* EU:C:2015:334.

they are viewed rather sceptically under the Rome I Regulation, Article 11, which provides very liberal rules for determining formal validity for contracts in general (recalling from Section 3.3.2, however, that the Rome I Regulation does not apply to jurisdiction agreements).

It should also be noted that the formality requirements under the Brussels I Regulation have long been understood to be exhaustive – the courts of EU Member States may not impose any additional formality requirements in determining the validity of jurisdiction agreements, as this would qualify their obligations under the Regulation.[16] This rule is very likely to continue to apply despite the reference to national law under Article 25 of the 2012 Recast, which potentially permits application of different national law doctrines to the question of the substantive validity of a jurisdiction agreement.[17] On the other hand, it is somewhat unclear what the effect of non-compliance with the formality requirements in Article 25 should be in relation to proceedings against a non-EU domiciled party in the Member State court chosen in the agreement.[18] One view is that the field of jurisdiction agreements (regardless of the domicile of the parties) is now covered by the Brussels I Regulation, and thus no basis of jurisdiction arises. The other is that non-compliance with the formality requirements of Article 25 means that the question of jurisdiction falls back on national law, under which it is possible that the jurisdiction agreement may be valid and effective.

5.2.1.2   The Brussels I Regulation in Reflexive Effect?

An important and difficult issue concerns what effect should be given to jurisdiction agreements in favour of non-Member States, where jurisdiction is taken under the Brussels I Regulation. As discussed in Section 3.4.2, the Brussels I Regulation is silent on the effects to be given to such agreements. The view that has generally attracted the support of courts and academic literature is that some 'reflexive effect' should be given to the exclusive jurisdictional rules adopted under the Regulation – applying them to non-Member State situations in a similar or identical manner to the way in which they are applied to Member State situations.[19] Thus, an exclusive jurisdiction agreement in favour of the courts of a non-Member State should (arguably) be given an equivalent (but possible discretionary) effect

---

[16] See e.g. Case 150/80 *Elefanten Schuh* v. *Jacqmain* [1981] ECR 1671. This was not clear, however, from the Jenard Report.
[17] See Section 3.3.2.
[18] See discussion in Hartley (2013).
[19] See e.g. Cheshire, North and Fawcett (2017), p.473ff; Nuyts (2007), p.81ff; Fentiman (2006b).

to that provided for exclusive jurisdiction agreements in favour of Member State courts under Article 25[20] – precluding any exercise of jurisdiction contrary to the agreement. Assuming such reflexive effect exists, the difficulty that arises for present purposes is whether the *formality* requirements under Article 25 should also be applied reflexively. For example, in the *Nile Rhapsody* case discussed further below,[21] an English defendant claimed that the English courts should stay proceedings on the basis of an oral exclusive jurisdiction agreement in favour of the Egyptian courts. The basis for this decision would not stand under current law, because the oral jurisdiction agreement was given effect under the *forum non conveniens* discretion, which (as discussed in Section 3.4.2) the CJEU has expressly ruled incompatible with the Brussels I Regulation.[22] If that case arose today, and the court were persuaded to apply a reflexive effect doctrine, there is some doubt whether the jurisdiction agreement would be given effect, because the agreement would not satisfy the formality requirements of Article 25. Although it is often argued that there should be a discretionary element to the reflexive effect doctrine, this is usually in relation to the question of whether proceedings *must* be stayed where an agreement satisfies the criteria in Article 25 (except that it is in favour of the courts of a non-EU Member State), or whether proceedings may continue despite the agreement (if, for example, the chosen non-Member State court is not practically available to the parties, or would not resolve the dispute fairly). If Article 25 is being given reflexive effect, even in a discretionary way, this does not appear to leave open the possibility that non-EU Member State jurisdiction agreements may be given effect in circumstances *beyond* those in which they are enforceable under the Brussels I Regulation.

It is not clear, however, whether this is the best approach. There is a strong argument that this would not be consistent with meeting the expectations of the parties, as they would not expect to have to satisfy the formal conditions of the Brussels I Regulation in order for a non-Member State jurisdiction agreement to be effective, and thus that any reflexive effect of Article 25 should include a degree of flexibility also with regard to its formality requirements. Arguably, in such cases the formality requirements of the law of the jurisdiction selected by the parties would be the most appropriate standard to apply to the formal validity of the agreement.[23] If

---

[20] See e.g. *Konkola Copper Mines* v. *Coromin* [2005] EWHC 898 (Comm).
[21] [1994] 1 Lloyd's Rep 382.
[22] C-281/02 *Owusu* v. *Jackson* [2005] ECR I-1383.
[23] Or perhaps it should be sufficient if the agreement satisfies the formality requirements of either EU law or the law of the chosen court – by analogy to Art.11 of the Rome I Regulation, discussed in Section 7.2.2.

two parties enter into an oral exclusive jurisdiction agreement in favour of the Hong Kong courts, and such agreements are generally effective under Hong Kong law, then the effectiveness of the agreement should arguably be recognised by the courts of EU Member States even if one or more of the parties is domiciled in an EU Member State. On this view, if proceedings are brought against the EU Member State domiciled party in the courts of their domicile it should thus be open to those courts to give the jurisdiction agreement reflexive effect and decline jurisdiction. On the other hand, at least some of the justifications for formality requirements noted above would militate against such an approach, perhaps making the formality requirements akin to mandatory rules.

As noted in Section 3.4.2, there is an argument that the failure to address the reflexive effect of jurisdiction agreements in Article 25 is intentional, and no reflexive effect is possible under the Brussels I Regulation. This argument is highly controversial (and somewhat doubtful), but it is strengthened under the 2012 Recast, because rules dealing with prior or related proceedings in a non-Member State have been introduced, partially addressing the reflexive effect issue. Even if this is the case, however, a similar issue may arise in relation to these new non-Member State *lis pendens* rules. The rules require the court to consider, among other things, whether the non-Member State court has taken jurisdiction "in circumstances where a court of a Member State would have exclusive jurisdiction".[24] If courts in Hong Kong, for example, are first seised of a dispute based on an oral jurisdiction agreement, and then the English courts are second seised (based on the domicile of the defendant), it is somewhat unclear whether this test would be satisfied – it depends on whether the formality requirements under Article 25 are also applied in evaluating whether a Member State court would have exclusive jurisdiction in the 'circumstances'. Again, there is an argument that applying these formality requirements strictly would not be consistent with meeting the expectations of the parties, who would arguably not expect a non-Member State jurisdiction agreement to have to satisfy the conditions of the Brussels I Regulation to be effective, and might therefore have neglected to document it in writing.

5.2.2 Common Law

By contrast to the position under EU law, under the common law no special formality requirements apply to choice of court agreements. This is true in relation to both jurisdiction agreements in favour of common law

---

[24] Recital 24.

courts (in this section, focusing on the English courts), and those in favour of foreign courts. It may be noted that this even applies to the effect of jurisdiction agreements as between the component parts of the United Kingdom – although the United Kingdom has generally adopted the rules of the Brussels I Regulation to determine the 'internal' allocation of jurisdiction, the rule governing jurisdiction agreements does not incorporate the formality requirements of the Brussels I Regulation.[25]

5.2.2.1   A Jurisdiction Agreement as a Basis of Jurisdiction

Under Practice Direction 6B of the Civil Procedure Rules, the English courts may give permission to commence proceedings outside the territory where "A claim is made in respect of a contract where the contract ... contains a term to the effect that the court shall have jurisdiction to determine any claim in respect of the contract".[26] As noted in Section 3.4.3, since the 2012 Recast the Brussels I Regulation has been extended to cover agreements in favour of the courts of a Member State between two non-EU domiciled parties – so in practice the common law rule is rarely likely to be applied in England (except to cases falling outside the scope of the Regulation), although this position may change if or when Brexit occurs. In any event, under the common law as traditionally applied in England and still applied in other common law states, there was (and continues to be) no requirement that a choice of court clause be in writing, or anything similar. Jurisdiction may be asserted purely on the basis of an oral choice of court agreement, or even (at least in theory) where such an agreement is identified as an implied term of a contract. As noted in Section 5.2, however, this has not arisen in practice, arguably because of the breadth of the common law rules on jurisdiction – there is no need to find, for example, that an English choice of law agreement implies an English jurisdiction agreement, if the fact that a contract is governed by English law is itself a basis of jurisdiction.[27]

5.2.2.2   Foreign Jurisdiction Agreements

Where the English courts are taking jurisdiction under the Brussels I Regulation (generally where claims are brought against EU Member State domiciled parties), or where a jurisdiction agreement is in favour of the

---

[25] Civil Jurisdiction and Judgments Act 1982, sch.4, s.12(1); see further e.g. Cheshire, North and Fawcett (2017), pp.320–21.

[26] Para 3.1(6)(d).

[27] Civil Procedure Rules, PD6B, Para 3.1(6)(c).

courts of another Member State, the effectiveness of the jurisdiction agreement will be governed by the Brussels I Regulation, including the formality requirements discussed above. Where, however, the English courts are taking jurisdiction based on the common law rules (generally where claims are brought against non-EU Member State domiciled parties), jurisdiction agreements in favour of non-EU Member States are usually given effect through the *forum conveniens* or *forum non conveniens* discretion, a flexible test under which there are no formality requirements. In *The Nile Rhapsody*,[28] for example, the English courts accepted the defendant's argument that an oral exclusive jurisdiction agreement in favour of the Egyptian courts had been entered into by the parties, in addition to the terms of their written contract. The Court even determined that it had the power to find "that the contract should be deemed to be rectified"[29] to reflect the jurisdiction agreement, despite holding that (pursuant to the agreement) the court did not have jurisdiction over the merits of the claim, although also determined that such rectification was unnecessary for the Court to give effect to the oral jurisdiction agreement. Thus, under the common law, the question of the validity of a jurisdiction agreement is an ordinary question of contract law, not subject to any special formality requirements. This may be considered to reflect the strong acceptance of party autonomy under the common law, and also the way in which under the common law questions of party autonomy are commonly viewed as substantive questions of contract law rather than matters involving state regulatory authority.

As noted in Section 3.4.3, under the common law (as indeed under many other legal orders) foreign jurisdiction agreements may also have an indirect effect through the rules on the recognition and enforcement of foreign judgments, in determining that the jurisdiction of a foreign court was properly established and thus its judgment is *prima face* capable of recognition and enforcement. Historically, there was some doubt over whether such an agreement needed to be express – that is, whether a formality requirement applied. In *Sirdar Gurdyal Singh* v. *Rajah of Faridkote* (1894),[30] it was held that "such obligation, unless expressed, could not be implied". It has, however, recently been clarified in *Vizcaya Partners Ltd* v. *Picard* (2016)[31] that an actual but unwritten foreign jurisdiction agreement

---

[28] [1994] 1 Lloyd's Rep 382.
[29] At [69].
[30] [1894] AC 670, 686 (Privy Council). See also e.g. *Vogel* v. *RA Kohnstamm Ltd* [1973] QB 133.
[31] [2016] UKPC 5, [56–8] (Gibraltar).

is sufficient. The authorities merely establish that such an agreement is not implied by a choice of foreign law, or through the act of entering into the contract in a particular place, or through agreeing to a particular place being the place of performance of the contract. Such actions may establish the jurisdiction of the foreign court (under its own rules), but do not constitute submission to its jurisdiction for the purposes of the rules on recognition and enforcement of judgments.

5.2.3   United States

As discussed in Chapters 3 and 4, there are a wide variety of US approaches to choice of court agreements, in the different state and federal courts. In federal law and under most state laws there are no formality requirements that apply to choice of court agreements, similarly to the common law approach discussed above. The validity of a jurisdiction agreement is treated as an ordinary contractual question, and a purely oral jurisdiction agreement may be given effect. However, certain US states do adopt a variety of different approaches, sometimes requiring that choice of court clauses be in a particular form to be effective.[32] This is reflective of the scepticism towards party autonomy in choice of court in some US states, as examined in Section 3.4.1.

A more uniform rule can be identified for contracts covered by the United Nations Convention on Contracts for the International Sale of Goods ('CISG'), which applies in the United States (in both federal and state courts) and most other major trading states, but not the United Kingdom, Hong Kong, India, or South Africa. The CISG does not directly regulate the validity of choice of court agreements. However, Article 11 does expressly provide that there are no formality requirements for the formation of a contract of sale. Some state parties to the CISG have entered reservations to this Article to preserve national law requirements for contracts to be in writing,[33] but the United States has not entered any such reservation. The prohibition of formality requirements under the CISG is also considered to extend to forum selection clauses – thus, purely oral jurisdiction agreements in international sale of goods contracts that fall under the CISG may be given effect.[34]

---

[32] See generally Yackee (2004), p.50ff; Yackee (2003).
[33] Pursuant to Article 96.
[34] *Chateau des Charmes Wines v. Sabate USA Inc.,* 328 F 3d 528 (9th Cir. 2003).

5.2.4   Hague Convention on Choice of Court Agreements 2005

The Hague Convention on Choice of Court Agreements 2005 does not expressly impose requirements for formal validity in relation to jurisdiction agreements. However, it may do so indirectly through the way in which jurisdiction agreements are defined. Under Article 3 of the Convention:

(a) 'exclusive choice of court agreement' means an agreement concluded by two or more parties that meets the requirements of paragraph *c)* and designates, for the purpose of deciding disputes which have arisen or may arise in connection with a particular legal relationship, the courts of one Contracting State or one or more specific courts of one Contracting State to the exclusion of the jurisdiction of any other courts;

...

(c) an exclusive choice of court agreement must be concluded or documented -
   (i) in writing; or
   (ii) by any other means of communication which renders information accessible so as to be usable for subsequent reference;[35]

The effect of these provisions is that a jurisdiction agreement that does not satisfy the formality requirements in Article 3(c) is not covered by the Convention, nor is the recognition and enforcement of a judgment based on such an agreement. A purely oral jurisdiction agreement will thus not be effective pursuant to the Convention, unless it is later documented in writing or in some other form in which it is accessible for subsequent reference (such as, for example, an audio recording).

If these requirements are not satisfied, the question arises as to what consequences follow. One possibility is that the jurisdiction agreement should be considered unenforceable – this is, for example, the effect of non-compliance with the formality requirements under the Brussels I Regulation in EU Member States. Another possibility is that the question of the enforceability of the jurisdiction agreement should be considered to fall outside the scope of the Hague Convention, and thus revert back to national law. It will then be a matter for the national law of each Convention state to determine whether to give effect to the agreement (or to recognise and enforce any judgment that has been obtained on the basis of the agreement). The latter approach is probably the better one, as it is likely not the intention of the Hague Convention to actively preclude the

---

[35] The Hague Convention Explanatory Report also observes that "The wording of this provision was inspired by Art.6(1) of the UNCITRAL Model Law on Electronic Commerce 1996" – at [13], n.40, and [112], n.144.

enforceability of jurisdiction agreements that do not comply with its for-mality requirements.[36] This is the approach taken by many states in rela-tion to the New York Convention 1958, which similarly imposes a writing requirement for arbitration agreements – a purely oral arbitration agree-ment is, under this approach, viewed simply as falling outside the scope of the New York Convention, and may potentially be enforced pursuant to national law.[37]

It is even clearer that the intention of the Hague Convention is that the formality requirements it contains be exhaustive. Thus, state parties are not permitted to impose any additional formality requirements to jurisdiction agreements (such as language or typeface requirements), as these would have the effect of qualifying their obligations under the Convention.[38] This is, again, consistent with the approach taken in relation to the New York Convention 1958.[39]

5.3   Requirement for an International Dispute?

If two parties entirely from one jurisdiction enter into a contract to be performed exclusively in that jurisdiction, and there are no relevant con-nections to any other state, and *no jurisdiction agreement* in favour of any other court, there is no doubt that only the courts of that place will be able to hear any disputes that may arise. There are, however, two ways of under-standing this result. The first is that rules of private international law do not apply to purely domestic cases – that such cases fall within the domain of a single legal order, and there is therefore no need to consider rules on jurisdiction. The second is that in such cases, the application of rules of jurisdiction has the result that only a single court – the court of the parties and the events – will have jurisdiction. These different approaches will, rather obviously, usually lead to identical outcomes. The possible excep-tion to this is where a purely domestic contractual arrangement contains a jurisdiction agreement in favour of a foreign court. There are four possible positions that may be adopted in response to such a situation.

A first possibility is to invalidate the choice, on the basis that there is no objective connection between the chosen court and the parties or their contractual relationship. As discussed in Chapter 3, there are some legal

---

[36] Hague Convention Explanatory Report, [13] and [110], n.150.
[37] See Section 6.3.2.
[38] Hague Convention Explanatory Report, [110].
[39] See Section 6.3.2.

systems (for example, some states in the United States) that only recognise a choice of forum where the dispute has some objective connection to that forum. Similar constraints exist under Chinese law – a choice of a foreign court is only permitted where there is a recognised connection with that court (such as where it is the place of domicile of one of the parties, or the place of performance of the contract).[40] Under such an approach, it will be impossible for the parties to validly select a foreign court for a purely domestic contract.

A second possibility is to invalidate (or not give effect to) the choice, on the basis that purely domestic relationships are not properly matters for private international law. It is notable, for example, that the Hague Convention on Choice of Court Agreements 2005 provides in Article 1 that it only applies in "international cases", and further that for the purposes of its rules on jurisdiction:

> a case is international unless the parties are resident in the same Contracting State and the relationship of the parties and all other elements relevant to the dispute, regardless of the location of the chosen court, are connected only with that State.[41]

This provision does not require a connection with the state whose courts are chosen, merely a connection with more than one state.[42] The meaning of 'resident' is not defined for natural persons; Article 4(2) provides that a legal person is resident in the place of their statutory seat, the place under whose law they were incorporated, the place of their central administration, and in their principal place of business.[43] The location of the chosen court is thus itself excluded as a relevant factor in determining whether the case is international – the act of choosing a foreign court does not itself internationalise the contract. It is unclear what other 'elements relevant to

---

[40] Civil Procedure Law, Art.34; Supreme People's Court 'Interpretation of Civil Procedure Law', Fa Shi [2015] No. 5, Art.531. See generally e.g. Bath (2016). In any case, a choice of a foreign court is not available for a contract that is not 'foreign-related'. This requires that either a party (in respect of either their nationality or habitual residence), the performance of the contract, or some other relevant factor (such as the subject matter of the contract, or the place of contracting) be outside Mainland China. See the Supreme People's Court 'Interpretation of Civil Procedure Law', Fa Shi [2015] No. 5, Art.522, and further discussion in Section 9.3

[41] See e.g. further discussion in Weller (2017), p.93ff; Hartley (2013b), pp.101–2.

[42] But see Article 19, discussed in Section 3.4.4.

[43] The term 'or' is used in the Convention rather than 'and', but the intention is evidently that multiple places of residence may be established under this test: see Hague Convention Explanatory Report, [120].

the dispute' may be relied on as factors making the contract international.[44] The place of formation of a contract, for example, could be viewed as a relevant factor, but this would enable the 'internationality' requirement to be readily established in otherwise domestic cases, and in cases of electronic contracting could be difficult to determine. A choice of foreign law could be viewed as sufficient to internationalise the contract, but for a contract otherwise connected with a single state that choice may also have limited effectiveness,[45] which perhaps suggests that it should not be sufficient to render the contract international for jurisdictional purposes. The exclusion of purely domestic relationships does not, of course, preclude Convention states from giving choice of court agreements effect for such relationships, but it does certainly carve out the space for Convention states to invalidate exercises of party autonomy in such cases, should they wish to do so.[46] The Convention curiously does not impose a similar internationality requirement for the rules on the recognition and enforcement of judgments, although it gives states the option to do so under Article 20 (but *only* as a defence to enforcement in the state objectively connected to the dispute).

A third possibility is to consider that ordinary rules of private international law apply, even to purely domestic cases. An alternative way of expressing this understanding might be to say that the choice by the parties itself internationalises the dispute, implicating rules of private international law. Under the Brussels I Regulation, for example, although it is generally considered that the Regulation only applies to questions of "international jurisdiction",[47] there is authority (although the point is not definitively settled) to the effect that a choice of court agreement in favour

---

[44] A similar issue arises in the context of choice of law – see discussion in Section 9.3. In the context of choice of law it is clear that this is based on connecting factors at the time of the choice – here the position is less certain, and there is an argument that the test should be based on connecting factors at the time of commencement of proceedings.

[45] See further Section 9.3.

[46] Although it is a curious omission that if, for example, a contract between two Singapore companies to be performed entirely in Singapore contains a choice of court agreement in favour of the Singapore courts, and litigation is commenced in England on the basis that one of the companies has a branch office in London, the Hague Convention will not require the English courts to stay the proceedings because the situation is purely domestic to one state. Of course, the English courts would be very likely to stay their proceedings under the doctrine of *forum non conveniens* in such circumstances, but the Convention perhaps missed an opportunity to add further certainty to such cases.

[47] The term comes from the pre-amble to the Brussels Convention 1968. See the Jenard Report, p.8 and pp.37–8; the Schlosser Report, p.123; C-281/02 *Owusu* v. *Jackson* [2005] ECR I-1383, [25]; Opinion 1/03 *Competence of the Community to conclude the new Lugano Convention* [2006] ECR I-1145, [143]–[145]. See e.g. further discussion in Weller (2017), p.93ff.

of a Member State is sufficient to internationalise the dispute.[48] The choice
by the parties of a Member State court that is unconnected to them or the
dispute will thus likely be effective, even if the parties and their dispute
are otherwise solely connected with a single state (whether or not it is a
Member State).[49]

A fourth possibility is opened up in those systems of law, such as the
common law and (generally) in the United States, in which the effectiveness of choice of court agreements is a matter of discretion, as examined
in Section 3.4. In those systems, the existence of a jurisdiction agreement
can be considered relevant but not necessarily binding. In a purely domestic case, it is likely that the choice of a foreign forum will receive greater
scrutiny – in the common law tradition, asking whether the chosen forum
really is clearly the most appropriate for the parties, and (generally) in the
United States, scrutinising the potential unfairness of the choice of court
agreement. The treatment of such cases will thus fall somewhere between
invalidating and enforcing choice of court agreements, depending on the
circumstances of the case.

5.4   Exclusive Subject-Matter Jurisdiction

A second major type of restriction on choice of court agreements is the
exclusion of certain categories of dispute based on their subject matter. In
most legal systems, it is recognised that certain categories of dispute are
so closely associated with a single legal order that only the courts of that
order should resolve the dispute,[50] and this frequently trumps the exercise
of party autonomy by invalidating any choice of court agreement in favour
of a different court.

5.4.1   EU Law (Brussels I Regulation, Article 24)

The only rules in the Brussels I Regulation that displace party autonomy
altogether are those exclusive grounds for jurisdiction established under

---

[48] *Provimiv Aventis Animal Nutrition SA* [2003] EWHC 961 (Comm) at [74]–[75]; *Snookes
v. Jani-King (GB) Ltd* [2006] EWHC 289 (QB), [39]–[45]. But see Hartley (2013b), p.102ff.

[49] This also seems to be supported by Article 3(3) and Recital 15 of the Rome I Regulation,
discussed in Section 9.3, which contemplates that an effective jurisdiction agreement may
be entered into in a purely domestic contract, but limits the effect of that agreement for
choice of law purposes.

[50] In addition to the examples discussed below, note e.g. the Chinese Civil Procedure Law,
Arts.33 (including real estate disputes) and 266 (including contracts for the exploration or
exploitation of natural resources in China); Supreme People's Court 'Interpretation of Civil
Procedure Law', Fa Shi [2015] No. 5, Art.531. See generally e.g. Bath (2016). Note also the
new Brazilian Code of Civil Procedure (L.13.105/15), Art.23.

Article 24. Article 24 provides for a number of situations under which the courts of a Member State are to have exclusive jurisdiction, regardless of any choice by the parties,[51] and regardless of whether any party is domiciled in a Member State.[52] Each of these operates therefore as 'subject-matter' restrictions on Article 25, which gives effect to jurisdiction clauses – defining types of disputes for which party autonomy will be ineffective. Article 24 may override both jurisdiction agreements in favour of the forum (the chosen court will be required to stay the proceedings in favour of the foreign court designated by Article 24),[53] as well as jurisdiction agreements in favour of a foreign court (if designated by Article 24, the court seised will be required to exercise jurisdiction despite the foreign jurisdiction agreement).[54]

5.4.1.1   Grounds of Exclusive Jurisdiction

Article 24(1) provides that "proceedings which have as their object" rights *in rem* in immovable property or tenancies of immovable property located in a Member State may only be heard in the courts of the territory in which the property is located, subject to an exclusion for "tenancies of immovable property concluded for temporary private use for a maximum period of six months". This rule takes priority over Article 25 of the Regulation, and thus choice of court agreements will never be effective in respect of (non-excluded) claims directly involving title to immovable property located in a Member State, whether or not these arise out of a contractual relationship. The rule in Article 25 is limited to jurisdiction agreements in favour of the courts of Member States, but even if jurisdiction agreements in favour of non-Member States may be given reflexive effect in some cases, as discussed in Section 3.4.2, this could not include cases in which the basis of jurisdiction was Article 24, because of the priority of Article 24 over Article 25.

One basis for the policy determination that party autonomy should not be applicable in this context might be that public state interests in the exclusive territorial control over title to immovable property justify overriding party autonomy. This in turn reflects the intimate connection between questions of statehood and title to land under public international law – the

---

[51] See Recital 19 to the Brussels I Regulation and Art.25(4).
[52] This seems clear from the text (and is implied in CJEU case law), but see *Choudhary* v. *Bhatter* [2009] EWCA Civ 1176 (now doubted by *Dar Al Arkan Real Estate Development Co* v. *Refai* [2014] EWCA Civ 715).
[53] See also Art.27, discussed further below.
[54] See e.g. *Speed Investments Ltd* v. *Formula One Holdings Ltd* [2004] EWCA Civ 1512.

very question of statehood is, in international law, tied up with questions of title to and control over territory. A further related justification is the more pragmatic point that a judgment of any State in respect of title to foreign immovable property would be unenforceable (as set out in Article 45(1)(e)(ii)) – although as the Brussels I Regulation might have dictated to the opposite effect, this justification returns to the basis that states would never agree to enforce foreign judgments over their own immovable property because of the connection between their statehood and territory. Finally, it is sometimes argued that the land law of each state is frequently complex and reflects particular local interests, and as disputes concerning title to land will be governed by the law of the location of the land, the court best placed to resolve those disputes most efficiently will always be the courts of the place of the land. The choice of a different court by the parties might therefore alternatively be invalidated on the basis that it can never be a better choice than that selected by the rule in Article 24(1) itself.

Article 24 provides four further grounds of exclusive jurisdiction, each of which may be justified on similar grounds. Article 24(2) provides that the courts of the Member State in which a company or other legal person has its seat have exclusive jurisdiction in respect of proceedings "which have as their object" the validity of its constitution or of the decisions of its organs, or its nullity or dissolution. This rule reflects the fact that legal persons are a product of a particular legal order, and questions of the existence or scope of that personality can be best resolved by its courts, which will have particular access to its corporate filings.[55] Article 24(3) provides that the courts of a Member State have exclusive jurisdiction over proceedings "which have as their object" the validity of entries in a public register kept in the territory of that Member State – again, clearly reflecting the unique position of those courts and the public interest in those registers. Article 24(4) similarly provides, in relation to registered intellectual property rights, that the courts of the Member State of (purported) registration have exclusive jurisdiction over claims "concerned with" their registration or validity.[56] It does not, therefore, encompass infringement claims – indeed this rule is considered to prevent the court hearing an infringement action from also determining questions of validity raised as a defence (as discussed in the following section). The public interests at stake here are a combination of those under Article 24(1), 24(2), and

---

[55] See e.g. C-372/07 *Hassett* v. *South Eastern Health Board* [2008] ECR I-7403, [21].
[56] Note also the similar rule in the Max Planck Principles for Conflict of Laws in Intellectual Property 2011, available at www.cl-ip.eu, Art.2:401.

24(3) – exclusive jurisdiction is justified by the fact that intellectual property rights are territorial in character and connected to sovereign grants of
monopoly, the product of a particular legal order, and also (in this case)
located in a register under the public supervision of the Member State in
which the register is located. It is notable that Article 24(4) extends only to
registered or registrable intellectual property rights ("patents, trade marks,
designs, or other similar rights"), and does not therefore apply to copyright. The exclusion of copyright suggests that it is territorial control over
the register that ultimately justifies the exclusive jurisdiction – since copyright otherwise shares with registrable intellectual property the qualities of
being territorial in character, connected to sovereign grants of monopoly,
and the product of a particular legal order. Finally, Article 24(5) provides
that proceedings "concerned with" the enforcement of a judgment may
only be heard in "the courts of the Member State in which the judgment
has been or is to be enforced". The justification for exclusivity of jurisdiction in this context perhaps echoes that in respect of Article 24(1) – public
international law provides for territorial limitations on enforcement jurisdiction (in the absent of consent or special arrangements), as the exclusive
exercise of public power within a territory is an inherent feature of statehood itself.[57] It would therefore be futile to confer jurisdiction over the
local enforcement of a judgment on a foreign court, even if this was by
agreement of the parties, as the foreign court would be powerless to make
any such enforcement orders.

5.4.1.2   Scope of Exclusive Jurisdiction

One central difficulty in the interpretation of Article 24 is the determination of which claims fall within the subject-matter restrictions. Articles
24(1), (2), and (3) state that they apply to proceedings "which have as their
object" the relevant subject matter, whereas Articles 24(4) and (5) state
that they apply to proceedings "concerned with" the relevant subject matter. As discussed below, it is not entirely clear whether this difference in
wording is intended to be legally significant, but in each case the wording
defines a connection which is required to justify the application of the relevant provision of Article 24.

The difficulty in applying this requirement is perhaps most evident with
respect to Article 24(1), but is equally applicable to the other sections.

---

[57] See further e.g. Mills (2014); *Masri* v. *Consolidated Contractors International Company SAL*
    [2008] EWCA Civ 303, [127]; *Kuwait Oil Tanker Company SAK* v. *Qabazard* [2002] EWCA
    Civ 34.

In respect of Article 24(1), the problem is distinguishing between claims *in rem* and claims *in personam* that simply happen to relate to immovable property – determining when proceedings "have as their object" rights *in rem* in immovable property. The restrictive jurisdictional rules of Article 24(1) may arguably be avoided through careful presentation or analysis of a claim as based on power over the person of the defendant, rather than over the subject matter of the dispute – ordering the defendant to do (or refrain from doing) a particular act, such as transfer title to the property, rather than making a direct determination concerning title. In this way, if the application of Article 24(1) is avoided, party autonomy may at least potentially be reintroduced for such claims. In practice, the English courts (with some support from the CJEU) have relied on this distinction in a number of cases to exercise jurisdiction over disputes relating to foreign immovable property, finding that Article 24(1) (or its predecessor under the Brussels Convention 1968) did not exclude jurisdiction.[58] The CJEU has similarly determined recently that a dispute over the validity of a contract for the gift of land did not concern title to the land, and so was not covered by Article 24(1).[59] This practice may seem an unsatisfactory evasion of Article 24(1), but simply reflects the fact that subject-matter and personal jurisdiction coexist as recognised grounds of jurisdictional authority. The fact that only one court may make orders directly concerning title to the immovable property does at least partially reduce the likelihood of a direct conflict of jurisdictional claims. However, an indirect conflict might arise where, for example, a local court (exercising jurisdiction under Article 24(1)) determines that the legal owner of immovable property retains title, while a foreign court (exercising jurisdiction under, for example, Article 25) determines that the legal owner should sign the documents required to execute a transfer.[60] Such conflicts may, at least in the eyes of the local court, be partially resolved by Article 45(1)(e)(ii), which (as noted above) permits the court to refuse to enforce a judgment from another Member State that has been obtained in breach of Article 24(1). However, another Member State court may well have power in a practical sense over the owner of the property (because, for example, they or their assets are located in the territory of that Member State) and be able to use that to require execution of a transfer, even if the property itself is

---

[58] See e.g. C-294/92 *Webb* v. *Webb* [1994] ECR I-1717; *Ashurst* v. *Pollard* [2000] EWCA Civ 291.

[59] C-417/15 *Schmidt* v. *Schmidt* EU:C:2016:881.

[60] See similarly C-294/92 *Webb* v. *Webb* [1994] ECR I-1717.

beyond their enforcement jurisdiction. In such cases the real question of the hierarchy between Articles 24 and 25 becomes more difficult to determine. There is a risk that a carefully drafted jurisdiction agreement combined with a carefully constructed statement of claim may undermine the intended effect of Article 24(1), even if the court chosen by the parties may not have formal control over the affected land.

A similar problem arises with respect to determining the scope of application of Article 24(2) – here again, the problem is determining when proceedings "have as their object" the relevant subject matter. The CJEU has given guidance on this issue, in a dispute in which a company sought to contest the enforcement of a contract against it on the grounds that the conclusion of the contract was the result of an act by its organs that was invalid because contrary to its statutes.[61] The issue was whether this brought the contractual dispute within what is now Article 24(2), and thus subject to the exclusive jurisdiction of the courts of the seat of the company (Germany), or whether the plaintiff could rely on the exclusive jurisdiction agreement in the contract in favour of the English courts. The CJEU first noted that:

> there is a certain divergence among the various language versions of that provision. According to some of the language versions, the courts where a company or other legal person or an association of natural or legal persons has its seat have exclusive jurisdiction 'in the matter of' the validity of its constitution, its nullity or its dissolution or of the validity of the decisions of its organs. By contrast, other language versions provide for such jurisdiction where proceedings have such a question as their 'object' or 'subject-matter'.[62]

The Court went on to emphasise, however, the "well-established case-law that the various language versions of a text of European Union law must be given a uniform interpretation",[63] and therefore that a purposive approach to interpreting the requirements of Article 22 (the predecessor to what is now Article 24) must be applied, holding that it is an exception to the usual rules on jurisdiction under the Regulation and must therefore be construed narrowly. In particular, the Court noted that:

> a strict interpretation of Article 22(2) which does not go beyond what is required by the objectives pursued by it is particularly necessary because the jurisdiction rule which it lays down is exclusive, so that its application

---

[61] C-144/10 *Berliner Verkehrsbetriebe* EU:C:2011:300.
[62] At [26].
[63] At [28].

would deny the parties to a contract all autonomy to choose another forum.[64]

The Court thus very clearly emphasised the importance of party autonomy in the scheme of the Regulation, as a justification for construing Article 24, a rule which overrides that autonomy, narrowly. This is of particular interest, because Article 24 may be viewed as adopting a policy that is just as strong as that expressed in Article 25, and indeed in hierarchical terms Article 24 is clearly superior to Article 25 because it invalidates contrary exercises of party autonomy. However, the Court considered that the policy of giving effect to party autonomy was so strong that it should justify a narrow interpretation of the hierarchically superior rule.

The Court's analysis concluded by finding that:

> in a dispute of a contractual nature, questions relating to the contract's validity, interpretation or enforceability are at the heart of the dispute and form its subject-matter. Any question concerning the validity of the decision to conclude the contract, taken previously by the organs of one of the companies party to it, must be considered ancillary. While it may form part of the analysis required to be carried out in that regard, it nevertheless does not constitute the sole, or even the principal, subject of the analysis.[65]

English courts have similarly determined that in the context of both Articles 24(2) and (3) the phrase "proceedings which have as their object" should be considered to mean "proceedings which are principally concerned with" the relevant subject matter,[66] or have it as the main subject matter of the dispute.[67] This interpretative approach is also supported by Article 27 of the Brussels I Regulation, which only obliges another court to stay its proceedings if it is seised of a claim "which is principally concerned with a matter over which the courts of another Member State have exclusive jurisdiction by virtue of Article 24". In such cases, however, it is clear that the rule precludes the validity of any jurisdiction agreement to the contrary entered into by the parties.[68] Conversely, a jurisdiction

---

[64] At [32].

[65] At [38].

[66] *Ferrexpo AG* v. *Gilson Investments Ltd* [2012] EWHC 721 (Comm), [144]-[147]. A slightly more nuanced approach is the proposition that if the "real subject-matter" of a dispute is a question of the internal management of a company then it does not matter that the "the main area of live dispute" is the validity of a contract: *Speed Investments Ltd* v. *Formula One Holdings Ltd* [2004] EWCA Civ 1512, [30]; see also *FKI Engineering Ltd* v. *Dewind Holdings Ltd* [2007] EWHC 72 (Comm).

[67] See also *Blue Tropic Ltd* v. *Chkhartishvili* [2014] EWHC 2243 (Ch); *Blomqvist* v. *Zavarco Plc* [2015] EWHC 1898 (Ch).

[68] *Speed Investments Ltd* v. *Formula One Holdings Ltd* [2004] EWCA Civ 1512.

agreement may be effective to cover issues that fall within the scope of Article 24(1), (2), or (3), to the extent that they arise incidentally as part of other proceedings and are not the principal subject matter of the dispute.

In contrast with the general approach set out above, it may be noted that Article 24(4) and its predecessors, dealing with disputes concerning the validity of registrable intellectual property, have been interpreted more strictly. Where a claim is made for breach of such intellectual property rights, and the invalidity of the rights is raised incidentally as a defence in the proceedings, it has been held by the CJEU that Article 24(4) will apply in relation to the issue of validity, precluding the court seised of the infringement claim from resolving this incidental question.[69] The words "irrespective of whether the issue is raised by way of an action or as a defence", which were added in the 2012 Recast (and Lugano Convention 2007), confirm this result. This could potentially provide a greater restriction on party autonomy in relation to intellectual property rights – a choice of court agreement between two parties could potentially be given effect for non-contractual claims (such as claims for breach of IP rights) arising out of the contract, but to the extent that the issue of the validity of the IP rights arose (even incidentally), the agreement would not be effective to confer jurisdiction over that issue on the chosen court. It is not entirely clear why intellectual property rights should justify such increased jurisdictional constraints, including limitations on party autonomy, when compared with (for example) title to land. Article 25(5), however, dealing with enforcement of judgments, has a stronger justification for being interpreted in this restrictive manner, because of the strictly territorial nature of enforcement jurisdiction.

5.4.1.3   'Reflexive Effect' of Exclusive Subject-Matter Jurisdiction

Article 24 establishes that where a dispute has one of the designated subject-matter connections with a Member State, the courts of that state are given exclusive jurisdiction. It is silent, however, on what should

---

[69] C-4/03 *Gesellschaft für Antriebstechnik mbH & Co. KG (GAT)* v. *Luk Lamellen und Kupplungsbau Beteiligungs KG* [2006] ECR I-6509; see similarly *Fort Dodge Animal Health Ltd* v. *Akzo Nobel NV* [1998] FSR 222, CA; *Coin Controls Ltd* v. *Suzo International (UK) Ltd* [1999] Ch 33; *Prudential Assurance Co. Ltd* v. *Prudential Insurance Co. of America* [2003] EWCA Civ 327; *Anan Kasei Co. Ltd* v. *Molycorp Chemicals & Oxides (Europe) Ltd* [2016] EWHC 1722 (Pat).

happen if such a connection exists in relation to a non-Member State. This is another aspect of the *Owusu* v. *Jackson* problem discussed in Section 3.4.2. For present purposes, focusing on the effectiveness of choice of court agreements, the key question is whether the English courts should accept or exercise jurisdiction if there is a jurisdiction agreement in favour of the English courts that satisfies the requirements of Article 25,[70] but the dispute has subject-matter connections with a non-Member State of the kind recognised under Article 24. For example, the dispute may concern title to immovable property located in a non-Member State. There is a strong argument that in this context all the subsections of Article 24 should be given a 'reflexive effect' to override party autonomy under Article 25, perhaps with a degree of discretion.[71] However, it is unclear whether this is what is provided by the Brussels I Regulation, and if anything the 2012 Recast of the Brussels I Regulation has made it more difficult to argue in favour of a reflexive effect approach, for the reasons explained in Section 3.4.2. If the reflexive effect doctrine is rejected and Article 25 jurisdiction is instead viewed as mandatory,[72] this could extend the effectiveness of party autonomy under the Brussels I Regulation. A choice of court agreement in favour of the courts of a Member State could potentially encompass, for example, disputes concerning title to non-Member State immovable property, although it could not encompass disputes concerning title to immovable property located in a Member State. However laudable may be the systemic goals of certainty and predictability for the benefit of the European internal market that led to the decision in *Owusu* v. *Jackson*, such a significant and novel enlargement of party autonomy would seem inappropriately dismissive of non-Member State public interests and the other policy justifications that support the application of Article 24 in relation to Member States. In view of the strong connections between title to property and territorial sovereignty, the rejection of this aspect of the reflexive effect doctrine might even risk being viewed as a violation of public international law.

---

[70] The issue also arises where jurisdiction is based on, for example, Article 4 or Article 7, but in those contexts it does not implicate questions of party autonomy.

[71] See e.g. *Masri* v. *Consolidated Contractors International Company SAL* [2008] EWCA Civ 303, [125]; *Ferrexpo AG* v. *Gilson Investments Ltd & Ors* [2012] EWHC 721 (Comm); but see *Catalyst Investment Group Ltd* v. *Lewinsohn* [2009] EWHC 1964 (Ch), [89].

[72] See e.g. *Equitas Ltd* v. *Allstate Insurance Company* [2008] EWHC 1671, [64]; *Skype Technologies SA* v. *Joltid Ltd* [2009] EWHC 2783 (Ch), [22]; *UBS AG* v. *HSH Nordbank AG* [2009] EWCA Civ 585, [102].

5.4.2   *Common Law*

Rules analogous to exclusive subject-matter jurisdiction that may trump exercises of party autonomy have also long been recognised as part of the common law. The most significant is known as the 'Mozambique rule', named after the decision in *British South Africa Co* v. *Companhia de Moçambique* (1893),[73] under which common law courts will not exercise jurisdiction over a dispute involving foreign immovable property (analogous to Article 24(1) of the Brussels I Regulation) even if there is a choice of court agreement in their favour. A similar doctrine has also (somewhat more controversially) been applied to intellectual property in some cases,[74] principally with regard to the question of the validity of a patent (analogous to Article 24(4) of the Brussels I Regulation)[75] – although some recent case law also suggests doubt on the point.[76] In general, the ambit of the doctrine has tended to be eroded over time, largely because it removes any discretion from the court as to whether it is appropriate to exercise jurisdiction in the particular facts of the case, but also perhaps in part because its effect is to override exercises of party autonomy. It would, for example, mean that a choice of court agreement in a complex contract including a transfer of land (or a patent) might be ineffective in respect of questions arising concerning title to the land (or patent), but effective for other questions, splitting the proceedings.

The Mozambique rule has traditionally been described as a rule of 'non-justiciability' – the argument being that the courts are incapable of resolving disputes involving title to foreign immovable property, or that it would be futile for them to do so. If this is indeed the correct characterisation of the rule, then it would clearly override any jurisdiction agreement entered into by the parties. It is, however, doubtful whether this characterisation is desirable – arguably, it reflects the peculiar facts of the Mozambique case itself, in which the dispute presented was in reality a question of territorial delimitation between the colonial interests of the United Kingdom and Portugal rather than a private property dispute, and so was non-justiciable

---

[73] *British South Africa Co* v. *Companhia de Moçambique* [1893] AC 602. See further Cheshire, North and Fawcett (2017), p.484ff.

[74] *Potter* v. *Broken Hill Pty Co. Ltd* (1906) 3 CLR 479 (Australia). In *Lucasfilm* v. *Ainsworth* [2011] UKSC 39 the application of the rule to registrable intellectual property was assumed by the parties, and tentatively accepted by the Supreme Court (at [107]), but its application to copyright was rejected (overruling *Tyburn Productions* v. *Conan Doyle* [1991] Ch 75). See further Cheshire, North and Fawcett (2017), p.494ff.

[75] See e.g. *Chugai Pharmaceutical Co. Ltd* v. *UCB Pharma SA* [2017] EWHC 1216 (Pat).

[76] *Regie Nationale des Usines Renault SA* v. *Zhang* (2002) 210 CLR 491, [76].

because it was a matter of public international law.[77] The better view is that the Mozambique rule is simply a rule of exclusive foreign jurisdiction, which common law courts recognise as trumping other rules of jurisdiction, including (at least ordinarily) jurisdiction agreements in their favour. This reflects the fact that the origins of the doctrine lie in part in a traditional distinction drawn in the common law between local and transitory actions, as discussed in Section 2.2.1, with local actions (such as those for title to land) only permitted at the location of the property, while transitory actions could alternatively be commenced at the location of the defendant. While this was a rule developed for the allocation of jurisdiction to different courts within England (in this respect it was abolished by the Judicature Act 1873), in practice it lead to the consequence that English courts could not hear disputes concerning title to foreign immovable property, because no English court was local to the property. The decision in *British South Africa Co* v. *Companhia de Moçambique* (1893)[78] can be viewed as simply confirming that this rule of jurisdiction survived the changes introduced by the Judicature Act 1873. The characterisation of the Mozambique rule as a rule of jurisdiction (not non-justiciability) is also supported by the fact that the rule has actually been abolished in some common law jurisdictions, such as New South Wales,[79] where the point is instead considered as a powerful factor in the exercise of the *forum conveniens* and *forum non conveniens* discretions. It is therefore possible that an exclusive jurisdiction agreement entered into in favour of the courts of New South Wales will be effective, despite the fact that the subject matter of the dispute concerns title to foreign immovable property – one effect of the abolition of the Mozambique rule is therefore the strengthening of party autonomy. The English courts have exercised jurisdiction based on an English jurisdiction agreement over a dispute concerning the scope of a foreign patent, requiring the application of foreign patent law.[80] This suggests that, at least in such cases (where validity was not directly in issue), any deference to foreign courts should not be viewed as a matter of non-justiciability, but merely as a connecting factor in the exercise of jurisdictional discretion, which may be overridden by concerns of giving effect to party autonomy.

---

[77] On which see generally *Belhaj* v. *Straw* [2017] UKSC 3.
[78] [1893] AC 602.
[79] Jurisdiction of Courts (Foreign Land) Act 1989 (NSW).
[80] *Celltech Chiroscience Ltd* v. *Medimmune Inc.* [2002] EWHC 2167 (Patents) and [2003] EWCA Civ 1008.

Common law courts have also long taken the view that where a dispute concerns local immovable property, jurisdiction should almost always be exercised – this may be considered the converse of the Mozambique rule, conferring something like 'exclusive' jurisdiction on the courts of the location of the property.[81] This aspect of the rule has been less clearly articulated, because it is given effect through the exercise of the *forum conveniens* and *forum non conveniens* discretions: the courts will give permission to commence proceedings or refuse to stay proceedings where the dispute concerns title to land located in the forum, in part because no foreign court will be likely to take jurisdiction. In England, this rule has been rendered largely redundant, because if a dispute concerns title to land in England the question of jurisdiction is covered by Article 24 of the Brussels I Regulation (and will thus clearly override any jurisdiction agreement to the contrary), but it still applies in other common law jurisdictions. It is sometimes contended that a similar rule applies for disputes concerning the internal management of a company (analogous to Article 24(2) of the Brussels I Regulation) or title to intellectual property (analogous to Article 24(4) of the Brussels I Regulation); most such cases in England will similarly now be covered by the Brussels I Regulation (and will clearly in such cases override jurisdiction agreements). In other common law jurisdictions the subject matter of such disputes is probably best analysed as a very strong connecting factor in the exercise of jurisdictional discretion. It has been considered, for example, that such connecting factors may support the claim that an anti-suit injunction should be awarded to support this basis of 'exclusive' jurisdiction, although this ground for an anti-suit injunction is not well developed.[82] If such a basis of 'exclusive' jurisdiction exists in favour of a common law court, it is unclear how it may interact with an exclusive choice of court agreement in favour of a different foreign court, particularly if that foreign court would not apply the Mozambique rule (and would thus hear the case). For example, if a dispute concerned title to land in New Zealand, but the parties had entered into an exclusive jurisdiction agreement in favour of the courts of New South Wales (in which jurisdiction the Mozambique doctrine will not be applied), it is unclear whether the jurisdiction agreement or the rule of 'exclusive' jurisdiction will be given priority in either court.

---

[81] See e.g. *Agnew* v. *Usher* (1884) 14 QBD 78; *Pakistan* v. *Zardari* [2006] EWHC 2411 (Comm), [171].

[82] But see, by analogy, *Samengo-Turner* v. *J&H Marsh & McLennan (Services) Ltd* [2007] EWCA Civ 723, discussed in Section 5.5.

The justification for each of these special rules of jurisdiction and their overriding effect on choice of court agreements is evident – party autonomy is viewed as inappropriate or inapplicable in the context of immovable property (and perhaps similarly certain registered intellectual property rights) because of the special connection or interest that the state has in the question of title to land. The usual justifications for party autonomy are overridden by the public interests requiring courts to exercise exclusive control over local property, and choice of court agreements are thus ineffective in this context. The exact contours of the doctrine remain, however, somewhat uncertain.

5.4.3   United States

As discussed in Section 2.2.1 and immediately above, the origins of the common law Mozambique doctrine lie in part in a traditional distinction drawn between local and transitory actions. This distinction was accepted as part of the common law in the United States in the famous case of *Livingston* v. *Jefferson* (1811),[83] in which former President Thomas Jefferson avoided suit in Virginia, for trespass to land in Louisiana, by relying on the doctrine. At the time, Louisiana did not permit lawsuits against absent defendants, and so the effect of the doctrine was that no proceedings could be brought against Jefferson unless he physically visited Louisiana territory, which he was careful not to do. While elsewhere in the common law world this distinction has generally disappeared (as for example under the Judicature Act 1873 (UK), discussed above), it has remained part of the law in most jurisdictions in the United States[84] and has been recognised numerous times by the Supreme Court,[85] although in a minority of US states it has been narrowed or abolished (at least in intra-US disputes).[86] In proceedings in a federal court exercising diversity jurisdiction, it is contentious whether on this question the court should apply

---

[83]   15 F.Cas. 660 (CCDVa. 1811). See further discussion in Section 2.2.1.

[84]   See generally e.g. *Trust Company Bank* v. *United States Gypsum Co.*, 950 F.2d 1144 (5th Cir. 1992); *Eldee-K Rental Properties, LLC* v. *DirecTV, Inc.*, 748 F.3d 943 (9th Cir. 2014).

[85]   See e.g. *Louisville & Nashville RR* v. *Western Union Telegraph Co.*, 234 US 369, 372 (1914); *Ellenwood* v. *Marietta Chair Co.*, 158 US 105, 107 (1895); *Greeley* v. *Lowe*, 155 US 58 (1894); *Huntington* v. *Attrill*, 146 US 657, 669–70 (1892); *Casey* v. *Adams*, 102 US 66 (1880); *McKenna* v. *Fisk*, 42 US 241 (1843).

[86]   See e.g. *Reasor-Hill Corp.* v. *Harrison*, 249 S.W.2d 994, 995–6 (1952); *St. Louis Smelting & Refining Co* v. *Hoban*, 209 S.W.2d 119, 123–4 (1948); *Little* v. *Chicago Etc Ry Co.*, 67 NW 846 (1896); *Archibald* v. *Mississippi & TR Co.*, 6 So. 238, 238–9 (1889); *Holmes* v. *Barclay*, 4 La.Ann. 63 (1849). See generally e.g. Weintraub (2008), p.305ff.

the law of the state in which the federal court is sitting[87] (in accordance with the general doctrine applicable to substantive common law questions established in *Erie Railroad Co.* v. *Tompkins* (1938)),[88] or whether federal procedural law governs. Federal law now provides that the doctrine has been abolished with regard to venue,[89] but it is unclear whether this actually affects questions of jurisdiction.[90]

In those jurisdictions in which the doctrine has not been abolished, its effect is to require that certain claims, such as those directly concerning title to real property, must be brought in the courts of the state in which the property is located. Personal actions such as claims under a contract that relate to immovable property are, however, likely to be classified as transitory. Actions in bankruptcy have also been excluded from the doctrine by statute.[91] Where a state has jurisdiction under the local action doctrine, jurisdictional 'long arm' statutes now generally permit proceedings to be brought against absent defendants, to ensure that the court may hear the case even if the defendant is not present in its territory.

It might be expected that the impact of the local action doctrine on party autonomy would be similar to the common law rules discussed above – that disputes concerning title to immovable property could only be heard exclusively in the courts of the location of the property, irrespective of any jurisdiction agreement between the parties. It is, however, unclear whether the requirements of the local action doctrine can be affected by a jurisdiction agreement. In some cases the courts have held that "The local action doctrine is best characterized as a rule of convenience which, like personal jurisdiction and venue, can be waived",[92] suggesting that a choice of court clause would be capable of overriding the usual rule. In other cases, however, the courts have held that if a claim falls under the local

---

[87] See e.g. *Trust Company Bank* v. *United States Gypsum Co.*, 950 F2d 1144 (5th Cir. 1992), reluctantly applying state law; *Bailey* v. *Shell Western E&P, Inc.*, 609 F.3d 710, 721 n.4 (5th Cir. 2010); *Eldee-K Rental Properties, LLC* v. *DirecTV, Inc.*, 748 F.3d 943 (9th Cir. 2014).

[88] 304 US 64 (1938).

[89] 28 US Code s.1391(a)(2): "the proper venue for a civil action shall be determined without regard to whether the action is local or transitory in nature".

[90] See e.g. *Eldee-K Rental Properties, LLC* v. *DirecTV, Inc.*, 748 F.3d 943 (9th Cir. 2014) (determining that the doctrine still applies to questions of federal subject-matter jurisdiction, and noting that "circuit courts generally agree that the local action doctrine is jurisdictional in nature, and not merely a rule of venue that can be waived").

[91] See e.g. *Kismet Acquisition, LLC* v. *Icenhower (In re Icenhower)*, 757 F.3d 1044 (9th Cir. 2014) (also refusing to give effect to a jurisdiction agreement in favour of the courts of Mexico, the place of the property).

[92] *Hallaba* v. *WorldCom Network Services*, 196 FRD 630, 648 (N.D.Okla. 2000).

action doctrine, it will override a jurisdiction agreement.[93] In those jurisdictions that do not apply the local action doctrine, the fact that a dispute
concerns title to foreign land will not prohibit the exercise of jurisdiction,
although it is likely to be given significant weight as a factor in the exercise of jurisdictional discretion. In such cases, it may be outweighed by a
choice of court clause, and may thus (depending on the facts) not serve as
a constraint on party autonomy.

Outside of the context of land, there is limited support for the existence of
other categories of overriding exclusive jurisdiction. To the contrary, there is,
for example, Supreme Court authority for the proposition that "There is no
rule of law ... which requires dismissal of a suitor from the forum on a mere
showing that the trial will involve issues which relate to the internal affairs
of a foreign corporation".[94] The court also noted, however, that "the ultimate
inquiry is where trial will best serve the convenience of the parties and the
ends of justice",[95] suggesting that this consideration has been subsumed as
part of the *forum non conveniens* discretion, similar to the way disputes concerning title to land are dealt with in jurisdictions in which the local action
doctrine has been abolished. Where proceedings concern matters internal
to a corporation, and this requires examination of difficult legal issues under
the law of incorporation, or inspection of documents located in the place
of incorporation, these factors would therefore point towards a refusal to
enforce a local forum selection agreement, and thus as limitations on party
autonomy. In general, US courts have recognised that disputes concerning
foreign registered intellectual property should be heard in the foreign court
of the place of registration.[96] This is given effect through the refusal to exercise discretionary jurisdiction, or through *forum non conveniens*. Where
there is a contrary exclusive jurisdiction agreement, it is possible that the
court may prefer to give effect to the agreement between the parties, giving
priority to party autonomy over the rule of (quasi-exclusive) subject-matter
jurisdiction.[97] Conversely, US courts have sometimes declined to hear cases
concerning US intellectual property, because of an exclusive choice of court
agreement in favour of a foreign court, although this appears to be limited to
cases concerning infringement (rather than validity) of the rights.[98]

---

[93] See e.g. *Incline Energy* v. *Weiner*, Case No.15-cv-03411-WHO (USDC, N.D.Cal.), Order
denying motion to dismiss, 20 November 2015.

[94] *Koster* v. *Lumbermens Mutual Casualty Co.*, 330 US 518, 527 (1947).

[95] Ibid.

[96] *Voda* v. *Cordis Corp*, 476 F.3d 887 (Fed. Cir. 2007).

[97] See e.g. *Fairchild Semiconductor* v. *Third Dimension*, 589 F.Supp.2d 84, 85 (D. Me. 2008).

[98] *Warner Swasey Co* v. *Salvagnini Transferica SpA*, 806 F.2d 1045 (Fed. Cir. 1986), affirming
633 F.Supp. 1209 (WDNY 1986).

5.4.4 Hague Convention on Choice of Court Agreements 2005

The Hague Convention on Choice of Court Agreements 2005 is a special-ised convention dealing only with the effect of jurisdiction agreements, which means it does not set out other rules of 'exclusive' subject matter jurisdiction that might directly override party autonomy. However, it leaves open the possibility for such rules to function through the exclu-sions from its scope. The Hague Convention Explanatory Report notes, in relation to these exclusions, that:

> There are various reasons why the matters referred to in Article 2(2) are excluded. In some cases, the public interest, or that of third parties, is involved, so that the parties may not have the right to dispose of the mat-ter between themselves. In such cases, a particular court will often have exclusive jurisdiction that cannot be ousted by means of a choice of court agreement.[99]

The exclusions therefore reflect likely limitations on the scope of party autonomy in choice of forum, although they are permissive rather than obligatory – they do not mandate that such limitations must be applied by Convention states. A number of the exclusions cover categories of dis-putes that are widely viewed as coming within exclusive subject-matter jurisdiction rules. For example, the Convention excludes "rights in rem in immovable property, and tenancies of immovable property",[100] "the validity, nullity, or dissolution of legal persons, and the validity of deci-sions of their organs",[101] "the validity of intellectual property rights other than copyright and related rights",[102] and "the validity of entries in pub-lic registers",[103] all reflecting grounds of exclusive jurisdiction recognised under the Brussels I Regulation. As discussed above, disputes concern-ing breach of intellectual property rights (as opposed to their validity) are generally not considered to fall within the scope of exclusive jurisdiction rules (as for example under Article 24(4) of the Brussels I Regulation). The Convention potentially supports a slightly distinct rule on this point, providing that it excludes "infringement of intellectual property rights other than copyright and related rights, except where infringement pro-ceedings are brought for breach of a contract between the parties relating

---

[99] At [53].
[100] Article 2(2)(l).
[101] Article 2(2)(m).
[102] Article 2(2)(n).
[103] Article 2(2)(p).

to such rights, or could have been brought for breach of that contract".[104]
This at least leaves open the possibility that states who are parties to the
Convention might view certain infringement proceedings as being matters so closely connected to a single member state (presumably the state of
registration) as to be subject to the exclusive jurisdiction of that state, and
in any case not to be potentially subject to a choice of forum agreement.

Also notably excluded from the scope of the Convention are "claims for
personal injury brought by or on behalf of natural persons"[105] and "tort
or delict claims for damage to tangible property that do not arise from
a contractual relationship".[106] In these cases it appears that the exclusion
is not necessarily justified because it is considered that another forum
would have exclusive jurisdiction, but rather because these are matters on
which states may wish to impose restrictions on party choice of forum.[107]
A final notable exclusion from the Convention is "anti-trust (competition)
matters",[108] which are probably excluded because states take different views
on whether such claims are matters of private law that might properly be
subject to a choice of forum by the parties or whether they engage public
interests such that proceedings should only take place in the courts whose
competition law is applicable.

In relation to all these exclusions, the Convention provides that:

> Notwithstanding paragraph 2, proceedings are not excluded from the scope
> of this Convention where a matter excluded under that paragraph arises
> merely as a preliminary question and not as an object of the proceedings. In
> particular, the mere fact that a matter excluded under paragraph 2 arises by
> way of defence does not exclude proceedings from the Convention, if that
> matter is not an object of the proceedings.

The effect of this is that the exclusions are likely to be viewed as relatively
narrowly defined, and it is possible that they may be defeated through
careful drafting of a statement of claim so that the excluded issues are not
presented as the object of the proceedings. The approach to these matters under the Convention is therefore likely to resemble fairly closely
the jurisprudence that has emerged relating to Article 25 of the Brussels
I Regulation (and its predecessor provisions), which also construe these

---

[104] Article 2(2)(o).
[105] Article 2(2)(j).
[106] Article 2(2)(k).
[107] See generally Chapter 4.
[108] Article 2(2)(h).

provisions relatively narrowly, in part to preserve the domain of party autonomy and give maximum effect to choice of court agreements. One exception, however, is where the validity of registrable IP rights arises incidentally in proceedings brought for breach of contract. As examined above, Article 25(4) has been held to preclude consideration of validity in any court other than the court of registration, while the Convention suggests that a jurisdiction agreement may be effective in these circumstances.

5.5   Special Jurisdictional Regimes

Further possible restrictions on the exercise of party autonomy in the context of choice of court agreements may arise under special jurisdictional regimes that apply based on the types of parties or disputes involved. The restriction here is not based on the claim that another court should have exclusive subject matter jurisdiction, but rather that giving effect to a choice of court agreement would not necessarily be appropriate because of the inequality of bargaining power between the parties. This typically means greater restrictions on party autonomy or greater scrutiny of choice of court agreements rather than a blanket prohibition on their effectiveness. The best known examples of these types of restrictions come from insurance, consumer, and employment law.[109]

In part these protections are motivated by the question of forum itself (for example, ensuring a consumer has access to their local court), but as discussed further below and in Section 9.4.1 they are also sometimes motivated by concerns about the applicable law. If a state wishes to protect consumer rights, it may do so through a statutory mandatory rule preventing (or limited the effect of) a choice of foreign law, but if the consumer is subject to an effective foreign choice of court agreement, the mandatory rule is unlikely to be applicable. Courts have thus frequently taken the view that a restriction on choice of forum may also be necessary to ensure substantive protection of weaker parties or the effectiveness of other similar provisions of domestic law.[110] Such restrictions should only apply, however, where the protection is considered to possess an internationally mandatory character, otherwise

---

[109] For consumer restrictions in China, see Supreme People's Court 'Interpretation of Civil Procedure Law' Zhu Shi [2015] No. 5, Art.31.

[110] See e.g. *Mitsubishi Motors Corp* v. *Soler Chrysler-Plymouth, Inc.*, 473 US 614, 637 n.19 (1985) ("in the event the choice-of-forum and choice-of-law clauses operated in tandem as a prospective waiver of a party's right to pursue statutory remedies for antitrust violations, we would have little hesitation in condemning the agreement as against public policy"). See further discussion in Basedow (2013b) and in Section 9.4.1.

invalidating a choice of foreign court to ensure the application of local law would excessively undermine party autonomy.[111]

5.5.1   EU Law (Brussels I Regulation)

The Brussels I Regulation includes three specialised sets of jurisdictional rules, designed to protect parties who are assumed to be in a weaker negotiating position, for three distinct types of claims – those relating to insurance, consumers and employees (respectively, in Sections 3, 4, and 5 of Chapter II of the Regulation). The rules set out for each of these types of claims override the general rules on jurisdiction, and thus potentially impose further restrictions on the application of party autonomy through Article 25.[112] (It is notable, however, that they do not serve as restrictions on submission to a forum under Article 26.)[113] As a consequence, weaker parties are also not subject to the modified *lis pendens* rules that reinforce party autonomy set out in Article 31 of the Regulation, as discussed in Section 3.4.2 – this is expressly provided for in Article 31(4). A jurisdiction agreement that is invalid because of Sections 3, 4, and 5 of Chapter II of the Regulation cannot thus be relied on to give primacy to the (invalidly) chosen court in the case of parallel proceedings. In addition to these constraints, a further indirect protection is offered in Article 45(1)(e)(i) of the Regulation, which allows the courts of one Member State to refuse enforcement of a judgment given by the courts of another Member State where the judgment conflicts with "Sections 3, 4 or 5 of Chapter II where the policyholder, the insured, a beneficiary of the insurance contract, the injured party, the consumer or the employee was the defendant". The effect of this rule is to allow the enforcing court to review whether the judgment court was in compliance with the protective rules in favour of the weaker party. As this function should already be carried out by the judgment court, it essentially means a double-checking of the protections offered to the weaker party, including in respect of the constraints on party autonomy. Each of these categories of weaker parties is examined in turn below. It should also be noted that there is a further source of potential EU law restrictions on choice of court agreements, derived from EU mandatory rules. This is discussed in the context of the common law below,

---

[111] See e.g. *Monster Cable*, Cour de Cassation (France), 07-15.823, Case No 1003 of 22 October 2008; *Richards* v. *Lloyd's of London*, 135 F.3d 1289 (9th Cir. 1998); *Rodriguez de Quijas* v. *Shearson/American Express, Inc.*, 490 US 477 (1989).

[112] See Article 25(4).

[113] See C-111/09 *Vienna Insurance Group* v. *Bilas* EU:C:2010:290, and now Article 26(2). See also Section 1.3.2.

because it is closely related to a technique traditionally applied by common law courts, but it is equally applicable in any EU Member State. It is also discussed further in Section 9.4.1, in the context of mandatory rules and choice of law.

5.5.1.1   Insurance (Articles 10–16)

General Rules   Article 10 of the Brussels I Regulation provides that jurisdiction over matters relating to insurance is determined by the specialised rules in Section 3 of Chapter II (Articles 10–16) rather than the general rules, without prejudice only to Article 6 (the application of national jurisdictional rules in respect of non-EU domiciled defendants) and Article 7(5) (the ability to sue a branch office in the location of the branch in respect of a claim arising out of its operations). Articles 11–13 set out various locations in which an insurer domiciled in a Member State may be sued – principally (but subject to various exceptions) in their place of domicile, or in the place of the harmful event, or if they are being sued by the policyholder, the insured or a beneficiary, in the domicile of the claimant. Article 14 provides that an insurer may (subject to limited exceptions) only sue a defendant (who might be the policyholder, the insured or a beneficiary) in the courts of the defendant's domicile. The effect of these rules is to preclude the usual application of Article 25, and thus generally to invalidate jurisdiction agreements, both in terms of prorogation (the English courts may not exercise jurisdiction in claims brought against a French insurance policyholder even if the insurance contract has an English exclusive jurisdiction agreement) and derogation (the English courts may exercise jurisdiction in claims brought by an English insurance policyholder even if the insurance contract has a French exclusive jurisdiction agreement).

Article 15, however, partially reintroduces the possibility of party autonomy, by providing for various limited ways in which the jurisdictional rules in Section 3 may be departed from by agreement.[114] The five circumstances in which an agreement is permissible are set out as follows:

> The provisions of this Section may be departed from only by an agreement:
>
> (1) which is entered into after the dispute has arisen;
> (2) which allows the policyholder, the insured or a beneficiary to bring proceedings in courts other than those indicated in this Section;
> (3) which is concluded between a policyholder and an insurer, both of whom are at the time of conclusion of the contract domiciled or habitually resident in the same Member State, and which has the effect of

---

[114] See Hartley (2013b), p.240ff.

conferring jurisdiction on the courts of that Member State even if the
harmful event were to occur abroad, provided that such an agreement
is not contrary to the law of that Member State;

(4)   which is concluded with a policyholder who is not domiciled in a
      Member State, except in so far as the insurance is compulsory or relates
      to immovable property in a Member State; or

(5)   which relates to a contract of insurance in so far as it covers one or
      more of the risks set out in Article 16.

The first of these permits only retrospective exercises of party autonomy.
In practice these are unlikely to be common, as if there are multiple potential venues for litigation, each will potentially favour one of the parties,
and thus it is unlikely that they would reach agreement giving jurisdiction exclusively to a different forum. Given that the restrictions on party
autonomy are generally motivated by the concern that the insured is a
weaker party, it must be queried whether these concerns do not continue
even for agreements after the dispute has arisen. One possible explanation for the rule would be that party autonomy is only restricted because
of doubts over the ability of the weaker party to foresee the disputes that
may arise – concerns that would evidently be addressed once a dispute
has in fact arisen. Foreseeability concerns alone do not, however, seem a
persuasive account of the reasons for protecting weaker parties in insurance contracts.[115] The second category permits a non-exclusive jurisdiction agreement for the benefit of the policyholder, insured or beneficiary,
allowing them to bring suit in an additional court (which might also be in
a non-Member State),[116] although again if these provisions are based on
the assumption that insurers are the dominant parties in negotiations such
unilateral concessions by insurers are unlikely to be common. The third
permits the conferral of jurisdiction on the court of common domicile
or habitual residence of the parties, although is unlikely to be commonly
applied in practice because such a court would ordinarily have jurisdiction pursuant to Articles 11 and 14 of the Regulation, unless the domicile
or habitual residence of the parties changes between the time the contract
is entered into and the dispute arises. The fourth permits party autonomy
in relation to non-EU domiciled policyholders, except in limited circumstances (discussed further below), which somewhat curiously excludes
them from the protection of weaker parties envisaged by the Regulation.

---

[115] Compare e.g. C-269/95 *Benincasa* v. *Dentalkit* [1997] ECR I-3767, [17] (the consumer
protection provisions are simply designed to protect "the weaker party economically").
See Sections 2.4.1 and 2.4.2.

[116] By analogy with C-154/11 *Mahamdia* v. *People's Democratic Republic of Algeria*
EU:C:2012:491.

Finally, the fifth covers narrowly defined categories of risk as set out in Article 16, including (essentially) loss of or damage to or caused by ships or aircraft, or goods in transit by ship or aircraft. It was considered that parties insuring such risks are unlikely to need special protection through restraints on their jurisdictional autonomy. The key point to note is that these provisions, which reintroduce the possibility of choice of court agreements for insurance contracts, are in fact very narrowly defined and unlikely to apply in the vast majority of cases. Although Article 15 does not state this, it has been held that for an agreement to satisfy Article 15 it should also be required to satisfy the formal criteria set out in Article 25,[117] discussed in Section 5.2.1. As noted in Section 5.2.1.2, it is, however, less clear whether this should be the case, or indeed what the effect will be in general, if the parties enter into an exclusive jurisdiction agreement in favour of a non-Member State court.

These rules generally appear to contemplate applying only to insurers domiciled (or deemed to be domiciled)[118] in a Member State.[119] This leaves unclear the scenario where an EU Member State domiciled party purchases insurance from a non-EU domiciled party; for example, where a French party purchases insurance from a New York company, subject to an exclusive New York jurisdiction agreement, but then sues in France. Although the drafting is not entirely clear,[120] the better view is probably that in this situation the rules in the Regulation do not apply, as they do not specify when proceedings may be brought against non-EU domiciled insurers, and Article 25 (operating to reflexive effect) should not be relied on as a fallback in this situation (even though it does apply regardless of the domicile of the parties).[121] This would leave the question to be covered by French national law, pursuant to the acknowledgment in Article 10 that it is "without prejudice to Article 6". A more difficult situation might arise if the exclusive jurisdiction agreement were in favour of the English

---

[117] Case 201/82 *Gerling Konzern Speziale Kreditversicherungs-AG* v. *Italian Treasury Administration* [1983] ECR 2503 (but holding that this condition only needs to be met between the insurer and the policyholder, as there does not need to be a contractual relationship between the insurer and the insured or beneficiary).

[118] Article 11(2).

[119] Article 11(1).

[120] Some uncertainty arises because Article 11 is limited to "an insurer domiciled in a Member State", but Article 14(1) only uses the expression "an insurer". In this scenario, however, the proceedings would be brought by the French policyholder, so Article 11 would be the only potentially relevant article.

[121] However, the fact that Article 10 omits to mention Article 25 does not definitively establish that this article is inapplicable, because Article 10 also omits to mention Article 26 which clearly operates as an exception pursuant to Article 26(2).

courts. If proceedings were brought by the New York party in England, it is possible that Article 14(1), permitting suit by "an insurer"[122] only in the policyholder's domicile, would be viewed as applicable and prevent application of Article 25. On the other hand, if the French party commenced proceedings in France, Article 14(1) would not be applicable, but nor would Article 11(1) as it only applies to claims against insurers domiciled in an EU Member State. The better approach may well be again that this situation is left to national law (in both England and France under this example), as it is not dealt with (satisfactorily) under the Regulation.

The rules also generally appear to apply only to insurance policyholders, insured parties or beneficiaries domiciled in a Member State.[123] An exception is, however, provided in Article 15(4), which covers an agreement concluded with a policyholder who is not domiciled in a Member State. Unless the insurance "is compulsory or relates to immovable property in a Member State",[124] the restrictions on party autonomy under Article 15 are expressly not applicable. Thus, the non-EU Member State domiciled policyholder can potentially agree to the exclusive jurisdiction of the courts of the Member State in which the insurance company has its domicile, allowing the EU domiciled insurer to sue in its home court. The fact that party autonomy is not apparently restricted in this context perhaps suggests the strength of the doctrine in EU law, although it may also merely reflect a favouring of the interests of EU insurers over their non-EU customers.[125] If the restrictions on party autonomy are genuinely motivated by concerns that it will not be properly exercised in contracts involving weaker parties, then it is difficult to see why they should not be applied to non-EU Member State domiciled weaker parties. Although a range of reasons may be offered for giving effect to party autonomy, as explored in Chapter 2, they all require that the choice made by the parties be a genuine agreement.[126]

Non-Contractual Claims   Article 10 of the Regulation states that the special rules in Section 3 apply to "matters relating to insurance". As no part of Section 3 expressly limits its application to claims *under* an insurance contract, it is at least arguable that this might extend beyond contractual claims, to non-contractual claims *relating to* insurance. Section 3 of the

---

[122] Not "an insurer domiciled in a Member State", as per Article 11, although it is not clear if the difference in language is significant.

[123] Article 14(1).

[124] Article 15(4).

[125] See further discussion in Mills (2016a).

[126] See in particular Section 2.4.1.

Regulation therefore appears to apply not just to contractual claims, but also to insurance-related non-contractual claims. Whether party autonomy is given effect for those non-contractual claims would thus depend on Article 15. The terms of Article 15 are, however, themselves silent on whether the limited party autonomy they allow for applies to both contractual and non-contractual claims – although Article 15 is expressed in broad enough terms to cover both, as it simply allows (in limited circumstances) the provisions of Section 3 to be departed from "by an agreement".

Two types of non-contractual claims should be distinguished here. First, those that engage the same policy concerns which justify the special protection provided for assumed weaker parties under the rules. For example, an insurance company that acted in such a way as to frustrate the entitlements of a beneficiary under an insurance policy might be subject to a claim for tortious interference with the insurance contract. Second, those that do not engage those policy concerns. For example, where there is a dispute over whether an insurance company has effectively assigned their rights under an insurance contract to another insurance company, which might give rise to a proprietary claim concerning ownership of those contractual rights.

The policy underlying the special restrictions on party autonomy provided for under the special regime applicable to insurance suggests that Section 3 (and thus the restrictions on party autonomy in Article 15) should apply to the first type of claim (which might otherwise, as discussed in Chapter 4, be affected by a choice of court agreement), but not to the second. To put this more generally, while Section 3 might apply to non-contractual disputes relating to insurance, it should be limited to disputes that replicate the inequality between parties which justifies the limitations on party autonomy under Article 15. A beneficiary under an insurance contract should not lose the benefit of their special protection because they are required or even choose to bring their claim in a non-contractual form. Thus, a jurisdiction agreement under an insurance contract that purported to give a court exclusive jurisdiction over both contractual and non-contractual claims should be as ineffective with respect to the non-contractual claims as it is with respect to the contractual claims, in accordance with Article 15.

Equally, the better view is that Section 3 should not apply to non-contractual claims that do not replicate such an inequality between parties. Whether this is in fact what is provided for by Section 3 of the Regulation is, however, somewhat unclear. The restrictions on party autonomy under

Article 15 do not themselves limit their application to claims between stronger and weaker parties, and the fact that Article 11(1)(b) is specifically limited to claims brought by the policyholder, the insured or a beneficiary appears to suggest that the other sections of Article 11 are not subject to this limitation. If a dispute between insurance companies over an assignment of rights under an insurance contract fell within Section 3, an exclusive jurisdiction agreement in the contract of assignment that designated a particular forum for both contractual and non-contractual claims arising under the contract could be ineffective. There seems little justification for such a rule, and the term "matters relating to insurance" should therefore be construed narrowly to exclude disputes (contractual or non-contractual) in which there is no inequality of bargaining power. The limits of party autonomy for such disputes should therefore be governed by the general rule set out in Article 25, as examined in Chapters 3 and 4.

5.5.1.2   Consumer Contracts (Articles 17–19)

Section 4 of Chapter II of the Brussels I Regulation (Articles 17–19) applies to "matters relating to a contract concluded by a person, the consumer, for a purpose which can be regarded as being outside his trade or profession", subject to certain conditions. As with insurance contracts, this is without prejudice only to Article 6 (the application of national jurisdictional rules in respect of non-EU domiciled defendants) and Article 7(5) (the ability to sue a branch office in the location of the branch in respect of a claim arising out of its operations). Article 18 provides the basic rules on jurisdiction, which are essentially that a consumer may sue the other party to a contract either in the courts of the other party's domicile, or in the courts of the consumer's own domicile (even if the other party is not domiciled in any EU Member State),[127] while a consumer may only be sued themselves in matters relating to a consumer contract in the courts of their own domicile[128] (a rule that appears to extend to claims brought by non-EU parties against EU Member State domiciled consumers).[129] One general effect of these rules is to preclude the effectiveness of jurisdiction agreements, both in terms of prorogation (the English courts may not exercise jurisdiction in claims brought against a French consumer even if the consumer contract has an English

---

[127] Article 18(1).

[128] Article 18(2).

[129] This comes from a combination of Article 18(1), which contemplates that the rules cover contracts between an EU Member State domiciled consumer and a non-EU Member State party, and Article 18(2).

exclusive jurisdiction agreement) and derogation (the English courts may exercise jurisdiction in claims brought by an English consumer even if the consumer contract has a French exclusive jurisdiction agreement). A limited possibility for party autonomy is, however, reintroduced through Article 19 of the Regulation,[130] which provides as follows:

> The provisions of this Section may be departed from only by an agreement:
>
> (1) which is entered into after the dispute has arisen;
> (2) which allows the consumer to bring proceedings in courts other than those indicated in this Section; or
> (3) which is entered into by the consumer and the other party to the contract, both of whom are at the time of conclusion of the contract domiciled or habitually resident in the same Member State, and which confers jurisdiction on the courts of that Member State, provided that such an agreement is not contrary to the law of that Member State.

These are very similar to the first three situations in which choice of court agreements are permitted for insurance contracts, and the analysis set out above in that context applies similarly here. The first two of these categories of agreements are unlikely in practice to arise, and the second is in any case limited to non-exclusive jurisdiction agreements for the benefit of the consumer. The first category also assumes dubiously that the weakness of consumers in negotiations (which ordinarily justifies limiting party autonomy) would not be replicated in any agreement reached after a dispute has arisen, and perhaps suggests instead (again dubiously) that party autonomy is only restricted for reasons of foreseeability. Similarly to the case with the rules governing insurance contracts discussed above, although Article 19 does not state this, it can safely be presumed that for an agreement to satisfy Article 19 it should also be required to satisfy the formal criteria set out in Article 25, as discussed in Section 5.2.1.

The fact that these rules apply to proceedings brought by a consumer regardless of the domicile of the defendant means that they extend these jurisdictional protections to EU domiciled consumers contracting with non-EU domiciled commercial parties. An English consumer who purchases goods from a Californian party under a contract that gives exclusive jurisdiction to the courts of California will not therefore be bound by the jurisdiction agreement, and may sue in England. If the consumer is sued in California, the English courts might even award an anti-suit injunction to restrain the proceedings.[131] A Californian judgment obtained against the

---

[130] See generally Hartley (2013b), Chapter 13.
[131] By analogy with *Samengo-Turner* v. *J&H Marsh & McLennan (Services) Ltd* [2007] EWCA Civ 723 (in relation to employment contracts, discussed below).

English consumer should in any case be refused enforcement under the national law of each Member State as a matter of public policy, by way of ensuring the effectiveness of the Regulation. On such facts the consumer may also not be sued in any Member State other than England, because the rules extend to all claims against EU domiciled consumers regardless of the domicile of the claimant. The rules do not, however, appear to cover non-EU domiciled consumers[132] – a New York consumer who purchases a product from a French retailer, subject to a contract with an exclusive French jurisdiction agreement in it, might find that they can be sued by the seller (if, for example, payment fails) in France. (Article 25 may apply, or alternatively the proceedings may be viewed as falling under residual national law rules by virtue of the exclusion in Article 17(1).)[133] Such proceedings may be unlikely unless the consumer has foreign assets, but nevertheless it is striking that the consumer protection provisions only appear to seek to protect EU Member State domiciled consumers – similarly to the rules for insurers, the fact that party autonomy is not apparently restricted for other parties perhaps suggests the strength of the doctrine in EU law, although it may also merely reflect an unprincipled favouring of the interests of EU businesses over non-EU consumers.[134]

Article 17 provides that Section 4 applies "in matters relating to a [consumer] contract", thus not limiting its application to claims *in* contract. It is thus strongly arguable that Section 4 will apply to some non-contractual claims – such as claims by a consumer in tort based on a misrepresentation that induced a consumer contract. The terms of Article 19, restricting party autonomy in respect of consumer contracts, are also expressed broadly enough to apply to both contractual and non-contractual claims. The better view (similar to the argument made above in relation to insurance contracts) is that the limitations under Article 19 should apply to the benefit of consumers regardless of whether the consumer chooses or is required to bring their claim in a non-contractual form. Section 4 should not, however, apply to disputes that relate to a consumer contract, but that do not themselves replicate the inequality of parties which justifies the restriction on party autonomy – such as a proprietary dispute between two companies over the effectiveness of a purported assignment of rights under a consumer contract.

---

[132] Articles 17(1) and 18(2) appear to assume that the consumer is domiciled in a Member State.

[133] The fact that Article 17(1) omits to mention Article 25 is not definitive, because it also omits Article 26 which clearly operates as an exception pursuant to Article 26(2).

[134] See further discussion in Mills (2016a).

5.5.1.3   Employment Contracts (Articles 20–23)

Article 20 of the Brussels I Regulation provides that jurisdiction for "matters relating to individual contracts of employment" is to be determined by Section 5 of Chapter II of the Regulation (Articles 20–23), without prejudice to Article 6 (the application of national jurisdictional rules in respect of non-EU domiciled defendants), Article 7(5) (the ability to sue a branch office in the location of the branch in respect of a claim arising out of its operations), and, for proceedings against an employer, Article 8(1) (the ability to bring closely connected claims against parties domiciled in different Member States in the courts of domicile of one of the parties). In general terms, the rules in Section 5 provide similar protections for employees as those that are provided for consumers – the employee may sue the employer in the employer's place of domicile or in the place of their habitual employment[135] (even if the employer is not domiciled in any EU Member State),[136] but the employer may only sue the employee in the place of employment[137] (also even if the employer is not domiciled in any EU Member State).[138]

The exclusion of the general rules on jurisdiction also excludes the rules on choice of court agreements under Article 25, both in terms of prorogation (the English courts may not exercise jurisdiction in claims brought against a French employee even if the employment contract has an English exclusive jurisdiction agreement) and derogation (the English courts may exercise jurisdiction in claims brought by an English employee even if the employment contract has a French exclusive jurisdiction agreement). A narrow degree of party autonomy is, however, reintroduced by Article 23, which provides:

> The provisions of this Section may be departed from only by an agreement:
>
> (1) which is entered into after the dispute has arisen; or
> (2) which allows the employee to bring proceedings in courts other than those indicated in this Section.

These rules are similar to the first two situations in which choice of court agreements may be permitted for insurance contracts or employment

---

[135] Article 21(1).
[136] Article 21(2).
[137] Article 22(1).
[138] This comes from a combination of Article 21(2), which contemplates that the rules cover contracts between an EU Member State domiciled employee and a non-EU Member State employer, and Article 22(1). On the EU jurisdictional rules for employment contracts, see generally Grusic (2015), Chapter 4; Hartley (2013b), Chapter 14; Merrett (2011), Chapter 4.

claims, and the analysis set out above applies equally to these rules. Agreements after a dispute has arisen are unlikely to arise in practice, and giving them effect is potentially undesirable because of the inequality of the parties that justifies the general exclusion of party autonomy (not the lack of foreseeability of the dispute). Article 23(2) is limited to non-exclusive jurisdiction agreements for the benefit of the employee.[139] Similarly to the case with the rules governing insurance and consumer contracts discussed above, although Article 23 does not state this, for an agreement to satisfy Article 23 it should also be required to satisfy the formal criteria set out in Article 25,[140] as discussed earlier in this chapter.

As noted above, these rules cover all EU domiciled employees, including where they are employed by non-EU domiciled parties. An exclusive jurisdiction agreement in an employment contract in favour of a non-Member State court is subject to the rules in Article 23, and thus such an agreement will ordinarily be viewed as invalid. This should prevent the enforcement of any non-Member State judgment in the courts of any Member State (as a matter of public policy to ensure the effectiveness of EU law), and may even (somewhat controversially)[141] justify an anti-suit injunction to restrain proceedings in the chosen jurisdiction.[142] The effect of this is that an employee in an EU Member State who is employed by a non-EU Member State party may not be prevented from suing in their Member State of employment – a US company is not able to include an enforceable US exclusive jurisdiction agreement in its employment contract if the employee works in, for example, England.[143] In the converse scenario, where an English company employs a US resident to work in the US and includes an exclusive choice of court agreement in favour of the English courts, a different analysis may follow. The rules that restrict party autonomy in employment disputes appear to apply only to employees domiciled in an EU Member State.[144] Thus, if the English company sues its employee in England, it is open to the English court to take jurisdiction. (Article 25 may apply, or alternatively the proceedings may be viewed as falling under residual national law rules by virtue of the exclusion in Article 20(1).)[145]

---

[139] C-154/11 *Mahamdia v. People's Democratic Republic of Algeria* EU:C:2012:491.

[140] *Simpson v. Intralinks Ltd* [2012] ILPr 34, [32].

[141] See e.g. Bergson (2017); Briggs (2007).

[142] *Samengo-Turner v. J&H Marsh & McLennan (Services) Ltd* [2007] EWCA Civ 723.

[143] See further e.g. *Petter v. EMC Europe Ltd* [2015] EWCA Civ 828 and [2015] EWHC 1498 (QB), discussed further below.

[144] Article 22(1).

[145] The fact that Article 20(1) omits to mention Article 25 is not definitive, because it also omits Article 26 which clearly operates as an exception pursuant to Article 26(2).

As similarly noted above with regard to insurance contracts and consumers (where equivalent limitations arise), this might be considered to reflect the strength of party autonomy, or simply an unprincipled favouring of EU Member State domiciled business interests over foreign employees.[146]

As noted above, Article 20 provides that Section 5 applies "in matters relating to individual contracts of employment", again not limiting its application to contractual claims. If an employee brings a claim against their employer in tort, and the claim relates to their contract of employment, the better view is that they should retain the benefit of the special protections under Section 5 including the limitations on party autonomy set out under Article 23.[147] Thus, a jurisdiction agreement under the employment contract should be as effective or ineffective with respect to non-contractual claims relating to the contract of employment as it is with respect to claims directly under the employment contract. Determining when a non-contractual claim is sufficiently related to the contract may in some cases pose a difficult threshold question – for example, if an employee suffers a tort at an after-work social function and sues their employer. The analysis of this particular problem should draw on the general analysis of the subject-matter limitations under Article 25, as discussed in Section 4.3.1. On the other hand, the better view is that the restrictions on party autonomy provided for under Section 5 should not apply to a dispute that relates to a contract of employment, but which does not replicate the inequality of parties that justifies the special restrictions on party autonomy in Section 5. A proprietary dispute over the assignment of employment contract rights, for example, should not be considered to be a matter "relating to individual contracts of employment".

5.5.2   Common Law

In England, most questions of jurisdiction involving special categories of disputes (such as those concerning insurance contracts, consumers or employees) will now be covered by the Brussels I Regulation, particularly as that Regulation applies to consumer or employment claims brought by the weaker party in an EU Member State regardless of whether the counter-party is domiciled in a Member State. However, in other common law states, and potentially in England following Brexit, the common

---

[146] See further discussion in Mills (2016a).
[147] See e.g. *Arcadia Petroleum Ltd* v. *Bosworth* [2016] EWCA Civ 818; *Alfa Laval Tumba AB* v. *Separator Spares International Ltd* [2012] EWCA Civ 1569.

law rules will be applicable. Traditionally, common law jurisdictional rules have not recognised distinct categories of disputes, such as insurance, consumer or employment disputes, in which party autonomy is limited. However, constraints on party autonomy do operate in these fields, through two main mechanisms.

First, as explored in Section 3.4.3, the common law gives effect to jurisdiction agreements as a basis of jurisdiction over non-present defendants, as a strong factor in favour of exercising that jurisdiction (pursuant to the *forum conveniens* discretion), and also as a strong factor in favour of not staying proceedings brought against defendants present in the territory (pursuant to the *forum non conveniens* discretion).[148] In the *forum conveniens* and *forum non conveniens* tests, it is open to the court to determine that it would not be in the interests of justice for a foreign jurisdiction agreement to be given effect to preclude proceedings brought by a local party, for example, because the local courts have an alternative basis of jurisdiction, and it would not in practice be possible for that party to pursue proceedings in the designated forum. This might take into account the limited resources or sophistication of, for example, a local consumer or employee. Alternatively or in addition, the effects of such agreements could be more closely scrutinised to reflect the fact that a foreign exclusive jurisdiction agreement, while contractually valid, was not freely negotiated and may reflect the interests of the stronger contracting party.[149] Such an approach has recently been endorsed by a majority of the Supreme Court of Canada in *Douez* v. *Facebook, Inc.* (2017),[150] which held that in consumer contracts a foreign exclusive jurisdiction agreement requires additional scrutiny because of the inequality of bargaining power of the parties. The court refused enforcement of the exclusive jurisdiction agreement on this basis, and also (interestingly) because the case involved quasi-constitutional privacy rights, raising the public interest in hearing the litigation locally. This approach ought to work symmetrically – it should affect the issue of whether an exclusive jurisdiction agreement *in favour of* a common law

---

[148] As noted in Section 3.4.3, there is some debate about whether cases involving foreign exclusive jurisdiction agreements fall under the general *forum conveniens* or *forum non conveniens* discretions, or are covered by a separate rule, but the point is not very significant as it does not appear to affect what factors are relevant to the discretion or how much weight is attached to them.

[149] See e.g. *Quinlan* v. *Safe International Försäkrings AB* [2005] FCA 1362, [46] (Australia); *Welex AG* v. *Rosa Maritime Limited ('The 'Epsilon Rosa')* [2003] EWCA Civ 938, [48]; *Sohio Supply Co.* v. *Gatoil (USA) Inc.* [1989] 1 Lloyd's Rep 588, 591–2; Pavlović (2016).

[150] 2017 SCC 33. In Quebec, however, foreign choice of court agreements in consumer and employment contracts are automatically ineffective under Article 3149 of the Civil Code.

court should be given effect by that court, where for example a New York consumer or employee is being sued in Singapore on the basis of such an agreement. However, it is doubtful whether this will be the case in practice, as it would be highly unusual for any court (common law or otherwise) to determine that it is unable to do justice to the parties.

Second, and more powerfully, various statutes in common law systems tend to provide for mandatory rules that may invalidate the effect of a choice of court clause. For example, in England an employee may not effectively enter into an exclusive choice of court agreement in favour of a foreign court,[151] and the Consumer Rights Act 2015 could potentially invalidate unfair exclusive choice of court clauses.[152] In Australia a choice of a foreign forum may similarly be invalidated as an attempt to evade the terms of a mandatory statute, such as the Insurance Contracts Act 1984 (Cth)[153] or the Franchising Code.[154] Importantly, in England and indeed any other EU Member State these mandatory rules may also be sourced from EU law – thus, a foreign party employing a commercial agent in the EU cannot avoid the Commercial Agents Directive through an exclusive jurisdiction agreement in favour of a foreign court that would not apply the Directive.[155] A choice of foreign law to govern the contract will not be effective to displace these mandatory rules.[156] Once again, however, such provisions are generally protective of local consumers or employees, and are unlikely to be effective to preclude, for example, the Singapore courts from exercising jurisdiction where there is an exclusive jurisdiction agreement in favour of the Singapore courts and a claim is brought against an English consumer or employee.

It is of interest to note that under the common law, therefore, the restrictions on party autonomy designed to protect a weaker party only generally appear to operate in favour of the forum, by way of invalidating a choice of a foreign court. As noted, this is a consequence of the fact that a court

---

[151] Employment Rights Act 1996, s.203(1). This is now largely redundant, however, because of the effect of the Brussels I Regulation.

[152] C-240/98 *Oceano Grupo Editorial SA* v. *Rocio Murciano Quintero* [2000] ECR I-4941; *Standard Bank London Ltd* v. *Apostolakis (No 2)* [2001] EWHC 493 (Comm).

[153] *Akai Pty Ltd* v. *People's Insurance Co.* (1997) 188 CLR 418; see e.g. Garnett (2013a).

[154] Competition and Consumer (Industry Codes – Franchising) Regulation 2014 (Australia), sch.1, s.21.

[155] See *Accentuate Ltd* v. *Asigra Inc* [2009] EWHC 2655 (QB) (arbitration clause invalidated because the arbitrators would not give effect to mandatory EU rules – see further discussion in Section 9.4.1). See also e.g. Rühl (2007b).

[156] See further discussion in Section 9.4.

will only very rarely view itself as incapable of delivering justice to the parties, even if one of them is a weaker foreign party, and thus restrictions on the ability of such parties to select the forum have not been developed. An argument could perhaps be made that in such cases a common law court should give effect to foreign statutory restrictions on choice of court agreements, thereby finding the choice of court agreement to be invalid. The Singapore courts, might, for example, in deciding whether they have jurisdiction over claims against an English consumer under an exclusive Singaporean jurisdiction agreement, take into account the rules of EU law in the Brussels I Regulation that would invalidate such an agreement. This would, however, be difficult to fit within existing legal categories. As discussed further in Section 9.4, the application of foreign mandatory rules under the common law is generally limited to cases in which the rule would make the performance of the contract unlawful in the territory of the foreign state itself[157] – cases involving a contract to do something in a foreign state that is illegal under the law of that place.[158] The effect of the Brussels I Regulation rule invalidating foreign choice of court agreements for English consumers would not be to prohibit doing anything in England, but only (if anything) to prohibit reliance on the choice of court agreement in the chosen state (Singapore, in our example). It is therefore not obvious that a foreign statute could provide a basis on which a common law court could refuse jurisdiction over a foreign consumer subject to a choice of court agreement in favour of the court.

5.5.3   United States

The situation under US law in relation to the protection of weaker parties such as insurance policyholders, consumers or employees is broadly comparable to that under the common law. Rules on jurisdiction do not themselves generally provide specialised treatment for such parties, include in respect of their exercises of party autonomy through choice of court clauses. However, special protection is potentially provided both through jurisdictional discretion and through mandatory rules or reliance on public policy.[159]

---

[157] See similarly Rome I Regulation, Art.9(3).
[158] See further Section 9.4.1.
[159] See generally e.g. Borchers (2008).

In relation to jurisdictional discretion, under US federal law (as set out in Section 3.4.1) any choice of forum clause may not be effective if "enforcement is shown by the resisting party to be 'unreasonable' under the circumstances",[160] in particular (although perhaps not exclusively) because of "fraud, undue influence, or overweening bargaining power".[161] This means that the fairness of choice of court clauses involving weaker parties is likely to be scrutinised, but it does not necessarily suggest that such clauses are likely to be invalidated.[162] The seminal Supreme Court decision in *Carnival Cruise Lines, Inc v. Shute* (1990)[163] was itself notably a case involving consumers purchasing cruise ship tickets, which had (printed on their reverse) an exclusive choice of court agreement. The Court held, however, that the parties should be bound by the jurisdiction agreement, notwithstanding the fact that the agreement was not and could not have been negotiated, noting in particular that the cruise line had a legitimate interest in limiting the courts in which it could potentially be sued, and that this interest would operate not only to the benefit of the cruise line but also its customers in the form of increased legal certainty and lower prices.[164] The Court's approach here does not appear to signify any special treatment of jurisdiction agreements – under US law, all form contracts ('contracts of adhesion') are generally subject to "scrutiny for reasonableness"[165] – and thus the decision does not appear to establish that 'overweening bargaining power' will frequently justify invalidating a forum selection agreement, even in the case of non-negotiable consumer contracts.[166] The Second Restatement of Conflict of Laws similarly provides that "The parties' agreement as to the place of the action cannot oust a state of judicial jurisdiction, but such an agreement will be given effect unless it is unfair or unreasonable."[167] As discussed in Section 3.4.1, however, the practice of US states is highly variable, some refusing to give effect to any jurisdiction agreements and others seeking to restrict their function only in certain contexts, pursuing a policy of protecting a range of weaker parties including consumers, employees, and franchisees.[168]

---

[160]   *The Bremen* v. *Zapata Off-Shore Co.*, 407 US 1, 9 (1972).

[161]   Ibid., at 12.

[162]   See e.g. *Barnett* v. *DynCorp International, LLC*, 831 F.3d 296 (5th Cir. 2016) (enforcing a choice of court agreement in favour of Kuwait in an employment contract).

[163]   *Carnival Cruise Lines, Inc.* v. *Shute*, 499 US 585 (1990). See further e.g. Brand (2013a), p.201ff; Borchers (1992); Mullinex (1992).

[164]   At 593–4.

[165]   Ibid., at 600 (1990), per Justice Stevens (dissenting, although not on this point).

[166]   See also e.g. *Wong* v. *PartyGaming Ltd*, 589 F.3d 821, 829–30 (6th Cir. 2009).

[167]   Second Restatement of Conflict of Laws, s.80.

[168]   See e.g. *Kubis & Perszyk Associates* v. *Sun Microsystems Inc.*, 680 A.2d 618, 627 (NJ 1996) ("we hold that forum-selection clauses in franchise agreements are presumptively invalid,

The diversity of approaches to choice of court agreements in the United States is also reflected in relation to mandatory rules. Some states have a range of mandatory statutes that operate to restrict the effectiveness of choice of court agreements.[169] Such restrictions may also apply in federal courts as part of federal law. In *Boyd v. Grand Trunk Western Railroad Co.* (1949),[170] for example, the Supreme Court held that a choice of forum clause was void because it was contrary to Section 6 of the Federal Employers' Liability Act, which gave federal employees the right to sue in their place of residence or business or the location where the cause of action arose. A foreign choice of court agreement may also be considered contrary to federal or state public policy, if the cause of action engages important public interests.[171]

As discussed under Section 5.5.2, these techniques appear focused primarily on ensuring that local weaker parties such as consumers or employees are unable to contract out of the protections of local law, by prohibiting selection of a foreign forum (and foreign law). If a consumer from outside the United States is sued in a US court in reliance on a choice of court agreement in favour of that court, the US court will not necessarily view the exercise of jurisdiction as unfair and to refuse to hear the case, even if the consumer's own jurisdiction would consider the choice of court agreement to be invalid. This is essentially what took place in the English decisions discussed under the EU law employment protection provisions in Section 5.5.1. In *Petter v. EMC Europe Ltd* (2015),[172] the English courts issued an anti-suit injunction to restrain US proceedings that had been commenced by the US employer of a party employed in England – proceedings had been commenced in Massachusetts in reliance on a jurisdiction agreement in the contract. The evident implication is that the court in Massachusetts would (or would likely) have exercised jurisdiction based on the choice of court agreement in its favour, even though this would have involved suit over a foreign employee in the home jurisdiction of their employer, contrary to the protections under the EU law rules applicable in England.

---

and should not be enforced unless the franchisor can satisfy the burden of proving that such a clause was not imposed on the franchisee unfairly on the basis of its superior bargaining position").

[169] For examples, see e.g. discussion in *Wong v. PartyGaming Ltd*, 589 F.3d 821, 826–7 (6th Cir. 2009) (with particular reference to the courts of Ohio); s.47.025, Fla. Stat. (1999) (prohibiting foreign jurisdiction agreements for construction contracts). See generally discussion in Symeonides (2016), Chapter 11.

[170] 338 US 263 (1949); see also e.g. *Krenger v. Pennsylvania Railroad Co.*, 174 F.2d 556 (1949).

[171] See e.g. *Red Bull Associates v. Best Western International*, 862 F.2d 963 (2nd Cir. 1988).

[172] [2015] EWCA Civ 828.

5.5.4   *Hague Convention on Choice of Court Agreements 2005*

The Hague Convention on Choice of Court Agreements 2005 does not provide for special jurisdictional rules to constrain the exercise of party autonomy in subject areas such as insurance, consumer or employment disputes. Such disputes are, however, generally excluded from its scope – Article 2(1)(a) excludes choice of court agreements to which a consumer is a party, and Article 2(1)(b) excludes choice of court agreements "relating to contracts of employment, including collective agreements". This leaves open the possibility that Convention states may determine, as a matter of their residual national (or regional) law, to impose restrictions on party autonomy for such disputes. In the European Union, for example, it preserves the effect of the protective rules for consumers and employees discussed above. The exclusion in the Convention may in some respects however be broader than the protective rules under the Brussels I Regulation – a contract between two natural persons "acting primarily for personal, family or household purposes" (two "consumers" for the purposes of the Convention) would be excluded from the scope of the Convention,[173] but would also not be covered by the protective rules under the Brussels I Regulation (because no party would be pursuing "commercial or professional activities").[174] The exclusion of contracts involving consumers from the Hague Convention should perhaps thus be understood as motivated not (only) because of a perceived inequality of bargaining power, but more broadly as a means of delimiting the scope of the Convention. Alternatively, the Hague Convention might be considered to have a more protective approach under which it is not inequality between the parties, but their lack of commercial sophistication, which justifies the exclusion of party autonomy.

It is further notable that insurance disputes are not excluded from the scope of the Convention, a point reinforced by the rule in Article 17, which provides that insurance disputes are (in particular) not excluded in cases in which the insurance relates to a matter excluded from the scope of the Convention. This suggests that the Convention takes a more sceptical position towards the question of whether insurance contracts do involve a negotiating disparity that would be deserving of particular constraints on party autonomy. However, Article 21 of the Convention does permit a state party to adopt a declaration at the time of ratification excluding particular

---

[173] Hague Convention Explanatory Report, [50].
[174] Article 17(1)(c).

categories of dispute from its scope (the Convention will not apply for such disputes where the choice of court agreement is in favour of the state making the declaration, or where the dispute is heard in the courts of that state). The European Union has indeed made such a declaration in relation to "insurance contracts", subject to exceptions that (broadly speaking) replicate the rules authorizing limited party autonomy under Article 15 of the Regulation, as discussed above.[175] Singapore has not, however, made any such declaration on its ratification of the Convention. If and when further states accede to the Hague Convention, it will be of interest to see whether the imposition of constraints on party autonomy for insurance contracts becomes broadly accepted, or whether the EU might revisit its own limitation on such contracts, a possibility expressly left open by its declaration.

5.6   Conclusion

The analysis in this chapter has examined four important types of constraints on the exercise of party autonomy in choice of forum. First, the imposition of formality requirements on jurisdiction agreements, which may render some choices of forum ineffective. Second, the exclusion of a choice of forum for purely domestic cases, suggesting either that a choice of a foreign forum is ineffective in such cases because unjustified, or that private international law as a whole is not engaged in such cases. Third, the exclusion of party autonomy in cases that engage exclusive subject matter jurisdictional rules, suggesting the recognition of overriding public interests for such cases. Fourth, the exclusion or restriction of party autonomy for contracts involving presumptively weaker parties, such as consumer, employment, or insurance contracts, reflecting doubts over whether a genuine exercise of party autonomy is possible for such contracts. The variety of these restrictions reflects the range of principled concerns with the exercise of party autonomy, set out in Section 2.4, including questions concerning the authenticity of a choice, the recognition of overriding or countervailing public interests, and the possible requirement for a cross-border element. A striking feature of the analysis in this chapter is that the means for recognising these concerns, or indeed whether they are recognised at all, is also significantly varied in the different legal systems under examination. Formality requirements may or may not be imposed; jurisdiction agreements may or may not be effective for purely domestic

---

[175] See www.hcch.net/en/instruments/conventions/status-table/notifications/?csid=1044&disp=resdn.

cases; exclusive subject-matter jurisdictional rules may differ in scope and may be recognised as mandatory or discretionary; and the special protections for weaker parties may also vary in the range of parties that are protected, and in the means through which they are protected. While the issues addressed in this chapter are undoubtedly widely recognised as matters of concern in party autonomy in choice of forum, there is far from consensus regarding the extent and means through which they should be accommodated.

6

Arbitration Agreements

6.1 Introduction

The resolution of disputes through arbitration is commonplace in international commerce.[1] (It is also commonplace in domestic commerce, although such disputes do not raise the same private international law issues and are thus not the subject of this chapter.) The widespread acceptance of the effectiveness of arbitration agreements has been established and reinforced through the adoption of the New York Convention on the Recognition and Enforcement of Foreign Arbitral Awards 1958, which has more than 150 state parties including all the major trading states.[2] The Convention has an even broader effect through defining the expectations of good international business practice on signatory and non-signatory states. While historically many legal systems were sceptical of arbitration (as an impermissible attempt by private parties to 'oust' the jurisdiction of the courts),[3] most large trading states now adopt a 'pro-arbitration' approach, which tends to favour the validity and effectiveness of arbitration agreements.[4] The fact that arbitration agreements (and as a consequence, arbitral awards) are recognised worldwide through a standardised

---

[1] This chapter is concerned only with arbitration between private parties. Although investor-state arbitration has been strongly influenced by the model of commercial arbitration, this model is perennially in tension with the international law origins of investment law and the inherently public regulatory concerns at stake, and investment arbitration thus raises distinct issues: see further e.g. Mills (2011). Nor does this chapter discuss other forms of arbitration between public and private entities, which may similarly engage broader public interests; see further Brekoulakis and Devaney (2017).

[2] www.uncitral.org/uncitral/en/uncitral_texts/arbitration/NYConvention_status.html.

[3] See Section 2.2.1. The common law history is helpfully set out in *Kulukundis Shipping Co.* v. *Amtorg Trading Corp.*, 126 F.2d 978 (2nd Cir. 1942); see also *Haskell* v. *McClintic-Marshall Co.*, 289 F.405 409 (9th Cir. 1923); *Kill* v. *Hollister* (1746) 95 ER 532 (KB).

[4] See e.g. *Moses H. Cone Memorial Hospital* v. *Mercury Construction Corp.*, 460 US 1 (1983); *Scherk* v. *Alberto-Culver Co.*, 417 US 506 (1974); *Fiona Trust* v. *Privalov* [2007] UKHL 40 (each discussed further below). Even Brazil, which has traditionally been notable for its scepticism towards party autonomy in choice of forum and choice of law, has become generally open to arbitration. See e.g. Stringer (2006).

set of international rules is a significant reason for the popularity of arbitration. It is well known that the Hague Convention on Choice of Court Agreements 2005 is an effort to replicate that success in the context of judicial dispute resolution, and thus to level the playing field between arbitration and litigation when it comes to the resolution of international commercial disputes.[5]

The New York Convention 1958 includes both rules governing arbitration agreements and rules governing the recognition and enforcement of arbitral awards. The focus in this chapter is on the issue of when an arbitration agreement will be valid and effective. On matters of jurisdiction, as the Convention is addressed to and binding on states, it is only concerned with the derogation effect of an arbitration agreement – the obligation on state courts not to exercise jurisdiction where this would be contrary to an arbitration agreement, which is the core of the agreement.[6] Of course, this only refers to the exercise of judicial jurisdiction on the merits. As arbitral tribunals lack the power to coerce the parties (except through the threat of adverse findings), national courts will generally act in support of an arbitration agreement, for example, through compelling arbitration,[7] making ancillary orders to obtain evidence or freeze assets,[8] issuing an anti-suit injunction to restrain the conduct of foreign proceedings brought in breach of the agreement (giving specific performance to the arbitration agreement),[9] or potentially through awarding damages for breach of an arbitration agreement.[10]

---

[5] See Hague Convention Explanatory Report, [1] ("The hope is that the Convention will do for choice of court agreements what the New York Convention on the Recognition and Enforcement of Foreign Arbitral Awards of 10 June 1958 has done for arbitration Agreements"); Teitz (2005).

[6] New York Convention 1958, Art.II(3); Arbitration Act 1996 (UK), s.9; 9 US Code s.3.

[7] See e.g. 9 US Code s.4.

[8] See e.g. Arbitration Act 1996 (UK), s.44; *Mobil Cerro Negro Ltd* v. *Petroleos De Venezuela SA* [2008] EWHC 532 (Comm).

[9] See e.g. *Ust-Kamenogorsk Hydropower Plant JSC* v. *AES Ust-Kamenogorsk Hydropower Plant LLP* [2013] UKSC 35; *Alfred C Toepfer International GmbH* v. *Societe Cargill France* [1997] EWCA Civ 2811. Such an injunction may not, however, be awarded by the courts of an EU Member State to restrain proceedings in another Member State, as this would violate the principle of mutual trust under EU law – see C-185/07 *Allianz SpA* v. *West Tankers Inc.* [2009] ECR I-663, and related discussion in Section 3.4.2. The position does not appear changed under the 2012 Recast of the Brussels I Regulation, despite the addition of Recital 12. An arbitral tribunal may itself issue an anti-suit injunction, although it remains unclear whether a national court could assist in its enforcement – see C-536/13 *Gazprom* EU:C:2015:316.

[10] See e.g. *National Westminster Bank Plc* v. *Rabobank Nederland* [2007] EWHC 1742. These may also be awarded by an arbitral tribunal – see e.g. *West Tankers Inc.* v. *Allianz SpA* [2012] EWHC 854 (Comm).

There are a variety of reasons why there is widespread consensus around at least the general enforceability of arbitration agreements. If parties are free to choose between different national courts as alternative forums in which to resolve their disputes, arbitration might be considered as an extension of that freedom which is consistent with each of the justifications for party autonomy examined in Chapter 2. If, for example, parties are viewed (from a party-sovereigntist perspective) as exercising an inherent autonomy, not derived from national law, in choosing between different state courts, there seems little reason why that autonomy should be constrained to selecting between formal judicial institutions. This is particularly the case if, as is commonly argued, arbitration offers the possibility of a dispute resolution method that is more efficient or suitable for the parties than any national court. If choice of court agreements are supported simply because they create greater certainty for the parties in conducting cross-border activity, either to their benefit or to the benefit of the economy more generally, then arbitration agreements may be viewed as equally creating such certainty. If, alternatively, enforcing choice of court agreements is considered to be justified because it creates regulatory competition which leads to improvements in national judicial institutions, such competition would appear to be enhanced if it is extended to include also privately constituted arbitral tribunals. From this perspective, the possibility for the parties to select an arbitral tribunal and potentially to customise its procedures would make courts work even harder and more efficiently to compete. Consistently with this approach, the acceptance of party autonomy in the context of arbitration is typically defined in broad terms. There is, for example, generally no need for any connection between the place of arbitration and the dispute. One effect of this is to create a further regulatory marketplace, creating competition not only between arbitration and national courts but also between different centres of arbitration, potentially either at the time of drafting an arbitration clause or at the time of commencing arbitration.

The policy of giving effect to arbitration agreements should not, however, be viewed as simply a natural extension of party autonomy in choice of court – as examined in Section 2.2.1, widespread support for arbitration in fact pre-dated support for foreign choice of court agreements in both England and the United States, and arbitration agreements create distinct issues from those that arise for choice of court agreements.[11] On the one

---

[11] Contrary to the words of the US Supreme Court, an arbitration agreement is not merely "a specialized kind of forum-selection clause that posits not only the situs of suit but also the procedure to be used in resolving the dispute" – *Scherk* v. *Alberto-Culver Co.*, 417 US 506, 519 (1974).

hand, there may be limits imposed on arbitration because certain types of private litigation engage public interests that are considered unsuitable for private dispute settlement. Private arbitrators, unlike judges, do not hold a public office or owe duties to greater public interests than the resolution of the dispute (unless required to do so by the parties) – this is reflected in a range of choice of law questions in arbitration examined in this chapter. Arbitral proceedings will frequently be confidential, which may limit (or eliminate) the opportunity for third parties either acting in their own interest or the public interest to scrutinise the subject matter of the dispute and potentially intervene – indeed that is one of the key attractions of arbitration for many parties. These aspects of arbitration raise concerns about its impact as a form of regulatory governance, including whether it provides a means for private parties to escape rules that give effect to public interests and values.[12] Concerns have also recently been raised by common law judges that the confidentiality of arbitral awards as well as their lack of precedential value may have harmful effects on the progressive public development of the law.[13]

On the other hand, there are public benefits to be gained from the privatisation of the costs of dispute resolution, taking the burden of such disputes away from courts, which may make arbitration a desirable form of exercise of party autonomy. As discussed in Chapter 3, one possible concern with choice of court agreements, particularly influential in the United States, is that party autonomy should be limited because of the burden it imposes on a particular judicial order which may not be closely connected to the dispute. Giving effect to party autonomy in individual jurisdictional disputes may impose a burden on particular court systems – in particular, the infrastructure costs of courts and court officials (and sometimes jurors) – but the issue is only *which* courts should bear the burden, not whether *any* courts should do so. This concern is less of an issue for arbitration agreements, which may relieve court congestion and impose the costs of resolving the dispute at least principally on the parties,[14] although a more limited burden may be imposed on the courts of the 'seat' of the arbitration in supervising the conduct of the arbitral proceedings and potentially reviewing the validity of the arbitral award (particularly if proceedings are brought to set it aside).[15] It is important to note that the concept of

---

[12] See Section 2.4.3.

[13] See e.g. French (2016); Thomas (2016).

[14] See e.g. *Mobil Oil* v. *Asamera Oil*, 43 N.Y.2d 276 (NYCA 1977).

[15] As (somewhat ironically) occurred in the case cited immediately above: *Mobil Oil* v. *Asamera Oil*, 487 F. Supp. 63 (SDNY 1980).

the 'seat' of the tribunal is itself no longer considered a question of fact (the place where the tribunal 'sits' to hold hearings), but rather a 'juridical' question[16] (essentially, identifying the legal order that provides the default and/or non-derogable procedural law for the tribunal, sometimes referred to as the *lex arbitri*) – it is now uncontroversial that the venue (or venues) for tribunal hearings may not be the same as the seat, although this is still unusual.[17] Determining the seat of an arbitration may itself be a difficult legal question.[18]

The popularity and widespread acceptance of arbitration does not mean that it is a settled area of law – the New York Convention leaves many questions unclear or unanswered, a significant number of which engage choice of law issues.[19] Five of the main disputed questions relating to party autonomy in arbitration are addressed in turn below. The first (addressed in Section 6.2) is an underlying theoretical issue, but one that has important practical implications across the law of arbitration – whether arbitration should be viewed as an internationalised system of dispute resolution, or whether it should be viewed as the product of the national legal order or orders governing the arbitration, or whether it has a distinct transnational character. The second (addressed in Section 6.3) is the closely related question of what law should be applied by either a court or an arbitral tribunal to determine the validity of an arbitration agreement. The third (addressed in Section 6.4), again related, is the question of when disputes concerning the validity of an arbitration agreement should be heard by national courts and when they should be heard by the arbitral tribunal itself. The fourth (addressed in Section 6.5) concerns the scope and effects of arbitration agreements, including their breadth of subject-matter scope, effect on third parties, exclusivity or non-exclusivity, and whether they may permit or exclude class arbitration. A fifth and final issue (addressed in Section 6.6) is whether certain types of disputes should be considered incapable of

---

[16] Dicey, Morris and Collins (2012), [16–035]; see e.g. the Arbitration Act 1996 (UK), s.3 (referring to the 'juridical seat'); *Bharat Aluminium Co.* v. *Kaiser Aluminium Technical Services, Inc.* (2012) 9 SCC 552 (Supreme Court of India).

[17] For discussion see e.g. *Shagang South-Asia (Hong Kong) Trading Co. Ltd* v. *Daewoo Logistics* [2015] EWHC 194 (Comm); *Bay Hotel and Resort Ltd* v. *Cavalier Construction Co. Ltd* [2001] UKPC 34.

[18] If the parties expressly or implicitly provide for a seat this will be determinative, reflecting the contractual foundations of arbitration. If not, however, a further complexity arises as to how (and under whose law) the seat should be determined. See generally Hill (2014).

[19] For a masterful overview, see Bermann (2015). For a more detailed treatment of the issues in this chapter see also Mills (2018).

settlement through arbitration, rendering arbitration agreements over such disputes invalid, and again what law should provide this standard.

As explained in Section 6.2, the basic structure of analysis for international arbitration agreements comes from the New York Convention 1958, an international law source, as augmented by national or transnational sources. For this reason, while certain features of national practice will be discussed in this chapter, the analysis is in general less comparative and more international in its approach compared with the chapters on choice of court agreements. However, it may be noted at this preliminary point that the European Union has not regulated questions of arbitration,[20] leaving these to national law and the New York Convention. It is also notable that in the United States the law governing arbitration clauses is more unified than the law governing choice of court agreements – the New York Convention is directly applicable in the majority of international disputes concerning arbitration, and in most other cases (cross-border commercial disputes involving non-Convention states or those internal to the United States) the governing law in both federal and state courts is the Federal Arbitration Act 1925.[21]

6.2 Is Arbitration International, National or Transnational?

Advocates for arbitration often point to its international character as a feature that makes it attractive to private parties, particularly multinational corporations. Doing business around the world leaves a party exposed to potential litigation risks. Choice of court clauses go some way to ameliorating those risks, but the analysis in Chapters 3, 4, and 5 has highlighted a range of ways in which choice of court clauses may be ineffective, and these differ significantly between different states. Choice of a national court also potentially raises the problem of the recognition and enforcement of foreign judgments, particularly if a party in a cross-border transaction negotiates to have disputes heard in their home courts. Although (as set out in Section 3.4) judgments based on choice of court agreements will be frequently enforceable across borders, this will again depend on variable rules of national law (unless governed by EU law or the Hague Convention on Choice of Court Agreements 2005). Arbitration offers the promise that a party doing business internationally can rely on a single set of familiar dispute resolution and enforcement rules and procedures

---

[20] Except as noted above, n.9.
[21] *Southland Corp. v. Keating*, 465 US 1 (1984).

regardless of where their business is conducted, as the effectiveness of an arbitration agreement is (according to this promise) a matter of international standardisation through the New York Convention 1958, supplemented by further soft law standardisations such as the UNCITRAL Model Law on International Commercial Arbitration that forms the basis for the national arbitration law of many states. An arbitration clause may, from this perspective, be viewed as a contractual clause governed (at least to some extent) by international law, because it is the New York Convention that sets out its (general) meaning and significance.

It is, however, often debated whether arbitration can really deliver on this promise. Arbitral tribunals do not have the coercive powers of national courts – they are not, for example, able to seize the person or property of a defendant. For this reason, arbitration agreements may require the support of national judicial bodies, to provide for protective or supportive injunctive orders or the enforcement of arbitral awards, or even where necessary to compel arbitration. When national judicial institutions exercise this supportive function, or are simply seised of proceedings contrary to an arbitration agreement, they will also be required to review the question of the validity and effectiveness of the arbitration agreement – in the words of the New York Convention, whether it is "null and void, inoperative or incapable of being performed".[22] In national courts, this traditionally means recourse to national rules or standards for a variety of questions, as discussed further in Section 6.3. Indeed, the New York Convention implies that national standards will govern the validity of an arbitration agreement, in the rules governing enforcement of arbitral awards, as it permits refusal of enforcement of an award where "the said agreement is not valid under the law to which the parties have subjected it or, failing any indication thereon, under the law of the country where the award was made".[23] As a consequence, in interpreting or determining the validity of an arbitration agreement, a court will have to identify the governing law of the agreement, which will (almost invariably) involve application of rules of private international law. These generally limit the court to identifying a system of national law, as discussed further below and in Chapter 10. The New York Convention also only obliges contracting states to give effect to arbitration agreements that cover "a subject matter capable of settlement by arbitration", but does not set out what subject matters are covered, leaving this (at least in the eyes of most national courts) as a matter for national

---

[22] Article II(3).
[23] Article V(1)(a).

law standards, as discussed further in Section 6.6. Finally, the New York Convention rules governing enforcement of arbitral awards also permit an award to be refused enforcement by national courts on the basis that "the recognition or enforcement of the award would be contrary to the public policy of that country",[24] appearing again to defer to national law standards.

Most commonly, proceedings in support of arbitration will be brought in the courts of the seat of the arbitration, which has led some theorists to view arbitration as a replication of the judicial function which is authorised by the legal system of the seat, thereby giving priority to the national law of the seat in determining questions that may arise concerning the validity or effectiveness of the arbitration agreement. This approach, perhaps most closely associated with F. A. Mann,[25] is referred to as 'monolocal' by Emmanuel Gaillard[26] and has also been described by Jan Paulsson as the 'territorialist' thesis.[27] The problem with this approach is that the issues may arise in any court (if, for example, proceedings are brought that may be contrary to an arbitration agreement), and it is not clear why the law of the seat should be prioritised over other national laws. Given these complexities, a second perspective is to see arbitration as anchored in 'a plurality of national legal orders'. In Gaillard's terminology this is a 'multilocal' approach;[28] Paulsson has similarly described this as the 'pluralistic' thesis, under which "arbitration may be given effect by more than one legal order, none of them inevitably essential".[29]

All this might be taken to indicate that it is national law, or national laws, which provides the foundation of arbitration.[30] However, the variability of national law standards on these questions is viewed as highly unsatisfactory by many in the arbitration community, who consider that it diminishes the effectiveness of international arbitration, and fails to reflect its independence from national legal orders. It has thus been proposed that instead of applying national standards to these questions, they should be considered to be governed by 'transnational law' standards developed and applied in the practice of arbitral tribunals themselves around the

---

[24] Article V(2)(b). See further the discussion of 'public policy' in Section 9.4.2.
[25] Mann (1967a); Mann (1967b).
[26] Gaillard (2010b), p.279.
[27] Paulsson (2011); Paulsson (2013).
[28] Gaillard (2010b), p.279.
[29] Paulsson (2011), p.292.
[30] See e.g. Radicati di Brozolo (2011a).

world, also known as the *lex mercatoria*.[31] This is a third approach to arbitration, endorsed by Gaillard, which conceives of international arbitration as functioning in an autonomous 'transnational' realm, rather than part of one or more national legal orders: "the juridicity of arbitration is rooted in a distinct, transnational legal order, that could be labeled as the arbitral legal order, and not in a national legal system, be it that of the country of the seat or that of the place or places of enforcement".[32] An arbitration may apply national law, but that does not mean that national law is the source of its authority, and under this view it may therefore equally be open to a tribunal to apply non-state sources of law.[33] Paulsson similarly describes this approach as postulating that "arbitration is the product of an autonomous legal order accepted as such by arbitrators and judges".[34] Horatia Muir Watt has also analysed, more critically, the process under which international commercial arbitration "has now established itself as a largely auto-poetic, parallel, world of private justice, supposedly secreted by a self-regulating transnational merchant community".[35]

This view has not been widely supported by national courts (with the exception of France, as discussed below), but has become popular among arbitrators themselves. There are limits to how 'independent' of national law an arbitrator can (or ought to) be – arbitrators are generally considered to have a duty to render an enforceable award,[36] and this may require them to take into account the practice of national courts in which their award is likely to be enforced. Thus, although the (apparent) requirements of the New York Convention 1958 to apply national law standards to various questions are addressed only to state parties and thus to national courts, in practice arbitrators may well also comply with those standards in order to ensure the effectiveness of their award. This influence should not, however,

---

[31] See also Section 10.4 on the application of *lex mercatoria* to the substance of an arbitration.

[32] Gaillard (2010a), p.35.

[33] See further e.g. Schultz (2014); Michaels (2014a), p.52 ("If the arbitral award is denationalized, then, functionally, the same is true for the arbitrator: he ceases to be part of a national state and instead becomes integrated in a 'global adjudication system.' The arbitrator is no longer obliged toward his or any other national state, nor only toward the parties themselves. Instead, he adopts a transnational role within a transnational system into which he is integrated").

[34] Paulsson (2011), p.292. Paulsson also describes a fourth approach under which "arbitration may be effective under arrangements that do not depend on national law or judges at all" (Paulsson (2011), p.292). This is not entirely distinguishable from the third approach, although he argues that in practice it collapses into the second (pluralistic) approach, as non-national law is simply another form of legal ordering.

[35] Muir Watt (2010), p.254.

[36] See e.g. ICC Rules of Arbitration, Art.42.

be overstated. It may be difficult to anticipate the place or places where an arbitral award will be enforced. In many contexts, compliance with arbitral awards will be driven by reputational concerns in the marketplace rather than by legal compulsion, and will thus be more free-standing than it may appear from a strictly legal perspective. Compliance with court judgments is frequently voluntary in the same way, and if not, their effectiveness may equally depend on the cooperation of foreign courts to seize available assets. Some arbitrators may freely apply transnational standards, in the confidence that their award will likely be complied with by the parties without recourse to any national court, or failing that, that it will receive the same cooperative support of national courts. The reality may be that in such cases, the arbitration agreement should be viewed as governed by transnational law standards rather than by international or national law – indeed, as examined in Section 10.4, many arbitrators may apply transnational law standards not merely to the arbitration agreement, but also to the merits of the dispute between the parties. If this view is accepted, the system of transnational private ordering provided by international arbitration thus co-exists with, and perhaps even competes with, the public system of states and their judicial bodies operating under or through national and public international law.[37] As explored in Section 1.1.2, the recognition of party autonomy under this perspective would appear to reflect a party-sovereigntist conception that it is an exercise of inherent powers by individuals, not a power given to private parties by national law.

Ultimately, the question of whether arbitration is international, national, or transnational cannot be definitively answered, and the realities of practice reflect a combination of these elements. The general framework and standards for arbitration are provided by international law through the New York Convention 1958; these standards leave many points still to be resolved, and national courts are likely to look to national law to address such points; arbitral tribunals may instead prefer to identify and rely on transnational legal standards, to avoid dependence on variable rules of national law. The remainder of this chapter examines a number of key legal questions concerning the exercise of party autonomy through arbitration agreements – the difficulties in answering these questions reflects the underlying uncertainty about the theoretical foundations of arbitration itself.

---

[37] See further e.g. Gélinas (2016); Brekoulakis (2013).

6.3   What Law Should Govern the Validity of an Arbitration Agreement?

A choice of court agreement is only one among a number of different possible grounds for the exercise of jurisdiction by a national court. By contrast, the sole basis for the exercise of jurisdiction by an arbitral tribunal is the consent of the parties,[38] usually expressed in a contract, in the form of an arbitration agreement.[39] (Consent to arbitration is required, rather than an *obligation* to arbitrate – this does not preclude the possibility that one or both parties may have an *option* to arbitrate their disputes or alternatively to commence proceedings in a court.)[40] The question of the scope and limits of party autonomy in relation to arbitration agreements is thus central to the functioning of arbitration in general. In the words of Lord Hope in the House of Lords:

> As everyone knows, an arbitral award possesses no binding force except that which is derived from the joint mandate of the contracting parties. Everything depends on their contract, and if there was no contract to go to arbitration at all an arbitrator's award can have no validity.[41]

The US Supreme Court has similarly observed that "arbitration is a matter of contract, and a party cannot be required to submit to arbitration any dispute which he has not agreed so to submit".[42] The Federal Arbitration Act provides that arbitration agreements shall be "valid, irrevocable, and enforceable, save upon such grounds as exist at law or in equity for the revocation of any contract",[43] which is understood to be a reference to state

---

[38]   Unusually, a form of dispute resolution referred to as 'arbitration' may be mandated by statute, but this is probably best considered not to be truly arbitration and in any case is not discussed in this chapter as it does not involve the exercise of party autonomy. See further Cuniberti (2008).

[39]   See generally e.g. Redfern and Hunter (2015), [2.01] ("The agreement to arbitrate is the foundation stone of international arbitration"); Born (2014), p.225 ("The foundation of almost every international arbitration – and of the international arbitral process itself – is an international arbitration agreement"); Steingruber (2012).

[40]   See generally e.g. Draguiev (2014); *PMT Partners Pty Ltd (In Liq)* v. *Australian National Parks & Wildlife Service* [1995] HCA 36 (Australia); *Pittalis* v. *Sherefittin* (1986) QB 868.

[41]   *Fiona Trust* v. *Privalov* [2007] UKHL 40, [34].

[42]   *Steelworkers* v. *Warrior & Gulf Co.*, 363 US 574, 582 (1960); see also *Gateway Coal Co.* v. *United Mine Workers*, 414 US 368, 374 (1974). The requirement for 'agreement' to the arbitration clause is interpreted strictly in many jurisdictions in the United States, and may for example invalidate arbitration clauses in contracts of adhesion (standard form contracts not subject to negotiation); see e.g. *Miner* v. *Walden*, 101 Misc.2d 814 (NY Sup Ct. 1979). The approach for arbitration clauses in the United States is thus similar to that for choice of court clauses – see Sections 3.4.1 and 5.5.3.

[43]   Section 2.

contract law doctrines (so long as they are not unduly restrictive of arbitration and do not single out arbitration clauses for disfavoured treatment).[44] However, the simple observation that an arbitration agreement is a contract masks two further complexities.

The first is that an arbitration agreement is not concerned with the substantive rights and obligations of the parties, but rather with the establishment of a mechanism to resolve legal disputes that arise between them, as a substitute for national courts, and thereby to determine their substantive rights and obligations. Consent to arbitration in effect involves opting in to a private alternative to the public functions of courts,[45] and it might thus be viewed as procedural or jurisdictional in character, rather than an ordinary substantive contractual obligation, as explored further below. Consent may thus be a necessary but not sufficient condition for the legitimacy of arbitration.[46] (Under this jurisdictional view, courts are more likely to scrutinise the fairness of contractually agreed dispute resolution processes, potentially viewing a process that does not meet judicial standards of procedural fairness as not genuinely arbitration – an issue that has recently been prominent in sports arbitration.)[47] The second complexity is that describing arbitration as a product of contract leaves ambiguous the question of whether there is a further foundation behind the 'contract', which in turn gives the 'contract' that status. Those who view arbitration as an autonomous international ordering would reject the contention that this status must be conferred by national law, but at least conventionally a contract must have a system of law behind it; without a governing law to give it the status of a contract, it is merely a "piece of paper".[48] Where a legal relationship crosses borders, this raises the difficulty of determining which system of law should determine whether an arbitration agreement is binding and effective. This may raise questions of substantive and formal validity (discussed immediately below), questions of the scope and effects of the agreement (discussed in Section 6.5), as well as the question of whether a valid agreement is legally effective for the dispute at hand (discussed in Section 6.6).

---

[44] See e.g. *AT&T Mobility LLC* v. *Concepcion*, 563 US 333 (2011), discussed further in Section 6.5.4 below. See also most recently *Kindred Nursing Centers Limited Partnership* v. *Clark*, 137 S.Ct. 1421 (2017).

[45] See classically, for example, Carlston (1952); Kronstein (1963); McConnaughay (1999).

[46] See e.g. Gélinas (2016).

[47] See e.g. Lewis et al. (2016), Chapter 4.

[48] *Amin Rasheed Shipping Corporation Appellants* v. *Kuwait Insurance Co.* [1984] AC 50, 65 (per Lord Diplock: "Contracts are incapable of existing in a legal vacuum. They are mere pieces of paper devoid of all legal effect unless they were made by reference to some system of private law"). See further Section 10.2 .

6.3.1   Substantive Validity

The starting point of this analysis is the widely adopted doctrine of 'separability', sometimes also referred to as 'severability'. This requires (unless the parties agree to the contrary) that the validity of the arbitration agreement be determined separately from that of any contract as part of which it may have been agreed.[49] Although the doctrine is widespread, it is not universal, which may itself raise a difficult applicable law issue. The question of whether a doctrine of separability applies may be viewed as a procedural question (governed by the law of the 'seat' of the arbitration) or as a substantive law question (governed by the law of the contract). The former is probably preferable, as the latter is somewhat question-begging.[50] Where separability applies, this in turn means that the law governing an arbitration agreement is determined separately from the law that governs the substantive contractual rights and obligations of the parties.[51] A choice of law clause in a contract will thus not necessarily determine the law that governs an arbitration agreement in the same contract. As noted above, the New York Convention 1958 provides that the enforcement of an arbitral award may be refused if the arbitration agreement is invalid "under the law to which the parties have subjected it or, failing any indication thereon, under the law of the country where the award was made".[52] The Convention curiously omits a rule for determining the law that governs the validity of an arbitration agreement directly, but the rule set out for enforcement of arbitral awards has also been influential in that context for obvious reasons. An express agreement on the law governing the arbitration agreement will thus almost invariably be given effect.[53] In the absence of such an agreement, arbitral tribunals and the courts of Convention states are left with a great deal of discretion in determining whether the parties should be considered to have implicitly 'subjected' the arbitration agreement to a particular system of law.

---

[49] See e.g. Arbitration Act 1996 (UK), s.7.

[50] The law on the point is surprisingly unclear in the United Kingdom. Section 2(5) of the Arbitration Act 1996 states that the separability rule in s.7 applies if English law governs the arbitration agreement, even if the seat of the arbitration is not in England – it is unclear if this is in addition to (or instead of) the general rule that the provisions of the Act apply where the seat of the arbitration is in England (s.2(1)). See e.g. *National Iranian Oil Company* v. *Crescent Petroleum Company International Ltd* [2016] EWHC 510 (Comm).

[51] See e.g. Dicey, Morris and Collins (2012), [16-011ff]; *Sulamérica CIA Nacional De Seguros SA* v. *Enesa Engenharia SA* [2012] EWCA Civ 638.

[52] Article V(1)(a).

[53] See e.g. Buys (2012); *Sulamérica CIA Nacional De Seguros SA* v. *Enesa Engenharia SA* [2012] EWCA Civ 638. See further, in relation to substantive law, Section 10.4.1.

6.3.1.1   Before a National Court

National courts generally rely on national choice of law rules to determine the law applicable to an arbitration agreement, and practice is variable.[54] It is, in particular, much debated whether to look to the law governing the substantive contractual terms, or the law of the seat of arbitration – the former as a presumed choice, and the latter either as a matter of presumed choice or a default rule in the absence of a choice by the parties (as suggested under the New York Convention). There are reasonable policy arguments in favour of either approach.

Many parties who enter into a contract containing an arbitration agreement and a choice of law clause are likely to presume that the choice of law clause would be effective for all its terms, including the arbitration agreement. There is something to be said for a (rebuttable) presumption that parties would have intended for a single law to govern their entire agreement – this is now the general approach in England.[55] This assumes, of course, that the choice of law clause is itself valid and effective – if it is not, it will evidently not determine the governing law for the arbitration agreement.[56]

On the other hand, the effectiveness of an arbitration agreement is sometimes viewed as a jurisdictional matter rather than a substantive one, and jurisdictional questions are always left to the law of the 'forum', which in this context might suggest the seat of the arbitration – that law will, in any case, be applied to procedural questions concerning the arbitration.[57] A party choosing arbitration in England, even as part of a contract otherwise governed by French law, may thus (alternatively) expect that the validity of the arbitration agreement will be a matter of English law even if proceedings are commenced in the French courts. This is the rule

---

[54] It may be noted in passing that arbitration agreements are excluded from the scope of the Rome I Regulation in the European Union. The choice of law rules are thus to be found in the national law of EU Member States, including the common law in England – see further Section 7.2.1.

[55] *Sulamérica Cia Nacional de Seguros SA* v. *Enesa Engenharia SA* [2012] EWCA Civ 638, [26]; *Arsanovia Ltd* v. *Cruz City 1 Mauritius Holdings* [2012] EWHC 3702 (Comm); see further Arzandeh (2013). A freestanding arbitration agreement, not entered into as part of a broader contract, may however require a distinct approach: see e.g. *BCY* v. *BCZ* [2016] SGHC 249 (Singapore).

[56] See generally Chapter 7; see e.g. *Dees* v. *Billy*, 357 Fed.Appx 813 (9th Cir. 2009) (also determining that the arbitration agreement was an invalid 'contract of adhesion' under Nevada law).

[57] See e.g. *FirstLink Investments Corp. Ltd* v. *GT Payment Pte Ltd* [2014] SGHCR 12 (Singapore); Goh (2015); *Abuja International Hotels Ltd* v. *Meridien Sas* [2012] EWHC 87 (Comm); *C* v. *D* [2007] EWCA Civ 1282.

generally applied by the English courts if the presumption that an arbitration agreement is governed by the substantive applicable law is rebutted,[58] or if there is no choice of substantive applicable law for the contract.[59] It is also the approach that has been adopted in China.[60] This approach will not work, however, if the parties have not designated a seat and a tribunal has not yet been established, in which case either the substantive applicable law or the law of the forum is likely to govern.[61]

Whichever approach is adopted, national choice of law rules will almost invariably (with France as a notable exception, as discussed below) point towards some system of national law to determine the validity of the arbitration agreement, even if the parties have purported to choose for it to be governed by non-state law.[62]

6.3.1.2   Before an Arbitral Tribunal

The analysis is somewhat more complicated if the question of what law governs an arbitration agreement arises before an arbitral tribunal.[63] The arbitral tribunal is not necessarily bound by national choice of law rules – national arbitration laws do not generally take a prescriptive approach to these questions. If the parties have specifically chosen a governing law for their arbitration agreement, that will almost invariably be applied by the tribunal, because the tribunal is contractually required to resolve the dispute in accordance with the agreement of the parties. The law chosen by the parties need not be the law of any state – arbitral tribunals are likely to recognise an express choice of non-state law to govern the arbitration

---

[58] *Sulamérica Cia Nacional de Seguros SA* v. *Enesa Engenharia SA* [2012] EWCA Civ 638, [32]. Somewhat controversially, the courts found in *Sulamérica* that the presumption can be rebutted if the substantive applicable law would render the arbitration agreement unenforceable – essentially adopting a presumption in favour of the effectiveness of the arbitration agreement. See e.g. Pearson (2013). See similarly the Swiss Law on Private International Law, Art.178(2).

[59] See e.g. *Habas Sinai Ve* v. *VSC Steel Company Ltd* [2013] EWHC 4071 (Comm).

[60] Law of the People's Republic of China on the Laws Applicable to Foreign-Related Civil Relations (2010), Art.18: "The parties may by agreement choose the law applicable to their arbitration agreement. Absent any choice by the parties, the law of the place where the arbitration institution locates or the law of the seat of arbitration shall be applied." See further discussion in Yang (2014).

[61] See e.g. 'Interpretation on Certain Issues Concerning PRC Law on the Application of Laws to Foreign-Related Civil Relations', Supreme People's Court, Fa Shi [2012] No. 24, 28 December 2012, Art.14 (defaulting to forum law in the absence of any agreement as to the law applicable to the arbitration agreement or the location or seat of arbitration).

[62] On the choice of non-state law see further Chapter 10.

[63] See generally e.g. Bermann (2015); Grigera Naón (2001).

agreement, as authorised for example under the UNCITRAL Model Law.[64] As discussed further in Section 10.4, the concept of party autonomy recognised by a tribunal applying this approach is thus notably different from that recognised by a national court – the 'contract' giving rise to the authority of the tribunal need not, from the point of view of the tribunal itself, depend on any system of national law, but on a recognised exercise of autonomy pursuant to transnational standards.

In the absence of an express choice of law for the arbitration agreement, an arbitral tribunal will need to apply a choice of law rule to identify the governing law, either through finding an implied choice of another law or through a default rule, or find an alternative to a choice of law methodology. A preliminary difficulty faced by the tribunal will thus be in identifying this choice of law rule. There are three basic approaches that tend to be taken.

The first is to apply a choice of law rule taken from national law. One obvious candidate would be the national law of the seat of arbitration – the validity of an arbitration agreement designating England as the seat of arbitration will thus be evaluated in the arbitral tribunal in the same way it would be evaluated by the English courts (which is not necessarily based on English law, as discussed above).[65] An arbitral tribunal may also consider the national choice of law rules of the place in which the arbitral award is likely to be enforced to be potentially relevant, as part of their duty to render an enforceable award. In many cases, however, this will not be influential because it will be difficult for the tribunal to anticipate where their award would be enforced, particular where the parties have assets in multiple jurisdictions.

The second approach is for the tribunal to apply choice of law rules that are not taken from a single national law, but rather based on a 'transnational' standard identified from the general practice of other arbitral tribunals or based on 'general principles' of private international law identified from the practice of states.[66] This approach is arguably supported by the UNCITRAL Model Law, which provides that "Failing any designation by the parties, the arbitral tribunal shall apply the law determined by the conflict of laws rules which it considers applicable".[67] This gives the tribunal itself the authority to determine the applicability of potential choice of law rules, rather than prioritising those of the seat, and allows the

---

[64] Article 28(1).
[65] See e.g. Mann (1967a).
[66] See generally e.g. Nazzini (2016).
[67] Article 28(2) – this provision is not directly concerned with the jurisdiction of the tribunal, but with the merits of the claim. See also e.g. the Arbitration Act 1996 (UK), s.46(3).

tribunal to consider a wide range of national and non-state law sources in reaching that determination, although may also lead the tribunal to adopt state choice of law rules and ultimately to apply national law. It may be noted that the Hague Principles on Choice of Law in International Commercial Contracts 2015 expressly exclude arbitration agreements from their scope,[68] however, because they are "commonly considered to be procedural issues".[69]

The third approach is for the tribunal to eschew choice of law rules, and simply apply 'transnational law' (in substance) to govern the arbitration agreement, in much the same way as arbitral tribunals may apply transnational law to govern the substantive legal obligations between the parties, as discussed further in Section 10.4. This approach is evidently based on the idea that arbitration forms an autonomous international legal order, not derivative from national law but establishing its authority directly from the agreement of the parties, discussed in Section 6.2. In the absence of a clause specifying that transnational law should govern the arbitration agreement, it is somewhat bold to suggest that the exclusion of national law (with all the uncertainty that encompasses) is what was agreed to by the parties, implicitly or by default. Yet this approach has, somewhat remarkably, also been adopted as part of French national law: if the parties to an arbitration agreement have not selected a governing law for the agreement, French courts will view the arbitration agreement as bound by principles of transnational law,[70] which may be identified from the practice of arbitral tribunals or through international codifications such as the UNIDROIT Principles of International Commercial Contracts. There are limited signs that such an approach may be growing in influence elsewhere – for example, in the Western Australian Supreme Court's decision that in interpreting an international arbitration agreement, "account should be taken of principles which are evident in international jurisprudence dealing with the construction of such agreements".[71] In general, however, viewing the validity of an arbitration agreement as governed by transnational law is much more likely to be adopted as an approach in arbitral tribunals than national courts.

---

[68] Article 1(3)(b).

[69] Commentary to the Hague Principles, [1.7].

[70] See e.g. Cour de Cassation, *Municipalité de Khoms El Mergeb* v. *Société Dalico*, 20 December 1993, 91-16828; Cour de Cassation, *Société d'études et représentations navales et industrielles (SOERNI)* v. *Société Air Sea Broker limited (ASB)*, 8 July 2009, 08-16025. See further discussion in *Dallah Real Estate and Tourism Holding Company* v. *Government of Pakistan* [2010] UKSC 46.

[71] *Cape Lambert Resources Ltd* v. *MCC Australia Sanjin Mining Ltd* [2013] WASCA 66, [55].

6.3.2   *Formal Validity*

The analysis above has focused primarily on the issue of what law governs the substantive validity of an arbitration agreement. Questions may also arise concerning the formal validity of arbitration agreements, analogous to the formal validity issues that may restrict choice of court agreements as discussed in Section 5.2. The most evident issue is that the New York Convention 1958 requires an arbitration agreement to be in writing.[72] The fact that the Convention deals with formal validity is generally understood to mean that no additional formality requirements may be imposed by Convention states, otherwise they would be adding conditions to their treaty obligations. Even the requirement for writing is less significant than it may at first seem, for two reasons. The first is that the trend is to interpret this 'writing' requirement flexibly, to accommodate the development of electronic communications.[73] The second is that a failure to satisfy this condition does not necessarily render the arbitration agreement invalid, but rather establishes only that the agreement falls outside the scope of the New York Convention. This means that whether unwritten arbitration agreements or arbitral awards based thereon[74] will nevertheless be enforced is a matter for national law. The question of what law governs the arbitration agreement, discussed above, will thus also potentially be critical for questions of formal validity. Although practice is not universal, many national legal systems will enforce unwritten arbitration agreements, as directed by the UNCITRAL Model Law.[75] Section 5 of the Arbitration Act 1996 (UK), for example, appears to require an arbitration agreement to be in writing (although this is interpreted flexibly), but oral arbitration

---

[72] Article II(1) and (2) (defining an agreement in writing to include "an arbitral clause in a contract or an arbitration agreement, signed by the parties or contained in an exchange of letters or telegrams"). For different interpretations of this requirement see e.g. *Sphere Drake Ins.* v. *Marine Towing*, 16 F.3d 666 (5th Cir. 1994); *Kahn Lucas Lancaster, Inc.* v. *Lark International Ltd*, 186 F.3d 210 (2nd Cir. 1999).

[73] See e.g. UNCITRAL Model Law, Art.7 (particularly Option I).

[74] Although the text is unclear, the better view is that the writing requirements in Article II apply equally to enforcement proceedings under Articles III, IV, and V – see e.g. Born (2014), pp.664–6. But note the UNCITRAL "recommended interpretation" of Articles II and VII, available at www.uncitral.org/uncitral/en/uncitral_texts/arbitration/2006recommendation.html, which suggests that the scope of the New York Convention may be extended by more favourable national laws.

[75] UNCITRAL Model Law, Art.7 (both Options I and II). One example is the French Code of Civil Procedure, Article 1507 ("An arbitration agreement shall not be subject to any requirements as to its form"), but contrast Article 1443 for domestic arbitration ("In order to be valid, an arbitration agreement shall be in writing"). See further Born (2014), pp.706–7.

agreements may still be enforced pursuant to the common law.[76] In the United States, in cases where the New York Convention does not apply, an arbitration agreement must be in writing to fall within the Federal Arbitration Act, otherwise its effectiveness is a matter of state law.[77] Where federal law applies, state law may not, however, impose additional formal validity requirements.[78]

As discussed in Section 5.2, rules of formal validity such as writing requirements may be introduced for a variety of reasons, including to ensure that contractual obligations are not entered into lightly or inadvertently, and are based on a genuine agreement rather than one imputed by law. Understood this way, the writing requirement in the New York Convention may be viewed as sceptical of arbitration – ensuring that no party loses their rights of access to a court without clear evidence. As in the context of jurisdiction agreements, however, the imposition of such formality requirements carries a degree of risk that the court will not be able to give effect to genuinely agreed (but unwritten) arbitration clauses – that it may serve as a restriction on party autonomy. The flexibility in interpreting such requirements and the approaches of many national courts to give effect to arbitration agreements even in the absence of compliance with these requirements suggests perhaps a move away from the scepticism that may have prompted the imposition of formality requirements in the New York Convention, towards a disposition in favour of arbitration as an increasingly common exercise of party autonomy.

6.4   Should Courts or Tribunals Resolve Disputes Concerning the Validity of an Arbitration Agreement?

As noted above, the approach to determining the validity of an arbitration clause may vary depending on whether the question is raised before an arbitral tribunal or before a court. This immediately raises the further question as to the circumstances in which tribunals or courts should address these matters. The question of who should decide on the jurisdiction of an arbitral tribunal is one that raises perennial difficulties.[79]

---

[76] Arbitration Act 1996 (UK), s.81(1)(b).

[77] It is, however, unclear whether the writing requirements under the Act are the same as those under the New York Convention: see e.g. Strong (2012a).

[78] *Doctor's Associates, Inc.* v. *Casarotto*, 517 US 681 (1996); *Threlkeld & Co. Inc.* v. *Metallgesellschaft Ltd (London)*, 923 F.2d 245 (2nd Cir. 1991).

[79] See generally e.g. Reisberg (2009); Barcelo (2003); Park (2000).

6.4.1 Distinguishing Jurisdiction and Admissibility

Before addressing the respective roles of courts and arbitral tribunals in determining the validity of an arbitration agreement, a preliminary point that must be addressed concerns the distinction between questions of jurisdiction and questions of admissibility. The terminology is unfortunately not used consistently in the arbitration literature, but for present purposes the concept of 'admissibility' (sometimes also referred to as conditions precedent to arbitration, or procedural arbitrability)[80] refers to whether or not a claim has been properly brought before an arbitral tribunal. This is a distinct question from whether the tribunal has or would have jurisdiction over the claim. For example, an arbitration agreement may require the parties to attempt to negotiate a settlement for a period of time before commencing arbitration,[81] or may impose a contractual limitation period (requiring that arbitration be commenced within a certain time period of a breach of contract arising).[82] Doubts may arise as to whether a party who has initiated arbitration has complied with such a condition. These doubts do not, however, affect the validity of the arbitration agreement. As a consequence, presuming there are no other reasons to question the arbitration agreement, the question of whether the condition has been satisfied is a matter that should be resolved by the arbitral tribunal (as a dispute arising out of the contract), not a matter for a court. Should there be additional doubts over the validity of the arbitration agreement, these would need to be resolved by either a court or the tribunal itself (as analysed further below) before the question of admissibility is addressed. This is not to say that drawing a line between questions of admissibility and questions of jurisdiction is always straightforward,[83] but where an issue falls on the admissibility side of the line, it should be heard only by an arbitral tribunal.[84] Where a valid arbitration agreement supports the arbitral

---

[80] See *Howsam v. Dean Witter Reynolds, Inc.*, 573 US 79, 83-86 (2002); for criticism of this terminology see Paulsson (2005).

[81] See generally Kayali (2010); Jones (2009); Jolles (2006); Jiménez Figueres (2003). See e.g. *HIM Portland LLC v. DeVito Builders, Inc.*, 317 F.3d 41 (1st Cir. 2003); *Channel Tunnel Group v. Balfour Beatty Construction Ltd* [1993] AC 334.

[82] See further Tweeddale and Tweeddale (2009).

[83] For a general, practically oriented guide to this distinction, see e.g. Chartered Institute of Arbitrators, 'International Arbitration Guidelines 2015/2016: Jurisdictional Challenges' (available at www.ciarb.org/guidelines-and-ethics/guidelines/practice-guidelines-protocols-and-rules). See further Born and Šćekić (2016), p.227; Gouiffès and Ordonez (2015); Paulsson (2005).

[84] See e.g. *BG Group plc v. Republic of Argentina*, 134 S.Ct. 1198 (2014); *Howsam v. Dean Witter Reynolds, Inc.*, 573 US 79, 83-86 (2002); but see *Wah (aka Alan Tang) v. Grant Thornton International Ltd* [2012] EWHC 3198 (Ch).

tribunal's determination of admissibility questions, that determination should be considered decisive, including by national courts.[85] As discussed below, by contrast, a tribunal's decision on its own jurisdiction cannot be decisive in determining whether such jurisdiction in fact exists.

6.4.2 Arbitral Tribunals

One of the foundational principles of international arbitration (and indeed of international dispute resolution more generally) is 'competence-competence'.[86] This principle has two fundamentally distinct components. The first component, uniformly adopted in any state that accepts arbitration, is the rule of 'positive competence-competence' – simply providing that an arbitral tribunal has the power to rule on its own jurisdiction.[87] Indeed, the exercise of this power is usually considered a necessary precondition to the exercise of any other powers by the tribunal. In some legal systems (including the United Kingdom)[88] this rule may, however, be departed from by agreement of the parties, which may instead require disputes over the validity of the arbitration agreement to be resolved exclusively by a court.

The second component is an additional rule of 'negative competence-competence'.[89] The negative aspect of competence-competence does not provide that a decision of an arbitral tribunal on its own jurisdiction is the *final word* on the matter[90] – if the tribunal does not have jurisdiction, then no decision made by the tribunal as to its own jurisdiction can be effective to determine that it does. It should follow from this that any decision of the tribunal as to its own jurisdiction does not require deference, although a court may nevertheless find the reasoning and conclusions of the tribunal

---

[85] Paulsson (2005).

[86] See generally e.g. Redfern and Hunter (2015), [5.105ff]; Born (2014), Chapter 7; Dicey, Morris and Collins (2012), [16-013]; Park (2007a), p.55; *Ust-Kamenogorsk Hydropower Plant JSC* v. *AES Ust-Kamenogorsk Hydropower Plant LLP* [2013] UKSC 35; *Dallah Real Estate and Tourism Holding Company* v. *Government of Pakistan* [2010] UKSC 46, [84] ("the principle that a tribunal in an international commercial arbitration has the power to consider its own jurisdiction is no doubt a general principle of law"); UNCITRAL Model Law, Art.16; Arbitration Act 1996 (UK), s.30.

[87] See e.g. Arbitration Act 1996 (UK), s.30.

[88] Arbitration Act 1996 (UK), s.30(1) ("Unless otherwise agreed by the parties, the arbitral tribunal may rule on its own substantive jurisdiction …").

[89] See generally e.g. Gaillard and Banifatemi (2008).

[90] This proposition, sometimes described as 'definite' or 'real' competence-competence, was at one time adopted under German law, but has apparently been abandoned: see Born (2014), [7.01]. It may however still be part of the law of some other states, at least if the parties have agreed to it. See e.g. Park (2007b).

persuasive.[91] The true effect of the adoption of negative competence-competence is that courts are required (at least in some circumstances) to give the tribunal the *first word* on determining its own jurisdiction. Negative competence-competence may be provided directly under national procedural law – potentially even, as in France, in a non-derogable form.[92] Alternatively, national law may permit the parties to agree to negative competence-competence by contract, making use of what is commonly known as a '*Scott* v. *Avery* clause'.[93]

Negative competence-competence reduces the complexities and potential conflicts that may arise where arbitral and judicial proceedings run in parallel. The downside of this is that it increases the risk that an arbitral tribunal's award will be denied recognition or enforcement after lengthy and costly arbitral proceedings, should one or more national courts ultimately disagree with the tribunal's determination of its own jurisdiction. National arbitration laws typically attempt to balance these considerations by providing that negative competence-competence only applies where a threshold standard is met for the validity of the arbitration agreement – that it only applies if, for example, there is a reasonable argument in favour of the validity of the arbitration agreement. In France, however, a stronger version of the doctrine applies.[94] Even if an arbitral tribunal has not yet been established, the French courts must nevertheless refuse to determine the validity of an arbitration agreement unless it is manifestly void or inapplicable[95] – as noted above, this rule cannot even be derogated from by agreement of the parties. If an arbitral tribunal has been established, the courts

---

[91] *Dallah Real Estate and Tourism Holding Company* v. *Government of Pakistan* [2010] UKSC 46, [30]–[31] ("The tribunal's own view of its jurisdiction has no legal or evidential value, when the issue is whether the tribunal had any legitimate authority ... at all ... This is not to say that a court seised of an issue ... will not examine, both carefully and with interest, the reasoning and conclusion of an arbitral tribunal which has undertaken a similar examination. Courts welcome useful assistance").

[92] French Code of Civil Procedure, Art.1448.

[93] From *Scott* v. *Avery* (1856) 10 ER 1121. See generally e.g. Tweeddale and Tweeddale (2011); *Alfred C Toepfer International GmbH* v. *Societe Cargill France* [1997] EWCA Civ 2811 (finding that a *Scott* v. *Avery* clause does not preclude the court from adopting measures to support and enforce the arbitration agreement).

[94] French Code of Civil Procedure, Arts.1448, 1455 and 1465. See e.g. Gaillard and Banifatemi (2008). See also similarly *Shin-Etsu Chemical Co. Ltd* v. *Optifibre Ltd* (2005) 7 SCC 234 (Supreme Court of India); *Pacific International Lines (Pte) Ltd* v. *Tsinlien Metals and Minerals Co. Ltd* [1993] 2 HKLR 249 (Hong Kong).

[95] See e.g. Cour de cassation, 1e civ, 12 February 2014, 13-18.059; Cour de cassation, 1e civ, 18 May 2011, 10-11.008; Cour de cassation, 1e civ, 12 November 2009, 09-10.575; Cour de cassation, civ, Chambre commerciale, 25 November 2008, 07-21.888; Cour de Cassation, 1e civ, 7 June 2006, 03-12.034.

are required to submit any dispute concerning the jurisdiction of the tribunal to the tribunal itself for determination. There is no possibility for the court to refuse to do so even if it views the arbitration agreement as manifestly invalid. By contrast, the English courts have traditionally insisted on a full hearing of questions concerning the validity of the arbitration agreement when deciding whether to stay proceedings,[96] although a more flexible approach appears to be supported by recent case law.[97] The position in the United States is perhaps less clear, although it has been argued that courts in practice draw a distinction between what are referred to as 'gateway' issues (which ought to be reviewed by the courts if and when they arise) and 'non-gateway' issues (which should at least initially be left to arbitral tribunals).[98] This essentially means applying negative competence-competence selectively depending on the jurisdictional issue raised. As noted further below, however, this can also be affected by an agreement by the parties to arbitrate questions that arise concerning the validity of the arbitration agreement – in other words, an arbitration clause for the arbitration clause itself.

6.4.3 Courts

Questions concerning the validity of an arbitration agreement may come before a court at a range of different stages. They may arise before any arbitral tribunal has been established (if proceedings are commenced in court, and an arbitration agreement is alleged to contest the jurisdiction of the court). They may equally arise after a tribunal has completed its work, when proceedings are brought to enforce the arbitral award. They are perhaps most likely to arise in the courts of the seat of the tribunal, for example in proceedings to compel the appointment of an arbitrator or to set aside an arbitral award, but in practice they may arise in any court in which proceedings may be commenced contrary to the agreement or in which enforcement of the arbitral award may be sought. It is contentious

---

[96] See e.g. *Law Debenture Trust Corporation Plc* v. *Elektrim Finance BV* [2005] EWHC 1412 (Ch). Under English law, a party that has participated in arbitral proceedings may not refer the question of the validity of the arbitration agreement to the courts without the permission of the other party or the tribunal, although it appears they may do so indirectly by commencing substantive proceedings, which will require the court to consider whether the proceedings should be stayed: see Arbitration Act 1996 (UK), s.9, s.32, and s.72(1).

[97] *Fiona Trust* v. *Privalov* [2007] EWCA Civ 20, [34] ("it will, in general, be right for the arbitrators to be the first tribunal to consider whether they have jurisdiction to determine the dispute").

[98] See e.g. Bermann (2012).

in the law and practice of arbitration whether decisions on the validity of an arbitration agreement made by the courts of the seat of arbitration should be given greater authority than those of other courts.[99] In practice, arbitrators may decide to continue with an arbitration notwithstanding the finding of a non-seat national court that the tribunal lacks jurisdiction, if the arbitrators take the view that the courts of the seat or the courts of the likely place of enforcement of the arbitral award would disagree. On the other hand, a decision by the courts of the seat of arbitration is more likely to be effective, particularly if the venue of the arbitration is the same as the seat, as the court may even restrain the arbitrators from continuing by injunction. However, even in that scenario it is possible for the arbitrators simply to move the arbitration venue. The issue is not only one of practicality, but again reflects distinct conceptions of whether the arbitration agreement derives its authority from national law. As discussed in Section 6.2, arbitrators who conceive of their authority as existing independent of the authority of states are more likely to take the view that they can and should form entirely their own view of the validity of the arbitration agreement, irrespective of the view taken by national courts. By contrast, arbitrators who view their authority as deriving from the recognition of arbitration agreements under national law are more likely to consider decisions by national courts as determinative of that authority. A similar issue arises in different national courts once an award has been rendered – if the award is set aside by the courts of the seat of arbitration, it may be viewed by other courts as thereby nullified, or as continuing to have validity on the basis of the arbitration agreement independently from its non-recognition under national law.[100]

A cardinal principle that must be applied in any judicial proceedings considering the validity of an arbitration agreement is the doctrine of separability. It was noted in Section 6.3 that this doctrine has the consequence

---

[99] See further discussion in *Dallah Real Estate and Tourism Holding Company* v. *Government of Pakistan* [2010] UKSC 46, [27ff].

[100] French practice views the arbitral award as 'free standing' and thus potentially enforceable even if purportedly 'set aside' by the courts of the seat – see e.g. Cour de cassation, 1e civ, *Hilmarton*, 23 March 1994, 92-15137; Cour de cassation, 1e civ, *PT Putrabali Adyamulia* v. *Rena Holding*, 29 June 2007, 05-18053. US practice suggests that an award is generally annulled if set aside by the courts of the seat: see e.g. *TermoRio SA ESP* v. *Electrificadora Del Atlantico SA ESP*, 487 F.3d 928 (DC Cir. 2007); *Baker Marine (Nig.) Ltd.* v. *Chevron (Nig.) Ltd.*, 191 F.3d 194 (2nd Cir. 1999); but for a counter-example see *In re Chromalloy Aeroservices*, 939 F.Supp. 907 (D.D.C. 1996). In English law enforcement of the award depends on the enforceability of the judgment setting it aside – see *Yukos Capital SARL* v. *OJSC Rosneft Oil Company* [2012] EWCA Civ 855. See further Mills (2016b); Van den Berg (2014); Gaillard (1999).

that the law governing an arbitration agreement may be different from the law governing the remainder of the contract. A second and related consequence of the doctrine is that the validity of the arbitration agreement is a question that must be addressed independently from that of the remainder of the contract.[101] In practice, this means that a court must consider issues of validity carefully. If the issue is one that only affects the substantive terms of the contract (the contract price, for example, was the product of bribery or misrepresentation), then it will have no impact on the validity of the arbitration agreement (or award). Issues concerning the validity of the substantive contractual terms (like questions of admissibility) should then be left for determination by the tribunal, in accordance with the arbitration agreement.[102] If the issue is one that specifically affects the arbitration agreement, it is clear that, at least generally, a court may reach its own conclusion on the matter.[103] This general rule may be affected, however, where the contract further specifies that disputes over the validity of the arbitration agreement are also matters exclusively for the arbitral tribunal – a possibility that US courts in particular have long contemplated,[104] and in many cases (somewhat controversially) appear to presume.[105] This is, in essence, a second arbitration agreement that specifically applies to the first arbitration agreement. In that case, questions of the validity of the first

---

[101] See e.g. Redfern and Hunter (2015), [5.100ff]; Born (2014), Chapter 3; Arbitration Act 1996 (UK), s.7; *Fiona Trust* v. *Privalov* [2007] UKHL 40; *Prima Paint Corp* v. *Flood & Conklin Mfg. Co.*, 388 US 395, 403–04 (1967); *Buckeye Check Cashing, Inc.* v. *Cardegna*, 546 US 440, 444–5 (2006); French Code of Civil Procedure, Art.1447; Leboulanger (2007), p.3; Rau (2003).

[102] See e.g. *Prima Paint Corp* v. *Flood & Conklin Mfg. Co.*, 388 US 395 (1967).

[103] See e.g. *Dallah Real Estate and Tourism Holding Company* v. *Government of Pakistan* [2010] UKSC 46, [24].

[104] *AT&T Technologies, Inc.* v. *Communications Workers*, 475 US 643, 649 (1986) ("Unless the parties clearly and unmistakably provide otherwise, the question of whether the parties agreed to arbitrate is to be decided by the court, not the arbitrator"); *First Options of Chicago, Inc.* v. *Kaplan*, 514 US 938, 943 (1995) ("the question 'who has the primary power to decide arbitrability' turns upon what the parties agreed about that matter. Did the parties agree to submit the arbitrability question itself to arbitration?"). See also e.g. *Dallah Real Estate and Tourism Holding Company* v. *Government of Pakistan* [2010] UKSC 46, [24] ("Of course, it is possible for parties to agree to submit to arbitrators (as it is possible for them to agree to submit to a court) the very question of arbitrability").

[105] *Oracle America* v. *Myriad Group*, 724 F.3d 1069 (9th Cir. 2013) (deciding that incorporation of UNCITRAL rules is clear evidence of an agreement to arbitrate questions of arbitrability, despite the fact that the UNCITRAL rules only provide for *positive* competence-competence); see similarly *Schneider* v. *Kingdom of Thailand*, 688 F.3d 68, 73 (2nd Cir. 2012). A similar approach is adopted where the American Arbitration Association's rules are incorporated: see e.g. *Petrofac, Inc.* v. *DynMcDermott Petroleum Operations Co.*, 687 F.3d 671, 675 (5th Cir. 2012); *Fallo* v. *High-Tech Institute*, 559 F.3d 874, 878 (8th Cir. 2009).

arbitration agreement must be arbitrated, but if an issue arises concerning the validity of the second arbitration agreement – the agreement to arbitrate disputes over the validity of the first arbitration agreement – that in turn needs to be resolved by a court.[106] The jurisdiction of the courts may thus not be precluded entirely, although it may be narrowed.

A further difficult question is how a court should deal with a challenge to the contract as a whole which contains an arbitration agreement – for example, an argument that no contract whatsoever would have been signed, except for misrepresentation or bribery. (This closely parallels the question of which court should determine the validity of an exclusive jurisdiction agreement, which is also separable from any contract in which it may be found.)[107] There is a lack of consistency in the way courts approach such questions. The leading authorities appear to require that the alleged invalidity has to be specifically targeted to the arbitration agreement for the court to consider the issue, otherwise it should be passed to the tribunal.[108] The difficulty with this argument is that the requirement for 'specific targeting' may not take sufficiently seriously the effect of the source of the invalidity on the arbitration agreement and thus on the authority of the tribunal. The deference to an arbitral tribunal under this approach appears to derive from the pro-arbitration disposition of the courts, rather than an exercise of party autonomy, as it is contested whether there is any such exercise. An alternative view is that such questions (challenges to the validity of the contract as a whole) should be viewed as potentially invalidating (separately) both the arbitration agreement and the substantive terms.[109] The court should then consider the issues as part of its evaluation of the validity of the arbitration agreement – asking, for example, whether the arbitration agreement itself was induced by a misrepresentation (as no contractual relationship whatsoever would have been entered into without the misrepresentation). Should the arbitration agreement be considered to be invalidated, it would then potentially be for the courts to conclude that the substantive terms of the contract were equally invalidated.

---

[106] *Rent-A-Center, West, Inc.* v. *Jackson*, 130 S.Ct. 2772 (2010).

[107] See Section 3.3.2.

[108] *Fiona Trust* v. *Privalov* [2007] UKHL 40, [19], [35]; *Rent-A-Center, West, Inc.* v. *Jackson*, 130 S.Ct. 2772 (2010).

[109] See e.g. *Hyundai Merchant Marine Company Limited* v. *Americas Bulk Transport Limited* [2013] EWHC 470 (Comm). See further discussion in Leboulanger (2007), p.22ff.

6.5   Issues Concerning the Scope and Effects of an Arbitration Agreement

Where a valid arbitration agreement exists, a range of further secondary questions may arise concerning the scope and effects of the agreement. This section focuses on four such questions – the types of disputes that will be covered by the agreement, the parties who will be bound by the agreement, whether the agreement will be considered exclusive or non-exclusive, and whether the agreement will permit or preclude class arbitration.

6.5.1   Subject-Matter Scope

The existence of a valid arbitration agreement binding on two disputing parties does not necessarily imply that every dispute that may arise between those parties must be arbitrated. There are two types of limits on what disputes will be covered. The first, covered in this section, is created by the parties through limits on the scope of their agreement. The second, examined in Section 6.6, is created by operation of the law through limits on what types of disputes are considered arbitrable. The two considerations should be carefully distinguished, although this is not always the case in practice, particularly as US scholarship and case law tends to use the term 'arbitrability' for both questions interchangeably.[110] One important reason for making this distinction is that interpretation of the scope of a valid arbitration agreement is a matter on which courts may defer to a determination of the arbitral tribunal,[111] while the legal limits on arbitrability are matters that should be determined by a court despite the parties having entered into an arbitration agreement.[112]

It is generally the case that parties will enter into an arbitration agreement in order to resolve disputes that may arise in connection with a 'defined legal relationship.'[113] Classically, an arbitration agreement is found as part of a contract, and almost invariably it will apply to disputes that arise out of the performance of the contract. Traditionally, the main areas of uncertainty

---

[110] For endorsement of the distinction, see *Mitsubishi Motors Corp.* v. *Soler Chrysler-Plymouth, Inc.*, 473 US 614, 628 (1985) (requiring "a two-step inquiry, first determining whether the parties' agreement to arbitrate reached the statutory issues, and then, upon finding it did, considering whether legal constraints external to the parties' agreement foreclosed the arbitration of those claims").

[111] See Section 6.4, with the possible exception of disputes in which it is unclear if any claim falls within the scope of the agreement.

[112] See Section 6.6.

[113] UNCITRAL Model Law, Art.7(1).

have been whether an arbitration agreement encompasses disputes concerning the validity and not merely the performance of the contract, and whether it encompasses non-contractual claims that relate to the contract, including statutory claims.[114] Issues may also arise concerning whether the agreement encompasses claims under other contracts between the parties – as noted in Section 4.2, particular difficulties emerge where those other contracts contain inconsistent dispute resolution clauses. The New York Convention 1958 itself notes that an arbitration agreement may contemplate disputes that arise "in respect of a defined legal relationship, whether contractual or not",[115] but does not offer any further guidance on how arbitration agreements should be construed. The exact subject-matter scope of an arbitration agreement is ultimately a matter of contractual interpretation, because an arbitral tribunal has only as much authority as the parties have conferred upon it – the sole basis of its jurisdiction is the exercise of party autonomy through the arbitration agreement. The approach adopted should thus depend on the law that governs the arbitration agreement, which must be determined as discussed in Section 6.3. National courts do not, however, always clearly acknowledge that this is a matter that may be governed by foreign law, as discussed further below.

Traditionally, some courts have approached the interpretation of an arbitration agreement as a matter requiring detailed technical analysis of the words used by the parties. The standpoint of this approach was arguably to presume that parties should only be understood to have excluded the jurisdiction of the courts where there is a clear agreement to do so – viewing this form of exercise of party autonomy as anomalous. The English courts, for example, traditionally distinguished between arbitration clauses that referred to disputes 'arising under' the contract, which were often considered to apply strictly to the performance of the contract, and clauses that referred to disputes 'relating to' the contract, which were considered to encompass a broader range of disputes.[116] This approach was decisively rejected by the House of Lords in *Fiona Trust* v. *Privalov* (2007). The Court considered that a 'fresh start' should be made on the issue, and held that:

> the construction of an arbitration clause should start from the assumption that the parties, as rational businessmen, are likely to have intended

---

[114] See generally Redfern and Hunter (2015), [2.63]–[2.70]; Born (2014), Chapter 9.
[115] Article II(1).
[116] See e.g. *Overseas Union Insurance Ltd* v. *AA Mutual International Insurance Co. Ltd* [1988] 2 Lloyd's Rep 63, 67.

any dispute arising out of the relationship into which they have entered or purported to enter to be decided by the same tribunal. The clause should be construed in accordance with this presumption unless the language makes it clear that certain questions were intended to be excluded from the arbitrator's jurisdiction.[117]

The Lords noted that this change brought the English courts more in line with the approach in the United States (discussed below), Germany,[118] and Australia.[119] In Australia, arbitration agreements have not only been interpreted broadly in terms of encompassing contractual or tortious actions, they have also been viewed as encompassing similar statutory claims (such as for misleading and deceptive conduct under the Trade Practices Act 1974), even if the statute would not necessarily be applied by the arbitral tribunal.[120] In the United States a similarly broad approach has long been endorsed by the Supreme Court, which held in 1960 that:

> An order to arbitrate the particular grievance should not be denied unless it may be said with positive assurance that the arbitration clause is not susceptible of an interpretation that covers the asserted dispute. Doubts should be resolved in favor of coverage ... In the absence of any express provision excluding a particular grievance from arbitration, we think only the most forceful evidence of a purpose to exclude the claim from arbitration can prevail.[121]

---

[117] *Fiona Trust* v. *Privalov* [2007] UKHL 40, [13], per Lord Hoffmann. See similarly e.g. *Sulamérica CIA Nacional De Seguros SA* v. *Enesa Engenharia SA* [2012] EWCA Civ 638, [40]; *Microsoft Mobile OY (Ltd)* v. *Sony Europe Ltd* [2017] EWHC 374 (Ch). In *Fiona Trust*, the contract was governed by English law and the seat of arbitration was in London, and there was no doubt that the arbitration agreement was itself governed by English law. As discussed above, the interpretation of an arbitration agreement should be a matter for the law governing the arbitration agreement. The ruling in *Fiona Trust*, strictly speaking, should be understood as a presumption that arises as part of English substantive law, and should not be applied by the English courts where the arbitration agreement is governed by foreign law (unless that foreign law applies the same presumption). It remains to be seen whether the courts will in fact follow this approach in practice.

[118] *Bundesgerichtshof Decision of 27 February 1970*, JZ 1970, 730, translated report at (1990) 6 Arbitration International 79.

[119] *Comandate Marine Corp* v. *Pan Australia Shipping Pty Ltd* [2006] FCAFC 192, [165]; *Walter Rau Neusser Oel und Fett AG* v. *Cross Pacific Trading Ltd* [2005] FCA 1102, [41]. See further discussion in Keyes (2009), p.186ff (suggesting that the Australian presumption may be weaker than that adopted by the House of Lords).

[120] See *Comandate Marine Corp* v. *Pan Australia Shipping Pty Ltd* [2006] FCAFC 192, [184], expressly rejecting the earlier approach in *Hi-Fert Pty Ltd* v. *Kiukiang Maritime Carriers Inc. (No 5)* [1998] FCA 1485. See also e.g. *Francis Travel Marketing Pty Ltd* v. *Virgin Atlantic Airways Ltd* (1996) 39 NSWLR 160.

[121] *Steelworkers* v. *Warrior & Gulf Navigation Co.*, 363 US 574, 582, 584–5 (1960). See further *Gateway Coal Co.* v. *Mine Workers*, 414 US 368, 377–8 (1974); *Mitsubishi Motors*

The Supreme Court claimed that this approach reflected the fact that arbitration required a basis in party autonomy – that "the judicial inquiry ... must be strictly confined to the question whether the reluctant party did agree to arbitrate the grievance or did agree to give the arbitrator power to make the award he made".[122] The reality, however, is that, like the new approach of the English courts, it is a presumption that is supportive of arbitration, tending to find that the parties have exercised their autonomy broadly even in the absence of evidence. This approach means, for example, that in the absence of clear evidence to the contrary an arbitral tribunal is to be presumed to have jurisdiction over non-contractual claims relating to the contract containing the arbitration agreement, as well as claims concerning the validity of that contract. The standpoint of this approach is thus the opposite of that traditionally (but no longer) adopted in England – it is presumed that parties who have selected arbitration intend for their arbitration agreement to encompass the broadest possible range of disputes, unless otherwise indicated. Although the English courts referred to this as based on the likely intentions of 'rational businessmen', this was not a proposition based on empirical evidence. Well-informed businessmen would in fact understand the laws applicable to the interpretation of arbitration agreements, and under the traditional approach, would have chosen their words carefully to indicate the precise intended scope of their agreement.[123] The change in rule is arguably more reflective of a change in attitude from the courts themselves, indicating a more positive disposition towards arbitration. The US Supreme Court almost acknowledged as much in finding that its broad approach was required "to be consistent with congressional policy in favor of settlement of disputes by the parties through the machinery of arbitration".[124] There is evidently a danger with

---

    Corp. v. *Soler Chrysler-Plymouth, Inc.*, 473 US 614 (1985); *AT&T Technologies Inc.* v. *Communications Workers of America*, 475 US 643, 650 (1986); *Threlkeld & Co. Inc.* v. *Metallgesellschaft Ltd (London)*, 923 F.2d 245 (2nd Cir. 1991); *Watson Wyatt & Co.* v. *SBC Holdings, Inc.*, 513 F.3d 646 (6th Cir. 2008). As discussed above, the interpretation of an arbitration agreement should be a matter for the law governing the arbitration agreement. This broad interpretative approach should thus arguably be followed only for an arbitration agreement governed by US federal law or a state law adopting an equally proarbitration policy.

[122] *Steelworkers* v. *Warrior & Gulf Nav. Co.*, 363 US 574, 582 (1960).

[123] See e.g. *Mediterranean Enterprises* v. *Ssangyong Corp.*, 708 F.2d 1458, 1464–5 (9th Cir. 1983).

[124] *Steelworkers* v. *Warrior & Gulf Nav. Co.*, 363 US 574, 582 (1960). See similarly *Moses H. Cone Memorial Hospital* v. *Mercury Construction Corp.*, 460 US 1, 24 (1983) (the interpretation

such presumptions that the law goes beyond the agreement of the parties, imputing to them a broader intention than is evidenced by their contract, giving rise to an arbitration that is legally binding but lacks a genuine foundation in party autonomy.[125]

This is not to say, however, that arbitration agreements will always be interpreted to encompass all disputes, even those unrelated to the contractual relationship that founded them. The US Supreme Court has clearly accepted the principle that the parties *may* limit the scope of their arbitration agreement to cover only certain disputes,[126] and some cases still appear to interpret arbitration agreements narrowly and technically,[127] even suggesting that parties are unlikely to intend for non-contractual claims to go to arbitration because arbitrators are not necessarily lawyers but may only have experience with contract law matters.[128] English courts have also limited the scope of arbitration agreements to claims sufficiently closely connected to (or arising out of) the contract as part of which the agreement was entered into.[129] Even the most broadly worded arbitration agreement is likely to have some limit on its scope. In one recent US case,[130] the arbitration clause in a loan agreement covered "any claim, dispute or controversy between you and us that in any way arises from or relates to this Agreement ... [including] disputes based upon contract, tort, consumer rights, fraud and other intentional torts, constitution, statute, regulation, ordinance, common law and equity". When the borrower defaulted on the loan, the lender's agents tried to take possession of security, and in the course of an altercation the borrower was shot and partially paralysed.

---

of an arbitration clause "must be addressed with a healthy regard for the federal policy favoring arbitration").

[125] Note e.g. *Watson Wyatt & Co.* v. *SBC Holdings, Inc.*, 513 F.3d 646, 649 (6th Cir. 2008) ("This policy ... is not so broad that it compels the arbitration of issues not within the scope of the parties' arbitration agreement"). For a cautious approach to relying on the *Fiona Trust* presumption in the context of the formation of arbitration agreements, see *Lisnave Estaleiros Navais SA* v. *Chemikalien Seetransport GmbH* [2013] EWHC 338 (Comm), [42].

[126] *Mitsubishi Motors Corp.* v. *Soler Chrysler-Plymouth, Inc.*, 473 US 614, 628 (1985).

[127] In *Cape Flattery Ltd* v. *Titan Maritime, LLC*, 647 F.3d 914 (9th Cir. 2011), the court held that an arbitration clause covering disputes "arising under" a contract did not cover a tort occurring during performance of the contract.

[128] See e.g. *Green Tree Financial Corp.* v. *Bazzle*, 539 US 444, 452–3 (2003); *Armada Coal Export, Inc.* v. *Interbulk, Ltd*, 726 F.2d 1566 (11th Cir. 1984).

[129] See e.g. *Microsoft Mobile OY (Ltd)* v. *Sony Europe Ltd* [2017] EWHC 374 (Ch); *The Angelic Grace* [1995] 1 Lloyd's Rep 87.

[130] *Clay* v. *New Mexico Title Loans, Inc.*, 288 P.3d 888 (N.M. Ct. App. 2012).

The court concluded that a claim in tort against the lender and their agents was not covered by the arbitration agreement, on the basis that:

> A party may be assumed to have intended to arbitrate issues that are closely related to those governed by the agreement itself, but not those that are unrelated to the agreement, out of the context of the agreement, or outrageous and unforeseeable.[131]

The limitation of the agreement to foreseeable disputes is consistent with the principles suggested by a consequentialist approach to party autonomy, as analysed in Section 2.4.2. It is notable that this limit of foreseeability is sometimes also applied in the context of choice of court agreements, as analysed in Chapter 4.

6.5.2   Effect on Third Parties

An arbitration agreement in a contract will ordinarily only be binding on the signatories to the agreement, as a matter of privity of contract.[132] A further question concerning the scope or effectiveness of an arbitration agreement is its effect on third parties – parties who may not be signatories to the agreement but become parties to a dispute related to the contract.[133] This is closely analogous to the question of the impact of a choice of court agreement on third parties, discussed in Section 3.6. Like that problem, it raises particularly difficult choice of law issues – the law governing whether a party is bound by an arbitration agreement may be considered to be different from the law governing the validity of the arbitration agreement in general. Courts have recognised that such parties may become bound by, or be able to benefit from, an arbitration agreement in a number of ways under various principles including contract, agency law or estoppel.[134] Three particular contexts may be highlighted.

---

[131] At 896.

[132] See e.g. *EEOC* v. *Waffle House, Inc.*, 534 US 279 (2002). An arbitration agreement in one contract may be incorporated by reference as part of the terms of another contract – this is not, however, strictly a third-party problem but rather a question of determining whether the terms of the agreement include an arbitration clause, so it is not covered in this section. But see e.g. *Exchange Mutual Insurance Co.* v. *Haskell Co.*, 742 F.2d 274 (6th Cir. 1984).

[133] See further e.g. Brekoulakis (2017); Redfern and Hunter (2015), [2.42ff]; Born (2014), Chapter 10; Park (2014); Steingruber (2012); Mayer (2012); Brekoulakis (2011); Hanotiau (2007), p.341.

[134] See generally analysis in *Merrill Lynch Investment Managers* v. *Optibase, Ltd.*, 337 F.3d 125 (2nd Cir. 2003); *EI Dupont de Nemours* v. *Rhone Poulenc Fiber*, 269 F.3d 187 (3rd Cir. 2001); *Thompson-CSF, SA* v. *American Arbitration Association*, 64 F.3d 773 (2nd Cir. 1995);

First, although the agreement is signed by one party, it may be considered to have been entered into on behalf of (or as agent for) another party.[135] The apparent third party is thus in reality a party to the agreement, and generally the agent is not.[136] A subsidiary may, for example, be acting as an agent for its parent company. Holding the parent to be bound by the arbitration agreement in this context is sometimes also categorised as falling under broader principles of corporate veil-piercing.[137] In the context of corporate groups, some courts and arbitral tribunals have (controversially)[138] extended this principle by taking the view that an arbitration agreement was entered into on behalf of the whole group of companies, and thus each member of the corporate group is both bound by and can benefit from the clause.[139] Such claims may go beyond traditional agency principles, either as a matter of national law, or even as a matter of transnational law (if arbitration agreements are viewed as independent exercises of party autonomy, separate from national law and courts). Doubts may thus be expressed as to whether they genuinely reflect the agreement of the parties, or whether they instead reflect a pro-arbitration policy that risks conferring authority on tribunals beyond that authorised by the exercise of party autonomy. Viewing an arbitral tribunal as having such authority for the purposes of resolving a complex dispute efficiently would require a fundamental change in the conceptualisation of arbitration, emphasising its public (quasi-judicial) function rather than private law foundations.[140]

Sunkist Soft Drinks, Inc. v. *Sunkist Growers, Inc.*, 10 F.3d 753 (11th Cir. 1993), cert. denied, 115 S.Ct. 190 (1994).

[135] See e.g. *Dallah Real Estate and Tourism Holding Company* v. *Government of Pakistan* [2010] UKSC 46 (considering whether the government of Pakistan was party to an arbitration agreement entered into by a trust established as a separate legal entity under the law of Pakistan, but finding that this argument did not succeed on the facts); *Pakistan* v. *Dallah Real Estate and Tourism Holding Co*, Cour d'Appel (Paris), 17 February 2011, 09-28533 (reaching the opposite conclusion); *Egiazaryan* v. *OJSC OEK Finance* [2015] EWHC 3532 (Comm).

[136] See e.g. *Covington* v. *Aban Offshore Ltd*, 650 F.3d 556 (5th Cir. 2011).

[137] See e.g. *Thompson-CSF, SA* v. *American Arbitration Association*, 64 F.3d 773, 777–8 (2nd Cir. 1995). These principles have, however, tended to be construed increasingly narrowly: see generally e.g. *Prest* v. *Petrodel Resources Ltd* [2013] UKSC 34. See also generally Kryvoi (2011).

[138] See e.g. *Sarhank Group* v. *Oracle Corporation*, 404 F.3d 657 (2nd Cir. 2005); *Peterson Farms Inc.* v. *C&M Farming Ltd* [2004] EWHC 121 (Comm).

[139] See e.g. *Dow Chemical* arbitration, ICC Case No. 4131, (1984) 9 Yearbook of Commercial Arbitration 131; Brekoulakis (2017); Hanotiau (2011); Ferrario (2009); Wilske, Shore and Ahrens (2006).

[140] For such an argument see e.g. Brekoulakis (2017).

Second, a contract may be entered into by two parties for the benefit of a third party. As a consequence of privity, the contract would traditionally not be enforceable by the third party, but in many legal systems reforms have been introduced permitting third party enforcement in certain circumstances (as discussed in relation to jurisdiction agreements in Section 3.6). However, as a matter of law or contract, it may be required that the third party accepts any procedural conditions attached to the exercise of the rights under the contract.[141] Thus, a third party enforcing rights given to them under a contract that contains an arbitration agreement which purports to apply also to third parties may find that they may only vindicate those rights through arbitration. However, problematically, they may also experience difficulty in enforcing any subsequent arbitral award, as they may not be considered to have been a party to the arbitration agreement for the purposes of the New York Convention.[142]

Third, rights under a contract, including in respect of an arbitration agreement, may later become exercisable by a third party. This may arise in a variety of ways, such as through assignment or novation of the rights, through a merger of companies,[143] or through the exercise of subrogation, such as where an insurance company makes a claim based on the rights of the insured under a contract containing an arbitration agreement. In any of these cases it may be difficult to determine whether the party exercising the substantive rights is also bound by the arbitration agreement – the issue has been particularly contentious in the context of subrogation.[144]

6.5.3   Exclusive or Non-Exclusive

Like jurisdiction agreements, arbitration agreements may be exclusive or non-exclusive – intending to preclude the jurisdiction of national courts, or to give the parties the option of arbitration in addition to recourse to the jurisdiction of national courts. The analysis in Section 3.3 highlighted a trend towards viewing jurisdiction agreements as exclusive unless clearly non-exclusive, set out expressly in the Brussels I Regulation as part

---

[141] See e.g. the *Contracts (Rights of Third Parties) Act* 1999 (UK), s.8; *Fortress Value Recovery Fund I LLC* v. *Blue Skye Special Opportunities Fund LP (A Firm)* [2013] EWCA Civ 367; *Nisshin Shipping Co. Ltd* v. *Cleaves & Co. Ltd* [2003] EWHC 2602 (Comm); *American Bureau of Shipping* v. *Tencara Shipyard*, 170 F.3d 349 (2nd Cir. 1999) (reaching a similar result through estoppel).

[142] See further Tweeddale (2011).

[143] See e.g. *John Wiley & Sons, Inc.* v. *Livingston*, 376 US 543 (1964).

[144] See e.g. C-185/07 *Allianz SpA* v. *West Tankers Inc.* [2009] ECR I-663; *West Tankers Inc.* v. *Ras Riunione Adriatica Di Sicurta Spa* [2005] EWHC 454 (Comm).

of EU law and in the Hague Choice of Court Convention 2005. Such a presumption should, if anything, operate more strongly in the context of arbitration agreements. Parties who include an arbitration agreement in a contract will usually be pre-judging that disputes which may arise in connection with the contract will be best settled through arbitration, and they will intend to exclude the possibility of judicial settlement for that reason. In the context of choice of court agreements, the presumption in favour of exclusivity reflects a presumed desire of commercial parties for legal certainty, and the same argument would apply even more strongly for the selection of an arbitration agreement. Interpreting a jurisdiction agreement as non-exclusive means the parties have recourse to a number of different courts; interpreting an arbitration agreement as non-exclusive means the parties have recourse not only to different courts but also to different modes of dispute resolution.

Despite these tendencies, however, it remains possible that courts may identify an arbitration agreement as non-exclusive, for two main reasons. The first is that some commercial parties wish to maximise flexibility, not certainty, particularly if they might anticipate a wide range of different possible disputes emerging in relation to a contract. The second is that, despite the generally pro-arbitration disposition adopted by many courts, as discussed above, there may remain a residual scepticism towards arbitration and the exclusion of the jurisdiction of courts. In the recent Privy Council decision of *Anzen Ltd* v. *Hermes One Ltd (British Virgin Islands)* (2016),[145] for example, the arbitration clause provided that in the event of an unresolved dispute "any party may submit the dispute to binding arbitration". Proceedings were commenced in the courts of the British Virgin Islands, and a key question was whether they should be stayed in light of the arbitration agreement – in other words, whether the agreement was exclusive or non-exclusive. Rather than simply adopting a strong presumption in favour of exclusivity, the Privy Council engaged in a wide-ranging analysis of the commercial practice around the use of the term 'may' rather than 'shall' in jurisdiction and arbitration agreements, including case law in Singapore, Canada, and the United States,[146] ultimately concluding that the arbitration agreement was non-exclusive. In the process, the court observed that "clauses depriving a party of the right to litigate should be expected to be clearly worded – even though the commercial community's evident preference for arbitration in many spheres makes any such

---

[145] *Anzen Ltd* v. *Hermes One Ltd (British Virgin Islands)* [2016] UKPC 1.
[146] At [22]–[28].

presumption a less persuasive factor nowadays than it was once".[147] This clearly suggests at least that no presumption arises in favour of exclusivity, and if anything a weak presumption may arise against it. The technical linguistic analysis in this decision does not appear very dissimilar to the type of analysis that was disapproved of in the *Fiona Trust* decision discussed above,[148] in the context of the subject-matter scope of an arbitration agreement, but it is consistent with the idea that the interpretive goal is to identify the intentions of the parties rather than to support arbitration.

The existence of a non-exclusive arbitration agreement raises a further potential complexity, in terms of the possibility of parallel judicial and arbitral proceedings, risking conflicting judgments. As in the context of jurisdiction agreements, the fact that the parties have entered into a non-exclusive agreement should not be taken as an indication that they contemplate the possibility of parallel proceedings, but only that they contemplate the possibility of proceedings in multiple alternative forums.[149] There are several possibilities as to how such parallel proceedings may be addressed. Perhaps the most obvious way would be simply to give priority to the court or tribunal first seised, taking the approach that the parties have not given priority to any particular forum in their agreement. In *Anzen Ltd v. Hermes One Ltd (British Virgin Islands)* (2016), this would have meant the court accepting jurisdiction, as no arbitral proceedings had yet been commenced. Alternatively, the court might take the view that proceedings could be stayed on a *forum non conveniens* analysis, but only if the dispute was more appropriate for settlement through arbitration rather than in the courts. However, these options were not argued before the Privy Council,[150] and the court instead focused on two alternative readings of the arbitration agreement. The first was that the court should stay its proceedings if and when arbitral proceedings were commenced, even if the court was first seised. The second was that the court should stay its proceedings if the defendant in those proceedings asked it to do because of a preference for the dispute to be submitted to arbitration. The Privy Council ultimately found that the second of these options was the correct

---

[147] At [13].

[148] *Fiona Trust v. Privalov* [2007] UKHL 40.

[149] See e.g. *Deutsche Bank Ag v. Tongkah Harbour Public Company Ltd* [2011] EWHC 2251 (Comm), and further Section 3.4.3. Exceptionally, however, an arbitration agreement may be drafted in such a way as to expressly contemplate parallel proceedings, as in *Royal Bank of Canada v. Cooperatieve Centrale Raiffeisen-Boerenleenbank BA* [2004] EWCA Civ 7 ("nor will the bringing of Proceedings in any one or more jurisdictions preclude the bringing of Proceedings in any other jurisdiction").

[150] *Anzen Ltd v. Hermes One Ltd (British Virgin Islands)* [2016] UKPC 1, [10].

interpretation of the clause at hand. In effect, the court found that the non-exclusive arbitration clause was nevertheless intended to create a priority in favour of arbitration over litigation in court, such that the stated preference of either party for arbitration would be enough to prevent judicial proceedings, even in the absence of an actual arbitration.[151] The arbitration clause thus gave each party the right to block litigation by the other party, even without themselves commencing arbitration. This conclusion was far from obvious from the text of the agreement, and arguably risks adopting a position where a pro-arbitration disposition determines the effect of the arbitration clause, rather than the intentions of the parties. It is curious that this case thus combined a sceptical approach towards whether an arbitration agreement was exclusive, with a pro-arbitration approach to the interpretation of the effects of a non-exclusive arbitration agreement.

6.5.4   Class Arbitration

An arbitration is typically a bilateral dispute between the two parties to an arbitration agreement. In recent years, the possibility and practice of 'class arbitration' has received increasing attention, particularly (in fact almost exclusively) in the United States, and has been the subject of a remarkable number of decisions of the US Supreme Court. The issue is particularly prominent in the United States because (as discussed further in Section 6.6) there are relatively limited restrictions on what disputes may be settled by arbitration, and so it is common to see arbitration clauses in employment and consumer contracts. Where a legal issue arises affecting a number of potential claimants against a single defendant, it is generally considered advantageous (certainly for the claimants, but also in the public interest) to facilitate settlement of all the issues together through 'class action' legal proceedings, and these have become particularly prominent in the legal landscape of the United States. Class action proceedings typically have two great benefits. The first is that they support the efficient resolution of a large number of disputes in a single set of proceedings. The second is that they support access to justice for weaker parties (such as consumers or employees), who may otherwise not be able to afford individualised dispute resolution (or to find lawyers willing to bring proceedings on their behalf). This second feature is also potentially an important check on the power of large corporations – for this reason, attempts to contract out of

---

[151] See also e.g. *Union Marine* v. *Government of Comoros* [2013] EWHC 5854 (Comm); *NB Three Shipping Ltd* v. *Harebell Shipping Ltd* [2004] EWHC 2001 (Comm).

the possibility of class action proceedings may be invalidated by national (or US state) law.[152]

For various reasons, many corporate actors have increasingly turned to arbitration to resolve their disputes rather than courts. As discussed above, some of these reasons relate to the widespread global enforceability of arbitration agreements and arbitral awards. Another less salutary reason is the potential confidentiality of arbitral proceedings, which may prevent a single claim against a company (for example, by one consumer) being relied on as a precedent by other claimants in a similar position. There is a danger here that individualised exercises of party autonomy through arbitration agreements have negative public consequences, in denying the potential public benefits associated with individual or class action judicial proceedings. As a consequence, some jurisdictions have developed a concept of class arbitration – permitting a large number of arbitral proceedings against a single defendant to be consolidated in a single claim, to mirror the benefits in efficiency and access to justice of class action litigation. In support of this approach, for example, the American Arbitration Association published 'Supplementary Rules for Class Arbitrations' in 2003. These developments are controversial, as class arbitration requires some adaptation of the traditional conceptions and procedures of arbitration, but it could be argued that as each individual bilateral dispute is supported by an individual arbitration agreement, consolidation of those disputes remains broadly consistent with giving effect to party autonomy. The initial response from the courts appeared to be supportive of this argument, with a plurality of the US Supreme Court in *Green Tree Financial Corp.* v. *Bazzle* (2003)[153] holding that the question of whether class arbitration was permissible was primarily a matter for arbitrators not courts, and those judges who addressed the issue appearing to find that an arbitration clause could be open to class arbitration even if it was silent on the point. However, the Supreme Court later emphasised in *Stolt-Nielsen SA* v. *AnimalFeeds International Corp* (2010)[154] that class arbitration could only be supported where the parties had consented to it as part of the terms of their arbitration agreement. Because class arbitration involved fundamentally different procedural questions, such consent could not be presumed or imputed to the parties as a matter of policy, but must be found in

---

[152] In California see e.g. *America Online, Inc.* v. *Superior Court*, 90 Cal.App.4th 1, 17–18 (2001).
[153] 539 US 444 (2003).
[154] 559 US 662 (2010).

the arbitration agreement as a matter of contractual interpretation.[155] The Court thus held that the Federal Arbitration Act required a strict approach to be taken to the enforcement of the arbitration agreement between the parties, limiting the availability of class arbitration. (It may be noted, however, that this was not a case involving unequal parties such as consumers or employees.) The later decision of the Court in *Oxford Health Plans* v. *Sutter* (2013)[156] found again that the availability of class arbitration was a matter of contractual interpretation, but emphasised that the decision of an arbitrator on the point should rarely be interfered with by the courts, even if (as in this case) the arbitrator found class arbitration to be available when the parties had not addressed the question expressly in their agreement. This appears to open the door again to a slightly looser approach to determining the availability of class arbitration, at least for arbitrators and in the absence of express provision on the point in the contract.[157]

In parallel, the development of class arbitration prompted a further backlash from corporations seeking to avoid these types of proceedings. This came through adopting revised arbitration clauses that specify that they only consent to individual arbitration, and expressly exclude or waive the possibility of class arbitration. The emergence of such clauses has created a difficult policy conflict. On the one hand, the underlying purpose of arbitration agreements is to give effect to the agreement of the parties, and class arbitration waiver clauses can be part of that agreement. For those who view arbitration agreements as reflecting an inherent autonomy of the parties, there seems little reason not to give effect to this particular form of exercise of that autonomy. On the other hand, it may be considered that at least part of the purpose of giving effect to arbitration agreements is because this is considered to have a public benefit – for example, increasing efficient dispute resolution through taking disputes and costs away from the courts. Those who see party autonomy in respect of arbitration as effective because national legal orders choose to support it may see class arbitration waiver clauses as taking away a significant part of the public benefit that can be achieved through arbitration (or class action litigation), and potentially raising questions about whether this form of

---

[155] See generally analysis in Strong (2012b).

[156] 133 S.Ct. 2064 (2013).

[157] As noted in note 2 of the Court's Opinion, the parties in this case treated the question of class arbitrability as (essentially) a matter of admissibility, submitting the point to the arbitrator. It may be questioned whether this approach is always correct, and if not, this may limit the significance of this decision to cases in which the parties have agreed to arbitrate questions of the validity of the arbitration agreement itself – see further Section 6.4.

autonomy should be supported by national law. As a consequence, some courts, including State courts in California, took the view that consumer arbitration clauses containing class arbitration waivers were invalid as a matter of unconscionability,[158] just as Californian law invalidates class action waivers in relation to litigation (as noted above).

The issue of the validity of such rules also came before the US Supreme Court in *AT&T Mobility LLC* v. *Concepcion* (2011).[159] A party to an arbitration agreement with a class arbitration waiver (in a cellular phone contract) sought instead to join a class action law suit in the Californian Federal District Court, relying on the decision of the Californian courts that the class arbitration waiver rendered the arbitration clause unconscionable and invalid. The Supreme Court concluded (by a five to four majority) that US states, at least generally, cannot invalidate class arbitration waiver clauses, because to do so would be inconsistent with the Federal Arbitration Act policy of giving effect to the agreement between the parties – "to ensure the enforcement of arbitration agreements according to their terms so as to facilitate streamlined proceedings".[160] (As noted above, a class action waiver would mean that a class arbitration could not proceed, because there would be no agreement between the parties permitting such an arbitration.) In this particular context, it appears that the US Supreme Court determined that the Federal Arbitration Act adopts a broad policy of supporting any exercise of party autonomy, irrespective of whether to do so achieves a public benefit – if anything, the emphasis in the majority judgment was on the benefits of arbitration to defendants, not to the public or the parties collectively. If any conditions were to be imposed on that support for party autonomy, they would require amendment of the Federal Arbitration Act or other legislation. Although the decision may thus be read on one level as simply a matter of federal law pre-empting state law, it is also arguably based on a reading of the Federal Arbitration Act as adopting a deontological or private consequentialist approach to the support for party autonomy, as the Act is considered to require enforcement

---

[158] *Discover Bank* v. *Superior Court*, 113 P.3d 1100 (Cal. 2005).

[159] *AT&T Mobility LLC* v. *Concepcion*, 563 US 333 (2011). See also the related decision in *DIRECTV* v. *Imburgia*, 136 S.Ct. 463 (2015). See further e.g. Strong (2012b); Bermann (2011); Stipanowich (2011); Resnik (2011).

[160] *AT&T*, at 344. The concern with 'streamlined proceedings' in the majority opinion (language that is not found in the Federal Arbitration Act) focused on a comparison between class arbitration and bilateral arbitration, not between class arbitration and potentially hundreds or thousands of bilateral arbitrations, which arguably ought to be the proper basis of comparison. On any analysis, class arbitration is more 'streamlined' than thousands of bilateral arbitrations, even if as a result it is less desirable for defendants.

of any exercise of that autonomy in strict terms, regardless of perceived negative public consequences. Support for the idea that there is an underlying deontological approach (the inherent exercise of party autonomy is supported rather than any form of consequential benefits) may perhaps be found in the later decision of the Supreme Court in *American Express v. Italian Colors Restaurant* (2013),[161] in which the Court held that a class arbitration waiver was enforceable even if it rendered the cost of proving the claim greater than the potential recovery. Some further clarification of these issues may be provided, as the Supreme Court has recently granted certiorari in three further cases involving the enforceability of arbitration agreements containing class action waivers, focused particularly on the question of whether such waivers are valid in employment contracts (as violating the rights of employees to engage in collective activities).[162] If class arbitration waiver clauses are effective (as they appear to be for most consumer contracts),[163] there is evidently a danger that such clauses will prevent any collective proceedings based on contractual relationships – the arbitration clause preventing class action in litigation, and the waiver preventing class arbitration – which would be a dramatic cultural change in US litigation practice. This risks undermining access to justice and would potentially necessitate greater state regulation as a counterbalance to the declining prospect of enforcing corporate responsibility through private law claims. However the issues are resolved, it is evident that the disputes around the availability of class arbitration, based on competing interpretations of the purpose of the Federal Arbitration Act, are also reflections of competing conceptions of why exercises of party autonomy through arbitration agreements should be given effect.

6.6   What Types of Disputes are Capable of Settlement through Arbitration?

The analysis above has been primarily concerned with the question of the validity and scope of the arbitration agreement. If a dispute falls within the scope of an arbitration agreement that is contractually binding, there

---

[161] 133 S.Ct. 2304 (2013).

[162] Docket number 16-307, argued 2 October 2017. *Murphy Oil USA, Inc. v. NLRB*, 808 F.3d 1013 (5th Cir. 2015); *Morris v. Ernst & Young LLP*, No. 13-16599 (9th Cir. 22 August 2016); *Lewis v. Epic Systems Corp.*, 823 F.3d 1147 (7th Cir. 2016).

[163] It may be noted that the Consumer Financial Protection Bureau adopted rules in July 2017 that preclude class arbitration waivers in consumer financial products: see www .consumerfinance.gov/arbitration-rule/.

remains the question of whether the agreement will be enforced for that type of dispute – whether, in the words of the New York Convention 1958, the dispute concerns "a subject matter capable of settlement by arbitration".[164] This is evidently a distinct issue from the question of the intended scope of the agreement, although in practice the two questions are not always carefully distinguished.[165] The term generally used to describe this issue is 'arbitrability'. Somewhat confusingly, in the United States the term 'arbitrability' is often used in a much broader sense to encompass questions concerning the validity of the arbitration agreement (sometimes referred to as 'subjective arbitrability')[166] or the admissibility of the dispute (sometimes referred to as 'procedural arbitrability').[167] The issue examined in this section is then sometimes referred to as either 'subject-matter arbitrability' or 'objective arbitrability', as it is focused on the subject matter or object of the dispute. Rules addressing this issue are comparable to certain aspects of non-justiciability that arise in national courts[168] – for example, the common law rule that disputes concerning title to foreign immovable property are non-justiciable, examined in Section 5.4.2. Like those rules, questions of subject-matter arbitrability thus function as limitations on party autonomy, as they constrain the power of parties to enter into an effective arbitration agreement.

6.6.1   Approaches to Subject-Matter Arbitrability

An exhaustive account of the types of disputes that may raise subject-matter arbitrability issues or the wide range of national approaches taken to this question is beyond the scope of this book.[169] For present purposes it is sufficient to identify two major categories of disputes that are commonly considered non-arbitrable.

The first are disputes in which there is a significant inequality between the parties, such as those involving consumers, employees, or insured

---

[164] Article II(1); see similarly Art.V(2)(a).

[165] See e.g. *Clough Engineering Limited* v. *Oil & Natural Gas Corporation Ltd* [2007] FCA 881, [39] and [41] (Australia); *ET Plus SA* v. *Welter* [2005] EWHC 2115 (Comm), [51].

[166] For further analysis see e.g. *Howsam* v. *Dean Witter Reynolds, Inc.*, 537 US 79 (2002); Shore (2009); Fortier (2005), pp.269–70.

[167] See e.g. Bermann (2012), p.10.

[168] See generally e.g. Cheshire, North and Fawcett (2017), p.484ff; McLachlan (2014), Chapter 6.

[169] For a wide-ranging comparative analysis, see the Study on Arbitrability (2016) of the International Bar Association Subcommittee on Recognition and Enforcement of Arbitral Awards. See further generally Redfern and Hunter (2015), [2.124ff]; Born (2014), Chapter 6; Mistelis and Brekoulakis (2009); Bantekas (2008).

parties[170] – the same categories of parties in which there are commonly restrictions on party autonomy through choice of court agreements, as discussed in Section 5.5. The restrictions on arbitration agreements for such parties may be viewed as reflecting the same concerns as those that arise in the context of choice of court agreements: that unequal bargaining power may lead to a dispute resolution mechanism which unfairly favours the stronger party. There are, however, also additional concerns that are particular to arbitration agreements. One feature of arbitration (commonly considered an advantage) is the power of the parties to customise the applicable procedural rules, which is usually not available in respect of national courts. This raises the possibility that the terms of an arbitration agreement may create unfairness not only in the venue and mode of dispute resolution, but also in its procedures. A further concern is that national legal systems commonly include special protections for weaker parties, such as implied terms in contracts, or mandatory statutes that override contrary contractual provisions. Arbitrators may be less likely to view those terms as part of the applicable law or as otherwise rules requiring application, because arbitrators are not (or at least may not perceive themselves to be) part of any national dispute resolution system.[171]

There are, however, countervailing reasons why arbitration may be considered a mechanism that is not only suitable but favourable for resolving disputes involving weaker parties. Some forms of arbitration may be cheaper, faster, and more informal than court proceedings, and they may therefore offer greater promise of real 'access to justice' for weaker parties.[172] (This may also be affected by the availability of class arbitration, as discussed in Section 6.5.4.) Arbitrators may also possess specialist expertise that enables them to resolve disputes (such as those arising from employment contracts)[173] more efficiently and with a greater understanding of

---

[170] See e.g. Consumer Rights Act 2015 (UK), Schedule 2, s.20(a); *Clyde & Co. LLP* v. *Van Winkelhof* [2011] EWHC 668 (statutory employment claims not arbitrable); Wilcke and Wildhaber (2010); Mistelis and Brekoulakis (2009).

[171] See further Section 6.2.

[172] But contrary to this point, some legal systems restrict arbitration for small claims – see e.g. the Arbitration Act 1996 (UK), s.91, and The Unfair Arbitration Agreements (Specified Amount) Order 1999, SI 1999/2167 (arbitration agreement not binding on a consumer if amount sought is less than £5,000).

[173] See e.g. Carbonneau (2009), p.144; *Circuit City Stores, Inc.* v. *Adams*, 532 US 105 (2001); *AT&T Technologies, Inc.* v. *CWA*, 475 US 643, 650 (1986) (the "presumption of arbitrability for labor disputes recognizes the greater institutional competence of arbitrators in interpreting collective bargaining agreements" – although note that in this case the Court did not distinguish clearly between subjective and objective 'arbitrability'); *Textile Workers* v. *Lincoln Mills*, 353 US 448 (1957).

industry practices.[174] For these reasons, some legal systems, particularly the United States, do not impose significant restrictions on the arbitrability of disputes involving weaker parties, and indeed at times appear positively to support the practice of arbitrating such disputes.[175] The fact that the Federal Arbitration Act provides that arbitration agreements are generally to be enforceable has been taken to preclude any state laws restricting any categories of disputes from being arbitrable, so it is only federal law that can impose any such restrictions.[176] Section 1 of the Act does exclude "contracts of employment of seamen, railroad employees, or any other class of workers engaged in foreign or interstate commerce" from arbitration, but the provision has been narrowly construed so that it is limited to transportation workers,[177] and other employment disputes have been clearly held to be arbitrable under the Act.[178] It has also recently been confirmed, for example, that the Act "includes no exception for personal-injury or wrongful-death claims."[179] These rules do leave open the possibility of federal law constraints on arbitrability, but even federal law providing consumers with a 'right to sue' has been interpreted as not precluding mandatory arbitration of consumer contracts.[180] These issues are sometimes controversial, and law reforms are occasionally proposed,[181] but the wealth of US authority is supportive of a broad approach to arbitrability even in disputes involving weaker parties.

The second reason why certain categories of dispute may be considered incapable of settlement through arbitration is because the dispute has effects beyond the parties. This may include effects on third parties, who

---

[174] This point might, however, work either for or against weaker parties, depending on whether arbitrators (consciously or otherwise) align themselves with more powerful actors, or are generally appointed from an industry background.

[175] See e.g. Schmitz (2013); C Smith and Moyé (2012). One notable exception, however, is the prohibition on arbitration clauses in residential mortgage loan agreements: see 15 US Code 1639c(e).

[176] See e.g. *Preston v. Ferrer*, 552 US 346, 353 (2008); *AT&T Mobility LLC v. Concepcion*, 563 US 333 (2011).

[177] *Circuit City Stores, Inc. v. Adams*, 532 US 105 (2001).

[178] See e.g. *Nitro-Lift Techs., LLC v. Howard*, 133 S.Ct. 500 (2012); *14 Penn Plaza LLC v. Pyett*, 556 US 247 (2009); *Gilmer v. Interstate/Johnson Lane Corp.*, 500 US 20 (1991).

[179] *Marmet Health Care Center, Inc. v. Brown*, 132 S.Ct. 1201 (2012).

[180] *CompuCredit Corp. v. Greenwood*, 132 S.Ct. 665 (2012).

[181] For critical commentary see e.g. Cole (2001); Sternlight (1996). Note e.g. the proposed Arbitration Fairness Act 2015 amendment to 9 US Code s.402(a): "Notwithstanding any other provision of this title, no predispute arbitration agreement shall be valid or enforceable if it requires arbitration of an employment dispute, consumer dispute, antitrust dispute, or civil rights dispute" (not enacted).

will typically be unable to intervene in arbitral proceedings without the consent of both disputing parties, but may intervene much more readily in judicial proceedings by order of the court.[182] A dispute may also have public effects or involve significant points of public interest or public order, which may be judged unsuitable for resolution by an arbitral panel that does not hold a public office but is rather purely contractually bound to the parties, and which may resolve the dispute confidentially. In general, criminal proceedings and other public law disputes such as administrative claims are considered non-arbitrable for these reasons.[183] Family law disputes are also commonly considered not to be arbitrable, either because of the issues of public policy involved or because of their effect on third parties. Article 2060 of the French Civil Code provides, for example, that "One may not enter into arbitration agreements in matters of status and capacity of the persons, in those relating to divorce and judicial separation, or on controversies concerning public bodies and institutions and more generally in all matters in which public policy is concerned."

The most contentious issues are those that involve elements of private and public law and whose very categorisation is contested. For example, intellectual property rights may on the one hand be categorised as private property rights, but may on the other be viewed as statutory monopolies granted for the public interest. Traditionally, the latter categorisation has led to doubts over their arbitrability,[184] although the trend in this area (and indeed in general) is probably towards viewing more disputes as capable of settlement through arbitration.[185] Similarly, disputes under corporate law (such as claims by shareholders against a company) have also been considered arbitrable, despite the significant public regulatory issues involved, with the exception of proceedings to wind up a company (because of their potential impact on third parties).[186] There is also an increasing trend towards the arbitration of trusts disputes, which raises particular issues concerning whether an arbitral tribunal can perform the

---

[182]   See e.g. the analysis of rights 'in rem' as non-arbitrable in *Booz Allen and Hamilton Inc.* v. *SBI Home Finance Limited* (2011) 5 SCC 532 (Supreme Court of India).

[183]   See e.g. Hiber and Pavić (2008).

[184]   See generally e.g. Grantham (1996).

[185]   See e.g. *Scherk* v. *Alberto-Culver Co.*, 417 US 506 (1974) (allowing arbitration of a dispute involving trademarks); *Desputeaux* v. *Éditions Chouette (1987) inc.* [2003] 1 SCR 178 (Supreme Court of Canada, permitting arbitration of a copyright dispute, and more generally favouring a narrow interpretation of arbitrability limitations). See further generally e.g. Keyes (2009), p.190ff; Bantekas (2008); McConnaughay (2001).

[186]   See e.g. *Fulham Football Club (1987) Ltd* v. *Richards* [2011] EWCA Civ 855; *ACD Tridon Inc.* v. *Tridon Australia Pty Ltd* [2002] NSWSC 896.

supervisory role traditionally carried out by the courts.[187] Another area of law in which questions of arbitrability have proven highly contentious is competition law (also known as anti-trust law). As is well known, different legal systems take different approaches towards the question of whether competition law rules are enforceable through regulatory action by public authorities or through private causes of action. Private claims pursuant to competition law may be viewed as a means of protecting public interests in prohibiting anti-competitive conduct, and it may therefore be considered that such claims should not be arbitrated. This was historically the position in the United States,[188] although the modern view is that the possibility for a court to review the validity of an arbitral award (to take a 'second look' at the dispute) provides sufficient protection of the public interest.[189] This may, however, also depend on whether the arbitral tribunal will apply the relevant US law, even if the parties have chosen foreign law in their contract – US statutory rules may thus (somewhat controversially) be viewed as mandatory by US courts (as discussed further below), and a failure to apply them may lead to a refusal of enforcement of any arbitral award.[190] Similar developments in favour of arbitrating competition law disputes have taken place in the European Union,[191] including the United Kingdom,[192] while the position remains contentious in other jurisdictions, such as Australia.[193]

6.6.2   The Applicable Law

The question of what law governs subject-matter arbitrability may arise both before an arbitral tribunal and in any court in which proceedings may be commenced contrary to an arbitration agreement or where enforcement or annulment of an arbitral award may be sought.[194] There

---

[187] See e.g. Strong (2012c).

[188] See e.g. *American Safety Corp.* v. *J.P. Maguire & Co.*, 391 F.2d 821 (2nd Cir. 1968).

[189] *Mitsubishi Motors Co.* v. *Solar Chrysler-Plymouth*, 473 US 614, 638 (1985); see further e.g. Korzun (2016); Radicati di Brozolo (2011b); Bridgeman (2008); L Smith (1986).

[190] See generally Korzun (2016) (suggesting that arbitrators may be compelled to apply anti-trust law, even if the parties have chosen a different law to govern the arbitration, by their duty to render an enforceable award); Force (2011).

[191] In C 126/97 *Eco Swiss China Ltd* v. *Benetton International NV* [1999] ECR I-3055, however, the CJEU held that national courts must set aside an arbitral award as contrary to public policy if it is contrary to certain provisions of EU competition law. See e.g. Lew (2009), p.252; Zekos (2008); Dempegiotis (2008); Bridgeman (2008).

[192] See e.g. *ET Plus SA* v. *Welter* [2005] EWHC 2115 (Comm). In the United Kingdom, the scope of 'arbitrability' was quite deliberately left undefined in the Arbitration Act 1996, s.81(1)(a), leaving it to the courts to develop guiding rules or principles.

[193] Downie (2013).

[194] Courts are, however, unlikely to defer to the decisions of arbitral tribunals on such matters, as they go to the power of the tribunal – see Section 6.4.

are a number of different laws that could potentially be applied by a court or tribunal to this question, and some arbitrators may also look to transnational standards rather than any national law.[195] The New York Convention 1958 itself provides limited guidance, requiring national courts to give effect to an arbitration agreement if it concerns "a subject matter capable of settlement by arbitration",[196] without defining either the content or the source of that standard. There is no uniform approach, which means that analysis of the issue can be complex and give rise to conflicting decisions.

One option is to apply the law governing the arbitration agreement to questions of subject-matter arbitrability. It might be argued that this approach should be adopted because the issue concerns the validity of the arbitration agreement, and issues of validity are usually resolved by the putative applicable law,[197] including most other questions that arise concerning the validity of the arbitration agreement. If there is a choice of law agreement (express or implied) governing the arbitration clause, a court or tribunal may also need consider whether that agreement should be interpreted as extending to questions of subject-matter arbitrability, otherwise such issues may be governed by a different law.[198] The difficulty with this approach is that the issue of subject-matter arbitrability is arguably distinct from other questions concerning the validity of the arbitration agreement, because it is not a contractual question (has an agreement been properly formed) but rather a question of public policy (is the agreement legally enforceable).

As a consequence, there is a tendency for national courts to view the question of subject-matter arbitrability as governed by the law of the forum – a second option for the law governing arbitrability – and not subject to a contrary choice of law by the parties or governed by foreign law. Courts may develop judicial standards for non-arbitrability, or look to statutes that expressly or implicitly grant a right of access to the courts. One potential implication of this approach arises where a forum statute would have effect in judicial proceedings, and an arbitral tribunal would not necessarily apply the statute as part of the governing law. This could be analysed as a question of the validity of the arbitration agreement, as discussed in Section 6.3.1, or as a question of subject-matter arbitrability. In such cases, the arbitration agreement may be refused enforcement to prevent evasion of the statute,[199] or may only be enforced subject to stipulations as to the governing law applied by the arbitral tribunal, an approach

---

[195]   See generally e.g. Hanotiau (2014); Danov (2008); Hanotiau (1999).
[196]   Article II(1).
[197]   See e.g. Article 10 of the Rome I Regulation (but noting that this does not apply to arbitration agreements).
[198]   See e.g. *Cape Flattery Ltd* v. *Titan Maritime LLC*, 647 F.3d 914 (9th Cir. 2011).
[199]   See traditionally e.g. *Wilko* v. *Swan*, 346 US 427 (1953) (subsequently overruled).

that has some judicial backing in the United States[200] and has gained recent support in England.[201] (This issue is analogous to the approach, discussed in Section 9.4.1, under which a foreign choice of court agreement may not be given effect because the foreign court would not apply a forum statute – although as noted there, this approach is not generally applied in the United States for choice of court agreements.) This approach may be criticised for not sufficiently respecting the autonomy of the parties, unless the forum statutes are classified as mandatory rules (in the private international law sense) that should not be evaded through the combination of a choice of foreign law and arbitration agreement.

A third potential source of arbitrability standards is the law of the seat of the arbitration (which may or may not be the same as the law that governs the arbitration agreement). As this law usually provides the procedure for arbitration, there is an argument that it should also determine subject-matter arbitrability, because those procedures will have been designed as a product of the legal system's own conceptions of what types of disputes may be arbitrated. If a legal system views employment disputes as incapable of settlement through arbitration, for example, its arbitration law is unlikely to establish procedures suitable for the arbitration of employment disputes. The courts of the seat of arbitration are particularly likely to look to their national law for the legal limits on subject-matter arbitrability, as it is both the law of the forum and the law governing the arbitration procedure.[202] It is less clear whether other courts or the arbitrators will recognise the primacy of the law of the seat in such questions. A decision by the courts of the seat of arbitration declaring that an arbitration agreement is

---

[200] See e.g. Force (2011), p.418; Kleinheisterkamp (2009); Cheng (2009). The approach derives from *Mitsubishi Motors Corp.* v. *Soler Chrysler-Plymouth, Inc.*, 473 US 614, 637 n.19 (1985) ("in the event the choice-of-forum and choice-of-law clauses operated in tandem as a prospective waiver of a party's right to pursue statutory remedies for antitrust violations, we would have little hesitation in condemning the agreement as against public policy."); see also *Rodriguez de Quijas* v. *Shearson/American Express, Inc.*, 490 US 477 (1989). In practice, however, US courts have generally adopted a 'wait and see' approach under which scrutiny of the law applied by the arbitral tribunal happens at least primarily at the award enforcement stage: see *Vimar Seguros y Reaseguros, SA* v. *M/V Sky Reefer*, 515 US 528, 540 (1995); *Lindo* v. *NCL (Bahamas) Ltd*, 652 F.3d 1257 (11th Cir. 2011).

[201] *Accentuate Ltd* v. *ASIGRA Inc.* [2009] EWHC 2655 (QB) (arbitration clause invalidated because the arbitrators would not give effect to mandatory EU rules – see further Section 9.4.1). See further e.g. Rühl (2007b).

[202] Note UNCITRAL Model Law, Article 34(2)(b)(i), permitting an award to be set aside if "the subject-matter of the dispute is not capable of settlement by arbitration under the law of this State" (meaning the law of the seat of arbitration).

invalid or setting aside an arbitral award on the same basis may not always be recognised by other national courts or even by arbitrators.[203]

A fourth national law that could be applied by a court or arbitral tribunal would be the law of the (likely) place of enforcement of the arbitral award, on the basis that the place of enforcement is unlikely to recognise an arbitral award in respect of subject matter that is viewed within its legal order as incapable of settlement by arbitration. Indeed, Article V(2)(a) of the New York Convention 1958 expressly provides that an award may be refused recognition in a Contracting State if "the subject matter of the dispute is not capable of settlement by arbitration under the law of that country".[204] The court where an arbitral award is being enforced is thus directed to apply the law of the forum to subject-matter arbitrability – not the law of the seat or the law governing the arbitration agreement. It may be, however, that the enforceability of the agreement and the enforceability of the award should be considered as separate issues, governed by separate applicable laws. These could be applied either disjunctively or conjunctively – a court in which an arbitral award is being enforced could refuse enforcement if the dispute was not arbitrable under *either* the law of the arbitration agreement *or* the law of the forum, or only if it was not arbitrable under *both* laws. The extent to which a court is favourably disposed towards arbitration is likely to determine which approach is adopted.[205] This approach is less likely to be influential if the issue of subject-matter arbitrability arises before an arbitral tribunal, or before the courts of the seat of arbitration if proceedings are brought to set aside an award, or before a court in which the arbitration agreement arises as a jurisdictional defence. Although it is often argued that arbitrators have a duty to render an enforceable award, in each such context it may be difficult to predict where an award might be enforced, and thus the law of the place of enforcement will be unlikely to influence questions of subject-matter arbitrability.

Each of these national legal orders has at least an arguable claim to regulate questions of subject-matter arbitrability, but none appears to have a clearly overriding interest, and each may apply widely varying standards. In the face of this complexity, it is no surprise that some arbitral authorities

---

[203] See further discussion in Section 6.4.3.
[204] Note also UNCITRAL Model Law, Article 36(1)(b)(i), permitting a court to refuse recognition or enforcement of an award on the basis that "the subject-matter of the dispute is not capable of settlement by arbitration under the law of this State" (meaning the law of the state where recognition or enforcement is sought).
[205] See further e.g. Smutny and Pham (2008).

and tribunals prefer (once again) to look to transnational standards rather than any particular national law, applying principles of 'transnational public policy'.[206] While this may appear to simplify the choice of applicable law task for the tribunal, the identification of such standards may itself be extremely difficult, particularly as different national legal orders evidently take different approaches to this important constraint on the autonomy of private parties to enter into arbitration agreements.

6.7 Conclusions

The exercise of party autonomy through an arbitration agreement, permitting a choice by the parties of a non-state private form of dispute resolution, is extremely widely accepted. A variety of different justifications may be offered as to why states are supportive of arbitration agreements. It can be argued that arbitration allows parties to choose and customise the most efficient dispute resolution system for their dispute, for example, or that a possible choice of arbitration makes courts work harder to compete. The acceptance of arbitration may also simply reflect the reality of the autonomy of powerful commercial parties, whose preference is to detach themselves from national judicial regulation. Supporting arbitration can also be attractive to states, as it takes some of the burden of resolving disputes away from public courts, reducing their drain on public resources. Although the foundations of arbitration remain in party autonomy, this chapter has also noted some contexts in which state support for arbitration agreements, in giving effect to a pro-arbitration policy, seems to go beyond enforcing the agreement of the parties.

Analysed more closely, however, the apparent consensus on arbitration is more questionable than it may appear. Fundamental disagreements remain concerning the theoretical characterisation of arbitration and its connection to national law. These are reflected in different approaches to the question of what law should govern the validity of an arbitration agreement, and when the decision on validity should be made by a court or by the tribunal itself. The scope and interpretation of arbitration agreements raises a range of further important issues, which again are treated differently in different national orders, as is the question of subject-matter arbitrability. The diversity of approaches to all these issues also reflects the difficulty of the foundational questions they raise – in the tension between the autonomy of private parties and the effectiveness of public interests and values, the law of arbitration provides some of the most keenly contested territory.

---

[206] See e.g. Pryles (2007); Lalive (1986).

7

Choice of Law in Contract

7.1 Introduction

This chapter begins consideration of the second major aspect of party autonomy in private international law – choice of law – which will be continued in Chapters 8–10. It focuses on choice of law in contractual disputes, that is, the effectiveness of a choice by parties as to which law will govern their contractual relationship. It is also focused on the choice of law question as it arises in courts, rather than before arbitral tribunals – as discussed further in Chapters 6 and 10, choice of law in arbitration raises distinct issues. Party autonomy has become widely (but not universally)[1] accepted in choice of law in contract, including under the common law, under EU regulation, in the United States, and under international codifications on choice of law. In choice of law in contract, it is generally considered the pre-eminent choice of law rule, with other considerations such as the location of the parties or the performance of their contract relegated to a subsidiary role. It may be stated generally that under the modern law of most states, express choice of law agreements are almost always given effect, although this is not without significant qualifications or limits in some states, as discussed throughout this chapter and in Chapters 8–10.

To explore the limits of this widespread acceptance, this chapter focuses on five key issues that arise in choice of law in contract. First, in Section 7.2, the distinction between party autonomy, which is a subjective choice of law rule based on agreement between the parties, and the objective choice of law rule which is applied in default of any choice – a distinction that is readily identifiable in theory, but which the courts have often found difficult to draw in practice. Second, in Section 7.3, the question of whether party autonomy should be unlimited, or whether the choice of the parties requires some objective connection or justification – an issue which has

---

[1] See discussion of Brazil below; note also the limited acceptance of party autonomy in the Middle East, discussed in Basedow (2013a), p.168ff.

been particularly contentious in the United States in recent years. Third, in Section 7.4, the question of the timing of a choice of law – whether it may be made after the contract itself, and if so under what conditions and with what effects. These three issues relate to the *effectiveness* or *permissibility* of a particular choice of law agreement, as a matter of private international law rules. They are therefore necessarily governed by the law of the forum in each jurisdiction in which they arise. The fourth issue discussed in this chapter, in Section 7.5, concerns the question of what law should govern the *validity* of a choice of law agreement itself. Questions of validity, which are a matter for contract law, must be distinguished from questions of permissibility, which are a matter for private international law. The choice of law question for choice of law agreements is a particularly difficult issue because applying the nominated law runs the risk of circularity or 'bootstrapping', denying parties protection which they may be otherwise given by law, but any other choice appears to risk undermining the apparent intentions of the parties. The fifth issue, in Section 7.6, concerns what effect should be given to a choice of law which invalidates the contract between the parties, which raises the difficult issue of whether the validity of the contract should be prioritised over the choice of law agreement.

7.2 The Effectiveness and Limits of Choice of Law Agreements: Subjective and Objective Choice of Law Rules in Contract

As explored in Section 2.2.2, historically the determination of the law applicable to a contract focused on objective territorial connecting factors. While the rules were often contentious, the debate principally concerned whether the place of contracting or the place of performance of the contract ought to determine the governing law. Party intentions were discussed by the courts, but principally as a justification for the adoption of one or other of these rules – an argument as to which was more suited to meeting party expectations. With the widespread adoption of party autonomy as a choice of law rule in its own right, such *objective* choice of law rules in contract have generally been demoted to a subsidiary role, with the parties' *subjective* expectations at the forefront, whether expressed in their contract or implied from its other terms. However, as the analysis below demonstrates, the boundary between objective and subjective considerations has often proven difficult to delineate in practice. This is particularly the case where there is no express choice of law, and the court is considering whether such a choice may have been made implicitly, or whether the court should apply the objective rule applicable in the absence of party choice. As discussed in Section 5.2, choice of court agreements are frequently subject to formality requirements (such as a need for the agreement to be in writing or evidenced in written form) – no such requirements generally apply for choice of law agreements, which opens the possibility for a court to identify an implied choice of law agreement.[2]

The influence of party autonomy in choice of law has become so great that it is sometimes suggested that party intentions are the very foundation of all choice of law rules in contract. Objective tests have thus sometimes been justified on the basis that they are meeting hypothetical party expectations – described as reflecting an 'imputed' agreement between the parties, or what the parties would have agreed on if they had thought about the issue. Party autonomy has thus become so successful as a principle that it has tended, somewhat confusingly, to shape the language of choice of law in contract, even in situations in which it does not apply.

This section examines the status of party autonomy in choice of law in contract under the common law, EU law, in the United States, and under international codifications, as well as under Chinese and Brazilian law (highlighted because of their traditional opposition to party autonomy). As a matter of principle party autonomy in choice of law in contract is generally well accepted, and thus the main focus is on exploring the limits of that autonomy by examining the boundary between the subjective test, where an express or implied agreement is identified between the parties as to the applicable law, and the objective test, which determines the law of the contract in the absence of any actual agreement between the parties. There are, in general, twin dangers in determining this boundary. If the rules giving effect to party autonomy are interpreted too restrictively, there is a danger that some genuine agreements will not be given effect, and the autonomy of the parties frustrated. If, on the other hand, the rules are interpreted too broadly, there is a danger that the court will identify imputed agreements rather than actual agreements, and thus that the rule purportedly giving effect to party autonomy will in such cases actually serve as a very flexible objective rule.

7.2.1   Common Law

In England, the common law choice of law rules in contract are now principally of historical interest, having been replaced first by the Rome Convention 1980 and now Rome I Regulation (both considered further

---

[2] See e.g. Pertegás and Marshall (2014), p.984ff.

below), although they will still apply to contracts entered into prior to the commencement date of the Rome Convention in the United Kingdom (1 April 1991), and it is unclear whether they may be revived if or when the United Kingdom leaves the European Union. They are analysed in this section primarily for four reasons. First, they provided an illuminating demonstration of the difficulties which courts have had in identifying exactly what role party intentions should place in choice of law in contract, and in particular in distinguishing between implied and imputed intentions. Second, they are part of the historical antecedent for the Rome Convention 1980, which drew on the common law experience, among others, in adopting its own approach. (The earlier historical context for the development of the modern common law is also discussed in Section 2.2.2.) Third, the common law rules continue to apply in England to certain contracts which are excluded from the scope of the Rome Convention 1980 and Rome I Regulation, such as jurisdiction and arbitration agreements. Fourth, the common law approach to choice of law in contract, as largely developed by courts in England, continues to be applied in other common law systems around the world.

7.2.1.1   Traditional Confusion between Implied and Imputed Intentions

The foundation of the modern common law approach to choice of law in contract is found in *Vita Food Products Inc. v. Unus Shipping Co.* (1939),[3] in which the Privy Council held that a contract is generally governed by "the law which the parties intended to apply".[4] The court went on to say that "where there is an express statement by the parties of their intention to select the law of the contract, it is difficult to see what qualifications are possible, provided the intention expressed is bona fide and legal".[5] The requirement that a choice be 'bona fide and legal' has not generally been interpreted as a significant qualification on choice of a governing law, although it is discussed further in Section 7.3. It may thus be stated that express choices of law are generally effective to determine the law applicable to a contract under the common law. The more difficult question has been what approach should be taken in the absence of an express choice.

---

[3] [1939] AC 237. The decision was in fact the culmination of a series of cases on the issue – see also *R* v. *International Trustee for the Protection of Bondholders AG* [1937] AC 500; *Mount Albert Borough Council* v. *Australasian Temperance and General Mutual Life Assurance Society Ltd* [1938] AC 224.

[4] At p.290.

[5] Ibid.

In *Vita Food Products*, the applicable law in the absence of an express choice was considered by the court to be still a matter of identifying the 'intention' of the parties. Such intention must, it was held, be "objectively ascertained, and, if not expressed, will be presumed from the terms of the contract and the relevant surrounding circumstances".[6] This description of both express and presumed intentions as "objectively ascertained" is somewhat confusing. In reference to an expressed intention, it probably just refers to the fact that such an intention must be determined based on objective evidence – the terms of the contract itself. In the absence of an express choice of law clause, however, the passage cited above suggests that 'intention' involves both subjective and objective considerations ("the terms of the contract and the relevant surrounding circumstances"), and that an 'intention' will be identified ('presumed') even if the parties did not actually have any genuine agreement on the applicable law.

According to this interpretation, *Vita Food Products Inc. v. Unus Shipping Co.* (1939), supported by other authorities,[7] adopted a two-stage test – the first stage looking for an express choice of law agreement (and giving it effect if it is found), and the second (in the absence of an express choice) looking at the contract and other circumstances to determine a 'presumed' choice. The combination of subjective and objective factors in the second stage of this test was, however, somewhat confusing – where an implied agreement is identified, it is unclear why it should be treated differently from an express agreement. The Privy Council also referred to the need "to give effect to the express or implied intention of the parties that the proper or substantive law of the contract ... should be English law",[8] and it had elsewhere long been held that "there is no difference as to effect between that which is expressed in terms and that which is implied and clearly understood".[9] Despite the *Vita Food Products* decision, it therefore remained somewhat unclear what role an unwritten but subjective intention should play in determining choice of law in contract. In particular, it was unclear whether an implied intention should be automatically given effect, or whether it was subject to being overruled by 'objective' factors. In *Bonython v. Commonwealth of Australia* (1951),[10] the Privy Council held that, in the absence of an express choice of law, "the question becomes

---

[6] At p.290. See similarly *R v. International Trustee for the Protection of Bondholders AG* [1937] AC 500, 529.

[7] See n.3 above.

[8] At p.299.

[9] *Peninsular and Oriental Steam Navigation Company v. Shand* (1865) 16 ER 103, 112.

[10] *Bonython v. Commonwealth of Australia* [1951] AC 201.

a matter of implication to be derived from all the circumstances of the transaction",[11] again appearing to conflate implied choices and objective connecting factors.[12]

The Court of Appeal revisited the choice of law rules for contract in the case of *The Assunzione* (1954),[13] largely following the above approach, but offering some further (and unfortunately again confused) analysis centred around the term 'intention'. It was suggested by Lord Justice Singleton that, in the absence of an express choice, "one must look at all the circumstances and seek to find what just and reasonable persons ought to have intended if they had thought about the matter at the time when they made the contract", and that "it may be said that just and reasonable persons would like the dispute determined in the most convenient way and in accordance with business efficiency".[14] The difficulty with this approach is that, once again, it seems to conflate subjective and objective considerations, encompassing an examination of both real and hypothetical intentions. The reference to 'business efficiency' suggests an influence from the approach taken towards implied terms under English contract law, which itself may be criticised for blurring the distinction between subjective and objective 'intentions'.[15]

In *The Assunzione*, Lord Justice Birkett suggested that "If the intention of the parties is not expressed in the contract itself, the court must ascertain as best it can what is the implied or the presumed intention to be gathered from the whole of the facts in the circumstances of the case after they have been fully considered".[16] It is unclear whether "implied" (suggesting a subjective test) and "presumed" (suggesting here an objective test) are offered as alternative descriptions of a single test, or as separate stages. Later in the judgment "presumed intention"[17] and "probable intention"[18]

---

[11] At p.221.

[12] The test was applied again in *In Re United Railways of Havana and Regla Warehouses Ltd* [1961] AC 1007, 1068. For a different (three-stage) interpretation of *Bonython*, see Jaffey (1984).

[13] [1954] P 150.

[14] At p.179. See further Jaffey (1984), p.536ff; Williams (1986), p.13.

[15] See e.g. *The Moorcock* (1889) 14 PD 64; *Hillas & Co.* v. *Arcos Ltd* [1932] UKHL 2; *Liverpool City Council* v. *Irwin* [1977] AC 239. The test was reformulated in *Attorney General of Belize* v. *Belize Telecom Ltd* [2009] UKPC 10, [16] (holding that the meaning of a contract "is not necessarily or always what the authors or parties to the document would have intended", but rather an "objective meaning which is conventionally called the intention of the parties"); see further *Marks and Spencer plc* v. *BNP Paribas Securities Services Trust Company (Jersey) Ltd* [2015] UKSC 72.

[16] At p.180. See similarly *National Thermal Power Corporation* v. *Singer Corporation* (1992) 3 SCC 551 (Supreme Court of India), relying on this authority.

[17] At p.185.

[18] At p.186.

are apparently used as synonyms for what must be determined in the absence of express choice, suggesting continuing uncertainty. Finally, Lord Justice Hodson contributes to this confusion by appearing to suggest that in determining the applicable law in the absence of an express choice "it was not legitimate to look at a matter which was outside the knowledge of both parties",[19] implying that the test is a purely subjective question of construction of the contract. By contrast, in the House of Lords decision of *Whitworth Street Estates (Manchester) Ltd* v. *James Miller & Partners Ltd* (1970)[20] it was suggested by Lord Reid (in a minority judgment) that, in the absence of an express choice of law:

> At one time it was thought that the problem could be solved by means of an implied term in the contract. But ... I think that the better view now is to apply a more objective test.[21]

The distinction between implied and imputed choices of law remained, therefore, a matter of significant contention. Some common law judges even remained sceptical of giving effect to party choices at all, particularly when it came to questions of the validity (rather than the interpretation) of the contract.[22]

7.2.1.2   The Modern Three Stage Test

The issue came before the House of Lords for consideration again in *Compagnie D'Armament Maritime SA* v. *Compagnie Tunisienne De Navigation SA* (1971).[23] Lord Wilberforce endorsed[24] the two-stage test set out in the seventh edition of Dicey and Morris (1958), which provided that:

> Where the intention of the parties to a contract with regard to the law governing the contract is not expressed in words, their intention is to be inferred from the terms and nature of the contract, and from the general circumstances of the case, and such inferred intention determines the proper law of the contract.[25]

This test once again conflated the questions of implied and imputed intention under the notion of an 'inferred' intention, and Lord Wilberforce on

---

[19]   At p.187.

[20]   [1970] AC 583.

[21]   At p.603; see similarly the judgment of Lord Wilberforce (at pp.614–5).

[22]   See e.g. *The Fehmarn* [1958] 1 WLR 159, 162 (per Lord Denning, "I do not regard the choice of law in the contract as decisive. I prefer to look to see with what country is the dispute most closely concerned"); *In Re Claim by Helbert Wagg & Co. Ltd* [1956] Ch 323.

[23]   [1971] AC 572.

[24]   At p.595. A similar two-stage test was advocated by North (1993), pp.105–6, which influenced the High Court of Australia in *Akai Pty Ltd* v. *People's Insurance Co. Ltd* (1996) 188 CLR 418, 441–2.

[25]   Dicey and Morris (1958), p.731.

this basis held that both subjective and objective factors "should be considered together as elements relevant to intention, inferred or presumed".[26]

Other members of the court, however, took the opportunity to distinguish three different aspects of the rule.[27] The first was the question of whether there was an express choice of law, which the facts established was not the case. The second was whether a provision in the contract implied a choice of law when, according to Lord Reid, "construed in light of the facts known to both parties at the time when it was agreed".[28] Here, facts unknown to the parties are (rightly) only excluded from consideration in relation to the question of the (subjective) interpretation of the contract to determine whether it contains an implied term choosing the applicable law. The third stage was to determine, "in the absence of any positive indication of intention in the contract", the objective question of "with what country or system of law the contract has the closest connection",[29] looking at all connecting factors (including those not known to the parties at the time of contracting).

This separation of three stages was followed by the Court of Appeal in *Coast Lines Ltd* v. *Hudig & Veder Chartering NV* (1972).[30] When the issue arose again in *Amin Rasheed Shipping Corporation* v. *Kuwait Insurance Co.* (1984),[31] the House of Lords divided on whether an implied intention was present on the facts, but the distinction between the second and third stages of the test in principle was reaffirmed.[32] This is despite Lord Wilberforce's expression of continued reluctance towards moving from a two-stage to a three-stage test, with the suggestion that "these situations merge into each other"[33] in practice.[34] This may, however, be more favourably interpreted

---

[26] At p.596.

[27] Lord Diplock applied a distinct two-stage test, with the first stage encompassing (subjective) express and implied choice of law agreements, and the second the (objective) close connection test – this approach is echoed in some Australian authority, discussed below.

[28] At p.583.

[29] Ibid.

[30] [1972] 2 QB 34, 46–50.

[31] [1984] AC 50. See discussion in Jaffey (1984); Mann (1980).

[32] At pp.61, 69.

[33] At p.69. This was acknowledged again but somewhat further clarified by Lord Justice Bingham in *The Komninos S* [1991] 1 Lloyd's Rep 370, 373–4.

[34] While the three-stage test is also part of Australian common law, there is regrettably some continued support for this 'merger' in Australian authorities – the Supreme Court of NSW has held that "In the absence of an express choice of law clause, courts search for an inferred intention, even in circumstances where it is unlikely that the parties gave the matter any thought at all" (*Ace Insurance Ltd* v. *Moose Enterprise Pty Ltd* [2009] NSWSC 724, [50]),

merely as an observation of a practical overlap in the factors under consideration under the different stages of the test, rather than an undermining of the distinction between the stages themselves. This practical intersection is illustrated, for example, by the decision in *Attock Cement Co. Ltd* v. *Romanian Bank* (1989).[35] In that case, in considering what implication as to the applicable law might arise out of related contracts (under the 'doctrine of infection'), the Court of Appeal observed:

> It is classified in Dicey & Morris as an example of an implied choice of law. While I do not quarrel with that classification, I wonder whether it may not equally be an example of the rule that, in the absence of an express or implied choice, the proper law of a contract is that system of law with which the contract has the closest and most real connection.[36]

The Court thus acknowledged that related contracts may be relevant to both the second and third stages of the test – suggesting an implied choice of law, or if no such choice is identifiable, serving as an objective connecting factor – without collapsing the distinction between those stages.

There is no definitive list of factors which may be relevant at the second or third stages, or indeed both – although it may be noted that the factors set out in the Giuliano-Lagarde Report on the Rome Convention 1980 as relevant to finding an implied choice under that instrument (discussed in Section 7.2.2) are all factors which may also be relied on under the second stage of the common law test. In practice, many factors may be relevant to both the second and third stages of the common law test. For example, if the court is determining whether the parties have (implicitly) chosen a governing law, the fact that the parties agreed on a place of performance for the contract may be influential, as parties may expect that system of law to apply. If the court determines that no implied choice of law has been made, the place of performance of the contract is likely also to be a very important element in the third stage of the test, as an objective connective factor. Again, the fact that certain factors are influential at more than one stage of the test does not affect the conceptual distinction between the subjective and objective elements of the test.[37] This is reflected in the fact that

---

finding support in the High Court of Australia's statement that finding an implied choice of law agreement "is not a question of implying a term as to choice of law" (*Akai Pty Ltd* v. *People's Insurance Co. Ltd* (1996) 188 CLR 418, 441).

[35] [1989] 1 Lloyd's Rep 572.

[36] At p.580; see further e.g. *Wahda Bank* v. *Arab Bank* [1996] 1 Lloyd's Rep 470, 472–3.

[37] See further e.g. *Sulamérica Cia Nacional de Seguros SA* v. *Enesa Engenharia SA* [2012] EWCA Civ 638, [25].

some factors are given much more weight in the second stage of the test than in the third, and some factors should probably only be relevant at the second state of the test.

One factor that is highly relevant at the second stage, but arguably less significant at the third, is the presence of an exclusive choice of court agreement. If the parties have selected a single forum to resolve any dispute arising under the contract, without specifying the applicable law, it may generally be assumed (in the absence of indications to the contrary) that they would have intended the forum to apply its own law. This presumption may derive from two points. First, parties are unlikely to have in mind the possibility that the court they have chosen may apply foreign law, as this is (except to lawyers familiar with private international law) not very widely understood. Second, a dispute is generally resolved most efficiently by a court applying its own law, as this reduces the expense and uncertainty of dealing with the proof of foreign law. This rule establishes a notable link between party autonomy in choice of court and choice of law – an exclusive choice of court is a strong factor indicating an implied choice of law. (It may be queried, however, whether this should apply if the exclusivity of the agreement arises by way of a legal presumption, as under the Brussels I Regulation and the Hague Convention on Choice of Court Agreements 2005 – although the legal presumption may itself be viewed as based on a presumed intention of the parties.)[38] A non-exclusive jurisdiction agreement is, however, much weaker evidence of an implied choice of law, as it does not establish a preference for the nominated court. If the court determines that an implied choice has not been made, it is less clear whether a choice of court clause is itself a factor connecting the contract to a particular system of law, which would support the application of that law. The better view is probably that it should be considered a weak factor (in either exclusive or non-exclusive forms), because it is the place of performance of at least some of the rights and obligations set out in the contract. A choice of court agreement is a right to bring proceedings in a particular forum, and an obligation to accept that forum, which is at least principally to be performed in the place of the chosen court (noting that an exclusive choice of court agreement also establishes an obligation not to bring proceedings in any other court). Although other performance obligations under a contract may lie elsewhere and give rise to other objective connections, a choice of court agreement should thus be considered at least relevant as a minor objective connecting factor. Again, it is therefore a

---

[38] See e.g. Marshall (2012), p.18ff; see further discussion in Section 3.3.1.

factor that affects both the second and third stages of the test, although its effect is different at each stage.

A further factor that probably ought to be relevant only to the second stage of the test, if at all, is the so-called 'presumption of validity'. If there is evidence that the parties may have implicitly chosen a particular governing law, but that law would render their contract invalid, then it is sometimes argued that this should indicate that in fact no implied choice of law exists, as the parties are presumed to intend to enter into binding legal relations. There are some doubts over whether this presumption should be given much weight – it seems to presume that the intention of the parties to enter into a binding contract is more important to them than their (apparent) intended choice of law for the contract. This issue is discussed further in Section 7.6. If it is to be given some weight, however, it seems clear that it should only apply in relation to the second stage of the test. The fact that a contract may be invalid under the law with which it is objectively most closely connected should not be considered a factor connecting it with a different system of law. The function of choice of law rules is not to maximise contractual validity in cross-border relations.

A final factor of note, which is likely to be relevant to the second but not the third stage, is the incorporation by reference of terms into the contract. As discussed in Section 1.3.6, an important distinction must be drawn between incorporation by reference, which is an exercise of contractual autonomy, and the selection of the governing law, which is an exercise of private international law party autonomy (which in fact determines the law governing the limits of contractual autonomy). However, the incorporation by reference of terms of law into a contract may be an indication that the parties expect their contract to be governed by that system of law (although it may potentially indicate the opposite if that would render the incorporation redundant). The use by the parties of clauses in their contract derived from a system of national law would not, however, be likely to be considered an objective connecting factor between the contract and that system of law.

By the time the Rome Convention 1980 came into effect in England in 1991 (as discussed below), the common law had thus developed an at least theoretically clear three-stage test (express choice, implied choice, and the closest and most real connection test), while acknowledging that there was a degree of overlap in the factors relevant to the second and third stages,[39] and that maintaining this clarity might therefore prove

[39] See further e.g. Dicey, Morris and Collins (2012), [32-006]–[32-007].

to be difficult in practice. The three-stage test was restated more recently in *Lexington Insurance Company* v. *AGF Insurance Limited* (2009),[40] in applying the common law test to a contract concluded in 1977 and thus falling outside the Rome Convention. Lord Justice Potter's suggestion in *Samcrete Egypt Engineers and Contractors SAE* v. *Land Rover Exports Ltd* (2001) that the common law test "compendiously involved the considerations now required to be looked at separately under Articles 3 and 4 of the Convention"[41] was thus not accurate, although it did describe some historical practice.

The modern English authorities, such as *Amin Rasheed Shipping Corporation* v. *Kuwait Insurance Co.* (1984),[42] are generally cited as precedent for the current position under Australian[43] and Canadian law, alongside 'restatements' such as *Akai Pty Ltd* v. *People's Insurance Co. Ltd* (1996)[44] in Australia. In the latter case, the majority emphasised the importance of clarity in the distinction between subjective and objective choices of law – almost to the point of suggesting a new 'two-stage' test, distinct from the old English approach, which combines the first two (rather than the last two) stages of the modern three-stage English test.[45] While supporting party autonomy and giving express and implied choice of law agreements effect, this approach also (helpfully) emphasises that the identification of an objective choice of law rule involves distinct considerations which risk being obscured if they are discussed through the language of an 'imputed intention'.

Perhaps innovatively, some Australian courts have expressed the view that a contractual choice of law is generally only 'declaratory' and not 'promissory' in character.[46] The significance of this determination is that litigating in a court which does not respect the choice of law agreement does not itself amount to a breach of contract (unless it is in breach of an exclusive jurisdiction agreement). A choice of law clause is thus not considered

---

[40] [2009] UKHL 40, [90].
[41] [2001] EWCA Civ 2019, [39].
[42] [1984] AC 50.
[43] See e.g. Attorney-General's Department, Private International Law Consultation, 'Discussion Paper – Reducing legal complexity of cross-border transactions and relationships' (2013), 26 (available in Dickinson, Keyes and John (2014)).
[44] (1996) 188 CLR 418.
[45] *Akai Pty Ltd* v. *People's Insurance Co. Ltd* (1996) 188 CLR 418, per Toohey, Gaudron and Gummow JJ. For further support for such an approach, see Marshall (2012); Nygh (1999), p.107ff.
[46] See e.g. *Ace Insurance Limited* v. *Moose Enterprise Pty Ltd* [2009] NSWSC 724, [41]–[53].

to be an undertaking to *ensure* that the chosen law applies, but merely an indication of agreed intention at the time of contracting. Another implication of this approach is that a court should not exercise jurisdiction merely in order to ensure that the law chosen by the parties applies (even where, as in England, a choice of forum law provides a basis of jurisdiction).[47] This issue has recently been dealt with similarly (although not identically) in the English courts.[48] It is unclear whether this approach will be accepted broadly in the common law world, but it has the virtue of recognising the distinctiveness of choice of law issues (which determine the application of rules of private law) from contractual issues that arise within private law systems.[49] The alternative approach, under which a court may or should exercise jurisdiction to ensure that a choice of law agreement is to be given effect, appears to unduly prioritise (i) the choice of law rules of the forum over those of other courts, and (ii) choice of law rules over the rules and principles governing the allocation of jurisdiction, unless the law applicable in a foreign court would be unjust.[50] Those who argue in favour of this alternative approach, however, may take the view that if a foreign court would fail to give effect to a choice of law agreement between the parties, that is itself an injustice – essentially, viewing party autonomy in choice of law as not merely a forum rule but a mandatory requirement of justice.

Under the common law it has long been accepted that the parties may choose different laws to govern different sections of their contract, or that they may choose a law which only governs certain sections, leaving the remainder to be determined under the 'objective' choice of law rule.[51] The choice of law rule in contract thus accommodates dépeçage where that reflects the intention of the parties. If the parties have made no choice of law at all, the objective choice of law rule will generally indicate a single governing law for the entire contract, unless a part of the contract is considered to be 'severable' and thus subject to distinct choice of law analysis. This issue often arises in the context of arbitration agreements, and is thus discussed further in Chapter 6.

---

[47] See discussion in Section 3.4.3.
[48] *Navig8 PTE Ltd* v. *Al-Riyadh Co. for Vegetable Oil Industry* [2013] EWHC 328 (Comm), [22]. See discussion in Hook (2014). But see *Tiernan* v. *The Magen Insurance Co. Ltd* [2000] ILPr 517, [18].
[49] But see Briggs (2016); Briggs (2008), [11.45]ff; *AMT Futures Ltd* v. *Marzillier, Dr Meier & Dr Guntner Rechtsanwaltsgesellschaft mbH* [2014] EWHC 1085 (Comm), [10] (overturned on appeal, but without addressing this point).
[50] Hook (2014); see further generally Hook (2016).
[51] See e.g. Dicey, Morris and Collins (2012), [32-025].

7.2.2   EU Law (1) – The Rome Convention 1980

In the European Union, choice of law rules in contract have been harmonised with universal effect – that is, the harmonised rules apply in Member State courts regardless of whether the dispute is connected with other Member States or with non-Member States, and whether or not the law identified is that of a Member State or non-Member State.[52] Unlike in the context of jurisdiction, there is no residual application of national law, except to those choice of law issues which fall outside the scope of the European instruments. The most notable of these are choice of court agreements and arbitration agreements – the law governing these types of agreements is discussed (respectively) in Sections 3.3 and 6.3.

European choice of law rules for contract were first harmonised by treaty, in the Rome Convention 1980. These rules remain applicable for many contracts entered into prior to 17 December 2009, when its successor, the Rome I Regulation, came into effect. The distinction between subjective and objective choice of law rules in contract under the Rome Convention is examined in this section, before the next section examines the equivalent issues as they arise under the Rome I Regulation.

7.2.2.1   Articles 3 and 4

The codification of choice of law in contract in the Rome Convention 1980 adopts an ostensibly clear distinction between subjective and objective tests, dealing with them in separate articles. This was a significant departure from the blurring of considerations which had, even more than the common law approach examined above, characterised the approaches of some Member States (at least according to the Giuliano-Lagarde Report).[53] Article 3(1) selects "the law chosen by the parties", which "must be expressed or demonstrated with reasonable certainty by the terms of the contract or the circumstances of the case" – it thus encompasses both express and implied choices of law. Despite the use of the word 'or', it is clear that "the correct approach ... is to consider both the terms of the contract and the circumstances of the case".[54] Article 4, which sets out the objective choice of law rule, applies only "To the extent that the law applicable to the contract has not been chosen in accordance with Article 3".

---

[52] Article 2 of the Rome Convention 1980 and Rome I Regulation.
[53] See Giuliano-Lagarde Report, p.19. See further e.g. Williams (1986), p.13.
[54] *Marubeni Hong Kong and South China Limited* v. *Mongolia* [2002] 2 All ER (Comm) 873, [42]; Giuliano-Lagarde Report, p.17 (the question of an implied choice of law must be determined "in the light of all the facts").

The primary rule is thus that party autonomy is given effect, whether based on an express or implied agreement. As discussed further below, there is no requirement in Article 3 for any objective connection between the chosen law and the parties or their contract, unlike the old law of some European Member States, or the present law of some states in the United States.[55] Article 4 itself draws only on objective factors connecting the contract with the law of a country. These factors are taken into account in two ways. First, under Article 4(1) or (5), which set out a broad flexible test seeking to identify the country with which a contract is "most closely connected" or "more closely connected". Second, in Article 4(2), (3), and (4), through more rigid presumptions looking, for example, to the habitual residence of the characteristic performer of the contract, or the location of the property for a contract concerning a right in immovable property. The balance between the flexible and rigid elements of Article 4 has been a matter of difficulty in practice as the rules appear contradictory[56] – for present purposes, it is sufficient to note that Article 4 is certainly to some extent more rigid than the traditional common law identification of the 'closest and most real connection', and that, however flexible Article 4 may be, the intentions of the parties should not be relevant to its application. A clear distinction is thus made, at least in principle, between the subjective test in Article 3 and the objective test in Article 4.

In practice, however, there has been some difficulty in determining the limits of the rule giving effect to party autonomy under Article 3 of the Rome Convention 1980, and thus of the appropriate balance between Articles 3 and 4, as discussed further below. One source of this uncertainty is the requirement in Article 3(1) that an implied choice must be "demonstrated with reasonable certainty", which is not entirely clear in its intention or effect. On one interpretation, it is simply a rule of evidence, requiring a level of proof of the implied choice. As an evidentiary requirement, it is likely to affect not merely the threshold of proof, but also to allocate the burden of proof – thus, although there is no specific textual basis for this, it has been generally accepted that the onus of establishing an implied choice of law agreement is on the party seeking to establish that the choice of law has been made.[57] On another interpretation, this requirement is substantive, and provides that only clearly demonstrable

---

[55] See Section 7.3.1.
[56] See e.g. Lando and Nielsen (2008), p.1700ff; Hill (2004); Atrill (2004); Jaffey (1984).
[57] See e.g. Clarkson and Hill (2016), p.218; *Lawlor v. Sandvik Mining & Construction Mobile Crushers and Screens Ltd* [2013] EWCA Civ 365.

implied agreements should be given effect. Thus, even if the parties have subjectively (albeit implicitly) agreed on a particular law being applicable, the agreement might not always be followed (if it cannot be demonstrated to the required standard). Put this second way, it seems more like a limitation on party autonomy – something like a formality requirement – than a rule of evidence. (It may be noted that the Rome Convention and Rome I Regulation do not otherwise impose formality requirements on choice of law agreements – although they appear to accept the possibility that national law may impose such requirements.)[58] Even if it is characterised as an evidentiary rule, it may clearly have substantive effects, potentially excluding the effectiveness of an implied choice of law agreement that is genuine (or appears to be on the balance of probabilities), but not "demonstrated with reasonable certainty".[59]

Although this operates as a potential limitation on party autonomy, one possible justification for this rule is that it operates in service of the policy objective of legal certainty, which is also (as examined in Section 2.3) sometimes relied on to justify party autonomy. If party autonomy is supported because it is considered to increase legal certainty for the parties, then it may be contended that the rules giving effect to party autonomy must themselves be certain in their application, which might justify excluding implied choices which are not clearly demonstrated. Another policy behind this requirement is arguably an attempt to prevent the blurring of the boundary between subjective and objective factors that was characteristic of some national law approaches. The concern it addresses is that a court might be prepared to find an implied choice of law in circumstances in which such a choice is not really subjectively demonstrated, but is rather being imputed to the parties by the court (as the law they *would have* chosen, not the law they *did* choose). The narrowing of Article 3 to require that the agreement be "demonstrated with reasonable certainty" is, from this perspective, an attempt to provide for a balance between Articles 3 and 4. It aims to ensure that the use of Article 3 is limited to *demonstrably*

---

[58] See e.g. Rome I Regulation, Art.3(5) and Art.11. The rule in Article 11 is, however, likely to minimise the effectiveness of national formality requirements, as in most cases it requires that only one of a number of laws be satisfied. It is not clear whether a requirement under national law for a choice of law agreement to be express and in writing would actually be consistent with the Rome I Regulation, which (as discussed) requires effect to be given to implied choices of law.

[59] See further e.g. *Lawlor* v. *Sandvik Mining & Construction Mobile Crushers and Screens Ltd* [2013] EWCA Civ 365.

subjective agreements, and to prevent it being used as a device to mask decisions by the courts which are based on other considerations. Thus, as discussed further below,[60] the limitations on Article 3 also serve to protect the role of Article 4.

Article 3(1) of the Rome Convention 1980 also notably provides that "the parties can select the law applicable to the whole or a part only of the contract". This form of intentional contractual dépeçage is much less problematic than the operation of dépeçage in tort, which was wisely excluded from the Rome II Regulation.[61] The application of a different governing law to a severable part of a contract is also expressly permitted under Article 4(1) of the Rome Convention, although it is difficult to see the circumstances in which it would be appropriate for a court to determine that different parts of a single contract should be governed by different applicable laws on an objective basis. One clause that is commonly governed by a different applicable law than other contractual terms is an arbitration agreement, as discussed in Section 6.3, but as arbitration agreements are excluded from its scope there was no need for the Rome Convention to deal with this issue. As noted below, there is no equivalent provision in the Rome I Regulation.

7.2.2.2   Giuliano-Lagarde Report

National courts may consult the Giuliano-Lagarde Report, prepared by the drafters of the Rome Convention 1980, for assistance in its interpretation.[62] The Report makes the distinction between the subjective nature of the test in Article 3 and the objective nature of the test in Article 4 very clear, stating that "The choice of law by the parties will often be express but the Convention recognizes the possibility that the Court may, in the light of all the facts, find that the parties have made *a real choice of law* although this is not expressly stated in the contract" (emphasis added).[63] Even more clearly, the Report clarifies the limitations of Article 3 by explaining that:

> This Article does not permit the court to infer a choice of law that the parties might have made where they had no clear intention of making a choice. Such a situation is governed by Article 4.[64]

---

[60] See Section 7.2.3.
[61] Rome II Regulation, Art.4; see further Mills (2009b); Nygh (1999), p.128ff; McLachlan (1990).
[62] See e.g. Contracts (Applicable Law) Act 1990 (UK), s.3(3)(a).
[63] Giuliano-Lagarde Report, p.17.
[64] Ibid.

The reference to "a real choice of law", as opposed to a choice that the parties "might have made", is clearly intended to indicate that Article 3 should remain purely subjective. Thus, it should be limited to an actual choice of law by the parties, rather than a choice being imputed by the courts based on an assumption or determination that it is what the parties might or would have chosen.

The Giuliano-Lagarde Report includes a range of illustrative examples of factual situations that might give rise to an implied choice of law. In each case, a slightly different formulation of wording is used to describe the standard of the test, but always emphasising that the implied choice must be clearly established in some way. According to the Report,[65] an implied choice of law might arise in any of the following (non-exhaustive) list of situations (with the key words italicised for emphasis):

- Standard form contracts: "the contract may be in a standard form which *is known to be* governed by a particular system of law even though there is no express statement to this effect, such as a Lloyd's policy of marine insurance".
- Previous course of dealing: "a previous course of dealing between the parties under contracts containing an express choice of law may leave the court *in no doubt* that the contract in question is to be governed by the law previously chosen where the choice of law clause has been omitted in circumstances which do not indicate a deliberate change of policy by the parties".
- Choice of court agreement: "In some cases the choice of a particular forum may show *in no uncertain manner* that the parties intend the contract to be governed by the law of that forum, but this must always be *subject to the other terms of the contract and all the circumstances of the case*".
- Reference to statutory provisions: "references in a contract to specific Articles of the French Civil Code may leave the court *in no doubt* that the parties have *deliberately chosen* French law, although there is no expressly stated choice of law".[66]
- Related transactions: "Other matters that may *impel the court* to the conclusion that *a real choice of law* has been made might include an express choice of law in related transactions between the same parties ..."

[65] Ibid. For discussion of these and other possible examples see Cheshire, North and Fawcett (2017), p.718ff; Nygh (1999), p.114ff.

[66] Although the incorporation by reference of provisions of a statute is not the same as a choice of law (see Section 1.3.6), it may thus evidence an implied choice.

- Arbitration agreement: (continuing from above) "... or the choice of a place where disputes are to be settled by arbitration in circumstances indicating that the arbitrator should apply the law of that place".

The diverse terminology used to describe the approach which should be taken to applying Article 3 uniformly emphasises the subjective nature of the test, and the high evidentiary threshold which must be overcome if a court is to find an implied choice of law agreement. It is not entirely clear, however, whether the exercise of paraphrasing this requirement in a variety of ways really helps clarify the test.

The fact that a choice of court agreement is an indicator of a possible implied choice of law is particularly notable. As discussed above in the context of the common law rules, this creates an evidentiary link between the exercise of party autonomy in choice of court and in choice of law, although the two remain conceptually distinct. The presence of an arbitration agreement may also serve as an indication that the parties intended the law of the place of arbitration to apply, but this indication is likely to be weaker. Arbitrators, unlike judges, are not necessarily experts in the law of the place in which they sit. The selection of a place of arbitration is also likely to be more influenced by the procedural arbitration law of that place than the substantive applicable law, as discussed in Section 6.3.

The reference in the Report to 'all the circumstances of the case' in the quote relating to choice of court agreements above, reiterating and perhaps broadening or strengthening the reference to "the circumstances of the case" in Article 3(1) itself, is also important to note. It acknowledges that the test for an implied agreement, however 'subjective' in character, must take place within a matrix of 'objectively' identified factual circumstances. This is a point also recognised in common law jurisprudence, although, as noted above,[67] it has sometimes been suggested that it should be limited to facts known to the parties at the time of entering into the contract, if it is to be truly a basis for determining their subjective intentions. The factors relevant to determining an implied agreement under Article 3 should thus be different from those relevant to applying Article 4, although there will be significant overlap. As discussed above, under the common law a presumption that the parties intend to enter into binding contractual relations has also been considered relevant to the determination of whether there is an implied choice of law agreement, directing the court away from an implied choice of a law that would invalidate the contract.[68]

---

[67]   See Section 7.2.1.
[68]   See further Section 7.6.

If this factor is to be given any weight under the Rome Convention (and Rome I Regulation), it should only be relevant to the application of Article 3, and not Article 4.

7.2.2.3   The Rome Convention 1980 in Practice

It was not automatically within the power of the CJEU to hear disputes over the interpretation of the Rome Convention 1980. The Brussels Protocol,[69] drafted in 1988 to give Member State courts the power to ask the CJEU for binding interpretations of the Rome Convention, did not come into effect in the United Kingdom until 2005.[70] For most of its history the Convention has thus had to be interpreted purely by national courts.

The Convention itself makes some attempt to 'Europeanise' its national interpretation through Article 33, which provides that the different language versions are "equally authentic", and in practice arguments based on foreign language texts have occasionally been raised before English courts.[71] The desirability of adopting an 'internationally minded' approach is further supported by Article 18 of the Rome Convention, which provides that "In the interpretation and application of the preceding uniform rules, regard shall be had to their international character and to the desirability of achieving uniformity in their interpretation and application", meaning that national rules of construction should not be applied.[72] In practice, however, the absence of CJEU supervision of the approaches of different Member State courts has led to different national traditions of interpretation of the Rome Convention.[73] This is evidently problematic, given that the purpose of the Convention is to create uniformity of approach between the different Member States, to improve the efficient functioning of the internal market.

Of course, the problem is now somewhat resolved by both the Brussels Protocol, giving Member State courts the power to ask the CJEU to interpret the Rome Convention 1980, and the introduction of the Rome I Regulation, which is automatically within CJEU jurisdiction. Nevertheless, the existence

---

[69] See Contracts (Applicable Law) Act 1990, Schedule 3; the Tizzano Report, OJ C 219, 3 September 1990.

[70] Contracts (Applicable Law) Act 1990, s.3; The Contracts (Applicable Law) Act 1990 (Commencement No. 2) Order 2004, SI 2004/3448.

[71] See e.g. *American Motorists Insurance Co. (AMICO)* v. *Cellstar Corporation* [2003] EWCA Civ 206, [43].

[72] See e.g. *Egon Oldendorff* v. *Libera Corporation* [1996] 1 Lloyd's Rep 380, 387; *Samcrete Egypt Engineers and Contractors SAE* v. *Land Rover Exports Ltd* [2001] EWCA Civ 2019, [24]; *Iran Continental Shelf Oil Company* v. *IRI International Corporation* [2002] EWCA Civ 1024, [14]–[15].

[73] See generally e.g. Hill (2004).

of different national traditions of interpretation remains an important feature of the jurisprudence that has developed under the Convention.

English Case Law   It is not surprising, in light of the similarity between the Rome Convention and common law tests for choice of law in contract, that English courts have readily recognised the distinction in the Convention between a (subjective) express or implied choice of law under Article 3 and the (objective) determination of the applicable law in the absence of choice under Article 4. The courts have, for example, adopted the Giuliano-Lagarde Report's suggestion that Article 3 requires a "real choice".[74] They have also recognised that the requirement that an implied choice must be "demonstrated with reasonable certainty", in the words of Article 3, "may have led to a change of emphasis" compared with the approach to implied terms under common law.[75] The implication is that Article 3 should be construed narrowly, in the interest of maintaining a clear distinction between the domains of Articles 3 and 4, but thereby restricting the scope of party autonomy.

It has, however, also been suggested that "The circumstances which may be taken into account when deciding whether or not the parties have made an implied choice of law under Article 3 of the Rome Convention ... range more widely in certain respects than the considerations ordinarily applicable to the implication of a term into a written agreement".[76] This enlargement of factors might suggest an expansion of situations in which an implied choice will be given effect by the courts – a broadening, not a narrowing, of the recognition of a subjective intention under Article 3, when compared with the common law.[77] It may thus reasonably be concluded that "If it involves a change of emphasis from the approach by the common law it is a small one".[78] While it must be doubted whether there are enough cases to generalise confidently, in practice English courts have not appeared reticent in finding an implied choice of law under the Rome Convention, particularly, it might be quietly observed, in favour of English law.[79]

---

[74] *Egon Oldendorff* v. *Libera Corporation* [1996] 1 Lloyd's Rep 380, 387–8.

[75] Ibid., p.389.

[76] *ISS Machinery Services Ltd* v. *The Aeolian Shipping SA* [2001] 2 Lloyd's Rep 641, 645; see further *American Motorists Insurance Co. (AMICO)* v. *Cellstar Corporation* [2003] EWCA Civ 206, [44]. In *The Aeolian*, the Court found, however, no implied choice of English law on the facts.

[77] It may, for example, including 'circumstances' arising subsequent to the contract – see e.g. Nygh (1999), pp.111–2.

[78] *Egon Oldendorff* v. *Libera Corporation* [1996] 1 Lloyd's Rep 380, 390.

[79] See also e.g. *Gan Insurance Co. Ltd* v. *Tai Ping Insurance Co. Ltd* [1999] CLC 1270; *Tiernan* v. *The Magen Insurance Co. Ltd* [2000] ILPr 517; *Marubeni Hong Kong and South China*

Rome I Regulation Green Paper   The Rome I Regulation Green Paper that preceded the adoption of the Regulation included its own analysis of practice under the Rome Convention 1980. This analysis critically observed that different national traditions of interpretation may have emerged in the approach to Article 3. Part of the explanation for this, it suggested, was that "some translations of the Convention seem to be more flexible than others",[80] noting in a footnote that, in Article 3(1), "Instead of 'with reasonable certainty' and 'mit hinreichender Sicherheit' in the English and German versions, the French version asks for 'de façon certaine'".[81] This apparent inconsistency is particularly problematic given that, as noted above, Article 33 provides that the different language versions are "equally authentic".

In a section headed "Difficulties encountered in applying this Article [Article 3]", the Green Paper made the following claims:

> The borderline between the tacit choice and the purely hypothetical choice is rather vague. Analysis of the case-law reveals a major difference of the solutions regarding this point: the German and English courts, perhaps under the influence of a slightly more flexible form of words, and under the influence of their previous solutions, are less strict about discerning a tacit choice than their European counterparts.[82]

The claim was therefore made in the Green Paper that the English (and German) courts have preserved at least partially the influence of their traditional approach to choice of law in contract, which (arguably) blurred the distinction between subjective and objective choices of law. The attempt by the Rome Convention to make this distinction clear, by raising the threshold for finding an implied choice of law, is thus criticised as unsuccessful. The Green Paper therefore identified a perceived risk that in England (and Germany) there is a continued conflation of the subjective and objective elements of the test.

As noted above, there is some basis for arguing that the case law suggests that English courts have indeed been quite open to finding implied choices of law under Article 3. If this has involved the courts drawing on objective factors rather than purely subjective intentions in Article 3, it may be viewed not only as an excessively expansive interpretation of Article 3, but

---

    Limited v. *Mongolia* [2002] 2 All ER (Comm) 873; *Tryg Baltica International (UK) Ltd* v. *Boston Compania De Seguros SA* [2004] EWHC 1186 (Comm), [8]. For an eyebrow-raising defence of this practice on economic grounds see Penadés Fons (2015).

[80] Rome I Regulation Green Paper, s.3.2.4.1.

[81] Ibid., at n.49.

[82] At s.3.2.4.2.

as undermining the boundary between subjective and objective considerations. It seems unlikely, however, if such a blurring exists in the English practice, that it should be attributed to the "previous solution" adopted under the common law. There is a stronger case for suggesting that the traditional use of 'hypothetical party intentions' ('hypothetischer Parteiwille') in German law, as an intermediate stage between an implied and imputed choice of law, might have influenced German national practice under the Rome Convention.[83] By contrast, the common law test immediately prior to the Rome Convention did not fail to distinguish between subjective and objective considerations, while recognising that the factors involved may overlap in practice. As examined in Section 7.2.1, it is true that English courts did at one stage adopt a two-stage test in which a 'presumed intention' of the parties would be determined based on a combination of subjective and objective factors. This had, however, long been rejected by the time of the adoption of the Rome Convention.

If English courts have used Article 3 excessively, finding an implied choice where one has not actually been made subjectively by the parties, the better explanation (explored further below) is that this is because it may serve as a mechanism to avoid the unfamiliar and somewhat unsatisfactory test which they would have to apply under Article 4 of the Rome Convention in the absence of finding an implied choice of law. An expansive approach to the interpretation of Article 3 thus offers an alternative 'objective' choice of law rule, one which leaves the courts with much greater discretion to look for the "closest and most real connection", unrestrained by the presumptions in Article 4. This is arguably the real danger identified in the Rome I Regulation Green Paper – that an expansive approach to the identification of implied choice of law agreements under Article 3 may go beyond party autonomy and undermine the certainty and predictability which are key objectives of the Rome Convention.

7.2.3   EU Law (2) – The Rome I Regulation 2008

In 2008, the Rome I Regulation was adopted to replace the Rome Convention 1980. There were essentially two main reasons behind this move. First, it brought choice of law in contract within the framework of European law, as a Regulation, and thus automatically within the jurisdiction of the CJEU. Second, it was at least initially intended to make significant changes to the rules adopted under the Rome Convention. It is well

---

[83] See e.g. Triebel (1988), p.943; Giuliano-Lagarde Report, p.19.

known that the changes in the final version of the Rome I Regulation are more modest than those originally proposed.[84] One possible explanation for this is that the United Kingdom initially expressed scepticism towards the Regulation and opted out of its process, although participated in the drafting of the Regulation on the basis that a later opt-in might be possible if the instrument was satisfactory. This appears to have proved a successful bargaining strategy in achieving a more attractive final text, evidenced by the ultimate decision of the United Kingdom to opt back in.

7.2.3.1   Articles 3 and 4

The Rome I Regulation maintains the Rome Convention's ostensibly clear distinction (and rule of priority) between the subjective and objective aspects of choice of law in Articles 3 and 4, with Article 4 applying only "To the extent that the law applicable to the contract has not been chosen in accordance with Article 3". The most significant change in the Rome I Regulation is in fact to Article 4, which is restructured around a series of rules (rather than presumptions) in Article 4(1) and 4(2), although with the possibility to apply a law "manifestly more closely connected" as an exception under Article 4(3), or the law "most closely connected" under Article 4(4) if the presumptions are unable to determine the applicable law.

There remains no general restriction on party autonomy under Article 3 – unlike the old law of some European Member States, or the present law of the United States, no need for a connection between the law chosen by the parties and the contract.[85] Such a restriction has, however, been introduced in the Rome I Regulation as a protective measure in relation to contracts for the carriage of passengers under Article 5(2) and certain insurance contracts under Article 7(3). This is a novel and somewhat surprising alternative (of doubtful effectiveness)[86] to the technique previously adopted under Articles 5(2) and 6(1) of the Rome Convention, and also continued under Articles 6(2) and 8(1) of the Rome I Regulation, which provide that the choice of a different applicable law cannot deprive consumers and employees (respectively) of the benefit of the mandatory laws of the country whose law would apply in the absence of that choice. This matter is discussed further in Section 9.2.2.

---

[84] See, generally, the Rome I Regulation Proposal; Solomon (2008).
[85] See Section 7.3.
[86] See e.g. Nielsen (2009), p.107; Gruber (2009), p.118ff; Heiss (2008), p.268ff.

Aside from these special qualifications of party autonomy, the Regulation introduces only a slight change of wording from the Rome Convention when it comes to implied choices of law. Where Article 3(1) of the Rome Convention required that the choice "must be expressed or demonstrated with reasonable certainty by the terms of the contract or the circumstances of the case", Article 3(1) of the Rome I Regulation requires that "The choice shall be made expressly or clearly demonstrated by the terms of the contract or the circumstances of the case".[87] It is difficult to detect what significance this nuancing of the language has – perhaps a choice which is 'clearly demonstrated' is more certain than a choice which has merely been shown with 'reasonable certainty', which suggests a marginal raising of the bar for finding an implied choice of law, and thus a narrowing of Article 3.[88] It must be questioned whether, if there really is a problem with the approaches of the German and English courts towards Article 3 (as the Rome I Regulation Green Paper suggests),[89] this subtle amendment in wording will go far towards addressing it.

It is notable, however, that the French language version of Article 3(1) of the Rome I Regulation has not been changed from the Rome Convention – it still refers to a choice which is "exprès ou *résulte de façon certaine* des dispositions du contrat ou des circonstances de la cause" (emphasis added), which (as noted above)[90] was the language version of the Rome Convention implicitly preferred by the Rome I Regulation Green Paper. The German language version has been changed in terms similar to the English.[91] Perhaps what is really sought, therefore, is not reform of the rules as a whole, but better 'harmonisation' of the different language texts,

---

[87] The Rome I Regulation Proposal originally suggested amending the wording of Article 3(1) to provide that a choice of law "must be expressed or demonstrated with reasonable certainty by the terms of the contract, *behaviour of the parties* or the circumstances of the case" (emphasis added). It is arguable that this change might have given further encouragement to an expansive use of Article 3(1), contrary to the narrowing effect of the amendments ultimately adopted in the Rome I Regulation, although the commentary to the Rome I Regulation Proposal emphasised (at p.5) the need to establish the "true tacit will of the parties rather than a purely hypothetical will".

[88] See further e.g. Penadés Fons (2015); Lando and Nielsen (2008), p.1698.

[89] See Section 7.2.2.3.

[90] See Section 7.2.2.3.

[91] In the Rome Convention 1980, "Die Rechtswahl muß ausdrücklich sein oder sich mit hinreichender Sicherheit aus den Bestimmungen des Vertrages oder aus den Umständen des Falles ergeben"; in the Rome I Regulation, "Die Rechtswahl muss ausdrücklich erfolgen oder sich eindeutig aus den Bestimmungen des Vertrags oder aus den Umständen des Falles ergeben."

on the French model[92] – although whether this is reform or merely greater consistency is evidently a question of perspective.

Article 3(1) of the Rome Convention, as noted above,[93] expressly permits a form of intentional contractual dépeçage, and this is continued unchanged under Article 3(1) of the Rome I Regulation. The provision for application of a different governing law to a severable part of a contract, expressly permitted under Article 4(1) of the Rome Convention, is not, however, included in the Rome I Regulation. It is difficult to anticipate what effect this exclusion will have in practice.[94] It should not prevent parts of a single document from being recognised as separate and severable contracts that should be subject to individual choice of law analysis and may thus be governed by different applicable laws. On the other hand, Article 4(2) suggests that a single applicable law should be found for contracts with multiple elements – it seeks to identify a single governing law even if a contract is covered by more than one of the rules set out in Article 4(1). In the vast majority of cases this is the preferable result, because the different elements of a contract generally need to be interpreted consistently, and this is also the approach that is ordinarily followed under the Rome Convention despite its express authorisation of dépeçage. The exclusion of dépeçage from Article 4 of the Rome I Regulation is thus unlikely to be greatly significant in practice, although may add a degree of legal certainty to the process of determining the applicable law in the absence of choice by reducing its potential complexity.

7.2.3.2   Recitals 11 and 12

There is no report on the drafting on the Rome I Regulation that might play an equivalent role to the Giuliano-Lagarde Report for the Rome Convention 1980. The Regulation instead includes numerous recitals which are intended to assist in its interpretation. It is, however, difficult to predict what weight will be given to them. Given the negotiating history of the Rome I Regulation, it is tempting to view at least some of them as the product of negotiated political compromise rather than coherent regulatory design. Nevertheless, they should at least be a starting point where the interpretation of one of the rules is unclear.

Recital 11 of the Rome I Regulation provides that "The parties' freedom to choose the applicable law should be one of the cornerstones of

---

[92] See e.g. Heiss (2009), p.1; Wilderspin (2008), p.263.
[93] See Section 7.2.2.
[94] See e.g. Magnus (2009), p.31.

the system of conflict-of-law rules in matters of contractual obligations". On its face this appears uncontroversial, reflecting the fact that party autonomy under Article 3 is the primary rule in the Regulation, with Article 4 operating as a fallback. If this recital is supposed to aid in interpretation of the Regulation, however, it does raise a difficult question. This affirmation of party autonomy is, at least arguably, in tension with the attempt under the Rome I Regulation to narrow the scope of Article 3. If party autonomy is "one of the cornerstones of the system", then this suggests that any genuine agreement on the applicable law should be given effect, whether express or implied. Is party autonomy really respected if the court is satisfied, on the balance of probabilities, that there is an implied choice of law agreement, but feels constrained to refuse to give it effect because it is not (in the language of Article 3) "clearly demonstrated"? As noted earlier,[95] even if the requirement for an implied choice to be "clearly demonstrated" is characterised as evidentiary, it may have substantive effects on the limits of party autonomy under Article 3, and thus on the balance between Articles 3 and 4.

The other Recital directly relevant to the scope of party autonomy under the Rome I Regulation (for present purposes) is Recital 12, which provides that "An agreement between the parties to confer on one or more courts or tribunals of a Member State exclusive jurisdiction to determine disputes under the contract should be one of the factors to be taken into account in determining whether a choice of law has been clearly demonstrated." This endorses the idea that an exclusive jurisdiction agreement is an indicator of a possible implied choice of law under Article 3, although does not offer any great clarification of how important it should be as a factor (except perhaps for excluding the possibility that it might be decisive) – an issue which had received variable treatment in national courts under the Rome Convention.[96] It is evident that under the Rome I Regulation, as under the Rome Convention, there is potentially a link between party autonomy in choice of court and choice of law – with a choice of court agreement being evidence of a possible implied choice of law – but the strength of this link is unclear. Recital 12 also does not explain whether in singling out exclusive jurisdiction agreements it is intended to indicate that they are given greater weight than the range of other factors that were also considered relevant under the Rome Convention, as discussed above. It is unclear why a choice of court agreement alone is elevated to the status of a recital, while

[95] See Section 7.2.2.
[96] See discussion in Wilderspin (2008), p.263ff.

the other factors discussed in Section 7.2.2 and in the Giuliano-Lagarde Report are ignored, and whether this is intended to have any implication concerning the relative weight to be given to those other factors. If, as examined above, the perceived problem with the Rome Convention was that certain courts were too ready to find an implied choice of law agreement, perhaps it is more likely that an interpretation giving exclusive jurisdiction agreements only weaker effect should be favoured, but the interests of legal certainty and perhaps the drafting history may favour giving jurisdiction agreements a stronger effect.[97] The fact that Recital 12 is limited to agreements in favour of "one or more courts or tribunals of a Member State" is also very puzzling.[98] It is difficult to identify any reason of principle why a choice of a non-Member State forum should be given any less weight in determining an implied choice of law – the surely unintended implication would be a structural bias within the rules in favour of a European Member State legal system being applicable.

It may thus be debated whether Recital 11 and 12 clarify or render more obscure the interpretation of Article 3 of the Rome I Regulation.

7.2.3.3   Policy Considerations

It may be argued that the technical debates set out above concerning the scope of party autonomy under the Rome Convention and Rome I Regulation to some extent obscure the real issue. The answer to the problem of how to interpret either version of Article 3 is not a purely analytical matter, but a question of determining the policy balance between Articles 3 and 4. Article 3 gives power over the allocation of regulatory authority to the parties; Article 4 determines the allocation of regulatory authority objectively based on a combination of territorial and personal connecting factors. The uncertainty about how extensively Article 3 should be used is therefore arguably a reflection of an underlying uncertainty as to how these two theories should be accommodated. Party autonomy is, in one sense, clearly given priority – under both the Rome Convention and Rome I Regulation, Article 4 only ever applies "To the extent that the law applicable to the contract has not been chosen in accordance with Article 3".

---

[97] The Rome I Regulation Proposal included in Article 3(1) the stronger provision that "If the parties have agreed to confer jurisdiction on one or more courts or tribunals of a Member State to hear and determine disputes that have arisen or may arise out of the contract, they shall also be presumed to have chosen the law of that Member State." The presence of this stronger draft of the clause may be viewed as evidence for or against a strong interpretation of the final version.

[98] See e.g. Heiss (2009), p.2.

The issue remains, however, how expansively Article 3 should be interpreted, and thus what scope of application the policy of party autonomy should be given.

Can an answer to this problem be found in the underlying objectives of the Rome Convention and Rome I Regulation? The core objective of the Rome I Regulation is, according to Recital 1, to enhance the "proper functioning of the internal market". Normally it might be expected that this would be favoured by legal certainty and thus by the application of party autonomy, suggesting an expansive interpretation of Article 3. But if a rule facilitating party autonomy is applied in too expansive a way, so that it goes beyond what the parties themselves have actually chosen, it ceases to reflect a real choice, and ceases to provide a certain and predictable guide to the parties as to the law which will apply to their contract. If that occurs, the decision by the courts as to an 'implied' (but actually 'imputed') choice of law becomes a more flexible substitute for Article 4. It thus risks undermining the efforts of Article 4 to provide an objectively predictable determination of the applicable law. On the other hand, the suggestion by some commentators (and some states in the negotiations for the Rome I Regulation)[99] that this should be resolved by abolishing the possibility of an implied choice of law is ultimately unsatisfactory. This would risk undermining genuine party autonomy and thus ultimately the internal market objectives it seeks to advance. A balanced approach that gives effect to a real, albeit unwritten, choice of law agreement should remain part of choice of law in contract.

None of this particularly explains why, at least according to the Rome I Regulation Green Paper, some courts have failed to strike such a balance in their interpretation of Article 3, finding too readily an implied choice of law agreement. Perhaps rather than a failure to interpret (and thus a need to amend) the language of Article 3, the real issue here is doubt over Article 4. A court may be drawn to Article 3 as a means of avoiding the well-known difficulties in interpreting Article 4,[100] although the Rome I Regulation does offer some clarification here over the unfortunate drafting in Article 4 of the Rome Convention.[101] A court faced with a choice between applying Articles 3 and 4 might also have doubts about the policy choices implicitly built into Article 4. It may doubt whether the

---

[99] See e.g. Clarkson and Hill (2016), pp.224–5; see similarly North (1993), pp.105–6.

[100] See e.g. Lando and Nielsen (2008), p.1700ff; Hill (2004); Atrill (2004).

[101] Some *very* limited assistance in interpreting Article 4 of the Rome Convention 1980 was finally offered by the CJEU in C-133/08 *Intercontainer Interfrigo SC (ICF)* v. *Balkenende Oosthuizen BV and MIC Operations BV* [2009] ECR I-9687.

allocation of regulatory authority made by Article 4, in favour (at least presumptively) of the characteristic performer's place of habitual residence[102] (and not, for example, the place of performance of the contract) is appropriate – whether it really "essentially links the contract to the social and economic environment of which it will form a part".[103] The use of this factor also has a tendency to connect the contract with the economically stronger party, contrary to the general policy of protection of weaker parties pursued under the Convention and Regulation.[104] These concerns with Article 4 may tempt courts to use Article 3 expansively as a more flexible escape mechanism to that contained in Article 4 itself.

Perhaps, therefore, the reforms in the Rome I Regulation may be criticised for misdiagnosing the problem – treating the symptom (Article 3) and not the cause (Article 4). If a broad approach to Article 3 has been adopted under the Rome Convention, it should arguably be taken as a critique of the logic of Article 4, and not merely a failure to interpret Article 3 correctly, under the 'bad influence' of antecedent national practice – at least not in the case of the common law. The apparent attempt to further narrow Article 3 in the Rome I Regulation is not likely to prove effective (in the absence of more significant reforms to Article 4), and may risk undermining the general policy of giving priority to party autonomy in choice of law in contract.

7.2.4   United States

The historical origins of party autonomy in choice of law in the United States were discussed in Section 2.2.2. That history highlighted that by the early twentieth century, party autonomy in contractual choice of law had been generally followed by the courts in practice, but rejected by some judges and theorists (including in Beale's First Restatement of Conflict of Laws). The rejection by theorists arose because it was difficult to reconcile the (at least perceived) underpinnings of the conflict of laws, in the

---

[102] Subject to exceptions under Article 4(2) of the Rome Convention 1980, and as defined in Article 19 of the Rome I Regulation.

[103] Giuliano-Lagarde Report, p.20; see further e.g. Morse (1982), p.131; D'Oliveira (1977); Collins (1976). To put these concerns another way, there may be doubts over whether the choice of law rule in Article 4 of the Rome I Regulation, like its predecessor in the Rome Convention 1980, genuinely complies with the horizontal effect of the subsidiarity principle – because it does not allocate regulatory authority over the contract to the system of law most closely affected by it (which would generally be the place of performance of the contract).

[104] Jaffey (1984), p.550.

limits on the law-making powers of states, with the apparent 'law-making' powers given to private parties under party autonomy. The gap between theory and practice in this matter was part of what prompted the 'conflict of laws revolution' in the middle part of the twentieth century, leading to the introduction of a range of new theoretical and doctrinal approaches to choice of law. The possibility of such a range of approaches was also facilitated by the US Supreme Court's decision, in *Klaxon Company* v. *Stentor Electric Manufacturing Company* (1941),[105] that choice of law was state law rather than federal law, and that federal courts exercising diversity jurisdiction[106] should apply the choice of law rules of the state in which they are sitting – itself a radical departure from the previous understanding that choice of law rules were part of federal common law under *Swift* v. *Tyson* (1842).[107] The combination of the theorists' revolution and the Supreme Court's revolution has meant that the United States has become a 'conflict of laws laboratory', with the fifty states potentially able and frequently willing to adopt different approaches to choice of law, although acting within broader constraints imposed by the US Constitution.[108] Federal courts also commonly apply their own conflict of laws rules when dealing with admiralty cases,[109] and sometimes (but not always)[110] do the same when exercising federal question jurisdiction,[111] usually following the Second Restatement approach.

---

[105] 313 US 487 (1941). See generally Mills (2010), p.438ff.

[106] See Section 3.4.1.

[107] 41 US 1 (1842). See generally Mills (2010), p.409ff.

[108] These have, however, been interpreted increasingly narrowly. See e.g. *Allstate Insurance* v. *Hague*, 449 US 302 (1981); *Philips Petroleum Co.* v. *Shutts*, 472 US 797 (1985); *Sun Oil Co.* v. *Wortman*, 486 US 717 (1988). See generally Mills (2009a), p.140ff. See further discussion in Section 7.3.1.

[109] See e.g. *Aqua-Marine Constructors, Inc.* v. *Banks*, 110 F.3d 663, 670 (9th Cir. 1997); *State Trading Corporation of India Ltd* v. *Assuranceforeningen Skuld*, 921 F.2d 409, [47] (2nd Cir. 1990) (noting that under federal law "a contractual choice of law clause generally takes precedence over choice of law rules").

[110] See e.g. *AI Trade Finance, Inc.* v. *Petra International Banking Corp.*, 62 F.3d 1454, [47] (D.C. Cir. 1995) (following *Klaxon*'s rule that the federal courts must apply the choice of law rules of the state in which the court sits); *In re Payless Cashways*, 203 F.3d 1081, 1084 (8th Cir. 2000).

[111] See e.g. *Huynh* v. *Chase Manhattan Bank*, 465 F.3d 992, 997 (9th Cir. 2006); *Edelmann* v. *Chase Manhattan Bank*, 861 F.2d 1291 n.14 (1st Cir. 1988); *Corporacion Venezolana de Fomento* v. *Vintero Sales Corp.*, 629 F.2d 786, 795 (2nd Cir. 1980). The Supreme Court has declined on several occasions to determine the correct approach: See e.g. *Automobile Workers* v. *Hoosier Cardinal Corp.*, 383 US 696, 705 n.8 (1966); *Richards* v. *United States*, 369 US 1, 7 (1962).

A complete analysis of the approaches to choice of law in each of these different jurisdictions is beyond the scope of this book.[112] This section analyses the effectiveness of choice of law agreements in contractual claims under four of the most important and widely followed approaches. The first is the approach under the Uniform Commercial Code, a model law that has supported party autonomy in contract since its adoption in 1952. The second is the Second Restatement of Conflict of Laws, adopted in 1969, which allows the court to look to a range of factors and considerations in identifying the applicable law, including any agreement reached by the parties. The third is the 'interest analysis' approach, also encompassing a variation that focuses on 'comparative impairment', under which the focus is on which system of law has the greatest interest in regulating the parties or their dispute. The fourth is the traditional 'lex loci contractus' approach, under which the court applies the law of the place of the contract (variously interpreted as the place where it was entered into or the place where it was or should have been performed). Under these latter two approaches, it remains unclear how and why a choice of law agreement between the parties should be given effect. Nevertheless, it is true that in contractual disputes, choice of law clauses are upheld in the vast majority of cases. The historical disconnect in the United States between the practice of the courts, which generally supports party autonomy, and the theory of conflict of laws, which (at least apparently and in significant part)[113] does not, thus remains a feature of contemporary US private international law.

7.2.4.1   Uniform Commercial Code

One important influence on choice of law in the United States is the Uniform Commercial Code, first promulgated by the National Conference of Commissioners on Uniform State Laws and the American Law Institute in 1952, which seeks to provide a model law for US states to follow in the field of commercial transactions. The UCC has been adopted in some form in every US state, although as a model law it can be (and frequently is) adopted with local modifications, and since its original drafting the NCCUSL and ALI have also made various modifications to its text that have not necessarily been universally adopted by US states. For cases

---

[112] For further information see e.g. Symeonides (2017) (including at p.33 a table setting out the choice of law approach of each US state); Coyle (2017); Zhang (2006a).

[113] A notable exception is the account of choice of law in Brilmayer (1989); see also Peari (2013).

falling within its scope (principally contracts for the sale or lease of goods and various financial contracts, but not services or employment contracts or contracts relating to land), the UCC trumps the Second Restatement or other choice of law approaches, because it is adopted and implemented through a state statute.

The UCC has, from its adoption in 1952, provided for party autonomy. In its current form (last amended in 2008, but essentially unchanged since 1958), Section 1-301 of the UCC provides that, subject to certain exceptions:

> (a) Except as otherwise provided in this section, when a transaction bears a reasonable relation to this state and also to another state or nation the parties may agree that the law either of this state or of such other state or nation shall govern their rights and duties.

The requirement that a 'reasonable relation' must exist with the law to be chosen is discussed in Section 7.3. Subject to this (important) qualification, the UCC essentially provides and has always provided that the parties may agree on the law to govern their contractual relations. Such an agreement may be express or implied. In the absence of agreement, the UCC directs the courts of a state to apply their own law, if the transaction bears a reasonable relation to that state, although in practice many states will apply other choice of law rules at this point to determine the applicable law, looking to a range of objective connecting factors such as the place where the contractual obligations were or should have been performed.

7.2.4.2   Second Restatement of Conflict of Laws

As discussed further in Section 2.2.2, the First Restatement of Conflict of Laws adopted in 1934 did not allow the parties to choose the law applicable to their contracts, on the basis that this "involves permission to the parties to do a legislative act."[114] Although there was some practice in US courts in support of this approach, it was (and became increasingly) a minority position that contributed to the dissatisfaction with the First Restatement. The Second Restatement of Conflict of Laws, unlike its predecessor, is open to party autonomy in choice of law, in two distinct ways.

First, the Restatement recognises a range of policy foundations for choice of law which are at least arguably compatible with party autonomy, such as "the needs of the interstate and international systems",[115]

---

[114] Beale (1935), p.1079; also in Beale (1910b), p.260; Beale (1896), p.170; see further discussion in Mills (2013); Yntema (1955), p.54ff.

[115] Second Restatement of Conflict of Laws, s.6(2)(a).

"the protection of justified expectations",[116] "the basic policies underlying the particular field of law",[117] "certainty, predictability and uniformity of result",[118] and "ease in the determination and application of the law to be applied".[119] These are all set out in section 6, which establishes the general principles of the Restatement. As discussed in Chapter 2, each of these considerations might play a role in arguments in favour of party autonomy – that application of the law chosen by the parties might benefit the interstate and international systems, protect the parties' expectations, be more compatible with the policies underlying contract law itself (holding the parties to their bargain), and lead to a choice of law rule which is more certain, predictable and easy to apply than traditional rules. In the Restatement, these policy considerations are, however, balanced against others under which it is less clear what role party autonomy might play – for example, "the relevant policies of the forum",[120] or "the relevant policies of other interested states and the relative interests of those states in the determination of the particular issue".[121] As explored further in the section below on 'interest analysis', it is not clear how party choices could be understood to affect the policies of states whose regulatory interests are potentially implicated by a relationship or dispute. Although section 9 of the Restatement generally suggests that a state should have 'jurisdiction' in the international law sense over a person or dispute before its law may be applied (which would generally require a territorial or personal connection), the comments to that section suggest that "A person's consent may provide another basis of jurisdiction", and "So if parties in their contract provide that their rights and obligations under the contract shall be determined in accordance with the local law of state X, this law may be so applied."[122] This suggests an important modification of public international law jurisdictional constraints to accommodate party autonomy, as discussed in Section 1.2.2.

The second way in which the Second Restatement accommodates party autonomy in contract is more directly through the applicable choice of law rule. Section 187 of the Restatement provides as follows:

> (1) The law of the state chosen by the parties to govern their contractual
> rights and duties will be applied if the particular issue is one which the

---

[116] Section 6(2)(d).
[117] Section 6(2)(e).
[118] Section 6(2)(f).
[119] Section 6(2)(g).
[120] Section 6(2)(b).
[121] Section 6(2)(c).
[122] Section 9, comment (f).

parties could have resolved by an explicit provision in their agreement directed to that issue.

(2) The law of the state chosen by the parties to govern their contractual rights and duties will be applied, even if the particular issue is one which the parties could not have resolved by an explicit provision in their agreement directed to that issue, unless either

    (a) the chosen state has no substantial relationship to the parties or the transaction and there is no other reasonable basis for the parties choice, or

    (b) application of the law of the chosen state would be contrary to a fundamental policy of a state which has a materially greater interest than the chosen state in the determination of the particular issue and which, under the rule of § 188, would be the state of the applicable law in the absence of an effective choice of law by the parties.

(3) In the absence of a contrary indication of intention, the reference is to the local law of the state of the chosen law.

If the parties have not chosen a governing law for their contract, section 188 applies, which directs a court to apply the law with the most significant relationship to the transaction and the parties, determined based on a range of objective connections including the place of contracting and place of performance as well as potentially an analysis of state interests (as discussed further below).

Several features of this essentially two-part choice of law rule are notable. First, party autonomy is clearly set out as the primary choice of law rule under section 187, with section 188 having only residual effect. Second, section 187 clearly encompasses both express and implied choices of law. The comments to section 187 note that "even when the contract does not refer to any state, the forum may nevertheless be able to conclude from its provisions that the parties did wish to have the law of a particular state applied",[123] identifying the use of particular legal expressions or doctrines peculiar to one system of law as possible indicators of such an implied choice.[124] They also go on to state that "It does not suffice to demonstrate that the parties, if they had thought about the matter, would

---

[123] Section 187, comment (a).

[124] It is not entirely clear whether a choice of forum clause might also indicate an implied choice of law, as is the case under the common law and EU law approaches above. The US Supreme Court has suggested that "Under some circumstances, the designation of arbitration in a certain place might also be viewed as implicitly selecting the law of that place to apply to that transaction." – *Scherk* v. *Alberto-Culver Co.*, 417 US 506, 519 n.13 (1974). But the better view is probably that an exclusive choice of court agreement is a much stronger indication of an implied choice of law, as the seat of an arbitration is generally selected for procedural or practical reasons rather than because of the substantive applicable law.

have wished to have the law of a particular state applied."[125] The boundary between the subjective and objective tests for choice of law in contract is thus relatively clearly established in principle, even if it may be more difficult to apply in practice.

Third, the rule in section 187 distinguishes between issues "which the parties could have resolved by an explicit provision in their agreement", and those which they could not.[126] It is unclear how this distinction should be determined. In any system of contract law, there will be rules which 'fill in the gaps' of a contract but which the parties can replace or alter through their agreement (default rules), as well as rules which the parties may not override (contractual mandatory rules). Section 187 appears to rely on this distinction in determining whether the parties have a free choice of law – but this distinction is itself different in different systems of law, so cannot obviously be identified in advance of that determination. There appears to be an underlying confusion here between the concepts of contractual party autonomy and private international law party autonomy – a distinction examined in Section 1.3.5 – as determining the scope of contractual autonomy ought to require a prior determination of the governing law. One approach would be for the court to determine the applicable law in the absence of choice (using section 188), and then use that system of law to determine the limits of party autonomy under section 187. Another might be for the court to apply the law of the forum to determine these limits, or the law chosen by the parties as a putative governing law. None of these approaches is straightforward or entirely satisfactory. The comments to section 187(1) themselves suggest that it "is a rule providing for incorporation by reference and is not a rule of choice of law",[127] further confusing matters,[128] but then goes on to say that "Whether the parties could have determined a particular issue by explicit agreement directed to that issue is a question to be determined by the local law of the state selected by application of the rule of s 188".[129] The comments to section 187(2) appear to contradict those in section 187(1), in explaining that rules which the parties cannot determine themselves may include "those involving capacity, formalities and substantial validity", which are examples of contractual mandatory rules (not incorporation by reference). There is a lack of clarity in two distinctions in this rule – the distinction

---

[125] Second Restatement of Conflict of Laws, s.187, comment (a).
[126] See e.g. discussion in Hay, Borchers, and Symeonides (2010), p.1088ff.
[127] Section 187, comment (c).
[128] See Section 1.3.6.
[129] Section 187, comment (c).

between a choice of law to govern the contract and the incorporation of terms by reference, and the distinction between contractual party autonomy and private international law party autonomy, both discussed further in Section 1.3.

Assuming that it can be identified (on some basis) that "the particular issue is one which the parties could not have resolved by an explicit provision in their agreement directed to that issue", there are two restrictions to party autonomy imposed under section 187(2). First, that the law chosen will not be applied if "the chosen state has no substantial relationship to the parties or the transaction and there is no other reasonable basis for the parties choice". This issue is discussed in Section 7.3. Second, that the law chosen will not be applied if "application of the law of the chosen state would be contrary to a fundamental policy of a state which has a materially greater interest than the chosen state in the determination of the particular issue and which, under the rule of § 188, would be the state of the applicable law in the absence of an effective choice of law by the parties". This rule allows for a form of recognition of mandatory rules – those establishing a fundamental policy of the state whose law would apply under section 188 in the absence of a choice by the parties – and is discussed in Section 9.2.4.

A final feature of section 187 of the Second Restatement which may be noted is that it provides for an 'issue by issue' analysis in the context of choice of law in contract. Thus, if the parties have made a choice of law for only part of their contract, or a choice of different laws for different sections of their contract, there is a possibility for the application of dépeçage by choice, just as there is under the common law and EU rules as examined above.

7.2.4.3   Interest Analysis

Aside from, or in conjunction with, the Second Restatement of Conflict of Laws, many US states apply an approach to choice of law issues known as 'interest analysis'.[130] The central tenet of this approach is that the law applicable to a dispute or relationship should be determined based on an analysis of the degree of interest which each state or government has in regulating the dispute or relationship. A common variant, known as the 'comparative impairment' approach, looks to the question from a slightly different perspective – the degree of impairment that would be suffered by each of the potentially interested states if its regulation were not applied

---

[130]   See e.g. Juenger (1984); Currie (1963).

to the dispute or relationship.[131] In either case, the central contested questions around this approach concern what to do if there are conflicting governmental interests (the different approaches generally either prioritise the law of the forum, or engage in a process of weighing and comparing interests) and how to identify interests. Identification of interests could take one of two forms. First, it might involve looking to see which state has the greatest objective connection with the dispute, and therefore the greatest interest in its regulation. Under this approach, interest analysis is similar to the objective approach under section 188 of the Second Restatement, as set out above. Second, it might involve an examination of the potentially applicable statutes and the policies behind them, to see whether the different legislators have expressed an 'interest' in regulating the dispute (or issue) at hand. It is this second form of interest analysis which is both most common and most distinctive – although its similarities with the medieval 'statutist' approach discussed in Section 2.2.2 have long been noted.[132] Like that approach, it focuses on determining the applicable law through statutory interpretation, based on a purposive analysis of the scope of application of each potentially applicable statute in light of the policy interests it is designed to serve. The two variations of interest analysis are, however, not always clearly distinguished – the comments to section 188 of the Second Restatement, for example, appear to conflate elements of both, stating that:

> The purpose sought to be achieved by the contract rules of the potentially interested states, and the relation of these states to the transaction and the parties, are important factors to be considered in determining the state of most significant relationship. This is because the interest of a state in having its contract rule applied in the determination of a particular issue will depend upon the purpose sought to be achieved by that rule and upon the relation of the state to the transaction and the parties.[133]

There is little apparent scope for party autonomy under either of these variations of interest analysis.[134] In one version, interest analysis is based on the objective connections between the dispute and each different potentially applicable legal order, and in the other it is based on the subjective intentions of the legislators, expressed through their statutes, rather than the subjective intentions of the parties. In either case, the law that the parties intend or wish to apply does not appear relevant. If the scope of application of the potentially applicable statutes should be identified through a

---

[131] Baxter (1963).
[132] See further e.g. Mills (2009a), p.139.
[133] Second Restatement of Conflict of Laws, s.188, comment (c).
[134] See e.g. discussion in Lehmann (2008), p.409ff; Zhang (2006a), p.538ff.

process of interpretation, then it is particularly unclear why parties should be given the power to extend that scope of application contractually.

This apparent incompatibility between interest analysis and party autonomy generally leads to one of two distinct approaches. First, some courts and scholars have hybridised interest analysis with a party autonomy approach, with party autonomy either serving as an overriding rule (as under the Second Restatement) or as a strong if not decisive connecting factor in addition to the analysis of governmental interests. These approaches recognise that the general policies underpinning party autonomy should also be given effect, alongside the policies behind particular state statutes, and either prioritise party autonomy or attempt to balance it alongside other policy considerations. The adoption of party autonomy may be viewed in part as a reaction against the state-focused approach of interest analysis, which appears to marginalise the interests of the parties. Second, some US scholars have remained sceptical of party autonomy.[135] There has, however, been limited support for such scepticism in the practice of the courts.

7.2.4.4   Lex loci contractus

A fourth major approach to choice of law followed in some US states is the traditional 'lex loci contractus' approach, essentially similar to that set out in the First Restatement of Conflict of Laws. The law of Oklahoma, for example, provides that:

> A contract is to be interpreted according to the law and usage of the place where it is to be performed, or, if it does not indicate a place of performance, according to the law and usage of the place where it is made.[136]

Similarly, the courts of Maryland apply the law of the place of contracting – thus it was recently held that an insurance policy entered into in California would be governed by Californian law, even though its coverage extended to events in Maryland.[137]

This approach on its face does not appear compatible with party autonomy. The rule it adopts appears derived from ideas of territorial state sovereignty, and Beale's concerns (discussed above and in Section 2.2.2) that private parties should not be able to override the limits on state sovereigns remain apparently relevant under this approach. Nevertheless, many states that adopt this approach also hybridise it with support for

---

[135] See e.g. Currie (1963), p.103; see further discussion in Nygh (1999), p.12.
[136] Oklahoma Statutes §15-162.
[137] *Francis* v. *Allstate Insurance Co.*, 709 F.3d 362 (4th Cir. 2013).

party autonomy, applying the law of the place of the contract only in the absence of an express or implied choice of law agreement,[138] without necessarily providing a coherent theoretical position to support such hybridisation.

7.2.5   China

In the analysis of the common law, EU law and US law above, it is clear that party autonomy in choice of law in contract, while not uncontested, has been widely adopted. This support is perhaps strongest in these (Western) jurisdictions, because of their traditional support for freedom of contract and the close associations which have been drawn between freedom of contract and party autonomy in choice of law,[139] but it is by no means limited to them. An illustration of how widely accepted party autonomy has become in choice of law is provided by its adoption as a choice of law rule in modern China – a legal system which has not traditionally been receptive towards freedom of contract, let alone free choice of law,[140] although has gone through a process of dramatic change in recent decades. With the introduction of a socialist market economy in the 1980s, party autonomy was accepted as part of contractual freedom under the 1985 Foreign Economic Contract Law and 1986 General Principles of Civil Law, although party autonomy was not permitted for Chinese citizens until the 1999 Contract Law,[141] and (as examined in Chapter 9) it remains subject to a number of exceptions and exclusions. In 2007, the Supreme People's Court promulgated Rules (judicial guidelines) on 'Related Issues concerning the Application of Law in Hearing Foreign-Related Contractual

---

[138] As in Maryland, e.g. *Francis v. Allstate Insurance Co.*, 709 F.3d 362 (4th Cir. 2013).

[139] As examined in Section 2.2.2.

[140] See further e.g. Zhang (2011a), p.116 ("For decades after the Communist Party of China took control of the nation in 1949, the country operated in the cage of a rigid planned economy, and no contracts were ever needed in any business transactions. During that period, freedom of contract was labeled as capitalist ideology, an enemy to the socialism that the country was determined to pursue, and party autonomy was not only remote in theory, but also impossible in practice" (footnote omitted)); Tang, Xiao and Huo (2016), Chapter 1; Zhang (2006b); Chen (1987).

[141] Tang, Xiao and Huo (2016), p.210ff; Liang (2012), p.79ff; Zhang (2011a), p.116. See also the 'Model Law of Private International Law of the People's Republic of China' (Sixth draft, 2000), Art.100 (an academic codification of Chinese Law prepared by the Chinese Society of Private International Law) (www.rucil.com.cn/admin/edit/UploadFile/200891911459766 .pdf).

Dispute Cases Related to Civil and Commercial Matters',[142] which including the following provisions:

> Article 3. To choose a law or alter a choice of law applicable to contractual disputes shall be done by the parties in an explicit manner.
> Article 4. The people's court shall permit the parties concerned to choose a law or alter a choice of law applicable to contractual disputes by agreement prior to the end of court debate of the first instance.

The meaning of the term 'Foreign-Related' in this context is discussed in Section 9.3. The current choice of law rules in China are (largely) set out in the Law of the People's Republic of China on the Laws Applicable to Foreign-Related Civil Relations (2010).[143] Article 3 establishes the general principle that:

> The parties may explicitly choose the law applicable to their foreign-related civil relation in accordance with the provisions of this law.

Article 41, which sets out the specific choice of law rule in contract, further provides that:

> The parties may by agreement choose the law applicable to their contract. Absent any choice by the parties, the law of the habitual residence of a party whose performance of obligation is most characteristic of the contract or the law most closely connected with the contract shall be applied.

A special rule also applies for certain agency relationships, under Article 16, which provides (in relevant part) that "The parties may by agreement choose the law applicable to their relation of commissioned agency."

It is notable that Article 3 of the 2010 law, like Article 3 of the 2007 Rules, allows for only express ('explicit') and not implied choices of law, thereby unusually adopting a formality requirement for choice of law agreements. Although Articles 41 and 16 would perhaps appear open to implied agreements on choice of law, in accordance with the approach taken in most other legal systems, the better view is probably that giving effect to such agreements is excluded by Article 3 – an approach which is apparently consistent with previous Chinese practice.[144] The rejection of implied choices of law (as noted above, a position which some scholars

---

[142] Fa Shi [2007] No. 14, 23 July 2007, available in translation at www.fdi.gov .cn/1800000121_39_2045_0_7.html

[143] See further generally e.g. Tang, Xiao and Huo (2016), Chapter 8; Liang (2012); Huo (2011); Zhang (2011a); Tu and Xu (2011).

[144] See Tang, Xiao and Huo (2016), pp.211–2; Zhang (2011a), p.118 ("no tacit choice is recognized in China ... the parties' intention with regard to the governing law of their contract may not be implied from the terms of the contract or from the course of dealing between

have advocated for reform of the Rome I Regulation)[145] limits the risk that a judge might inappropriately find an implied choice of law where none is justified. On the other hand, it risks excluding party choices which are genuine but undocumented. A limited form of implied choice is arguably recognised, however, under Article 4 of the 2007 Supreme Court Rules, which provides that:

> In case the parties concerned fail to choose a law applicable to contractual disputes but both invoke the law of a same country or region and neither has raised any objection to the choice of law, the parties concerned shall be deemed as having made the choice of a law applicable to contractual disputes.

As discussed in Section 7.4.1, this might also be interpreted as a rule relating to the proof of foreign law – that a failure to plead foreign law leads to the application of Chinese law in default – although it is in fact not limited to an implied choice of the law of the forum. The status of this rule is now unclear given its absence from the 2010 law. Similarly, the status of dépeçage under Chinese choice of law in contract is now somewhat unclear, as it is not expressly endorsed under the 2010 law, although it was formerly recognised as part of Chinese law.[146]

7.2.6   Brazil

As noted in Section 2.2.2, Latin American jurisdictions were generally slow to endorse party autonomy, as it was considered to conflict with the assertion of their emergent territorial sovereignty in the nineteenth century, by potentially allowing European companies trading in Latin America to evade the application of local law.[147] There remains significant resistance to party autonomy in choice of law in Latin America, although the trend is probably away from this position, as the status of party autonomy has increasingly been endorsed in national reforms and indeed (as discussed further below) in an Inter-American Convention in 1994.[148]

---

the parties ... [The] requirement of express choice of law by the parties ... has become a well-settled rule in practice since 1987" (footnote omitted)).

[145] See Sections 7.2.2 and 7.2.3.

[146] See Zhang (2011a), pp.120–1; see also the 'Model Law of Private International Law of the People's Republic of China' (Sixth draft, 2000), Art.100.

[147] See further e.g. Albornoz (2010); Pereznieto Castro (1985).

[148] Albornoz (2010).

Brazilian law may be highlighted as illustrative of this situation.[149] Brazil's choice of law rules in contract, set out in the Introductory Law to the Civil Code of 1942, do not expressly recognise party autonomy.[150] While there is scholarly debate over whether the law does actually exclude party autonomy,[151] and some Brazilian state courts have apparently accepted party choices of law on occasion,[152] only the law of the place of contracting (and perhaps the place of performance) is recognised as a valid connecting factor in the 1942 choice of law rules, and the general position appears to be that party autonomy is excluded by its omission from the rules.

It might be tempting, but would not be entirely accurate, to describe this as maintaining a traditional Latin American perspective on this issue.[153] The reason this would be inaccurate is that the choice of law rules in place in Brazil before 1942, adopted in the 1916 Introduction to the Civil Code, actually (with broad exceptions) permitted party autonomy in choice of law, although there are doubts over how effectively these provisions were applied in practice.[154] It has been argued that the 1942 change was in fact the product of "a territorial and nationalist approach to conflict of laws" prompted by the arrival of large numbers of immigrants during the Second World War.[155] It is perhaps notable that Brazil has also traditionally refused to consent to investor–state arbitration through Bilateral Investment Treaties.[156] Both positions may be ascribed to a similar sentiment – the desire to maintain legal control over the regulation of private parties through local state courts. However, Brazil does accept the permissibility of a choice of arbitration in commercial disputes under the Arbitration Law of 1996 (as amended in 2015), and (under Article 2) allows for arbitration to be governed by the law freely chosen by the parties, which is not entirely consistent with this objective. The UN Convention on Contracts for the International Sale of Goods 1980 also came into effect in Brazil in 2014, which (as discussed in Section 10.3.1) appears to endorse a broad form of party autonomy in choice of law in contract. As noted in Section 3.1, Brazil has also recently accepted party autonomy in relation

---

[149] Note similarly the law of Uruguay – see Basedow (2013a), p.168.
[150] See generally e.g. Basedow (2013a), pp.166–7; Albornoz (2010), p.44ff; Stringer (2006), pp.968–77.
[151] De Araujo (2013), p.78ff; Tiburcio (2013), p.23.
[152] See De Aguilar Vieira (2013), p.183ff; De Araujo (2013), p.80ff.
[153] See further Albornoz (2010).
[154] De Araujo (2013), p.77.
[155] Ibid.
[156] See e.g. Kalicki and Madeiros (2008).

to choice of court agreements. While for now Brazil remains a prominent qualification to the claim that the principle of party autonomy in choice of law in contract has achieved universal acceptance, from these developments and certain case law[157] it may hesitantly be suggested that even Brazil appears to be moving towards acceptance of the principle.

7.2.7   International Codifications

The major international codifications relating to choice of law in contract all adopt party autonomy as their primary choice of law rule. Two of the most significant are highlighted below. Party autonomy was also recognised as long ago as the Hague Convention of 15 June 1955 on the law applicable to international sales of goods.[158] It may also be noted that in 1991 the International Law Association adopted the Basel Principles on 'The Autonomy of the Parties in International Contracts Between Private Persons or Entities', a soft law instrument advocating giving broad effect to party autonomy.

7.2.7.1   Mexico City Convention 1994

In 1994, the Mexico City Convention was adopted at the Fifth Inter-American Specialized Conference on Private International Law, seeking to harmonise choice of law rules in contract in the Americas. It includes the following choice of law rule:

> Article 7 – The contract shall be governed by the law chosen by the parties. The parties' agreement on this selection must be express or, in the event that there is no express agreement, must be evident from the parties' behavior and from the clauses of the contract, considered as a whole. Said selection may relate to the entire contract or to a part of same.

While this Convention has only been ratified by Mexico and Venezuela (although also signed by Bolivia, Brazil, and Uruguay), it has nevertheless been influential in the debate and development of choice of law rules both regionally and further afield.[159] It evidently permits not only express but also implied choices of law, as well as the operation of intentional dépeçage to choice of law in contract.

---

[157] See further Albornoz (2010), p.45.
[158] www.hcch.net/en/instruments/conventions/full-text/?cid=31. Note also the similar 1986 Convention, not in force: www.hcch.net/en/instruments/conventions/full-text/?cid=61.
[159] See further e.g. Moreno Rodriguez and Albornoz (2011); Albornoz (2010), p.26ff; Juenger (1997), p.203ff; Juenger (1994).

Article 7 concludes by stating that "Selection of a certain forum by the parties does not necessarily entail selection of the applicable law." The conceptual distinction between choice of court and choice of law is thus clearly recognised, and a choice of court cannot have decisive effect in determining the applicable law. However, the Convention is silent on whether a choice of court agreement is a relevant factor in determining the existence of an implied choice of law agreement, and if so how much weight should be given to it – as discussed above, this has also been a point of uncertainty under the common law and under the Rome Convention and Rome I Regulation.

7.2.7.2 Hague Principles on Choice of Law in International Commercial Contracts 2015

A broader international consensus on the adoption of party autonomy in the context of choice of law in contract may also be suggested by the Hague Principles on Choice of Law in International Commercial Contracts, prepared under the auspices of the Hague Conference on Private International Law and formally approved in 2015.[160] These are a set of soft law rules (accompanied by detailed and helpful commentary) intended to influence international practice, although they may also be adopted directly as national choice of law rules (as they have been in Paraguay).[161] It is notable that the Principles are addressed not only to states but also to arbitral tribunals,[162] and their support for party autonomy in this context reflects the contractual foundations of arbitration, discussed further in Chapters 6 and 10. The Principles have as their primary focus the effectiveness of choice of law agreements – they do not set out any 'objective' choice of law rule to be applied in the absence of a choice by the parties. The main rule set out in Article 2 is entitled 'Freedom of choice', and provides as follows:

(1) A contract is governed by the law chosen by the parties.
(2) The parties may choose –
    (a) the law applicable to the whole contract or to only part of it; and
    (b) different laws for different parts of the contract.

It is notable that this rule, like that under the Mexico City Convention 1994 set out above, expressly supports dépeçage in choice of law in contract

---

[160] www.hcch.net/en/instruments/conventions/full-text/?cid=135. For further background see the Preparatory Work available at www.hcch.net/en/instruments/contracts-preparatory-work; Boele-Woelki (2016); Pertegás and Marshall (2014); Symeonides (2013a).
[161] www.hcch.net/en/publications-and-studies/details4/?pid=6300&dtid=41.
[162] See e.g. Basedow (2017).

where that reflects the intentions of the parties.[163] Article 4 further provides that:

> A choice of law, or any modification of a choice of law, must be made expressly or appear clearly from the provisions of the contract or the circumstances. An agreement between the parties to confer jurisdiction on a court or an arbitral tribunal to determine disputes under the contract is not in itself equivalent to a choice of law.

The rule thus provides for both express or implied choice of law agreements.[164] The Commentary to the Hague Principles emphasises, however, that "There must be a real intention of both parties that a certain law shall be applicable", and that "A presumed intention imputed to the parties does not suffice",[165] thus clearly distinguishing between (subjective) implied and (objective) imputed choices of law. The requirement that an implied agreement must 'appear clearly from the provisions of the contract or the circumstances' raises similar issues to those discussed above in relation to the Rome Convention and Rome I Regulation – while it serves a principally evidentiary purpose, its practical effect may be to exclude some genuine implied choices of law which nevertheless do not 'appear clearly' to have been made. Although this operates as a potential limitation on party autonomy, it is arguably justifiable as it operates in service of other policy objectives including particularly legal certainty, which are also often raised in support of party autonomy itself. The commentary to Article 4 provides that "By limiting tacit choice of law to situations in which the choice appears clearly, Article 4 promotes predictability of results by lessening the likelihood of disputes as to whether there has been a choice of law."[166]

The commentary to Article 4 of the Principles further provides that, in determining whether there is an implied choice of law:

> One has to take into account both the terms of the contract and the circumstances of the case. However, either the provisions of the contract or the circumstances of the case may conclusively indicate a tacit choice of law.[167]
>
> ...
>
> A choice of law is found to appear clearly from the provisions of the contract only when the inference drawn from those provisions, that the parties intended to choose a certain law, is strong. There is no fixed list of criteria that determines the circumstances under which such an inference is strong enough to satisfy the standard that a tacit choice must "appear clearly"; rather, the determination is made on a case-by-case basis.[168]

---

[163] See further discussion in Pertegás and Marshall (2014), p.994ff.
[164] See e.g. Gama (2017).
[165] Commentary to the Hague Principles, [4.6].
[166] Ibid., [4.1].
[167] Ibid., [4.7].
[168] Ibid., [4.8].

The commentary does, however, note that the use of a standard form of contracting typically governed by a particular system of law can be a strong indicator of tacit choice, as can the use of terminology characteristic of a particular national legal system, or the existence of related contracts.[169] It is perhaps curious that Article 4 of the Principles mentions a choice of court or arbitration agreement only to emphasise that such an agreement is not equivalent to a choice of law clause. This clearly implies that a choice of court or arbitration clause cannot be conclusive of a choice of law, and perhaps might suggest that such clauses should not be given much or any weight as a factor indicating a choice of law. However, the commentary notes that "a choice of court agreement between the parties to confer jurisdiction on a court may be one of the factors to be taken into account in determining whether the parties intended the contract to be governed by the law of that forum".[170] In practice, as analysed above in relation to the common law and European choice of law rules, such clauses are often given significant weight because parties are likely to assume or intend that a court will apply its own law. It may be expected that this approach will continue under the Principles, although the emphasis on "a real intention" might suggest that an exclusive jurisdiction agreement should be given less weight if its exclusivity arises from a legal presumption, as provided for under the Brussels I Regulation and the Hague Convention on Choice of Court Agreements 2005,[171] rather than from its own terms. Although choice of forum and choice of law clauses are thus clearly distinguished conceptually under the Principles, a link of uncertain strength between them is nevertheless recognised. The commentary similarly notes that "an arbitration agreement that refers disputes to a clearly specified seat may be one of the factors in determining the existence of a tacit choice of law",[172] again without indicating how much weight should be attributed to this factor. In practice, however, courts and tribunals applying the Principles are likely to give significantly less weight to an arbitration agreement than a choice of court clause as an indicator of an implied choice of law, because (as examined in Section 6.3) the seat of an arbitration is more commonly chosen due to the arbitration law of the seat, rather than indicating a desire to apply its substantive applicable law, and (unlike judges) arbitrators sitting in a particular location are not necessarily experts in the law of that place.

It may finally be noted that Article 5 of the Hague Principles provides that "A choice of law is not subject to any requirement as to form unless

---

[169] Ibid., [4.9], [4.10], and [4.13].
[170] Ibid., [4.11].
[171] See further discussion in Section 3.3.1.
[172] Commentary to the Hague Principles, [4.12].

otherwise agreed by the parties." This is consistent with the usual practice of not imposing any formality requirements on a choice of law agreement. The mooted exception (that the parties might themselves impose such a requirement) is presumably focused on a possible change in applicable law (discussed in Section 7.4) rather than an initial choice, and deals with the situation in which a contract provides, for example, that it may only be modified in writing.

7.3   Does a Choice of Law Require an Objective Connection?

As explored in Section 2.2.2, the historical origins of party autonomy in choice of law in contract arose in the context of competition between the selection of the law of the place of contracting and the law of the place of performance. References to party intentions by the courts were principally justifications for selecting the law of the place of performance, as the law that the parties had in mind when making their contract, rather than the (increasingly arbitrary) place where the contract was made. Thus, party autonomy was invoked to decide between potentially applicable *objective* choice of law rules, not as a *subjective* choice of law rule in itself. Over time, the intention of the parties moved from being a justification for the selection of an objective rule, to being a rule in its own right – with an express indication of those intentions overriding any presumptions which the law might otherwise apply. Different legal systems have, however, continued to take different views as to whether party autonomy is entirely free of any requirement for an objective connection, or whether some objective link between the chosen system of law and the parties or their dispute is necessary for the choice to be permissible.

7.3.1   *Systems in which an Objective Connection Is Required*

There are a number of legal systems in which a choice of law by the parties requires an objective connection or some other justificatory factor in order to be valid.[173] The most prominent among these may be found in the United States.[174] As discussed above, there are a range of different US

---

[173] See e.g. Albornoz and González Martín (2016), p.445ff; Symeonides (2014), p.118ff; Nygh (1999), p.55ff.

[174] An objective connection was also traditionally required under the national law of some European Member States. These rules have, however, now been almost entirely displaced by the Rome Convention 1980 and Rome I Regulation, under which (as discussed below) such a connection is not required. See e.g. Lando (1987), p.171ff.

approaches to choice of law in contract. Although some of these are not obviously compatible with party autonomy – for example, an interest analysis approach that focuses on the policy objectives of potentially applicable statutes – it is nevertheless true that in general choice of law clauses will be given effect under US law. Where party autonomy is given effect under these approaches, the limits of the effectiveness of choice of law agreements are often not well articulated. As discussed further below, in the two major codifications of choice of law, however – the Second Restatement and the Uniform Commercial Code – an objective connection between the parties or their dispute and the chosen law of their contract may be considered necessary. In other states, practice is variable – some jurisdictions take different approaches depending on the value of the transaction, permitting a choice without a 'reasonable relation' for higher value transactions.[175] As noted in Section 7.2.4, there are, however, constitutional constraints on choice of law in the US. Although the position is not certain, it has been suggested that these require 'sufficient contacts' between the law chosen by the parties and their dispute.[176]

A requirement for an objective connection in order for a choice of law to be valid may seem like a minor constraint on party autonomy, particularly as it might be thought parties are not likely to choose unconnected laws with great frequency. However, the practice is not in fact as uncommon as might be supposed, as the choice might be made for reasons of neutrality or expertise, and it suggests a major distinction in approach. Under this approach, party autonomy is a significantly less radical development, as it does not suggest that a law may be applied without a traditional jurisdictional link (a territorial or personal connection which would justify the application of law under traditional public international law, as well as under traditional objective connecting principles in private international law). Instead, party autonomy functions only to choose between the systems of law indicated by those territorial or personal connections. Party autonomy effectively does not function as a *new* basis for determining the applicable law to a contract, but rather as a rule of

---

[175] See e.g. New York Code, s.5-1401 (no reasonable relation required for transaction valued at more than $250,000), note also s.5-1402 (relating to jurisdiction, as discussed in Section 3.4.1); California Civil Code, s.1646.5 (no reasonable relation required for a transaction valued at more than $250,000); Texas Business and Commerce Code, s. 271 (no reasonable relation required for transaction valued at more than $1m). See e.g. Zhang (2006a), p.541ff.

[176] See e.g. *Allstate Insurance* v. *Hague*, 449 US 302 (1981) (requiring sufficient contacts, but doing so in the absence of party choice and for the purpose of ensuring 'fairness' – a requirement which would seem unnecessary in the context of a choice of law agreement). See discussion in Zhang (2006a), p.557ff.

priority – similarly to the traditional role of party intentions in the nineteenth century. Where the laws of more than one state might apply because each has a sufficiently strong objective connection to the parties or the transaction, it is the parties' choice (under this approach) that determines which law is applied. This perspective on party autonomy thus does not recognise the agreement of the parties as overriding traditional objective justifications for the application of a particular law, but as operating within the framework of those justifications.

7.3.1.1   United States – Second Restatement of Conflict of Laws

As discussed in Section 7.2.4, section 187 of the Second Restatement of Conflict of Laws distinguishes between issues which the parties can resolve through a particular provision in their contract, where the system of law is only providing default rules, and those which they cannot (although, as discussed above, determining what law should govern this question is not straightforward). In respect of the former, dealt with in section 187(1), there is no requirement for the chosen law to have any connection to the parties or their dispute. In respect of the latter, section 187 provides (in relevant part) that:

> (2) The law of the state chosen by the parties to govern their contractual rights and duties will be applied, even if the particular issue is one which the parties could not have resolved by an explicit provision in their agreement directed to that issue, unless either
> (a) the chosen state has no substantial relationship to the parties or the transaction and there is no other reasonable basis for the parties choice

There remains some uncertainty as to whether this test actually requires an objective connection.[177] It might be argued, for example, that the choice of a neutral law unconnected with the parties or their contract might be a deliberate compromise, which would in itself be a 'reasonable basis for the parties choice'. However, where the Second Restatement is fused with an interest analysis approach (as is often the case), the absence of an objective connection is likely to mean a lack of interest in the state whose law has been chosen, potentially invalidating the choice.[178]

The comments to section 187 of the Second Restatement include the following explanation of this requirement:

---

[177] See e.g. Hay, Borchers, and Symeonides (2010), p.1090ff.

[178] See e.g. discussion in *Hatfield* v. *Halifax PLC*, 564 F.3d 1177 (9th Cir. 2009); *Hambrecht & Quist Venture Partners* v. *American Medical International, Inc.*, 38 Cal.App.4th 1532 (1995).

The forum will not, for example, apply a foreign law which has been chosen by the parties in the spirit of adventure or to provide mental exercise for the judge. Situations of this sort do not arise in practice. Contracts are entered into for serious purposes and rarely, if ever, will the parties choose a law without good reason for doing so.

...

The parties to a multistate contract may have a reasonable basis for choosing a state with which the contract has no substantial relationship. For example, when contracting in countries whose legal systems are strange to them as well as relatively immature, the parties should be able to choose a law on the ground that they know it well and that it is sufficiently developed. For only in this way can they be sure of knowing accurately the extent of their rights and duties under the contract. So parties to a contract for the transportation of goods by sea between two countries with relatively undeveloped legal systems should be permitted to submit their contract to some well-known and highly elaborated commercial law.[179]

These comments appear to suggest that the restriction might only prevent choices made in bad faith, but on the other hand appear to accept a choice made with a view to evading the otherwise applicable law – an issue discussed further below. In practice, however, the 'substantial relationship' test has been considered by the courts in at least some cases to require an objective connection to justify the choice of law by the parties.[180] For example, the courts have refused to recognised a choice of law which was made on the sole basis that one of the parties' lawyers was from that jurisdiction.[181] There would seem to be sensible arguments of economic efficiency which might support such a choice, but nevertheless the courts appear in this case to have required an objective connection rather than merely a rational policy basis for the choice. In other cases, however, the courts have recognised that economic considerations may justify a choice even in the absence of any objective connection – finding, for example, that a franchisor had a reasonable basis for choosing a single law to govern all its franchise agreements (even if that law was unconnected to the

---

[179] Second Restatement of Conflict of Laws, s.187, comment (f).

[180] See also e.g. *Don King Productions, Inc. v. Douglas*, 742 F.Supp. 786 (S.D.N.Y. 1990). The courts tend, however, to accept any objective connection, even a fairly marginal one: see e.g. Rühl (2007a). For a proposal to abandon the need for an objective connection altogether in international cases see Silberman and Yaffe (2017), p.424ff.

[181] *Contour Design, Inc. v. Chance Mold Steel Co., Ltd.*, 693 F.3d 102, n.5 (1st Cir. 2012). Similar doubts have been expressed as to the choice of the law of the place of negotiating or entering into the contract, or the mere place of incorporation of one of the parties – see Hay, Borchers, and Symeonides (2010), p.1093ff.

franchise), and also for choosing the law of Washington state because of its proximity to the franchisor's headquarters in Vancouver, Canada.[182]

7.3.1.2   United States – Uniform Commercial Code

In its present version, section 1-301 of the UCC provides as follows:

> (a) Except as otherwise provided in this section, when a transaction bears a reasonable relation to this state and also to another state or nation the parties may agree that the law either of this state or of such other state or nation shall govern their rights and duties.

The Official Comment explains the requirement for a 'reasonable relation' in the following terms:

> In general, the test of "reasonable relation" is similar to that laid down by the Supreme Court in *Seeman v. Philadelphia Warehouse Co.* (1927). Ordinarily the law chosen must be that of a jurisdiction where a significant enough portion of the making or performance of the contract is to occur or occurs. But an agreement as to choice of law may sometimes take effect as a shorthand expression of the intent of the parties as to matters governed by their agreement, even though the transaction has no significant contact with the jurisdiction chosen.[183]

The final sentence of this passage would seem to undermine the need for any objective connection – it is difficult to reconcile with the actual text of the UCC. The decision of *Seeman v. Philadelphia Warehouse Co.* (1927)[184] concerned the question of whether the parties to a contract could choose between the place of contracting and the place of performance of the contract when it came to specifying interest rates under the contract, where (as was common at the time among US states) one or both of those places capped the permissible interest rates. The court held that the parties could make such a choice, although also noted that there should be limits on party freedom to choose the governing law:

> A qualification of these rules, as sometimes stated, is that the parties must act in good faith, and that the form of the transaction must not 'disguise its real character' ... The effect of the qualification is merely to prevent the evasion or avoidance at will of the usury law otherwise applicable, by the parties' entering into the contract or stipulating for its performance at a place which has no normal relation to the transaction and to whose law they would not otherwise be subject.[185]

---

[182] *1-800-Got Junk? LLC v. Superior Court*, 189 Cal.App.4th 500 (2010).
[183] Citation omitted. See discussion in Hay, Borchers, and Symeonides (2010), p.1153ff.
[184] 274 US 403 (1927).
[185] At p.408.

This passage might seem to support the position, similar to that applicable under some interpretations of the Second Restatement, that the limitation is not one of 'objective connection', but rather one of good faith – a requirement similar to that under the doctrine of *fraude à la loi*, discussed in Section 7.3.1.3. It is notable, however, that this decision actually predates the application of modern party autonomy – the court was relying on party intentions only to select between the place of contracting or place of performance. In context, the decision is probably not authority for the proposition that an objective connection is not required.

This provision of the UCC has a notable recent history which offers stronger evidence that the requirement for an objective connection remains significant. In 2001, the UCC was amended to remove the requirement for an 'objective connection' for a permissible exercise of party choice of law in contract, except in respect of consumer contracts, with revised section 1-301 providing that:

(1) an agreement by parties to a domestic transaction that any or all of their rights and obligations are to be determined by the law of this State or of another State is effective, whether or not the transaction bears a relation to the State designated; and

(2) an agreement by parties to an international transaction that any or all of their rights and obligations are to be determined by the law of this State or of another State or country is effective, whether or not the transaction bears a relation to the State or country designated.[186]

The change was, however, very controversial, was not widely implemented, and was indeed reversed in further May 2008 amendments to the Code.[187] The reinstatement of the old test under the current version of the UCC strongly suggests that the UCC and Second Restatement approach is not merely an anachronistic continuation of an old approach towards party autonomy (under which party intentions were used to justify a choice between objective rules), but is instead a genuine policy choice under which party autonomy in choice of contract is significantly restricted. Under this approach, it appears that party choice of law agreements are not on their own sufficient to justify the application of a particular law, but may be sufficient to elect between the potentially applicable laws where a contract has objective connections with more than one legal system. Party autonomy is understood as a rule of priority or selection rather than as a basis for the application of law in its own right.

[186] Section 1-301(c).
[187] See e.g. http://www.ali.org/doc/uccamendment.pdf; http://ali.org/_news/reporter/08june/08june.html. See further e.g. Burge (2015); Borchers (2008); Solomon (2008), p.1723ff; Zhang (2006a); Graves (2005).

7.3.1.3   Fraude à la loi

As noted above, the requirement that the law chosen by the parties have some objective connection with them or their transaction is often combined or conflated with a requirement that there be some rational or 'good faith' basis for their choice. This brings to mind the civil law doctrine of *fraude à la loi*, under which parties are not permitted plan their affairs in such a way as to evade the application of otherwise mandatory provisions of law.[188] In some versions, this might encompass actions by the parties which would affect objective choice of law rules – it might, for example, be relied on as an exception to a law of the place of contracting or law of the place of performance rule, where a contract for sale was deliberately entered into in a foreign location or the place of delivery was deliberately specified for a foreign territory, purely to prevent the application of local law.[189] Classically, under French law, it would encompass parties who travel to a foreign jurisdiction in order to marry or divorce, where this would not be permitted under their law of nationality or domicile – it thus emerged as a general exception to the preference for the law of the place of the ceremony. In the context of choice of law agreements, the doctrine might be relied on to deny effect to a choice of law by the parties where their selection was viewed as 'illegitimate' or as having been made in 'bad faith'. Whether this acts as a constraint on party autonomy will thus still depend, however, on what is considered a legitimate choice. If a legal system permits free choice by the parties of the law to govern their contract, there is no reason to impugn any choice as one made in bad faith or lacking legitimacy – the better view is that the doctrine thus has no continuing place under the Rome Convention or Rome I Regulation.[190] It may be noted, however, that the concept of 'abuse of law' is arguably a general principle of European Union law, and it is difficult to predict what influence it will ultimately have on EU private international law.[191]

While the generally considered view is that "The concept of 'fraude à la loi' has traditionally had little place in Anglo-American thinking about

---

[188] See generally e.g. Basedow (2013a), p.282ff; Parra-Aranguren (1988), p.102ff; Audit (1974). For discussion of a similar doctrine in Chinese law, see Xiao and Long (2009), p.205ff, although it is not clear whether this remains the current position except in relation to the factors which determine whether a contract is foreign-related – see Section 9.3.

[189] See further the discussion of 'indirect choice' through control over objective connecting factors in Section 1.3.1.

[190] See e.g. Nygh (1999), p.264.

[191] See e.g. de la Feria and Vogenauer (2011), particularly Chapters 18 and 19.

the choice-of-law problem",[192] it may be that it has had an indirect influence through the requirement that a choice by the parties be in good faith. If this doctrine has indeed influenced US law, in its requirement for some objective connection or other rational basis for a choice of law by the parties, this is a curiosity – it is difficult to see how it makes sense in a system of contract law which is premised on freedom of contract, in which courts seldom if ever second-guess whether the parties had good reasons to adopt particular contractual terms. This is particularly the case because, as explored in Chapter 9, local interests may be more straight-forwardly protected through application of mandatory rules which may not be evaded by the selection of a foreign law by the parties, particularly in a situation in which the contract is entirely connected to a single legal system but the parties choose a foreign system of law to govern. The pos-sible role of good faith restrictions in relation to choice of law agreements under US law may reflect a residual scepticism towards party autonomy in choice of law.

7.3.2   Systems in which no Objective Connection Is Required

In most other legal systems, the development of party autonomy has led to the conclusion that there is no need for any objective connection between the law chosen and the parties or their dispute or relationship.[193] The law is applied simply because it is the law under which the parties have expressly or impliedly agreed to contract. This point was, for example, recently clari-fied in an Interpretation of Chinese Law by the Supreme People's Court.[194] As discussed in Section 9.3, where no objective connection is required, this raises the related issue of whether purely 'domestic' contracts (internal to one legal system) are capable of being subject to a choice of foreign law. For example, it is notable that party autonomy in choice of law is only available in China for 'foreign-related' contracts – thus, a foreign law may not be chosen to govern a contract between two Chinese parties to be performed in China.

---

[192]   Von Mehren (1977), p.420.
[193]   See generally Nygh (1999), p.57ff. Although to suggest that the contrary position is "no longer seriously argued" (Nygh (1999), p.57) goes too far, particularly in light of the recent US history discussed above.
[194]   'Interpretation on Certain Issues Concerning PRC Law on the Application of Laws to Foreign-Related Civil Relations', Supreme People's Court, Fa Shi [2012] No. 24, 28 December 2012, Art.7; see Tang, Xiao and Huo (2016), p.212.

7.3.2.1 Common Law

In *Vita Food Products Inc.* v. *Unus Shipping Co.* (1939)[195] the Privy Council held that "where there is an express statement by the parties of their intention to select the law of the contract, it is difficult to see what qualifications are possible, provided the intention expressed is bona fide and legal".[196] It has sometimes been questioned whether this requirement for a 'bona fide and legal' choice imposes some type of restriction on a choice of law by the parties. In practice, it is not clear what this criteria could mean, except that the choice of law agreement must be valid, that is, a genuine agreement not obtained through, for example, fraud or coercion (matters to be determined applying the law governing the validity of the agreement, as explored in Section 7.5) – although it might also be considered to indicate the possible application of a doctrine of *fraude à la loi*, as discussed above. This criteria has not, in any event, been applied by the English courts, which have preferred to limit the effect of a choice of foreign law through the recognition of mandatory rules. The Canadian courts have however on a number of occasions appeared to consider the 'bona fide' limitation as a further condition for the enforceability of a choice of law agreement, suggesting that it prohibits choices of law which are made for the purpose of 'evading' the otherwise applicable law.[197] One interpretation of this approach is that it requires examining the objective connecting factors which would determine the applicable law in the absence of any choice by the parties, and potentially invalidating a choice of law which is unsupported by those connecting factors, although it is possible that other justifications for a choice of a particular national law (such as its neutrality or expertise) might also be accepted. The evident danger in this approach is that it requires the court to 'second-guess' the reasons behind the agreement between the parties. In other common law jurisdictions a choice of law agreement does not require any more justification than any other term of the contract between the parties – but its effect is subject to the protection given through mandatory rules, as discussed in Section 9.4.

Whatever the exact meaning of 'bona fides' in this context, *Vita Food Products* has generally been taken to provide that there is no 'objective' limit on the parties' choice – indeed, the Privy Council also expressly

---

[195] [1939] AC 237.

[196] At p.290.

[197] See e.g. *Nike Infomatic Systems Ltd* v. *Avac Systems Ltd* (1979) 105 DLR (3d) 455 (BCSC); *United Nations* v. *Atlantic Seaways Corp.* (1979) 99 DLR (3d) 609 (FCA); *Bank of Montreal* v. *Snoxell* (1982) 143 DLR (3d) 349 (AB QB).

stated that "Connection with English law is not as a matter of principle essential".[198] Thus, the parties may expressly choose English law as a neutral or preferred law even if it is entirely unconnected with their contract. The will of the parties is therefore clearly given priority over objective connecting factors, and operates regardless of and unconstrained by such objective connections. As a result, and contrary to the position suggested under some isolated older English authorities,[199] the generally accepted position is that party autonomy in choice of law is not subject to any limitation under the common law which requires any objective connection between the law chosen and the parties or their relationship.

7.3.2.2   Rome Convention 1980 and Rome I Regulation

The national law of some European member states, unlike English law, traditionally did require a connection between the law chosen by the parties and their dispute or relationship.[200] However, this connection was rejected in the process of European codification of choice of law in contract, under which no connection between the parties or their dispute and the law they have chosen is necessary in order for that choice to be effective. This is clear by implication from Article 3(3) of the Rome Convention and Rome I Regulation, each of which (as discussed in Section 9.3) provides for the additional application of non-derogable rules where the contract is entirely internal to a single legal system but a foreign law is chosen by the parties. Such a provision would be redundant if the choice by the parties would be ineffective in the absence of an objective connection. Article 3 of the Rome I Regulation, like its predecessor under the Rome Convention, is thus not a rule determining the priority between objective bases for determining the applicable law, but a rule which *trumps* the otherwise applicable choice of law rules which are based on territorial or personal connections.

7.3.2.3   International Codifications

International codification efforts in choice of law in contract have also tended to adopt the position that a party choice of law does not require any objective connecting factor or rational basis to be effective. Article 2 of the Basel Principles (1991), a soft law instrument adopted by the International

---

[198] At p.290.
[199] See e.g. *In Re Claim by Helbert Wagg & Co. Ltd* [1956] Ch 323, 341 ("This court will not necessarily regard [the parties' expression of intention] as being the governing consideration where a system of law is chosen which has no real or substantial connexion with the contract looked upon as a whole").
[200] See e.g. Lando (1987), p.171ff.

Law Association, provides that the parties may freely choose the law of any state, implicitly rejecting any objective connection requirement. The Mexico City Convention 1994 is silent on the issue, thus apparently leaving party autonomy unconstrained. Unlike the Rome Convention 1980 and Rome I Regulation, however, this cannot be deduced as a necessary implication of other terms of the Convention, because (as discussed further in Section 9.3) the Mexico City Convention only applies if a contract has objective connections to more than one legal system (and so does not deal with a possible choice of foreign law for a contract entirely internal to a legal system). In the absence of the Convention applying, it would be up to national law whether a party choice of law was nevertheless respected in such circumstances. A clearer position is adopted in the Hague Principles on Choice of Law in International Commercial Contracts 2015, which expressly state in Article 2(4) that "No connection is required between the law chosen and the parties or their transaction."[201]

7.4   The Timing of a Choice of Law

Ordinarily, parties choosing a system of law to govern their contractual relations would do so as a term of the contract, and thus the choice is contemporaneous with the formation of the remainder of the contract. As discussed in Chapter 8, more complex issues arise in relation to choice of law in other subject areas – in relation to choice of law in tort, for example, a contractual agreement on the governing law is likely to be entered into either before the tort (as part of establishing a pre-existing contractual relationship) or after the tort (to vary or clarify the governing law), but seldom at the same time. In relation to choice of law in contract, the issues are likely to concern only a subsequent choice by the parties – a variation or clarification of the law governing their contract.

7.4.1   Permissibility of a Subsequent Choice of Law

As far as the relationship between the contracting parties goes, there does not seem to be any essential reason not to permit a subsequent choice of law, at least to the extent that the choice would have been permissible at the time of entering into the agreement. Like any other term of the contract, a choice of law clause may be varied by the parties by agreement, or a contract between the parties may be varied through the addition of

---

[201] See discussion in Pertegás and Marshall (2014), p.988ff.

such a clause. A contract might even give the power of making the subsequent choice to one party unilaterally (known as a 'floating' choice of law clause),[202] although it may be queried whether this could have retrospective effect (for example, if it rendered past conduct of the other party in breach of contract) and whether an unrestricted choice would render the terms of the contract too uncertain.[203]

It could be argued that when or whether variations in a contract are permitted is a contractual issue, and thus whether a subsequent choice of law is possible should depend on the law governing (i) the contract, (ii) the original choice of law agreement (if there is one), or (iii) the new chosen law. Particular questions might be raised, for example, concerning whether a subsequent implied agreement on the applicable law is capable of varying the terms of a written contract between the parties. A further concern would be that such a change could prejudice the rights of third parties, such as a guarantor of a party's contractual obligations or assignee of a party's contractual rights. Again, this might be viewed as a private law issue, as an assignor or beneficiary of a guarantee may be considered to have undertaken not to make such a variation. Arguments have thus been made that the effectiveness of a subsequent choice of law should therefore depend on substantive contract law – potentially the original governing law, new governing law, or even both.[204]

In practice, however, these issues have tended to be viewed not as contract law questions, but as either (i) private international law questions, where the subsequent choice is made prior to the commencement of proceedings, or (ii) procedural questions, where the choice is made in the course of proceedings. Each of these issues is considered below.

Where a subsequent choice of law is made prior to the commencement of proceedings, the validity of that choice should arguably be analysed as a distinct private international law question, governed by choice of law rules themselves (specifically, the choice of law rules applied by the forum state), rather than a contractual issue to be resolved by a substantive law. This is a consequence of the fact that it is rules of private international law, not rules of contract law, which determine whether any choice of law agreement is

---

[202] This could vary the law previously chosen by the parties, or if no such law had been chosen, designate a law to replace that applicable under the objective choice of law rule. Such a power may be subject to implied restrictions of good faith. See e.g. *BP Plc* v. *National Union Fire Insurance Co.* [2004] EWHC 1132 (Comm), [35].

[203] See e.g. Nygh (1999), p.98ff; Howard (1995); Beck (1987); Briggs (1986).

[204] Cheshire North and Fawcett (2017), p.709ff; Nygh (1999), p.101; Diamond (1979), pp.162–5.

permissible, because the choice is (importantly) a special matter of private international law party autonomy rather than ordinary contractual autonomy. The issue of the permissibility of a variation of a choice of law clause should thus similarly be a matter for private international law, which is indeed typically the case in practice. For example, in the European Union Article 3(2) of the Rome Convention 1980 provides that:

> The parties may at any time agree to subject the contract to a law other than that which previously governed it, whether as a result of an earlier choice under this Article or of other provisions of this Convention. Any variation by the parties of the law to be applied made after the conclusion of the contract shall not prejudice its formal validity under Article 9 or adversely affect the rights of third parties.

The Convention does not directly address the question of whether a choice of law made after a contract has been entered into may be implied as well as express. The Giuliano-Lagarde Report offers some support for the argument that an implied choice after contracting is indeed permitted as part of the "maximum freedom"[205] given to the parties under Article 3(2). First, in support of the adoption of Article 3(2) it observes that:

> In the Federal Republic of Germany and in France the choice of applicable law by the parties can apparently be made even after the contract has been concluded, and the courts sometimes deduce the applicable law from the parties' attitude during the proceedings when they refer with clear agreement to a specific law. The power of the parties to vary the choice of law applicable to their contract also seems to be very widely accepted.[206]

This seems to conflate somewhat the procedural issue of whether a choice of law may be made during proceedings with the private international law issue of whether a subsequent choice may be made prior to proceedings, but there is at least an implication (particularly in the reference to a choice deriving from "the parties' attitude") that an implied choice of law based on conduct after contracting (but before proceedings are commenced) is permitted. It should be noted that the Report does generally distinguish between the two contexts, as it goes on to note that:

> If the choice of law is made or changed in the course of proceedings the question arises as to the limits within which the choice or change can be effective. However, the question falls within the ambit of the national law of procedure, and can be settled only in accordance with that law.[207]

---

[205] Giuliano-Lagarde Report, p.17.
[206] Ibid., footnote omitted.
[207] Ibid., p.18.

This suggests that the effectiveness of an implied choice of law during the course of proceedings is a procedural matter, and therefore excluded from the scope of the Rome Convention under Article 1(2)(h) – it is not a matter for either substantive law or even private international law. Thus, although the point is perhaps arguable,[208] the Rome Convention (and Rome I Regulation) should probably not be viewed as having an effect on the common law approach to proof of foreign law, under which such proof is traditionally, although perhaps decreasingly, considered optional.[209] Under this approach, a failure to plead or prove the content of foreign law by both parties is considered to lead to the application of forum law. One way of analysing this is as an implied choice of law by the parties – this is probably preferable to the explanation that foreign law is presumed to be the same as local law, which is an unsatisfactory legal fiction. The permissibility of such a choice is not a question of private international law, but of procedural law. Such a procedural law is, nevertheless, a means of facilitating a further exercise of party autonomy – it gives effect to an implicit agreement by the parties as to the governing law of their dispute – but one that is limited to the law of the forum. Common law courts have increasingly recognised that the procedural rules on the proof of foreign law may function as limited choice of law rules, and have thus increasingly constrained the freedom of the parties in line with other constraints on party autonomy – recognising, for example, that a court may apply foreign mandatory rules to evaluate the lawfulness of a contract even if the parties have defaulted to the law of the forum.[210] Giving effect to such constraints is likely to require a degree of procedural innovation, as it challenges the role of the common law judge as a passive arbiter of the dispute. Although the rules on the proof of foreign law thereby have substantive effects, they are, however, undoubtedly also motivated by their particular national procedural context, and a full treatment of this form of implicit choice of law is beyond the scope of this book.

The possibility that under rules of private international law (prior to the commencement of proceedings) the parties may make an implied subsequent choice of law through conduct is, on its face, in tension with the usual suspicion of the English courts towards using subsequent conduct as evidence for the interpretation of a contract.[211] The obvious

---

[208] See e.g. *Parker* v. *Tui UK Ltd* [2009] EWCA Civ 1261, [22]–[23].

[209] See e.g. Mills (2008a); Fentiman (2006a); Fentiman (1998); Hartley (1996).

[210] See e.g. *Shaker* v. *Al-Bedrawi* [2002] EWCA Civ 1452, [64]. See further Section 9.3.

[211] See e.g. *James Miller & Partners Ltd* v. *Whitworth Street Estates (Manchester) Ltd* [1970] AC 583.

reconciliation of these two principles would be to require proof of the existence of a new implied contract varying the applicable law, rather than just evidence of a mere change of understanding of the parties – the issue is not one of contractual interpretation, but formation or variation. This may, however, be somewhat objectionable in theory, if choice of law agreements are (as was recently suggested by the Supreme Court of New South Wales) "declaratory of the parties' intention, not promissory".[212] In any case, proving the existence of a new unwritten contract varying the applicable law of a prior contract may be very difficult in practice.[213] In the United States, the Second Restatement of Conflict of Laws does not address the issue of a subsequent choice of law – it thus appears to be left to general rules of contract law – but it is notable that the Oregon Codification of choice of law permits a subsequent choice but requires it to be in the form of an "express agreement", essentially imposing a (rare) formality requirement for the validity of such a choice of law, rather than leaving this issue as an evidentiary question.[214]

The same issue arises in respect of the Rome I Regulation, which does not materially alter the rule set out in Article 3(2), except that it refers to "Any change in the law to be applied that is made after the conclusion of the contract" rather than (in the Rome Convention) "Any variation by the parties of the law to be applied made after the conclusion of the contract". The justification for and effects of this change, in particular, whether it is intended to favour a more or less formal reading of the requirements of Article 3(2), are somewhat obscure.

As explored above, the approach to choice of law adopted in the EU has influenced and reflected broader practice in other jurisdictions – this is also true on the issue of the timing of a choice of law. The Law of the People's Republic of China on the Laws Applicable to Foreign-Related Civil Relations (2010), which sets out the presently applicable choice of law rules in China, does not directly address the issue of the timing of a choice of law in contract, simply providing that "The parties may by agreement choose the law applicable to their contract."[215] However, as noted above, in 2007 the Chinese Supreme People's Court promulgated Rules on 'Related

---

[212] *Ace Insurance Ltd* v. *Moose Enterprise Pty Ltd* [2009] NSWSC 724, [51]; see Section 7.2.1.

[213] The point was argued unsuccessfully in *ISS Machinery Services Ltd* v. *The Aeolian Shipping SA* [2001] 2 Lloyd's Rep 641; see also *Attock Cement Co. Ltd* v. *Romanian Bank* [1989] 1 Lloyd's Rep 572 (rejecting evidence of an oral choice of law agreement in respect of a written contract, under the common law). See discussion in Hill (2004), p.332ff.

[214] Oregon Revised Statutes, s.15.350(3); Hay, Borchers, and Symeonides (2010), p.1133.

[215] Article 41.

Issues concerning the Application of Law in Hearing Foreign-Related Contractual Dispute Cases Related to Civil and Commercial Matters',[216] which provided as follows:

> Article 4 The people's court shall permit the parties concerned to choose a law or alter a choice of law applicable to contractual disputes by agreement prior to the end of court debate of the first instance.
>
> In case the parties concerned fail to choose a law applicable to contractual disputes but both invoke the law of a same country or region and neither has raised any objection to the choice of law, the parties concerned shall be deemed as having made the choice of a law applicable to contractual disputes.

This Article thus combined a rule of private international law permitting a subsequent choice of law (up to the commencement of proceedings) with a rule of procedural law permitting a choice (up to the end of the first instance proceedings) – interestingly, the latter was not limited to the choice of the law of the forum. An almost identical approach was endorsed in a 2012 Interpretation of the 2010 Law, issued by the Supreme People's Court.[217] It may also be noted that Article 100 of the 'Model Law of Private International Law of the People's Republic of China' (Sixth draft, 2000)[218] (an academic codification of Chinese Law prepared by the Chinese Society of Private International Law) provided for a slightly more detailed rule on this issue. It stated, in relevant part, that:

> Parties to a contract can make a choice of law when or after the contract is concluded but before the court holds hearing. And after the contract is concluded, parties can also vary the law chosen at the time of the conclusion of the contract. The variation has retrospective effect, but without prejudice to the rights and benefits of the third party.

Aside from specifying that a variation must have retrospective effect, which is arguably unsatisfactory if the parties are intending only to change their legal relationship prospectively, this approach appears generally consistent with that in the EU, and it is difficult to see any reasons why a modern Chinese court would depart from it. It is notable that it addresses only the private international law question of a choice prior to the commencement of proceedings, leaving aside the procedural question of a choice during proceedings. The question of a procedural choice of

---

[216] Available in translation at www.fdi.gov.cn/1800000121_39_2045_0_7.html.

[217] 'Interpretation on Certain Issues Concerning PRC Law on the Application of Laws to Foreign-Related Civil Relations', Supreme People's Court, Fa Shi [2012] No. 24, 28 December 2012, Art.8.

[218] www.rucil.com.cn/admin/edit/UploadFile/200891911459766.pdf.

law is perhaps addressed implicitly in a separate Article 10 of the Law of the People's Republic of China on the Laws Applicable to Foreign-Related Civil Relations (2010), which provides in relevant part that:

> Where the parties have chosen a foreign law to be applicable, they shall adduce the law of that country. Where the foreign law cannot be ascertained or the law of that country does not have a relevant provision, the PRC law shall be applied.[219]

If a failure by the parties to plead foreign law is understood to be a reason the law cannot be ascertained by the court, this rule will in effect be very similar to the common law procedural rule recognising an implied choice of forum law.

A consistent approach also seems to be taken in international codifications of choice of law in contract. Article 6 of the Basel Principles (1991), a soft law instrument adopted by the International Law Association, provides that the parties may choose the law applicable to a contract or modify that choice at any time, and may give their choice retrospective effect subject to rights acquired by third parties. Article 8 of the Mexico City Convention 1994 equivalently provides that:

> The parties may at any time agree that the contract shall, in whole or in part, be subject to a law other than that to which it was previously subject, whether or not that law was chosen by the parties. Nevertheless, that modification shall not affect the formal validity of the original contract nor the rights of third parties.

The Hague Principles on Choice of Law in International Commercial Contracts 2015 similarly provides, in Article 2(3), that:

> The choice may be made or modified at any time. A choice or modification made after the contract has been concluded shall not prejudice its formal validity or the rights of third parties.

The approaches in the legal systems examined above broadly coalesce around the (logical) idea that once a free choice of law is permitted, a variation in that choice should also be permitted at any point in time. The better view is that such choices may (unless otherwise specified) be implied as well as express, although demonstrating that the parties have made an implied choice may be difficult as an evidentiary matter. This rule should

---

[219] Note also Article 9 of the Rules on 'Related Issues concerning the Application of Law in Hearing Foreign-Related Contractual Dispute Cases Related to Civil and Commercial Matters', providing (in part) that "In case neither the parties concerned nor the people's court can ascertain the content of the foreign law through proper channels, the people's court may apply the law of the People's Republic of China." Available in translation at www.fdi.gov.cn/1800000121_39_2045_0_7.html

not, however, affect questions of the pleading and proof of foreign law, which should remain governed by national procedural law. More contentious issues arise concerning what effects a subsequent choice of law should be given, which is the subject of the following section.

7.4.2   Effect of a Subsequent Choice of Law

As noted above, parties are likely to enter into a subsequent choice of law agreement either to clarify or vary the law that governs their contractual relations. These two different motivations are likely to mean two different desired effects. If the parties are clarifying the law of their contract, it may be expected that their intention is to effect this change retrospectively – such that any prior performance of the contract will now be evaluated according to the new (or newly certain) law. A similar effect would likely be intended by parties who are entering into an implied agreement at the time of litigation, or indeed any parties reaching such an agreement after all contractual obligations have been performed. For parties who have an ongoing business relationship pursuant to the contract, however, a variation of the law governing their contractual relations may be intended to have a purely prospective effect. Indeed, it is arguably unlikely that such parties would intend for their past contractual performance to be re-evaluated retrospectively under a new governing law, particularly if there is no prior uncertainty as to that law (for example, because the original contract contains an initial choice of law which is now being varied). In practice, identifying whether parties intend a subsequent choice of governing law to have retrospective or purely prospective effect should be a matter of contractual interpretation, and thus governed by the law which governs the choice of law agreement – the subject of the next section of this chapter.

Under most of the codified rules noted above it is expressly provided that any subsequent choice of law may not prejudice the formal validity of the original contract. This is generally justified on the basis that the choice made by the parties should not have the effect of retrospectively invalidating their agreement – as in the Giuliano-Lagarde Report on the Rome Convention 1980, which states that:

> The purpose of the reservation concerning the formal validity of the contract is to avoid a situation whereby the agreement between the parties to subject the contract to a law other than that which previously governed it could create doubts as to the validity of the contract during the period preceding the agreement between the parties.[220]

---

[220] At p.18.

It is somewhat unclear, however, why such a rule should be adopted. It has the effect of allowing the parties to evade formality requirements which exist under their own laws and the laws which they would like to govern their contract – they simply need to make an initial choice of a law which renders their contract formally valid, and then a subsequent choice of their actual preferred law. The temporary selection of a law with no (or weaker) formality requirements is enough to circumvent any such requirements that form part of other potentially applicable laws. Why parties should be permitted to evade formality requirements in this way is not explained in the Report – such requirements are presumably adopted in pursuit of certain policy objectives which are frustrated if the requirements are not met. This is, however, at least arguably consistent with the general approach of the Rome Convention and Rome I Regulation towards formality requirements, which is to minimise their effect by requiring the parties to comply with only one of various possible governing laws (the law governing the contract, the law of the place of contracting, or the law of the place where either party or their agent is present or habitually resident at the time of contracting).[221] While such a presumption works in favour of the validity of contracts, it undermines formality requirements adopted as part of national legal systems for national policy purposes. It is somewhat curious that this issue, essentially a matter of substantive contract law policy, has been addressed in this way as part of European choice of law rules – perhaps the acquiescence of Member States suggests a declining commitment to their formality requirements.

In various choice of law rules discussed above, including under the Rome Convention and Rome I Regulation, it is provided that any subsequent choice of law may not 'prejudice' the formal validity of the original contract. Under each of these rules, it is clear that (in accordance with the justification discussed above) the contract may not be *invalidated* by the subsequent choice, but it is less clear whether it may also not be *validated* by the subsequent choice.[222] The better view is probably that the issue can only arise in the former situation, as in the latter a valid contract does not exist based on the original choice of law. Where the parties in that context purport to 'vary' the law governing the contract, and do so in favour of a law which renders the contract formally valid, they are essentially entering into a new contract, and this contract should be treated as formally valid pursuant to the usual rules in order to give effect to their intentions.

---

[221] Rome I Regulation, Art.11; Rome Convention 1980, Art.9.
[222] See Giuliano-Lagarde Report, p.18.

The various rules discussed above are silent on how a subsequent choice of law may affect the material or substantive validity of the contract. It is therefore possible that the parties may choose a law that renders their contract materially invalid, either prospectively or retrospectively. For this to be the effect of their choice, the subsequent choice of law agreement must itself be materially valid – a different issue from the *permissibility* of a subsequent choice. The material validity of a subsequent choice of law will generally be governed by the newly chosen law, the 'putative law of the agreement', as discussed further below.

7.5 The Law Governing a Choice of Law Agreement

The permissibility of a choice of law agreement is a matter for private international law rules, as discussed in the various sections above. However, once it is established that a choice is permissible, there are various other questions that may arise regarding choice of law agreements, including questions as to their interpretation and their formal and material validity. The question of interpretation will include what disputes are covered by the choice of law agreement, including the question of whether it might apply to non-contractual disputes – a matter discussed further in Section 8.2. The issue of formal validity could arise particularly if a legal system imposes formality requirements on choice of law agreements, such as requiring them to be in writing – this is rarely seen in practice,[223] although it was proposed (and not adopted) in the course of negotiations for the Rome I Regulation,[224] and (as noted in Section 7.2.5) has been adopted in China. The material validity of a choice of law agreement will include questions concerning whether the agreement was entered into pursuant to misrepresentation, duress, undue influence, or a mistake. These questions should be resolved through identification and application of the law or laws governing the choice of law agreement.

When it comes to determining the law governing jurisdiction and arbitration agreements, matters discussed above in Sections 3.3 and 6.3 respectively, a doctrine of severability is applied under which the jurisdiction or arbitration agreement is treated as an independent contract. If the validity and applicability of that independent contract is established,

---

[223] See generally Albornoz and González Martín (2016), p.443ff.
[224] As discussed above, the Rome I Regulation recognises that formality requirements may be adopted as part of national law, but adopts a rule that minimises their effectiveness: see Art.3(5) and Art.11.

it then determines which court or tribunal has the power to determine the substantive issues between the parties. Although choice of law agreements are not invariably analysed in the same way, it might be argued that they should be.[225] The law governing the substantive issues between the parties (including the validity of their substantive contractual terms) depends on whether they have made a valid and effective choice of law; this depends on whether the choice of law agreement is itself valid in accordance with its governing law. The validity and applicability of the choice of law agreement should thus, under this approach, be examined independently from the other contractual issues between the parties, as a preliminary question. The validity or otherwise of the choice of law agreement will then determine what governing law should be applied to evaluate the validity of the substantive contractual terms. There is an express suggestion that such an approach should be adopted in Article 7 of the Hague Principles on Choice of Law in International Commercial Contracts 2015, which provides that "A choice of law cannot be contested solely on the ground that the contract to which it applies is not valid." The commentary to the Principles further explains that this is indeed intended to introduce a doctrine of severability similar to that applied to choice of court agreements and arbitration clauses, on the basis that the choice of law agreement has "a distinct subject matter and possesses an autonomous character from the contract to which it applies".[226] The approach is justified on the basis of the claim that "This is consistent with the approach followed in international and European instruments, such as Article 10 of the Rome I Regulation, according to which the parties' choice of law should be subject to an independent assessment that is not automatically tied to the validity of the main contract". It is not clear, however, whether Article 10 of the Rome I Regulation actually supports this approach – it merely provides that "The existence and validity of a contract, or of any term of a contract, shall be determined by the law which would govern it under this Regulation if the contract or term were valid". This does not necessarily require that the validity of a choice of law clause be evaluated prior to and separately from questions of general contractual validity. The adoption of severability in this context is more novel than the Hague Principles themselves suggest.

Whether or not analysed as a prior question, it may be necessary to determine what law governs the validity of (and indeed interpretation of) a choice of law agreement. In determining that law, however, there is a logical problem.[227] A choice of law clause is an attempt to choose the law

---

[225] See e.g. Hook (2016), Chapter 4.
[226] Commentary to the Hague Principles, [7.2].
[227] See e.g. Nygh (1999), p.95.

that governs the contract between the parties, including the clause itself. Ignoring that law when it comes to determining the validity and applicability of the choice of law clause would seem to depart from the intentions and expectations of the parties. But applying the law chosen in the clause to the clause itself would seem to presume its validity for the purposes of determining that validity – an apparent exercise in 'bootstrapping'. The parties have made a valid choice of law, because they have chosen a system of law under which they are viewed as having made a valid choice of law.

The danger this presents is that the parties may choose a system of law under which a contract (including the choice of law clause) is created unreasonably. For example, imagine under the law of Utopia an offer to contract is (in certain circumstances) deemed to be accepted if it is not expressly refused. A person resident in England receives such an offer, including a clause selecting the law of Utopia. Not being aware of Utopian law, they ignore the offer, and are later sued in England for non-performance of the contract. If the choice of Utopian law is effective, there would appear to be a binding contract between the parties. If Utopian law is applied to the question of the validity of the choice of law clause, that would also appear to be binding, and such a choice is permitted under the Rome I Regulation.

There are two approaches that might be adopted to respond to this concern. The first is to accept the effectiveness of the choice of law, but adopt additional safeguards regarding the proper formation of a contract. The second is to hold that the validity of the choice of law clause should be governed by a different system of law – which could be either forum law, or the law which would apply to the contract in the absence of choice (the law most closely connected to the contract).

7.5.1   Validity of Choice of Law Clause
Governed by the Chosen Law

An example of the first approach is adopted in the EU, as part of the Rome Convention 1980 and Rome I Regulation. Article 3(5) of the Rome I Regulation[228] provides as follows:

> The existence and validity of the consent of the parties as to the choice of the applicable law shall be determined in accordance with the provisions of Articles 10, 11 and 13.

The referenced Articles set out the usual rules governing material validity, formal validity, and incapacity. As noted above, the effect of Article

---

[228]   See similarly the Rome Convention 1980, Art.3(4).

10(1) is that a choice of law clause is presumed valid and applied when determining the law which governs its own validity. However, this is made subject to a safeguard set out in Article 10(2), which states that:

> Nevertheless, a party, in order to establish that he did not consent, may rely upon the law of the country in which he has his habitual residence if it appears from the circumstances that it would not be reasonable to determine the effect of his conduct in accordance with the law specified in paragraph 1.

A similar approach is adopted in the Mexico City Convention 1994, in which Article 12 provides that:

> The existence and the validity of the contract or of any of its provisions, and the substantive validity of the consent of the parties concerning the selection of the applicable law, shall be governed by the appropriate rules in accordance with Chapter 2 of this Convention.
>
> Nevertheless, to establish that one of the parties has not duly consented, the judge shall determine the applicable law, taking into account the habitual residence or principal place of business.

Similarly again, the Hague Principles on Choice of Law in International Commercial Contracts 2015 provide in Article 6(1)(a) that "whether the parties have agreed to a choice of law is determined by the law that was purportedly agreed to", but qualify this in Article 6(2) by stating that:

> The law of the State in which a party has its establishment determines whether that party has consented to the choice of law if, under the circumstances, it would not be reasonable to make that determination under the law specified in paragraph 1.

While these rules rely on slightly different connecting factors (the habitual residence, principal place of business, and/or establishment of a party), they are otherwise to similar effect.[229] Questions of capacity may similarly be governed by a different law than that chosen by the parties for their contract – for example, corporate capacity is generally determined by the law of the place of incorporation.[230]

There are two possible ways in which these provisions might be applied to the hypothetical 'Utopia' scenario set out above. The first would be simply to apply the safeguard provision to the contract as a whole. The party habitually resident in England could thus rely on the provision to establish that no contract was formed based on their failure to expressly refuse the offer. No contract would exist between the parties.

---

[229] A similar approach was also adopted under Article 4 of the Basel Principles (1991).
[230] *Integral Petroleum SA v. SCU-Finanz AG* [2015] EWCA Civ 144.

The second would be to apply it to the formation of the choice of law agreement separately as a preliminary step – this would seem to be required by the Hague Principles, which *only* apply to the issue of consent to the choice of law agreement, not the issue of consent to the contract as a whole. The party habitually resident in England could thus rely on the provision to establish that there is no choice of Utopian law under the contract. This would mean that the law governing the remainder of the contract should be determined pursuant to the rules which apply in the absence of party choice, for example under Article 4 of the Rome I Regulation. This might be Utopian law – for example, if the contract concerns the sale of goods by a Utopian party to an English party, because the seller's habitual residence is presumed to determine the law governing the contract under Article 4(1)(a). Applying Article 10(1) would point to Utopian law governing the validity of the contract, and thus there would be a valid contract between the parties. However, Article 10(2) could be applied again in relation to the contract (without the choice of law clause), to establish that there was no consent to the substantive agreement. In this scenario, it therefore does not generally matter whether the choice of law agreement is analysed separately as a preliminary question, or whether the rule is simply applied to the contract as a whole – in either case, the contract should be invalidated.

It is, however, possible that there are cases in which the adoption of this second approach *could* make a difference. For example, the law chosen in the contract might be Utopian law, but the law that would apply in the absence of choice might be Ruritanian law instead (for example, because the seller's habitual residence is Ruritania). Ruritanian law might similarly find that a contract is established in the circumstances outline above. Under the second approach, whether the English party could rely on Article 10(2) to invalidate the contract (minus the already invalidated choice of Utopian law clause) would depend on whether "it appears from the circumstances that it would not be reasonable to determine the effect of his conduct in accordance with" Ruritanian law – which is a distinct question from whether it would not be reasonable to apply Utopian law. It is possible, for example, that the English party is well aware of Ruritanian law and has entered into contracts governed by that system of law before, but has no such knowledge of Utopian law. But it is difficult to argue that a valid Ruritanian contract between the parties should be formed here – the intention of the seller was only to enter into a contract governed by Utopian law.

Which approach should be adopted is not a straightforward question. However, the complexity of the issues raised by the second approach would perhaps suggest that the first would be preferable, contrary to the approach which seems to be required by the Hague Principles on Choice of Law in International Commercial Contracts 2015. In other words, the validity of the choice of law clause should arguably not be considered as a distinct and severable contract between the parties. Either the contract including the choice of law clause is valid, or the contract as a whole is invalid. Invalidating only the choice of law clause would leave the possibility that a valid contract is nevertheless otherwise formed, which would risk imposing a bargain on the parties that neither of them wished to enter.

A further difficulty with relying on the chosen law to determine the validity of the choice of law clause may arise if the parties have made inconsistent choices of law in the course of contractual negotiations, such as where each party has provided to the other their standard terms and conditions. The question then arises as to whose law should govern the question of which standard terms and conditions apply, and thus which choice of law clause is effective. Different solutions may be adopted under national systems of contract law in the absence of particular rules of private international law dealing with this problem, favouring the terms of the 'offer', or the 'acceptance', or some combination of the two, or instead the law objectively determined.[231] Article 6(1)(b) of the Hague Principles provides that in this scenario:

> if the parties have used standard terms designating two different laws and under both of these laws the same standard terms prevail, the law designated in the prevailing terms applies; if under these laws different standard terms prevail, or if under one or both of these laws no standard terms prevail, there is no choice of law.

This rather innovative rule would be a positive development – by adopting a private international law solution it reduces the risk of inconsistent decisions being reached as to the applicable law. It is also an interesting rule, as it first identifies whether there is a true or merely a false conflict (if both potentially applicable laws would lead to the same outcome), and in the case of a true conflict, abandons party autonomy rather than imposing a legal solution on the situation which would favour one of the choices of law.[232] It remains to be seen, however, whether states will find it beneficial to have a distinct rule of contract formation applicable to choice of law clauses – this raises the possibility that the standard terms of one party

---

[231] See e.g. discussion in Pertegás and Marshall (2014), p.992ff; Nygh (1999), pp.95–6.

[232] See the Commentary to the Hague Principles for analysis of how this rule should be applied in different scenarios; see also Graziano (2017).

might apply without their choice of law clause, rendering some of those substantive terms inappropriate or even invalid.

7.5.2   Validity of Choice of Law Clause Governed by Residual or Forum Law

The second option that might be taken to determine which law should govern the validity of a choice of law clause is not to apply the chosen law, even presumptively – at the risk of applying some other law which the parties would not have had in mind. It might be suggested that the law most closely connected to the contract should be applied, as determined by the choice of law rules that would apply in the absence of a choice by the parties.[233] This is used as a partial test under the Second Restatement of Conflict of Laws (as examined in Section 7.2.4), in two ways. First, section 187 of the Restatement applies different limitations to party autonomy based on a decision as to whether "the particular issue is one which the parties could have resolved by an explicit provision in their agreement directed to that issue" – a matter which is (at least apparently) judged according to the law applicable in the absence of choice by the parties.[234] Second, if it is determined that the issue is one which the parties could not have resolved by an explicit provision in their agreement, their chosen law may be excluded if it would be contrary to the public policy of the state which "would be the state of the applicable law in the absence of an effective choice of law by the parties".[235]

However, among other concerns, this approach has the disadvantage that it adds unnecessary complexity to the issues, similarly to the approach outlined above, as different foreign laws may govern the validity of the choice of law agreement and the remainder of the contract. It also undermines the certainty and efficiency benefits from party autonomy, because it means that a court may well still have to determine what law would apply in the absence of a choice.[236] An alternative approach is simply to apply forum law to determine the validity of the choice of law clause – this

---

[233] There is also (somewhat unclear) support for this approach under the common law: in *The Hollandia* [1983] 1 AC 565, 576 (a choice of law should be invalidated "if the particular choice of substantive law made by the express clause is such as to make the clause null and void under the law of the place where the contract was made, or under what, in the absence of such express clause, would be the proper law of the contract").

[234] Comment (c).

[235] Section 187(2)(b).

[236] See e.g. Hay, Borchers, and Symeonides (2010), p.1130.

approach has some support in the Australian case law,[237] is also commonly applied in US courts to the question of interpretation of the clause,[238] and has traditionally been applied in China.[239] It might be queried whether this approach distinguishes sufficiently between the question of the effectiveness of a valid choice of law (a matter for the law of the forum) and the question of the validity of the choice of law agreement (which is at least ostensibly contractual in nature and could be governed by another system of law).[240] There is, however, support for this approach in other parts of the Second Restatement of Conflict of Laws. The Restatement provides special rules which state that the chosen law determines issues relating to capacity and other questions of substantive and formal validity[241] – a similar approach to that under the Rome I Regulation, as discussed above. However comment (b) to section 187 explains further that:

> A choice-of-law provision, like any other contractual provision, will not be given effect if the consent of one of the parties to its inclusion in the contract was obtained by improper means, such as by misrepresentation, duress, or undue influence, or by mistake. Whether such consent was in fact obtained by improper means or by mistake will be determined by the forum in accordance with its own legal principles.

The reference to the forum resolving issues of the validity of the choice of law clause applying "its own legal principles" is clearly intended to indicate the application of local contract law, rather than merely local choice of law rules.[242]

This approach was followed, albeit somewhat opaquely, by the Eighth Circuit court in *John T. Jones Construction Co. v. Hoot General Construction Co., Inc.* (2010).[243] In this case, a clause in the contract selected the law of North Dakota, but the court found that a choice of law clause "can have no effect until the court determines the validity of the contract itself", and thus the validity of the contract as a whole should be examined as a preliminary question. The court held that forum law (the law of Iowa) should be

---

[237] See e.g. *Oceanic Sun Line Special Shipping Co. Inc. v. Fay* (1988) 165 CLR 197, 261 (per Gaudron J).

[238] See (critical) discussion in Coyle (2017), p.680ff.

[239] See e.g. Xiao and Long (2009), p.200.

[240] Harris (2000) argues (at p.252) that this distinction is not always clearly drawn in Nygh (1999).

[241] Sections 198, 199, and 200.

[242] Hay, Borchers, and Symeonides (2010), pp.1129–30.

[243] 613 F.3d 778 (8th Cir. 2010).

applied to that question. If the contract is valid under forum law, this will include the choice of law clause, which will then be applied as a further test for the validity of the contract as a whole. This somewhat confused analysis in truth simply involves applying forum law (the law of Iowa, in this case) to determine the validity of the choice of law clause, which (if valid) will then determine the law that governs the validity of the remainder of the contract. It therefore in practice gives effect to the approach suggested in comment (b) of section 187 of the Second Restatement.

7.6   The Validity of a Choice of Law that Invalidates the Contract

As discussed earlier in this chapter, choice of law rules may impose various constraints on the validity of a choice of law clause. The parties might only be permitted, for example, to choose legal systems with an objective connection to their relationship or to the parties themselves. These constraints do not derive from the law governing the choice of law clause, but from choice of law rules themselves – a purported choice of law agreement thus may be invalidated not only by the contract law that governs it, but also by the rules of private international law that determine its permissible effectiveness. Another possible such constraint is the question of what effect should be given to a choice by the parties that invalidates their contract.

One approach that appears to have had an influence in the English courts under the common law and also potentially in applying the Rome Convention 1980 is a presumption of validity, as already noted in Section 7.2. If there is no express choice of law in a contract, but there are factors that might indicate an implied choice of law, the court may nevertheless find that the parties cannot be understood to have made an implied choice of a law that would invalidate their contract.[244] In this approach, the potential invalidity is relied on as an indicator of the intentions of the parties, presuming them to have an intention to form valid contractual relations. Some doubt may be expressed over how much weight should be attached to this presumption, as it assumes that the intention of the parties to enter into a valid contract outweighs their intended governing law; the other terms of the agreement are prioritised over the (apparent) choice of law. In any case this is not, strictly speaking, a factor that *invalidates* a choice of law agreement, but is rather evidence that such an agreement does not exist.

---

[244]   See also e.g. *Sulamérica Cia Nacional de Seguros SA* v. *Enesa Engenharia SA* [2012] EWCA Civ 638, discussed in Section 6.3.

A distinct approach, adopted in the Second Restatement of Conflict of Laws, is explained in the comments as follows:

> On occasion, the parties may choose a law that would declare the contract invalid. In such situations, the chosen law will not be applied by reason of the parties' choice. To do so would defeat the expectations of the parties which it is the purpose of the present rule to protect. The parties can be assumed to have intended that the provisions of the contract would be binding upon them (cf. § 188, Comment b). If the parties have chosen a law that would invalidate the contract, it can be assumed that they did so by mistake. If, however, the chosen law is that of the state of the otherwise applicable law under the rule of § 188, this law will be applied even when it invalidates the contract. Such application will be by reason of the rule of § 188, and not by reason of the fact that this was the law chosen by the parties.[245]

This approach will invalidate even an express choice of law that renders the contract invalid. A similar rule was endorsed under Article 3(3) of the Basel Principles (1991), adopted by the International Law Association, which provides that "Whenever the contract is not valid under the law chosen by the parties, that choice shall have no effect". A curiosity of this approach is that it suggests that the parties have an underlying intention (to form a contract) which is more important than even their *express* choice of law intention (to have their contract governed by a particular law).[246] It is equally plausible that parties might wish to enter into a contract governed by a particular law, and that if they are unable to do so because of a provision of that chosen law, they would wish their contract to fail rather than have it potentially validated and governed by an objectively determined law. This is a similar issue to that discussed above in relation to the potential invalidity of the choice of law clause under its governing law. The alternative view is that the choice of law clause may be an essential term of the contract, and thus a choice of law clause that leads to an invalid contract should not be itself viewed as invalid and 'severed' from the contract on that basis.

7.7 Conclusions

The international codifications and national and EU rules examined in this chapter (with the notable exception of Brazil) clearly permit the parties to

---

[245] Second Restatement of Conflict of Laws, s.187, comment (e).
[246] See discussion in Hay, Borchers, and Symeonides (2010), pp.1134–5; Nygh (1999), pp.59–60.

choose the law governing their contract. Party autonomy in choice of law is firmly established as a general principle. In most legal systems, there are no formality requirements for a choice of law, which has created the possibility for implied choices to be identified. Although a clear distinction between situations of implied choice and the objective choice of law rule applicable in the absence of choice can be identified in theory, in practice the line between the two is sometimes blurred, as courts may find an implied choice based on the weight of factors objectively connecting a contract to a particular legal system, potentially going beyond giving effect to party autonomy. Restricting implied choices too greatly, however, runs the opposite risk of not giving effect to party autonomy in some cases.

An important point of variation in different legal systems relates to the question of whether an objective connection is required between the chosen law and the parties or their contract, or some other rational basis for their choice. Some legal systems provide for an entirely free choice, while others constrain the choice of the parties in various ways. Where an objective connection is required, party autonomy in choice of law appears to function more as a rule of priority (determining which objective connection is decisive) rather than as a basis for the applicable law in its own right. Different approaches have also been adopted to the complex issue of whether an implied choice of a different law may be made after a contract has been entered into, whether before or after legal proceedings have been commenced, and whether such a variation has retrospective or prospective effect, and what impact it might have on third parties and on the validity of the contract.

While private international law rules determine the permissibility of a choice of law, further questions may arise concerning the validity of a choice of law agreement as a contractual term. This requires identifying the law that should govern the choice of law agreement, where again a variety of different approaches may be identified in practice, applying for example the chosen law to the clause itself, or the law that would be applicable in the absence of choice, or forum law. A choice of a law that invalidates the contract also gives rise to varying effects in different legal systems.

The firm establishment of party autonomy as a general principle in choice of law in contract is thus perhaps more questionable on closer examination. While there is close to consensus on the basic question of the effectiveness of choice of law agreements, there is divergent practice on a range of issues which reflects strikingly distinct perspectives on why and when party choices of law should be given effect.

Choice of Law in Non-Contractual Relations

8.1 Introduction

This chapter continues the analysis of party autonomy with respect to the applicable law, looking at choice of law in non-contractual relations. Party autonomy has traditionally had a very limited role outside of choice of law in contract. Two main reasons might be suggested for this. First, it could reflect an assumption or determination that there are greater public interests or policies involved in non-contractual claims. To the extent that tort law is concerned with the regulation of harmful behaviour, for example, it could be argued that parties should not be able to 'opt out' of local standards. Second, in non-contractual disputes there will frequently be no pre-existing relationship between the parties and thus no opportunity for the exercise of prior party autonomy – although, as discussed below, this is not always the case, and also does not preclude the possibility of a choice of law entered into after the events giving rise to the claim.

The modern trend is for party autonomy to play an increasing role in non-contractual choice of law, but one that is still subject to special limits. Party autonomy has perhaps had the greatest impact in relation to tortious claims, for example under the Rome II Regulation in the European Union. It has also, for example, been recognised as having a potential role in the assignment of debts, under the Rome Convention 1980 and now Rome I Regulation. Beyond these fields, the role of party autonomy has been limited and largely indirect, although the trend appears to be towards a greater influence for the parties themselves in determining the law governing their legal relations. This chapter explores the extent to which there is an emerging trend towards the broader recognition of party autonomy in non-contractual disputes, and the particular constraints which are commonly recognised as operating to restrict party autonomy in this context.

In examining choice of law in non-contractual relations, two separate questions must be distinguished. First, the scope of the choice of law agreement – whether the exercise of autonomy by the parties should be understood to encompass non-contractual claims. This is essentially a question of contractual interpretation, examined in Section 8.2 below. Second, the effectiveness of a choice of law agreement that encompasses or may otherwise indirectly affect non-contractual claims. This is essentially a question for the rules of private international law examined in the other sections of this chapter, dealing with tort and delict (Section 8.3), unjust enrichment and related issues (Section 8.4), property (Section 8.5), equitable claims (Section 8.6), trusts (Section 8.7), and succession and family law (Section 8.8). This second question may also be approached through the analytical framework of characterisation (also known as classification, and discussed further below).[1] A non-contractual claim may, for example, have to be characterised to determine whether it should be covered by the choice of law rule for tort or property, which may affect the scope of permitted party autonomy. Such a claim might alternatively be viewed by the court as actually concerned with contractual rights, and thereby covered by the choice of law rules in contract (examined in Chapter 7) under which party autonomy is strongly effective, or potentially by one of the special regimes that limit or exclude party autonomy (examined in Chapter 9).

8.2   The Scope of Choice of Law Agreements

Before examining the extent to which private international law rules permit a choice of law in relation to a non-contractual claim, a preliminary question arises: how should it be determined whether a choice of law agreement *intends* to cover non-contractual claims? The issues here are analogous to those explored in Section 4.2, in relation to the question of whether a choice of court agreement should be understood as intending to apply to non-contractual claims. As in that context, two separate questions need to be distinguished. First, the scope of the agreement, which is a matter of contract law and the subject of this section. Second, the effectiveness of the agreement, which is a matter of private international law and the subject of the remainder of this chapter.

Three alternative formulations of a choice of law clause might be compared.

> Disputes concerning the interpretation or breach of this contract will be governed by English law. *(Clause 8A)*

---

[1]   See generally e.g. Cheshire, North and Fawcett (2017), Chapter 3; Forsyth (1998).

> Any disputes between the parties, whether contractual or non-contractual, which arise out of this contractual relationship, are to be governed by English law. *(Clause 8B)*
>
> Any disputes arising between the parties, whether contractual or non-contractual, whether or not connected with this contractual relationship, are to be governed by English law. *(Clause 8C)*

Each of these is formulated as a choice that relates to 'disputes' arising between the parties, which is a common way for these clauses to be drafted in practice, although of course the intention and effect of these clauses is to determine the law that governs at least some aspects of the legal relationship between the parties, whether or not a formal legal dispute arises. Choice of law clauses may thus alternatively be simply expressed as applicable to the contract ('This contract is governed by English law') rather than the types of disputes – in that form they resemble most closely *Clause 8A*, although with greater ambiguity as to their scope.

If the parties enter into *Clause 8A*, no apparent question of the possible impact of this clause on non-contractual claims arises. The parties appear to have chosen the law only for contractual claims. As discussed below, it is however possible that, despite this wording, the clause may be interpreted as encompassing related non-contractual claims, along the lines of *Clause 8B*. Even if this is not the case, a clause limited to claims in contract does not preclude the possibility that such a choice may have an indirect impact on determining the law that governs non-contractual claims (as under Article 4(3) of the Rome II Regulation, and explored further below), but does preclude the possibility that the parties have purported to make a direct choice of the governing law that might be given effect. Put simply, if the parties have not made a choice of law in relation to the dispute that arises between them, there can be no direct question of party autonomy.

If the parties enter into *Clause 8B* or *Clause 8C*, however, it is clear that their intention is that their choice should have effect for (respectively) some or all non-contractual claims. The exact scope of the choice – whether it requires some direct connection between the performance of the contract and the non-contractual claim – will still be a matter of interpretation, although different presumptive rules may be adopted in different jurisdictions on this point.[2] Whether private international law rules can or should give effect to this intention – either directly or indirectly – is the subject of the remainder of this chapter.

---

[2] See generally Coyle (2017).

The more difficult issue is what approach should be taken if the parties have entered into a choice of law agreement that does not address these questions clearly, such as a contractual clause which simply states:

> Governing Law: English *(Clause 8D)*

As noted above, *Clause 8A* might similarly be viewed as ambiguous, or as strictly limited to contractual claims. Should *Clause 8D* be understood as limited to contractual disputes (as per a strictly construed *Clause 8A*), extending to some non-contractual disputes (as per *Clause 8B*), or extending to all non-contractual disputes (as per *Clause 8C*)? This is ultimately a question of contractual interpretation, which will require application of the law that governs the choice of law clause. The complexities of determining that law are discussed in Section 7.5. Different national systems may take different approaches to this issue, although a common core of these approaches should be a search for the intentions of the parties.

The better view is arguably that *Clause 8D* should generally (and in the absence of evidence to the contrary regarding the intentions of the parties) be understood to have the same intentions as *Clause 8B* – that it should encompass non-contractual disputes that arise out of the contractual relationship, but not other non-contractual disputes. Interpreting *Clause 8D* to exclude all non-contractual claims (a strict *Clause 8A*) is likely to be contrary to the shared intentions of the parties. If parties were asked whether, for example, they wanted a choice of law clause to apply if a claim were brought in tort for negligent performance of contractual obligations rather than directly for a breach of contract it is strongly likely that they would answer positively – parties are generally unlikely to have intended legalistic distinctions regarding forms of action to constrain their autonomy.[3] On the other hand, interpreting *Clause 8D* to encompass all non-contractual claims (*Clause 8C*) is likely to go beyond the expectations or intentions of the parties, which would generally be to establish the legal framework for a particular relationship, rather than for all legal issues between the parties, even those entirely unrelated to the terms of the contract. Although this issue is not frequently litigated, it may be noted that at least some courts have in practice been cautious before finding that a choice of law clause in a contract is sufficiently broad to encompass non-contractual claims that arise between the parties.[4] Since *Knieriemen* v. *Bache Halsey Stuart*

---

[3] See empirical analysis in Coyle (2017), p.696ff.
[4] See e.g. Coyle (2017), p.667ff.

Shields (1980),[5] the New York courts (and thus also New York federal courts exercising diversity jurisdiction)[6] have tended to construe ambiguous choice of law clauses narrowly in terms of their subject scope, and some other courts have followed suit.[7] In *Hawk Enterprises*, Inc. v. *Cash America International*, Inc. (2012),[8] for example, a clause providing that Texas law would govern a franchise agreement including "all matters relating to its validity, construction, performance, and enforcement" was held not to cover a claim for tortious interference with rights under the contract. However, many courts, including for example those in California,[9] tend to interpret ambiguous choice of law agreements as encompassing at least closely related non-contractual claims.[10]

The interpretation of ambiguous choice of law clauses as including non-contractual claims, but only those arising out of the contract, arguably also fits best with the theoretical justifications for party autonomy explored in Chapter 2. The parties to a contract can more readily be understood as exercising a genuine choice if that choice is constrained to matters related to the contractual relationship. To the extent that their choice encompassed unforeseeable non-contractual matters, it would be unlikely to be efficient or a genuine exercise of autonomy or to have any positive 'law-market' generating effects. The main advantage that such a choice might present to the parties is legal certainty – that should a non-contractual claim arise between them, even one that was entirely unexpected, they would not have to face the uncertainty of the usual application of choice of law rules, because they would have chosen the governing law. This argument depends, however, on whether the choice of law clause would actually be given effect in this way as a matter of private international law. As explored in the remainder of this chapter, this is not necessarily the case.

---

[5] 427 N.Y.S.2d 10 (1980).

[6] *Krock* v. *Lipsay*, 97 F.3d 640 (2nd Cir. 1996); but cf *Turtur* v. *Rothschild Registry International, Inc.*, 26 F.3d 304 (2nd Cir. 1994).

[7] See e.g. *Cooper* v. *Meridian Yachts, Ltd.*, 575 F.3d 1151 (11th Cir. 2009); *Benchmark Electronics.* v. *JM Huber Corp.*, 343 F.3d 719 (5th Cir. 2003); *Green Leaf Nursery* v. *El DuPont De Nemours & Co.*, 341 F.3d 1292 (11th Cir. 2003).

[8] (2012) 282 P.3d 786.

[9] *Nedlloyd Lines BV* v. *Superior Court*, 834 P.2d 1148, 1155 (1992) ("a valid choice-of-law clause, which provides that a specified body of law 'governs' the 'agreement' between the parties, encompasses all causes of action arising from or related to that agreement, regardless of how they are characterized, including tortious breaches of duties emanating from the agreement or the legal relationships it creates"); see similarly *Northwest Airlines* v. *Astraea Aviation Services*, 111 F.3d 1386 (8th Cir. 1997); *Hatfield* v. *Halifax PLC*, 564 F.3d 1177 (9th Cir. 2009).

[10] Coyle (2017), p.672ff.

8.3   Tort and Delict

Although contractual autonomy must be distinguished from private international law party autonomy (as discussed particularly in Section 1.3.5), there is something intuitive about the choice of law rule in contract looking to and depending on the agreement, obligations, and common expectations of the parties – particularly but not only where the parties have themselves agreed on a governing law. Our understanding of the function of choice of law rules in contract is thus informed by our underlying understanding of the function of contract law itself. Obligations arising out of the law of tort are by contrast generally accidental, and they are not created partly by the intentions of the parties themselves but by operation of law. It is thus more difficult to conceptualise the purpose of tort law as giving effect to the expectations of the parties. Finding any single theoretical underpinning for tort law has proven a difficult, some might say impossible, task. This difficulty has, naturally enough, also been reflected in choice of law in tort, where a variety of choice of law rules and approaches have been adopted in an effort to encompass the competing substantive objectives of tort law. Choice of law in tort has thus fairly been described as "one of the most vexed questions in the conflict of laws".[11] Traditional approaches have provided little scope for recognition of party autonomy, but as will be discussed below, there have been significant innovations in recent years that have seen party autonomy exercise an increasing influence in this field.

8.3.1   Traditional Territorial Rules:
No Scope for Party Autonomy

Perhaps the most obvious function of tort law is the regulation of harmful behaviour in a territory. By imposing civil liability for breach of certain behavioural standards, tort law is intended to influence that behaviour. This 'conduct regulation' function of tort conceptualises it as comparable (broadly speaking) to the conduct regulating effects of criminal law, with tort law working alongside criminal regulation to reinforce behavioural norms.[12] Conceived in this way, there is a strong connection, or at least a strong presumption of a connection, between tort law and territory, as the public regulatory function of tort law will generally be territorial in application. The analogy between tort and criminal law historically led to

---

[11] *Boys* v. *Chaplin* [1968] 2 QB 1 (CA), 20, per Lord Denning M.R.
[12] See further e.g. Symeonides (2008), p.188.

the adoption of a pure *lex fori* rule in choice of law in tort[13] – that is, the English courts would always apply their own tort law, regardless of where the relevant events took place,[14] just as English courts will only ever apply their own public law.[15] The conduct regulating function of tort law was considered to establish that it possessed a 'public' regulatory character that took it outside the ordinary realm of private international law – and thus outside the scope of the emerging doctrine of party autonomy in the late nineteenth century. More recent choice of law rules in tort tend to view this role of conduct regulation as a question of private law, and take the significance of this function to be the need for a territorial choice of law rule. In most modern legal systems, the starting point for choice of law in tort has thus been the *lex loci delicti* rule – that a tort is governed by the law of the place of the tort.

Although it has received a degree of clarification and modification in subsequent cases, the basic traditional common law choice of law rule in tort – a rule that still applies to choice of law in defamation today – was established in the 1870 decision of *Phillips* v. *Eyre*.[16] The court held as follows:

> As a general rule, in order to found a suit in England for a wrong alleged to have been committed abroad, two conditions must be fulfilled. First, the wrong must be of such a character that it would have been actionable if committed in England ... Secondly, the act must not have been justifiable by the law of the place where it was done.[17]

In so doing, the court hybridised the two traditional influences on choice of law in tort, as discussed above – the first viewing tort law as comparable

---

[13] As the Law Commission and Scottish Law Commission expressed it:

> the law of tort and delict was formerly seen, much more than it is today, as having a punitive rather than a compensatory function. As such it was more closely allied to criminal law, an area of the law where there is no question of a court in this country applying anything other than the domestic law of England or Scotland

(Joint Report of the Law Commission (No.193) and the Scottish Law Commission (No.129) on 'Private International Law: Choice of Law in Tort and Delict' (1990), [2.6]. Available at www.bailii.org/ew/other/EWLC/1990/193.pdf.)

[14] See e.g. *The Halley* (1868) LR 2 PC 193 (although this case also suggests a variant of the double-actionability rule – that English courts should apply their own law, but liability also depends on the law of the place of the tort). This 'public' conception of tort law can arguably be traced to Savigny (who was cited by the Appellants in *The Halley*, p.195) – see further Von Hein (2008), p.1669.

[15] See e.g. *The United States Securities and Exchange Commission* v. *Manterfield* [2009] EWCA Civ 27.

[16] *Phillips* v. *Eyre* (1870) LR 6 QB 1. See further generally Mills (2015); Handford (2008).

[17] *Phillips* v. *Eyre* (1870) LR 6 QB 1, 28.

to criminal law, and thus as a matter of public law governed by the law of the forum, and the second viewing tort law as a matter of territorial conduct regulation. The peculiarity of this rule was to insist on the application of both principles, requiring that liability be established under both sets of laws, the *lex fori* and the *lex loci delicti* – thus it is widely known as the rule of 'double-actionability'. For torts occurring in England, English law is always applied[18] – this is sometimes considered a distinct rule, and sometimes merely a special application of double-actionability.

The double-actionability rule established in *Phillips* v. *Eyre* has received significant further development by the courts. In the case of *Boys* v. *Chaplin*,[19] the court held that exceptionally the double-actionability requirement could be disapplied in favour of the exclusive application of English law. While the court described the exception to double-actionability as a discretion that was necessary to avoid an injustice, arguably the real reasoning behind this decision was that the two parties were English (members of the UK military temporarily posted overseas), and the key issue in the proceedings was the question of the allocation of loss between those parties – what types of damages were recoverable.[20] In the case of *Red Sea Insurance Co* v. *Bouygues SA*,[21] the Privy Council held that a claim in tort brought before the courts of Hong Kong (against a company incorporated in Hong Kong, but with its head office in Saudi Arabia) arising out of problems with construction work in Saudi Arabia could be governed exclusively by the law of Saudi Arabia, similarly applying a law common to the parties.

In the history of the development of the common law rule on choice of law in tort, there have thus been a number of influences – first, the idea that the law of the forum should apply because tort has a public function; second, the idea that the law of the place of the tort should apply because tort has a conduct regulating function; and third, the idea that the law common to the parties should apply because tort law has the function of determining the allocation of loss between the parties. In the common law development and application of these ideas there has been no role for party autonomy. The third of these ideas, however, could arguably be viewed as opening the door to a possible recognition of party autonomy in choice of law in tort. The acceptance that the law of an underlying relationship between the parties might govern torts that arise between them

---

[18] *Szalatnay-Stacho* v. *Fink* [1947] KB 1.
[19] *Boys* v. *Chaplin* [1971] AC 356.
[20] This was determined to be a question of substance rather than procedure, and thus governed by the double-actionability rule rather than exclusively the law of the forum.
[21] *Red Sea Insurance Co.* v. *Bouygues SA* [1995] 1 AC 190.

could lead to the parties indirectly selecting the law to govern claims in tort, if it is considered that the parties can choose the law that governs their relationship, as in the case of a contractual relationship. This potential role for party autonomy was developed in England under the influence of the Private International Law (Miscellaneous Provisions) Act 1995, which is discussed below.

The double-actionability rule was subject to widespread criticism, as being 'chauvinist' and 'parochial'[22] – it provided, at least viewed from one perspective, that English law should be applied to any tort, regardless of where in the world it was committed. The response to these criticisms culminated in the 1995 UK statutory reform discussed below. The double-actionability rule has also been abandoned in both Canada and Australia in recent decades, with the reforms led by the courts rather than legislature.

In *Tolofson* v. *Jensen* (1994),[23] a case concerning an inter-provincial tort, the Canadian Supreme Court addressed the choice of law rules to be applied in both inter-provincial and international tortious disputes. In respect of inter-provincial torts, the Court drew on the idea that the sovereign power of the Canadian provinces is subject to territorial limitation. As a result, the Court held that the character of the constitutional system mandated the application of a *lex loci delicti* rule for inter-provincial torts, rejecting the double-actionability rule. In respect of international torts, the Court held that "it is to the underlying reality of the international legal order ... that we must turn if we are to structure a rational and workable system of private international law",[24] and that "on the international plane, the relevant underlying reality is the territorial limits of law under the international legal order".[25] Thus, the *lex loci delicti* rule was held to be equally applicable in international tort disputes. The Court did recognise that it is possible that "a rigid rule on the international level could give rise to injustice"[26] and thus that there remained in international cases "a discretion in the court to apply our own law to deal with such circumstances".[27]

---

[22] See e.g. Joint Report of the Law Commission (No.193) and the Scottish Law Commission (No.129) on 'Private International Law: Choice of Law in Tort and Delict' (1990) (*supra* n 13), [2.7].

[23] [1994] 3 SCR 1022; Blom (2002), p.109ff; Wai (2001); Tetley (1999), p.156; Herbert (1998); McClean (1996), p.80ff.

[24] *Tolofson* v. *Jensen* [1994] 3 SCR 1022, 1047–8.

[25] At p.1047.

[26] At p.1054.

[27] At p.1054. The exception was applied in e.g. *Wong* v. *Wei* (1999) 65 BCLR 3d 222; *Hanlan* v. *Sernesky* (1998) 38 OR 3d 479.

The Court observed that the exception might particularly apply in favour of the law of the forum where both parties are nationals or residents of the forum state.[28]

In *Pfeiffer* v. *Rogerson* (2000),[29] the Australian High Court similarly held that the constitutional idea of a unitary federal system with territorially limited State sovereigns implied a strict *lex loci delicti* rule for choice of law in Australian inter-State tort disputes, rejecting the double-actionability rule. In *Regie National des Usines Renault SA* v. *Zhang* (2002)[30] the *lex loci delicti* rule was extended to international torts. The extension of the new approach beyond the inter-State context was largely based on a general preference for the predictability and territoriality of the *lex loci delicti* rule, and the pragmatic basis that it is better to have a consistent single approach for both inter-State and international choice of law disputes.[31] As noted above, in inter-State cases the court rejected the possibility of a flexible exception operating to modify the possible injustice caused in individual cases by such a mechanical rule. Unlike the approach recently adopted in Canada, the Australian High Court extended this inflexibility to the international sphere, rejecting the idea that in the international context the court should reserve the right to apply the *lex fori* or another more closely connected law.[32]

In strict application, neither the Canadian nor Australian approaches would appear to be compatible with party autonomy. The application of the law of the place of the tort, with or without a flexible exception in favour of the law of the forum or common home law of the parties, does not encompass the wishes of the parties for their relationship to be governed by another system of law. The Canadian Supreme Court did note the possibility for the parties themselves to select the law governing the tort indirectly through the rule that the law of the forum would be applicable if the parties failed to plead the content of foreign law, but that rule provides a very limited procedural recognition of party autonomy – only

---

[28]   *Tolofson* v. *Jensen* [1994] 3 SCR 1022, 1057; *Hanlan* v. *Sernesky* (1998) 38 OR 3d 479.

[29]   203 CLR 503; see generally Stellios (2005); Princi (2002); Tilbury, Davis and Opeskin (2002), p.533ff; James (2001).

[30]   210 CLR 491; Duckworth (2002); Princi (2002); Lindell (2002).

[31]   Kirby J at [125]ff. But contrast, however, the approach taken by the High Court in respect of torts occurring on the high seas in *Blunden* v. *Commonwealth* (2004) 203 ALR 189; see Mutton (2004).

[32]   One of the consequences of this rigid approach is that the courts may tend to employ 'escape devices' where its results are unattractive. The High Court, for example, adopted (somewhat unsatisfactorily) the doctrine of *renvoi* in *Neilson* v. *Overseas Projects Corporation of Victoria* (2005) [2005] HCA 54; see further Mills (2006b).

permitting an *ex post facto* choice, and only the selection of the law of the forum.[33]

In the United States, many states apply a more flexible 'proper law of the tort' approach, often framed by the parameters of the Second Restatement of Conflict of Laws, as discussed further below. Other US states, however, follow a more traditional approach and apply a straightforward law of the place of the tort rule, similar to that applied in Canada or Australia. This was the general approach set out in the First Restatement of Conflict of Laws, which placed particular reliance on objective territorial connecting factors – in this context, the 'place of the wrong'.[34] In modern application sometimes this rule is qualified by a common domicile rule – where the two parties are from the same domicile (generally the forum) that law may be applied in preference, on the basis that it is the law that governs the relationship between the parties. As discussed above in relation to Canada and Australia, these rules are unlikely to permit consideration of any choice of law by the parties – they focus solely on the objective connections between the dispute or the parties and the states whose laws may be applicable.

8.3.2   Private International Law (Miscellaneous Provisions) Act 1995 (UK)

As noted above, the traditional common law double-actionability rule was subject to widespread criticism. In the United Kingdom, the response to these criticisms came not from the courts (as in Canada and Australia), but legislatively through the Private International Law (Miscellaneous Provisions) Act 1995. The Act essentially established a two stage test for determining the law applicable to a claim in tort (with the notable exception of defamation claims, which remain subject to the double-actionability rule).[35] It did not adopt direct party autonomy, although it is notable that this had been a recommendation of the Law Commission in its critical review of the existing law.[36]

Section 11(1) of the Act established the general rule, "that the applicable law is the law of the country in which the events constituting the tort or delict in question occur", offering further guidance in section 11(2) on how that place should be determined where "elements of those events

---

[33] See Section 7.5.
[34] See First Restatement of Conflict of Laws, s.377 et seq.
[35] See further Mills (2015).
[36] Law Commission, 1984 Consultation 265, para 7.3.1(a). See discussion in Carruthers and Crawford (2005), p.83.

occur in different countries". Essentially, the basic rule adopted here is a *lex loci delicti* rule – the law of the place of the tort. There is no scope for application of party autonomy in this aspect of the test, as it relies entirely on an objective connecting factor.

The second stage of the test, set out in section 12, provided for a flexible exception under which a different law may be applied if this appears substantially more appropriate on the basis of a comparison of the connecting factors between the tort and different countries. While this rule is expressed in very general terms, in practice the courts have tended to use it almost exclusively for cases in which the relationship between the parties is centred around a different legal order. In *Edmunds* v. *Simmonds*,[37] for example, two English parties were involved in a car accident in Spain while on holiday there – the court found that English law should be applicable, emphasising that both parties were English, and that most of the damages were suffered in England. Again, there would be little scope for party autonomy if the application of section 12 were limited to situations where objective connecting factors such as common residence determined the governing law.

The courts have, however, also applied section 12 in situations where the relationship between the parties does not come from their common residence or domicile, but from a contract. The Court of Appeal somewhat hesitantly considered the issue in the case of *Morin* v. *Bonhams and Brooks* (2003).[38] This case concerned a claim in tort arising out of an alleged negligent misstatement contained in the advertising material for a vintage car auction. It was argued by the claimant that English law should apply to his claim in tort, on the basis that the auction materials were first received and read by him in England. The Court decided, however, that Monegasque law was applicable to the dispute under section 11 of the Act, because the most significant elements of the tort occurred in Monaco. This was sufficient to decide the case. However, the defendant had argued that even if section 11 pointed to English law, section 12 should be applied in favour of the law of Monaco. One of the considerations relied on to support this claim was that the auction contract was governed by the law of Monaco (and also included an exclusive jurisdiction agreement in favour of the Monaco courts). The Court noted but did not decide the question of whether a contract between the parties governed by a different system of law could be viewed as a factor connecting the tort with that system of law,

---

[37] *Edmunds* v. *Simmonds* [2001] 1 WLR 1003.
[38] [2003] EWCA Civ 1802; Carruthers and Crawford (2005), p.84ff.

observing only that "In general terms, it would seem odd, if an express choice of law were not at least relevant to the governing law of a tort".[39]

The issue was later addressed more directly by the High Court in *Trafigura Beheer BV* v. *Kookmin Bank Co* (2006).[40] In that case, section 11 of the Act would point to the application of the law of Singapore. In considering whether section 12 might apply to displace that selection, the Court held that factors relating to the parties under that section could include "the fact of a pre-existing relationship between the parties, whether contractual or otherwise".[41] The Court went so far as to suggest that "when the law governing all the contractual relationships between relevant parties ... is English law, it would seem bizarre to hold that the applicable law to determine issues arising in relation to Kookmin's tort claim against Trafigura should be the law of another country".[42]

This decision establishes an important way in which party autonomy may indeed play a role in choice of law in tort, despite its traditional absence from choice of law analysis in this field. The role is not direct – party autonomy is not itself part of the choice of law rule under the Act – but it is a powerful indirect influence, through recognition that the law chosen by the parties to govern their contractual relations may well be the law which is most closely connected with claims in tort that arise out of that contractual relationship.[43] In any legal system in which a flexible choice of law rule in tort is applied, it may well be open to the court to find similarly that a tort that arises between parties to a contract will be governed by the law chosen by them to govern their contractual relations, at least where the tort relates to the performance of the contract. Although the 1995 Act has generally now been replaced in the UK by the Rome II Regulation (except for claims for breach of privacy), the approach adopted by the English courts in the development of section 12 of the Act has been broadly followed under the Regulation, as will be examined in Section 8.3.3.

In New Zealand, a new statutory choice of law rule has recently been adopted pursuant to the Private International Law (Choice of Law in Tort) Act 2017. The Act is closely modelled on the Private International Law

---

[39] At [23].

[40] [2006] EWHC 1450 (Comm).

[41] At [103].

[42] At [113].

[43] A contract entered into by the parties as a *consequence* of a tort, however, should not be relied on in a similar way: see *VTB Capital plc* v. *Nutritek International Corp* [2012] EWCA Civ 808 (overturned on other grounds at [2013] UKSC 5).

(Miscellaneous Provisions) Act 1995 (UK), but with one important point of distinction for present purposes. Section 11(2)(c) of the New Zealand statute provides that nothing in the Act "precludes recognition or development of a choice of law rule giving effect to an agreement as to the applicable law". The Act thus expressly leaves open the possibility of a more direct recognition of party autonomy in choice of law in tort, without itself providing for that as a rule.

8.3.3   Rome II Regulation: General Rule for Torts and Delicts

Regulation of choice of law in tort has long been on the agenda of the European Union. The Rome II Regulation on the law applicable to non-contractual obligations was finally enacted on 11 July 2007, coming into force from 11 January 2009 and applying to events occurring after that date.[44] The motivation for the Rome II Regulation was less a matter of modifying the choice of law rule of any particular state, and more a question of ensuring that the same choice of law rule would be applied in all Member States – the principal goal of the Rome II Regulation was harmonisation, itself in pursuit of improving the efficient functioning of the internal market (as set out in Recital 6). A notable feature of the Regulation is that it contains a number of specific choice of law rules for particular torts, implicitly determining that different torts may indeed have different policy interests and concerns that ought to be reflected in specialised choice of law rules. A second notable feature is the significant potential role for party autonomy under the Regulation, which takes two forms.

The first recognition of party autonomy arises most prominently under the general choice of law rule set out in Article 4 of the Regulation. Article 4(1) specifies that a tort is generally governed by the law of the place of the tort, which is defined as the place in which direct damage is suffered. Article 4(2) specifies that this general rule is displaced in favour of the law of common habitual residence of the parties, should they have one. Thus far, the rule relies solely on objective connecting factors, leaving no scope for party autonomy. However, Article 4(3) finally specifies that if another law is "manifestly more closely connected" than the law chosen under Article 4(1) or (2), then that law applies instead, expressly providing that "A manifestly closer connection with another country might be based in particular on a pre-existing relationship between the parties, such

---

[44]   The date of commencement of the Regulation was unclear from its text, but was settled in C-412/10 *Homawoo* v. *GMF Assurances* EU:C:2011:747.

as a contract, that is closely connected with the tort/delict in question". Although not entirely clear from the text, the better view is that this refers to possible application of the law governing the pre-existing relationship (such as the law of an underlying contract) rather than the objective connections of the relationship (such as the place of contractual performance). Such an underlying contract may be governed by a law chosen by the parties (through application of the Rome I Regulation, as examined in Section 7.2), and if so, this rule provides an indirect recognition of party autonomy in a similar form to that adopted by the English courts under section 12 of the 1995 Act (as discussed above).[45] In Article 4 of the Rome II Regulation, party autonomy is not itself adopted as a choice of law rule in tort, but it is given an indirect effect through recognising that the tort may arise out of a contractual relationship whose law, which may have been chosen by the parties themselves, should also govern the claim in tort. Article 5 of the Regulation, dealing with product liability claims, is structured similarly to Article 4, and has an identically worded exception in Article 5(2) which allows for the possibility of identifying a manifestly closer connection based on an underlying contractual relationship.

The second and more innovative[46] recognition of party autonomy in the Rome II Regulation arises under Article 14, which gives direct recognition to choices of law by the parties. It applies to all non-contractual claims, except those covered by Article 6 (unfair competition)[47] or Article 8 (infringement of intellectual property rights), where it is expressly excluded. Article 14 permits the parties to choose the law to govern non-contractual obligations in certain circumstances. The choice of law by the parties is required to be "expressed or demonstrated with reasonable certainty by the circumstances of the case", and "shall not prejudice the rights of third parties". These qualifications are similar to those that apply to a choice of law under the Rome I Regulation, as discussed in Section 7.2. The choice by the parties is also expressly subject to national or European mandatory rules, as set out in Articles 14(2) and (3) and discussed further in Section 9.4. Article 14 does not require any connection between the obligations or the parties and the chosen law, and thus a law without

---

[45] Similar rules are adopted in many other states – see Symeonides (2014), p.81ff.

[46] Although with some national precedent – see e.g. Introductory Act to the Civil Code, Art.42 (Germany); see further Symeonides (2014), p.100ff; Kramer (2008). For further background see Zhang (2011b); De Boer (2007); Carruthers and Crawford (2005).

[47] Note, however, that Article 6(3)(b) gives the claimant a limited choice of law, similarly to the unilateral choice given to claimants for environmental tort claims under Article 7, as discussed below.

any objective connection to the dispute may be chosen.[48] It also does not require any connection between the contract containing the choice of law clause and the non-contractual obligation, and thus it appears that contracting parties may choose the law to govern even unrelated non-contractual claims, if their choice of law clause is expressed in sufficiently broad terms. The direct recognition of party autonomy under Article 14 is novel, but it is also quite restrictive, on the apparent basis (discussed further in Chapter 9) that "Protection should be given to weaker parties by imposing certain conditions on the choice."[49] In setting these conditions, the rule distinguishes between choice of law agreements entered into before or after the event giving rise to the damage has occurred.

In relation to choice of law agreements entered into before the event giving rise to the damage, dealt with under Article 14(1)(b), the rule is subject to restrictive conditions. Such a choice is only permitted if "all the parties are pursuing a commercial activity" and the agreement is "freely negotiated". There is no guidance in the Regulation itself as to the meaning of these terms, which have not previously been used in EU codifications of choice of law, and they are likely to require significant judicial clarification. The reasons for these qualifications are relatively easy to understand, although they are potentially problematic in application.

The requirement that the agreement be 'freely negotiated' is apparently intended to indicate that the choice of law clause is the product of genuine agreement, rather than imposed through one party's standard terms and conditions. This idea, however, appears to require further explanation and justification. If the parties have reached a genuine contractual agreement as to the governing law, then why should it matter how that agreement was reached? This rule seems to require a higher standard for the formation of a choice of law agreement in tort than applies elsewhere for the formation of a contract or even for a choice of law clause more generally. As a consequence, there will be choice of law clauses in contracts that will be binding terms as a matter of contract law and effective under the Rome I Regulation, but nevertheless ineffective under the Rome II Regulation because they have not been 'freely negotiated'. It is notable that this appears to imply that a choice of law agreement is somehow qualitatively different from other contractual terms, at least in the context of tortious claims, and that enforcement of choice of law clauses requires a greater justification than being merely the enforcement of the contract between the parties.

[48] See also Section 7.3.
[49] Recital 31.

A standard form contract with an English exclusive jurisdiction agreement and English choice of law clause, purporting in both cases to cover non-contractual claims arising out of the contract, is likely to be effective with regard to the jurisdiction agreement but ineffective with regard to the choice of law clause (unless indirectly enforced through Article 4(3) – a point discussed further below). Such inconsistency is hardly likely to respect party intentions or lead to efficient dispute resolution.

The second major requirement applicable to Article 14(1)(b) is that the parties must 'be pursuing a commercial activity'. It is clear that the intention here is to limit the application of this part of Article 14 to 'business-to-business' contracts, to protect weaker parties,[50] although the lack of a definition of 'commercial activity' will no doubt lead to practical difficulties in some cases. While this provision may protect, for example, consumers and employees, it would not protect other weaker parties such as small businesses or franchisees. The justification for this rule would appear to reflect a consideration of the different policy interests that are at stake in giving effect to party autonomy in this field. On the one hand, allowing for party autonomy increases certainty for the parties, as it enables them to predict in advance the law which will govern non-contractual disputes that arise between them, particularly where the choice of law rule which would otherwise apply has an open-textured element whose application may be difficult to predict (as is the case with Article 4(3) of the Rome II Regulation). On the other hand, parties may not be able to anticipate the range of non-contractual obligations that might arise between them, and thus may not always make a sensible or desirable choice in terms of the governing law for those obligations. As discussed in Section 2.4.2, this may be reflected in the idea of 'foreseeability' as a constraint on party autonomy, a consideration which is often applied in a jurisdictional context, as particularly discussed in Chapter 4. In this area, a distinct decision is made – instead of limiting choice of law in tort to foreseeable torts, a restriction is imposed on the *parties* who may make such a choice, but there is no requirement of foreseeability. The justification for this is that commercial parties are likely to value certainty more than they are to value the appropriateness or desirability of a particular law applying for non-contractual obligations. The benefit of knowing in advance that a single law will govern all claims arising between the parties is considered to outweigh the costs of the fact that such a law may govern unforeseen non-contractual liability. Commercial parties for whom this is not the case

---

[50] See Rome II Regulation, Recital 31.

may, of course, simply not enter into such choice of law agreements, or may constrain their choice of law agreements to cover only a limited category of non-contractual liabilities.

As noted above, Article 14 also deals separately with choice of law agreements entered into by the parties after the event giving rise to the damage has occurred. Under Article 14(1)(a), such agreements are effective without any restriction as to the parties or requirement that their terms be 'freely negotiated'. At first glance, this enhanced scope of autonomy may seem appropriate and beneficial, as the parties should be free to vary their non-contractual rights and responsibilities through a choice of law clause, as they would be free to settle non-contractual liability through a contractual agreement. However there are three concerns that arise with this provision.

The first is that doubts may be expressed over whether it is necessary at all. Why would the parties wish to choose a different law to govern non-contractual obligations arising between them? The law they are selecting will either be different from the law that would apply in default of a choice, or it will be the same. If it is different, then it will benefit one of the parties, and it is unclear why the other party would consent to the change. If it is the same, then there is no justification for the choice, unless the chosen law is the law of the forum and the parties have selected it to avoid the cost of pleading and proving foreign law. (It may also be that the foreign law is different from forum law, but insufficiently different to justify the expense of proving it.) In this case, however, the situation is already dealt with at least in common law systems through the rules on the pleading and proof of foreign law,[51] although for other systems where the burden of establishing foreign law falls on the court this rule may perhaps prove useful to the parties.

A second concern that arises in relation to this provision is the fact that it permits choice of law after the event giving rise to the damage has occurred, but before the damage itself. The rule would thus seem to permit the parties to vary the terms of a non-contractual obligation *without* full knowledge of their non-contractual rights or liabilities, which seems contrary to the restrictions otherwise imposed in Article 14(1)(b). This is particularly important because questions of damage – both in terms of types of damages and quantification – are governed by the substantive applicable law, under Article 15 of the Rome II Regulation. To give an example, consider a patient who undergoes a flawed medical procedure. The doctor

---

[51] See further Section 7.4.

admits negligence, but the nature and extent of damage has not yet been determined. Is it appropriate that the patient be able to agree contractually to a particular governing law for the negligence action (remembering that under Article 14 there is no requirement that the claim be connected with the law that is chosen), when that law will determine what damage – known and unknown – is going to be recoverable? Given the logic behind this rule, it would perhaps arguably have been better if it had been restricted to agreements entered into after damage has occurred and been identified, and specified that such agreements could only apply to damage prior to the agreement.

A third concern with the way that Article 14(1)(a) permits a free choice of law, albeit only after the events giving rise to the tort have occurred, is whether this achieves the intended effect of protecting weaker parties. Even after damage has occurred, weaker parties who do not obtain legal advice may be persuaded to enter into an agreement, such as a consent to mediation, which includes a binding choice of law clause. Such concerns are, however, perhaps best left to the general law of contract.

The recognition of party autonomy under Article 14 is distinct from that under Article 4(3), although the relationship between these two provisions raises some difficult questions. In general, the direct recognition of party autonomy under Article 14 is clearer and more decisive than the indirect role party autonomy has under Article 4(3). In the latter, party choice in a contract is only one factor to be taken into consideration as part of a discretionary test. The choice by the parties is also slightly distinctive, in that Article 14 is concerned with choice of law clauses that are intended to apply to non-contractual obligations, whereas Article 4(3) is concerned with choice of law clauses intended to govern a contract – giving them an extended indirect effect to cover non-contractual obligations. Under Article 14, unlike Article 4(3), there is thus no requirement that the non-contractual claim be 'closely connected' to the contract – indeed Article 14 does not require that there be a contract between the parties at all other than the choice of law agreement, although it would be highly unusual for that to be the case.

There are, however, also some ways in which Article 4(3) is broader than Article 14. For example, there is no requirement that the choice of law clause in an underlying contract has to be expressed in terms broad enough to cover non-contractual obligations for it to be given effect indirectly through Article 4(3). The chosen law is not applied because it purports to govern the claim in tort, but because it governs the contract. There is also no requirement for the purposes of Article 4(3) that the agreement be freely negotiated, or that it be between parties pursuing a commercial activity. A somewhat difficult question thus arises as to what effect agreements that do not satisfy the requirements of Article 14 might have under Article 4(3). A choice of law agreement in one party's standard terms and conditions that purported to cover both contractual and non-contractual issues, for example, would not appear to satisfy Article 14, but could well be relied on for the purposes of Article 4(3) as a factor connecting a non-contractual claim arising out of the contract with the chosen system of law.[52] Whether this will be permitted, in furtherance of the policy objectives of Article 4(3), or rejected, as it risks undermining the restrictions on Article 14, is a difficult issue that will require judicial clarification.

8.3.4   *Rome II Regulation: Environmental Protection*

A further important and distinctive form of party autonomy arises under Article 7 of the Rome II Regulation, which provides that:

> The law applicable to a non-contractual obligation arising out of environmental damage or damage sustained by persons or property as a result of such damage shall be the law determined pursuant to Article 4(1), unless the person seeking compensation for damage chooses to base his or her claim on the law of the country in which the event giving rise to the damage occurred.

This rule allows for the possibility of a choice of law. It is distinctive in that the choice is unilateral (solely within the power of the claimant), and limited to a single option – the law of the place in which the event giving rise to the damage occurred – as an alternative to the default rule under Article 4(1), which selects the place of the direct damage. This rule clearly contemplates such a choice being made by the claimant after the damage has occurred, at the time when proceedings are commenced, which would obviously be expected to lead to the application of whichever of the two options provides for greater liability or damages. It is evident that this rule therefore embodies a substantive policy objective – an increase in environmental protection – which is unusual in the European tradition of private international law.[53] Although not the principal subject of present concern, this is an interesting and somewhat controversial development – it is unclear whether choice of law rules are necessarily an appropriate device to achieve environmental objectives, rather than simply the adoption of

---

[52] See e.g. Cheshire, North and Fawcett (2017), pp.855–6.
[53] See Recital 25; see further e.g. Cheshire, North and Fawcett (2017), p.828ff.

minimum environmental standards. Given the Rome II Regulation has universal application, the effect of the rule may be to adopt a preference between non-EU systems of environmental regulation, thus exporting EU values internationally.[54] For example, consider a UK company operating a mine in Africa in Country A. The mine pollutes a river, causing environmental damage downstream in Country B. The company can clearly be sued in the English courts, under Article 4 of the Brussels I Regulation. The Rome II Regulation's choice of law rule then permit the claimant to choose between the laws of Country A and Country B – effectively imposing an EU preference for greater environmental regulation extraterritorially. At the same time, the rule seeks to achieve this objective in a limited way that respects the limits on national regulatory authority, by requiring the claimant to choose between two states that have territorial power over the tort in question.

For present purposes, it is of particular interest that the rule uses the device of individual party choice to achieve its objective of increasing environmental protection, rather than simply requiring the court to apply the system of law most favourable to the claimant. The effect of giving the claimant a choice in this context is to delegate the cost of making this determination to the claimant, rather than imposing it on the court, who might otherwise have to undertake a difficult and potentially awkward comparative analysis of the benefits of different legal orders. The form of party autonomy adopted in this rule is thus strikingly distinctive from other forms. It is not designed to allow the parties to define and meet their shared expectations, or even to determine between themselves the law that would be most appropriate to resolve their dispute, but rather to allow one party to serve a European policy objective, and to bear the costs of doing so (at least temporarily, as the costs of obtaining legal advice on such questions may ultimately be recoverable if the claim is successful). Party autonomy in this provision empowers a single private party, but does so on the presumption that their choice – no doubt exercised in their own favour – will also serve a public benefit that would otherwise have to be meet by public resources.

8.3.5   Modern US Approaches: Interest Analysis, Proper Law of the Tort, and the Second Restatement of Conflict of Laws

As already noted above, a number of US states follow a traditional approach to choice of law in tort, and continue to apply a straightforward law of the

---

[54] Mills (2016a).

place of the tort rule. Sometimes this rule is qualified by application of the law of the common domicile of the parties, particularly if that common domicile is the forum state – the perceived need to apply the law common to the parties in some cases was indeed the primary reason for the rejection of the traditional territorial approach.[55] In either case, these rules do not permit consideration of choices of law by the parties themselves, as they rely exclusively on objective connecting factors. Other US states, however, generally apply one of three non-traditional approaches, each of which is considered in turn below – interest analysis, the proper law of the tort, or the approach under the Second Restatement of Conflict of Laws.[56]

As discussed in Section 7.2.4, the central tenet of interest analysis approaches is that the law applicable to a dispute or relationship should be determined based on an analysis of the degree of interest that each state or government has in regulating the dispute or relationship. A common variant, known as the 'comparative impairment' approach, looks similarly to the degree of impairment that would be suffered by each of the potentially interested states if its regulation were not applied to the dispute or relationship. This approach permits the court to consider in a more flexible manner the regulatory interests of the states whose laws may potentially be applicable. Those interests might be analysed objectively, based on consideration of the factual connections between the dispute and the states whose laws might apply, or they might be analysed subjectively, usually through focusing on the policy objectives of the particular statutes that might be applicable. It is, however, only the interests or intentions of the potentially governing laws or their states that are taken into consideration under this approach – interest analysis does not encompass the expressed or imputed interests or intentions of the parties, including as might have been established through a choice of law clause.

A second approach that is applied in some US states is to apply the 'proper law of the tort' – taking into account a range of potential connecting factors, and determining the governing law through application of a flexible and fact-sensitive test. Whether such an approach permits consideration of choices made by the parties themselves depends on how broad a range of factors is taken into account. A proper law of the tort approach might limit itself to considering objective connecting factors, such as the

---

[55] See e.g. *Babcock* v. *Jackson*, 12 N.Y.2d 473 (1963); *Neumeier* v. *Kuehner*, 31 N.Y.2d 121 (1972). Subsequent New York cases have adopted a broader interest analysis style approach: see e.g. *Cooney* v. *Osgood Machinery*, 81 N.Y.2d 66 (1993); *Edwards* v. *Erie Coach Lines Co.*, 17 N.Y.3d 306 (2011).

[56] See generally e.g. Zhang (2011b); Hay, Borchers, and Symeonides (2010), p.1141ff.

place of the wrongful act, the place of direct damage, the place of consequential loss, and the places of residence of the parties. Alternatively,
it may take into account a connection between the tort and the system
of law governing a contract – where the contract is related to the claim
in tort. This is similar to the approaches under section 12 of the Private
International Law (Miscellaneous Provisions) Act 1995 and Article 4(3)
of the Rome II Regulation examined in Section 8.3.3. It is also possible
(although perhaps less likely) that under this approach a direct expression
of the wishes or intentions of the parties in relation to the law applicable to
torts between them would be taken into consideration, as under Article 14
of the Rome II Regulation. Where such intentions or wishes fall within the
broad range of factors to be taken into consideration, a proper law of the
tort approach would not necessarily be subject to the types of important
restrictions that apply under Article 14 of the Rome II Regulation, and the
courts would need to be sensitive to the policy considerations expressed
in those restrictions when it comes to attaching weight to those intentions
or wishes.

A third popular approach followed in many US states is the approach set
out under the Second Restatement of Conflict of Laws. The rule that gives
effect to party autonomy in contract, as examined in Section 7.2.4, is in
section 187 – but that rule governs only "The law of the state chosen by the
parties to govern their *contractual* rights and duties" (emphasis added).
The rule applicable to choice of law in tort is similar to a proper law of the
tort approach in that it encompasses a wide range of factors, but some clarity is provided through partial codification of the type and range of factors
to be taken into account. The general choice of law rule in tort (which is
supplemented by other rules for specific torts) is set out in section 145(1),
providing that "The rights and liabilities of the parties with respect to an
issue in tort are determined by the local law of the state which, with respect
to that issue, has the most significant relationship to the occurrence and
the parties under the principles stated in § 6". Section 145(2) details contacts to be taken into consideration in making that determination, including objective connecting factors between the tort and the parties, but also
including "the place where the relationship, if any, between the parties is
centered" as a factor. This would potentially permit the court to take into
account a prior contractual relationship between the parties governed by
a law determined through a choice of law clause – thus allowing for the
same indirect effect of party autonomy as adopted under Article 4(3) of
the Rome II Regulation. The choice of law rules provided for particular
torts generally presumptively select the law of the place of the tort, defined

for example in section 146 as the law of the place of the injury for personal injury claims, but this is subject to the qualification that the law of another state will be applied if it has a more significant relationship applying the principles in section 6. Under section 6 of the Second Restatement, as examined in Section 7.2.4, the courts can take into account a wide range of factors, including "the protection of justified expectations", which could further support giving weight to any expressed agreement between the parties, particularly one that would encompass claims in tort (comparable to the approach under Article 14 of the Rome II Regulation). However, the Second Restatement is alive to the potential problems that might be raised by such an approach, and a note of caution is adopted in the comments on section 6, which provide as follows:

> There are occasions, particularly in the area of negligence, when the parties act without giving thought to the legal consequences of their conduct or to the law that may be applied. In such situations, the parties have no justified expectations to protect, and this factor can play no part in the decision of a choice-of-law question.[57]

This might be viewed as requiring an element of foreseeability before a choice of law agreement is able to encompass claims in tort – it at least suggests that the courts should be hesitant before giving direct or indirect effect to choice of law agreements that govern claims in tort which would not have been anticipated by the parties. This hesitancy may be given effect in one of two ways – by finding either that the clause (properly interpreted) does not extend to non-contractual claims,[58] or that if it does, it is ineffective as a matter of private international law. In practice the two questions do not necessarily appear to be clearly distinguished.[59] The confusion between these points may sometimes also work in favour of party autonomy – even courts whose choice of law rules do not appear to permit exercises of party autonomy in tort may give effect to such a choice on the basis of a broad interpretation of a choice of law agreement, without closely analysing whether this is actually permissible under applicable tort choice of law rules.

---

[57] Second Restatement of Conflict of Laws, s.6(2), comment (g). See similarly in s.145, comment (b): "the protection of the justified expectations of the parties, which is of extreme importance in such fields as contracts, property, wills and trusts, is of lesser importance in the field of torts".

[58] See Section 8.2.

[59] See further Hay, Borchers, and Symeonides (2010), p.1142, identifying a wide range of inconsistent case law on whether a choice of law clause encompasses non-contractual claims, even those arising from the same contractual relationship.

8.3.6   China

Another recent extension of party autonomy into the field of choice of law in tort and delict comes – perhaps surprisingly – in the Law of the People's Republic of China on the Laws Applicable to Foreign-Related Civil Relations (2010).[60] As discussed in Section 7.2.5, Article 3 of the Law establishes the general principle that:

> The parties may explicitly choose the law applicable to their foreign-related civil relation in accordance with the provisions of this law.

Article 44 of the Law sets out the general rule dealing with tortious liability, establishing that:

> Tortious liability is governed by the law of the place of tortious act. Where the parties have common habitual residence, the law of their common habitual residence shall be applied. Where the parties have chosen by agreement an applicable law after the tortious act occurs, the agreement shall be followed.

Although the drafting (or perhaps translation) is not entirely clear, the better view is probably that (despite the general terms of Article 3) the final sentence of Article 44 means that party autonomy does not apply to tortious liability, except for agreements entered into after the tortious act has occurred.[61] This is similar to the rule set out in Article 14(1)(a) of the Rome II Regulation. As discussed further in Section 8.3.3, there is some doubt as to how useful such a rule will be in practice, as any change in the law is likely to benefit one party, and thus reaching agreement would be unlikely in practice. The parties might agree to apply the law of the forum where it did not differ significantly or at all from the otherwise applicable law, in order to save on costs, but such agreements can often be given effect through the election not to plead foreign law.[62] As under Article 14(1)(a) of the Rome II Regulation, the possibility of a choice after the tortious act has occurred, but before the extent of damage has been determined, also raises potential concerns, as discussed again in Section 8.3.3. As in other legal systems, the applicability of contractual or non-contractual choice of law rules under Chinese law is, however, affected by the question of characterisation – it is possible that a claim that is tortious in form may be

---

[60] See further generally e.g. Tang, Xiao and Huo (2016), Chapter 9; Sun (2016); Huo (2011); Zhang (2011a).
[61] See discussion in Tang, Xiao and Huo (2016), p.256ff; Huo (2011), p.1089ff.
[62] See further Section 7.4.1.

characterised as contractual because it requires determination of contractual rights.[63]

8.3.7   *International Codifications*

Both the Mexico City Convention 1994 and the Hague Principles on Choice of Law in International Commercial Contracts 2015 (each of which is discussed in Chapter 7) are focused exclusively on contractual claims. The primary rule set out in Article 2(1) of the Hague Principles, for example, is that "A contract is governed by the law chosen by the parties." Neither convention thus addresses the question of whether a choice of law agreement in a contract may affect non-contractual claims, either directly or indirectly, with the arguable exception of Article 9(1)(g) of the Hague Principles which extends the applicable law to "pre-contractual obligations". (These are not always characterised as contractual – see for example under Article 12 of the Rome II Regulation, discussed in Section 8.4.2). As examined above, this is an issue on which practice is highly variable, and thus international harmonisation would be particularly helpful, but also particularly unlikely.

8.4   Unjust Enrichment and Related Issues

This section considers the potential role of party autonomy in relation to questions of unjust enrichment and related areas of law. A central difficulty here is that the treatment of these issues is markedly different in different legal systems, but choice of law rules require an internationally minded approach towards the question of characterisation, and European choice of law rules in particular must be interpreted to have a harmonised EU meaning. The definition of a term such as 'unjust enrichment' under the Rome II Regulation is thus, for example, unlikely to be identical to the definition under English law, although finding a clear international definition of unjust enrichment for the purposes of characterisation is likely to be highly problematic when the concept is so contested within and between national systems.[64]

---

[63] See e.g. Liang (2012), p.81ff.
[64] See Sherborne (2017); Pitel (2004); Dicey, Morris and Collins (2012), [36-014]; Chong (2008); Rushworth and Scott (2008); Rose (1995).

8.4.1   Common Law

Choice of law rules for unjust enrichment have been slow to develop, even in the common law world in which such claims are increasingly common. There are two main reasons for this. First, the undoing of an unjust enrichment was historically often viewed as a remedy (under the name 'restitution')[65] rather than a substantive cause of action. Traditionally (although now somewhat debatably) remedies were viewed as a procedural matter for the law of the forum, rather than a matter determined by choice of law rules – thus, there was no need for a separate choice of law rule for unjust enrichment. Even if remedies are viewed as a matter of substance rather than procedure (as required now under the distinction adopted in EU choice of law rules),[66] this would not require a special choice of law rule – the law governing remedies is the law governing the substantive claim.

For those who, by contrast, viewed unjust enrichment as a substantive claim rather than remedy, it was commonly considered that the claim still depended on an underlying basis for the unjustness of the enrichment, or 'causa'. One choice of law rule that has traditionally been advocated is that the claim should be exclusively governed by the law of the causa underlying the enrichment (which might be, for example, a contract or a tort). Under this approach, there is again no need for a separate choice of law rule for unjust enrichment claims. The question of what law will apply to the issue of unjust enrichment will simply (again) depend on another choice of law rule. Thus, the applicability of party autonomy will equally depend on whether it is permitted under that choice of law rule – the choice of law rule for the 'causa' underlying the enrichment. The argument for this approach is particularly strong where unjust enrichment takes the form of restitution in response to a wrong – even if it is not merely a remedy, it should be treated as similarly dependent on the law governing the underlying wrong.[67] (On the other hand, proprietary restitution – which involves a claim for title to the affected property, for example on the basis of a constructive trust, not merely a right for it to be returned – may be better analysed as a claim in property, a subject that is dealt with in

---

[65] For a discussion of the uses of the terms 'unjust enrichment' and 'restitution' in this context, see further Chong (2008). A distinct approach has developed in Australia – see e.g. Sherborne (2017); *Australian Financial Services and Leasing Pty Ltd* v. Hills Industries (2014) 253 CLR 560.

[66] See e.g. Rome II Regulation, Art.15.

[67] See e.g. Yeo (2004), p.315; Panagopoulos (2000), p.174.

Section 8.5.)[68] The argument for applying the law of the 'causa' is evidently weaker in those cases in which unjust enrichment arises without any underlying relationship existing or wrong having been committed – to the extent that unjust enrichment recognises a claim in such circumstances.

These views (and the long-running and unresolved debates about the nature of unjust enrichment and restitution in the common law) have limited the development of choice of law rules for unjust enrichment. As such views are no longer generally adopted, however, such choice of law rules have increasingly emerged. The modern view is that unjust enrichment is not merely concerned with remedies, but is its own distinct branch of the law of obligations,[69] which requires its own choice of law rule – a rule that may, but need not necessarily, depend on the law applicable to an underlying causa.

One traditional choice of law rule that has been proposed for unjust enrichment claims is to apply the law of the place of enrichment. Section 453 of the First Restatement of Conflict of Laws, for example, provides that "When a person is alleged to have been unjustly enriched, the law of the place of enrichment determines whether he is under a duty to repay the amount by which he has been enriched". Such a strict territorial rule would evidently leave no scope for the application of party autonomy. This approach has, however, been criticised on the basis that, in cases of cross-border unjust enrichment, it does not clearly select between the place in which the enriching act occurs (or the place of impoverishment, which might be different) and the place in which the enrichment occurs (and whether this is the place of immediate enrichment, or ultimate enrichment, if for example received money is transferred to one or more other jurisdictions). If it is considered to select between these laws (favouring for example the place of direct enrichment), a further concern is that the selected system of law may only be peripherally connected to the claim.[70]

Unjust enrichment claims have also sometimes been categorised for domestic purposes as 'quasi-contract' actions. Indeed, the first proposal for distinct English choice of law rules for unjust enrichment claims, in the 1949 edition of *Dicey on the Conflict of Laws*, dealt with them under the heading of 'quasi-contract'. This categorisation (whose helpfulness has

---

[68] Stevens (2000); Chong (2005), pp.873–80.

[69] *Pavey & Matthews Pty Ltd* v. *Paul* (1987) 162 CLR 221 (High Court of Australia); *Lipkin Gorman* v. *Karpnale* [1991] AC 548 (House of Lords).

[70] See e.g. Sherborne (2017), p.29 ("the law of the place of enrichment will often have no connection to the restitutionary issue"); Chong (2008), p.885ff.

been much criticised)[71] might suggest a role for party autonomy in choice of law for unjust enrichment. The solution adopted in 1949 was to apply the 'proper law of the obligation', and if the obligation arose in connection with a contract, that was defined to be the 'proper law of the contract'. What this meant is perhaps not entirely clear – the term 'proper law' is now sometimes used under the common law to indicate the rule applicable to contracts in the *absence* of party choice (although the terminology is used inconsistently). If the use of this term in Dicey indicated a possible scepticism towards giving a role to party autonomy in the context of unjust enrichment, this was shared with a range of other scholars, on the apparent basis that the "restitutionary obligation is imposed by law and is not of the parties' volition".[72] The characterisation of unjust enrichment as based on quasi-contract has, however, since been rejected,[73] although the law continues to recognise that unjust enrichment claims may be closely connected to a contract. By the 14th edition of *Dicey and Morris on the Conflict of Laws* in 2006, the common law choice of law rule for unjust enrichment had evolved to suggest more simply and clearly application of the law governing any underlying contract, thus potentially giving indirect effect to party autonomy in relation to the unjust enrichment claim,[74] in the following terms:

> (a) If the obligation arose in connection with a contract, its proper law was the law applicable to the contract;
> (b) If it arose in connection with a transaction concerning an immovable (land), its proper law was the law of the country where the immovable was situated (lex situs);
> (c) If it arose in any other circumstances, its proper law was the law of the country where the enrichment occurred.[75]

In England these developing common law rules have now (except for matters excluded from its scope)[76] been replaced by those adopted under the Rome II Regulation. Those rules share some characteristics with the common law approach, and some of the issues to which they give rise are discussed below. For other common law jurisdictions, however, the rules

---

[71] See e.g. Bennett (1990).

[72] Chong (2008), p.874 (describing rather than endorsing this position, with further references).

[73] *Westdeutsche Landesbank Girozentrale* v. *Islington London Borough Council* [1996] AC 669.

[74] See also *Arab Monetary Fund* v. *Hashim* [1993] 1 Lloyd's Rep 543.

[75] At [36-008] in Dicey, Morris and Collins (2012) (the 15th edition).

[76] See e.g. Section 8.6 (on equitable claims).

discussed above remain applicable, giving effect to party autonomy only where an unjust enrichment claim derives from a contract.[77] It is notable that the rule set out above does not include particular provision for unjust enrichment claims arising out of torts or delicts (which, analogous to the rule for contracts, would look to the law of the underlying causa) – although such a rule would not provide significant additional scope for party autonomy to have an indirect effect on the law applicable to such claims, as there is limited scope for party choice of law in tortious claims under the common law (as discussed in Section 8.3).

8.4.2 Rome II Regulation

In Section 8.3, dealing with claims in tort, it was noted that the Rome II Regulation recognises party autonomy in two ways. First, it gives a direct effect to party choices under Article 14, but subject to some important restrictions. Second, it potentially gives an indirect effect to a choice of law clause in a contract, through extending that choice of law to apply to non-contractual claims in tort (under Article 4), including for product liability (under Article 5), that arise out of the contract.

The direct form of party autonomy recognised under Article 14 also applies to claims dealt with in Chapter III of the Rome II Regulation, which are not claims in tort but those arising out of various other forms of non-contractual obligation – unjust enrichment (Article 10), 'negotiorum gestio' (claiming payment from a party for unauthorised acts that benefited that party) (Article 11), and 'culpa in contrahendo' (liability arising out of pre-contractual dealings, such as "the violation of the duty of disclosure and the breakdown of contractual negotiations")[78] (Article 12). The discussion in Section 8.3 regarding the limits and problems of Article 14 is thus equally applicable for these claims. The direct recognition of party autonomy in the context of these forms of claim is as innovative as it is in relation to choice of law in tort – perhaps even more so.

The indirect recognition of party autonomy found in Article 4(3) (in relation to general claims in tort arising out of a contractual relationship) is also similarly present in Article 10(1), dealing with unjust enrichment, and Article 11(1), dealing with 'negotiorum gestio'. In each case, the rule

---

[77] See e.g. discussion in Sherborne (2017); Millett (1997).
[78] Recital 30.

allows for the identification of the governing law based on an underlying relationship between the parties. Article 10(1), for example, provides that:

> If a non-contractual obligation arising out of unjust enrichment, including payment of amounts wrongly received, concerns a relationship existing between the parties, such as one arising out of a contract or a tort/delict, that is closely connected with that unjust enrichment, it shall be governed by the law that governs that relationship.

These rules essentially take the view (discussed above) that unjust enrichment should be viewed as incidental to this underlying relationship, if 'closely connected' to it – that it is the choice of law rules of the underlying relationship that should determine the governing law for the unjust enrichment claim. (If there is no such relationship or the claim is not 'closely connected' to it, then the rule selects the common habitual residence of the parties (Article 10(2) and 11(2)), or if no such law exists, the law of the country in which the unjust enrichment took place (Article 10(3)) or the unauthorised act was performed (Article 11(3)) – thus falling back ultimately on a law of the place of enrichment rule.)[79] Where the parties have an underlying contractual relationship, the effect of an exercise of party autonomy in relation to that underlying contract (given effect through application of the Rome I Regulation) is thus potentially extended to also apply to these non-contractual claims (through application of the Rome II Regulation).

Where the underlying contract has been invalidated or frustrated (thus leading to a claim for unjust enrichment for part or full performance of payment or delivery obligations), it is not entirely clear how this should be approached under these rules, because it is not entirely clear whether the rules under the Rome II Regulation require that the underlying contractual relationship be *valid*. This could be viewed as an issue concerned with "the consequences of nullity of the contract" under the Rome I Regulation,[80] governed by the law of the contract, or as a claim for unjust enrichment arising out of the (failed) contractual relationship, governed by the Rome II Regulation. Normally these would point to the same law, but if it is the latter, the Rome II Regulation might point to a different law than the law governing the contract through an escape clause, as noted

---

[79] The point was somewhat contentious in the drafting of the Regulation – see further Chong (2008), p.883. See further e.g. *Banque De Genève* v. *Polevent Ltd* [2015] EWHC 1968 (Comm).

[80] Article 12(1)(e).

below. Although the position is not clear,[81] the better view is probably that the governing law should be determined by the Rome I Regulation rather than the Rome II Regulation, in accordance with the expectations of the parties. Such claims would therefore clearly be governed by any choice the parties may have made in relation to the nullified contract[82] – although this may not apply if the reason for nullifying the contract also invalidates the choice of law clause.[83]

Both Articles 10(1) and 11(1) also contemplate the possibility that these forms of non-contractual liability might concern a relationship between the parties arising out of a claim in tort, as well as in contract. To the extent that the law applicable to such claims in tort may have been determined through an exercise of party autonomy (directly under Article 14 of the Rome II Regulation, or indirectly under Article 4(3) of the Rome II Regulation), as examined in Section 8.3.3, that choice by the parties may thereby be extended to cover these additional forms of non-contractual liability. The effect given to party autonomy in these circumstances may potentially be doubly indirect – a choice of law in an underlying contract might determine the law that governs a claim in tort (under Article 4(3)), which in turn might determine the law that governs a claim for unjust enrichment arising out of the tort (under Article 10(1)).

A notable difference between Articles 10(1) and 11(1) and the approach under Article 4(3) is that the selection of the law of an underlying relationship, if such a relationship exists, is the *primary* choice of law rule rather than serving as part of an escape clause. Although Articles 10 and 11 also contain escape clauses that may here work to depart from the law chosen by the parties in some circumstances,[84] these are unlikely to be applied frequently, and thus the enhanced 'status' given to indirect party autonomy in relation to these types of claims (as a primary rule rather than an exception) is likely to mean an enhanced effect.

Under Article 12(1), dealing with '*culpa in contrahendo*', the treatment of the issues is quite distinct again. If the contractual dealings lead to a contract (for which the parties may have chosen the applicable law), or if they do not but the law that would have governed such a contract is identifiable (including perhaps from a draft choice of law clause accepted in negotiations), then the law governing the contract governs the obligations

---

[81] See e.g. Dicey, Morris and Collins (2012), [36-023].
[82] See similarly e.g. *Dimskal Shipping Co. SA* v. *International Transport Workers Federation* [1992] 2 AC 152, under the common law.
[83] See further Section 7.5.
[84] Under Articles 10(4) and 11(4).

arising out of the pre-contractual dealings. In this case, the rule is not subject to any escape clause – the actual or putative contractual choice of law by the parties is automatically extended to cover non-contractual liability. However, Recital 30 clarifies that:

> Article 12 covers only non-contractual obligations presenting a direct link with the dealings prior to the conclusion of a contract. This means that if, while a contract is being negotiated, a person suffers personal injury, Article 4 or other relevant provisions of this Regulation should apply.

This concept of requiring a 'direct link' between the dealings and the non-contractual obligations also essentially functions to limit the effect of the law chosen (or proposed) by the parties in their contractual negotiations. The requirement for such a connection perhaps suggests a foreseeability restriction on the scope of party autonomy, an issue discussed in Section 2.4.2.

8.4.3   US Second Restatement of Conflict of Laws

As noted above, the First Restatement of Conflict of Laws provided in section 453 for a 'law of the place of enrichment' rule – vulnerable to criticism on the grounds that fixing a territorial location for a cross-border enrichment can be difficult or arbitrary. As part of the greater flexibility generally introduced into US choice of law rules during the mid-twentieth century, this rule was substantially revised under the Second Restatement,[85] section 221 of which provides:

(1) In actions for restitution,[86] the rights and liabilities of the parties with respect to the particular issue are determined by the local law of the state which, with respect to that issue, has the most significant relationship to the occurrence and the parties under the principles stated in § 6.

(2) Contacts to be taken into account in applying the principles of § 6 to determine the law applicable to an issue include:

(a) the place where a relationship between the parties was centred, provided that the receipt of enrichment was substantially related to the relationship,

(b) the place where the benefit or enrichment was received,

(c) the place where the act conferring the benefit or enrichment was done,

(d) the domicil, residence, nationality, place of incorporation and place of business of the parties, and

---

[85] See generally Hay (1978).

[86] This rule generally applies to unjust enrichment claims – see e.g. *Powers* v. *Lycoming Engines*, 328 Fed.Appx. 121 (3rd Cir. 2009).

(e) the place where a physical thing, such as land or a chattel, which was substantially related to the enrichment, was situated at the time of the enrichment.

These contacts are to be evaluated according to their relative importance with respect to the particular issue.

The principles to be taken into account under section 6 are discussed in Section 7.2.4 and Section 8.3.5. Essentially this approach requires the court to take into account a very wide range of factors and evaluate the law most closely connected to the unjust enrichment. Although one of the factors under section 6 of the Restatement relates to the expectations of the parties, there is no provision for a choice of law by the parties to be given direct effect under this rule. The comments to this section emphasise that the expectations of the parties will frequently not be a significant factor in this analysis, on the basis that "the purpose of restitution is to do justice to the parties after an event whose occurrence one of the parties, at least, will usually not have foreseen".[87] The link between foreseeability and giving effect to party expectations is notable, and consistent with the analysis in Section 2.4.2.

However, in practice the Second Restatement approach is likely to lead to indirect party autonomy effects where the parties have an underlying contractual relationship connected with the claim for unjust enrichment, pursuant to section 221(2)(a). Indeed this subsection is described in the comments as "the contact that … is given the greatest weight in determining the state of the applicable law".[88] The comments go on to explain that:

> When the enrichment was received in the course of the performance of a contract between the parties, the law selected by application of the rules of §§ 187–188 will presumably govern one party's rights in restitution against the other. The applicable law will be that chosen by the parties if they have made an effective choice under the circumstances stated in § 187.

These rules are thus clearly intended to permit party autonomy to play a significant indirect role in choice of law in unjust enrichment, although the cost of the added flexibility in the Second Restatement rule may well be a degree of unpredictability in its application.[89]

---

[87] Comment (b).

[88] Comment (d); see e.g. *Casa Orlando Apartments, Ltd* v. *Federal National Mortgage Association*, 624 F.3d 185 (5th Circ. 2010).

[89] See e.g. *Caton* v. *Leach Corporation*, 896 F.2d 939 (5th Circ. 1990) (problematically finding that the choice of law clause in an employment contract did not determine the governing law for an unjust enrichment claim brought by an employee whose contract was terminated, because the clause was drafted narrowly).

8.4.4   China

Article 47 of the Law of the People's Republic of China on the Laws Applicable to Foreign-Related Civil Relations (2010)[90] provides as follows:

> Unjust enrichment and *Negotiorum gestio* are governed by the law chosen by the parties by agreement. Absent any choice by the parties, the law of their common habitual residence shall be applied. Absent common habitual residence, the law of the place where the unjust enrichment or *Negotiorum gestio* occurs shall be applied.

It is somewhat unclear from this text whether this contemplates an agreement entered into by the parties before or after liability has emerged. The reference to the law 'chosen by the parties by agreement' perhaps suggests the latter (comparable to the limited autonomy permitted under Article 44). However, the similarity of these rules to the equivalent rules in the Rome II Regulation (Articles 10 and 11, as discussed above), which may have influenced drafting of these provisions, might suggest a broader approach under which the law of any underlying contract between the parties determines the law governing these forms of non-contractual liability, as is clear under the Rome II Regulation. If this is the correct analysis, an exercise of contractual party autonomy would thereby be extended to these forms of non-contractual liability arising out of the contractual relationship.

8.5   Property

A further distinct category of choice of law rules applies where claims concern title to property. As discussed further below, such claims are almost invariably governed by the law of the location of the property, the *lex situs*, a strict rule based on an objective factor which leaves no scope for party autonomy. However, the traditional imperviousness of proprietary claims to party autonomy is being eroded in a range of ways.[91] There are no European rules directly applicable to choice of law in property, although the Rome I and Rome II Regulations may affect certain specialised questions, as examined below.

8.5.1   Characterisation Issues

Classifying claims that relate to property may be difficult in practice, and this may mean that some claims categorised as proprietary in a domestic

---

[90] See discussion in Tang, Xiao and Huo (2016), Chapter 10; Huo (2011), p.1091ff.
[91] See generally Westrik and Van der Weide (2011).

legal system are governed by other choice of law rules under which party autonomy is recognised.[92] Where questions of title to property arise between the parties to a contract, for example, the issues raised might be characterised as contractual (whether the defendant is contractually obliged to recognise the claimant's claim to title) and thus subject to a choice of law clause under the contract. Similarly, tortious claims that concern interference with property rights are generally governed by choice of law rules in tort, not property, and may therefore be affected by party choice of law agreements in the variety of ways discussed in Section 8.3.[93] Characterisation may however be more complex where proceedings raise both proprietary and tortious issues, such as where a claim in trespass is defended on the grounds that the claimant is not the owner of the property. In such cases, the question of title to property still needs to be determined using the choice of law rule for property, even if that issue is being raised as an ancillary or incidental question (usually under a defence) to a claim in tort.[94] These difficulties in characterisation remain somewhat unresolved in relation to the Rome I Regulation and Rome II Regulation in the European Union – although neither is expressly applicable to proprietary questions, it is unclear to what extent they may extend to such questions through their characterisation as matters of contractual or noncontractual obligation. Other proceedings may however raise strictly proprietary issues, particularly those affecting parties not subject to any contractual relationship, giving rise only to questions that must be determined using the choice of law rules for property. These are the primary focus of this section.

8.5.2 Traditional Territorial Rule: No Scope for Party Autonomy

As noted above, the law that governs proprietary claims has traditionally been the law of the location of the property – the *lex situs* – in regard to both movable and immovable property.[95] For movable property, the relevant location is the place at which the transfer or creation of proprietary rights has allegedly occurred, not the location of the property at the time

---

[92] See e.g. *Macmillan v. Bishopsgate Investment Trust (No 3)* [1995] EWCA Civ 55; Cheshire, North and Fawcett (2017), Chapter 3.

[93] The tort of conversion, however, raises the opposite question, as it deals with issues which are often characterised as proprietary. See e.g. Cheshire, North and Fawcett (2017), p.808ff; Dicey, Morris and Collins (2012), [34-021].

[94] See e.g. Cheshire, North and Fawcett (2017), Chapter 4.

[95] See generally Cheshire, North and Fawcett (2017), Chapters 30–31.

the proceedings are commenced or the issue is considered. This remains the rule under the common law, which still applies in English courts because proprietary claims are not covered by European choice of law rules (with the exception of contractual rights, discussed below).[96] Under the common law, the *lex situs* rule also applies for claims in proprietary estoppel, which are characterised (for choice of law purposes) as claims in property, as they seek to establish rights to land.[97] The *lex situs* rule was also (unsurprisingly) the rule adopted under the First Restatement of Conflict of Laws, which generally relied on objective territorial connecting factors. In section 257, for example, it was provided that "Whether a conveyance of a chattel which is in due form and is made by a party who has capacity to convey it is in other respects valid, is determined by the law of the state where the chattel is at the time of the conveyance".

The justification for the strict *lex situs* rule is clearest in regard to immovable property – although this rule is rarely applied in this context, because courts will rarely hear cases involving title to foreign immovable property, as discussed in Section 5.4. Control over land is usually considered to be integral to a state's sovereign interests, giving rise to a claim for exclusive regulatory control both as a matter of jurisdiction and applicable law. (The application of the *lex situs* was also proposed in *Dicey* to govern unjust enrichment claims arising out of transactions concerning immovable property, before such issues were regulated by the Rome II Regulation.)[98]

For movable property the issues are more complex. For example, consider a painting stolen from England and taken to Italy, where it is sold to a third party, who brings it back to England, where the original owner sues for title.[99] It is clear that Italian law applies under the *lex situs* rule, although there is no reason why the claimant should have known or anticipated that title to their property would be subject to foreign law in this way. The *lex situs* rule is justified on the basis that the interests of the claimant are, however, outweighed by those of the defendant, who should be able to assume that purchase of the property in Italy will be governed by local law.[100] The claimant is in the position to protect their property rights

---

[96] See generally e.g. Carruthers (2005).
[97] See Dicey, Morris and Collins (2012), [36-095].
[98] See Dicey, Morris and Collins (14th edition, 2008), [36-008].
[99] As in *Winkworth* v. *Christie, Manson and Woods Ltd* [1980] Ch 496.
[100] "A purchaser ought to satisfy himself that he obtains good title by the law prevailing where the chattel is ... but should not be required to do more than that" – *Macmillan* v. *Bishopsgate Investment Trust (No 3)* [1995] EWCA Civ 55, [46].

through securing their property from theft.[101] Arguments have been made that property questions should sometimes be governed by the 'proper law of the property', particularly in situations in which the location of property is fortuitous or incidental (such as property in transit),[102] although the simplicity and relative certainty of the *lex situs* rule is a strong point in its favour.

The application of the law of the location of property evidently leaves no room for party autonomy to determine the applicable law. For movable property, the parties might affect the governing law by choosing the location where a transfer of title is to take place, but this indirect selection of the applicable law is not strictly what is meant by party autonomy, as discussed in Section 1.3.1. For claims concerning title to immovable property even this is not possible, although it is rarely suggested that such claims should be governed by any law other than the *lex situs*. The possibility of applying the law chosen by the parties in relation to movable property is, however, certainly worthy of further consideration.

8.5.3 *Party Autonomy in Choice of Law in Property?*

A rule under which the parties were able to choose the law that governs claims in property that arise between them would not always be practically relevant to proprietary claims, which are often brought in this form because of the absence of a contractual or other relationship between the parties (such as in the example of the painting discussed above). However, where parties do have a prior contractual relationship, there seems to be little reason why they should not be able to determine the law that would govern proprietary claims between them which arise out of that relationship. This is particularly the case where the contract concerns the transportation of goods, and the location of the goods at the time when questions of title arise may be fortuitous.[103] In the common law, as noted above, such an effect may be achieved through characterisation of the claim as contractual rather than proprietary, where it concerns the question of title to property transferred pursuant to contract, as between the contracting parties (such as the effectiveness of a retention of title clause). This effect may not be achieved, however, in relation to agreements entered into after

---

[101] "And an owner, if he does not wish to be deprived of his property by some eccentric rule of foreign law, can at least do his best to ensure that it does not leave the safety of his own country" – *Macmillan* v. *Bishopsgate Investment Trust (No 3)* [1995] EWCA Civ 55, [46].

[102] *Winkworth* v. *Christie, Manson and Woods Ltd* [1980] Ch 496, 501.

[103] See further various chapters in Westrik and Van der Weide (2011).

a dispute concerning movable property has arisen. Although the parties might make an effective choice of forum law through failing to plead or prove foreign law, as discussed in Section 7.4, it is again unclear why a broader party autonomy should not apply in these (relatively unusual) circumstances, as would, for example, ordinarily be possible for claims in tort pursuant to Article 14 of the Rome II Regulation.

The possibility for party autonomy to be applied in cases of claims for property was opened up in the United States in the Second Restatement of Conflict of Laws. The general principle for the choice of law rules for claims in property is set out in section 222 in the following terms:

> The interests of the parties in a thing are determined, depending upon the circumstances, either by the "law" or by the "local law" of the state which, with respect to the particular issue, has the most significant relationship to the thing and the parties under the principles stated in § 6.

As discussed earlier in this chapter, this raises the possibility for party autonomy to influence the applicable law for claims in property, at least indirectly. Section 244, dealing with the validity and effect of a conveyance of movable property, acknowledges this directly in providing as follows:

> (1) The validity and effect of a conveyance of an interest in a chattel as between the parties to the conveyance are determined by the local law of the state which, with respect to the particular issue, has the most significant relationship to the parties, the chattel and the conveyance under the principles stated in § 6.
> (2) In the absence of an effective choice of law by the parties, greater weight will usually be given to the location of the chattel, or group of chattels, at the time of the conveyance than to any other contact in determining the state of the applicable law.

Party autonomy is thus potentially permitted in the context of choice of law in movable property, at least in part on the basis that in cases where there is a conveyance of movable property "there is no clear line of distinction ... between property and contractual rights".[104] However, this analysis evidently only applies for the contracting parties. Where the dispute concerns the effect of a conveyance on third party interests, section 245 specifies that the applicable law will 'usually' be the law applied by the courts at the location of the property. In other words, it applies a flexible *lex situs* rule, but modified through the adoption of renvoi. As a general point, if or where party autonomy is adopted in choice of law in property, it is indeed very likely to remain necessary to invoke the *lex situs* (with or without

---

[104] Comment (c).

renvoi) to govern third party interests, as third parties will not necessarily know which law the property has been subjected to through an exercise of contractual choice of law.

Under the Second Restatement the limited effectiveness of party autonomy is not extended to claims concerning immovable property. Section 223, applicable to disputes concerning the validity and effect of a conveyance of immovable property, provides that the law applicable to such claims is the law that would be applied by the courts of the location of the property, which would normally be the local law of that place. In other words, it applies a strict *lex situs* rule, but modified through the adoption of renvoi. Under this rule there is evidently no scope for the application of party autonomy. Section 224, applicable to the construction of an instrument of conveyance, permits the parties to choose the applicable law for that purpose (applying the *lex situs* as a default rule in the absence of such choice), but this should be viewed as a contractual choice of law rather than an exercise of party autonomy in relation to property, as there is no doubt that interpretation of a conveyancing instrument is a contractual rather than proprietary issue.

In the Law of the People's Republic of China on the Laws Applicable to Foreign-related Civil Relations (2010),[105] a similar but rather clearer approach is taken that also gives a direct effect to party autonomy in relation to movable property. Article 37 of the Law provides that:

> The parties may by agreement choose the law applicable to rights *in rem* in movable property. Absent any choice by the parties, the law of the place where the property locates when the legal fact occurs shall be applied.

Article 38 similarly provides that:

> The parties may by agreement choose the law applicable to the change of the rights *in rem* in movable property which is in transit. Absent any choice by the parties, the law of the destination of transportation shall be applied.

Under both of these rules, it appears clear that agreements may be reached prior to the time of the disputed event or transaction, and thus these rules are likely to assist parties to achieve certainty in the law applicable to their legal relationship. A contractual choice of law clause, drafted in broad enough terms, will be effective to cover not merely contractual disputes but also proprietary disputes arising between the parties, particularly concerning the subject matter of the property. While (as noted above) other legal systems may well use devices such as characterisation to resolve such

---

[105] See discussion in Tang, Xiao and Huo (2016), Chapter 11; Huo (2011), p.1083ff.

problems in a similar way in practice, the innovation of the Chinese law on this point appears to achieve the same objectives with arguably greater clarity and certainty. It may also be noted that Article 38 addresses the issue of property in transit in the absence of choice, by selecting the law of the destination, which is probably as good a solution as any to this difficult issue. As noted above, in many cases claims are brought in proprietary form because of the lack of a contractual relationship between the parties – in such cases, a choice of law agreement might also be possible after the event under the Chinese rule. Also as noted above, in the common law this does not appear possible under the *lex situs* rule, which does not leave any scope for the parties to agree on the law governing movable property claims, even after the event giving rise to the dispute.

8.5.4   Party Autonomy and Contractual Rights?

One particular context in which a potential role for party autonomy has developed in choice of law in property is in relation to contractual rights. In some legal systems (such as under the common law tradition), such rights are characterised as a form of property. The assignment of contractual rights by one of the contracting parties can create issues concerning the relationship between the assignee and the other contacting party (typically a debtor), as well as potentially between competing assignees. If the contractual rights are analysed as proprietary in character, as is traditionally the case under the common law, these issues are viewed as governed by the *lex situs* – the law of the location of the contractual rights – which is (under the common law) generally identified as the location of the party obliged to perform them (being the place at which they could be enforced).[106] This rule has, however, been criticised because this location is not necessarily clear to the assignees, and may in any case change over time. Another approach was adopted in the First Restatement of Conflict of Laws, which in section 348 applied the law of the place of contracting to the question of the assignability of contractual rights; but that place may have no real connection to the parties or their contract.

A different rule has been developed in the European Union under the Rome Convention 1980 and now (to very similar effect) under the Rome I Regulation.[107] Under Article 14(2) of the Rome I Regulation, the

---

[106] See generally Cheshire, North and Fawcett (2017), pp.1280–2.
[107] See generally Westrik and Van der Weide (2011); Cheshire, North and Fawcett (2017), Chapter 32.

assignability of contractual rights and the relationship between the assignee and the debtor are governed by the law applicable to the underlying contract, not the situs of the contractual rights. The rule does not clearly specify whether it applies to the question of priority between assignees where there are multiple assignees, but it is also likely to be applied in that context.[108] The law applicable to the contract may, of course, be chosen by the contracting parties, pursuant to Article 3 of the Rome Convention 1980 and Rome I Regulation, as analysed in Section 7.2. This means that the exercise of party autonomy by those contracting parties determines not only the relationship between them, but also the proprietary effect of an assignment of those contractual rights, at least as between the debtor and the assignee and potentially also between assignees.[109] One way of understanding this change is that it effects a re-characterisation of these issues as contractual rather than proprietary, and thus governed by the law applicable to the contract rather than the *lex situs* rule.[110] In any case, the clear consequence is that the law chosen by the initial contracting parties governs also the potential rights of third party assignees.

This rule is limited to the question of the assignability of contractual rights – whether the assignee can enforce their rights against the debtor. As between assignor and assignee, Article 14(1) of the Rome I Regulation specifies that it is the law of the contract of assignment that governs. Under Recital 38, it is stated that "Article 14(1) also applies to the property aspects of an assignment, as between assignor and assignee, in legal orders where such aspects are treated separately from the aspects under the law of obligations". The effect of this rule is once again to characterise what in the common law could be potentially a proprietary question as a contractual question. Thus, proprietary questions relating to an assignment of contractual rights, as between the assignor and assignee, are governed by the law of the contract of assignment. If the parties have chosen a governing

---

[108] For analysis, see generally the British Institute of International and Comparative Law, 'Study on the question of effectiveness of an assignment or subrogation of a claim against third parties and the priority of the assigned or subrogated claim over a right of another person', available at http://ec.europa.eu/justice/civil/files/report_assignment_en.pdf.

[109] The Hague Securities Convention 2006 (in force 2017 in Mauritius, Switzerland, and the United States), Art.4, similarly gives indirect effect to party autonomy for certain proprietary questions arising from dealings with securities – but only if the law chosen to govern the account is the law of a place in which the relevant intermediary has an office. Thus, an objective connection is required to support the subjective choice of law (on which see further Section 7.3). See www.hcch.net/en/instruments/conventions/full-text/?cid=72.

[110] See generally e.g. *Raiffeisen Zentralbank Osterreich AG v. Five Star General Trading* [2001] EWCA Civ 68.

law for their contract of assignment, the effect of that exercise of party autonomy is extended to govern proprietary questions (including whether title to the contractual rights has been passed). In two distinct ways, choice of law clauses in contracts are thus given direct effect under the Rome I Regulation for what would at least traditionally be characterised under the common law as proprietary questions.

The Second Restatement of Conflict of Laws gives less clear answers to these questions, but also potentially opens up the possibility for indirect exercises of party autonomy. Under section 208, the assignability of a contractual right is said to be governed by the "law of the state which has the most significant relationship to the contract and the parties with respect to the issue of assignability". Under section 209, the relationship between assignor and assignee is similarly referred to the law with the most significant relationship to the issue, and under section 210 the effect of the assignment on the obligor is referred to the laws applicable under either section 208 or section 209. Questions of priority between multiple assignees are also potentially governed by the law applicable under either section 208 or section 209, depending on the circumstances. These rules all essentially refer a judge to the various factors in section 6 of the Restatement, examined in Sections 7.2.4 and 8.3.5, which will in turn take into consideration the intentions of the parties as a factor. The court may well thus give effect to any exercises of party autonomy in the underlying contract or contract of assignment in determining the governing law for these (at least traditionally) proprietary questions.

8.5.5   Party Autonomy and Intellectual Property?

Choice of law rules in the context of intellectual property have not traditionally been well developed – there are, for example, no special rules in the First or Second Restatements of Conflict of Laws dealing with intellectual property claims.[111] This is largely a consequence of the fact that intellectual property is inherently territorial (as a sovereign monopoly), and there was a perception at least that cross-border intellectual property claims were and ought to be infrequent as cases would be litigated solely in the place of the intellectual property. This perception is certainly no

---

[111] The First Restatement did have a rule dealing with "intangible things created by law", in section 213, pointing to the law of the state under which the thing was created, but this was principally addressed to debts and contractual rights.

longer accurate, if it ever was,[112] particularly in light of how easily intellectual property rights are exploited and infringed on the internet. As a consequence, there have been a number of recent efforts to develop choice of rules in this area, including under the Rome II Regulation, the American Law Institute Principles of the Law on 'Intellectual Property: Principles Governing Jurisdiction, Choice of Law & Judgments in Transnational Disputes' 2008 ('ALI Principles'),[113] and the Max Planck Principles for Conflict of Laws in Intellectual Property 2011 ('CLIP Principles').[114] These issues are complex, and only a basic analysis can be provided here.[115]

As in the context of jurisdiction, when it comes to choice of law it is commonly considered that intellectual property rights require distinct treatment from other forms of property. In Section 5.4.1 it was noted that a distinction is drawn in the Brussels I Regulation between claims concerning title to registered intellectual property, for which the courts of the location of the property are given exclusive jurisdiction, and those concerning breach of any intellectual property (and title to non-registered intellectual property), which are subject to the general rules of jurisdiction (as claims in tort or property), including the possible application of a choice of court clause. In the context of choice of law, a similar distinction may be drawn between proprietary issues that concern the title to or validity of the intellectual property, and personal issues (potentially including infringement proceedings) that may arise between the parties to an intellectual property transaction or dispute. A further distinction may be drawn between registrable intellectual property rights, such as patents and trademarks, and those that do not require registration, such as copyright.

For issues concerning the title to or validity of intellectual property, the territoriality of intellectual property may suggest a *lex situs* rule similar to that applied in the context of immovable property, and similarly no scope for the application of party autonomy. Indeed, the traditional approach adopted in relation to intellectual property is to view the law of the 'location' of the property as covering all issues that arise, excluding any scope for party autonomy. The applicable law for validity questions might thus be

---

[112] See further Section 5.4.

[113] These were not given the title of a 'Restatement' because it was considered that the existing law was too unsettled for the principles to be described as 'restating' the law. They are therefore more *lex ferenda* and more international than most of the work of the American Law Institute.

[114] Available at www.cl-ip.eu.

[115] For further detail see e.g. Torremans (2015); Matulionyte (2013); Kono (2012); Fawcett and Torremans (2011).

identified as the place of registration of the property for registrable intellectual property rights, or for non-registrable intellectual property as the place where infringement has occurred or may occur.[116] In either case this is the system of law whose protection is being invoked (as registrable intellectual property can only be relied on within the territory in which it is registered), and thus this is often thus referred to as the *lex loci protectionis*.

The basic rule in section 301 of the ALI Principles is therefore that:

> (1) The law applicable to determine the existence, validity, duration, attributes, and infringement of intellectual property rights and the remedies for their infringement is:
>   (a) for registered rights, the law of each State of registration.
>   (b) for other intellectual property rights, the law of each State for which protection is sought.

A similar rule is adopted under Article 3:102 of the CLIP Principles. It may at first glance perhaps be surprising to see 'infringement' in the list of issues covered exclusively by the *lex loci protectionis* of the intellectual property under the ALI Principles, as such issues could be viewed as personal matters between the parties rather than concerning title to the property itself.[117] In this respect, however, section 301 is essentially providing a default rule. Section 302(1) of the ALI Principles provides that "the parties may agree at any time, including after a dispute arises, to designate a law that will govern all or part of their dispute". The permissible scope of their agreement is strictly limited under section 302(2), and it may not cover any of the following:

> (a) the validity and maintenance of registered rights;
> (b) the existence, attributes, transferability, and duration of rights, whether or not registered; and
> (c) formal requirements for recording assignments and licenses.

Comment (a) to this section explains that "In general, the public-law aspects of intellectual property must be adjudicated under the laws that give rise to the rights in each jurisdiction concerned" – clearly recognising that an exercise of party autonomy would be inappropriate where public interests are concerned. This does leave the parties free to choose the law that governs any claims which arise (or have arisen) between them

---

[116] The law of the country of origin of the intellectual property has also sometimes been relied on as a potentially applicable law, but this is not widely supported.

[117] Similarly, under the CLIP Principles, the law governing infringement is "the law of each State for which protection is sought" – Art.3:601. This is subject to a limited party autonomy in relation to remedies – Art.3:606.

concerning infringement of intellectual property rights, as well as certain issues arising in relation to the transfer or license of intellectual property rights.[118] Thus, for example, two contracting parties to an IP licensing agreement may, through a choice of law clause, determine the law that governs both contractual issues and also various claims relating to the transfer, license or infringement of intellectual property rights arising from the agreement. This is subject to various restrictions, such that the agreement may not adversely affect the rights of third parties,[119] and that standard form agreements are valid only if the choice of law clause was 'reasonable', based in part on the connections between the parties and their relationship with the chosen law.[120] It appears therefore that there is likely to be a requirement for an objective connection between the chosen law and the parties or their relationship.[121] Puzzlingly, however, comment (b) to this section goes on to state that:

> The principle of unfettered party autonomy is widely recognized in business-to-business transactions. It admits the choice of a third legal order, not being that of the grantor or of the recipient, even when the chosen law lacks any relationship to the parties, to the right, or to the territory of use.

Whether there is any requirement for an objective connection is therefore somewhat unclear under the Principles. Nevertheless, subject to these constraints, the exercise of autonomy by the parties is clearly permitted at least in relation to questions of infringement of intellectual property rights. An exercise of autonomy is also expressly permitted under the Law of the People's Republic of China on the Laws Applicable to Foreign-Related Civil Relations (2010),[122] Article 49 of which provides that "The parties may by agreement choose the law applicable to the transfer and license of intellectual property rights", although this is limited to contractual issues rather than infringement proceedings.

By contrast, under Article 8 of the Rome II Regulation, which deals solely with claims for infringement of intellectual property rights (questions of title falling outside the scope of the Regulation), a more traditional and restrictive approach is adopted. A broad rule in favour of the *lex loci protectionis* is set out in Article 8 for both registered and non-registered

---

[118] Under the CLIP Principles, some of these issues would be classified as contractual, and dealt with under a separate rule which permits a broad exercise of party autonomy – Art.3:501.

[119] Section 302(3).

[120] Section 302(5).

[121] See generally Section 7.3.

[122] See further generally e.g. Tang, Xiao and Huo (2016), Chapter 12; Zhang (2011a).

intellectual property rights, providing in subsection (1) that "The law applicable to a non-contractual obligation arising from an infringement of an intellectual property right shall be the law of the country for which protection is claimed", and in subsection (3) that "The law applicable under this Article may not be derogated from by an agreement pursuant to Article 14". In respect of non-contractual claims for infringement of intellectual property rights, the Rome II Regulation thus expressly excludes the possibility for the parties to exercise autonomy over the applicable law. In relation to infringement of intellectual property rights, Chinese law is also more circumspect about the exercise of party autonomy. Article 50 of the Law of the People's Republic of China on the Laws Applicable to Foreign-Related Civil Relations (2010) provides that "Liability for infringing intellectual property rights is governed by the law of the place where protection is sought", qualified only by the possibility that "The parties may also choose to apply the law of the forum after the infringement occurs." This latter rule permits a narrow exercise of party autonomy, although also in many legal systems this would equally be possible where the parties agreed not to plead or prove foreign law, as there would be a default to forum law,[123] and the rule may be simply intended to acknowledge this possibility.

8.6   Equitable Claims

Common law systems recognise equitable claims as a distinct legal category from contract, tort, unjust enrichment, or property. This category includes, for example, claims for breach of a fiduciary duty, breach of confidence, dishonest assistance in breach of trust, and knowing receipt of trust property. The existence of such a category domestically does not, however, necessarily require or suggest that a separate choice of law rule would be appropriate for such claims. As the category is unknown to civil law systems and largely a product of historical factors in the common law, the better view is that equitable claims should be characterised as falling under one of the other choice of law rules considered above or in Chapter 7, rather than (as has sometimes been argued) subject to their own choice of law rules or the law of the forum.[124] This is arguably supported by the fact that the First and Second Restatements of Conflict of Laws do not

---

[123] See Section 7.5.
[124] See generally Yeo (2004); Dicey, Morris and Collins (2012), [34-083] ("there is no reason to suppose that the domestic law distinction between equity and the common law is necessarily reflected in the rules of characterisation and choice of law in the conflict of laws; there is therefore no need for a separate choice of law rule for 'equitable obligations' generally").

include separate choice of law rules for equitable claims. Exactly how such claims should be characterised is, of course, a challenging question, perhaps particularly for the purposes of the Rome I and Rome II Regulations, under which terms must generally be given a common European definition. This section can only offer a relatively brief analysis of these complex questions, focusing on the potential impact of party autonomy under the different possible characterisations.

Breach of confidence (except in the context of claims arising from misuse of personal information, which are likely to be excluded from the Rome II Regulation under Article 1(2)(g)) and dishonest assistance in breach of trust are likely to be characterised as falling within the scope of the general rule for tortious claims under Article 4 of the Rome II Regulation.[125] The position in relation to knowing receipt of trust property is perhaps less clear, although a case can be made that the choice of law rule regarding unjust enrichment should apply at least in some situations (and in any case some argue that knowing receipt should be viewed as a species of unjust enrichment rather than a separate equitable claim).[126] Whichever approach is adopted, for each of these doctrines there is thus the potential for party autonomy to have both direct (under Article 14) and indirect (under Article 4(3) or Article 10(1)) effects on the applicable law, as discussed in Section 8.3.3.

With regard to a breach of confidence arising from misuse of personal information, because of the exclusion from the Rome II Regulation the issues would likely be governed by common law choice of law rules. Although the position is not certain, a breach of confidence arising from misuse of personal information has, under the common law, been characterised as a question of unjust enrichment.[127] Such a claim would therefore, unusually, still require application of the (somewhat unclear) common law choice of law rule for unjust enrichment (which has otherwise generally been replaced by the Rome II Regulation). The common law rule has not traditionally been considered to permit any direct exercise of party autonomy regarding choice of law for unjust enrichment, unlike under the Rome II Regulation, pursuant to Article 14 (as discussed in Section 8.4). However, indirect effects for party autonomy have traditionally been accepted under the common law rule – for example, if an unjust

---

[125] Dicey, Morris and Collins (2012), [36-058]–[36-061].

[126] Dicey, Morris and Collins (2012), [34-090]; Clarkson and Hill (2016), pp.289–91. See e.g. *Alliance Bank JSC* v. *Aquanta Corporation* [2011] EWHC 3281 (Comm), [43].

[127] Dicey, Morris, and Collins (2012), [34-091]; *Douglas* v. *Hello! Ltd (No.3)* [2005] EWCA Civ 595.

enrichment arose out of a contractual relationship, the unjust enrichment claim would be governed by the law of the contract, including any law chosen by the parties.

For breach of fiduciary duties, the position is potentially more context-sensitive.[128] If such a duty arises in the course of a contractual relationship, the issue may be best characterised as a contractual question governed by the law of the contract, determined (potentially by the parties themselves, if their contract contains a choice of law clause) pursuant to the Rome I Regulation. In other cases, it may be that the breach of duty is better considered to be governed by the Rome II Regulation, and viewed as a claim in tort or in restitution – in either case, there is potential for a direct selection of law by the parties, pursuant to Article 14. In the absence of an underlying contractual relationship a further indirect effect could arise under Article 4(3) or Article 10(1) of the Rome II Regulation if the breach related to a claim in tort (Article 10(1) expressly permits consideration of "a relationship existing between the parties, such as one arising out of a contract or a tort/delict"), and the parties had made a direct or indirect choice of law to govern the tort, as discussed in Section 8.3.

8.7   Trusts

The trust is a common law innovation under which the law recognises, in various circumstances, that the legal owner of property holds that property on behalf of another. A trust may arise through an express and voluntary declaration by a party either holding property or when transferring it to another party. It may also arise by operation of law, contrary to the wishes of the party holding or receiving property, such as where a fiduciary profits improperly from their position. In between these categories, the law also recognises trusts as arising through an implied or imputed intention, but (in general) difficulties arise in drawing a clear dividing line between cases in which the intention is implied as a matter of fact (and therefore can be refuted by evidence of a contrary actual intention), and where it is imputed as a matter of law (and therefore cannot be refuted by evidence of a contrary actual intention). The categorisation of types of trusts is not clearly settled in common law systems as a matter of domestic law as well as a matter of choice of law, but for present purposes they may be divided into express (or voluntary) trusts, and implied (or involuntary) trusts, each of which is considered in turn below.

---

[128] See e.g. Dicey, Morris, and Collins (2012), [34-087] and [36-069]–[36-072].

A wide range of legal issues may arise in relation to a trust, including the validity of its establishment, variation or termination, the appointment or removal of trustees, the rights and duties of trustees, and the relationships between trustees and beneficiaries. Where a trust involves parties or property in different jurisdictions, it will be necessary to determine the law that governs these issues. The purpose of this section is to explore the extent to which this determination may give effect to choices made by the parties themselves.

8.7.1   Express/Voluntary Trusts

A voluntary trust will ordinarily be created through a deed, contract or will executed by the settlor. The validity of the legal instrument creating the trust is a separate preliminary issue,[129] and the law that governs that issue is determined by the choice of law rules for that instrument, which will generally give effect to an exercise of party autonomy.[130] A trust will also often (but not always) require a valid transfer of property to be established, and the question of whether such a transfer has taken place will be governed by the choice of law rules for property (as discussed in Section 8.5), under which a choice of law by the parties has not traditionally been recognised as directly effective.

Assuming those preliminary conditions are met, it is then necessary to determine the law that governs the trust, in order to determine the validity of the trust as well as the various legal issues that govern its operation. At common law, it was accepted that the settlor could choose the law governing a trust, both expressly and also implicitly[131] – this is thus another context in which party autonomy is firmly established. In the absence of a choice, the law would be the system of law with the closest and most real connection to the trust.[132] Choice of law issues concerning trusts are generally excluded from the Rome I and Rome II Regulations, and thus have not received European harmonisation.[133] These issues have however been addressed in an international convention, the Hague Trusts Convention

---

[129] See e.g. Hague Trusts Convention 1985, Art.4 (excluding these matters).

[130] Under English law a deed is a form of contract, and a choice of law by the party or parties executing the deed will be given effect under the principles examined in Chapter 7. Choice of law for wills is discussed in Section 8.8.1.

[131] Cheshire, North and Fawcett (2017), p.1386; *Saliba v. Falzon* [1998] NSWSC 302.

[132] Cheshire, North and Fawcett (2017), p.1388.

[133] Rome II Regulation, Art.1(2)(e) excludes non-contractual obligations arising out of the relations between the settlors, trustees and beneficiaries of a trust created voluntarily. See similarly but more narrowly Rome I Regulation, Art.1(2)(h).

of 1985. The convention is intended to provide rules for choice of law and the recognition of trusts for both common law and civil law systems, and it has been ratified in the common law systems of the United Kingdom,[134] Australia,[135] Canada (but only for some provinces),[136] Cyprus and Hong Kong, as well as civil law systems such as Italy, the Netherlands, and Switzerland.[137]

The basic choice of law rule under the Hague Trusts Convention 1985 is set out in Articles 6 and 7, and is similar to the common law rule. Article 6 provides as follows:

> A trust shall be governed by the law chosen by the settlor. The choice must be express or be implied in the terms of the instrument creating or the writing evidencing the trust, interpreted, if necessary, in the light of the circumstances of the case.
>
> Where the law chosen under the previous paragraph does not provide for trusts or the category of trust involved, the choice shall not be effective and the law specified in Article 7 shall apply.

The rule thus clearly recognises the autonomy of the settlor to choose the governing law. In the absence of such a choice, Article 7 selects the law with which the trust is most closely connected, and indicates certain factors that should be taken into consideration in making that determination. Under either provision, the law selected governs a wide range of issues, including "the validity of the trust, its construction, its effects, and the administration of the trust".[138]

It is notable that Article 6 does not allow the settlor to choose a law that renders the trust invalid – this is a similar rule to that applied in some legal systems, such as under the Second Restatement of Conflict of Laws, that a choice of law by the parties in a contract cannot have the effect of invalidating the contract.[139] This is perhaps curious because it suggests that a choice of law by the settlor is secondary to their intention to create a (valid) trust – although the choice of law may be invalidated, their broader intention should be given effect (if the law that would govern in the absence of choice renders the trust valid). It is not always clear that this

---

[134] Recognition of Trusts Act 1987.
[135] Trusts (Hague Convention) Act 1991.
[136] Under the Uniform International Trusts Act.
[137] The other state parties are Lichtenstein, Luxembourg, Malta, Monaco, Panama, and San Marino: see www.hcch.net/index_en.php?act=conventions.status&cid=59.
[138] Article 8.
[139] See Section 7.6.

would actually be the intention of the settlor concerned – it is perfectly possible that they might wish to establish a trust under a particular legal system, but if the type of trust they wish to establish is not recognised they would rather the trust fail than that it be governed by a different system of law. To put this another way, the Hague Trusts Convention views a choice of law clause as a non-essential and severable term of the instrument establishing the trust – if the trust would be invalid under the chosen law, the choice of law clause is invalidated but the consent to the establishment of the trust is not.

The acceptance of party autonomy for voluntary trusts under the Hague Trusts Convention is also followed under the Second Restatement of Conflict of Laws, in which the law chosen in the trust instrument governs issues of construction,[140] and also has a role to play (but only for trusts over moveable property) in questions of validity[141] and administration.[142] In relation to questions of validity, this is subject to the chosen law having 'a substantial relation to the trust'.[143] This is consistent with the restrictive approach to choice of law in contract under some US approaches (including section 187 of the Second Restatement), which recognise only a choice of a law that is objectively connected to the contract, as discussed in Section 7.3. Under this approach, the choice made in the trust instrument acts as a rule of priority between different systems of law objectively connected to the trust, rather than the choice itself justifying the application of the chosen law.

Article 17 of the Law of the People's Republic of China on the Laws Applicable to Foreign-related Civil Relations (2010) provides that:

> The parties may by agreement choose the law applicable to trust. Absent any choice by the parties, the law of the place where the trust asset locates or where the trust relation is established shall be applied.

The effect given to party autonomy under this provision is consistent with other approaches discussed above, as well as with the general effectiveness of choice of law agreements in relation to both contractual and non-contractual issues in China under the 2010 law.

---

[140] Sections 268 and 277.
[141] Sections 269 and 270.
[142] Sections 271 and 272.
[143] Sections 269(b)(i) (trusts created by a will) and 270(a) (trusts inter vivos).

8.7.2   Implied/Involuntary Trusts

The potential role of party autonomy in relation to so-called 'implied' (or involuntary) trusts is rather more complex, because of the more contested nature of such trusts. Implied trusts are generally divided into two categories, resulting and constructive trusts.

A resulting trust arises where the law determines that a trust is necessary to give effect to what is assumed to be the intentions of the parties. Although a resulting trust emerges by operation of law, the emergence of a trust in such circumstances is defeated by evidence of a contrary intention. Resulting trusts are generally considered to arise in one of two circumstances – as presumed resulting trusts and automatic resulting trusts.

A presumed resulting trust arises where there is no actual evidence of an intention to create a trust, but the law recognises a presumption of such an intention in the circumstances – for example, where there is a transfer of property in circumstances in which it appears unlikely that a gift would be intended. Although such a trust is therefore arguably voluntary (albeit implied), there is no scope for the parties to choose a law to govern the trust, since there is no evidence of their intention to create a trust at all. There is thus no scope for party autonomy in such cases.

An automatic resulting trust arises where a trust has been intentionally created, but does not deal fully with the property of the settlor (for example, because the declaration of trust omits certain property that evidently ought to have been included, or because there is an excess of trust property once the purposes of the trust are fulfilled that the trust instrument does not purport to cover). The courts in such circumstances may recognise a resulting trust that covers the additional property. As the settlor has (once again) failed to expressly create the trust, there is no scope for direct party autonomy. However, a strong argument may be made that in such cases indirect effect should be given to any choice of law made by the settlor in the establishment of the original trust. As the court is essentially extending that trust, the new resulting trust recognised by the court should also be governed by the law chosen by the settlor.

The concept of constructive trusts is a particularly contentious issue in the law of trusts. In some jurisdictions (such as Australia), a constructive trust may be viewed as 'remedial' – it is a trust established by order of the court, normally (but not necessarily) without retrospective effect, usually in response to a wrong that constitutes a tort or unjust enrichment (for example, property lent and not returned on request, or money mistakenly paid). The principal advantage of a constructive trust as a remedy (over a claim in damages) is that it gives the claimant a proprietary entitlement and therefore priority over unsecured creditors, as well as potentially a greater ability to trace the proceeds of the wrong. If a constructive trust is conceived as a remedy in this way, there is a strong argument that it should not have its own choice of law rule, but that it should be simply governed by the law of the forum under whose power it is established. It would be somewhat curious, for example, if a New South Wales court creating a trust as a remedy were to do so subject to foreign law, as the court would be making a judicial order under forum law. However, perhaps curiously, remedial trusts may apparently nevertheless be included within the scope of the rules of Hague Trusts Convention 1985, as discussed below.

In other jurisdictions (such as England), constructive trusts are not viewed as 'remedial' but rather as 'institutional' – arising by operation of law based on a particular set of events or facts.[144] Under this type of trust, the focus is not on the intention of the settlor but on the wrongful conduct of a party which means that they should be viewed as a trustee rather than owner of property to which they have apparent title (such as a party accepting bribes, or otherwise profiting from a crime or breach of fiduciary duties). An institutional constructive trust is recognised and not created by the courts, and will therefore always take effect from the time of the conduct or receipt of the property in the relevant circumstances, rather than from the date of any subsequent court judgment recognising the trust. In any case, as the trust is not created by intention of any party, there is no scope for party autonomy. The choice of law rule that should apply to such trusts is uncertain – there is at least an argument that a constructive trust recognised in this way may be best viewed as a proprietary claim (for an interest in the trust property), and governed by the choice of law rules for property examined in Section 8.5.

The Hague Trusts Convention of 1985 (discussed above) states in Article 3 that it "applies only to trusts created voluntarily and evidenced in writing". On its terms, it is therefore highly likely not to cover presumed resulting trusts or constructive trusts, but could arguably cover an automatic resulting trust (a written trust instrument establishing the original trust may be viewed as evidence in writing of the resulting trust covering inadvertently omitted property).

---

[144] See e.g. *Westdeutsche Landesbank Girozentrale* v. *Islington London Borough Council* [1996] AC 669, 714.

Somewhat curiously, however, Article 20 of the Hague Trusts Convention gives state parties the power to extend the operation of the rules to "trusts declared by judicial decisions". Perhaps even more curiously, this power has been exercised by the United Kingdom, through section 1(2) of the Recognition of Trusts Act 1987, to extend the operation of the rules under the convention to any trust arising "by virtue of a judicial decision". The formulation in the 1987 Act would, taken literally, appear to be confined to remedial constructive trusts – the only situation in which the trust arises *by virtue of* the judicial decision (as opposed to other forms of trust that are *recognised* by the court). However, remedial constructive trusts are not accepted in English law, and Article 20 of the Hague Trusts Convention is itself expressed more broadly as covering trusts 'declared' by judicial decisions, which could potentially (although not unambiguously) cover all resulting and constructive trusts. The better view is probably that both the Convention and 1987 Act should be read as following this broader approach, and thus that for the purposes of UK law, resulting and constructive trusts should also be considered as falling within the scope of the Hague Trusts Convention rules.[145] However, although Article 6 of the Convention provides for party autonomy, as analysed above there will still be no prospect of such autonomy being recognised for these types of trusts, as they arise in the absence of any express intention (with the possible exception of automatic resulting trusts, as discussed above). The rule applied in Article 7 of the Convention probably does not differ significantly from the rule that would be applied under the common law, so the uncertain scope of the 1987 Act is unlikely to be a particularly significant problem in practice.

8.8   Succession and Family Law

The primary focus of this book is on civil and commercial matters, including contractual obligations as well as the various non-contractual issues examined above. In a book on party autonomy it would be remiss, however, not to discuss developments in choice of law relating to succession and family law. Although these are areas of law in which party autonomy has not traditionally played a significant role, largely because of the public interests involved, in recent years a greater role for party autonomy has

---

[145] See further Dicey, Morris and Collins (2012), [29-007]; Chong (2005); Harris (2002).

been recognised, albeit subject to particular constraints.[146] It may particularly be noted that in this context, party choice is frequently limited by a requirement for there to be an objective connection between the chosen law and the parties or their relationship – party autonomy appears to be adopted not as a basis for the application of law in itself, but rather as a means of choosing between the potentially applicable objectively connected laws.

A choice of law in these contexts takes on a different light than an exercise of party autonomy in a contract, which suggests that the economic justifications that are foregrounded in that context (focused on efficiency for the parties, or the creation of a law market – as discussed in Section 2.3) are less significant.[147] Some of the rules below essentially provide, for example, that a national of one state may choose to live in another state, but have their succession, divorce, or matrimonial property relations governed by their law of nationality. The autonomy that is thus facilitated is a form of multicultural identity, under which an individual may choose which aspect of their personal identity is most significant (or simply preferred) for the purposes of their family relations.[148] This suggests a 'deontological libertarian' approach, under which party autonomy is an expression of the inherent freedoms of individuals. This approach is most convincing in the context of personal relations (rather than commercial contracts), but still requires accepting an inherent individual autonomy 'prior to' the state, justifying the power of choice between state laws, which remains highly controversial. The European Parliament has, for example, voiced concerns that "the emphasis laid on party autonomy in recent EU initiatives on the sensitive issue of family law with transnational implications entails the risk, unless clear restrictions are applied, of opening the door to the unacceptable practice of forum shopping".[149]

---

[146] See generally e.g. Kohler (2013), p.398ff; Nagy (2012); Carruthers (2012); Yetano (2010); Jayme (2009); P Gannagé (1992).

[147] But see Yetano (2010), critically evaluating whether a market is being generated in 'family law products' (although somewhat conflating party autonomy with party control over objective factors determining the applicable law – see Section 1.3.1).

[148] See e.g. Maultzsch (2016), p.478; L Gannagé (2013); Smits (2013a); Knop, Michaels and Riles (2012), p.629 ("the value of this party autonomy lies in the agency it gives the parties to decide whether to situate themselves within one culture or another on a particular issue" – although making this point in the context of the 'autonomy' facilitated by optional proof of foreign law rules, discussed further in Section 7.5); Jayme (1995).

[149] European Parliament resolution of 23 November 2010 on civil law, commercial law, family law and private international law aspects of the Action Plan Implementing the Stockholm Programme (2010/2080(INI)), at para Q.

Another perspective on party autonomy in this context, focusing more on a private consequentialist justification, is its potential as a cross-border solution. Harmonisation of rules of private international law in the areas of succession and family law is particularly important, because of the harmful consequences for individuals if their personal affairs may be subject to inconsistent regulation in different legal systems. But achieving such harmonisation has been difficult, in part because of the major fracture between those states (particularly civil law systems) which tend to rely on nationality as the primary connecting factor, and those (particularly common law systems) which tend to rely on a more factual concept of domicile, only partially resolved by the development of a hybrid concept of 'habitual residence' at the Hague Conference on Private International Law.[150] If party autonomy can be agreed on as an overriding choice of law rule, it creates the possibility that this impasse can be overcome through giving the parties the power to determine which connection is given priority, with the great benefit of increasing consistent treatment of private legal relations across borders. This function of party autonomy is also arguably reflected in the limited choice offered to parties in this context – a choice of which objective criteria is determinative, rather than a free choice of law – as examined further below.

8.8.1 Succession

Where a person dies intestate an exercise of party autonomy in relation to succession issues is not likely, for rather obvious reasons. Where an individual with connections to more than one state makes a will, however, it may include a choice of law clause. The question arises therefore as to what effect that choice of law may have.

Under the common law traditionally a distinction is drawn between two issues.[151] First, the interpretation of the will, which is governed by the law intended by the testator. An express or potentially implied choice of law in the will is thus given effect in relation to questions of interpretation – a limited recognition of party autonomy. In the absence of any indication to the contrary the law of the testator's domicile at the date the will was made is presumed to be the law intended by the testator. Despite the language of intention, this is in reality an objective choice of law rule rather than a

---

[150] For background see Van Loon (2016), p.31ff; Basedow (2013a), p.246ff; Mills (2006a), pp.39–41.
[151] See generally e.g. *Dellar* v. *Zivy* [2007] EWHC 2266 (Ch).

subjective exercise of party autonomy, as this is an intention imputed to the testator on the basis of an objective connection, albeit one they may have freely determined.[152]

The second and more significant issue is the material validity of the will – whether it distributes the testator's property in a manner that is permissible under law. Here, under the common law, a distinction is drawn between the testator's immovable property, succession to which is governed exclusively by the *lex situs* of the property, and the testator's other property, which is governed by the law of the testator's domicile at the date of their death. Under this rule, no exercise of party autonomy is permissible (again, even if that domicile might be freely chosen).[153]

Choice of law rules in succession have recently been harmonised in the European Union through the Succession Regulation that came into effect in 2015, although the United Kingdom has opted out and remains subject to the common law rules. The Regulation provides that succession issues will generally be governed by the law of the habitual residence of the deceased at the time of death,[154] but this is subject to a limited exercise of party autonomy. Article 22(1) provides that "A person may choose as the law to govern his succession as a whole the law of the State whose nationality he possesses at the time of making the choice or at the time of death", and that a person with multiple nationalities may choose the law of any one of them. The choice may be made expressly in a will or may be implicit in its terms.[155] The law determined through these choice of law rules governs a wide range of issues (set out in Article 24), including questions of whether the distribution of property is legally permissible. The effect is therefore that a limited form of party autonomy is provided for the law of succession (as indeed existed under the national law of some European states prior to harmonisation,[156] and under Article 5 of the Hague Convention on the Law Applicable to Succession to the Estates of Deceased Persons 1989 (not in force)).[157] A person may choose the law of their nationality (or any of their nationalities) in preference to the law of their habitual residence, to govern not only issues of interpretation of their will but also its effectiveness, with the exception of certain rules regarding immovable property.[158]

---

[152] See Section 1.3.1

[153] See Section 1.3.1.

[154] Article 21(1).

[155] Article 22(2).

[156] See further e.g. Dutta (2009), p.569.

[157] www.hcch.net/en/instruments/conventions/full-text/?cid=62.

[158] Article 30.

It is notable that an entirely free choice is not possible, only the choice of a law with an objective connection to the testator (based on nationality) – thus party autonomy is used to select between different laws with strong objective connections, rather than establishing a connection in its own right.[159] If a choice of law is made by the testator under the Succession Regulation, this also creates the possibility that two disputing parties may agree that the courts whose law applies will have jurisdiction over disputes arising concerning the estate – the choice of law by the testator may thus have an indirect potential effect on a possible future choice of forum by other parties.[160]

8.8.2 Divorce

In 2010, an EU Regulation was adopted dealing with questions of the law applicable to divorce and legal separation, known as the Rome III Regulation.[161] As an 'enhanced cooperation' measure, it is only binding on those Member States that have agreed to it, which does not include the United Kingdom.[162]

Article 5 of the Rome III Regulation provides as follows:

> (1) The spouses may agree to designate the law applicable to divorce and legal separation provided that it is one of the following laws:
>   (a) the law of the State where the spouses are habitually resident at the time the agreement is concluded; or
>   (b) the law of the State where the spouses were last habitually resident, in so far as one of them still resides there at the time the agreement is concluded; or
>   (c) the law of the State of nationality of either spouse at the time the agreement is concluded; or
>   (d) the law of the forum.

Such an agreement may be concluded at any time, including (if the law of the forum permits) during the course of the proceedings.[163] The effect of this rule is to permit once again a limited form of party autonomy, under which the spouses are able to determine themselves which connecting factor – habitual residence or nationality – is relied on as the most

---

[159] See further Section 7.3.
[160] Article 5.
[161] See discussion in Kruger (2014); Boele-Woelki (2010).
[162] The adoption of party autonomy under the Rome III Regulation was a significant factor in the United Kingdom's decision not to opt in to the regulation – see further Carruthers (2012), p.889.
[163] Article 5(2) and (3).

significant to determine the legal regime governing the terms of their divorce or legal separation. Once again, these choices may be viewed as giving parties greater freedom over how the law views their identity – allowing an individual (or couple) to self-identify as part of a particular legal order for a particular purpose. The possibility to choose the law of the forum is also provided, but in the European Union the forum would be determined by application of the Brussels II *bis* Regulation, which does not itself allow for a free choice of court but looks (in general terms) to the habitual residence of one or both parties.[164] This rule, therefore, does not greatly extend the possible scope of party autonomy. An effective choice of forum law may, in any case, also be possible under some legal systems as a procedural consequence of a failure for either party to adduce evidence of foreign law.[165]

The Recitals to the Rome III Regulation offer some interesting comments on its provisions. First, it may be noted that Recital 15 offers the following justification for the adoption of party autonomy in this field:

> (15) Increasing the mobility of citizens calls for more flexibility and greater legal certainty. In order to achieve that objective, this Regulation should enhance the parties' autonomy in the areas of divorce and legal separation by giving them a limited possibility to choose the law applicable to their divorce or legal separation.

The claim is thus made that party autonomy enhances both flexibility and certainty. While this may be debatable, it is clear that it suggests that the justification for party autonomy is the ability for the parties themselves to resolve difficult choice of law questions – the private consequentialist approach examined in Section 2.3.1. This in turn is viewed as serving a greater public consequentialist goal, the increased mobility of citizens, which is both cause and intended effect of the adoption of these rules.

Second, Recitals 16 and 18 offers some notable caution in regard to the adoption of party autonomy. Recital 16 provides that "The law chosen by the spouses must be consonant with the fundamental rights recognised by the Treaties and the Charter of Fundamental Rights of the European Union", essentially codifying a rule of public policy as a constraint on party autonomy (discussed further in Section 9.4.2). Recital 18 more broadly provides that:

> (18) The informed choice of both spouses is a basic principle of this Regulation. Each spouse should know exactly what are the legal and social

---

[164] Article 3(1).
[165] See Section 7.5.

implications of the choice of applicable law. The possibility of choosing the applicable law by common agreement should be without prejudice to the rights of, and equal opportunities for, the two spouses. Hence judges in the participating Member States should be aware of the importance of an informed choice on the part of the two spouses concerning the legal implications of the choice-of-law agreement concluded.

Although the implications of this Recital are not clear, it suggests that choice of law agreements under the Regulation should be closely scrutinised by courts, to ensure fairness between the parties. This invites the courts to invalidate a choice that is to the advantage of one of the parties as a consequence of the other party not being fully informed. It is thus addressed to the concern as to whether there is a genuine agreement reached between the two parties, arguably again reflecting a consequentialist approach to party autonomy, as noted in Section 2.4.1.

The influence of party autonomy in the context of divorce is not unique to the European Union. It may also be noted, for example, that Article 26 of the Law of the People's Republic of China on the Laws Applicable to Foreign-related Civil Relations (2010)[166] provides that "In respect of consented divorce, the parties may by agreement choose to apply the law of a party's habitual residence or nationality", once again giving the parties a limited freedom to determine which legal regime governs their relationship.

8.8.3   Matrimonial Property

The Hague Convention on the Law Applicable to Matrimonial Property Regimes 1978,[167] while attracting few ratifications,[168] is a notable early example of the movement of party autonomy into the realm of family law. The choice of the parties is limited by a requirement that there be a substantive connection with the chosen law, which (as already noted above) is typical of the adoption of party autonomy in the field of family law. Article 3 of the Convention provides a substantive but also significantly limited choice of law for the parties before their marriage, as follows:

> The matrimonial property regime is governed by the internal law designated by the spouses before marriage.

---

[166] See discussion in Huo (2011), p.1080.
[167] See www.hcch.net/en/instruments/conventions/full-text/?cid=87.
[168] The Convention has only three contracting parties – see www.hcch.net/en/instruments/conventions/status-table/?cid=87.

The spouses may designate only one of the following laws –

(1) the law of any State of which either spouse is a national at the time of designation;
(2) the law of the State in which either spouse has his habitual residence at the time of designation;
(3) the law of the first State where one of the spouses establishes a new habitual residence after marriage.

The law thus designated applies to the whole of their property.

Nonetheless, the spouses, whether or not they have designated a law under the previous paragraphs, may designate with respect to all or some of the immovables, the law of the place where these immovables are situated. They may also provide that any immovables which may subsequently be acquired shall be governed by the law of the place where such immovables are situated.

Article 6 of the Convention provides a similar range of options in relation to a choice made during the marriage.

This innovative recognition of party autonomy has been followed in the EU Matrimonial Property Regulation, adopted in 2016. This is again an 'enhanced cooperation' measure, only binding on those Member States that have agreed to it, which does not include the United Kingdom. Recital 45 to the Regulation notes that:

> To facilitate to spouses the management of their property, this Regulation should authorise them to choose the law applicable to their matrimonial property regime, regardless of the nature or location of the property, among the laws with which they have close links because of habitual residence or their nationality. This choice may be made at any moment, before the marriage, at the time of conclusion of the marriage or during the course of the marriage.

The Regulation includes (in Article 22(1)) the possibility for spouses (or prospective spouses) to agree on a law to govern their matrimonial property regime, but only if it is either:

(a) the law of the State where the spouses or future spouses, or one of them, is habitually resident at the time the agreement is concluded, or
(b) the law of a State of nationality of either spouse or future spouse at the time the agreement is concluded.

Such an agreement only has prospective effect unless specifically agreed otherwise, and in any case this will not affect the rights of third parties.[169]

---

[169] Article 22(2) and (3).

The Regulation also sets out rules governing questions of formal and material validity for a choice of law agreement.[170] It is again notable that party autonomy in this area has also been recognised in the Law of the People's Republic of China on the Laws Applicable to Foreign-related Civil Relations (2010), Article 24 of which provides that "In respect of spousal property, the parties may by agreement choose to apply the law of a party's habitual residence or nationality, or the law of the place where the main property locates".

8.8.4   Maintenance

A further influence of party autonomy in the area of family law may be found in the EU Maintenance Regulation, which is modelled on the Hague Maintenance Convention 2007 (to which the EU is a party). A limited party autonomy in relation to choice of court agreements is recognised in Article 4 of the Maintenance Regulation (the choice may only be in favour of a court with an objective connection to the parties or their relationship), but is not effective with regard to disputes concerning maintenance obligations owed to a child under the age of eighteen. On questions of applicable law, the Maintenance Regulation directs the courts of EU Member States to apply the choice of law rules in the Hague Maintenance Protocol 2007 (to which the EU is also a party), for states bound by that protocol (which is all EU Member States except Denmark and the United Kingdom). The Protocol permits, in Article 8(1), a limited choice of law in relation to maintenance obligations, between:

(a) the law of any State of which either party is a national at the time of the designation;

(b) the law of the State of the habitual residence of either party at the time of designation;

(c) the law designated by the parties as applicable, or the law in fact applied, to their property regime;

(d) the law designated by the parties as applicable, or the law in fact applied, to their divorce or legal separation.

Under Article 9, common law systems may elect to apply 'domicile' instead of 'nationality' as the test for the purposes of Article 8(1)(a). There are significant constraints on the choice of the parties. For example, a choice may

---

[170] Articles 23 and 24.

not be made in respect of maintenance obligations owed towards a child or impaired adult.[171] Article 8(5) also provides more generally that:

> Unless at the time of the designation the parties were fully informed and aware of the consequences of their designation, the law designated by the parties shall not apply where the application of that law would lead to manifestly unfair or unreasonable consequences for any of the parties.

The rule thus requires the courts to scrutinise the fairness of the process under which a party agrees to a particular governing law, to ensure that the choose is indeed a genuine exercise of party autonomy.[172]

8.9   Conclusions

Party autonomy in choice of law has undoubtedly had its greatest influence in contract. However, parties may also intend to determine the law for non-contractual disputes that arise between them – whether they have done so may present a difficult question of interpretation of their choice of law agreement. If the parties do indeed seek to make such a choice, the question then arises whether the various non-contractual choice of law rules will give it effect. Although the influence of party autonomy in non-contractual matters has traditionally been very limited, it has clearly increased, in two ways. First, in some legal systems party autonomy has been recognised as having a direct effect for some non-contractual claims, although it may be subject to particular constraints (for example, permitting only retrospective choices, or limiting party autonomy to torts between parties pursuing a commercial activity). A choice of law by the parties in a voluntary trust is also frequently given direct effect. Second, in other contexts a choice of law by the parties may be given an indirect effect, influencing or determining the law applicable to a non-contractual dispute. For example, a choice of law in a contract from which a tort has arisen may affect the law governing the tort. A choice of law for a contract or tort may similarly affect equitable claims, claims in unjust enrichment, or claims for involuntary trusts that arise from the contract or tort. While party autonomy has traditionally had a limited affect in respect of property claims, the Second Restatement approach in the United States is notably more open to the influence of party choices, and in the European

---

[171] Article 8(3).
[172] See Section 2.4.1.

Union some effect is established through the characterisation of certain property disputes as contractual (and therefore subject to party choices). Finally, this chapter has noted a number of innovative ways in which party autonomy has had an influence in choice of law in relation to questions of succession and family law, generally as a means of allowing the parties to select themselves which objective connection determines the applicable law. While overall a trend towards an expanded recognition of party autonomy in choice of law may be identified, there is a notable variety of forms in which it emerges and restrictions to which it may be subject, both in terms of the different non-contractual causes of action, and in the examined legal systems and international codifications.

9

Limits on Party Autonomy in Choice of Law

9.1 Introduction

This chapter continues the analysis of party autonomy in choice of law, examining the various general limitations that restrict the ability of the parties to choose the governing law for their legal relations. Four main issues are examined. First, in Section 9.2, rules that limit or exclude a choice of law by the parties based on the subject matter of the contract or the characteristics of the contracting parties, such as for consumer or employment contracts. Second, in Section 9.3, restrictions which may apply based on the need for the contract to have a cross-border element – whether a choice of foreign law may be made for a purely domestic contract between local parties. Third, in Section 9.4.1, the possibility that mandatory rules, either those of the forum or of a foreign state, may partially or entirely override the law chosen by the parties. Fourth, in Section 9.4.2, the possibility that the law chosen by the parties may be excluded because of the application of forum public policy. Formality restrictions on choice of law agreements are noted in Section 7.2 – in practice these are much rarer than the formality restrictions on choice of court agreements examined in Section 5.2.

Although not examined in detail in this chapter, it may be noted that other constraints on party autonomy based on the good faith (or *bona fides*) of a choice of law have at times been suggested. As discussed in Sections 7.2 and 7.3, for example, some common law authority appears to suggest that only a *bona fide* choice of law by the parties will be respected,[1] and some Canadian courts have interpreted this as a potentially significant constraint on the exercise of party autonomy. Similarly, in the Montevideo Convention 1979 (the Inter-American Convention on General Rules of Private International Law), Article 11 provides that "The law of a State Party shall not be applied as foreign law when the basic principles of the

---

[1] *Vita Food Products Inc* v. *Unus Shipping Co.* [1939] AC 237.

law of another State Party have been fraudulently evaded".[2] In French law, the doctrine of *fraude à la loi* (discussed in Section 7.3.1) serves a similar purpose (as does the equivalent doctrine in many other civil law systems), seeking to invalidate a choice that has been made purely for the purpose of avoiding the objectively applicable law.[3] These approaches evidently involve second-guessing the exercise of party autonomy in choice of law, with the court reviewing whether the parties had exercised their autonomy for a proper purpose. In general, however, most private international law rules do not inquire into whether there are good reasons why a particular law may have been chosen – this is certainly the case with the rules which are the main focus of this comparative study, except where noted below. However, rules of private international law may nevertheless constrain either the choice or the effectiveness of the choice using one or more of the techniques discussed in this chapter – subject-matter or party restrictions on choice of law, constraints on the availability of choice in purely domestic contracts, and the application of mandatory rules or public policy.

9.2   Subject-Matter or Party Restrictions

As in the context of jurisdiction, examined in Section 5.5, the autonomy of the parties in choice of law is frequently restricted where the subject matter of the contract or the characteristics of the parties suggest an inequality that could leave a weaker party vulnerable to having a disadvantageous choice imposed upon it. Obvious examples of these types of contracts are consumer or employment contracts, in which there would be a risk that the weaker party might agree on a governing law under which their legal rights may be restricted.[4] Such a choice would neither be a true agreement, nor would it necessarily select the most appropriate law for the legal relationship between the parties, and thus (as noted in Section 2.4.1) the various justifications for party autonomy would not support giving it effect.

A measure to offer additional protection to weaker parties in the choice of law context might take a variety of forms. In some cases those forms of protection accept the validity of a choice of law by the parties, but seek to limit its potentially harmful consequences. Statutes providing for

[2]   Available at www.oas.org/juridico/english/treaties/b-45.html.
[3]   See e.g. discussion in Pertegás and Marshall (2014), p.991ff; see generally Parra-Aranguren (1988), p.102ff; Audit (1974).
[4]   For further comparative analysis of the justifications and techniques for restricting party autonomy in choice of law, see Rühl (2011); Symeonides (2014), p.125ff; Mahmoud (2005); Nygh (1999), p.139ff.

consumer or employee rights may, for example, be given mandatory effect, so that they are applicable even if there is a choice of foreign law (as discussed further in Section 9.4.1). Alternatively, if a foreign law is chosen under which the weaker party has very limited rights, that substantive law might be viewed as contrary to forum public policy (as discussed further in Section 9.4.2). In other cases, examined in this section, the protection of weaker parties involves a more direct restriction on party autonomy itself – this could comprise giving the parties a more limited choice of law, precluding a possible choice of law altogether, or scrutinising closely the fairness of a particular choice of law in a given case.

9.2.1   International Codifications

The concerns raised by party autonomy in certain contexts of bargaining inequality are widely recognised. Consumer and employment contracts were, for example, excluded under Article 1(2) of the Basel Principles (1991), a soft law instrument adopted by the International Law Association, although curiously no such exclusion was adopted as part of the Mexico City Convention 1994. Consumer and employment contracts are however excluded from the scope of the Hague Principles on Choice of Law in International Commercial Contracts 2015 under Article 1(1), again reflecting the controversy of applying party autonomy in this context, at least in an unrestricted manner.

Although only consumer and employment contracts are specifically excluded from the Hague Principles, the scope of the Principles is more broadly limited (also in Article 1(1)) to contracts "where each party is acting in the exercise of its trade or profession", and thus the Principles also do not purport to apply to contracts between non-commercial private parties (for example, a private sale of second hand goods through an online auction site). The concern in this context is evidently not with the relative strength of the parties, but rather their lack of sophistication and therefore uncertainty about whether they are capable of making an informed choice of law. The effect of the exclusion of contracts between non-commercial parties is of course not to preclude party autonomy for such contracts but only to preclude the application of the Hague Principles – other rules of law would be left to determine whether party autonomy applies, and if so how it is constrained. It is notable, however, that there is no restriction on party autonomy for contracts between non-commercial private parties under many national choice of law rules, such as under the Rome I Regulation.

9.2.2   EU Law – Rome I Regulation

In the European Union, the issue of protecting weaker parties arises most evidently in the Rome I Regulation, in the context of choice of law in contract. Under the Regulation, special choice of law rules affecting party autonomy are set out for contracts of carriage of passengers (Article 5(2)), consumer contracts (Article 6), insurance contracts (Article 7), and individual employment contracts (Article 8). The approach taken to limiting party autonomy is, however, different in these different contexts.

9.2.2.1   Carriage of Passengers and Insurance[5]

For contracts for the carriage of passengers, for example, a choice of law is permitted, but only if it is one of a number of specified laws (in Article 5(2)) – the law of the habitual residence of either party, the carrier's place of central administration, or the place of departure or destination. Party autonomy is not precluded as such, but (exceptionally in the Rome I Regulation) an objective connection between the chosen law and the parties or the contract is required. A similar approach is adopted for insurance contracts – except for those covering 'large risks', for which (under Article 7(2)) party autonomy is not restricted.[6] For other insurance contracts a limited list of laws which may be chosen by the parties is provided in Article 7(3), including (a) the law of any Member State in which the risk is situated at the time of the conclusion of the contract, (b) the law of the policy holder's habitual residence, and (passing over (c) and (d) for present purposes) (e) a more complex rule for cross-border commercial or professional insurance essentially permitting a choice of the place of any risk or of the policy holder's habitual residence. Article 7(3) further provides that "Where, in the cases set out in points (a), (b) or (e), the Member States referred to grant greater freedom of choice of the law applicable to the insurance contract, the parties may take advantage of that freedom". The meaning of this provision is rather obscure. The Rome I Regulation generally displaces any national choice of law rules within its scope, but this would make this section of Article 7(3) meaningless. What is presumably intended here is to permit Member States to continue to adopt their own national choice of law rules for these types of insurance contracts, provided they are compatible with the Rome I Regulation, accepting that this may allow for a broader choice of law than that specified under the

---

[5] See e.g. Nielsen (2009), p.107; Gruber (2009), p.118ff; Merrett (2009b); Heiss (2008), p.268ff.
[6] It is notable that these rules provide a different scope for party autonomy than those for choice of court agreements, as examined in Section 5.5.1.

Rome I Regulation. But it does not explain when these residual broader rules should apply. The "cases set out in points (a), (b) or (e)" are (essentially) situations where the parties have chosen the law of the location of the risk or of the policy holder's habitual residence. But obviously if the parties have chosen that law they cannot 'take advantage' of the freedom to choose any other law. Presumably (again) what is intended here is that the connecting factors identified in points (a), (b), and (e) have a double-role. First, they can be relied on by the parties to choose one of the designated laws. Second, the parties may instead rely on the national choice of law rules of the Member States designated under points (a), (b), or (e), to choose another system of law, if that choice is permitted under one of those national choice of law rules. The approach is thus only very mildly restrictive of party autonomy, as it still leaves it open for Member States to adopt much broader approaches to party autonomy under their national law that remain effective under the Rome I Regulation – but (in a curious double-autonomy or renvoi approach) only if the parties could choose the substantive law of that Member State.

9.2.2.2   Consumer and Employment Contracts

A different approach to restricting party autonomy applies in relation to consumer[7] and employment[8] contracts. Article 6(2) of the Regulation provides that the parties to a consumer contract have an unrestricted choice of the law to govern that contract, but goes on to state that "Such a choice may not, however, have the result of depriving the consumer of the protection afforded to him by provisions that cannot be derogated from by agreement by virtue of the law which, in the absence of choice, would have been applicable" (in the absence of the choice, as set out in Article 6(1)). Article 8(1) adopts a very similar approach in the context of employment contracts, permitting a free choice of law, but providing that the choice may not "have the result of depriving the employee of the protection afforded to him by provisions that cannot be derogated from by agreement under the law that, in the absence of choice, would have been applicable" (as set out in Article 8(2)–(4)). There are two ways of understanding these rules, to similar (but not identical) effect.

The first is that they mean that a choice of law which would lead to reduced protection for the consumer or employee – protection less than that to which they would be entitled under the law that would be

---

[7] See generally Garcimartin Alferez (2009); Hill (2008).
[8] See generally Grusic (2015), Chapter 5; Merrett (2011), Chapter 6.

applicable in the absence of choice – will be invalidated. The applicable law will instead be that determined by the rules in the absence of choice – party autonomy is excluded where its exercise would reduce the legal protection offered to the consumer or employee (but not where it would increase that protection).

The second way of understanding these provisions is that they do not in fact modify party autonomy itself, but rather modify the concept of what is considered to be a 'mandatory rule', applicable regardless of the choice by the parties.[9] Their effect is to transform 'mandatory' rules of contract law, which would ordinarily only be applicable if the contract is governed by the system of national law containing those rules, into rules which are 'mandatory' in a private international law sense (discussed further in Section 9.4) – applicable even though the contract is governed by a different system of law. Importantly, these rules are 'mandatory' even where they are not the law of the forum – any court hearing a consumer or employment dispute will be required to apply the non-derogable rules of the legal system designated in the absence of choice (essentially, the home law of the consumer or employee), in addition to the law actually chosen in the contract, to the extent that the non-derogable rules are more favourable to the consumer or employee than the chosen law.

Under both approaches, there is a burden on the court to determine which system of law is more advantageous to the consumer or employee. The key difference between these approaches is whether a choice of law that leads to the application of certain unfavourable rules is entirely or only partially invalidated. Under the first approach, a choice of New York law in a consumer contract with an English party may not deprive the party of their English consumer rights, and if it would lead to reduced rights, the contract should be considered instead to be governed by English law. Under the second, a choice of New York law in a consumer contract with an English party may not deprive the party of their English consumer rights, and if it would lead to reduced rights, the contract will remain governed by New York law but with the additional application of English consumer protection rules as mandatory rules.[10] The difference between these approaches may be significant, because the different governing laws

---

[9] This approach is arguably supported by C-29/10 *Koelzsch* v. *État du Grand Duchy of Luxemburg* [2011] ECR I-01595.

[10] See Rühl (2014), p.352 (describing this as a 'law mix' approach). It is unclear how the rule should be applied if the chosen law is favourable in some respects and unfavourable in others – the better approach is probably that a court should review the favourability of the law as a whole rather than combine the most favourable elements of different legal systems.

may affect other questions relating to the contract, such as its interpretation. Complicating matters somewhat, a choice of law clause in a consumer contract may also be scrutinised under general rules that invalidate unfair or misleading contractual terms, such as the Unfair Contract Terms Directive.[11] A clause which specified that the commercial party's home law applied exclusively may also therefore be invalidated because it misrepresents the consumer's rights[12] – thus, even if the second approach is correct, it may in practice lead to the same outcome as the first, depending on the drafting of the choice of law agreement. In any case, it is evident that the technique adopted to restrict choice of law party autonomy in the context of consumer and employment contracts is clearly distinct from that adopted for carriage of passengers and insurance contracts.

9.2.2.3 A Diversity of Techniques

It is not obvious why these two different techniques are both adopted in the Rome I Regulation. Both have the effect of providing additional protection for parties while partially preserving party autonomy, but do so in quite distinctive ways – limiting the scope of party autonomy, by constraining the choices available, or limiting the effect of party autonomy, by requiring the application of rules of law from a system other than that chosen by the parties, or potentially invalidating the parties' choice of law. Perhaps the variation reflects different conceptions of why party autonomy is constrained in these different contexts. In the context of consumer or employment contracts, the intent is to ensure that the weaker party gets the benefit of protective provisions of their home law, but otherwise to permit a free exercise of party autonomy to the maximum extent possible. In the context of transport or insurance contracts, the apparent intent is to ensure that the weaker party is not subject to a system of law chosen purely because it favours the other party, but rather one of the systems of law objectively connected to the contract – party autonomy is here arguably reconceived as a rule of priority between the different connected legal systems, rather than a matter of free choice. The different constraints on party autonomy thus notably appear to reflect different conceptions of its function, even in a single Regulation.

---

[11] Council Directive 93/13/EEC of 5 April 1993 on unfair terms in consumer contracts, OJ L 95/29.
[12] C-191/15 *Verein für Konsumenteninformation* v. *Amazon EU Sàrl* EU:C:2016:61; see further discussion in Mankowski (2017a).

9.2.3   EU Law – Rome II Regulation

In each of the examples above, it is striking that some form of party autonomy is preserved, even if it is constrained or its effect modified, suggesting
the centrality of the principle in the context of choice of law in contract.
Party autonomy is not quite as central in the context of non-contractual
obligations, as analysed in Chapter 8, and in the Rome II Regulation this is
reflected in the fact that the subject-matter restrictions on party autonomy
are stronger. Although a limited party autonomy is adopted as a general
principle in Article 14 of the Rome II Regulation (as discussed in Section
8.3), it is expressly excluded from effect in relation to unfair competition
claims (under Article 6(4)) and claims for infringement of intellectual
property rights (under Article 8(3)). Claims based on violations of privacy
or defamation are excluded from the Rome II Regulation altogether, and
thus whether party autonomy plays a role is left to national choice of law
rules, but in general these will not permit the parties a free choice of law.[13]
In these contexts, the exclusion of party autonomy is not motivated by the
desire to protect a weaker party, but rather by the degree of public interest involved in the type of dispute – it is state regulatory interests, rather
than private party interests, which are balanced against (and in these cases
trump) party autonomy. The concern is not that a free choice of law may
not be possible because of the inequality between the parties, but rather
than a free choice is undesirable because it is not only the interests of the
parties at stake in the dispute, as discussed in Section 2.4.3.

9.2.4   United States

As examined above, principally in Sections 7.2.4 and 8.3.5, there are a variety of approaches to choice of law in the United States. These approaches
are sometimes expressed in broad terms (such as government interest analysis, or comparative impairment), which (unlike the European approaches
discussed above) do not tend to include specific exceptions for contracts
involving weaker parties, such as consumer or employment contracts.[14] In
some cases weaker parties are protected using other techniques discussed
below, particularly mandatory rules. Another protective technique is to
require that choice of law clauses in contracts of adhesion (non-negotiated

---

[13] See for example the discussion of the common law choice of law rules in tort in Section 8.3.
[14] See generally Brand (2011); Healy (2009); Borchers (2008); Rühl (2007a).

contracts) be given sufficient prominence.[15] However, there are more general protections built into US contract law that may be relevant to the validity of a choice of law clause. Although the choice of law rules in the Second Restatement of Conflict of Laws do not expressly modify party autonomy to protect weaker parties or recognise public interests for particular types of contracts,[16] choice of law clauses may nevertheless be invalidated in various circumstances. As explained in comment (b) to section 187:[17]

> A factor which the forum may consider is whether the choice-of-law provision is contained in an "adhesion" contract, namely one that is drafted unilaterally by the dominant party and then presented on a "take-it-or-leave-it" basis to the weaker party who has no real opportunity to bargain about its terms. Such contracts are usually prepared in printed form, and frequently at least some of their provisions are in extremely small print. Common examples are tickets of various kinds and insurance policies. Choice-of-law provisions contained in such contracts are usually respected. Nevertheless, the forum will scrutinize such contracts with care and will refuse to apply any choice-of-law provision they may contain if to do so would result in substantial injustice to the adherent.

The validity of a choice of law clause in (for example) a consumer or employment contract is thus not determined categorically, but rather as a matter of scrutiny of the fairness of the terms of each particular clause and the impact of the choice.[18] Particular weight may be given to the question of whether the system of law which is chosen has an interest in regulating the dispute or relationship – keeping in mind that in US choice of law scholarship, 'interest' may be interpreted either subjectively (a state has purported to pass a law regulating the relationship) or objectively (the relationship is connected to the state). Under section 187(2)(b) of the Second Restatement, for example, as discussed in Section 7.2.4, a choice of law (for an issue which the parties may not resolve by contract) may be invalidated if:

> application of the law of the chosen state would be contrary to a fundamental policy of a state which has a materially greater interest than the chosen state in the determination of the particular issue and which, under the rule

---

[15] See, for example, 2015 Oregon Revised Statutes, s.15.350(2): "The choice of law must be express or clearly demonstrated from the terms of the contract. In a standard-form contract drafted primarily by only one of the parties, any choice of law must be express and conspicuous."

[16] This extends, for example, to contracts concerning a transfer of interests in land (s.189) and contracts for life insurance (s.192).

[17] Section 187 is discussed in Section 7.2.4.

[18] See e.g. *Brown & Brown, Inc.* v. *Johnson*, 980 N.Y.S.2d 631 (N.Y.App.Div. 2014). See further e.g. Hay, Borchers, and Symeonides (2010), p.1105ff; Healy (2009); Rühl (2007a).

of § 188, would be the state of the applicable law in the absence of an effective choice of law by the parties.

A choice of law may thus not be permitted where the state whose law would apply in the absence of the choice has a greater interest in the determination of the particular issue and considers its law to be a matter of 'fundamental policy'. This comparison of interests may thus permit the court to invalidate a choice of law that would deprive a weaker party of the protections of their local law, thereby constraining party autonomy. Comment (g) to section 187 notes expressly that:

> Fulfillment of the parties' expectations is not the only value in contract law; regard must also be had for state interests and for state regulation. The chosen law should not be applied without regard for the interests of the state which would be the state of the applicable law with respect to the particular issue involved in the absence of an effective choice by the parties.

The comment further notes that "a fundamental policy may be embodied in a statute which makes one or more kinds of contracts illegal or which is designed to protect a person against the oppressive use of superior bargaining power", inviting use of this provision to invalidate choices of foreign law in consumer or employment contracts. In practice, it has been observed that:

> under Section 187 of the Restatement (Second), which is followed in most states, a choice-of-law clause will not be enforced if the chosen law contravenes a fundamental policy of a state that has a greater interest in applying its law and whose law would have been applicable in the absence of the clause. This exception is often invoked, and usually applied, in employment contract cases.[19]

This approach is evidently more flexible and adaptable than the approach under the Rome I Regulation. It may have the effect, for example, that choice of law clauses in contracts between large and small businesses are considered to be invalid, or even sometimes those between equal negotiating parties. The downside of this approach, however, is evidently its unpredictability, and the difficulty in determining whether a choice of law clause is likely to be held valid may encourage litigation and frustrate efforts to resolve disputes through more efficient settlements.

A notable exception to this general flexibility was (temporarily) adopted in 2001 revisions to the Uniform Commercial Code. As discussed in

---

[19] Symeonides (2013b), pp.242–3. See e.g. *Ruiz* v. *Affinity Logistics Corp.*, 667 F.3d 1318 (9th Cir. 2012); *Cardoni* v. *Prosperity Bank*, 805 F.3d 573 (5th Cir. 2015); *Hackney* v. *Lincoln National Fire Insurance Co.*, 657 F.Appx 563 (6th Cir. 2016).

Section 7.3.1, section 1-301(c) of the 2001 UCC provided a general rule that parties may choose the law applicable to their contractual relations, and dropped the traditional requirement that the law chosen must bear a 'reasonable relation' to the transaction. Under section 1-301(f), this freedom was limited in a manner very similar to that adopted under the Second Restatement:

> An agreement otherwise effective under subsection (c) is not effective to the extent that application of the law of the State or country designated would be contrary to a fundamental policy of the State or country whose law would govern in the absence of agreement under subsection (d).

As discussed in Section 7.3.1, the 2001 revisions to the UCC were not widely adopted in US states, and have since been withdrawn. However, it remains of interest that the possibility of an unrestricted choice under the 2001 revisions was counterbalanced by specific provision for consumer contracts in subsection (e), as follows:

> (e) If one of the parties to a transaction is a consumer, the following rules apply:
> (1) An agreement referred to in subsection (c) is not effective unless the transaction bears a reasonable relation to the State or country designated.
> (2) Application of the law of the State or country determined pursuant to subsection (c) or (d) may not deprive the consumer of the protection of any rule of law governing a matter within the scope of this section, which both is protective of consumers and may not be varied by agreement:
> (A) of the State or country in which the consumer principally resides, unless subparagraph (B) applies; or
> (B) if the transaction is a sale of goods, of the State or country in which the consumer both makes the contract and takes delivery of those goods, if such State or country is not the State or country in which the consumer principally resides.[20]

The effect of these provisions would be to constrain party choice in the context of consumer contracts, using a combination of techniques. First, the choice is limited to a system of law objectively connected to the transaction. Second, the consumer retains the benefit of the protective rules of law of either their place of residence or the place of the transaction, depending on the circumstances. The techniques adopted here are more similar to those adopted in the Rome I Regulation (discussed in Section 9.2.2) than those traditionally adopted as part of US law. As in the

---

[20] 2001 version of the UCC: no longer available online, but see Burge (2015); Graves (2005).

case of the Rome I Regulation equivalent, it is not clear whether the second part of this rule invalidates a choice of law which would deprive the consumer of the benefits of the law designated in s.1-301(e)(2), or whether the choice remains valid but is overridden by the protective provisions of that law. Although these UCC amendments were rejected, they remain a notable variation on the usual methodologies of consumer protection in relation to choice of law in the United States.

9.2.5   Common Law

Under common law choice of law rules, similarly to the general approach under US law, no specific provision is made for different categories of contracts. The acceptance of party autonomy in choice of law is thus, as a general matter, extended to contracts involving weaker parties, such as consumer or employment contracts. The primary protections offered to such parties are those found in mandatory statutes, a distinct technique of protection for weaker parties that is discussed further in Section 9.4.1. In addition or as an alternative technique, choice of law agreements in consumer contracts may also be invalidated under consumer protection law if they are unfair or unreasonable terms. This is a form of substantive review rather than a private international law constraint, similar to the US fairness review of choice of law agreements discussed above. Such rules of consumer protection law are mandatory rules that cannot themselves be evaded through a choice of foreign law. Australian courts have, for example, determined that a choice of law clause in a contract between an Australian consumer and a US company that purported to apply the law of Washington State was ineffective, because it was an invalid attempt to exclude the application of Australian consumer protection law.[21] Statements in the contract purporting to limit the company's liability were also found to be misleading and deceptive conduct, because they misrepresented the rights of the consumer under Australian law. As a further technique, specific choice of law rules for consumer contracts may also be adopted in common law systems, which can involve more direct constraints on party autonomy (rather than substantive review of the fairness of particular rules). One notable example of such a rule is in the Canadian Uniform Jurisdiction and Choice of Law Rules for Consumer Contracts

---

[21] *Australian Competition and Consumer Commission* v. *Valve Corporation (No. 3)* [2016] FCA 196; see Australian Consumer Law, s.276 (Schedule 2, Competition and Consumer Act 2010).

2003, which requires in section 7(1) that a choice of law agreement in a consumer contract be in writing – a rare example of a formality constraint for choice of law, which would thus also prevent the finding of an implied choice of law in consumer contracts.

Statutory rules in common law systems that preclude choices of foreign law are relatively uncommon outside of consumer law, but not unknown. One prominent Australian example is the Insurance Contracts Act 1984 (Cth), which precludes both any choice of foreign law (in section 8(2)) and foreign forum (in section 52) to resolve disputes arising under insurance policies covered by the Act.[22]

9.2.6 China

As examined in Section 7.2.5 and in various parts of Chapter 8, Chinese choice of law rules include broad support for party autonomy as a matter of general principle – undoubtedly a significant development in the internationalisation of party autonomy. These principles are, however, modified in two important ways.

The first is the familiar idea that party autonomy is limited for certain categories of contracts based on the protection of weaker parties. For example, in employment contracts party autonomy appears to be entirely precluded under Article 43 of the Law of the People's Republic of China on the Laws Applicable to Foreign-Related Civil Relations (2010).[23] More distinctively, Article 42 provides that:

> A consumer contract is governed by the law of the consumer's habitual residence. Where the consumer chooses the law of the place where the commodity or the service is provided, or where the business operator does not engage in any business activity in the habitual residence of the consumer, the law of the place where the commodity or service is provided shall be applied.[24]

The meaning of 'foreign-related' in this context is discussed in Section 9.3. This is a further and distinct technique to protect consumers from a choice of a disadvantageous foreign law. (A similar rule is adopted in Article 45 for product liability claims.)[25] The apparent implication of this rule is that party autonomy is generally excluded, however, the consumer is given a

---

[22] *Akai Pty Ltd v. People's Insurance Co. Ltd* (1996) 188 CLR 418.
[23] See Tang, Xiao and Huo (2016), p.236ff.
[24] See discussion in Tang, Xiao and Huo (2016), p.231ff; Liang (2012), p.98ff; Huo (2011), p.1087ff.
[25] See Tang, Xiao and Huo (2016), p.258ff.

limited unilateral choice of law – they may select between the law of their habitual residence or the law of the place of provision of the goods or services – provided the business operator does business in the place of habitual residence. Evidently the consumer is likely to choose the law that offers them greater protection. This form of limited unilateral party autonomy is comparable to the rule under Article 7 of the Rome II Regulation, dealing with environmental torts[26] – like that provision, it may probably be best understood not as motivated by the principle of party autonomy, but rather as a means of outsourcing to the claimant the cost of determining which of the potentially applicable laws is best for them to apply, but with the objective of maximising the protection of the interests of the claimant. It is not clear whether consumers are likely to be capable of making this determination, or whether consumer claims are likely to be sufficiently large to justify this 'cost'.

A second distinctive modification of party autonomy under Chinese law is the exclusion of a range of contracts based on their subject-matter connection with China.[27] Under Article 126 of the Chinese Contract Law, for example:

> Article 126 The parties to a foreign-related contract may choose those laws applicable to the settlement of contract disputes, unless stipulated otherwise by law ...
> For the contracts to be fulfilled in the territory of the People's Republic of China on Chinese-foreign equity joint ventures, on Chinese-foreign contractual joint ventures and on Chinese-foreign cooperation in exploring and exploiting natural resources, the laws of the People's Republic of China shall apply.[28]

This rule identifies three types of contracts for which a choice of foreign law is not permissible. In the Rules on 'Related Issues concerning the Application of Law in Hearing Foreign-Related Contractual Dispute Cases Related to Civil and Commercial Matters',[29] promulgated by the Supreme People's Court in 2007, Article 8 expands on this list as follows:

> The performance of any of the following contracts within the territory of the People's Republic of China shall be subject to the law of the People's Republic of China:

---

[26] See Section 8.3.4.
[27] See generally e.g. Tang, Xiao and Huo (2016), p.56ff; Liang (2012), p.88ff.
[28] Available in translation at www.npc.gov.cn/englishnpc/Law/2007-12/11/content_1383564.htm.
[29] Available in translation at www.fdi.gov.cn/1800000121_39_2045_0_7.html.

(1) Contract on a Chinese-foreign equity joint ventures;
(2) Contract on a Chinese-foreign contractual joint ventures;
(3) Contract on Chinese-foreign cooperation in the exploration or exploitation of natural resources;
(4) Contract on the transfer of shares in a Chinese-foreign equity joint venture, Chinese-foreign contractual joint venture or wholly foreign-funded enterprise;
(5) Contract on the operation by a foreign natural person, foreign legal person or any other foreign organization of a Chinese-foreign equity joint venture or a Chinese-foreign contractual joint venture established within the territory of the People's Republic of China;
(6) Contract on the purchase by a foreign natural person, foreign legal person or any other foreign organization of share equity held by a shareholder in a non-foreign-funded enterprise within the territory of the People's Republic of China;
(7) Contract on the subscription by a foreign natural person, foreign legal person or any other foreign organization to the increased registered capital of a non-foreign-funded limited liability or company limited by shares within the territory of the People's Republic of China;
(8) Contract on the purchase by a foreign natural person, foreign legal person or any other foreign organization of assets of a non-foreign-funded enterprise within the territory of the People's Republic of China; and
(9) Other contracts subject to the law of the People's Republic of China as prescribed by a law or administrative regulation of the People's Republic of China.

Article 2 of the Law of the People's Republic of China on the Laws Applicable to Foreign-Related Civil Relations (2010) provides that "Where other statutes have a special and different provision on the law applicable to a foreign-related civil relation, that provision shall be followed", preserving the above restrictions from the general rules of party autonomy adopted under the 2010 law. The restrictions on party autonomy imposed by these rules are evidently significant. They are also clearly not based on the idea that party autonomy would be undesirable for the parties in these cases – the concern is not that the parties would be unable to make a balanced or efficient choice, but that there are broader public interests that would not be sufficiently protected by that choice.[30] These constraints are thus perhaps more comparable to those under the Rome II Regulation rather than those in the Rome I Regulation (both as discussed above), although framed with a wider conception of national interest which substantially limits party autonomy.

[30] See further Section 2.4.3.

9.3   Choice of Foreign Law in 'Domestic' Cases

A recurring issue in delimiting the scope of party autonomy is the question of whether it requires that the relationship between the parties have an international element – whether it applies to purely domestic contracts.[31] Another way of formulating this issue is to ask whether a choice of foreign law is itself sufficient to 'internationalise' a contract otherwise connected entirely to one legal order. The issue is recurrent because the position taken on the point is likely to differ depending on the underlying theoretical approach that is adopted to party autonomy. On one view, if a contractual relationship is entirely connected to a single system of law, there is no need for rules of conflict of laws to apply at all, let alone to give a free choice to the parties to resolve the choice of law problem more appropriately or efficiently than through the adoption of an objective choice of law rule. On another view, if party autonomy permits parties to select a law based on its appropriateness for them, creating regulatory competition, or involves the exercise of an autonomy inherent in private parties, then there is little reason why it should be precluded merely because a given relationship is objectively entirely connected with a different legal order than the law selected by the parties.

This issue is evidently connected to the question, examined in Section 7.3, of whether the law chosen by the parties must have an objective connection to their relationship. If such a requirement is adopted, as is for example the case under the law of some US states, then the problem logically cannot arise. If a relationship is entirely connected to a single legal order, and a foreign system of law is chosen by the parties, that choice will be invalidated because it is not supported by any objective connection. For states that do not require an objective connection between the relationship and the chosen law, however, the question remains as to whether a choice should be available in the narrower situation of a relationship entirely internal to one legal order.

Under the Basel Principles (1991), this issue is not addressed directly, but purely domestic contractual relationships were probably not contemplated by the focus of the Principles on 'international contracts'. The Mexico City Convention 1994 addressed the point in Article 1, which provides as follows:

> This Convention shall determine the law applicable to international contracts.

---

[31]   See e.g. Albornoz and González Martín (2016), p.440ff; Symeonides (2014), p.116ff; Harris (2000), p.250ff; Nygh (1999), p.47ff.

> It shall be understood that a contract is international if the parties thereto have their habitual residence or establishments in different States Parties or if the contract has objective ties with more than one State Party.

Similarly, Article 1 of the Hague Principles on Choice of Law in International Commercial Contracts 2015 provides that:

(1) These Principles apply to choice of law in international contracts where each party is acting in the exercise of its trade or profession. They do not apply to consumer or employment contracts.

(2) For the purposes of these Principles, a contract is international unless each party has its establishment in the same State and the relationship of the parties and all other relevant elements, regardless of the chosen law, are connected only with that State.

The exclusion of purely 'domestic' contracts from these international codifications recognises that the question of party autonomy in this context is controversial. It does not, of course, preclude the operation of party autonomy, but merely leaves the point to national law. In some national systems, party autonomy does, however, appear to be precluded in this context. In the Second Restatement of Conflict of Laws, the commentary to section 187 (which, as analysed in Section 7.2.4 gives general effect to party autonomy) provides that:

> The rule of this Subsection applies only when two or more states have an interest in the determination of the particular issue. The rule does not apply when all contacts are located in a single state and when, as a consequence, there is only one interested state.[32]

Under Article 126 of the Chinese Contract Law,[33] similarly, the rules governing party autonomy apply only to 'foreign-related contracts'.[34] This requires that either a party (in respect of either their nationality or habitual residence), the performance of the contract, or some other relevant factor (such as the subject matter of the contract, or the place of contracting) be outside Mainland China; otherwise the contract is automatically governed by Chinese law. In relation to the place of contracting in particular, it is

---

[32] Second Restatement of Conflict of Laws, s.187, comment (d).

[33] Available in translation at www.npc.gov.cn/englishnpc/Law/2007-12/11/content_1383564.htm.

[34] See 'Interpretation on Certain Issues Concerning PRC Law on the Application of Laws to Foreign-Related Civil Relations', Supreme People's Court, Fa Shi [2012] No. 24, 28 December 2012, Art.1. These principles also apply in the context of jurisdiction, and have also been articulated in the Supreme People's Court 'Interpretation of Civil Procedure Law', Fa Shi [2015] No.5, Art.531. See also discussion in Liang (2012), p.86ff.

notable that a foreign element may not be created for the purpose of avoiding PRC Law.[35]

Under the common law, the question of whether a choice of foreign law is permissible where a contractual relationship is entirely connected with a single legal system does not appear to have been addressed directly. It might be argued, on the one hand, that because there is no developed exception to the principle of party autonomy in choice of law, it should also be applied in this context, or that the choice of foreign law itself internationalises the contract. On the other hand, it might be argued that choice of law rules are not even engaged if the relationship lacks a foreign element, as there is no applicable law problem to resolve, and domestic law should receive automatic application.

The situation is clearer under the Rome Convention 1980 and now Rome I Regulation and Rome II Regulation in the European Union. Article 3(3) of the Rome I Regulation (based closely on Article 3(3) of the Rome Convention,[36] and also mirrored in Article 14(3) of the Rome II Regulation) provides that:

> Where all other elements relevant to the situation at the time of the choice are located in a country other than the country whose law has been chosen, the choice of the parties shall not prejudice the application of provisions of the law of that other country which cannot be derogated from by agreement.

By implication, this provision establishes that the parties are able to make a choice of foreign law in a case that is entirely internal to one legal system. To put this another way, the choice of law itself internationalises the contract, bringing private international law into play.[37] The rule does, however, impose special limitations on the effectiveness of such a choice.

---

[35] 'Interpretation on Certain Issues Concerning PRC Law on the Application of Laws to Foreign-Related Civil Relations', Supreme People's Court, Fa Shi [2012] No. 24, 28 December 2012, Art.11.

[36] For background see the Giuliano-Lagarde Report, p.18. Note that an equivalent protection of mandatory rules does not appear to arise under the Insolvency Regulation, EC Regulation 1346/2000, Art.13: see C-54/16 *Vinyls Italia SpA* v. *Mediterranea di Navigazione SpA* EU:C:2017:433.

[37] See e.g. Nygh (1999), p.53. Under the Rome Convention 1980, this was subject to an element of uncertainty because Article 1(1) specified that it applied to "any situation involving a choice between the laws of different countries", and the Giuliano-Lagarde Report suggested (at p.10) that this limited it to "situations which involve one or more elements foreign to the internal social system of a country". The Rome I Regulation removed the uncertainty by simply providing (in Article 1(1)) that it applies "in situations involving a conflict of laws".

A court applying these rules is expected to apply the provisions of the system of law objectively connected to the relationship "which cannot be derogated from by agreement". Importantly, this must be understood to be a broader category of rules than the mandatory rules that are applicable under Article 9(2) of the Rome I Regulation, as discussed in Section 9.4.1.[38] The reference here must be to rules of domestic private law – in particular, the rules that set the limits on contractual party autonomy.[39] An example might be the requirement for consideration under English contract law, which the parties evidently cannot overcome through a 'contractual' provision rejecting its application. A contract between two English parties to be performed entirely in England thus also cannot overcome this requirement merely by specifying that it is governed by French law – the choice will be effective for some matters (such as interpretation of the contract) but not for non-derogable matters including the rules of consideration. The effect of Article 3(3) is that a choice of foreign law in a purely domestic case is treated as if it were the incorporation by reference of all the rules of the system of foreign law as terms of the contract – such incorporation will only be effective to the extent that non-derogable rules of the otherwise applicable law permit.[40] Article 3(3) is also, unlike Article 9(2), not limited to the application of forum law – it thus may in some cases have an effect similar to but much broader than Article 9(3), also discussed in Section 9.4.1. A contractual relationship entirely internal to Australia, for example, might be subsequently litigated in France (because the defendant has moved to Paris) – the French courts would be obliged to apply non-derogable rules of Australian law under this provision, including the (Australian) common law rules governing consideration.[41]

One point that Article 3(3) leaves problematically unclear is the meaning of "elements relevant to the situation".[42] Although not unambiguous, the use of 'situation' suggests that this is a broader category of factors than those which might be relevant in determining which system of law has the closest connection to the contract under Article 4 of the

---

[38] This is supported by Recital (37) of the Rome I Regulation, which provides that "The concept of 'overriding mandatory provisions' should be distinguished from the expression 'provisions which cannot be derogated from by agreement' and should be construed more restrictively."

[39] See discussion in Section 1.3.5.

[40] On the distinction between incorporation by reference and choice of law, see Section 1.3.6.

[41] In the converse situation, of course, the Australian courts would not be bound by the Rome I Regulation – the effectiveness of this provision may thus depend on the limits on choice of forum, as discussed in Section 9.4.1.

[42] A similar issue arises in the context of jurisdiction – see Section 5.3.

Rome I Regulation.[43] However, if this is interpreted too broadly, it could undermine the effectiveness of this provision. Almost any contract has *some* international connection – negotiations carried out by email are, for example, likely to involve servers located around the world. While that is unlikely to be considered a sufficiently relevant element to internationalise the contract, other factors are likely to raise greater difficulties. The place of contracting might, for example, be considered relevant, and was indeed of great significance in some traditional choice of law methodologies,[44] but if this is sufficient it may allow parties to evade Article 3(3) too readily. (As noted above, Chinese law accepts that the place of contracting may make a contract 'foreign-related', but applies a good faith restriction – such an approach could also potentially be adopted in this context.) The same concern would arise if the use of a foreign language were considered sufficient to establish an international connection.[45] The use of a standard form international contract is a more difficult case – on the one hand, it clearly suggests an intention to avoid local mandatory rules, but on the other, national restrictions on party autonomy are precisely what is at stake in making this evaluation, and the use of an international form does not on its own suggest that the situation is substantively connected with another legal system.[46] It is not the intention of the parties that must be determined here, but the objective connections that their contract has with different legal orders. Another difficult issue may arise if the single contract at hand is purely domestic (aside from a choice of foreign law), but it is part of a series of related contracts with international links and common choice of law provisions. The English courts have determined that this should be sufficient to negate the application of Article 3(3), to ensure that all the related contracts are interpreted consistently.[47] An exclusive jurisdiction agreement in favour of a foreign court should not, however, be construed as an element relevant to the situation.[48] If a contract entirely internal to

---

[43] See e.g. *Banco Santander Totta SA* v. *Companhia Carris De Ferro De Lisboa SA* [2016] EWCA Civ 1267, [53].

[44] As discussed in Section 2.2.2.

[45] But see *Dexia Crediop SPA* v. *Comune Di Prato* [2017] EWCA Civ 428, [132].

[46] But see again *Dexia Crediop SPA* v. *Comune Di Prato* [2017] EWCA Civ 428, [132].

[47] *Dexia Crediop SPA* v. *Comune Di Prato* [2017] EWCA Civ 428, [134].

[48] This is also supported by Recital (15), which notes that

> Where a choice of law is made and all other elements relevant to the situation are located in a country other than the country whose law has been chosen, the choice of law should not prejudice the application of provisions of the law of that country which cannot be derogated from by agreement. This rule should apply whether or not the choice of law was accompanied by a choice of court or tribunal.

France has an English exclusive jurisdiction agreement and English choice of law clause, under Article 3(3) the English court may well be required to apply the non-derogable rules of French contract law.

The technique adopted here is very similar to that adopted under the Rome I Regulation in relation to consumer and employment contracts, as discussed in Section 9.2.2. It is notable that Article 3(3) (and similarly Article 14(3) in the Rome II Regulation) does not, however, appear designed primarily to constrain party autonomy to be protective of weaker parties – rather, it appears to seek a balance between the interests of private parties and the regulatory interests of states. The autonomy of the parties is constrained because it is considered that, in a purely domestic case, the state objectively connected has an overriding interest in the mandatory provisions of its contract law governing the relationship between the parties, although otherwise the parties remain free to make a choice of foreign law. The interpretation of Article 3(3) is thus not merely a technical question, but defines the scope of economic activity for which state regulation is given special protection. If Article 3(3) is interpreted strictly, with a wide range of international connecting factors disapplying its effect, this implies a shrinking domain of 'domestic' contracting, and a broadening domain of 'international' activity from which the state disclaims an overriding regulatory interest.[49]

In the Rome I Regulation, a further related provision has been added in Article 3(4) (mirrored again in the Rome II Regulation, in Article 14(4)), which provides that:

> Where all other elements relevant to the situation at the time of the choice are located in one or more Member States, the parties' choice of applicable law other than that of a Member State shall not prejudice the application of provisions of Community law, where appropriate as implemented in the Member State of the forum, which cannot be derogated from by agreement.

The effect of this is to replicate Article 3(3), but at the level of the European Union rather than individual states. If a relationship is entirely 'domestic' to the European Union, the parties are free to choose a non-EU Member State law, but this will be subject to non-derogable rules of EU law if the case is litigated in an EU Member State court.[50] Exactly what such rules may be is, however, unclear. It is, for example, notable that this provision

---

[49] Muir Watt (2010), p.261 (noting that Article 3(3) "presupposes a bright line separating the parochial, closely regulated world of the domestic ... economy, from the area of freedom where, beyond national ... frontiers, state policies relax their grip").

[50] The effectiveness of this approach will thus also be dependent on the limits on choice of forum, as discussed further in Section 9.4.1.

would not cover the category of EU mandatory rules identified in the *Ingmar*[51] decision of the CJEU, as discussed in Section 9.4.1, because in that case one of the parties was domiciled outside the European Union (and thus the case was covered only by Article 9(2)). The significance of Article 3(4) (and similarly Article 14(4) in the Rome II Regulation) is that it requires the application of EU rules that are not mandatory, but are non-derogable – a distinction that is unlikely to be clearly addressed in EU regulations themselves. This rule thus imposes a significant analytical burden on the courts, and may provide significant uncertainty for the parties.

9.4   Mandatory Rules and Public Policy

The operation of choice of law rules, outside those exceptional US approaches that favour the 'better law' or prioritise the application of forum law, is premised on the idea that the rules of private law of different national systems are equally legitimate. The determination of the applicable law may be based on the choice of the parties or on the objective connections between the relationship and different states, but in either case does not in general depend on a court evaluating the merits of the potentially applicable laws.[52] Choice of law rules start from the presumption that the rules of private law of each national legal order have equal status – they accept, in essence, an international pluralism of private law.[53] In some cases, however, this pluralism may come up against other national or even international values, and may be outweighed by those other values. It is an almost universally recognised feature of choice of law rules that they include two 'safety-nets' to the usual application of foreign law – mandatory rules and public policy – which are discussed in turn below.[54] These are limits on the choice of law process in general rather than specifically targeted constraints on party autonomy, but they also thereby serve as limits on the power of the parties to choose a particular law.

---

[51] C-381/98 *Ingmar GB Ltd* v. *Eaton Leonard Technologies Inc.* [2000] ECR I-9305.

[52] But note e.g. Section 9.2.2.2, under which the Rome I Regulation requires the courts to evaluate the relative merits of the chosen law and the law that would apply in the absence of choice in consumer and employment contracts.

[53] See generally Mills (2009a), Chapter 1.

[54] The impact of mandatory rules and public policy on the applicable law in arbitration is also discussed further in Chapters 6 and 10.

9.4.1 *Mandatory Rules*

Under almost all choice of law rules, 'mandatory' rules of national law may override the application of the law that is otherwise designated.[55] As discussed in Section 1.3.5, the rules under consideration in this context are not mandatory rules of contract law (which only apply if they are part of the governing law), but rather mandatory rules of private international law (which apply in addition to or instead of the governing law). The only exception is under some US choice of law approaches, which rely on other techniques (such as conducting an interest analysis) that already take into account the intent or policy of potentially applicable statutes in determining the governing law.[56] In more traditional approaches, private international law rules select the governing law (or allow the parties to do so) without requiring a court to consider the content of the potentially applicable laws, but then recognise that certain rules of law (typically statutes) may require application regardless of the law governing the dispute. As discussed above, under the Second Restatement of Conflict of Laws a somewhat hybridised approach is adopted, generally giving effect to party autonomy, but accepting that a choice of foreign law may be invalidated because it would be contrary to a fundamental policy of the state whose law would be applicable in the absence of that choice.[57] While mandatory rules are not specifically targeted at choices of foreign law, and may equally serve as a limit on the effect of objective choice of law rules, they thus frequently operate as a practical constraint on party autonomy.

Most commonly, mandatory rules involve the application of special provisions of the law of the forum, even when the substantive applicable law is foreign. Thus, in a dispute in the English courts, even if the parties have selected French law to govern their contract, and even if English choice of law rules validate that choice, the effect of that choice may be partially overridden by application of an English mandatory statute.

Determining whether a mandatory rule is applicable to the particular case, or whether it falls outside the territorial or other scope of the statute, may involve questions of statutory interpretation. However, this should be carefully distinguished from other questions of statutory interpretation that may arise in the choice of law process. In the context of employment

---

[55] See generally e.g. Nygh (1999), p.199ff.

[56] See Guedi (1991). But the practice of adopting mandatory rules continues in many US states – see Symeonides (2014), p.294ff; Symeonides (2017), p.26ff.

[57] For recent illustrative cases see e.g. Symeonides (2017), p.47ff; see also Zhang (2006a), p.533ff.

claims based on rights under UK statutes, courts in the UK have even gone so far as to ignore a choice of law analysis and focus entirely on the question of statutory interpretation,[58] but this approach is flawed. A full analysis should involve three distinct considerations.

First, determining the applicable law through choice of law rules, which may include the exercise of party autonomy. Second, if English law governs, determining whether a particular English statute applies to the case as part of that law, which may involve interpreting the scope of application of the statute or applying presumptions of statutory interpretation. The better view, however, is that this should not be approached as a general question of interpretative scope, but rather an inquiry to determine whether or not the statute is 'self-limiting' in its scope of application[59] – the statute should be presumed to apply to all cases governed by English law, unless the contrary is established as the legislative intention. In any case, this is the process of determining the *content* of the applicable law, rather than the choice of law process or the operation of mandatory rules.[60] (The same process should obviously be applied in determining the content of foreign law.) Third, if foreign law governs, determining whether an English statute nevertheless applies as a mandatory rule, which would again require interpreting its scope of application (as well as whether it has a mandatory status) – in this case, however, with a more traditional approach to statutory interpretation, including a focus on whether the statute is intended to have extraterritorial effect.

Under this analysis, the application of traditional conflict of laws rules may still require a secondary question of interpreting the scope of potentially applicable statutes, a technique more strongly associated with modern US approaches to choice of law (as discussed in Section 7.2.4), or the historical 'statutist' approach.[61] The UK employment cases noted above may perhaps best be interpreted as presuming that the relevant

---

[58] See e.g. *Lawson v. Serco* [2006] UKHL 3; *Ravat v. Halliburton* [2012] UKSC 1. For further discussion see e.g. Grusic (2015), Chapter 6; Grusic (2012).

[59] For US examples see e.g. *Red Lion Hotels Franchising, Inc. v. MAK, LLC*, 663 F.3d 1080 (9th Cir. 2011); *Taylor v. 1-800-Got-Junk?, LLC*, 387 Fed.Appx 727 (9th Cir. 2010); *Gravquick A/S v. Trimble Navigation International Ltd*, 323 F.3d 1219, 1233 (9th Cir. 2003).

[60] See further discussion in Nygh (1999), p.215ff; Lipstein (1977); Mann (1973); Morris (1946). Contrary to Nygh's view, if the choice of law agreement of the parties purports to *modify* the scope of application of a statute, this should be analysed as either incorporation by reference or a (generally impermissible) choice of non-state law – see further discussion in Section 10.1.

[61] For criticism of the relevance of statutory interpretation in choice of law, see e.g. Hook (2017); Bisping (2012).

statutes were *mandatory* forum rules, and therefore applicable regardless of whether English or foreign law governed, which left the question of statutory interpretation as determinative.

It is characteristic of the technique of applying mandatory rules that it does not invalidate the choice of foreign law (unlike some of the techniques discussed earlier in this chapter), but rather partially overrides its effects – it does not constrain the exercise of party autonomy, but rather its consequences. This possibility has been recognised in every international codification of choice of law, including Article 9 of the Basel Principles (1991), Article 11 of the Mexico City Convention 1994, and Article 11 of the Hague Principles on Choice of Law in International Commercial Contracts 2015.[62] It is also widely recognised in national and supranational choice of law codifications, including Article 9(2) of the Rome I Regulation,[63] Article 16 of the Rome II Regulation,[64] and Article 4 of the Law of the People's Republic of China on the Laws Applicable to Foreign-Related Civil Relations (2010),[65] as well as under the common law.[66] The CJEU has suggested that, as a departure from the general rule of party autonomy, the provisions relating to mandatory rules in the Rome I Regulation should be interpreted restrictively.[67] There is, however, an argument that this wrongly characterises Article 9(2) as an 'exception'. It might be said instead that the Rome I Regulation includes a balance of competing policies, recognising both party autonomy and state regulatory interests, and no presumption should arise as to how that balance should be resolved. It is notable that in support of its approach the CJEU has

---

[62] "These Principles shall not prevent a court from applying overriding mandatory provisions of the law of the forum which apply irrespective of the law chosen by the parties." See Dickinson (2017b).

[63] "Nothing in this Regulation shall restrict the application of the overriding mandatory provisions of the law of the forum."

[64] "Nothing in this Regulation shall restrict the application of the provisions of the law of the forum in a situation where they are mandatory irrespective of the law otherwise applicable to the non-contractual obligation."

[65] "Where a mandatory provision of the law of the People's Republic of China ('PRC') exists with respect to a foreign-related civil relation, that mandatory provision shall be applied directly." See also 'Interpretation on Certain Issues Concerning PRC Law on the Application of Laws to Foreign-Related Civil Relations', Supreme People's Court, Fa Shi [2012] No. 24, 28 December 2012, Art.10. See discussion in Tang, Xiao and Huo (2016), p.240ff; Liang (2012); Huo (2011).

[66] See e.g. Keyes (2008); Hartley (1997).

[67] C-135/15 *Republik Griechenland (the Hellenic Republic)* v. *Gregorios Nikiforidis*, EU:C:2016:774; C-184/12 *United Antwerp Maritime Agencies (Unamar) NV* v. *Navigation Maritime Bulgare*, EU:C:2013:663. See also Nygh (1999), pp.211–2.

referred to party autonomy as "the cornerstone" of the Rome Convention 1980 and now Rome I Regulation,[68] although in fact Recital (11) to the Rome I Regulation observes only that party autonomy is "one of the cornerstones of the system of conflict-of-law rules in matters of contractual obligations". Nevertheless, the approach of the CJEU evidently places great significance on the adoption of party autonomy as the key principle of the Rome I Regulation.

In EU Member States, the source of mandatory rules may come not only from national law, but also from EU law.[69] In the *Ingmar* case,[70] a commercial agency agreement was entered into between a Californian company and a UK-based agent, for work to be carried out in the United Kingdom. A dispute arose in the English courts. The contract contained a choice of law clause in favour of Californian law which was valid and effective under the Rome I Regulation. The Court of Justice determined that the provisions of UK law implementing the EU Directive on commercial agents[71] must nevertheless be applied as a mandatory rule – the choice of law by the parties was not invalidated, but it was not effective to evade the application of the Directive.[72] It may be queried whether, in the eyes of the CJEU, the 'cornerstone' of party autonomy remains as secure where competing provisions of EU law are concerned, rather than those of national law. The existence of EU mandatory rules may also, however, inhibit a Member State from adopting mandatory rules that go beyond EU requirements. If the parties to a commercial agency contract to be performed in one Member State choose for their contract to be governed by the law of another Member State which implements EU law but offers less protection to commercial agents, the choice of the parties should ordinarily be respected.[73] A similar approach has been adopted under

---

[68] C-184/12 *United Antwerp Maritime Agencies (Unamar) NV* v. *Navigation Maritime Bulgare* EU:C:2013:663, [49].

[69] This is distinct from the effect of Article 3(4), which requires all 'elements relevant to the situation' to be in the European Union, and leads to the application of a broader category of rules, as discussed in Section 9.3.

[70] C-381/98 *Ingmar GB Ltd* v. *Eaton Leonard Technologies Inc.* [2000] ECR I-9305. See e.g. Verhagen (2002).

[71] Council Directive 86/653/EEC of 18 December 1986 on the coordination of the laws of the Member States relating to self-employed commercial agents, OJ 1986 L 382/17.

[72] See also *Fern Computer Consultancy Ltd* v. *Intergraph Cadworx & Analysis Solutions Inc.* [2014] EWHC 2908 (Ch), generally following *Accentuate Ltd* v. *ASIGRA Inc.* [2009] EWHC 2655 (QB) but clarifying that the EU law does not invalidate the choice of law clause, only overrides its effect.

[73] C-184/12 *United Antwerp Maritime Agencies (Unamar) NV* v. *Navigation Maritime Bulgare* EU:C:2013:663. See Rühl (2016).

certain provisions of EU consumer protection law. In the United Kingdom, for example, Article 32 of the Consumer Rights Act 2015 (which implements EU law in this respect),[74] provides that:

(1) If –
  (a) the law of a country or territory other than an EEA State is chosen by the parties to be applicable to a sales contract, but
  (b) the sales contract has a close connection with the United Kingdom,

this Chapter, except the provisions in subsection (2), applies despite that choice.

If the application of mandatory rules is restricted to the rules of the forum, this technique of constraining party autonomy may only be of limited effect. This is because its effectiveness will depend on the forum in which the litigation is being conducted. Whether this technique is able to prevent parties from contracting out of mandatory rules may thus be dependent on whether a choice of forum by the parties is considered to be effective.[75] For example, if in a commercial contract closely connected to England the parties have entered into an exclusive choice of court agreement in favour of the French courts, as well as a choice of law agreement in favour of French law, the English courts are highly unlikely to hear the case, and the French courts will not apply English mandatory rules under Article 9(2) of the Rome I Regulation, as this is limited to the application of mandatory rules of the forum. It should not be presumed that a judgment would need to come back to the English courts for enforcement, nor that the English courts would necessarily be willing or able to rely on the non-application of English mandatory rules as a defence against enforcement of the judgment.[76] The constraint on party autonomy offered by mandatory rules under this approach is thus to some extent dependent on whether the parties are permitted a free choice of forum – for mandatory rules on consumer protection to be effective, for example, it will be necessary to have both a limited choice of forum (ensuring the litigation takes place in the consumer's home court)[77] as well as provision for the application of mandatory rules. There is otherwise a risk that the exercise of party autonomy in choice of forum and choice of law, in conjunction, will undermine the

---

[74] Directive 1999/44/EC of the European Parliament and of the Council of 25 May 1999 on certain aspects of the sale of consumer goods and associated guarantees, OJ L 171/12, Art.7(2).
[75] See discussion in Muir Watt (2010), p.267ff; Keyes (2008), p.28ff.
[76] For a US example, see *Richards* v. *Lloyd's of London*, 135 F.3d 1289 (9th Cir. 1998). See further discussion in Muir Watt (2003).
[77] See e.g. Section 5.4.

constraints on party autonomy in choice of law. The European Parliament has, for example, raised the concern that "the promotion by the Hague Conference of party autonomy in contractual relations worldwide has such serious implications from the point of view of the evasion of mandatory rules as to warrant its being debated and reflected upon in democratic fora worldwide".[78]

In this context, the approach under Australian law to the question of whether Australian state or federal court proceedings should be stayed in light of a foreign exclusive choice of court agreement (as discussed previously in Section 3.4.3) is notable. Australian courts have refused to stay proceedings despite a foreign exclusive jurisdiction agreement in some cases in which it is established that the foreign court would not recognise rights under Australian law – such as where the cause of action is based on an Australian statute that would not be applied by the foreign court.[79] Australian practice on this point has been viewed critically by some commentators,[80] and there is at best mixed support for this approach in the United States,[81] but it should perhaps only be criticised to the extent that the Australian statutes concerned are not categorised as mandatory rules. If they are merely rules of private law, it is not consistent with the basic approach of private international law for a choice of a foreign forum to be invalidated to ensure their application. If, however, they are mandatory rules in the private international law sense, intending to insist on their application by Australian courts, then invalidating a foreign choice of court agreement may be necessary to ensure that they are not readily evaded through the combination of a choice of foreign law and foreign forum. This

---

[78] European Parliament resolution of 23 November 2010 on civil law, commercial law, family law, and private international law aspects of the Action Plan Implementing the Stockholm Programme (2010/2080(INI)), [38].

[79] See e.g. *Hume Computers Pty Ltd* v. *Exact International BV* [2006] FCA 1439; *Reinsurance Australia Corporation Ltd* v. *HIH Casualty & General Insurance Ltd (in Liquidation)* [2003] FCA 56; *Commonwealth Bank of Australia* v. *White* [1999] 2 VR 681. See also discussion in Mills (2017); Keyes (2009), p.199ff.

[80] See e.g. Garnett (2009), p.166.

[81] See e.g. *Lipcon* v. *Underwriters at Lloyd's, London*, 148 F.3d 1285, 1295 (11th Cir. 1998); *Estate of Myhra* v. *Royal Caribbean Cruises, Ltd*, 695 F.3d 1233 (11th Cir. 2012). But see however *Mitsubishi Motors Corp* v. *Soler Chrysler-Plymouth, Inc.*, 473 US 614, 637 n.19 (1985) ("in the event the choice-of-forum and choice-of-law clauses operated in tandem as a prospective waiver of a party's right to pursue statutory remedies for antitrust violations, we would have little hesitation in condemning the agreement as against public policy"); *AOL* v. *Superior Court (Mendoza)*, 90 Cal.App.4th 1 (2001); *Hall* v. *Superior Court (Imperial Petroleum, Inc)*, 150 Cal.App.3d 411 (1983). See discussion in Basedow (2013b); Force (2011); Lowenfeld (1994), p.283ff.

may then involve an inquiry into whether the choice of foreign courts and law was justifiable or merely an effort to evade those mandatory rules.[82] If understood in this narrow form, the Australian law approach could be viewed as an extension of the French law doctrine of *fraude à la loi* (and similar rules in other civil law jurisdictions) discussed in Sections 7.3.1 and 9.1, although the French courts themselves have accepted the validity of a foreign choice of court agreement even if it leads to the non-application of forum mandatory rules.[83] There is, however, German authority which supports the adoption of an approach similar to the Australian case law – invalidating a choice of court agreement in favour of a non-Member State because it would lead to the non-application of mandatory rules of EU law under the *Ingmar* principle discussed above.[84] As discussed in Section 6.6.2, the English courts have also adopted this approach in relation to foreign arbitration agreements combined with choices of foreign law,[85] and it has been accepted that in principle this extends to foreign jurisdiction agreements.[86] A similar approach has been contemplated in Indian law.[87] The Hague Convention on Choice of Court Agreements 2005 is also arguably open to this possibility (as discussed in Section 3.4.4); the position under the Brussels I Regulation is however unclear.[88]

The key issue at stake is whether the effectiveness of the mandatory rules should be prioritised over the effectiveness of the jurisdiction agreement, which is a difficult policy question and may depend on the particular interests at stake in the dispute and under the relevant mandatory rule. The better view is that this issue requires a flexible approach, respectful of party autonomy but taking into account the importance of the mandatory

---

[82] A similar issue may arise in the context of arbitration agreements, as discussed in Section 6.6.2. See e.g. *Wilko v. Swan*, 346 US 427 (1953), but see *Rodriguez de Quijas v. Shearson/ American Express, Inc.*, 490 US 477 (1989).

[83] *Monster Cable*, Cour de Cassation (France), 07-15.823, Case No 1003 of 22 October 2008.

[84] See Weller (2017), p.104ff; BGH, VII ZR 25/12, 5 October 2012.

[85] *Accentuate Ltd v. ASIGRA Inc.* [2009] EWHC 2655 (QB), [88] ("The decision in *Ingmar* requires this court to give effect to the mandatory provisions of EU law, notwithstanding any expression to the contrary on the part of the contracting parties. In my judgment this must apply as much to an arbitration clause providing for both a place and a law other than a law that would give effect to the Directive, as it does to the simple choice of law clause that was under consideration in *Ingmar*").

[86] *Fern Computer Consultancy Ltd v. Intergraph Cadworx & Analysis Solutions Inc.* [2014] EWHC 2908 (Ch).

[87] *British India Steam Navigation Company v. Shanmughavilas Cashew Industries* (1990) 3 SCC 481.

[88] Weller (2017), p.107ff.

rule and the proximity of the dispute to the forum, similar to the approach that should be adopted in relation to the doctrine of public policy.[89]

A further way in which choice of law rules might address the concern about evading mandatory rules is through providing for the application of foreign mandatory rules – thus an effective choice of a foreign forum and foreign law would not necessarily evade application of local mandatory rules, should the foreign forum permit or require their application.[90] If in a contract closely connected to England, the parties enter into an effective exclusive choice of court agreement in favour of the French courts, this may not preclude the application of English mandatory rules if French choice of law rules so provide. This has, however, proven a highly contentious issue in the development of choice of law rules, primarily because it could potentially create significant uncertainty around the selection of the applicable law.[91] The most well-known debate centred around Article 7(1) of the Rome Convention 1980, which provided that:

> When applying under this Convention the law of a country, effect may be given to the mandatory rules of the law of another country with which the situation has a close connection, if and in so far as, under the law of the latter country, those rules must be applied whatever the law applicable to the contract. In considering whether to give effect to these mandatory rules, regard shall be had to their nature and purpose and to the consequences of their application or non-application.

The controversy around this very broad provision for the application of foreign mandatory rules meant that Article 7(1) was made optional, and a number of Member States, including the United Kingdom, Ireland, and Germany opted out of its application. In drafting the equivalent provision under the Rome I Regulation, a distinct and more limited approach was taken in order to ensure unanimity. Under Article 9(3) of the Rome I Regulation:

> Effect may be given to the overriding mandatory provisions of the law of the country where the obligations arising out of the contract have to be or have been performed, in so far as those overriding mandatory provisions render the performance of the contract unlawful. In considering whether to give effect to those provisions, regard shall be had to their nature and purpose and to the consequences of their application or non-application.

---

[89] Mills (2008b).

[90] See generally e.g. Nygh (1999), p.217ff. In the context of arbitration, see Hochstrasser (1994).

[91] See generally e.g. Hellner (2009); Bonomi (2008); Dickinson (2007); Chong (2006); Bonomi (2001).

This rule is much more limited in two ways – it applies only to the mandatory rules of the place of performance of contractual obligations, and it applies those rules only to the extent that they render the performance of the contract unlawful. The rule is based closely on the common law rules on foreign illegality, under which common law courts have long refused to enforce contracts whose performance is or becomes unlawful under the law of the place of performance.[92] In the common law, it was somewhat uncertain whether this rule was properly viewed as part of private international law or as part of the law of contract, dealing with frustration through illegality. In each of the major cases, the contract between the parties was governed by English law, so the court might have been simply developing a rule of English contract law. Under this approach, foreign law would be taken into account more as a matter of fact (a fact that renders performance of the contract essentially impossible) rather than applied as a matter of law. If the rule is classified in this way, and there is a reasonable argument that it should be, then it perhaps should not have been adopted as part of the Rome I Regulation but rather left for national contract law, although it is admittedly beneficial that the Rome I Regulation provides for a harmonised solution across the EU Member States. If, on the other hand, the rule is classified as a special choice of law rule, as is it under the Rome I Regulation, it may be viewed as a residue of the traditional emphasis in choice of law rules on the law of the place of performance as the law which has the strongest interest in regulating the contractual relationship[93] – a recognition that this interest has, to some extent, survived the adoption of party autonomy.[94]

The controversy over the potential application of foreign mandatory rules is reflected in each of the major international codifications governing choice of law. Article 9(2) of the Basel Principles (1991) provides, for example, that:

> If regard is to be had to mandatory provisions … of a law other than that of the forum or that chosen by the parties, then such provisions can only prevent the chosen law from being applied if there is a close link between the contract and the country of that law and if they further such aims as are generally accepted by the international community.

---

[92] *Ralli Bros v. Compania Naviera* [1920] 2 KB 287; *Foster v. Driscoll* [1929] 1 KB 470; *Regazzoni v. KC Sethia (1944) Ltd* [1958] AC 301; *Soleimany v. Soleimany* [1999] QB 785.

[93] See Section 2.2.2.

[94] The application of section 187(2)(b) of the Second Restatement of Conflict of Laws may also be similarly interpreted as preserving a role for the mandatory rules of the objectively applicable law – see further Section 9.2.4.

The requirements for a 'close link' and that the mandatory rules further 'such aims as are generally accepted by the international community' suggest a different conception of the context in which mandatory rules should be applied. Article 11 of the Mexico City Convention 1994 provides more neutrally that:

> Notwithstanding the provisions of the preceding articles, the provisions of the law of the forum shall necessarily be applied when they are mandatory requirements.
>
> It shall be up to the forum to decide when it applies the mandatory provisions of the law of another State with which the contract has close ties.

This preserves the requirement of a close link, but leaves to national law any other criteria. Finally, Article 11 of the Hague Principles on Choice of Law in International Commercial Contracts 2015 provides only that:

> The law of the forum determines when a court may or must apply or take into account overriding mandatory provisions of another law.

If the Hague Principles are taken to reflect the international consensus on party autonomy in choice of law, it appears this point is not part of the consensus. The application of foreign mandatory rules remains a potential way in which a choice of foreign law may be constrained, even when it is combined with an effective choice of a foreign forum, but principle and practice on the point evidently remain diverse and contested.

9.4.2   Public Policy

The public policy exception provides another important safety-net to the choice of law process – it allows a court to recognise that in certain cases foreign law may be inherently unjust or unjust in its application, and thus should not be applied despite the direction of choice of law rules. The existence of a public policy exception to the application of foreign law is, like the recognition of mandatory rules, an almost universally recognised feature of choice of law. The qualification 'almost' is necessary because under some modern US interest analysis approaches, "the need for a public policy exception in the negative sense has diminished because a state's public policy, especially the forum's, has become an integral, affirmative factor in a court's decision to apply or not apply that state's law."[95] A public policy exception nevertheless forms part of all the major

---

[95] Symeonides (2017), p.25. But see, however, the Second Restatement of Conflict of Laws, s.90, retaining a public policy defence in an approach that incorporates elements of interest analysis.

international codifications of choice of law. For example, under Article 5 of the Montevideo Convention 1979, "The law declared applicable by a convention on private international law may be refused application in the territory of a State Party that considers it manifestly contrary to the principles of its public policy (*ordre public*)". Under Article 8 of the Mexico City Convention 1994, "Application of the law designated by this Convention may only be excluded when it is manifestly contrary to the public order of the forum". Finally, under Article 11(3) of the Hague Principles on Choice of Law in International Commercial Contracts 2015, "A court may exclude application of a provision of the law chosen by the parties only if and to the extent that the result of such application would be manifestly incompatible with fundamental notions of public policy (*ordre public*) of the forum".[96] Public policy is also clearly recognised under the common law, in Article 21 of the Rome I Regulation[97] and (identically) in Article 26 of the Rome II Regulation, and in Article 5 of the Law of the People's Republic of China on the Laws Applicable to Foreign-Related Civil Relations (2010).[98]

Public policy is, like mandatory rules, not an exception specifically targeted at party autonomy – it may equally operate to exclude the effect of foreign law that is chosen as a result of an objective choice of law rule. It nevertheless frequently provides a significant constraint on the operation of party autonomy in choice of law, because it limits the effectiveness of the law chosen by the parties. The effect is not to invalidate the choice – public policy does not invalidate the exercise of party autonomy – but rather to give only partial effect to the law chosen by the parties, where applying the chosen law would be contrary to fundamental values of the forum.

There is a significant literature in private international law on public policy, and for present purposes it is not necessary to deal with the subject exhaustively.[99] It is important to note in this context that the 'public policy' that is referred to in private international law is distinct from 'public policy' as that term is used within the context of a national system of contract law. Certain types of contracts may be considered contrary to public policy under particular rules of national law, but private international law is concerned with the higher level question of which system of national

---

[96] See generally e.g. Dickinson (2017); De Vareilles-Sommières (2016).

[97] "The application of a provision of the law of any country specified by this Regulation may be refused only if such application is manifestly incompatible with the public policy (ordre public) of the forum."

[98] "Where the application of a foreign law will be prejudicial to the social and public interest of the PRC, the PRC law shall be applied." See discussion in Huo (2011).

[99] For further reference see e.g. Mills (2008b).

contract law applies.[100] If a state were to apply its contract rules of public policy in every case, it would not be respecting the choice of law process, as it would always be applying its own contract law. To illustrate the point, the English courts long ago recognised that although loan agreements for gambling were (at the time) void as contrary to English *contractual* public policy, such an agreement made in Monte Carlo under the law of Monte Carlo in order to allow gambling in Monte Carlo should not be considered contrary to English *private international law* public policy, and should thus be enforced by the English courts.[101] This reflects two fundamental principles of public policy.

The first is that it must be interpreted restrictively – foreign law cannot be viewed as contrary to local public policy merely because it is different from local law, otherwise choice of law would be entirely undermined. The public policy must be either fundamental to the forum, or potentially shared bilaterally[102] or internationally,[103] to override the choice of law. The European Convention on Human Rights may provide an important source of public policy in Convention states, although as between EU Member States the principle of mutual trust provides a counter-balancing force which suggests that public policy must be interpreted narrowly (it should be presumed that the law of another Member State is consistent with the ECHR unless this is manifestly not the case).[104]

The second principle is that whether public policy should apply will depend in part on the connections between the relationship concerned and the forum – this is sometimes known as the doctrine of proximity. In the Monte Carlo example above, it was evidently significant that the contract had been entered into in a foreign territory for the purposes of gambling in a foreign territory, and if this had not been the case, the English court may well have been minded to invalidate the contract through application of English public policy, even if the law of Monte Carlo had been expressly selected by the parties.

It is an almost invariable feature of public policy that it refers only to the public policy of the forum, albeit a policy which may be sourced from broader international norms. The caveat 'almost' is necessary,

---

[100] See similarly Section 1.3.5.

[101] *Saxby* v. *Fulton* [1909] 2 KB 208.

[102] See e.g. *Lemenda Trading* v. *African Petroleum Ltd* [1988] QB 448.

[103] See e.g. *Oppenheimer* v. *Cattermole* [1976] AC 249; *Kuwait Airways* v. *Iraqi Airways* [2002] UKHL 19.

[104] See e.g. C-7/98 *Krombach* v. *Bamberski* [2000] ECR I-1935, [21]; C-38/98 *Régie Nationale des Usines Renault* v. *Maxicar* [2000] ECR I-2973, [26]. See further e.g. Oster (2015).

however, because of Article 11(4) of the Hague Principles on Choice of Law in International Commercial Contracts 2015, which provides that:

> The law of the forum determines when a court may or must apply or take into account the public policy (*ordre public*) of a State the law of which would be applicable in the absence of a choice of law.

At first glance it is perhaps not clear in what circumstances this provision would be operative – the doctrine of public policy recognised under each of the choice of law rules discussed above refers only to forum (and not foreign) public policy.[105] It can be understood, however, as a reference to those US approaches, such as the Second Restatement of Conflict of Laws, discussed earlier in this chapter, in which the exercise of party autonomy may be invalidated where "application of the law of the chosen state would be contrary to a fundamental policy of a state which has a materially greater interest than the chosen state in the determination of the particular issue and which ... would be the state of the applicable law in the absence of an effective choice of law by the parties".[106] This provision in the Hague Principles is thus an effort to reconcile US approaches that fuse public policy concerns into the choice of law rule with those more traditional approaches under which public policy is a separate consideration, applied subsequent to the choice of law process.

9.5 Conclusions

This chapter has examined three of the most significant constraints on party autonomy in choice of law. First, limitations based on the subject matter of the contract or the nature of the parties, which are for example frequently used to protect consumers or employees. A number of different techniques are adopted – these limitations may preclude the exercise of party autonomy altogether, limit the possible choices for the parties, limit the effectiveness of a choice, or provide for a more discretionary review of the fairness of applying the chosen law. A second significant limitation on party autonomy in choice of law is whether a choice is available in a purely domestic case, or whether an international connection is required. Different approaches are again identifiable – precluding the choice altogether, limiting its effectiveness, or possibly not imposing any constraints at all. A third limitation may arise through recognition that there are

---

[105] In the common law the point was expressly addressed in *Peer International* v. *Termidor Music Publishers* [2003] EWCA Civ 1156.

[106] Second Restatement of Conflict of Laws, s.187(2)(b).

values which may trump the usual choice of law process, including where that process involves the exercise of party autonomy. This recognition may take the form of mandatory rules which are given effect regardless of the law which governs the contract, or rules of public policy which may block application of the selected law. In either case, a choice by the parties is not invalidated, but its effectiveness may be restricted. The principles governing the application of public policy are perhaps relatively settled, but the same cannot be said for some of the difficult issues arising in the context of mandatory rules. One such issue is whether effect should be given to foreign mandatory rules in some circumstances; another related issue is whether a foreign choice of court agreement should be invalidated in some circumstances to protect the application of forum mandatory rules.

In the legal systems and international codifications examined in this chapter, a core of agreement may be identified: that party autonomy should be subject to constraints that recognise a range of countervailing interests. However, there are a variety of methodologies adopted to give effect to these constraints, and a variety of views as to the extent to which they should limit the power of the parties to select a governing law.

10

Choice of Non-State Law

10.1 Introduction

The analysis of party autonomy in choice of law finishes in this chapter with an examination of the possible choice of non-state law. This is a perennial issue in choice of law, because one of the clear battle-lines between state interests and party autonomy is the question of whether individuals may choose non-state law, and thus avoid having their relationship governed by the law of any national legal system. This issue emerges in a range of contexts. It may arise where two parties select a religious law to govern an agreement, such as, for example, an instrument of Sharia-compliant finance, or in the application of Jewish law by rabbinical courts. Parties may also purport to have their contracts governed by reference to general principles of international business, particularly as applied in international commercial arbitration, which are often referred to as the *lex mercatoria*. Alternatively, they may adopt as a governing law one of the efforts to codify such rules or principles, for example, the UNIDROIT Principles of International Commercial Contracts, first adopted in 1994, and most recently revised in 2016.[1] Theoretically, a choice of non-state law may arise in any area of law which at least partially recognises party autonomy – as discussed in Chapter 8, this is not limited to contract law, and so the parties might also purport to select principles of non-state law to govern non-contractual disputes such as torts. In practice, however, the application of non-state law has largely focused on situations arising within contract law where party autonomy has had its strongest influence and principles of non-state law are most readily identifiable, and these will be the primary focus of this chapter. The question of applicable law is conceptually an independent issue from the choice of a state or non-state forum – a contract with a choice of non-state law may or may not also

---

[1] See generally e.g. Vogenauer (2015); Saumier (2012); Oser (2008); Bonell (2005); Baron (1999).

contain a clause conferring jurisdiction on a court or arbitral tribunal – although in practice, as discussed below, the most common context for a choice of non-state law has been arbitration.

This chapter examines the effectiveness of a choice of non-state law in both national court litigation (Sections 10.2 and 10.3) and arbitration (Section 10.4, and also introduced in Chapter 6). It continues the approach adopted in Chapters 7–9, examining a range of comparative and international sources, including the common law, the Rome I and Rome II Regulations in the European Union, US law, as well as under international codifications such as the Mexico City Convention 1994 and the Hague Principles on Choice of Law in International Commercial Contracts 2015.

There are three preliminary points to note before this analysis begins. First, it is particularly important in this context to recall the distinction drawn in Section 1.3.6 between a choice of law and the incorporation by reference of rules of law. The incorporation by reference of rules of law is, essentially, a shorthand technique for drafting a contract – instead of setting out all its terms in a single document, those terms may be included by reference from another source. That source may be state law, non-state law, or indeed any other source. There are few limitations on the origins of contractual provisions which might be incorporated by reference, provided the terms of the contract are clear and readily ascertainable to both parties. Whether it is lawful for the contract to include the terms that are thus incorporated as part of its text is an entirely different question, which is a matter of *contractual* party autonomy governed by the applicable law of the contract.[2] The applicable law of the contract may in turn be a matter of private international law party autonomy. Thus, even where choice of law rules do not permit a choice of non-state law as the governing law for a contract, the parties may be able to give effect to those rules through their incorporation as terms of the contract, if those rules are valid contractual terms under the national law which governs the contract. This is undoubtedly a matter of great significance, and the incorporation by reference of common terms in various contracts can benefit both contractual certainty and international standardisation, but it is not a matter of party autonomy in private international law.[3]

Second, whether the parties are choosing non-state law is sometimes far from self-evident, because it is possible for choices to be made which are

---

[2] See further Section 1.3.5.
[3] See e.g. discussion of the use of Incoterms and the standardisation of letters of credit in Basedow (2013a), p.142ff.

something of a hybrid of state and non-state law.[4] For example, the parties might select for their contract to be governed by the law of New York, as it stood at 1 January 2017 (sometimes known as a 'stabilisation clause'). In one sense this is state law, because evidently it is a freeze-frame of the law of a recognised sub-national legal order. In another sense, however, this is non-state law, because it is an attempt by the parties to select to govern their contract a system of law which will likely not be the law of any state as and when it applies – it will not be the law of New York, because New York law will have been modified by subsequent developments. Whether the parties are able to make such a choice is thus closely related to the questions examined in this chapter, and inextricably linked to the underlying conception of party autonomy that is adopted, as discussed further below.[5] A similar point may arise if the parties purport to modify the content of the chosen applicable law inconsistently with the non-derogable rules of that law. For example, a clause providing that "This contract is governed by English law without the doctrine of consideration" would in reality be a choice of non-state law rather than a choice of state law. The mere fact that the parties might have chosen a legal system in which no doctrine of consideration applies does not necessarily mean that they can derogate contractually from that aspect of English contract law.[6] A further related question is whether the parties, in making a choice of law, can affect the scope of application of potentially applicable statutes.[7] For example, consider an insurance contract made between Hong Kong and Singapore parties relating to a risk located in Beijing, but with a choice of English law clause.[8] Imagine that there is an English statute setting mandatory terms for insurance contracts, which states expressly that it applies only to contracts for risks located in England. A court (including but not only an English court) applying English law to the contract has to determine whether this should include the statute, despite its purported scope.[9] If the choice of law is considered to be limited strictly to state law, there is a

---

[4] This is a distinct issue from the question of whether the *lex mercatoria* is itself really non-state law, or rather a hybrid of national and non-national sources – on which see Michaels (2007).

[5] See also discussion in Hay, Borchers, and Symeonides (2010), p.1133; Nygh (1999), p.63ff.

[6] But see Albornoz (2010), p.24.

[7] See further e.g. Buxbaum (2017).

[8] It is presumed for the purposes of this example that the risk is a 'large risk' and thus party autonomy is not restricted under the Rome I Regulation, as discussed in Section 9.2.2.

[9] See e.g. *Boissevain* v. *Weil* [1950] AC 327; Mann (1973), p.135ff. If an English court is determining the issue, it will also need to consider whether the statute is potentially a forum mandatory rule – see further discussion in Section 9.4.1.

strong argument (despite some practice to the contrary)[10] that it should not include application of the statute, because this is not what is provided by English law – unlike the general rules of English contract law, which are not territorially or otherwise limited and whose scope is therefore determined only by choice of law rules. In support of this approach, where statutory interpretation remains part of determining the applicable rules of law, comment (b) to section 6(1) of the Second Restatement of Conflict of Laws provides that:

> The court should give a local statute the range of application intended by the legislature when these intentions can be ascertained and can constitutionally be given effect. If the legislature intended that the statute should be applied to the out-of-state facts involved, the court should so apply it unless constitutional considerations forbid. On the other hand, if the legislature intended that the statute should be applied only to acts taking place within the state, the statute should not be given a wider range of application.

If a choice of non-state law is not permitted, the statute in the example above should remain ineffective even if the parties expressly stated that they wish their contract to be governed by English law *including the statute*, as the statute on its terms can have no effect on their relationship (although indirect effect might be given to such a clause through the device of incorporation by reference, as noted above).[11] On the other hand, if the choice of law available to the parties is not limited to state law, there seems little reason why it could not extend to state law as modified by agreement of the parties, which would be in reality a particular form of non-state law.

The third and final preliminary point is to note that this chapter does not take a view on the jurisprudential question of whether non-state law is 'law'.[12] Under traditional 'positivist' definitions of law as the command of

---

[10] See e.g. *405341 Ontario Limited* v. *Midas Canada Inc.* (2010) 322 DLR (4th) 177 (choice of Ontario law required application of Ontario franchise law even though it was territorially limited); *1-800-Got Junk? LLC* v. *Superior Court*, 189 Cal.App.4th 500 (2010) (choice of Washington law required application of Washington franchise law even though it was territorially limited). The opposite conclusion was, however, reached in relation to the same franchise agreement in *Taylor* v. *1-800-Got-Junk?, LLC*, 387 Fed.Appx 727 (9th Cir. 2010), following the precedent set in *Gravquick A/S* v. *Trimble Navigation International Ltd*, 323 F.3d 1219, 1233 (9th Cir. 2003). See also *Red Lion Hotels Franchising, Inc.* v. *MAK, LLC*, 663 F.3d 1080 (9th Cir. 2011). More classically, a similar territorial limitation was also applied in *Mutual Life Insurance Company of New York* v. *Tine Cohen*, 179 US 262 (1900).

[11] See also *Vita Food Products* v. *Unus Shipping Co. Ltd* [1939] AC 277, 291 (incorporation by reference of a repealed statute).

[12] See generally Schultz (2014); Michaels (2009); Schultz (2008). For traditional scepticism, see Mann (1980).

a sovereign,[13] non-state law would clearly not satisfy the criteria for being 'law'. Modern theorists, however, including 'positivists', frequently take the view that the legal status of a norm is conferred through a collective understanding of a community that the norm is binding, typically because it satisfies certain procedural and potentially substantive criteria (with regard to state law, for example, it has been adopted by a parliament and does not violate the constitution). These approaches emphasise the importance of the internal perspective (how a norm is viewed by a member of the affected community) rather than identifiable objective characteristics of the norm.[14] This idea of law is more open to the possibility that law may be found in contexts other than the state, and this possibility has given rise to a flourishing literature on 'global legal pluralism', or 'law beyond the state'.[15] In a particular community (for example, a business community, or a religious community), it may be that certain behavioural rules become so embedded that they are viewed by the participants in that community as having the same bindingness as legal rules, even though they are not part of any national legal system. From this perspective, non-state law may be considered law if a sufficient number of its subjects and officials (arbitrators, lawyers, perhaps even academics) understand and accept it to be law. Different views may be taken on whether this alone is sufficient for rules to be called 'law', but there is no doubt that as a question of social fact, non-state regulatory systems have an influence on the behaviour of parties which is comparable to that of law, both within states and across state boundaries. These social facts can exist irrespective of their recognition by national courts or other institutional bodies, but their effectiveness does to some extent depend on this recognition, because state law is backed by the potential for the lawful application of coercive force. The question of whether non-state law is also recognised by courts is thus not *determinative* of the existence of non-state law, but it is important in evaluating the effectiveness of non-state law. One form in which this recognition can take place is through accepting the power of private parties to choose non-state law to govern their legal relations as a matter of private international law, which is the subject of this chapter. Whether non-state law is accepted as law is thus not just a question for jurisprudence, but also a practical question addressed through choice of law rules.

---

[13] Most closely associated with Austin (1832).
[14] Perhaps most closely associated with Hart (1961).
[15] See e.g. Helfand (2015); Schultz (2014); Brekoulakis (2013); Berman (2012); Zumbansen (2010); Gaillard (2010a); Michaels (2009).

10.2   Traditional Approaches: Applicable Law Means State Law

In private international law it has traditionally been clear that any contract has to be governed by the law of a state.[16] Choice of law rules are generally themselves part of national legal systems,[17] and as such it is perhaps unsurprising that they have traditionally been committed to what might be called a regulatory monopoly of the state.[18] As Ralf Michaels has argued, "while the recognition of foreign laws enhances the role of any state's law, because it creates a cartel of lawmakers, this cartel is almost necessarily hostile to outsiders".[19] This monopoly of the state as a sovereign actor has also (again traditionally) been supported by public international law. Classically, this position was expressed in the decision of the Permanent Court of International Justice in the *Serbian Loans Case* (1929), which included the determination that:

> Any contract which is not a contract between States in their capacity as subjects of international law is based on the municipal law of some country.[20]

Through choice of law rules, states have thus traditionally recognised each other's systems of law (commonly applying the laws of a foreign state in civil disputes), as part of recognising their coexisting sovereignties, but have not recognised purely private sources of rules. This approach thus implicitly requires that the public interests of at least one state must have a role to play in defining the relationship, and in resolving the dispute, between the parties. States have also thereby traditionally made a determination that the usual justifications for party autonomy do not extend to choice of non-state law in litigation. To the extent that party autonomy

---

[16] 'State' for these purposes should be understood as meaning 'territorial legal order' – obviously parties may choose the law of California or New South Wales to govern their contracts, even though these are not 'states' in the international law sense of the term. The tradition noted here is, however, a relatively modern one. In European international legal ordering, for example, there was evidently a significant role for ecclesiastical (canon) law in regulating legal relations prior to the dominance of the state. Under modern canon law, contracts are generally governed by the applicable civil law: 1983 Code of Canon Law, Canon 1290.

[17] Which is not to deny that they may reflect underlying obligations or limitations of public international law – see generally Mills (2009a).

[18] It is perhaps notable that (as discussed further below) a different position was adopted under the Hague Principles on Choice of Law in International Commercial Contracts 2015, prepared by an expert group rather than government representatives, although later approved by the Members of the Hague Conference.

[19] Michaels (2007), p.462. See also Muir Watt (2010), p.264.

[20] *Serbian Loans Case, France v. Yugoslavia* (1929) PCIJ Ser A, No 20, Judgment 14, p.41.

confers a power on individual parties or recognises such a power as inherent, this is understood to mean freedom to choose between state laws, but not freedom from *any* state laws; non-state law is not trusted to resolve disputes effectively and efficiently; and regulatory competition between *state* legal orders is viewed as competition enough. Party autonomy is constructed as a limited choice between the laws of states, accepting the pluralism of state legal orders, but not of legal orders beyond the state.

This position was (and continues to be) adopted in the common law approach to choice of law. This was perhaps put most expressively in the UK House of Lords decision in *Amin Rasheed Shipping Corporation* v. *Kuwait Insurance Co.*, which held that:

> contracts are incapable of existing in a legal vacuum. They are mere pieces of paper devoid of all legal effect unless they were made by reference to some system of private law which defines the obligations assumed by the parties to the contract by their use of particular forms of words and prescribes the remedies enforceable in a court of justice for failure to perform any of those obligations[21]

This reference to a 'system of private law' has long been understood to be limited to state law.[22] A choice of religious law is only possible to the extent that such religious law has been adopted as the law of a particular state.[23] The position is the same under the Rome Convention 1980[24] and now Rome I Regulation[25] in the European Union – it has long been established that choice of law rules require the designation of the law of a state, and thus a choice by the parties of non-state law is ineffective.[26] Non-state law is also excluded from selection in China.[27] It is true that courts have endeavoured in at least some cases to give effect to the intentions of parties who purport to choose non-state law (such as, for example, religious law),

---

[21] [1984] AC 50, 65 (Lord Diplock); see further Mann (1980). See also e.g. *Bank Mellat* v. *Helliniki Techniki SA* [1984] QB 291, 301.

[22] See e.g. *Musawi* v. *RE International (UK) Ltd* [2007] EWHC 2981 (Ch).

[23] This is arguably the basis for the decision in *Al Midani* v. *Al Midani* [1999] 1 Lloyd's Rep 923, although Justice Rix did hold that "the proper law of the agreement is either Shari'a law or such law as modified by Saudi law", and that "I regard Islamic or Shari'a law as a branch of foreign law", suggesting (contrary to other authorities) that Islamic law might have been the proper law independently of its national adoption. But see *Halpern* v. *Halpern* [2007] EWCA Civ 291, [24].

[24] Rome Convention 1980, Art.3.

[25] Rome I Regulation, Art.3. See further Nielson and Lando (2008).

[26] See e.g. *Beximco Pharmaceuticals Ltd* v. *Shamil Bank of Bahrain EC* [2004] EWCA Civ 19.

[27] Tang (2011).

by taking into consideration the rules of their chosen system of law in the *interpretation* of their contract.[28] However, this secondary role for the chosen law can only be of limited effect – it cannot, for example, affect questions of the validity of the terms of the contract. It is, rather, the equivalent of finding that parties have incorporated by reference certain (non-state) rules or principles of contractual interpretation as terms of their contract, as discussed above. This is expressly permitted under Recital 13 of the Rome I Regulation, which provides that parties are not precluded "from incorporating by reference into their contract a non-State body of law or an international convention". While this may appear to be about choice of non-state law, in fact it is simply an acknowledgement of the uncontroversial fact that the parties may incorporate terms into their contract from whatever source they wish (subject to the state law applicable to the contract), as discussed further in Section 1.3.6.

In the United States, while conflict of laws rules vary between states, it is generally similarly accepted that a contract is governed by the law of a state,[29] a position adopted under both the Second Restatement of Conflict of Laws[30] and the Uniform Commercial Code.[31] It has occasionally been argued that these rules do not preclude a choice of non-state law to govern a contract, but these arguments conflate the incorporation by reference of non-state law as terms of the contract (which may be permissible) with the application of non-state law as the law governing the contract (which is not recognised). Those states which have adopted an interest analysis approach to determining the applicable law, instead of or in conjunction with the approach under the Second Restatement, are also strongly likely to reject the possible application of non-state law, as under this approach the analysis is focused exclusively on the interests of the states whose law may potentially be applicable.[32]

One notable exception to the principle that choice of law rules select only 'state' law may arise in the case of unrecognised states.[33] In general, the non-recognition of an entity as a state should exclude the application of its law. However, it has now become firmly established that this should not be to the detriment of the people of the territory, who in practice may

---

[28] See e.g. *Halpern* v. *Halpern* [2007] EWCA Civ 291.

[29] See e.g. Hay, Borchers, and Symeonides (2010), pp.1135–6. One arguable exception – the choice of law codification in Oregon – is discussed below.

[30] See ss.187–8, and the definition of 'state' in s.3.

[31] Section 1-301.

[32] See e.g. *Trans Meridian Trading Inc.* v. *Empresa Nacional De Comercializacion De Insumos*, 829 F.2d 949 (9th Cir. 1987).

[33] See generally Mills (2017b); Dickinson (2013), p.102ff; McLachlan (2014), Chapter 10.

have no choice but to live their lives in accordance with the 'law' of the unrecognised state. The English courts have held, for example, that:

> the courts of this country can recognise the laws or acts of a body which is in effective control of a territory even though it has not been recognised by Her Majesty's Government de jure or de facto: at any rate, in regard to the laws which regulate the day to day affairs of the people, such as their marriages, their divorces, their leases, their occupations, and so forth.[34]

The New York courts have similarly recognised that:

> A foreign government, although not recognized by the political arm of the United States Government, may nevertheless have de facto existence which is juridically cognizable. The acts of such a de facto government may affect private rights and obligations arising either as a result of activity in, or with persons or corporations within, the territory controlled by such de facto government.[35]

This approach has also received support from the International Court of Justice in its *Advisory Opinion on Legal Consequences for States of the Continued Presence of South Africa in Namibia Notwithstanding SC Res. 276* (1971).[36] While the need to apply rules of non-state private law in such circumstances is clearly recognised as a matter of policy, it is not always clear whether choice of law rules in fact permit this, as they tend to expressly provide that they are limited to a choice of state law. An expansive interpretation of 'state' law may be required to overcome these limitations. The justification for this approach is that it would be an injustice not to recognise in some way the practical reality of the system of private law that holds sway over the lives of people in an unrecognised territory. There is, however, less justification to apply such law where the body of law has been chosen by the parties, and it may be that a choice of law agreement entered into by the parties should therefore not be permitted to extend to the law of an unrecognised state[37] – that, somewhat ironically, this form of non-state law may be applied only if it is *not* chosen by the parties.

10.3   The Emerging Possibility of a Choice of Non-State Law?

As discussed in Section 1.1, the classical model of international law that underlies the traditional perspective on choice of law, under which states are the exclusive subjects of international law and thus the sole possible

---

[34] *Hesperides Hotels* v. *Aegean Turkish Holidays* [1978] QB 205, 218, reversed on other grounds at [1979] AC 508.
[35] *Upright* v. *Mercury Business Machines Co.*, 13 A.D.2d 36, 38 (App.Div.N.Y. 1961).
[36] (1971) ICJ Reports 16.
[37] See e.g. Dickinson (2013), p.106 and p.129ff.

sources of law-making authority, has more recently been contested.[38] Many argue, for example, that individuals are bearers of direct rights under human rights law, and that investors are the bearers of direct rights under international investment treaties.[39] The (still much-debated) emergence of this 'new' international law, which recognises the importance of private as well as public actors and interests, raises questions about the traditional exclusivity of states as sources of normative authority – if states are not the only actors whose agency is recognised and valued in international law, then why should they claim a monopoly over law-making? These broader developments thus link back to the question of whether non-state law generated by private actors should be accepted as a valid form of law. The application of non-state law is not, strictly speaking, limited to cross-border cases. A state might choose, for example, to recognise religious law for purely domestic cases, as an alternative or supplement to state law. The focus in this section is, however, on the potential application of non-state law to cross-border cases, through rules of private international law.

At the outset, it must be stated that it remains exceptional that national rules of private international law accept a possible choice of non-state law.[40] One particular exception, the application by French courts of non-state law to govern arbitration agreements, was discussed in Section 6.3. The Oregon Choice of Law codification is another potential exception, at least according to the Reporter's comments on the draft,[41] although the statute itself seems to undermine the claim as it defines 'law' as the law of a state.[42] Aside from these examples, the exclusion of non-state law is almost

---

[38] See further e.g. Mills (2014). As noted in Section 1.1, it was also historically contested prior to the nineteenth-century dominance of the state over other forms of international legal ordering.

[39] See references in Section 1.1.2; see further e.g. *Occidental Exploration & Production Company* v. *Republic of Ecuador* [2005] EWCA Civ 1116, [17]–[19]; *Corn Products International* v. *Mexico*, Decision on Responsibility, 15 January 2008, ICSID Case No. ARB(AF)/04/01, at [168] ("It is now clear that States are not the only entities which can hold rights under international law; individuals and corporations may also possess rights under international law").

[40] It is notable that the web page recording use of the UNIDROIT Principles cites to very few decisions of national courts applying the Principles as the governing law of a contract. See www.unilex.info/article.cfm?pid=2&pos=1&iid=1208#IID1208, but note for example www.unilex.info/case.cfm?id=1864. For an argument in favour of a more expansive approach see Radicati di Brozolo (2012a). For further discussion see Nygh (1999), p.185ff.

[41] Nafziger (2002), p.421 ("In exercising this autonomy, parties may select model rules or principles. For example, parties to an international contract may choose to have it governed by the Unidroit Principles of International Commercial Contracts").

[42] See now 2015 Oregon Revised Statutes, 15.300 and 15.350.

invariable in those choice of law rules developed by state law-makers for application in national courts, a context in which state interests are likely to be most strongly influential. A greater scope for a potential choice of non-state law may be recognised where choice of rules are developed by private actors or contemplate application in arbitral tribunals as well as or instead of national courts. As an illustration, in addition to the developments discussed below, it may be noted in passing that the American Law Institute Principles of the Law on 'Intellectual Property: Principles Governing Jurisdiction, Choice of Law and Judgments in Transnational Disputes', adopted in 2008, included the following comment:

> The principle of unfettered party autonomy is widely recognized in business-to-business transactions. It admits the choice of a third legal order, not being that of the grantor or of the recipient, even when the chosen law lacks any relationship to the parties, to the right, or to the territory of use. Indeed, the chosen law could be "soft law" such as the UNIDROIT Principles for international commercial contracts.[43]

This appears to constitute recognition of a potential choice of non-state law in an influential statement of US choice of law principles, albeit one developed by private parties rather than state law-makers and focused particularly on intellectual property. It remains to be seen whether this is indicative of a broader trend in the US or other national legal systems, or perhaps merely symptomatic of a common confusion (discussed in Section 10.1) between the determination of the applicable law and the incorporation by reference of terms of non-state law.

10.3.1   UN Convention on Contracts for the International Sale of Goods 1980

The UN Convention on Contracts for the International Sale of Goods 1980 is a codification of rules of substantive contract law set out in a treaty, rather than a codification of choice of law rules. It essentially sets out rules of substantive law which must be incorporated into the national legal systems of Contracting states. Under Article 1(1), these must be applied in cross-border sale of goods cases either (a) where the place of business of each party is in a different Contracting state, or (b) "when the rules of private international law lead to the application of the law of a Contracting State". In the latter case, this might be through application of party autonomy, but if so, the law is applicable as part of the national law of a Contracting State,

---

[43]   Section 302, comment (b). See further Section 8.5.5.

and so this would not constitute a choice of non-state law.[44] However, the Explanatory Note to the Convention contains the further statement that:

> the Convention may also apply as the law applicable to the contract if so chosen by the parties. In that case, the operation of the Convention will be subject to any limits on contractual stipulations set by the otherwise applicable law.[45]

This is something of a curiosity. There is no provision in the Convention that deals with this point, so the 'explanation' appears to be simply an assertion that a choice of the Convention will be possible under national choice of law rules, even in those states that are not parties to the Convention. As discussed above, this is evidently not the case, as most national legal systems permit only a choice of national law. There are two ways the statement might be understood. First, it may be considered that parties can choose to be governed by the Convention by choosing the law of a state that has incorporated the Convention in its law. If so, however, this appears to replicate Article 1(1)(b), noted above. Second, it may be considered to be merely indicating the possibility of incorporation by reference of the terms of the Convention. The second sentence quoted above – that in such a case the operation of the Convention is subject to any limits on contractual stipulations under the otherwise applicable law – suggests that this is in fact what is contemplated here (contrary to the claim that in such situations the Convention is 'the law applicable to the contract'). If the Convention is not the applicable law but rather incorporated by reference, the effectiveness of the Convention would indeed be subject to the rules on contractual party autonomy set out in the actual applicable law. The better view is therefore probably that the CISG does not, despite appearances, directly contemplate the possibility that it may be chosen by the parties as a non-state governing law, although the position is far from clear.

10.3.2   Mexico City Convention 1994

A further openness to the possible application of non-state law was arguably envisaged under the Mexico City Convention 1994.[46] As noted in Section 7.2.7, while this Convention has only been ratified by Mexico and

---

[44] Whether or not such a choice was effective would, in any case, be a matter for the choice of law rules of the forum.

[45] Explanatory Note, [7].

[46] www.oas.org/juridico/english/treaties/b-56.html. See further e.g. Moreno Rodriguez and Albornoz (2011); Albornoz (2010), p.26ff; Symeonides (2014), pp.143–4; Juenger (1997); Juenger (1994).

Venezuela (although also signed by Bolivia, Brazil, and Uruguay), it has nevertheless been influential in the debate and development of choice of law rules both regionally and further afield. Article 7 of the Convention provides that the parties may freely choose the law applicable to their contract – although not unambiguous, the choice appears limited to state law. If no choice is made, Article 9 points to the law of the state most closely connected to the contract, and further provides that:

> The Court will take into account all objective and subjective elements of the contract to determine the law of the State with which it has the closest ties. It shall also take into account the general principles of international commercial law recognized by international organizations.

It is not clear how a court could or should take into account 'the general principles of international commercial law recognized by international organizations' when determining the closeness of the ties which a contract has with different states. Principles of international commercial law do not themselves connect a contract with any particular jurisdiction. It may be that the intention here is that the analysis of connecting factors may itself be influenced by general international approaches – that international commercial law may include choice of law rules or principles on which a court may draw. If so, this would involve not the application of non-state contract law, but rather the application of non-state choice of law rules in order to determine the applicable law (an approach which is sometimes taken in the context of arbitration, as discussed further in Section 10.4).

The clearest reference to non-state law in the Convention is in Article 10, which provides that, in addition to the state law which governs the contract, "the guidelines, customs, and principles of international commercial law as well as commercial usage and practices generally accepted shall apply in order to discharge the requirements of justice and equity in the particular case". This is again a rather curious rule, as it is not based on a choice of non-state law by the parties, but rather gives the court the discretion to apply non-state law in addition to the applicable national law. Where the parties have chosen a national law to govern their contract under Article 7, the application of non-state law in addition under Article 10 would seem potentially to *undermine* party autonomy, rather than broaden it, as it invites a court to apply rules of law which have not been chosen by the parties – one might expect that the selection of a national law by the parties would be presumed to be exclusive. It may be that Article 10 should be interpreted as principally modifying Article 9 rather than Article 7, allowing the court to apply non-state law in the absence of a choice of law by the parties. In any case, Article 10 of the

Mexico City Convention 1994 is often considered as influentially opening the door to the possible application of non-state law, despite Article
17 of the Convention expressly providing that "For the purposes of this
Convention, 'law' shall be understood to mean the law current in a State".

10.3.3   Hague Principles on Choice of Law in
International Commercial Contracts 2015

The traditional view that private international law rules could and should
only designate state law to govern cross-border disputes has been chal-
lenged more directly by the adoption in March 2015 of the Hague Principles
on Choice of Law in International Commercial Contracts, at the Hague
Conference on Private International Law.[47] As discussed in Section 7.2.7,
Article 2(1) of the Principles provides that "A contract is governed by the
law chosen by the parties". More uniquely, Article 3 goes on to state that:

> The law chosen by the parties may be rules of law that are generally accepted
> on an international, supranational or regional level as a neutral and bal-
> anced set of rules, unless the law of the forum provides otherwise.

The use of the term 'rules of law' is clearly intended to permit a choice of
non-state law,[48] but this is evidently subject to a number of complex conditions.[49] Those conditions can be understood as reflecting reservations
about potential sources of non-state law – they are essentially 'legitimacy'
conditions that are imposed on non-state law. There are four principal criteria identified in Article 3 of the Hague Principles, each of which raises
considerable uncertainty concerning the application of this rule.

The first criterion is that the law chosen must be a 'set of rules' of law.
This reflects concerns that non-state law must be sufficiently 'complete'
to provide determinative rules for questions concerning the interpretation or validity of the terms of the contract. This is a difficult question to
evaluate – clearly it is not required that the set of rules provides a determinative answer to *any* question of law, as no national law would satisfy that
condition. The commentaries suggest that the rules must provide answers
to 'common problems'.[50]

---

[47] www.hcch.net/en/instruments/conventions/full-text/?cid=135.

[48] The drafting history is unambiguous – see www.hcch.net/en/instruments/contracts-
preparatory-work. See also Mankowski (2017b); Saumier (2017); Boele-Woelki (2016);
Saumier (2014); Pertegás and Marshall (2014), p.996ff; Michaels (2014b); Saumier (2012);
Gama and Saumier (2011).

[49] See further e.g. Mankowski (2017b); Michaels (2014b).

[50] Commentary to the Hague Principles, [3.10] ("the 'rules of law' must be a set of rules and
not merely a small number of provisions. While comprehensiveness is not required, the

The second is that the rules must be 'generally accepted' on an international, supranational or regional level. The commentary to the Principles provides that:

> the "rules of law" chosen by the parties must have garnered general recognition beyond a national level. In other words, the "rules of law" cannot refer to a set of rules contained in the contract itself, or to one party's standard terms and conditions, or to a set of local industry-specific terms.[51]

As non-exhaustive examples of rules that would satisfy this condition, the commentaries suggest the UN Convention on Contracts for the International Sale of Goods 1980, the UNIDROIT Principles of International Commercial Contracts, and the Principles of European Contract Law (an academic codification of general rules of contract law in the European Union published between 1995 and 2002).[52] It is notable that it is not considered sufficient that the parties *themselves* have accepted the rules – party autonomy is not, on its own, considered a sufficient justification to support the application of rules of non-state law. The parties may not simply design a set of rules themselves; the rules may be private in origin, but they require some kind of collective recognition process to establish their legitimacy, rather than merely the consent of the particular parties. It is unclear if this also means that the parties may not modify the rules of non-state law, but must select an existing accepted set of rules, or indeed whether this depends on what the rules of non-state law say about this question. Acceptance on an 'international, supranational or regional level' is required, but what this means is opaque. It is unclear, for example, whether this condition requires acceptance only by those subject to the non-state rules, or by society in general – the former might not be enough to establish that the rules are generally considered legitimate, but the latter might be too difficult to satisfy. Islamic law, for example, is certainly accepted by Muslims (albeit subject to different interpretations), but its application is broadly rejected in most Western states – it is unclear whether it would satisfy this test. If not, because a broader public acceptance is required, then this would mean that technical rules of international commercial law are also unlikely to qualify, because they may be unknown (and therefore not accepted) outside the particular community in which they operate.

The third condition in the Principles is that the non-state rules must be (or perhaps must be accepted as being – the point is unclear) neutral and

---

chosen 'rules of law' must be such as to allow for the resolution of common contract problems in the international context").

[51] Commentary to the Hague Principles, [3.4].

[52] Commentary to the Hague Principles, [3.5]–[3.7]; see further Section 10.3.4.

balanced. This suggests a minimum substantive criterion for the 'justness' of the rules – rules which systematically favour certain parties over others are not to be considered as sufficiently balanced to be legitimate non-state law which may be chosen by the parties. This criterion is again likely to present difficulties in application. If a legal system provides no special rights for weaker parties – for example, franchisees[53] – it may be queried whether it is 'balanced' (no party receives special treatment) or 'unbalanced' (weaker parties are not protected). However, there is some ambiguity in the provision as to whether the rules must actually be neutral and balanced, or whether it is sufficient that they are 'accepted as' neutral and balanced on an international, supranational, or regional level. The commentaries provide that:

> The third attribute – that the set of "rules of law" be generally accepted as balanced – is justified by: (i) the assumption underlying party autonomy in commercial contracts according to which parties have relatively equal bargaining power; and (ii) the fact that the presumption that State laws are balanced is not necessarily transferrable to "rules of law". This requirement would likely preclude the choice of a set of rules that benefit one side of transactions in a particular regional or global industry.

It is curious that the presumed 'equal bargaining power' of the parties, said to underlie party autonomy, is considered to justify a restriction on their choice of law. It might be thought that the equal bargaining power of the parties would instead justify giving effect to their choice of law – that whatever law they chose should be presumed to be balanced, without further scrutiny by a court. This is generally the case in the context of party autonomy in choice of law; absent a concern of unequal bargaining power, there is generally no scrutiny of whether a *state* law chosen by the parties is fair and balanced, other than the limited review based on public policy discussed in Section 9.4.2, as the terms of that law are simply understood to reflect the agreement of the parties.

A fourth condition is that non-state law be chosen "unless the law of the forum provides otherwise". The commentary further notes that:

> arbitration statutes and arbitration rules commonly allow for the contractual choice of "rules of law". However, national laws have not allowed the same choice in disputes brought before courts. The Principles recognise this in Article 3 by deferring to the law of the forum if that law confines the parties' freedom to a choice of State law.[54]

---

[53] Noting that employment and consumer contracts are excluded from the Principles: see discussion in Section 9.2.1.

[54] Commentary to the Hague Principles, [3.14].

This condition is entirely redundant, because the Principles are soft-law rules that may be adopted as they are or modified by any national legal system. A state not wishing to adopt Article 3 of the Principles would simply not include this rule in its national law, rather than include it but prohibit elsewhere a choice of non-state law. The condition evidently reflects, however, a hesitancy in the drafting of the Principles – an acknowledgment that the choice of non-state law was a controversial matter, and that states would ultimately have power to determine whether it was possible in national courts.

The Hague Principles were initially prepared by an expert Working Group, although later approved (with some modifications) by a Special Commission of state representatives and then (unanimously) by the members of the Hague Conference.[55] They were also prepared for application not only by courts but also potentially by arbitral tribunals. It may be suggested that these two factors contribute to the openness of the Principles to the application of non-state law.[56] Indeed, it is notable that the legitimacy conditions attached to the application of non-state law were imposed late in the drafting process, under the influence of the state representatives in the Special Commission, after the potential for a choice of non-state law "proved to be the subject of much debate".[57] The Principles are soft law – it is notable that they are therefore *themselves* an example of non-state law, although they are non-state private international law rather than non-state private law, and therefore not open to choice by the parties directly, but rather aim to influence state choice of law rules or the practice of arbitral tribunals.[58] It remains to be seen whether their openness to non-state law will prove an enduring influence, although it is notable that they have been adopted as part of the law of Paraguay, including in respect of their permitting a choice of non-state law.[59]

10.3.4   Choice of European Contract Law?

One further recent possible innovation in the recognition of non-state sources of governing law may be identified in the proposal for a European contract law. For many years, there have been academic initiatives

[55] See generally www.hcch.net/en/instruments/contracts-preparatory-work.
[56] See e.g. Gama and Saumier (2011).
[57] Report of the November 2012 Special Commission meeting, [12], published February 2013, available at www.hcch.net/en/instruments/contracts-preparatory-work.
[58] See further discussion in Albornoz and González Martín (2016), p.457ff.
[59] www.hcch.net/en/publications-and-studies/details4/?pid=6300&dtid=41.

(sometimes supported by European Union institutions) to develop rules of European substantive private law, including perhaps most prominently the work carried out by the Commission on European Contract Law (which adopted the Principles on European Contract Law ('PECL') published between 1995 and 2002),[60] and more recently the Study Group on a European Civil Code (which published a broader private law codification further developing the PECL under the name 'Draft Common Frame of Reference' in 2009).[61] Although some supporters of these projects have proposed the adoption of substantive private law as a matter of EU law, replacing national private law (or aspects of national private law) altogether, there are serious doubts over whether this is legally and politically feasible.[62] As an alternative, and more relevantly for present purposes, it has at various times been proposed that an EU codification of contract law (or parts thereof) could be in some way adopted as a system of law in addition to those of the Member States, and made available for choice by private parties.[63] Such a possibility was contemplated in the drafting of the Rome I Regulation, Recital 14 of which provides that:

> Should the Community adopt, in an appropriate legal instrument, rules of substantive contract law, including standard terms and conditions, such instrument may provide that the parties may choose to apply those rules.

This possibility has also been reflected in the various codification projects. Article 1:101 of the PECL, for example, provides (in relevant part) that:

(2) These Principles will apply when the parties have agreed to incorporate them into their contract or that their contract is to be governed by them.

(3) These Principles may be applied when the parties:
    (a) have agreed that their contract is to be governed by "general principles of law", the "lex mercatoria" or the like; or
    (b) have not chosen any system or rules of law to govern their contract.

There are several different issues raised in this provision. Article 1:101(2) contemplates the possible incorporation by reference of the Principles, which (as discussed in Sections 1.3.6 and 10.1) is clearly distinct from a

---

[60] Available at www.trans-lex.org/400200/_/pecl/.

[61] Available at ec.europa.eu/justice/contract/files/european-private-law_en.pdf. See also the Common Core of European Private Law project, www.common-core.org. See generally Basedow (2013a), p.229ff.

[62] See generally Mills (2010), p.388ff.

[63] See further Green Paper from the Commission of 1 July 2010 on policy options for progress towards a European Contract Law for consumers and businesses, COM(2010) 348 final.

choice of non-state law. However, it also recognises as an alternative the choice of the Principles to govern a contract, which would clearly be a broadening of the scope of party autonomy. It also provides that the Principles may be applied where the parties have chosen the *lex mercatoria* or 'general principles of law'. This implicitly assumes that party autonomy may effectively include such choices, and asserts that the Principles have sufficient status to meet the expectations of the parties where such a choice is made. Finally, and most controversially, Article 1:101(3)(b) asserts that the Principles may apply even if they are not chosen by the parties, if no national law has been chosen. This would therefore not be based on an exercise of party autonomy at all, but is rather the bold assertion that non-state law might be applied instead of state law in the absence of party choice. Although Article 1:101 evidently contains a complex choice of law rule, it must be noted that this rule is itself somewhat circular. It is an Article in the Principles that declares that the Principles may be relied on as a source of law – thereby purporting to confer legal status on itself.[64] For a choice of the Principles to be possible in national courts, it would require the law of the forum to adopt a choice of law rule which permits that choice, which could (but need not) be based on Article 1:101. The Principles have, however, ultimately been left as a soft law instrument.

The Draft Common Frame of Reference was somewhat more neutral in the position it adopted on its potential application. It did not purport to set out when it could or would apply, but rather presented itself as an academic codification that might be drawn on for a variety of purposes. However, the commentary introducing the Draft CFR made the following observations:

> It is still unclear whether or not the CFR, or parts of it, might at a later stage be used as the basis for one or more optional instruments, i.e. as the basis for an additional set of legal rules which parties might choose to govern their mutual rights and obligations. In the view of the two Groups such an optional instrument would open attractive perspectives, not least for consumer transactions.[65]

A more formal and more narrowly targeted proposal to adopt standardised EU rules of contract law was made in relation to a Common European

---

[64] The same point may be noted about the Preamble to the UNIDROIT Principles of International Commercial Contracts, which purports to specify when the Principles shall or may be applied.

[65] Draft Common Frame of Reference, p.38.

Sales Law (CESL) in 2011.[66] This proposal was withdrawn in 2016,[67] although there are suggestions that it may be revived in an alternate form.[68] In any case, Article 3 of the CESL proposal provided that:

> The parties may agree that the Common European Sales Law governs their cross-border contracts for the sale of goods, for the supply of digital content and for the provision of related services within the territorial, material and personal scope as set out in Articles 4 to 7.

This is evidently once again a (proposed) rule of party autonomy, under which the parties may select as a governing law a set of non-state rules.

It is unclear whether any of these proposals are likely to be adopted – as the United Kingdom was generally an opponent of these initiatives, there may be greater possibility for this if or when Brexit occurs. The various initiatives are, in any case, worth analysing as potentially signalling a greater willingness to open up party autonomy to the application of non-state law.

The first point that must be made in analysing these initiatives is that the rules developed do not have an entirely private character. This would be most obviously the case in relation to the proposed Common European Sales Law, which would (under the proposal) have been formally adopted by the European Union. These rules are non-state law, but (unlike the *lex mercatoria*) are not private law made by private parties, because they would derive their authority from the European Union. They would represent a distinctive form of non-state law – rules of private law enacted by an international organisation, albeit one with a *sui generis* character possessing many of the characteristics of a state.

A second point to note is that the potential expansion of party autonomy to encompass EU private law rules is an innovation in European regulatory technique. Instead of adopting a Common European Sales Law as a mandatory Regulation or Directive (which would raise concerns of EU regulatory competence), it would be adopted indirectly as a new potential source of law facilitated by an expanded conception of party autonomy. The EU may not be able to create binding European contract law, but it may be able to give individuals the power to choose it – thus, EU law would expand its scope by bypassing the sovereignty of states, and relying on the sovereignty of individuals to confer authority on its private law (should any of them choose to do so).[69]

---

[66] Proposal for a Regulation of the European Parliament and of the Council on a Common European Sales Law, COM/2011/0635 final.
[67] European Commission Work Programme 2015, COM(2014) 910 final, Annex 2, [60].
[68] See e.g. ec.europa.eu/justice/contract/digital-contract-rules/index_en.htm; Norris (2016).
[69] See Smits (2013b); Rühl (2012).

A consequentialist justification for party autonomy is evidently operative here – there is no intuitive sense that parties should have a 'right' or 'freedom' to have their contracts governed by an invented European contract law, that this should be among their inherent liberties under a 'deontological libertarian' approach.[70] Creating such an entitlement would instead be about deliberately affecting the 'law market', through introducing additional regulatory competition.[71] Such competition could aim either to improve Member State contract laws, or ultimately to replace them through private choice. It would thus seek to override national legal systems not through traditional European legal methods of direct or indirect effect, but through the promotion of EU contract law in an expanded 'law market' as an alternative to national systems, relying on the autonomy of the parties themselves to give force and even priority to the EU rules. It consciously positions private parties as the ultimate determinants of whether a European contract law succeeds alongside or instead of national contract law – implicitly adopting an extremely strong conception of party autonomy.

10.4   Non-State Law in Arbitration

This section examines two issues concerning non-state law in arbitration. The first is the practice of arbitral tribunals themselves – whether and when non-state law may be applied by a tribunal to determine the merits of a dispute. The second is the practice of courts in relation to arbitration – including whether decisions of arbitral tribunals based on the application of non-state law will be recognised and enforced. As in Chapter 6, the focus in this section is on private arbitration rather than international arbitration involving one or more state parties, although some particular issues arising in respect of such disputes are noted below.

10.4.1   The Applicable Law in Arbitration

The law applicable to arbitration agreements was examined in Section 6.3. This section focuses on a distinct issue – the law applicable to the *merits* of arbitral proceedings, rather than the agreement upon which the *jurisdiction* of the tribunal is based. However, the analysis of the law applicable to the merits question is strongly influenced by similar factors to the analysis set out in Chapter 6.

---

[70]   See Section 2.3.
[71]   For a sceptical perspective, see Posner (2013).

The first point to note is that an arbitral tribunal is not an institution of a national legal system and does not, therefore, have a forum law. This means that there is ordinarily no substantive law or choice of law rules which it is institutionally bound to apply. A tribunal will apply the law of the seat of arbitration to procedural questions, but arbitration laws seldom dictate choice of law rules to be followed by tribunals.[72] If the parties have chosen an applicable national law to govern their contract, there is, however, a strong argument that arbitrators are inherently obligated to apply the designated law, because their authority is itself contractual (although this may be subject to qualifications relating to mandatory rules and public policy).[73] For the same reason, where the parties have chosen the *lex mercatoria* (or the principles of international business law, or a codification such as the UNIDROIT Principles of International Commercial Contracts) to govern their contract, or another source of non-state law such as a body of religious law, the practice of many arbitral tribunals will be to give effect to that choice and apply the selected non-state law as the law governing the merits of the dispute.[74] The choice of non-state law in the contract may be viewed as part of the contract conferring power on the tribunal – the arbitrators may consider themselves contractually bound to apply a non-state law chosen by the parties.[75] Another reason for giving effect to a choice of non-state law is that, as discussed in Section 6.2, arbitrators may view themselves as part of a transnational dispute resolution system, rather than functioning under the auspices of any national legal order. The application of transnational rules of substantive law reflects

[72] It may, however, be noted that in the context of investor-state arbitration, the ICSID Convention provides (in Article 42(1)) that "The Tribunal shall decide a dispute in accordance with such rules of law as may be agreed by the parties", thus recognising party autonomy in choice of law including the possibility of a choice of non-state law or international law.

[73] See generally e.g. Bermann and Mistelis (2011); Radicati di Brozolo (2012b); Nygh (1999), p.226ff; Blessing (1997); Voser (1996); Hochstrasser (1994); Mayer (1986); see further discussion in Section 9.4.

[74] ICC Arbitration Rules 2017, Art.21; UNCITRAL Rules on International Commercial Arbitration, Art.33; UNCITRAL Model Law on International Commercial Arbitration, Art.28; 1961 European Arbitration Rules; Art.VII. This is also reflected in the Resolution on Transnational Rules adopted at the 65th International Law Association Conference, Cairo, 26 April 1992. This practice has prompted a voluminous literature. See generally e.g. Bermann (2016); Basedow (2013a), p.140ff; Cuniberti (2013); Liukkunen (2013); Dessemontet (2012); Berger (2010); Hatzimihail (2008); Michaels (2007); Stone Sweet (2006); Howarth (2004); Pryles (2003); Juenger (2000); Nygh (1999), p.191ff; Carbonneau (1998); Teubner (1997); Lowenfeld (1990); Mustill (1988); Lando (1985).

[75] This raises the questions of what law governs the contract between the parties and the arbitrator(s), and whether this might itself be non-state law – which are beyond the scope of this book.

this conceptual approach, allowing the parties to contract out of not only national courts and procedural laws, but also national substantive laws.[76]

Even if the parties have made a choice of (state or non-state) law, some arbitral tribunals may, however, approach the applicable law not as a question of the contractual foundations of the tribunal, but take the view that the 'contractual' foundations require the identification of a national law that gives the agreement between the parties the status of a 'contract'.[77] For such tribunals, determining the applicable law is itself a matter of identifying and applying relevant choice of law rules, as a step prior to determining the validity and effectiveness of the choice of law agreement. A tribunal will also generally have to take this approach in the absence of party choice of law, or for issues falling outside the scope of any choice of law agreement.[78] A variety of different approaches to choice of law in this context may be followed.[79] A tribunal may, of course, simply apply the substantive law of the seat, but this approach is unlikely to be adopted as a rule unless the dispute is entirely internal to the seat of the arbitration. If a dispute touches more than one legal order, the tribunal will need to apply a set of choice of law rules to determine the substantive applicable law, and thus a preliminary question is what choice of law rules to apply.

One approach is for the tribunal to apply the choice of law rules of the seat – typically, the choice of law in contract rules examined in Chapter 7. If this approach is adopted by an arbitral tribunal, then the question of whether non-state law may be applied by the tribunal is dependent on the approach of the national law of the seat of the arbitration. An arbitration following this approach in any EU Member State, for example, would apply the Rome I Regulation, under which non-state law could never be the applicable law even if chosen by the parties. However, an arbitration in a state which had adopted the Hague Principles on Choice of Law in International Commercial Contracts 2015 could, following those principles, recognise a choice of non-state law (as discussed further in Section 10.3.3). A disadvantage of this approach is that it is not clear that the seat should have such a strong role in determining the substantive applicable law, as the seat of the arbitration is generally chosen for procedural or practical reasons, and it is not necessarily apparent that choice of law rules designed for courts should be followed strictly by arbitral tribunals.

---

[76] This may be particularly important where one or both parties are governments or state-owned, and the reason for choosing arbitration is to ensure the dispute is resolved without state interference in process or substance.

[77] See further Section 6.3.1.

[78] See further Section 8.2.

[79] See generally e.g. Bermann (2015); Cordero-Moss (2014); Grigera Naón (2001).

A second approach is for the tribunal to determine which national choice of law rules to apply based on a preliminary analysis of the connections the dispute has with different legal systems. Under this approach, a tribunal conducts what might be described as a 'choice of choice of law' determination. A tribunal sitting in London may decide that the dispute it is resolving, which centres around a contract to be performed in Singapore, should be resolved by applying whatever law would be applied by the courts of Singapore, and thus look to the choice of law rules of Singapore to determine the governing law. Once again, under this approach, the question of whether non-state law may be applied by the tribunal is dependent on the approach of the national law whose choice of law rules are chosen by the tribunal (including the possibility that the tribunal refers to a state which has adopted the Hague Principles). The main disadvantages of this approach are its complexity, the uncertainty around the test for determining which national choice of law rules to apply, and again the question of whether a tribunal should be applying choice of law rules developed for national courts.

A third approach is for the tribunal to apply 'transnational' choice of law rules. Under this approach, the tribunal would not look to any particular system of national law to determine the governing law, but would rather look to the standards and practices of other arbitral tribunals, or to 'general principles' of private international law derived from the practice of states.[80] The question for present purposes then becomes whether these standards permit the application of non-state law, either where this is chosen by the parties or in the absence of party choice.[81] Practice is by no means uniform on the point. If a tribunal were to derive transnational choice of law rules from the practice of states, as set out in national choice of law rules, there is very limited support for applying non-state law, as discussed in Section 10.2. However, the Hague Principles could be referred to directly by a tribunal in this context as a model of 'best practice', whether or not adopted by any state connected to the dispute, permitting a choice of non-state law. The practice thus reflected is not the practice of states, but of arbitral tribunals. Some arbitral tribunals have also found that the detachment of arbitration from national law permits or requires the application of non-state

---

[80] For a recent argument in favour of such an approach, see e.g. Hayward (2017).

[81] There are a few examples of the application of the UNIDROIT Principles by arbitral tribunals in the absence of party choice at www.unilex.info/article.cfm?pid=2&pos=1&iid=1224&cid=23#IID1224.

law, even in the absence of party choice (which would not, of course, be an exercise of party autonomy).[82]

Whether arbitration can be detached from national law in this way (with or without party choice of non-state law) is one of its most hotly contested questions, as discussed further in Section 6.2. Some arbitrators and scholars, perhaps most prominent amongst them Emmanuel Gaillard, have argued strongly that arbitration is transnational in character. As a consequence, it is argued, arbitration routinely can and should apply non-state law, and in so doing it does not depend on national law, because it is practically self-enforcing in the community of international business – "the legally binding nature of arbitration is rooted in a distinct, trans-national legal order, that could be labelled as the 'arbitral legal order', and not in a national legal order".[83] Some have even gone so far as to suggest that in arbitration a contract does not need a law at all (often referred to by the French 'contrat sans loi'),[84] although this is perhaps just a misleading way of saying that it does not need a state law.[85] In Gaillard's conception, the application of non-state law may be viewed as a methodology that replaces traditional choice of law approaches (rather than being recognised within them) – arbitral tribunals should, under this approach, determine the substantive rule for a given issue through a process of comparative law analysis rather than a choice of law process.[86] The *lex mercatoria* may thus be viewed not only as an alternative to national contract law, but also to private international law itself, although it may also be recognised within private international law (as is the case with the Hague Principles, as discussed in Section 10.3.3).

Of course arbitrators will frequently apply or draw on national laws to resolve contractual disputes, and this is even true of those contractual relationships in which the parties have designated the *lex mercatoria*. The application of national law may be in the form of applying rules of public

---

[82] It has been argued (somewhat tenuously), however, that the absence of party choice of law may imply that the parties each wished to avoid the application of the other party's law, suggesting instead an implied choice of non-state law: see e.g. *Ministry of Defence and Support for Armed Forces of the Islamic Republic of Iran v. Westinghouse Electric Corp.*, ICC Award No. 7375, 5 June 1996.

[83] Gaillard (2010b).

[84] See generally e.g. Michaels (2007); Gannagé (2007); Nygh (1999), Chapter 8; Teubner (1997).

[85] See discussion in Nygh (1999), p.172ff; Highet (1989).

[86] Gaillard (2000); see discussion in Schultz (2008), p.671ff. See similarly Lando (1985), p.752ff; Croff (1982). See also Redfern and Hunter (2015), [3.156ff].

policy or mandatory rules, either in a private international law sense (as examined further in Section 9.4) or where those rules form part of a system of national private law connected to the dispute.[87] To some extent this may be a recognition of the existence of state interests that override party autonomy, although it may also be simply a pragmatic recognition by the arbitrators that their award, in order to be ultimately enforceable, must be accepted by at least one national court system (although it may not be predictable *which* national court system will be asked to enforce the award). Other arbitrators, however, look to transnational standards even for questions of public policy, finding that the practice of arbitration has itself generated a 'transnational public policy' (sometimes described as 'truly international public policy').[88] The content of this policy is unclear, as is the 'public' whose interests are supposedly represented by these policies, and the authority under which that representation is carried out.

The general conclusion from this analysis is that there are contrasting conceptions of arbitration, under which it should be governed either entirely by national law or entirely by transnational law, and neither of them ultimately seems sustainable. The national law model is not sustainable because ultimately an arbitral tribunal does not have forum choice of law rules and must at some point apply some form of transnational law. This may be transnational substantive law, or it may be simply transnational choice of law rules that point to a national substantive law, or it may even be transnational rules to determine which national choice of law rules to apply. The transnational model is also arguably not entirely sustainable because although many arbitral awards may be complied with voluntarily for reputational reasons, ultimately an arbitral award is dependent on national courts for enforcement. When national courts review the validity of an arbitral award, they will generally look to national standards of public policy or mandatory rules, and an award that has ignored those standards may thereby be rendered ineffective. This issue is examined further in Section 10.4.2.

Although not the principal concern of this chapter, it may be noted that international courts and tribunals (dealing with disputes involving one or more states) may also adopt a transnational approach if required to determine the law governing a contract (as is commonly the case, for example, in investor–state arbitration).[89] An international court or tribunal, once again, will generally have no forum choice of law rules, and

---

[87] See generally e.g. the various articles in (2007) 18 *American Review of International Arbitration* 1–228.

[88] See classically e.g. Lalive (1986); Burger (1984); Dolinger (1982).

[89] See generally e.g. Kjos (2013); Salacuse (2013); Sasson (2010); Spiermann (2008).

reference to the choice of law rules of a particular state may be unsatisfactory. This was already arguably recognised by the Permanent Court of International Justice in the *Serbian Loans Case*,[90] discussed in Section 10.2. The increased judicialisation of international dispute resolution, with a range of international courts and tribunals dealing with disputes that are likely to touch on a variety of issues of national law, potentially opens up a new field for private international law – a direct need for the development of transnational private international law. The development of internationalised rules of private international law by institutions such as the Hague Conference could thus have the added benefit of crystallising transnational rules of private international law, which would assist in the work of international courts and tribunals.

10.4.2 *National Courts and Arbitration under Non-State Law*

As noted above, arbitral tribunals frequently recognise a choice of non-state law by the parties as valid, principally because of the contractual nature of arbitral jurisdiction and the transnational conception of arbitration as a dispute resolution system. A supporting role is also played by a further factor – the role that national courts may play in indirectly endorsing the application of non-state law by an arbitral tribunal. This issue arises in two contexts – first, the supervision by the courts of the seat of the conduct of an arbitration, including in applications to set aside an arbitral award; and second, the recognition and enforcement of arbitral awards.

It might be thought that national courts would be sceptical of the application of non-state law in arbitration, given that national choice of law rules generally view such a choice as invalid. This is, however, in fact generally not the case. Arbitrations based on the application of the UNIDROIT Principles, for example, have been widely recognised and enforced around the world.[91] This is facilitated by national arbitration laws that expressly or implicitly authorise the application of non-state law. In the United Kingdom, for example, Article 46 of the Arbitration Act 1996 provides as follows:

> Rules applicable to substance of dispute.
>
> (1) The arbitral tribunal shall decide the dispute –
>   (a) in accordance with the law chosen by the parties as applicable to the substance of the dispute, or
>   (b) if the parties so agree, in accordance with such other considerations as are agreed by them or determined by the tribunal.

---

[90] *Serbian Loans Case, France v. Yugoslavia* (1929) PCIJ Ser A, No 20, Judgment 14.
[91] This practice is documented with the support of UNIDROIT at www.unilex.info/.

This Act affirmed the practice of the courts, which has long been to enforce arbitral awards based on a variety of non-state law sources (provided the parties intend to create legally binding relations, and designate a sufficiently certain 'law' that does not violate forum public policy).[92]

There may appear at first glance to be an inconsistency here in UK law, and indeed in most national legal systems. Even though an arbitral award may be based on a law that the courts would not themselves recognise as a valid legal system, it is nevertheless entitled (at least presumptively) to judicial recognition and enforcement. A court which is itself interpreting a contract that purports to be governed by the *lex mercatoria* must (applying state choice of law rules, like the Rome I Regulation) find that this is an invalid choice of law, and that the contract is governed by some national law. A court which is determining the validity of an arbitral award based on the interpretation of the very same contract, in which the arbitrators applied the *lex mercatoria*, must (under for example the Arbitration Act 1996) recognise that this is a *valid* choice of law. The validity of the choice of law depends, it seems, on the context in which the question arises.

There are, however, sensible reasons of principle and policy behind this distinction. As a matter of principle, provisions of national law such as Article 46 of the Arbitration Act 1996 (UK) essentially recognise that arbitration is a creature of contract rather than national law, and it must be conducted according to the wishes of the parties. If the parties have contracted for non-state law to govern, arbitrators will at least presumptively view that contractual provision as binding on themselves as well as the parties. There is nothing necessary about this determination, as a national legal system could readily pass a law to the contrary (prohibiting parties from choosing or arbitrators from applying non-state law), but given the practices and perceptions of arbitration as independent from national law this would be undoubtedly viewed as hostile to arbitration. As a matter of policy, as examined in Chapter 6, there are good reasons for national legal systems to accept arbitration agreements in general – essentially, arbitration resolves disputes efficiently and without using public resources. There are also respectable reasons why states generally refuse to accept a choice of non-state law in national courts – essentially, it would put their public resources at the service of what may be characterised as purely 'private'

---

[92] *Deutsche Schachtbau- und Tiefbohrgesellschaft mbH v. R'as Al Khaimah Oil Company* ('the Rakoil Case') [1987] 2 All ER 769 (reversed on other grounds at [1990] 1 AC 295); *Channel Tunnel Group Ltd v. Balfour Beatty Constructions Ltd* [1993] AC 334; *Musawi v. RE International (UK) Ltd* [2007] EWHC 2981 (Ch); *Dallah Real Estate & Tourism Holding Co. v. Pakistan* [2010] UKSC 46. See further generally Schultz (2014).

norms. When it comes to the enforcement of arbitral awards based on non-state law, these policies must be weighed against each other. Enforcement of an arbitral award based on non-state law does involve using some public resources (through court proceedings to enforce the award) to serve private norms. But those resources are less than what would be required in full litigation of the dispute, and they give support to an efficient, flexible, and party-centred system of arbitration that is attractive to private commercial actors and relieves the caseload of the courts. And in determining the enforceability of an arbitral award, there is the opportunity to bring public policy to bear, if there are public interests in the case.

This supportive attitude of national law is to some extent a matter of respecting the practice of arbitral tribunals, but it also reinforces that practice. While an arbitrator is bound to apply the law chosen by the parties, this may sometimes be in tension with their duty to render an enforceable award, where the arbitrator is aware that the courts of the seat of arbitration or the place where the award is likely to be enforced might view the choice of the parties as invalid. Provisions such as Article 46 of the Arbitration Act 1996 (UK) give arbitrators comfort that they may apply non-state law as directed by the parties, without being concerned that to do so will render the award unenforceable. As a result, they offer indirect support to the common practice in arbitration of accepting a choice of non-state law as a valid exercise of party autonomy in choice of law.

10.5   Conclusion

The possibility for the parties to choose non-state law to govern their contract is a question that seems perennially to be at the frontiers of the development of party autonomy. In recent decades, it has become fairly commonplace for arbitral tribunals to give effect to a choice of non-state law by the parties, and even (exceptionally) to apply non-state law in the absence of party choice. This practice has to some extent been recognised and affirmed through national arbitration laws, which provide for the enforcement of arbitral awards based on non-state law. Arguments have been increasingly made that choices of non-state law should also be recognised by national courts, and the Hague Principles on Choice of Law in International Commercial Contracts 2015 are the clearest and strongest recognition that these arguments are gaining acceptance. Caution should be exercised, however, before declaring that the expansion of party autonomy to permit a choice of non-state law is imminent or even likely. The Hague Principles themselves are designed partly to be applied by arbitral tribunals, which may explain their particular openness to non-state law. National choice of law rules are, almost without exception, not open to a choice of non-state law by the parties. Allowing such a choice without any limitations could create concerns regarding the legitimacy of the body of private law chosen by the parties, but as the experience of the Hague Principles shows, drafting legitimacy criteria to constrain the application of non-state law is far from being a simple task.

The possibility of a choice of non-state law is notably an issue for which the different justifications for party autonomy examined in Section 2.3 appear to have different implications. Those who view party autonomy as deriving from an inherent exercise of private freedom might well be open to a choice beyond national law, as might those who look to party autonomy to create regulatory competition. On the other hand, those who view party autonomy as a rule that can choose efficiently between different potentially applicable laws by delegating that decision to the parties may not see any benefit in expanding that choice beyond national law, and those who view party autonomy as creating public benefit would generally recognise that this must be weighed against the other public interests protected by national legal systems, which may not be recognised in non-state law. The issue of non-state law in party autonomy thus reflects an underlying uncertainty as to the justifications for party autonomy, and is likely to remain highly contentious.

11

Conclusions

11.1 Introduction

This book has analysed a broad range of aspects of party autonomy in private international law, looking at both its historical and theoretical foundations (the focus of Chapter 2) and its application in legal practice, across both choice of forum (the focus of Chapters 3–6) and choice of law (the focus of Chapters 7–10), including state and non-state forms of law and dispute-resolution (both courts and arbitral tribunals, and state and non-state law), and dealing with contractual and non-contractual disputes. This final chapter concludes the analysis, first, by returning to the five questions of consistency identified in Section 1.4, and second, with a final appraisal of the role of party autonomy in private international law.

11.2 Five Questions of Consistency

As noted in Chapter 1, party autonomy is sometimes (and perhaps increasingly) described as a universal or at least general principle in private international law, and the analysis in this book confirms that it is undoubtedly true that choice of court and choice of law agreements are commonly given effect. Different aspects of party autonomy in private international law have, however, tended to be examined separately in the academic literature. The wide focus of this book permits it to address a fundamental issue: whether party autonomy is or should be consistent across the range of different contexts in which it arises. Five questions of consistency were identified in Section 1.4, and each is now examined in turn.

11.2.1 Consistency between Party Autonomy in Choice of Forum and Choice of Law

Choices of forum and law may be made independently, or in conjunction. In some respects the issues that they raise are different (a choice of law will always be exclusive, for example, while as examined in Sections 3.2 and 3.5 a choice of court may be non-exclusive or asymmetrical), but there are some common issues that arise concerning their effectiveness. If the parties choose both a forum and its law to govern their legal disputes, it might be expected that both choices would be effective in the same circumstances and to the same extent, so that the chosen forum will always apply its own law, and conversely, that only the courts whose law is chosen will have jurisdiction. There are some important linkages between choice of forum and choice of law in practice that might reflect this – for example, the fact that a choice of law may serve as a potential basis of jurisdiction under the common law, and may affect the exercise of jurisdiction more broadly under the common law and in the United States (as examined in Section 3.4), and the converse fact that an exclusive choice of court agreement is often relied on as establishing an implied choice of law (as examined in Section 7.2).

The analysis in this book suggests, however, that party autonomy in choice of forum and choice of law are not dealt with consistently in a number of important respects. This is at least in part because, as examined in Section 2.2, the origins of party autonomy in each context are clearly distinct. Party autonomy in choice of forum derived from the emergence of jurisdiction based on submission and a focus on questions of fairness rather than state power in the law of jurisdiction. Party autonomy in choice of law derived from justifications for particular contractual choice of law rules that relied on the imputed and then actual expectations of the parties. Although in both contexts choices by the parties are generally recognised, there are important differences. The law governing the validity of a jurisdiction agreement (see Section 3.3) will, for example, often be different from that governing the validity of a choice of law agreement (see Sections 7.5 and 7.6). Formality requirements are common in the context of choice of court agreements (see Section 5.2), and rare in the context of choice of law agreements (see Section 7.2). Distinct approaches are also often taken in choice of forum and choice of law to the question of whether an objective connection is required between the dispute and the court or law chosen by the parties (see Sections 5.3 and 7.3), and the related question of whether a choice is available in a purely domestic legal situation (see Section 9.3). While both rules of jurisdiction and choice of law rules constrain party autonomy in a range of subject matter contexts or in special regimes relating to weaker parties such as consumers or employees, the techniques applied to limit party autonomy in each context are different – in jurisdiction (see Section 5.5) tending to prevent a choice altogether and in choice of law (see Section 9.2) tending to permit a choice but potentially limit its effectiveness. This significant variation in practice suggests that, while there are undoubtedly common theoretical justifications for party autonomy in the context of both choice of forum and choice of law, it may be at best premature to suggest that treatment of these questions is guided by a single consistent set of principles.

11.2.2   Consistency between Party Autonomy in Contract and in Other Areas of Law

Party autonomy is almost always exercised as a term of a contract, in the form of a choice of court or choice of law clause, and naturally enough it has emerged primarily through the private international law of contracts (see Chapters 3 and 7). Choice of court and choice of law clauses may, however, intend to encompass non-contractual disputes – determining the subject-matter scope of such clauses can itself be a complex question (examined in Sections 4.2 and 8.2). Where such an intention is expressed, this invites a further question of consistency: is the treatment of party autonomy consistent whether a claim is brought in contract or in another form (such as a tort or a proprietary claim)?

In the jurisdictional context, an exercise of party autonomy is likely to be effective for a range of non-contractual claims if they have a link to the contract establishing the choice of court, often expressed through a foreseeability test (Section 4.3). An exclusive jurisdiction agreement will thus usually be effective to ensure that a single forum hears all claims arising from a contractual relationship, but not necessarily those beyond. In the context of choice of law, the analysis is more nuanced – choices of law are given varying degrees of effect (ranging from none at all to full effect) in respect of the variety of non-contractual causes of action (examined in Sections 8.2–8.7). The exercise of party autonomy in choice of law is thus often not effective in ensuring that all claims are governed by the chosen law, although the breadth and weight of influence of choice of law agreements appears to be expanding. These variations in approach suggest another distinction between choice of court and choice of law – in the former context, consistency of treatment through an expansive interpretation and enforcement of the jurisdiction agreement is generally favoured, while in the latter, the different policy considerations at stake in different causes of action take priority as specialised choice of law rules give varying degrees of effect to an exercise of party autonomy.

A further distinctive approach may be identified in the context of matters of personal law, such as family law and succession (examined in Section 8.8). Party autonomy is generally limited in such contexts to a choice between a number of objectively connected laws, but the choice itself takes on a different quality – it allows an individual or a couple to self-determine which connecting factor is most significant in their legal relations, and thus gives greater power to individuals in controlling legal aspects of their personal identity.

11.2.3   Consistency between the Choice of Non-State Forums or Law and the Choice of State Forums or Law

This book has also examined the extension of choice of forum beyond state courts, and the much-debated potential extension of choice of law beyond state law. The former development concerns arbitration (the subject of Chapter 6) – the extent to which parties can opt out of national courts in favour of private dispute resolution mechanisms. The latter (the subject of Chapter 10) concerns whether a court or arbitral tribunal should accept and recognise a choice of non-state law. This then invites a third question of consistency – whether a choice of a non-state forum or law is or should be treated consistently with a choice of a state court or law.

Some of the issues that arise concerning choice of court agreements and arbitration agreements are closely related. Each raises, for example, a difficult choice of law question for the determination of the validity of the agreement, as a severable contract, or the interpretation of its scope (examined in Sections 3.3 and 6.3). When these issues should be addressed by courts or left to arbitral tribunals raises further complexities (examined in Section 6.4). The issues that arise concerning the effect of choice of court or arbitration agreements on third parties (see Sections 3.6 and 6.5) are also very similar, as frequently is the treatment of formal validity requirements (see Sections 5.2 and 6.3), and the question of the exclusivity of the agreement (see Sections 3.3 and 6.5). In other respects, however, quite distinctive rules govern choice of court and arbitration agreements. Where a jurisdiction agreement is ineffective, this is commonly based on a very close connection between the subject matter of the dispute and a particular state (see Section 5.4). Where an arbitration agreement is ineffective, this is commonly based on a concern as to whether the subject matter is capable of settlement through arbitration (see Section 6.6) – the concern is focused on the absence of any public interest represented in arbitral proceedings, rather than the privileging of the public interests of a particular state. The effectiveness of a choice of court agreement is frequently constrained by strict or discretionary protections for weaker parties such as consumers and employees (see Section 5.5), while in at least some legal systems arbitration of consumer or employment disputes is positively encouraged. Arbitration may distinctively be characterised as a transnational dispute resolution process, and an arbitration agreement as thus governed by non-state law (explored in Section 6.2). The consensual basis of arbitration raises further difficulties concerning the possibility of class arbitration proceedings (examined in Section 6.5).

The treatment of a choice of state or non-state law is even more strikingly disparate. In national courts, almost without exception, a choice of non-state law is not considered a valid choice of law (see Section 10.2), although there are possible signs of a relaxation of this approach (see Section 10.3). In the context of arbitration, however, such a choice may freely be made, at least under some of the approaches taken to choice of law questions (see Section 10.4). The conflict between these perspectives is perhaps not as stark, however, as this would suggest, as national courts commonly recognise and enforce arbitral awards based on non-state law. It remains to be seen whether the acceptance of a choice of non-state law in the Hague Principles on Choice of Law in International Commercial Contracts 2015 signifies a broader trend towards greater consistency in the treatment of state and non-state law, or merely the fact that this instrument is aimed at both national legal development and application by arbitrators – two constituencies who may have irreconcilable interests.

11.2.4   Consistency between Party Autonomy in Practice and Party Autonomy in Theory

Practice and theory need not be coextensive – they may deal with distinct problems – but the rules of party autonomy need to be evaluated based on whether they achieve desired policy goals, and theoretical accounts of party autonomy need to be evaluated not only on their normative desirability but on their descriptive accuracy. This raises a further question concerning whether the limits on party autonomy in practice are consistent with its theoretical justifications.

The answer to this question is complicated by the fact that there are a number of distinct theoretical justifications for party autonomy, explored particularly in Section 2.3. In general terms, these various arguments are each supportive of the effectiveness of choice of court and choice of law agreements, but they suggest different potential limits or constraints on party autonomy. Five of these were identified in Section 2.4 – concerns of authenticity, foreseeability, public interests and values, justifiability, and the possible requirement for a cross-border element. Each of these constraints is identifiable in aspects of legal practice, as explored throughout this book. Concerns of authenticity particularly arise in the exercise of party autonomy by weaker parties, although these are treated differently in different legal systems and in the contexts of choice of court and choice of law. A limitation based on foreseeability is identifiable in certain aspects of the law in some legal systems, particularly relating to the scope of effect of party agreements, but is by no means universal. Public interests and values are frequently balanced against the exercise of party autonomy, but in a variety of ways and to a variety of extents. The possible requirement for an objective connection between the parties or their dispute and the court or law chosen by the parties, justifying the choice by the parties, is again present in the practice of some legal systems but not in others, and in certain aspects of party autonomy and not in others. A cross-border element is in some contexts required for an exercise of party autonomy, while in some contexts the engagement of private international law rules is triggered by the exercise of party autonomy itself. The general conclusion here is that each of the theoretical justifications for party autonomy is reflected in some aspects of practice, but no theoretical justification offers a complete explanation for practice across different jurisdictions or across different aspects of party autonomy. This suggests that the idea of party autonomy as a unifying principle of private international law may be more shallow than is sometimes contended.

11.2.5   Consistency between Legal Systems

A final and related question of consistency is whether the approaches to party autonomy in the various legal systems examined comparatively in this book (introduced in Section 1.2) are the same. As foreshadowed above, while the principle of party autonomy is broadly supported across the jurisdictions examined in this book (with some limited exceptions), the detailed rules governing its application in practice vary significantly between states (and indeed between the legal systems within the United States). For example, party autonomy may be significantly constrained by requirements for an objective connection in some US courts, or in some cases entirely ineffective, because (particularly state) courts may view foreign choice of court agreements as an impermissible attempt to oust the jurisdiction of the court, and may view foreign choice of law agreements as outweighed by the analysis of competing state interests. On the other hand, under US federal law and the law of other US states party autonomy is often recognised as effective even in relation to consumer or employment contracts. In the European Union, by contrast, party autonomy is generally unconstrained by requirements for any objective connection, but excluded or significantly constrained for consumer and employment contracts. Under the common law, choice of court agreements are also generally given effect without objective constraints, but this is ultimately subject to judicial discretion, while the techniques to constrain party autonomy for weaker parties rely more on the use of mandatory rules, raising challenging questions of whether these may be evaded through a combination of a choice of a foreign court and law (examined in Section 9.4).

The Hague Convention on Choice of Court Agreements 2005 and the Hague Principles on Choice of Law in International Commercial Contracts 2015 are undoubtedly impressive attempts to identify and articulate an international consensus or best practice in the context of party autonomy. It must be noted, however, that in excluding consumer and employment contracts they avoid some of the more contested issues in party autonomy, in other respects they raise some complex and as yet unresolved questions, and in a number of ways they do not reflect the existing practice of the legal systems examined in this book (nor could they, because of the variability of that practice). In most states, at least in many respects, they are therefore more of a model for law reform than a codification of existing rules. There would be evident benefits to harmonisation of the rules governing party autonomy in terms of ensuring consistent treatment of choice of court and law agreements between jurisdictions, and thereby increasing legal certainty for the parties to such agreements. The benefits of party autonomy are maximised if a choice of court or law agreement is given identical effect in different forums. Given the currently limited adoption of the Hague instruments, it must at this time be concluded that it is unclear whether the rules they propose and the prospect they offer of reaching internationally harmonised solutions will be enough to motivate states to compromise the local policies and preferences embodied in their presently diverse approaches to party autonomy.

11.3   Appraising Party Autonomy

At first glance, party autonomy in private international law may seem to have become ubiquitous and uncontroversial. Choice of court and choice of law agreements are commonplace in contracts, sometimes even included as boilerplate clauses without detailed consideration or careful drafting. Such clauses are also generally given effect in various direct and indirect ways, and lauded as providing efficient solutions to complex problems through empowering individuals. Party autonomy is undoubtedly here to stay as an approach to private international law problems in an increasingly globalised economy, reinforced by recent international and national codifications, and comes with undisputed benefits.

On closer examination, however, both the theoretical and practical aspects of party autonomy are more complex and more contested that this would suggest. Party autonomy is supported by several different justifications, but these suggest distinct approaches to the limits of choice of court and choice of law, each of which is reflected in aspects of the legal practice examined in this book. The cohesiveness of party autonomy as a principle across jurisdictions and across the various issues it encompasses is open to question, as noted in Section 11.2 and explored throughout this book. Particular questions may be raised as to whether party autonomy in jurisdiction and choice of law, often discussed as a unified phenomenon but with distinct historical origins, should really be encompassed under a single doctrine – the issues arising in the two contexts are often distinctive, and even where they are comparable, the approaches adopted are often not consistent. There are also various contexts in which the values inherent in party autonomy must be weighed against competing values and interests. The rules governing party autonomy in private international law are in some ways an exemplification of the perennial tension between the private and the public, the individual and the collective, which is characteristic of liberal societies, but with an international dimension that raises challenging questions as to which public interests (if any) should be involved. The benefits provided by giving effect to choice of court and choice of law agreements must particularly be weighed against the costs to the effectiveness of state substantive law. Enabling a free choice of law may, for example, increase the efficiency of economic activity, but risks undermining the policies inherent in the laws objectively connected to the parties or their legal relations. Enabling a free choice of an exclusive court or arbitral tribunal may facilitate better calculation of litigation risk, but itself risks undermining the safety net of state mandatory rules, and may in practical terms affect whether access to justice is real or illusory.

Private international law has long been understood as being concerned with the allocation of regulatory authority in matters of private law between states, both in terms of institutional authority (jurisdiction) and substantive regulatory authority (applicable law). In empowering individuals to choose which court or law regulates them, party autonomy essentially privatises the global governance function of allocating regulatory authority that has been traditionally carried out by rules based on objective connecting factors operating within the framework of public international law rules of jurisdiction. In some cases party autonomy removes altogether the territorial or nationality-based requirements for prescriptive jurisdiction, potentially de-linking private law from traditional regulatory constraints – allowing economic activity to disconnect from the law of the places or people affected by that activity. Party autonomy is a challenge to the framework of public international law jurisdiction, but the values and principles embodied in that framework are also a challenge to party autonomy. Both choice of arbitration and non-state law raise further fundamental questions about the scope of party autonomy. They raise the possibility that private parties might not only choose between different national courts or legal systems, but might also choose privately constituted alternatives. This would be a double-privatisation under which it is not just the power of choice given to private parties, but the power of creating the object of choice as a substitute for state-provided courts or law – not just a privatisation of the regulatory function of private international law, but a privatisation of the regulatory functions of substantive private law and national courts.

The issues raised by party autonomy in private international law are varied and complex. They include difficult technical questions, but they should not be dismissed as technicalities or as boilerplate issues. The power of private parties to choose their own court or their own law is firmly established as a general principle. The foundations and limits of that principle deserve close examination, however, because there remain many contested issues in both theory and practice, and because party autonomy raises fundamental questions concerning the effectiveness of state law and the justness and legitimacy of the functioning of private law and dispute resolution in the global legal order.

BIBLIOGRAPHY

Treaties, Regulations, Statutes, Reports, and Other Documents

Abbreviation	Full reference
Accession Convention 1978	Council Convention on the accession of the Kingdom of Denmark, Ireland and the United Kingdom of Great Britain and Northern Ireland to the Convention on jurisdiction and the enforcement of judgments in civil and commercial matters and to the Protocol on its interpretation by the Court of Justice (Signed on 9 October 1978) (78/884/EEC)
Accession Convention 1989	Convention on the accession of the Kingdom of Spain and the Portuguese Republic to the Convention on jurisdiction and the enforcement of judgments in civil and commercial matters and to the Protocol on its interpretation by the Court of Justice with the adjustments made to them by the Convention on the accession of the Kingdom of Denmark, of Ireland and of the United Kingdom of Great Britain and Northern Ireland and the adjustments made to them by the Convention on the accession of the Hellenic Republic (89/535/EEC)
Basel Principles (1991)	Principles on 'The Autonomy of the Parties in International Contracts Between Private Persons or Entities', International Law Association, adopted in Basel 1991. Available at www.idi-iil.org/app/uploads/2017/06/1991_bal_02_en.pdf.
Brussels Convention	Convention of 27 September 1968 on Jurisdiction and the Enforcement of Judgments in Civil and Commercial Matters (consolidated version), EU OJ 98/C 27/1, 26 January 1998
Brussels I Regulation 2001	Council Regulation (EC) No 44/2001 of 22 December 2000 on Jurisdiction and the Recognition and Enforcement of Judgements in Civil and Commercial Matters, EU OJ L 12/1, 16 January 2001

Brussels I Regulation (or Recast Regulation, where necessary for disambiguation)	Regulation (EU) No 1215/2012 of the European Parliament and of the Council of 12 December 2012 on jurisdiction and the recognition and enforcement of judgments in civil and commercial matters (recast), EU OJ L 351/1, 20 December 2012
Brussels II *bis* Regulation	Council Regulation (EC) No 2201/2003 of 27 November 2003 concerning jurisdiction and the recognition and enforcement of judgments in matrimonial matters and the matters of parental responsibility, repealing Regulation (EC) No 1347/2000, EU OJ L 338/1, 23 December 2003
Commentary to the Hague Principles	Commentary to the Hague Principles Principles on Choice of Law in International Commercial Contracts 2015. Available at www.hcch.net/en/instruments/conventions/full-text/?cid=135#text
First Restatement of Conflict of Laws	Restatement of the Conflict of Laws, adopted by the American Law Institute on 11 May 1934
Giuliano-Lagarde Report	Report on the Convention on the law applicable to contractual obligations, EU OJ C 282/1, 31 October 1980
Hague Convention on Choice of Court Agreements 2005	Convention of 30 June 2005 on Choice of Court Agreements, Hague Conference on Private International Law. Available at www.hcch.net/en/instruments/conventions/full-text/?cid=98
Hague Convention Explanatory Report	Explanatory Report, Hague Convention on Choice of Court Agreements 2005. Available at www.hcch.net/upload/expl37e.pdf
Hague Maintenance Convention 2007	Convention of 23 November 2007 on the International Recovery of Child Support and Other Forms of Family Maintenance, Hague Conference on Private International Law. Available at www.hcch.net/en/instruments/conventions/status-table/?cid=131
Hague Maintenance Protocol 2007	Protocol of 23 November 2007 on the Law Applicable to Maintenance Obligations, Hague Conference on Private International Law. Available at www.hcch.net/en/instruments/conventions/full-text/?cid=133
Hague Principles on Choice of Law in International Commercial Contracts 2015	Principles on Choice of Law in International Commercial Contracts 2015, Hague Conference on Private International Law. Available at www.hcch.net/en/instruments/conventions/full-text/?cid=135
Hague Succession Convention 1989	Convention of 1 August 1989 on the Law Applicable to Succession to the Estates of Deceased Persons, Hague Conference on Private International Law (not in force). Available at www.hcch.net/en/instruments/conventions/full-text/?cid=62.

Jenard Report	Report by Mr P. Jenard on the Convention of 27 September 1968 on jurisdiction and the enforcement of judgments in civil and commercial matters, EU OJ C 59/1, 5 March 1979
Law of the People's Republic of China on the Laws Applicable to Foreign-Related Civil Relations (2010)	Law of the People's Republic of China on the Laws Applicable to Foreign-Related Civil Relations (2010). English translation by L U Song, China Foreign Affairs University. Available at http://conflictoflaws.net/News/2011/01/PIL-China.pdf.
Maintenance Regulation	Council Regulation (EC) No 4/2009 of 18 December 2008 on jurisdiction, applicable law, recognition and enforcement of decisions and cooperation in matters relating to maintenance obligations, EU OJ L 7, 10 January 2009
Matrimonial Property Regulation	Council Regulation (EU) 2016/1103 of 24 June 2016 implementing enhanced cooperation in the area of jurisdiction, applicable law and the recognition and enforcement of decisions in matters of matrimonial property regimes, EU OJ L 183, 8 July 2016
Mexico City Convention 1994	Inter-American Convention on the Law Applicable to International Contracts 1994, signed in Mexico City on 17 March 1994
New York Convention 1958	New York Convention on the Recognition and Enforcement of Foreign Arbitral Awards 1958
Rome Convention 1980	Convention on the Law Applicable to Contractual Obligations, opened for signature in Rome on 19 June 1980 (consolidated version), EU OJ 98/C 27/2, 26 January 1998
Rome I Regulation	Regulation (EC) No 593/2008 of the European Parliament and of the Council of 17 June 2008 on the law applicable to contractual obligations (Rome I), EU OJ L 177, 4 July 2008
Rome I Regulation Green Paper	Green Paper on the conversion of the Rome Convention of 1980 on the law applicable to contractual obligations into a Community instrument and its modernisation, Brussels, COM (2002) 654 final, 14 January 2003
Rome I Regulation Proposal	Commission Proposal for a Regulation on the Law Applicable to Contractual Obligations (Rome I), COM (2005) 650 final, 15 December 2005
Rome II Regulation	Regulation (EC) No 864/2007 of the European Parliament and of the Council on the law applicable to non-contractual obligations (Rome II), EU OJ L 199, 31 July 2007
Rome III Regulation	Council Regulation (EU) No 1259/2010 of 20 December 2010 implementing enhanced cooperation in the area of the law applicable to divorce and legal separation (Rome III), EU OJ L 343, 29 December 2010

Second Restatement of Conflict of Laws	Restatement (Second) of the Conflict of Laws, adopted by the American Law Institute on 23 May 1969
Succession Regulation	Regulation (EU) No 650/2012 of the European Parliament and of the Council of 4 July 2012 on jurisdiction, applicable law, recognition and enforcement of decisions and acceptance and enforcement of authentic instruments in matters of succession and on the creation of a European Certificate of Succession, EU OJ L 201/107, 27 July 2012
UNCITRAL Model Law	UNCITRAL Model Law on International Commercial Arbitration (1985), as amended in 2006. Available at www.uncitral.org/uncitral/en/uncitral_texts/arbitration/1985Model_arbitration.html

Books, Book Chapters, and Journal Articles

Albornoz (2010)	M. M. Albornoz, 'Choice of Law in International Contracts in Latin American Legal Systems' (2010) 6 *Journal of Private International Law* 23
Albornoz and González Martín (2016)	M. M. Albornoz and N. González Martín, 'Towards the Uniform Application of Party Autonomy for Choice of Law in International Commercial Contracts' (2016) 12 *Journal of Private International Law* 437
Ancel, Marion, and Wynaendts (2013)	M. E. Ancel, L. Marion, and L. Wynaendts, 'Reflections on One-Sided Jurisdiction Clauses in International Litigation' (2013) 148 *Banque & Droit* 3. English version available at SSRN: https://ssrn.com/abstract=2258419
Andrews (2001)	N. Andrews, 'Strangers to Justice No Longer: The Reversal of the Privity Rule under the Contracts (Rights of Third Parties) Act 1999' (2001) 60 *Cambridge Law Journal* 353
Anon (2005)	Anon, 'Note: Recent International Agreement' (2005) 119 *Harvard Law Review* 931
Arzandeh (2013)	A. Arzandeh, 'The Law Governing Arbitration Agreements in England' [2013] *Lloyd's Maritime and Commercial Law Quarterly* 31
Atrill (2004)	S. Atrill, 'Choice of Law in Contract: The Missing Pieces of the Article 4 Jigsaw?' (2004) 53 *International and Comparative Law Quarterly* 549
Audit (1974)	B. Audit, *La Fraude à la Loi* (Dalloz, 1974)
Austin (1832)	J. Austin, *The Province of Jurisprudence Determined* (J. Murray, 1832)

Ballarino (2002)	T. Ballarino, 'From *Centros* to *Überseering*: EC Right of Establishment and the Conflict of Laws' (2002) 4 *Yearbook of Private International Law* 203
Bantekas (2008)	I. Bantekas, 'The Foundations of Arbitrability in International Commercial Arbitration' (2008) 27 *Australian Year Book of International Law* 193
Barcelo (2003)	J. J. Barcelo III, 'International Commercial Arbitration – Who Decides the Arbitrators' Jurisdiction? Separability and Competence-Competence in Transnational Perspective' (2003) 36 *Vanderbilt Journal of Transnational Law* 1115
Baron (1999)	G. Baron, 'Do the UNIDROIT Principles of International Commercial Contracts Form a New Lex Mercatoria?' (1999) 15 *Arbitration International* 115
Basedow (2000)	J. Basedow, 'The Communitarization of the Conflict of Laws under the Treaty of Amsterdam' (2000) 37 *Common Market Law Review* 687
Basedow (2013a)	'The Law of Open Societies – Private Ordering and Public Regulation of International Relations' (2013) 360 *Recueil des Cours* 9
Basedow (2013b)	'Exclusive Choice-of-Court Agreements as a Derogation from Imperative Norms', in P. Lindskoug et al. (eds.), *Essays in Honour of Michael Bogdan* (Juristförlaget, 2013)
Basedow (2017)	'The Hague Principles on Choice of Law: their addressees and impact' (2017) 22 *Uniform Law Review* 304
Basedow et al. (2017)	J. Basedow, G. Rühl, F. Ferrari, and P. de Miguel Asensio (eds.), *Encyclopaedia of Private International Law* (Edward Elgar, 2017)
Bath (2016)	V. Bath, 'Overlapping Jurisdictions and the Resolution of Disputes Before Chinese and Foreign Courts' (2015–16) 17 *Yearbook of Private International Law* 111
Baxter (1963)	W. Baxter, 'Choice of Law and the Federal System' (1963) 16 *Stanford Law Review* 1
Beale (1896)	J. H. Beale, 'Book Review: Dicey's "Confict of Laws"' (1896) 10 *Harvard Law Review* 168
Beale (1909a)	'What Law Governs the Validity of a Contract. I' (1909) 23 *Harvard Law Review* 1
Beale (1909b)	'What Law Governs the Validity of a Contract. II. The Present Condition of the Authorities' (1909) 23 *Harvard Law Review* 79
Beale (1910a)	'What Law Governs the Validity of a Contract. II. The Present Condition of the Authorities [Continued]' (1910) 23 *Harvard Law Review* 194

Beale (1910b)	'What Law Governs the Validity of a Contract. III. Theoretical and Practical Criticisms of the Authorities' (1910) 23 *Harvard Law Review* 260
Beale (1914)	*Bartolus on the Conflict of Laws* (Harvard University Press, 1914)
Beale (1935)	*A Treatise on the Conflict of Laws* (Baker Voorhis and Co., 1935)
Beaumont (2009)	P. Beaumont, 'Hague Choice of Court Agreements Convention 2005: Background, Negotiations, Analysis and Current Status' (2009) 5 *Journal of Private International Law* 125
Beck (1987)	A. Beck, 'Floating Choice of Law Clauses' [1987] *Lloyd's Maritime and Commercial Law Quarterly* 523
Bell (2003)	A. Bell, *Forum Shopping and Venue in Transnational Litigation* (Oxford University Press, 2003)
Bennett (1990)	T. W. Bennett, 'Choice of Law Rules in Claims of Unjust Enrichment' (1990) 39 *International and Comparative Law Quarterly* 136
Berger (2010)	K. P. Berger, *The Creeping Codification of the New Lex Mercatoria* (Kluwer, 2nd edn, 2010)
Bergson (2017)	I. Bergson, 'A New Frontier for Brussels I – Private Law Remedies for Breach of the Regulation?' (2017) 13 *Journal of Private International Law* 365
Berman (2012)	P. S. Berman, *Global Legal Pluralism: A Jurisprudence of Law Beyond Borders* (Cambridge University Press, 2012)
Bermann (1990)	G. A. Bermann, 'The Use of Anti-suit Injunctions in International Litigation' (1990) 28 *Columbia Journal of Transnational Law* 589
Bermann (2005)	(ed.), *Party Autonomy: Constitutional and International Law Limits in Comparative Perspective* (Juris, 2005)
Bermann (2011)	'The Supreme Court Trilogy and Its Impact on U.S. Arbitration Law' (2011) 22 *American Review of International Arbitration* 551
Bermann (2012)	'The "Gateway" Problem in International Commercial Arbitration' (2012) 37 *Yale Journal of International Law* 1
Bermann (2015)	'Arbitration and Private International Law' (2015) 381 *Recueil des Cours* 41
Bermann (2016)	'"International Standards" as a Choice of Law Option in International Commercial Arbitration' (2016) 27 *American Review of International Arbitration* 423
Bermann and Mistelis (2011)	G. A. Bermann and L. Mistelis (eds.), *Mandatory Rules in International Arbitration* (Juris, 2011)

Bisping (2012)   C. Bisping, 'Avoid the Statutist Trap: The International Scope of the Consumer Credit Act 1974' (2012) 8 *Journal of Private International Law* 35

Black and Pitel (2016)   V. Black and S. G. A. Pitel, 'Forum-Selection Clauses: Beyond the Contracting Parties' (2016) 12 *Journal of Private International Law* 26

Blessing (1997)   M. Blessing, 'Mandatory Rules of Law versus Party Autonomy in International Arbitration' (1997) 14 *Journal of International Arbitration* 23

Blom (2002)   J. Blom, 'Private International Law in a Globalizing Age: The Quiet Canadian Revolution' (2002) 4 *Yearbook of Private International Law* 83

Boele-Woelki (2010)   K. Boele-Woelki, 'For Better or for Worse: The Europeanization of International Divorce Law' (2010) 12 *Yearbook of Private International Law* 1

Boele-Woelki (2016)   'Party Autonomy in Litigation and Arbitration in View of the Hague Principles on Choice of Law in International Commercial Contracts' (2016) 379 *Recueil des Cours* 35

Bonell (2005)   M. J. Bonell, *An International Restatement of Contract Law: The UNIDROIT Principles of International Commercial Contracts* (Brill, 3rd edn, 2005)

Bonomi (2001)   A. Bonomi, 'Article 7(1) of the European Contracts Convention: Codifying the Practice of Applying Foreign Mandatory Rules' (2001) 114 *Harvard Law Review* 2462

Bonomi (2008)   'Overriding Mandatory Provisions in the Rome I Regulation on the Law Applicable to Contracts' (2008) 10 *Yearbook of Private International Law* 285

Borchers (1992)   P. J. Borchers, 'Forum Selection Agreements in the Federal Courts after Carnival Cruise' (1992) 67 *Washington Law Review* 55

Borchers (2008)   'Categorical Exceptions to Party Autonomy in Private International Law' (2008) 82 *Tulane Law Review* 1645

Born (2014)   G. Born *International Commercial Arbitration* (Kluwer Law International, 2nd edn, 2014)

Born and Šćekić (2016)   G. Born and M. Šćekić, 'Pre-Arbitration Procedural Requirements: 'A Dismal Swamp'', in D. Caron, S. Schill, A. Cohen Smutny, and E. Triantafilou (eds.), *Practising Virtue: Inside International Arbitration* (Oxford University Press, 2016)

Brand (2002)   R. A. Brand, 'Forum Selection and Forum Rejection in US Courts', in J. Fawcett (ed.), *Reform and Development of Private International Law* (Oxford University Press, 2002)

Brand (2011)　　　　'The Rome I Regulation Rules on Party Autonomy for Choice of Law: A US Perspective' (2011) University of Pittsburgh Legal Studies Research Paper Series No. 2011–29, available at SSRN: https://ssrn.com/abstract=1973162

Brand (2013a)　　　　'Transaction Planning Using Rules on Jurisdiction and the Recognition and Enforcement of Judgments' (2013) 358 *Recueil des Cours* 9

Brand (2013b)　　　　'Implementing the 2005 Hague Convention: The EU Magnet and the US Centrifuge', in J. Forner Delaygua, C. González Beilfuss and R. Viñas i Farré (eds.), *Entre Bruselas y La Haya, Estudios sobre la unificación internacional y regional del derecho internacional privado: Liber Amicorum Alegría Borrás* (Marcial Pons, 2013), available at http://ssrn .com/abstract=2288708

Brand and Herrup (2008)　　　R. A. Brand and P. Herrup, *The 2005 Hague Convention on Choice of Court Agreements: Commentary and Documents* (Cambridge University Press, 2008)

Brekoulakis (2007)　　　S. Brekoulakis, 'The Notion of the Superiority of Arbitration Agreements over Jurisdiction Agreements' (2007) 24 *Journal of International Arbitration* 341

Brekoulakis (2011)　　　*Third Parties in International Commercial Arbitration* (Oxford University Press, 2011)

Brekoulakis (2013)　　　'International Arbitration Scholarship and the Concept of Arbitration Law' (2013) 36 *Fordham International Law Journal* 745

Brekoulakis (2017)　　　'Rethinking Consent in International Commercial Arbitration: A General Theory for Non-signatories' (2017) 8 *Journal of International Dispute Settlement* 610

Brekoulakis and Devaney (2017)　　　S. Brekoulakis and M. M. Devaney, 'Public-Private Arbitration and the Public Interest under English Law' (2017) 80 *Modern Law Review* 22

Bridgeman (2008)　　　J. Bridgeman, 'The Arbitrability of Competition Law Disputes' (2008) 19 *European Business Law Review* 147

Briggs (1986)　　　A. Briggs, 'The Validity of "Floating" Choice of Law and Jurisdiction Agreements' [1986] *Lloyd's Maritime and Commercial Law Quarterly* 508

Briggs (2004)　　　'Anti-suit Injunctions and Utopian Ideals' (2004) 120 *Law Quarterly Review* 529

Briggs (2005)　　　'The Death of Harrods: Forum Non Conveniens and the European Court' (2005) 121 *Law Quarterly Review* 535

Briggs (2007)　　　'Decisions of British Courts During 2006: B. Private International Law' (2007) 78 *British Yearbook of International Law* 615

Briggs (2008)	*Agreements On Jurisdiction and Choice of Law* (Oxford University Press, 2008)
Briggs (2012)	'The Subtle Variety of Jurisdiction Agreements' [2012] *Lloyd's Maritime and Commercial Law Quarterly* 364
Briggs (2013)	'One-Sided Jurisdiction Clauses: French Folly and Russian Menace' [2013] *Lloyd's Maritime and Commercial Law Quarterly* 137
Briggs (2016)	'The Nature or Natures of Agreements on Choice of Court and Choice of Law' (2016) ASIL Webinar paper, available at www.asil.org/sites/default/files/pdfs/Which%20Law%20 Governs%20Forum%20Selection%20Clauses.pdf
Brilmayer (1989)	L. Brilmayer, 'Rights, Fairness, and Choice of Law' (1989) 98 *Yale Law Journal* 1277
Burge (2015)	M. E. Burge, 'Too Clever By Half: Reflections on Perception, Legitimacy, and Choice of Law Under Revised Article 1 of the Uniform Commercial Code' (2015) 6 *William and Mary Business Law Review* 357
Burger (1984)	D. C. Burger, 'Transnational Public Policy as a Factor in Choice of Law Analysis' (1984) 5 *New York Law School Journal of International and Comparative Law* 370
Buxbaum (2004)	H. L. Buxbaum, 'Forum Selection in International Contract Litigation: The Role of Judicial Discretion' (2004) 12 *Willamette Journal of International Law and Dispute Resolution* 185
Buxbaum (2017)	'Determining the Territorial Scope of State Law in Interstate and International Conflicts: Comments on the Draft Restatement (Third) and on the Role of Party Autonomy' (2017) 27 *Duke Journal of International and Comparative Law* 381
Buys (2012)	C. G. Buys, 'The Arbitrators' Duty to Respect the Parties' Choice of Law in Commercial Arbitration' (2012) 79 *St. John's Law Review* 59
Camilleri (2011)	P. Camilleri, 'Article 23: Formal Validity, Material Validity or Both?' (2011) 7 *Journal of Private International Law* 297
Carbonneau (1998)	T. E. Carbonneau (ed.), *Lex Mercatoria and Arbitration: A Discussion of the New Law Merchant* (Kluwer, 1998)
Carbonneau (2009)	'Liberal Rules of Arbitrability and the Autonomy of Labor Arbitration in the United States', in L. A. Mistelis and S. L. Brekoulakis (eds.), *Arbitrability: International and Comparative Perspectives* (Kluwer Law International, 2009)
Carlston (1952)	K. S. Carlston, 'Theory of Arbitration Process' (1952) 17 *Law and Contemporary Problems* 631
Carruthers (2005)	J. M. Carruthers, *The Transfer of Property in the Conflict of Laws* (Oxford University Press, 2005)

Carruthers (2012)	'Party Autonomy in the Legal Regulation of Adult Relationships: What Place for Party Choice in Private International Law?' (2012) 61 *International and Comparative Law Quarterly* 881
Carruthers and Crawford (2005)	J. M. Carruthers and E. B. Crawford, 'Variations on a Theme of Rome II: Reflections on Proposed Choice of Law Rules for Non-Contractual Obligations' (2005) 9 *Edinburgh Law Review* 65
Chan (2016)	F. W. H. Chan, 'Anti-suit Injunctions and the Doctrine of Comity' (2016) 79 *Modern Law Review* 341
Chen (1987)	T. P. Chen, 'Private International Law of the People's Republic of China: An Overview' (1987) 35 *American Journal of Comparative Law* 445
Cheng (2009)	T. H. Cheng, 'New Tools for an Old Quest: A Commentary on Jan Kleinheisterkamp, the Impact of International Mandatory Laws on the Enforceability of Arbitration Agreements' (2009) 3 *World Arbitration and Mediation Review* 121
Cheshire, North and Fawcett (2017)	P. Torremans et al., *Cheshire, North and Fawcett's Private International Law* (Oxford University Press, 15th edn, 2017)
Chong (2005)	A. Chong, 'The Common Law Choice of Law Rules for Resulting and Constructive Trusts' (2005) 54 *International and Comparative Law* 855
Chong (2006)	'The Public Policy and Mandatory Rules of Third Countries in International Contracts' (2006) 2 *Journal of Private International Law* 27
Chong (2008)	'Choice of Law for Unjust Enrichment/Restitution and the Rome II Regulation' (2008) 57 *International and Comparative Law Quarterly* 863
Clarkson and Hill (2016)	J. Hill and M. N. Shúilleabháin, *Clarkson & Hill's Conflict of Laws* (Oxford University Press, 5th edn, 2016)
Clermont (2015)	K. M. Clermont, 'Governing Law on Forum-Selection Agreements' (2015) 66 *Hastings Law Journal* 643
Cole (2001)	S. R. Cole, 'Uniform Arbitration: "One Size Fits All" Does Not Fit' (2001) 16 *Ohio State Journal on Dispute Resolution* 759
Collins (1976)	L. Collins, 'Contractual Obligations – The EEC Preliminary Draft Convention on Private International Law' (1976) 25 *International and Comparative Law Quarterly* 35
Cordero-Moss (2014)	G. Cordero-Moss, 'Limitations on Party Autonomy in International Commercial Arbitration' (2014) 372 *Recueil des Cours* 131

Coyle (2011)	J. F. Coyle, 'Rethinking the Commercial Law Treaty' (2011) 45 *Georgia Law Review* 343
Coyle (2017)	'The Canons of Construction for Choice-of-Law Clauses' (2017) 92 *Washington Law Review* 631
Croff (1982)	C. Croff, 'The Applicable Law in an International Commercial Arbitration: Is It Still a Conflict of Laws Problem?' (1982) 16 *International Lawyer* 613
Cuniberti (2005)	G. Cuniberti, 'Forum Non Conveniens and the Brussels Convention' (2005) 54 *International and Comparative Law Quarterly* 973
Cuniberti (2008)	'Beyond Contract – The Case for Default Arbitration in International Commercial Disputes' (2008) 32 *Fordham International Law Journal* 417
Cuniberti (2013)	'Three Theories of Lex Mercatoria' (2013) 52 *Columbia Journal of Transnational Law* 369
Cuniberti (2014)	'The International Market for Contracts: The Most Attractive Contract Laws' (2014) 34 *Northwestern Journal of International Law and Business* 455
Currie (1963)	B. Currie, *Selected Essays on the Conflict of Laws* (Duke University Press, 1963)
Cutler (1985)	M. R. Cutler, 'Comparative Conflict of Laws: Effectiveness of Contractual Choice of Forum' (1985) 20 *Texas International Law Journal* 97
Danov (2008)	M. Danov, 'The Law Governing Arbitrability under the Arbitration Act 1996' [2008] *Lloyd's Maritime and Commercial Law Quarterly* 536
De Aguilar Vieira (2013)	I. de Aguilar Vieira, 'The CISG and Party Autonomy in Brazilian International Contract Law' (2013) 1 *Panorama of Brazilian Law* 173
De Araujo (2013)	N. de Araujo, 'Recent Developments and Current Trends on Brazilian Private International Law Concerning International Contracts' (2013) 1 *Panorama of Brazilian Law* 73
De Boer (2007)	T. M. de Boer, 'Party Autonomy and Its Limitations in the Rome II Regulation' (2007) 9 *Yearbook of Private International Law* 19
De By (1989)	R. A. de By, 'Note: Forum Selection Clauses: Substantive or Procedural for *Erie* Purposes' (1989) 89 *Columbia Law Review* 1068
De la Feria and Vogenauer (2011)	R. de la Feria and S. Vogenauer (eds.), *Prohibition of Abuse of Law: A New General Principle of EU Law?* (Hart, 2011)

De la Torre (2013)	J. de la Torre, 'The Hague Choice of Court Convention and Federal Power over State Courts' (2013) 45 *Georgetown Journal of International Law* 219
Dempegiotis (2008)	S. Dempegiotis, 'EC Competition Law and International Arbitration in the Light of EC Regulation 1/2003' (2008) 25 *Journal of International Arbitration* 365
Dessemontet (2012)	F. Dessemontet, 'Emerging Issues in International Arbitration: The Application of Soft Law, Halakha and Sharia by International Arbitral Tribunals' (2012) 23 *American Review of International Arbitration* 545
De Vareilles-Sommières (2016)	P. De Vareilles-Sommières, 'Notes on an Unstable Couple: Party Autonomy and Public Policy in the Hague Principles on Choice of Law in International Commercial Contracts' (2015–16) 17 *Yearbook of Private International Law* 49
Diamond (1979)	A. L. Diamond, 'Conflict of Laws in the EEC' (1979) 32 *Current Legal Problems* 155
Dicey (1896)	A. V. Dicey, *A Digest of the Law of England with reference to the Conflict of Laws* (Stevens and Sons, 1896)
Dicey and Keith (1922)	A. V. Dicey and A. B. Keith, *A Digest of the Law of England with reference to the Conflict of Laws* (Stevens and Sons, 3rd edn, 1922)
Dicey and Morris (1958)	A. V. Dicey and J. H. C. Morris, *Dicey's Conflict of Laws* (Stevens and Sons, 7th edn, 1958)
Dicey, Morris and Collins (2012)	L. Collins et al., *Dicey, Morris and Collins on The Conflict of Laws* (Sweet and Maxwell, 15th edn, 2012)
Dickinson (2007)	A. Dickinson, 'Third Country Mandatory Rules in the Law Applicable to Contractual Obligations – "So Long, Farewell, Auf Wiedersehen, Adieu?"' (2007) 3 *Journal of Private International Law* 53
Dickinson (2013)	'Territory in the Rome I and II Regulations' [2013] *Lloyd's Maritime and Commercial Law Quarterly* 86
Dickinson (2015)	'Once Bitten – Mutual Distrust in European Private International Law' (2015) 131 *Law Quarterly Review* 186
Dickinson (2017a)	'Keeping up Appearances: The Development of Adjudicatory Jurisdiction in the English Courts' (2017) 86 *British Yearbook of International Law* 6
Dickinson (2017b)	'Oiling the Machine: Overriding Mandatory Provisions and Public Policy in the Hague Principles on Choice of Law in International Commercial Contracts' (2017) 22 *Uniform Law Review* 402
Dickinson, Keyes and John (2014)	A. Dickinson, M. Keyes, and T. John (eds.), *Australian Private International Law for the 21st Century: Facing Outwards* (Hart, 2014)

D'Oliveira (1977)   H. U. J. D'Oliveira, 'Characteristic Obligation in the Draft EEC Obligation Convention' (1977) 25 *American Journal of Comparative Law* 303

Dolinger (1982)   J. Dolinger, 'World Public Policy – Real International Public Policy in the Conflict of Laws' (1982) 17 *Texas International Law Journal* 167

Downie (2013)   C. Downie, 'Will Australia Trust Arbitrators with Antitrust? – Examining the Challenges in International Antitrust Arbitrations to Develop a Competition Arbitration Model for Australia' (2013) 30 *Journal of International Arbitration* 221

Draguiev (2014)   D. Draguiev, 'Unilateral Jurisdiction Clauses: The Case for Invalidity, Severability or Enforceability' (2014) 31 *Journal of International Arbitration* 19

Druzin (2009)   B. Druzin, 'Buying Commercial Law: Choice of Law, Choice of Forum, and Network Externalities' (2009) 18 *Tulane Journal of International and Comparative Law* 1

Duckworth (2002)   M. Duckworth, 'Certainty or Justice? Bringing Choice of Law Rules for International Torts into the Modern Era' (2002) 24 *Sydney Law Review* 569

Dutta (2009)   A. Dutta, 'Succession and Wills in the Conflict of Laws on the Eve of Europeanization' (2009) 73 *RabelsZ* 547

Eidenmüller (2011)   H. Eidenmüller, 'The Transnational Law Market, Regulatory Competition, and Transnational Corporations' (2011) 18 *Indiana Journal of Global Legal Studies* 707

Eidenmüller (2013)   (ed.), *Regulatory Competition in Contract Law and Dispute Resolution* (Beck/Hart, 2013)

Faulkner (2016)   T. Faulkner, *Law and Authority in the Early Middle Ages* (Cambridge University Press, 2016)

Fawcett and Torremans (2011)   J. J. Fawcett and P. Torremans, *Intellectual Property and Private International Law* (Oxford University Press, 2nd edn, 2011)

Fentiman (1998)   R. Fentiman, *Foreign Law in English Courts* (Oxford University Press, 1998)

Fentiman (2005)   'Case C-116/02, *Erich Gasser GmbH* v. *MISAT Srl*' (2005) 42 *Common Market Law Review* 241

Fentiman (2006a)   'Laws, Foreign Laws and Facts' (2006) 59 *Current Legal Problems* 391

Fentiman (2006b)   'Civil Jurisdiction and Third States: *Owusu* and After' (2006) 43 *Common Market Law Review* 705

Fentiman (2013)   'Unilateral Jurisdiction Agreements in Europe' (2013) 72 *Cambridge Law Journal* 24

Ferrario (2009)   P. Ferrario, 'The Group of Companies Doctrine in International Commercial Arbitration: Is There Any Reason for This Doctrine to Exist?' (2009) 26 *Journal of International Arbitration* 647

Force (2011) R. Force, 'The Position in the United States on Foreign Forum Selection and Arbitration Clauses, Forum Non Conveniens, and Antisuit Injunctions' (2011) 35 *Tulane Journal of Maritime Law* 401

Forsyth (1998) C. Forsyth, 'Characterisation Revisited: An Essay in the Theory and Practice of the English Conflict of Laws' (1998) 114 *Law Quarterly Review* 141

Fortier (2005) L. Y. Fortier, 'Arbitrability of Disputes', in G. Aksen et al. (eds.), *Global Reflections on International Law, Commerce and Dispute Resolution: Liber Amicorum in Honour of Robert Briner* (ICC Publishing, 2005)

French (2016) R. French, 'Transnational Dispute Resolution', speech delivered at Supreme and Federal Court Judges' Conference, Brisbane, 25 January 2016. Available at www.hcourt.gov .au/assets/publications/speeches/currentjustices/frenchcj/ frenchcj25Jan2016.pdf

Gaillard (1999) E. Gaillard, 'The Enforcement of Awards Set Aside in the Country of Origin' (1999) 14 *ICSID Review* 16

Gaillard (2000) 'Transnational Law: A Legal System or a Method of Decision-Making?' (2000) 17 *Arbitration International* 59

Gaillard (2010a) *Legal Theory of International Arbitration* (Nijhoff, 2010)

Gaillard (2010b) 'The Representations of International Arbitration' (2010) 1 *Journal of International Dispute Settlement* 271

Gaillard and Banifatemi (2008) E. Gaillard and Y. Banifatemi, 'Negative Effect of Competence-Competence: The Rule of Priority in Favour of the Arbitrators', in E. Gaillard and D. Di Pietro (eds.), *Enforcement of Arbitration Agreements and International Arbitral Awards: The New York Convention in Practice* (Cameron May, 2008)

Gama (2017) L. Gama Jr, 'Tacit Choice of Law in the Hague Principles' (2017) 22 *Uniform Law Review* 336

Gama and Saumier (2011) L. Gama and G. Saumier, 'Non-State Law in the (Proposed) Hague Principles on Choice of Law in International Contracts', in D. P. Fernández Arroyo and J. J. Obando Peralta (eds.), *El Derecho Internacional Privado en los Procesos de Integracion Regional* (Editorial Juridica Continental, 2011), available at SSRN: https://ssrn.com/abstract=1971302.

P Gannagé (1992) P. Gannagé, 'La pénétration de l'autonomie de la volonté dans le droit international privé de la famille' [1992] *Revue critique de droit international privé* 425

L Gannagé (2007)   L. Gannagé, 'Le contrat sans loi en droit international privé' (2007) 11.3 *Electronic Journal of Comparative Law*. Available at www.ejcl.org/113/article113-10.pdf

L Gannagé (2013)   'Les méthodes du droit international privé à l'épreuve des conflits de cultures' (2013) 357 *Recueil des Cours* 223

Garcimartin Alferez (2009)   F. J. Garcimartin Alferez, 'The Rome I Regulation: Exceptions to the Rule on Consumer Contracts and Financial Instruments' (2009) 5 *Journal of Private International Law* 85

Garnett (1998)   R. Garnett, 'The Enforcement of Jurisdiction Clauses in Australia' (1998) 23 *University of New South Wales Law Journal* 1

Garnett (2009)   'The Hague Choice of Court Convention: Magnum Opus or Much Ado About Nothing?' (2009) 5 *Journal of Private International Law* 161

Garnett (2013a)   'Jurisdiction Clauses since *Akai*' (2013) 87 *Australian Law Journal* 134

Garnett (2013b)   'Coexisting and Conflicting Jurisdiction and Arbitration Clauses' (2013) 9 *Journal of Private International Law* 361

Gélinas (2016)   F. Gélinas, 'Arbitration as Transnational Governance by Contract' (2016) 7 *Transnational Legal Theory* 181

Goh (2015)   N. Goh, 'A More Valid Presumption in the Implied Choice of Law Governing Arbitration Agreements' [2015] *Lloyd's Maritime and Commercial Law Quarterly* 161

Goodwin (2013)   J. Goodwin, 'Reflexive Effect and the Brussels I Regulation' (2013) 129 *Law Quarterly Review* 317

Gouiffès and Ordonez (2015)   L. Gouiffès and M. Ordonez, 'Jurisdiction and Admissibility: Are We Any Closer to a Line in the Sand?' (2015) 31 *Arbitration International* 109

Grantham (1996)   W. Grantham, 'The Arbitrability of International Intellectual Property Disputes' (1996) 14 *Berkeley Journal of International Law* 173

Graves (2005)   J. M. Graves, 'Party Autonomy in Choice of Commercial Law: The Failure of Revised UCC s.1-301 and a Proposal for Broader Reform' (2005) 36 *Seton Hall Law Review* 59

Graziano (2017)   T. K. Graziano, 'The Hague Solution on Choice-of-Law Clauses in Conflicting Standard Terms: Paving the Way to More Legal Certainty in International Commercial Transactions?' (2017) 22 *Uniform Law Review* 251

Grigera Naón (2001)   H. A. Grigera Naón, 'Choice-of-Law Problems in International Commercial Arbitration' (2001) 289 *Recueil des Cours* 1

Gruber (2009) U. P. Gruber, 'Insurance Contracts', in F. Ferrari and S. Leible (eds.), *Rome I Regulation* (Sellier European Law Publishers, 2009)

Grusic (2012) U. Grusic, 'The Territorial Scope of Employment Legislation and Choice of Law' (2012) 5 *Modern Law Review* 722

Grusic (2015) *The European Private International Law of Employment* (Cambridge University Press, 2015)

Guedi (1991) T. G. Guedj, 'The Theory of the Lois de Police: A Functional Trend in Continental Private International Law – A Comparative Analysis with Modern American Theories' (1991) 39 *American Journal of Comparative Law* 661

Guzman (2002) A. T. Guzman, 'Choice of Law: New Foundations' (2002) 90 *Georgetown Law Journal* 883

Handford (2008) P. Handford, 'Edward John Eyre and the Conflict of Laws' (2008) 32 *Melbourne University Law Review* 822

Hanotiau (1999) B. Hanotiau, 'The Law Applicable to Arbitrability', in A. J. van den Berg (ed.), *Improving the Efficiency of Arbitration Agreements and Awards: 40 Years of Application of the New York Convention* (ICCA Congress Series, vol 9, Kluwer Law International, 1999)

Hanotiau (2007) 'Non-Signatories in International Arbitration: Lessons from Thirty Years of Case Law', in A. J. van den Berg (ed.), *International Arbitration 2006: Back to Basics?* (ICCA Congress Series, vol 13, Kluwer Law International, 2007), 341

Hanotiau (2011) 'Consent to Arbitration: Do We Share a Common Vision?' (2011) 27 *Arbitration International* 539

Hanotiau (2014) 'The Law Applicable to Arbitrability' (2014) 26 *Singapore Academy of Law Journal* 874

Harris (2000) J. Harris, 'Contractual Freedom in the Conflict of Laws' (2000) 20 *Oxford Journal of Legal Studies* 247

Harris (2002) *The Hague Trust Convention: Scope, Application and Preliminary Issues* (Hart, 2002)

Hart (1961) H. L. A. Hart, *The Concept of Law* (Oxford University Press, 1961)

Hartley (1996) T. C. Hartley, 'Pleading and Proof of Foreign Law: The Major European Systems Compared' (1996) 45 *International and Comparative Law Quarterly* 271

Hartley (1997) 'Mandatory Rules in International Contracts: The Common Law Approach' (1997) 266 *Recueil des Cours* 337

Hartley (2005) 'The European Union and the Systematic Dismantling of the Common Law of Conflict Laws' (2005) 54 *International and Comparative Law Quarterly* 813

Hartley (2013a)   'Choice-of-Court Agreements and the New Brussels I Regulation' (2013) 129 *Law Quarterly Review* 309

Hartley (2013b)   *Choice-of-Court Agreements Under the European and International Instruments* (Oxford University Press, 2013)

Hatzimihail (2008)   N. E. Hatzimihail, 'The Many Lives – and Faces – of Lex Mercatoria: History as Genealogy in International Business Law' (2008) 71 *Law and Contemporary Problems* 169

Hay (1978)   P. Hay, 'Unjust Enrichment in the Conflict of Laws: A Comparative View of German Law and the American Restatement 2d" (1978) 26 *American Journal of Comparative Law* 3

Hay, Borchers and Symeonides (2010)   P. Hay, P. J. Borchers and S. C. Symeonides, *Conflict Of Laws* (West, 5th edn, 2010)

Hayek (1960)   F. A. Hayek, *The Constitution of Liberty* (University of Chicago Press, 1960)

Hayek (1973)   *Law, Legislation and Liberty* (University of Chicago Press, 1973)

Hayton (1987)   D. Hayton, 'The Hague Convention on the Law Applicable to Trusts and on their Recognition' (1987) 36 *International and Comparative Law Quarterly* 260

Hayward (2017)   B. Hayward, *Conflict of Laws and Arbitral Discretion: The Closest Connection Test* (Oxford University Press, 2017)

Healy (2009)   J. J. Healy, 'Consumer Protection Choice of Law: European Lessons for the United States' (2009) 19 *Duke Journal of International and Comparative Law* 535

Heiser (1993)   W. W. Heiser, 'Forum Selection Clauses in State Courts: Limitations on Enforcement After *Stewart* and *Carnival Cruise*' (1993) 45 *Florida Law Review* 361

Heiser (2010)   'The Hague Convention on Choice of Court Agreements: The Impact on Forum Non Conveniens, Transfer of Venue, Removal, and Recognition of Judgments in United States Courts' (2010) 31 *University of Pennsylvania Journal of International Law* 1013

Heiss (2008)   H. Heiss, 'Insurance Contracts in Rome I: Another Recent Failure of the European Legislature' (2008) 10 *Yearbook of Private International Law* 261

Heiss (2009)   'Party Autonomy', in F. Ferrari and S. Leible (eds.), *Rome I Regulation* (Sellier European Law Publishers, 2009)

Helfand (2015)   M. A. Helfand, *Negotiating State and Non-State Law: The Challenge of Global and Local Legal Pluralism* (Cambridge University Press, 2015)

Hellner (2009)	M. Hellner, 'Third Country Overriding Mandatory Rules in the Rome I Regulation: Old Wine in New Bottles?' (2009) 5 *Journal of Private International Law* 447
Hepple (1970)	B. A. Hepple, 'Intention to Create Legal Relations' (1970) 28 *Cambridge Law Journal* 122
Herbert (1998)	J. Herbert, 'The Conflict of Laws and Judicial Perspectives on Federalism: A Principled Defence of *Tolofson* v. *Jensen*' (1998) 56 *University of Toronto Faculty of Law Review* 3
Herranz Ballesteros (2014)	M. Herranz Ballesteros, 'The Regime of Party Autonomy in the Brussels I Recast: The Solutions Adopted for Agreements on Jurisdiction' (2014) 10 *Journal of Private International Law* 291
Hiber and Pavić (2008)	D. Hiber and V. Pavić, 'Arbitration and Crime' (2008) 25 *Journal of International Arbitration* 461
Highet (1989)	K. Highet, 'The Enigma of the Lex Mercatoria' (1989) 63 *Tulane Law Review* 613
Hill (2004)	J. Hill, 'Choice of Law in Contract under the Rome Convention: The Approach of the UK Courts' (2004) 53 *International and Comparative Law Quarterly* 325
Hill (2008)	*Cross Border Consumer Contracts* (Oxford University Press, 2008)
Hill (2014)	'Determining the Seat of an International Arbitration: Party Autonomy and the Interpretation of Arbitration Agreements' (2014) 63 *International and Comparative Law Quarterly* 517
Hochstrasser (1994)	D. Hochstrasser, 'Choice of Law and "Foreign" Mandatory Rules in International Arbitration' (1994) 11 *Journal of International Arbitration* 57
Holmes (1897)	O. W. Holmes Jr, 'The Path of the Law' (1897) 10 *Harvard Law Review* 457
Hook (2014)	M. Hook, 'The Choice of Law Agreement as a Reason for Exercising Jurisdiction' (2014) 63 *International and Comparative Law Quarterly* 963
Hook (2016)	*The Choice of Law Contract* (Hart, 2016)
Hook (2017)	'The "Statutist Trap" and Subject-Matter Jurisdiction' (2017) 13 *Journal of Private International Law* 435
Howard (1995)	M. N. Howard, 'Floating Choice of Law Clauses – The Star Texas' [1995] *Lloyd's Maritime and Commercial Law Quarterly* 1
Howarth (2004)	R. J. Howarth, 'Lex Mercatoria: Can General Principles of Law Govern International Commercial Contracts?' (2004) 10 *Canterbury Law Review* 36

Huo (2011)   Z. Huo, 'An Imperfect Improvement: The New Conflict
                      of Laws Act of the People's Republic of China' (2011) 60
                      International and Comparative Law Quarterly 1065

Jaffey (1984)   A. J. E. Jaffey, 'The English Proper Law Doctrine and the
                      EEC Convention' (1984) 33 *International and Comparative
                      Law Quarterly* 531

James (2001)   E. James, '*John Pfeiffer Pty. Ltd.* v. *Rogerson*: The "Certainty"
                      of Federal Choice of Law Rules for International Torts:
                      Limitations, Implications and a Few Complications' (2001)
                      23 *Sydney Law Review* 145

Jayme (1991)   E. Jayme, 'L'autonomie de la volonté des parties dans les
                      contrats internationaux entre personnes privées' (1991)
                      64-I *Annuaire de l'Institut de Droit International* 7

Jayme (1995)   'Identité culturelle et intégration – Le droit international
                      privé postmoderne' (1995) 251 *Recueil des Cours* 9

Jayme (2009)   'Party Autonomy in International Family and Succession
                      Law: New Tendencies' (2009) 11 *Yearbook of Private
                      International Law* 1

Jiménez   D. Jiménez Figueres, 'Multi-Tiered Dispute Resolution
Figueres (2003)   Clauses in ICC Arbitration' (2003) 14 *ICC Bulletin* 71

Johns (2008)   F. Johns, 'Performing Party Autonomy' (2008) 71 *Law and
                      Contemporary Problems* 243

Jolles (2006)   A. Jolles, 'Consequences of Multi-Tier Arbitration Clauses:
                      Issues of Enforcement' (2006) 72 *Arbitration* 329

Jones (2009)   D. Jones, 'Dealing with Multi-Tiered Dispute Resolution
                      Process' (2009) 75 *Arbitration* 188

Juenger (1984)   F. K. Juenger, 'Conflict of Laws: A Critique of Interest
                      Analysis' (1984) 32 *American Journal of Comparative Law* 1

Juenger (1985)   'General Course on Private International Law' (1985)
                      193 *Recueil des Cours* 119

Juenger (1992)   *Choice of Law and Multistate Justice* (Martinus Nijhoff,
                      1992)

Juenger (1994)   'The Inter-American Convention on the Law Appli-
                      cable to International Contracts: Some Highlights and
                      Comparisons' (1994) 42 *American Journal of Comparative
                      Law* 381

Juenger (1997)   'Choice of Law in the Americas' (1997) 45 *American
                      Journal of Comparative Law* 195

Juenger (2000)   'The Lex Mercatoria and Private International Law'
                      (2000) 60 *Louisiana Law Review* 1133

Juenger (2001)   'A Historical Overview', in *Selected Essays on the Conflict
                      of Laws* (Transnational Publishers, 2001)

Kalenský (1971)	P. Kalenský, *Trends of Private International Law* (Springer, 1971)
Kalicki and Madeiros (2008)	J. Kalicki and S. Madeiros, 'Investment Arbitration in Brazil: Revisiting Brazil's Traditional Reluctance Towards ICSID, BITs and Investor-State Arbitration' (2008) 24 *Arbitration International* 423
Karayanidi (2017)	M. Karayanidi, 'Reassessing the Approach to Jurisdiction in Civil and Commercial Matters: Party Autonomy, Categorical Equality and Sovereignty' (2017), PhD thesis, *Trinity College Dublin* (on file with author)
Karayanni (1996)	M. M. Karayanni, 'The Public Policy Exception to the Enforcement of Forum Selection Clauses' (1996) 34 *Duquesne Law Review* 1009
Kayali (2010)	D. Kayali, 'Enforceability of Multi-Tiered Dispute Resolution Clauses' (2010) 27 *Journal of International Arbitration* 551
Kegel and Schurig (2004)	G. Kegel and K. Schurig, *Internationales Privatrecht* (C. H. Beck, 9th edn, 2004)
Kenny and Hennigan (2015)	D. Kenny and R. Hennigan, 'Choice-of-Court Agreements, the Italian Torpedo, and the Recast of the Brussels I Regulation' (2015) 64 *International and Comparative Law Quarterly* 197
Keyes (2008)	M. Keyes, 'Statutes, Choice of Law, and the Role of Forum Choice' (2008) 4 *Journal of Private International Law* 1
Keyes (2009)	'Jurisdiction under the Hague Choice of Courts Convention: Its Likely Impact on Australian Practice' (2009) 5 *Journal of Private International Law* 181
Keyes and Marshall (2015)	M. Keyes and B. A. Marshall, 'Jurisdiction Agreements: Exclusive, Optional and Asymmetrical' (2015) 11 *Journal of Private International Law* 345
Kjos (2013)	H. E. Kjos, *Applicable Law in Investor-State Arbitration: The Interplay between National and International Law* (Oxford University Press, 2013)
Kleinheisterkamp (2009)	J. Kleinheisterkamp, 'The Impact of Internationally Mandatory Rules on the Enforceability of Arbitration Agreements' (2009) 3 *World Arbitration and Mediation Review* 91
S Knight (1977)	S. M. Knight, 'Avoidance of Foreign Jurisdiction Clauses in International Contracts' (1977) 26 *International and Comparative Law Quarterly* 664
C Knight (2008)	C. J. S. Knight, 'The Damage of Damages: Agreements on Jurisdiction and Choice of Law' (2008) 4 *Journal of Private International Law* 501

Knop, Michaels and Riles (2012)	K. Knop, R. Michaels and A. Riles, 'From Multiculturalism to Technique: Feminism, Culture and the Conflict of Laws Style' (2012) 64 *Stanford Law Review* 589
Kohler (2013)	C. Kohler, 'L'autonomie de la volonté en droit international privé: un principe universel entre libéralisme et étatisme' (2013) 359 *Recueil des Cours* 285
Kono (2012)	T. Kono (ed.), *Intellectual Property and Private International Law: Comparative Perspectives* (Hart, 2012)
Korzun (2016)	V. Korzun, 'Arbitrating Anti-Trust Claims: From Suspicion to Trust' (2016) 48 *New York University Journal of International Law and Politics* 867
Kramer (2008)	X. E. Kramer, 'The Rome II Regulation on the Law Applicable to Non-Contractual Obligations: The European Private International Law Tradition Continued' (2008) 26 *Nederlands Internationaal Privaatrecht (NIPR)* 414
Kronstein (1963)	H. Kronstein, 'Arbitration is Power' (1963) 38 *New York University Law Review* 661
Kruger (2004)	T. Kruger, 'The Anti-suit Injunction in the European Judicial Space: *Turner* v. *Grovit*' (2004) 53 *International and Comparative Law Quarterly* 1030
Kruger (2014)	'Rome III and Parties' Choice' (2014) *Family & Law*, available at www.bjutijdschriften.nl/tijdschrift/fenr/2014/01/FENR-D-13-00010.
Kryvoi (2011)	Y. Kryvoi, 'Piercing the Corporate Veil in International Arbitration' (2011) 1 *Global Business Law Review* 169
Kuhn (1918)	A. K. Kuhn, 'Local and Transitory Actions in Private International Law' (1918) 66 *University of Pennsylvania Law Review* 301
Lalive (1986)	P. Lalive, 'Transnational (or Truly International) Public Policy and International Arbitration', in P. Sanders (ed.), *Comparative Arbitration Practice and Public Policy in Arbitration* (ICCA Congress Series, vol 3, Kluwer Law International, 1986)
Lando (1985)	O. Lando, 'The Lex Mercatoria in International Commercial Arbitration' (1985) 34 *International and Comparative Law Quarterly* 747
Lando (1987)	'The EEC Convention on the Law Applicable to Contractual Obligations' (1987) 24 *Common Market Law Review* 159
Lando and Nielsen (2008)	O. Lando and P. A. Nielsen, 'The Rome I Regulation' (2008) 45 *Common Market Law Review* 1687

Leboulanger (2007)   P. Leboulanger, 'The Arbitration Agreement: Still Autonomous?', in A. J. van den Berg (ed.), *International Arbitration 2006: Back to Basics?* (ICCA Congress Series, vol 13, Kluwer Law International, 2007)

Lee (1997)   Y. Lee, 'Note: Forum Selection Clauses: Problems of Enforcement in Diversity Cases and State Courts' (1997) 35 *Columbia Journal of Transnational Law* 663

Leflar (1966a)   R. A. Leflar, 'Choice-Influencing Considerations in Conflicts Law' (1966) 41 *New York University Law Review* 267

Leflar (1966b)   'Conflicts Law: More on Choice-Influencing Considerations' (1966) 54 *California Law Review* 1584

Lehmann (2008)   M. Lehmann, 'Liberating the Individual from Battles between States: Justifying Party Autonomy in Conflict of Laws' (2008) 41 *Vanderbilt Journal of Transnational Law* 381

Lenhoff (1961)   A. Lenhoff, 'The Parties' Choice of a Forum: "Prorogation Agreements"' (1961) 15 *Rutgers Law Review* 414

Lew (2009)   J. Lew, 'Competition Laws: Limits to Arbitrators' Authority', in L. A. Mistelis and S. L. Brekoulakis (eds.), *Arbitrability: International and Comparative Perspectives* (Kluwer Law International, 2009)

Lewis et al. (2016)   A. Lewis, J. Taylor, N. De Marco and J. Segan, *Challenging Sports Governing Bodies* (Bloomsbury Professional, 2016)

Liang (2012)   J. Liang, 'Statutory Restrictions on Party Autonomy in China's Private International Law of Contract: How Far does the 2010 Codification Go?' (2012) 8 *Journal of Private International Law* 77

Lindell (2002)   G. Lindell, 'Choice of Law in Torts and Another Farewell to *Phillips* v. *Eyre* but the *Voth* Test Retained for *Forum Non Conveniens* in Australia' (2002) 3 *Melbourne Journal of International Law* 64

Lipstein (1977)   K. Lipstein, 'Inherent Limitations in Statutes and the Conflict of Laws' (1977) 26 *International and Comparative Law Quarterly* 884

Liukkunen (2013)   U. Liukkunen, 'Lex Mercatoria in International Arbitration', in J. Klabbers and T. Piiparinen (eds.), *Normative Pluralism and International Law* (Cambridge University Press, 2013)

Lorenzen (1919)   E. G. Lorenzen, 'Huber's *De Conflictu Legum*' (1919) 13 *Illinois Law Review* 375

Lorenzen (1921)   'Validity and Effect of Contracts in the Conflict of Laws (Part II)' (1921) 30 *Yale Law Journal* 655

Lorenzen (1928)   'The French Rules of the Conflict of Laws' (1928) 38 *Yale Law Journal* 165

Lorenzen (1930)   'Pan-American Code of Private International Law' (1930) 4 *Tulane Law Review* 499

Lorenzen (1934)   'Commercial Arbitration – International and Interstate Aspects' (1934) 43 *Yale Law Journal* 716

Low (2013)   G. Low, 'A Psychology of Choice of Laws' [2013] *European Business Law Review* 363

Lowenfeld (1990)   A. F. Lowenfeld, 'Lex Mercatoria: An Arbitrator's View' (1990) 6 *Arbitration International* 133

Lowenfeld (1994)   'International Litigation and the Quest for Reasonableness' (1994) 245 *Recueil des Cours* 1

Lunts (1952)   L. A. Lunts, *Mezinárodní právo soukromé* (Orbis, 1952)

Magnus (2009)   U. Magnus, 'Article 4 Rome I Regulation: The Applicable Law in the Absence of Choice', in F. Ferrari and S. Leible (eds.), *Rome I Regulation* (Sellier European Law Publishers, 2009)

Mahmoud (2005)   M. S. M. Mahmoud, 'Loi d'autonomie et méthodes de protection de la partie faible en droit international privé' (2005) 315 *Recueil des Cours* 141

Mankowski (2017a)   P. Mankowski, 'Just How Free Is a Free Choice of Law in Contract in the EU?' (2017) 13 *Journal of Private International Law* 231

Mankowski (2017b)   'Article 3 of the Hague Principles: The Final Breakthrough for the Choice of Non-State Law?' (2017) 22 *Uniform Law Review* 369

Mann (1967a)   F. A. Mann, 'State Contracts and International Arbitration' (1967) 42 *British Yearbook of International Law* 1

Mann (1967b)   'Lex Facit Arbitrum', in P. Sanders (ed.), *International Arbitration – Liber Amicorum for Martin Domke* (Martinus Nijhoff, 1967)

Mann (1973)   'Statutes and the Conflict of Laws' (1972–73) 46 *British Yearbook of International Law* 117

Mann (1980)   'England Rejects "Delocalised" Contracts and Arbitration' (1980) 33 *International and Comparative Law Quarterly* 193

Marshall (2012)   B. A. Marshall, 'Reconsidering the Proper Law of the Contract' (2012) 13 *Melbourne Journal of International Law* 1

Marshall and Keyes (2017)   B. A. Marshall and M. Keyes, 'Australia's Accession to the Hague Convention on Choice of Court Agreements' (2017) 41 *Melbourne University Law Review* 246

Matulionyte (2013)   R. Matulionyte, 'Calling for Party Autonomy in Intellectual Property Infringement Cases' (2013) 9 *Journal of Private International Law* 77

Maultzsch (2016)	F. Maultzsch, 'Party Autonomy in European Private International Law: Uniform Principle or Context-Dependent Instrument?' (2016) 12 *Journal of Private International Law* 466
Mayer (1986)	P. Mayer, 'Mandatory Rules of Law in International Arbitration' (1986) 2 *Arbitration International* 274
Mayer (2012)	'The Extension of the Arbitration Clause to Non-Signatories – The Irreconcilable Positions of French and English Courts' (2012) 27 *American University International Law Review* 831
McClean (1996)	D. McClean, 'A Common Inheritance? An Examination of the Private International Law Tradition of the Commonwealth' (1996) 260 *Recueil des Cours* 9
McConnaughay (1999)	P. J. McConnaughay, 'The Risks and Virtues of Lawlessness: A "Second Look" at International Commercial Arbitration' (1999) 93 *Northwestern University Law Review* 453
McConnaughay (2001)	'The Scope of Autonomy in International Contracts and Its Relation to Economic Regulation and Development' (2001) 39 *Columbia Journal of Transnational Law* 595
McLachlan (1990)	C. McLachlan, 'Splitting the Proper Law in Private International Law' (1990) 61 *British Yearbook of International Law* 311
McLachlan (2014)	*Foreign Relations Law* (Cambridge University Press, 2014)
Merrett (2006)	L. Merrett, 'The Enforcement of Jurisidiction Agreements within the Brussels Regime' (2006) 55 *International and Comparative Law Quarterly* 315
Merrett (2009a)	'Article 23 of the Brussels I Regulation: A Comprehensive Code for Jurisdiction Agreements?' (2009) 58 *International and Comparative Law Quarterly* 545
Merrett (2009b)	'Choice of Law in Insurance Contracts Under the Rome I Regulation' (2009) 5 *Journal of Private International Law* 40
Merrett (2011)	*Employment Contracts in Private International Law* (Oxford University Press, 2011)
Merrett (2018)	'The Future Enforcement of Asymmetric Jurisdiction Agreements' (2018) 67 *International and Comparative Law Quarterly* 37
Michaels (2006)	R. Michaels, 'EU Law as Private International Law? Reconceptualising the Country-of-Origin Principle as Vested-Rights Theory' (2006) 2 *Journal of Private International Law* 195
Michaels (2007)	'The True Lex Mercatoria: Law Beyond the State' (2007) 14 *Indiana Journal of Global Legal Studies* 447

Michaels (2009)   'Global Legal Pluralism' (2009) 5 *Annual Review of Law & Social Science* 243

Michaels (2014a)   'Roles and Role Perceptions of International Arbitrators', in W. Mattli and T. Dietz (eds.), *International Arbitration and Global Governance: Contending Theories and Evidence* (Oxford University Press, 2014)

Michaels (2014b)   'Non-State Law in the Hague Principles on Choice of Law in International Commercial Contracts', in K. Purnhagen and P. Rott (eds.), *Varieties of European Economic Law and Regulation: Liber Amicorum for Hans Micklitz* (Springer, 2014)

Millett (1997)   P. Millett, 'Jurisdiction and Choice of Law in the Law of Restitution', in T. Sood et al. (eds.), *Current Issues in International Commercial Litigation* (National University of Singapore, 1997).

Mills (2006a)   A. Mills, 'The Private History of International Law' (2006) 55 *International and Comparative Law Quarterly* 1

Mills (2006b)   'Renvoi and the Proof of Foreign Law in Australia' (2006) 65 *Cambridge Law Journal* 37

Mills (2008a)   'Arbitral Jurisdiction and the Mischievous Presumption of Identity of Foreign Law' (2008) 67 *Cambridge Law Journal* 25

Mills (2008b)   'The Dimensions of Public Policy in Private International Law' (2008) 4 *Journal of Private International Law* 201

Mills (2009a)   *The Confluence of Public and Private International Law* (Cambridge University Press, 2009)

Mills (2009b)   'The Application of Multiple Laws under the Rome II Regulation', in W. Binchy and J. Ahern (eds.), *The Rome II Regulation* (Brill, 2009)

Mills (2010)   'Federalism in the European Union and the United States: Subsidiarity, Private Law and the Conflict of Laws' (2010) 32 *University of Pennsylvania Journal of International Law* 369

Mills (2011)   'Antinomies of Public and Private at the Foundations of International Investment Law and Arbitration' (2011) 14 *Journal of International Economic Law* 469

Mills (2013)   'The Identities of Private International Law – Lessons from the US and EU Revolutions' (2013) 23 *Duke Journal of Comparative and International Law* 445

Mills (2014)   'Rethinking Jurisdiction in International Law' (2014) 84 *British Yearbook of International Law* 187

Mills (2015)   'The Law Applicable to Cross-Border Defamation on Social Media: Whose Law Governs Free Speech in "Facebookistan"?' (2015) 7 *Journal of Media Law* 1

Mills (2016a)	'Private International Law and EU External Relations: Think Local Act Global, or Think Global Act Local?' (2016) 65 *International and Comparative Law Quarterly* 541
Mills (2016b)	'The Principled English Ambivalence to Law and Dispute Resolution Beyond the State', in J. C. Betancourt (ed.), *Liber Amicorum for the Chartered Institute of Arbitrators: Selected Topics in International Arbitration* (Oxford University Press, 2016)
Mills (2017a)	'The Hague Choice of Court Convention and Cross-Border Commercial Dispute Resolution in Australia and the Asia-Pacific' (2017) 18 *Melbourne Journal of International Law* 1
Mills (2017b)	'States, Failed and Non-recognized', in J. Basedow, F. Ferrari, P. Asensio and G. Rühl (eds.), *Encyclopaedia of Private International Law* (Edward Elgar, 2017)
Mills (2018)	'Arbitral Jurisdiction', in T. Schultz and F. Ortino (eds.), *Oxford Handbook of International Arbitration* (Oxford University Press, 2018)
Mistelis and Brekoulakis (2009)	L. A. Mistelis and S. L. Brekoulakis (eds.), *Arbitrability: International and Comparative Perspectives* (Kluwer Law International, 2009)
Moreno Rodriguez and Albornoz (2011)	J. A. Moreno Rodriguez and M. M. Albornoz, 'Reflections on the Mexico Convention in the Context of the Preparation of the Future Hague Instrument on International Contracts' (2011) 7 *Journal of Private International Law* 491
Morris (1946)	J. H. C. Morris, 'The Choice of Law Clause in Statutes' (1946) 62 *Law Quarterly Review* 170
Morse (1982)	C. G. J. Morse, 'The EEC Convention on the Law Applicable to Contractual Obligations' (1982) 2 *Yearbook of European Law* 107
Muir Watt (2003)	H. Muir Watt, 'Choice of Law in Integrated and Interconnected Markets: A Matter of Political Economy' (2003) 9 *Columbia Journal of European Law* 383
Muir Watt (2004)	'Aspects économiques du droit international privé' (2004) 307 *Recueil des Cours* 1
Muir Watt (2005)	'European Integration, Legal Diversity and the Conflict of Laws' (2005) 9 *Edinburgh Law Review* 6
Muir Watt (2010)	'"Party Autonomy" in International Contracts: From the Makings of a Myth to the Requirements of Global Governance' (2010) 6 *European Review of Contract Law* 250
Muir Watt (2016)	'Conflicts of Laws Unbounded: The Case for a Legal-Pluralist Revival' (2016) 7 *Transnational Legal Theory* 313

Muir Watt and Fernández Arroyo (2014)	H. Muir Watt and D. P. Fernández Arroyo (eds.), *Private International Law and Global Governance* (Oxford University Press, 2014)
Mullinex (1992)	L. S. Mullinex, 'Another Easy Case, Some More Bad Law: *Carnival Cruise Lines* and Contractual Personal Jurisdiction' (1992) 27 *Texas International Law Journal* 323
Mustill (1988)	M. Mustill, 'The New Lex Mercatoria: The First Twenty-Five Years' (1988) 4 *Arbitration International* 86
Mutton (2004)	A. Mutton, 'Choice of Law on the High Seas: *Blunden* v. *Commonwealth*' (2004) 26 *Sydney Law Review* 427
Nafziger (2002)	J. A. R. Nafziger, 'Oregon's Conflicts Law Applicable to Contracts' (2002) 38 *Willamette Law Review* 397
Nagy (2012)	C. I. Nagy, 'What Functions May Party Autonomy Have in International Family and Succession Law? An EU Perspective' (2012) 30 *Nederlands Internationaal Privaatrecht* 576
Nazzini (2016)	R. Nazzini, 'The Law Applicable to the Arbitration Agreement: Towards Transnational Principles' (2016) 65 *International and Comparative Law Quarterly* 681
Niboyet (1927)	J. P. Niboyet, 'La Théorie de l'Autonomie de la Volonté' (1927) 16 *Recueil des Cours* 1
Nielsen (2009)	P. A. Nielsen, 'The Rome I Regulation and Contracts of Carriage', in F. Ferrari and S. Leible (eds.), *Rome I Regulation* (Sellier European Law Publishers, 2009)
Nielson and Lando (2008)	P. A. Nielson and O. Lando, 'The Rome I Regulation' (2008) 45 *Common Market Law Review* 1687
Nishitani (2016)	Y. Nishitani, 'Party Autonomy in Contemporary Private International Law' (2016) 59 *Japanese Yearbook of International Law* 300
Norris (2016)	K. Norris, 'Common European Sales Law: A Missed Opportunity or Better Things to Come?' (2016) 37 *Business Law Review* 29
North (1993)	P. North, *Private International Law Problems in Common Law Jurisdictions* (Kluwer Law International/M. Nijhoff, 1993)
Nozick (1974)	R. Nozick, *Anarchy, State, and Utopia* (Basic Books, 1974)
Nuyts (2007)	A. Nuyts, *Study on Residual Jurisdiction: General Report* (2007), European Commission Study JLS/C4/2005/07-30-CE
Nygh (1995)	P. E. Nygh, 'The Reasonable Expectations of the Parties as a Guide to the Choice of Law in Contract and in Tort' (1995) 251 *Recueil des Cours* 1

Nygh (1999) *Autonomy in International Contracts* (Oxford University Press, 1999)

Ogus (1999) A. Ogus, 'Competition between National Legal Systems: A Contribution of Economic Analysis to Comparative Law' (1999) 48 *International and Comparative Law Quarterly* 405

O'Hara and Ribstein (2000) E. A. O'Hara and L. E. Ribstein, 'From Politics to Efficiency in Choice of Law' (2000) 67 *University of Chicago Law Review* 1151

O'Hara and Ribstein (2009) *The Law Market* (Oxford University Press, 2009)

Oser (2008) D. Oser, *The UNIDROIT Principles of International Commercial Contracts: A Governing Law?* (Brill, 2008)

Oster (2015) J. Oster, 'Public Policy and Human Rights' (2015) 11 *Journal of Private International Law* 542

Panagopoulos (2000) G. Panagopoulos, *Restitution in Private International Law* (Hart, 2000)

Park (2000) W. W. Park, 'Determining Arbitral Jurisdiction: Allocation of Tasks Between Courts and Arbitrators' (2000) 9 *Arbitration and Dispute Resolution Law Journal* 19

Park (2007a) 'The Arbitrator's Jurisdiction to Determine Jurisdiction', in A. J. van den Berg (ed.), *International Arbitration 2006: Back to Basics?* (ICCA Congress Series, vol 13, Kluwer Law International, 2007)

Park (2007b) 'Determining an Arbitrator's Jurisdiction: Timing and Finality in American Law' (2007) 8 *Nevada Law Journal* 135

Park (2014) 'Non-Signatories and International Arbitration', in L. W. Newman and R. D. Hill (eds.), *Leading Arbitrators' Guide to International Arbitration* (Juris Publishing, 3rd edn, 2014)

Parra-Aranguren (1988) G. Parra-Aranguren, 'General Course of Private International Law: Selected Problems' (1988) 210 *Recueil des Cours* 9

Paulsson (2005) J. Paulsson, 'Jurisdiction and Admissibility', in G. Aksen et al. (eds.), *Global Reflections on International Law, Commerce and Dispute Resolution: Liber Amicorum in Honour of Robert Briner* (ICC Publishing, 2005)

Paulsson (2011) 'Arbitration in Three Dimensions' (2011) 60 *International and Comparative Law Quarterly* 291

Paulsson (2013) *The Idea of Arbitration* (Oxford University Press, 2013)

Pavlović (2016) M. Pavlović, 'Contracting Out of Access to Justice: Enforcement of Forum-Selection Clauses in Consumer Contracts' (2016) 62 *McGill Law Journal* 389

Peari (2013) S. Peari, 'The Choice-Based Perspective of Choice-of-Law' (2013) 23 *Duke Journal of Comparative & International Law* 477

Peari (2014)   'Savigny's Theory of Choice of Law as a Principle of "Voluntary Submission"' (2014) 64 *University of Toronto Law Journal* 106

Pearson (2013)   S. Pearson, '*Sulamérica* v. *Enesa*: The Hidden Pro-validation Approach Adopted by the English Courts with Respect to the Proper Law of the Arbitration Agreement' (2013) 29 *Arbitration International* 115

Penadés Fons (2015)   M. Penadés Fons, 'Commercial Choice of Law in Context: Looking Beyond Rome' (2015) 78 *Modern Law Review* 241

Pereznieto Castro (1985)   L. Pereznieto Castro, 'La tradition territorialiste en Droit International Privé dans les pays d'Amérique Latine' (1985) 190 *Recueil des Cours* 271

Pertegás and Marshall (2014)   M. Pertegás and B. A. Marshall, 'Party Autonomy and Its Limits: Convergence through the New Hague Principles on Choice of Law in International Commercial Contracts' (2014) 39 *Brooklyn Journal of International Law* 975

Petch (2016)   T. Petch, 'The Treatment of Asymmetric Jurisdiction Clauses in Financial Contracts in France and England' (2016) 5 *UCL Journal of Law and Jurisprudence* 313

Peters (2009)   A. Peters, 'Humanity as the A and Ω of Sovereignty' (2009) 20 *European Journal of International Law* 513

Petsoulas (2001)   C. Petsoulas, *Hayek's Liberalism and Its Origins: His Idea of Spontaneous Order and the Scottish Enlightenment* (Routledge, 2001)

Piggott (1892)   F. T. Piggott, *Service Out of the Jurisdiction* (W Clowes and Sons, 1892)

Pitel (2004)   S. G. A. Pitel, 'The Characterisation of Unjust Enrichment in the Conflict of Laws', in J. W. Neyers, M. McInnes, and S. G. A. Pitel (eds.), *Understanding Unjust Enrichment* (Hart, 2004)

Pontier (1998)   J. A. Pontier, 'The Justification of Choice of Law: A Liberal-Political Theory as a Critical and Explanatory Model, and the Field of International Consumer Transactions as an Example' (1998) 45 *Netherlands International Law Review* 388

Posner (2013)   E. Posner, 'The Questionable Basis of the Common European Sales Law: The Role of an Optional Instrument in Jurisdictional Competition' (2013) 50 *Common Market Law Review* 261

Princi (2002)   J. Princi, 'In Pursuit of Justice for Tort Choice of Law' [2002] *Australian International Law Journal* 237

Pryles (2003)   M. Pryles, 'Application of the Lex Mercatoria in International Commercial Arbitration' (2003) 18 *International Arbitration Report* 21

Pryles (2007)   'Reflections on Transnational Public Policy' (2007) 24
                             Journal of International Arbitration 1
Radicati di   L. G. Radicati di Brozolo, 'The Impact of National Law
Brozolo (2011a)   and Courts on International Commercial Arbitration:
                             Mythology, Physiology, Pathology, Remedies and Trends'
                             (2011) 3 *Paris Journal of International Arbitration* 663
Radicati di Brozolo   'Arbitration and Competition Law: The Position of
(2011b)   the Courts and of Arbitrators' (2011) 27 *Arbitration
                             International* 1
Radicati di Brozolo   'Non-national Rules and Conflicts of Laws' (2012) 48
(2012a)   *Rivista di diritto internazionale privato e processuale 841*,
                             available at SSRN: https://ssrn.com/abstract=2089822
Radicati di Brozolo   'Mandatory Rules and International Arbitration' (2012)
(2012b)   23 *American Review of International Arbitration* 49
Raphael (2008)   T. Raphael, *The Anti-Suit Injunction* (Oxford University
                             Press, 2008)
Ratković and   T. Ratković and D. Zgrabljić Rotar, 'Choice-of-Court
Zgrabljić Rotar (2013)   Agreements under the Brussels I Regulation (Recast)'
                             (2013) 9 *Journal of Private International Law* 245
Rau (2003)   A. S. Rau, 'Everything You Really Need to Know About
                             "Separability" in Seventeen Simple Propositions' (2003) 14
                             American Review of International Arbitration 121
Redfern and   N. Blackaby et al., *Redfern and Hunter on International
Hunter (2015)   Arbitration* (Oxford University Press, 6th edn, 2015)
Reese (1960)   W. L. M. Reese, 'Power of Parties to Choose Law Governing
                             Their Contract' (1960) 54 *Proceedings of the American
                             Society of International Law at Its Annual Meeting* 49
Reese (1964)   'The Contractual Forum: Situation in the United States'
                             (1964) 13 *American Journal of Comparative Law* 187
Reimann (1999)   M. Reimann, 'Savigny's Triumph? Choice of Law in
                             Contracts Cases at the Close of the Twentieth Century'
                             (1999) 39 *Virginia Journal of International Law* 571
Reisberg (2009)   S. H. Reisberg, 'The Rules Governing Who Decides
                             Jurisdictional Issues: *First Options* v. *Kaplan* Revisited'
                             (2009) 20 *American Review of International Arbitration* 159
Resnik (2011)   J. Resnik, 'Fairness in Numbers: A Comment on *AT&T*
                             v. *Concepcion*, *Wal-Mart* v. *Dukes*, and *Turner* v. *Rogers*'
                             (2011) 125 *Harvard Law Review* 78
Ribstein (1993)   L. E. Ribstein, 'Choosing Law by Contract' (1993) 18 *Journal
                             of Corporation Law* 245
Ritchie (2010)   J. Z. Ritchie, 'A Tie That Binds: Forum Selection Clause
                             Enforceability in West Virginia' (2010) 113 *West Virginia
                             Law Review* 95

Rose (1995) F. Rose (ed.), *Restitution and the Conflict of Laws* (Mansfield Press, 1995)

Roth (2003) W. Roth, 'From *Centros* to *Überseering*: Free Movement of Companies, Private International Law, and Community Law' (2003) 52 *International and Comparative Law Quarterly* 177

Rowan (2017) S. Rowan, 'The New French Law of Contract' (2017) 66 *International and Comparative Law Quarterly* 805

Rühl (2007a) G. Rühl, 'Party Autonomy in the Private International Law of Contracts: Transatlantic Convergence and Economic Efficiency', in E. Gottschalk et al. (eds.), *Conflict of Laws in a Globalized World* (Cambridge University Press, 2007)

Rühl (2007b) 'Extending *Ingmar* to Jurisdiction and Arbitration Clauses: The End of Party Autonomy in Contracts with Commercial Agents?' (2007) 6 *European Review of Private Law* 891

Rühl (2011) 'Consumer Protection in Choice of Law' (2011) 44 *Cornell International Law Journal* 569

Rühl (2012) 'The Common European Sales Law: 28th Regime, 2nd Regime or 1st Regime?' (2012) 19 *Maastricht Journal of European and Comparative Law* 148

Rühl (2014) 'The Protection of Weaker Parties in the Private International Law of the European Union: A Portrait of Inconsistency and Conceptual Truancy' (2014) 10 *Journal of Private International Law* 335

Rühl (2016) 'Commercial Agents, Minimum Harmonization and Overriding Mandatory Provisions in the European Union: Unamar' (2016) 53 *Common Market Law Review* 209

Rushworth and Scott (2008) A. Rushworth and A. Scott, 'Rome II: Choice of Law for Non-Contractual Obligations' [2008] *Lloyd's Maritime and Commercial Law Quarterly* 274

Salacuse (2013) J. W. Salacuse, *The Three Laws of International Investment: National, Contractual and International Frameworks for Foreign Capital* (Oxford University Press, 2013)

Samuel (2010) G. Samuel, *The Law of Obligations* (Edward Elgar, 2010)

Sanchez Fernandez (2010) S. Sanchez Fernandez, 'Choice of Court Agreements: Breach and Damages within the Brussels I Regime' (2010) 12 *Yearbook of Private International Law* 377

Sasson (2010) M. Sasson, *Substantive Law in Investment Treaty Arbitration: The Unsettled Relationship Between International and Municipal Law* (Kluwer Law International, 2010)

Saumier (2012) G. Saumier, 'Designating the UNIDROIT Principles in International Dispute Resolution' (2012) 17 *Uniform Law Review* 533

Saumier (2014)   'The Hague Principles and the Choice of Non-State "Rules of Law" to Govern an International Commercial Contract' (2014) 40 *Brooklyn Journal of International Law* 1

Saumier (2017)   'Article 3 of the Hague Principles: A Response to Peter Mankowski' (2017) 22 *Uniform Law Review* 395

Savigny (1849)   F. K. von Savigny, *Private International Law. A Treatise on the Conflict of Laws, and the Limits of Their Operation in Respect of Place and Time* (originally published 1849, trans. W. Guthrie, Stevens and Sons, 1869)

Schmitz (2013)   A. J. Schmitz, 'American Exceptionalism in Consumer Arbitration' (2013) 10 *Loyola University Chicago International Law Review* 81

Schneewind (1997)   J. B. Schneewind, *The Invention of Autonomy: A History of Modern Moral Philosophy* (Cambridge University Press, 1997)

Schultz (2008)   T. Schultz, 'Some Critical Comments on the Juridicity of Lex Mercatoria' (2008) 10 *Yearbook of Private International Law* 667

Schultz (2014)   *Transnational Legality: Stateless Law and International Arbitration* (Oxford University Press, 2014)

Sherborne (2017)   A. K. E. Sherborne, 'Restitution in the Conflict of Laws: Characterization and Choice-of-Law in Australia' (2017) 13 *Journal of Private International Law* 1

Shore (2009)   L. Shore, 'The United States' Perspective on "Arbitrability"', in L. A. Mistelis and S. L. Brekoulakis (eds.), *Arbitrability: International and Comparative Perspectives* (Kluwer Law International, 2009)

Silberman and Yaffe (2017)   L. J. Silberman and N. D. Yaffe, 'The Transnational Case in Conflict of Laws: Two Suggestions for the New Restatement Third of Conflict of Laws – Judicial Jurisdiction over Foreign Defendants and Party Autonomy in International Contracts' (2017) 27 *Duke Journal of Comparative & International Law* 405

C Smith and Moyé (2012)   C. Smith and E. V. Moyé, 'Outsourcing American Civil Justice: Mandatory Arbitration Clauses in Consumer and Employment Contracts' (2012) 44 *Texas Tech Law Review* 281

L Smith (1986)   L. M. Smith, 'Determining the Arbitrability of International Antitrust Disputes' (1986) 8 *Journal of Comparative Business and Capital Market Law* 197

Smits (2011)   J. M. Smits, 'Plurality of Sources in European Private Law, or: How to Live With Legal Diversity?', in R. Brownsword

	et al. (eds.), *The Foundations of European Private Law* (Hart, 2011)
Smits (2013a)	'A Radical View of Legal Pluralism', in L. Niglia (ed.), *Pluralism and European Private Law* (Hart, 2013)
Smits (2013b)	'Party Choice and the Common European Sales Law, or: How to Prevent the CESL from Becoming a Lemon on the Law Market' (2013) 50 *Common Market Law Review* 51
Smutny and Pham (2008)	A. C. Smutny and H. T. Pham, 'Enforcing Foreign Arbitral Awards in the United States: The Non-Arbitrable Subject Matter Defense' (2008) 25 *Journal of International Arbitration* 657
Sohn (1982)	L. B. Sohn, 'The New International Law: Protection of the Rights of Individuals Rather Than States' (1982) 32 *American University Law Review* 1
Solomon (2008)	D. Solomon, 'The Private International Law of Contracts in Europe: Advances and Retreats' (2008) 82 *Tulane Law Review* 1709
Spiermann (2008)	O. Spiermann, 'Applicable Law', in P. Muchlinski, F. Ortino and C. Schreuer (eds.), *The Oxford Handbook of International Investment Law* (Oxford University Press, 2008)
Steingruber (2012)	A. M. Steingruber, *Consent in International Arbitration* (Oxford University Press, 2012)
Steinle and Vasiliades (2010)	J. Steinle and E. Vasiliades, 'The Enforcement of Jurisdiction Agreements under the Brussels I Regulation: Reconsidering the Principle of Party Autonomy' (2010) 6 *Journal of Private International Law* 565
Stellios (2005)	J. Stellios, 'Choice of Law and the Australian Constitution: Locating the Debate' (2005) 33 *Federal Law Review* 7
Sternlight (1996)	J. R. Sternlight, 'Panacea or Corporate Tool?: Debunking the Supreme Court's Preference for Binding Arbitration' (1996) 74 *Washington University Law Quarterly* 637
Stevens (2000)	R. Stevens, 'Resulting Trusts in the Conflict of Laws', in P. Birks and F. Rose (eds.), *Restitution and Equity, Vol 1, Resulting Trusts and Equitable Compensation* (Mansfield Press, 2000)
Stipanowich (2011)	T. J. Stipanowich, 'The Third Arbitration Trilogy: *Stolt-Nielsen, Rent-a-Center, Concepcion* and the Future of American Arbitration' (2011) 22 *American Review of International Arbitration* 323
Stone Sweet (2006)	A. Stone Sweet, 'The New Lex Mercatoria and Transnational Governance' (2006) 13 *Journal of European Public Policy* 627

Story (1834)   J. Story, *Commentary on the Conflict of Laws* (Hilliard, Gray and Co, 1834)

Stringer (2006)   D. Stringer, 'Choice of Law and Choice of Forum in Brazilian International Commercial Contracts: Party Autonomy, International Jurisdiction, and the Emerging Third Way' (2006) 44 *Columbia Journal of Transnational Law* 959

Strong (2012a)   S. I. Strong, 'What Constitutes an "Agreement in Writing" in International Commercial Arbitration? Conflicts between the New York Convention and the Federal Arbitration Act' (2012) 48 *Stanford Journal of International Law* 47

Strong (2012b)   'Does Class Arbitration Change the Nature of Arbitration? *Stolt-Nielson, AT&T*, and a Return to First Principles' (2012) 17 *Harvard Negotiation Law Review* 201

Strong (2012c)   'Arbitration of Trust Disputes: Two Bodies of Law Collide' (2012) 45 *Vanderbilt Journal of Transnational Law* 1157

Sun (2016)   J. Sun, 'A Comparative Analysis of the Special Limitations to Party Autonomy in Non-Contractual Obligation in EU and China' (2016) 13 *US-China Law Review* 399

Symeonides (2008)   S. C. Symeonides, 'Rome II and Tort Conflicts: A Missed Opportunity' (2008) 56 *American Journal of Comparative Law* 173

Symeonides (2013a)   'The Hague Principles on Choice of Law for International Contracts: Some Preliminary Comments' (2013) 61 *American Journal of Comparative Law* 873

Symeonides (2013b)   'Choice of Law in the American Courts in 2012: Twenty-Sixth Annual Survey' (2013) 61 *American Journal of Comparative Law* 217

Symeonides (2014)   *Codifying Choice of Law Around the World: An International Comparative Analysis* (Oxford University Press, 2014)

Symeonides (2015)   'Choice of Law in the American Courts in 2014: Twenty-Eighth Annual Survey' (2015) 63 *American Journal of Comparative Law* 299

Symeonides (2016)   *Choice of Law* (Oxford University Press, 2016)

Symeonides (2017a)   'Choice of Law in the American Courts in 2016: Thirtieth Annual Survey' (2017) 65 *American Journal of Comparative Law* 1

Symeonides (2017b)   'What Law Governs Forum Selection Clauses?' (2017) *Louisiana Law Review* forthcoming. Available at SSRN: https://ssrn.com/abstract=3014070

Takahashi (2008)   K. Takahashi, 'Damages for Breach of a Choice of Court Agreement' (2008) 10 *Yearbook of Private International Law* 57

D Tan (2005a)	D. Tan, 'Anti-suit Injunctions and the Vexing Problem of Comity' (2005) 45 *Virginia Journal of International Law* 283
D Tan (2005b)	'Damages for Breach of Forum Selection Clauses, Principled Remedies, and Control of International Civil Litigation' (2005) 40 *Texas International Law Journal* 623
P Tan (2011)	P. Tan, 'Between Competing Jurisdiction Clauses: A Pro-Arbitration Bias?' [2011] *Lloyd's Maritime and Commercial Law Quarterly* 15
Tan and Yeo (2003)	D. Tan and N. Yeo, 'Breaking Promises to Litigate in a Particular Forum: Are Damages an Appropriate Remedy?' [2003] *Lloyd's Maritime and Commercial Law Quarterly* 435
Tang (2011)	Z. S. Tang, 'Non-State Law in Chinese Choice of Law Rules' (2011). Available at SSRN: https://ssrn.com/abstract=2079244
Tang (2012)	'Effectiveness of Exclusive Jurisdiction Clauses in the Chinese Courts' (2012) 61 *International and Comparative Law Quarterly* 459
Tang, Xiao and Huo (2016)	Z. S. Tang, Y. Xiao, and Z. Huo, *Conflict of Laws in the People's Republic of China* (Edward Elgar, 2016)
Taylor (1993)	D. H. Taylor, 'The Forum Selection Clause: A Tale of Two Concepts' (1993) 66 *Temple Law Review* 785
Teitel (2011)	R. Teitel, *Humanity's Law* (Oxford University Press, 2011)
Teitz (2005)	L. E. Teitz, 'The Hague Choice of Court Convention: Validating Party Autonomy and Providing an Alternative to Arbitration' (2005) 53 *American Journal of Comparative Law* 543
Tesón (1992)	F. R. Tesón, 'The Kantian Theory of International Law' (1992) 92 *Columbia Law Review* 53
Tetley (1999)	W. Tetley, 'Current Developments in Canadian Private International Law' (1999) 78 *Canadian Bar Review* 152
Teubner (1997)	G. Teubner, *Global Law Without a State* (Ashgate, 1997)
Tham (2004)	C. H. Tham, 'Damages for Breach of English Jurisdiction Clauses: More than Meets the Eye' [2004] *Lloyd's Maritime and Commercial Law Quarterly* 46
Thomas (2016)	Lord Thomas of Cwmgiedd, 'Developing Commercial Law through the Courts: Rebalancing the Relationship between the Courts and Arbitration', The Bailii Lecture, London, 9 March 2016. Available at www.judiciary.gov.uk/wpcontent/uploads/2016/03/lcjspeechbaillilecture20160309.pdf
Tiburcio (2013)	C. Tiburcio, 'Private International Law in Brazil: A Brief Overview' (2013) 1 *Panorama of Brazilian Law* 11
Tilbury, Davis and Opeskin (2002)	M. Tilbury, G. Davis and B. Opeskin, *Conflict of Laws in Australia* (Oxford University Press, 2002)

Torremans (2015)	P. Torremans (ed.), *Intellectual Property and Private International Law* (Edward Elgar, 2015)
Trakman (2011)	L. E. Trakman, 'A Plural Account of the Transnational Law Merchant' (2011) 2 *Transnational Legal Theory* 309
Triebel (1988)	V. Triebel, 'The Choice of Law in Commercial Relations: A German Perspective' (1988) 37 *International and Comparative Law Quarterly* 935
Tu (2007)	G. Tu, 'The Hague Choice of Court Convention: A Chinese Perspective' (2007) 55 *American Journal of Comparative Law* 347
Tu and Xu (2011)	G. Tu and M. Xu, 'Contractual Conflicts in the People's Republic of China: The Applicable Law in the Absence of Choice' (2011) 7 *Journal of Private International Law* 179
Tweeddale (2011)	A. Tweeddale, 'Arbitration under the Contracts (Rights of Third Parties) Act 1999 and Enforcement of an Award' (2011) 27 *Arbitration International* 653
Tweeddale and Tweeddale (2009)	A. Tweeddale and K. Tweeddale, 'Commencement of Arbitration and Time-Bar Clauses' (2009) 75 *Arbitration* 480
Tweeddale and Tweeddale (2011)	'*Scott v Avery* Clauses: O'er Judges' Fingers, Who Straight Dream on Fees' (2011) 77 *Arbitration* 423
Van den Berg (2014)	A. J. van den Berg, 'Should the Setting Aside of the Arbitral Award be Abolished?' (2014) 29 *ICSID Review* 263
Van Loon (2016)	J. H. A. Van Loon, 'The Global Horizon of Private International Law' (2016) 380 *Recueil des Cours* 9
Verhagen (2002)	H. L. E. Verhagen, 'The Tension between Party Autonomy and European Union Law: Some Observations on *Ingmar GB Ltd* v *Eaton Leonard Technologies Inc*' (2002) 51 *International and Comparative Law Quarterly* 135
Vischer (1992)	F. Vischer, 'General Course on Private International Law' (1992-I) 232 *Recueil des Cours* 4
Vogenauer (2013)	S. Vogenauer, 'Regulatory Competition through Choice of Contract Law and Choice of Forum in Europe: Theory and Evidence' (2013) 21 *European Review of Private Law* 13
Vogenauer (2015)	(ed.), *Commentary on the UNIDROIT Principles of International Commercial Contracts (PICC)* (Oxford University Press, 2nd edn, 2015)
Von Bar (1892)	L. Von Bar, *The Theory and Practice of Private International Law* (trans. G. R. Gillespie, W Green & Sons, 2nd edn, 1892)
Von Hein (2008)	J. von Hein, 'Something Old and Something Borrowed, but Nothing New? Rome II and the European Choice-of-Law Evolution' (2008) 82 *Tulane Law Review* 1663
Von Mehren (1977)	A. T. von Mehren, 'Review of Bernard Audit, *Fraude à la loi*' (1977) 25 *American Journal of Comparative Law* 420

Voser (1996)	N. Voser, 'Mandatory Rules of Law Applicable in International Commercial Arbitration' (1996) 7 *American Review of International Arbitration* 319
Wai (2001)	R. Wai, 'In the Name of the International: The Supreme Court of Canada and the Internationalist Transformation of Canadian Private International Law' (2001) 39 *Canadian Yearbook of International Law* 117
Wai (2002)	'Transnational Liftoff and Juridical Touchdown: The Regulatory Function of Private International Law in an Era of Globalization' (2002) 40 *Columbia Journal of Transnational Law* 209
Weintraub (2008)	R. J. Weintraub, *Commentary on the Conflict of Laws* (Foundation Press, 5th edn, 2008)
Weller (2015)	M. Weller, 'Mutual Trust: In Search of the Future of European Union Private International Law' (2015) 11 *Journal of Private International Law* 64
Weller (2017)	'Choice of Court Agreements under Brussels Ia and under the Hague Convention: Coherences and Clashes' (2017) 13 *Journal of Private International Law* 91
Westlake (1880)	J. Westlake, *A Treatise on Private International Law with Principal Reference to its Practice in England* (W. Maxwell, 1880)
Westrik and Van der Weide (2011)	R. Westrik and J. van der Weide (eds.), *Party Autonomy in International Property Law* (Sellier, 2011)
Whincop and Keyes (2001)	M. J. Whincop and M. Keyes, *Policy and Pragmatism in the Conflict of Laws* (Ashgate, 2001)
Wicker (1925)	W. H. Wicker, 'The Development of the Distinction between Local and Transitory Actions' (1925) 4 *Tennessee Law Review* 55
Wilcke and Wildhaber (2010)	A. J. Wilcke and I. Wildhaber, 'Arbitrating Labor Disputes in Switzerland' (2010) 27 *Journal of International Arbitration* 631
Wilderspin (2008)	M. Wilderspin, 'The Rome I Regulation: Communitarisation and Modernisation of the Rome Convention' (2008) 9 *ERA Forum* 259
Williams (1986)	P. R. Williams, 'The EEC Convention on the Law Applicable to Contractual Obligations' (1986) 35 *International and Comparative Law Quarterly* 1
Wilske, Shore and Ahrens (2006)	S. Wilske, L. Shore, and J. M. Ahrens, 'The "Group of Companies Doctrine" – Where is it heading?' (2006) 17 *American Review of International Arbitration* 73
Wolff (1950)	M. Wolff, *Private International Law* (Clarendon Press, 2nd edn, 1950)

Wright (2011)　　M. J. Wright, 'Enforcing Forum-Selection Clauses: An Examination of the Current Disarray of Federal Forum-Selection Clause Jurisprudence and a Proposal for Judicial Reform' (2011) 44 *Loyola of Los Angeles Law Review* 1625

Xiao and Long (2009)　　Y. Xiao and W. Long, 'Contractual Party Autonomy in Chinese Private International Law' (2009) 11 *Yearbook of Private International Law* 193

Yackee (2003)　　J. W. Yackee, 'A Matter of Good Form: The (Downsized) Hague Judgments Convention and Conditions of Formal Validity for the Enforcement of Forum Selection Agreements' (2003) 53 *Duke Law Journal* 1179

Yackee (2004)　　'Choice of Law Considerations in the Validity & Enforcement of International Forum Selection Agreements: Whose Law Applies?' (2004) 9 *UCLA Journal of International Law and Foreign Affairs* 43

Yang (2014)　　F. Yang, 'Applicable Laws to Arbitration Agreements under Current Arbitration Law and Practice in Mainland China' (2014) 63 *International and Comparative Law Quarterly* 741

Yeo (2004)　　T. M. Yeo, *Choice of Law for Equitable Doctrines* (Oxford University Press, 2004)

Yetano (2010)　　T. M. Yetano, 'The Constitutionalisation of Party Autonomy in European Family Law' (2010) 6 *Journal of Private International Law* 155

Yntema (1952)　　H. E. Yntema, '"Autonomy" in Choice of Law' (1952) 1 *American Journal of Comparative Law* 341

Yntema (1955)　　'Contract and Conflict of Laws: "Autonomy" in Choice of Law in the United States' (1955) 1 *New York Law Forum* 46

Yntema (1966)　　'The Comity Doctrine' (1966) 65 *Michigan Law Review* 9

Zekos (2008)　　G. Zekos, 'Antitrust/Competition Arbitration in EU versus U.S. Law' (2008) 25 *Journal of International Arbitration* 1

Zhang (2006a)　　M. Zhang, 'Party Autonomy and Beyond: An International Perspective of Contractual Choice of Law' (2006) 20 *Emory International Law Review* 511

Zhang (2006b)　　'Choice of Law in Contracts: A Chinese Approach' (2006) 26 *Northwestern Journal of International Law & Business* 289

Zhang (2011a)　　'Codified Choice of Law in China: Rules, Processes and Theoretic Underpinnings' (2011) 37 *North Carolina Journal of International Law and Commercial Regulation* 83

Zhang (2011b)　　'Party Autonomy in Non-Contractual Obligations: Rome II and Its Impacts on Choice of Law' (2011) 39 *Seton Hall Law Review* 861

Zumbansen (2010)　　P. Zumbansen, 'Transnational Legal Pluralism' (2010) 1 *Transnational Legal Theory* 141

INDEX

CPSIA information can be obtained
at www.ICGtesting.com
Printed in the USA
LVHW082142190219
608124LV00008B/46/P

9 781107 079175